Surburg's Works

Vol. II
Bible

Edited by
Herman J. Otten

LUTHERAN NEWS, INC., New Haven, Missouri

Surburg's Works

Library of Congress Card
Lutheran News, Inc.
684 Luther Lane
New Haven, MO 63068
Published 2017
Printed in the United States of America
IngramSpark, TN
ISBN #978-0-9864232-5-3

Table of Contents

How Dependable is the Bible? A Conservative Roman Catholic
Looks at Surburg 353

A Book Review Article of "The Battle for the Bible" 355

Why Should A Christian Study the Old Testament? 403

Jesus and the Canon - Did Jesus and the New Testament Writers
Recognize - Apocryphal and Pseudepigraphical Books As Canonical?......432

Member Beck Revision Committee 437

Defending the Book of Daniel 437

Liberal Lutheran Pastor Challenges Inerrancy and 6th Century
B.C. Dating of Daniel - ERRORS IN GOD'S WORD......................... 449

The Sources of the Pentateuch... 452

An Evaluation of Genesis 1:1-2:4a As Interpreted from an Historic
Historical-Critical Framework - Raymond F. Surburg's Response
to Brueckner.. 458

Lindsell's Bible in the Balance 472

Lindsell and Henry Hamman from Australia 472

Foundations of Biblical Inerrancy - Review by Raymond Surburg 474

A Book Review Article of Harold Lindsell's - "The Bible in the Balance"..... 476

Does the Lutheran Church-Missouri - Synod's Doctrine on the Nature of
the Bible Promote Fundamentalism? 515

The Theology of the Apocalypse or Revelation 522

The Sermon on the Mount... 534

Is the Bible Inerrant? 557

125th Anniversary of Walther's Birth - The Influence of Luther's
Principles of Interpretation on C.F.W. Walther's Hermeneutics 562

The Relationship of Genesis 3:15 - To The Incarnation of God's Son 578

The Resurrection of Christ from a Historical-Critical Lutheran Perspective
- As Compared with a Biblical and Confessional Lutheran Stance 592

The Meaning of 'Fullness of Time' in Galatians 4:4 and Its Relationship
to - Christ's Incarnation 607

An Evaluation of the Divergent Interpretations of the Lord's Mount
Olive Discourse 625

The Relationship of Isogogics to Effective Communication of God's
Word 643

The Presuppositions of the Historical-Grammatical Method 657

In Defense of Luther 667

A Rebuttal of Winrod's Attack Upon Luther as "the Fore-runner of
Anti-Christ" 667

Answering Winrod 679

Correction and Supplementation on the Vulgate 679

The Hermeneutics of Theodore Laetsch, Professor of Concordia
Seminary, St. Louis From 1927-1947 686

The Life and Writings of Carl Manthey Zorn 701

The Influence of Eugene Nida On Bible Translators And Bible
  Translations 712
A Jewish Book - The Jewishness of the New Testament: Jews and
  Judaism in the New Testament 723
The Contribution of Biblical Archaeology to Biblical Studies 740
The Hermeneutics of Robert Preus 753
What Significance Do - The Dead Sea Scrolls (DSS) Have for the
  Understanding of the New Testament? 770
Method in the Study of the Bible 781

Index 1868

How Dependable is the Bible?
A Conservative Roman Catholic Looks at Surburg

Dr. Surburg is professor of Hebrew and Old Testament interpretation at Concordia Seminary, Springfield, Illinois. He has done graduate work at Columbia, Fordham, and other universities.

Although the Bible continues to head best-seller lists, Dr. Surburg observes, it is strange how little it is read today. Even in seminaries and among teachers of religion, there is great ignorance of the Bible. Lack of interest in the Bible, he believes, has various causes, most of them having to do with the way people look at the Bible. Many scholars have been influenced by evolution and have debased the Bible to a purely human document. Other negative influences are destructive biblical criticism and humanistic modernism.

The author is entirely in favor of valid biblical criticism, which has in many cases cleared up difficulties and reconciled apparent discrepancies. But there are other forms of criticism, he points out, which have been extremely destructive to belief. He traces biblical criticism through the centuries, noting both its accomplishments and its mistakes.

The study of the ancient texts has serve to strengthen belief in the authenticity of the Scriptures. While there are variants, they prove, on examination, to be so small as to be of no significance. The Scriptures have come down to us substantially as they were written. The discovery of the Qumran scrolls has helped to confirm this.

There are schools of criticism, however, which have been very destructive, since their procedures are based on rejection of the supernatural. Critics who proceed from this assumption do not believe in direct revelation from God, and do not believe in the historicity of Scripture. They defend their highly subjective interpretations on grounds that the sacred writers did not intend to set forth facts, but to teach religious truths.

Dr. Surburg deals briefly with the documentary hypothesis of the composition of the Pentateuch, and in more detail with form and redaction criticism. The documentary hypothesis is, in short, the theory that the first five books of the Bible are composed of four or more different documents which were put together long after the Mosaic era. Form criticism has a somewhat different approach, postulating a long period of oral transmission during which traditions became interwoven with myth and legend, with the final writing reflecting the memory of a people rather than revelation or history. These methods completely alter the resultant interpretation of Scripture. Dr. Surburg says for example: "McKenzie in his *Dictionary of the Bible* sets forth views . . . which reject the position formerly held by Jewish, Roman Catholic and Protestant scholars regarding the historical character of large portions of the Old Testament books, and he presents a completely different understanding of the concept of history in the Old Testament."

Dr. Surburg discusses the higher critics' views of the psalms, the wisdom literature, prophecy (from which they eliminate all possibility of predictive prophecy), and the Gospels. Bultmann, one of the main proponents of form criticism, he writes, "has dissolved the Christian faith in the acids of demythologizing."

The destructive critics continue to undermine the Bible, says Dr. Surburg, at a time when archaeological discoveries have in a hundred or more cases supported the reliability of the scriptural record, and when more prudent scholars uphold its inspiration and inerrancy.

The book gives a brief but useful history of destructive biblical criticism, and points up the disbelief, to which it quite logically leads. Among the destructive ideas which are discussed, the Catholic reader will recognize many which, in spite of their considerable age, are now being freely dispensed among Catholics as the fruit of "modern scholarship."

– Edith Myers
(*The Wanderer*, a Roman Catholic publication)

A Book Review Article of
"The Battle for the Bible"
Christian News, November 1, 1976

The book, "The Battle for the Bible," written by Dr. Harold Lindsell, editor of the fortnightly journal "Christianity Today," is a book that will and has started a great controversy among a number of scholars representing a number of so-called evangelical denominations. "The Battle for the Bible" was published on April 26, 1976 and by June there was already 20,000 copies in print. This is one of the most important books to have been published in a long time, because it deals with an issue that is central to the survival of Biblical Christianity. For a number of years this book will occupy the attention of Christian scholars because the doctrine of the inerrancy of the Holy Scriptures is the bedrock on which a sound Scriptural theology rests and one which does justice to the claims of Christ, who said of the Old Testament "Scriptures cannot be broken" (John 10:35). This book contains a mine of information on the whole battle between fundamentalists and liberals with which many of this current generation of evangelicals are only partially aware.

In the foreword to the volume Dr. Harold J. Ockenga, president of Gordon-Conwell Theological Seminary, stated that there was a great need for Lindsell's book "in the burgeoning evangelical branch of Protestantism. If evangelicalism bids to take over the historic mainline leadership of nineteenth century Protestantism, as Dr. Martin Marty suggests, this question of biblical errancy must be settled. It is time for an evangelical historian to set forth the problem."

In this eleven-chapter book Lindsell discusses the current problem concerning the inerrancy of the Bible as it has developed in the last decades among evangelicals. After this he sets forth the truth of inerrancy of the Bible as a Scriptural doctrine. Then he gives the history of the doctrine of inerrancy as it has been held and taught throughout the centuries in Christendom. In the next four chapters (Numbers 4, 5, 6, and 7) he shows what has been happening in the Lutheran Church-Missouri Synod, in the Southern Baptist Convention, adduces the strange case of Fuller Theological Seminary, as well as a listing of a number of paragroups and denominations that have experienced deviations relative to Biblical inerrancy. In chapter 9 Lindsell takes up the arguments of those who reject total inerrancy and only advocate "limited infallibility" because of alleged errors and discrepancies in the Bible. In the second last chapter Lindsell shows what follows when individuals are permitted to challenge the complete reliability of the Word of God. The eleventh chapter contains a summary of what has been presented.

Ten years ago John Warwick Montgomery referred to an assertion of James Orr in his book The Progress of Dogma, in which the European scholar claimed that in each of the great epochs of church history, Christianity has been forced to come to grips with some important facet of divine truth, one which involved serious implications for the Christian faith and its adherents in the Christian Church. During the early church period the key issue of the church concerned the persons of the Godhead, especially as it involved the relation of the humanity to the deity in Jesus Christ. The great ecumenical creeds, the Apostle's, the Nicene and the Athanasian Creeds set forth the orthodox stance on the relationship of the three persons of the Godhead to each other. During the Middle Ages the controversy and discussion centered in the atonement of Jesus Christ. Anselm's "Latin doctrine" "gave solid expression to the biblical-salvation history as explicated in the Epistle to the Hebrews." During the Reformation it was justification by faith that occupied the center of the ecclesiastical stage. The three solas set forth the Pauline doctrine of salvation over against an anthropological interpretation in the Roman Catholic Church. Thus in the sixteen centuries since the ascension of Jesus Christ the church faced and overcame controversies in the areas of Christology, soteriology and the Reformation issues about the true way of salvation, by grace, without works. In the twentieth century the great watershed is the argument about the nature and complete inerrancy of the Bible as the inspired Word of God. Lindsell claims that "the struggle over Scripture is unique in the history of the church. How the issue is settled remains to be seen. But if it is finally settled that Scripture can err, then the church and its theologians will learn that no source and no standard remains to solve further doctrinal problems that may arise" (p. 201).

Charles Haddon Spurgeon grasped the seriousness of the issue that now divided "evangelicals," when he wrote:

Believers in Christ's atonement are now declared in union with those who make light of it; believers in holy Scripture are in confederacy with those who deny plenary inspiration; those who hold evangelical doctrine are in open alliance with those who call the Fall a fable, who deny the personality of the Holy Ghost, who call justification by faith immoral, and hold there is another probation after death; to be very plain, we are unable to call these things Christian Unions, they begin to look like confederacies in evil.

Pinnock, a defender of the inerrancy of the Bible quoted to the Southern Baptists Martin Luther, who wrote as follows:

If I profess with loudest voice and clearest exposition every portion of the truth except precisely that little which the world and the devil are at the moment attacking, I am not confessing Christ, however, boldly I may be professing Christ. Where the battle rages, there the loyalty of the soldier is proved, and to be steady on all the battlefield besides, is merely flight and disgrace if he flinches at THAT point.

What is occurring in the second half of the twentieth century is in some respect not new. In the 1880's B. B. Warfield of Princeton Theological Seminary fought vigorously for the teaching of Biblical inerrancy in The Presbyterian Church. Fifty years later another leading light of Princeton, J. Gresham Machen in the 1930's fought for the doctrine of Biblical inerrancy against the liberalism and neo-orthodoxy which had begun to dominate the Princeton faculty, once a bastion for Biblical inerrancy in the Presbyterian church in the U.S.A.

The doctrine of the inerrancy and infallibility of the Holy Scriptures is a teaching tied up with the Biblical doctrine of divine revelation. Man can never know more about God than God chooses to reveal. Whatever we do know about God, about the plan of salvation, what the end and purpose of human existence is, we owe to God's self-revelation. Revelation has come to mankind in two forms: natural revelation and special revelation, a truth taught in the canonical books of the Old and New Testament Scriptures.

The revelation of God has become inscripturated in the Bible, which in all of its parts constitutes the written Word of God to man. The Holy Scriptures are inspired of God. Lindsell defines inspiration "as the inward work of the Holy Spirit in the hearts and minds of chosen men who then wrote the Scriptures so that God got written what He wanted to man" (p. 30). Because of this fact the Bible in all its parts is the Word of God and does not merely contain the Word of God. While the phenomenon of revelation preceded that of inscripturation, still the Bible written by holy men of God as they were carried along by the Holy Spirit, are also a revelation of God. The Bible does give us a record of revelation that were vouchsafed to Adam, Noah, Abraham, Isaac, Jacob, Joseph, Moses, Joshua, Samuel, Gideon, David, Solomon and many other individuals, yet the Bible also is a revelation from the true God to mankind.

Because the Bible is from God "it is free from all error in its original autographs it is wholly trustworthy in matters of history and doctrine" (p. 30). Lindsell correctly contends that "however limited may have been their knowledge, and however much they may have erred when they were not writing sacred Scripture, the authors of Scripture, under the guidance of the Holy Spirit, were preserved from making factual, historical, scientific, or other errors. The Bible does not purport to be a textbook of history, science, or mathematics; yet when the writers of Scripture spoke of matters embraced in these disciplines, they did not incite error; they wrote what was true" (p. 31).

God cannot deceive men. The Bible is inerrant in that it is not false, mistaken or defective. Inspiration extends to all parts of the Bible and "it includes the guiding hand of the Holy Spirit even in the selection of the words of Scripture" (p. 31). The Holy Scriptures are the product of the Holy Spirit and chosen human beings. "The authors of Scripture retained their own styles of writing and the Holy Spirit, operating within this human context, so superintended the writing of the Word of God that the end product was God's."

Infallibility flows from the fact of the Bible's inspiration. God does not lie nor deceive mankind. Any part of the Scripture which is not infallible and inerrant therefore would not be from God. "If inspiration allows for the possibility of error then inspiration ceases to be inspiration" (p. 31). Even though the Bible was written over 1600 years ago by human beings who are fallible, yet when these same men were caused by the Holy Spirit to record the words that the Spirit wanted them to record, God prevented them from making errors and mistakes and thus their writings — **theopneustos** (God-spirited or God-breathed) are infallible and inerrant.

Limited Inerrancy Rejected

Like others before him who have written on the Bible's inspiration, Lindsell rejects as a misunderstanding of the position of these holding to total inspiration that the holy writers were merely machines who received the Bible by dictation. The so-called dictation theory, which attempts to caricature the Bible position, is shown to be a view imputed to orthodox writers, but a view neither held or defended. Other erroneous notions concerning inspiration that are completely unacceptable are those that only the ideas are inspired but not the words. Or that by inspiration is meant "genius of a high order," just as Milton, Shakespeare, Muhammad, Confucius, Beethoven and other gifted persons were inspired, so Biblical writers had a special genius for the expression of religious truth. Again Lindsell finds totally unacceptable the view that inspiration is to be equated with illumination.

While critical scholars speak about theories of inspiration, Lindsell contends that the infallibility of the Bible is a doctrine. Do the Holy Scriptures support the historic teaching of Christendom that the Bible, "God-spirited" is God's Word in its entirety and that as such it is reliable in all that it asserts? 2 Timothy 3:16, 17 reads: "All Scripture is inspired by God and profitable for teaching, for reproof, for correction, and for training in righteousness, that the man of God may be complete, equipped for every good work." The word translated "inspired" does not accurately render the Greek **theopneustos**, which means "God-spirited," "God-breathed out." This means that God is the author and source of the Bible and the Holy Writ is the product of God. This emphasizes the fact that the Scriptures are the product of God. "This is not to suggest," declares Lindsell, "that the Holy Spirit did not move on the writers themselves, but that the writers produced a product, which, while it was their own, was also the Word of the living God" (p. 34).

Another important passage is 2 Peter 1:21: "No prophecy ever came by the impulse of man, but men moved by the Holy Spirit spake from God." Here the apostle Peter suggests that the impulse to write came from the Holy Spirit. It was God Himself who caused the hearts and minds of men to accomplish, as instruments of God, what under normal conditions man could not have done or written the kind of Scripture, which because God was its author, was and is inerrant: and reliable in all that it asserts.

In his first letter to the Thessalonians Paul made it clear that they had not regarded his preaching as merely the words of men. No it was for the Thessalonians the Word of God. "And we also thank God constantly for this, that when you received the word of God which you heard from us you accepted it not as the word of men but as what it really is, the word of God, which is at work in you believers" (I Thess. 2:13). Concerning Paul's instructions and admonitions in I Corinthians, Paul averred: "If anyone thinks he is a prophet, or spiritual, he should acknowledge what I am writing to you is a command of the Lord." The Gospel Paul proclaimed to the Galatian churches is said by Paul that "it came through a revelation of Jesus Christ."

358

In the Old Testament there are more than 2,000 occurrences of the phrase and concept: "Thus says the Lord," which certainly means that God is speaking, and that we are not merely dealing with human ideas, opinions or theories. Fulfilled prophecy is one of the most powerful proofs for the infallibility of the Bible. Lindsell and many other evangelical writers associate the concept of inerrancy and infallibility with the autographs of Holy Writ. These no longer exist. Since the manuscripts of various Biblical books have transcriptional errors, the opponents of inerrancy claim it is an academic question and that the only real evidence we have supports the contention that the Bible has mistakes and errors. Why did God not see to it that the original biblical books survived if God wished people to believe in the Scripture's complete inerrancy? Lindsell responds: "No doubt, God did not intend for the autographs to be preserved. They would have been accorded a treatment similar to that given to the *Granth*, the sacred Scriptures of Sikhism. That writing is virtually worshiped and kept encased in such a way as to place the emphasis on the book rather than on God who lies behind it. Idolatry is hardly new, and we may be sure that the possession of the original books of Scripture would have been an incipient temptation to idolatrous worship" (p. 36).

The fact that there are copyist's errors does not per se argue for mistakes and errors in the autographs. God did not shield the Bible in history from errors, otherwise each time a copyist anywhere in Asia, Africa or Europe who happened to copy a Biblical manuscript, each and every time God would have to have watched over all copyists and restrained them from making those mistakes that are common to the part of copyists when reproducing another exemplar from the one being used as the basic for the version of the text.

Opponents of total and complete infallibility have made much of the numerous copyists mistakes in the thousands of Biblical manuscripts at the disposal of the students of lower or textual criticism. However, the science of textual criticism has analyzed and worked through thousands of textual variants and has reconstructed a text that may be labelled as representing the true Word of God. Lindsell contends that "textual problems today in no way make the doctrine of biblical inerrancy impossible. It must be remembered, too, that those who scoff at the inerrancy of the autographs because they cannot be produced for examination have no better case for arguing for the errancy of texts they cannot produce either. At worst, it is a standoff" (p. 37).

Related to the inerrancy of the Bible is the truth that the Scripture constitutes the authority men are to believe and which sets forth how they are to live. It is the Christian's only rule of faith and life and all the opinions of men and women are to be tested against it. The authority of the Bible is only viable if the Scripture is true. Those who destroy the trustworthiness of Holy Writ thereby remove its authoritative character. It is a contradiction to claim the Bible is authoritative and at the same time insists on its errancy and fallibility.

Lindsell correctly and effectively shows that the new type of hermeneutics that has come into vogue has destroyed the infallibility of

God's Word. The new hermeneutic, which operates with anti-supernaturalistic presuppositions, and resorts to a negative type of literary criticism, to form, tradition and redaction criticism, has made it impossible to hold to an inerrant Bible, because the historical-critical methodology finds and artificially creates many discrepancies, errors and mistakes.

The opposition to miracle and prophecy has forced critical scholars into the rejection of statements of the Bible with which past believing generations had no difficulty.

Erroneous ideas about revelation, inspiration, illumination, authorship and interpretation have been responsible for the defection and apostasy which has occurred in many main-line Protestant churches as well as in Roman Catholicism, where the new hermeneutic has also found many advocates.

In chapter three of his book, Lindsell starts with the New Testament and shows how critical scholars admit the New Testament writers held to the concept of an inerrant Scripture. Then he shows from the writings of Josephus, Clement of Alexandria, from the Letters of Polycarp, from the Apologists, The Letter of Barnabas, from the writings of Ireneus, Tertulian, Cyprian, Origen, Athanasius, Gregory of Nazianzus (c. 329-388), Basil the Great (330-379), Chrysostom, Theodoret, Jerome, Augustine, from the traditional stance of the Roman Catholic Church that all these held and taught the doctrine of the inerrancy and infallibility of the Bible.

During the Reformation the Protestant reformers like Luther, Calvin, Knox, Zwingli and others held the same view as did the Roman Church before and during their time. The Westminster Confession sets forth in Chapter I its position, namely, that the Bible is called "the only infallible rule of faith and practice." While some have endeavored to support the idea of limited inerrancy in the Westminster Confession, Lindsell claims that two expressions, descriptive of the nature of the Bible reject limited inerrancy, and these are the phrases: "the entire Scriptures are perfect," and the phrase "the consents of all the parts." Many of the Lutheran and Reformed Confessions have no statement about the inerrancy and infallibility of the Bible, because this was not a matter of dispute between Roman Catholic and Lutherans and other Protestants. Lindsell asserts that "no one can deny that in the United States, so far as the Reformed denominations are concerned, wherever the Westminster Confession was the controlling creed, it was understood to mean that the Scripture in all of its parts was without error. This was true of the northern and southern Presbyterian churches, as well as the United Presbyterian Church" (p. 63). During the days of the Fundamentalist-Modernist Controversy, the General Assembly, under the moderatorship of Clarence McCartney, voted to endorse Biblical infallibility. The Assembly was merely affirming the commonly accepted understanding of Presbyterianism on this topic. The former Dean of Princeton Theological Seminary, Dr. Elmer Homrighausen asserted:

Few intelligent Christians can still hold to the idea that the Bible is an infallible Book, that it contains no linguistic errors, no historical discrepancies, no antiquated scientific assumptions, not even had eth-

360

ical standards. Historical investigation and literary criticism have taken the magic out of the Bible and made it a composite human book, written by many hands in different ages. The existence of thousands of variations of texts makes it impossible to hold the doctrine of a book verbally infallible.

Dr. Homrighausen here clearly shows that he is advocating a position which is different from the one traditionally held by the Presbyterian Church. He asserted among other things: "Few **intelligent** Christians can still hold to the idea..." Those accepting the teaching of the infallibility of the Bible are categorized as making Christian apologetics "more ridiculous in the eyes of **sincere** men" (bold supplied).

Questions
1. Who wrote *"The Battle for the Bible?"* ____
2. Why was this book important? ____
3. The doctrine of the inerrancy of the Bible is ____.
4. The so-called dictation theory attempts to ____.
5. In the Old Testament there are more than ____ occurrences of the phrase "Thus says the Lord."
6. Possession of the original manuscripts would have led to ____.
7. The science of textual criticism has a reconstructed text which may be labeled as ____.
8. The "new hermeneutic" operates with ____.
9. Many of the Lutheran and Reformed Confessions have no statement about the inerrancy and infallibility of the Bible because ____.

Part II

The founding of Westminster Theological Seminary of Philadelphia was occasioned by the rejection of the inerrancy of the Bible. Dr. Edward J. Young, a professor at Westminster for many years, declared in his book *Thy Word is Truth*: "If the autographs of the Scripture are marred by flecks of mistake, God has simply not told us the truth concerning His Word. To assume that He could breathe forth a word that could contain mistakes is to say, in effect, that God Himself can make mistakes. We must maintain that the original of Scripture is infallible for the simple reason that it came to us direct from God Himself."

What has been true of the Presbyterians of the South and the North was also true of American and British Baptists. Both Baptists of the North and South have espoused the doctrine of Scriptural infallibility. The New Hampshire Confession of Faith declares that the Bible "has God for its author, salvation for its end, and truth, without any mixture of error, for its matter." The Southern Baptist Convention until recently, held to verbal inerrancy of Holy Writ. It was during the Fundamentalist-Modernistic controversy that a battle raged around differing viewpoints relative to the nature of the Bible, which resulted in schism and the formation of the General Association of Regular Baptists (dating from 1932) and the Conservative Baptist Association of America (originating in 1947). The latter group remained in the Northern Baptist Convention, convinced that the overwhelming majority of Northern Baptists held to the infallibility of the Bible. Two seminaries, the Eastern and Northern Baptist Theological Seminaries, were founded in order to combat and counteract liberal Baptist seminaries like Crozer, Andover-Newton, Chicago Divinity School and Colgate-Rochester.

Alvah Hovey, president of Newton Theological Institute defended Biblical inerrancy. In his book, *Manual of Systematic Theology and Christian Ethics* (Phil., 1880), he wrote: "... infallibility in the original languages requires for its compliment the infallibility in all copies, translations, and, some would say, interpretation of them. For otherwise, we are told, the benefit of infallibility is lost to all but primitive readers. But this, again, is a mistake; for the errors from transcription, translations, etc., are such as can be detected, or at least estimated, and reduced to a minimum; while errors in the original revelation could not be measured" (p. 65). On page 85 of his book Hovey responded to those who raised questions about the inerrancy of the Scripture by alluding and discussing questions of historical and scientific errors.

Lindsell claims that what was true about American Baptists was also true about British Baptists in years gone by. Charles Haddon Spurgeon is cited and quoted as a staunch defender of Biblical inerrancy (pp. 66-67). However, the same retreat from Biblical inerrancy that occurred in the nineteenth and twentieth centuries in America also took place in Great Britain, especially after the appearance of Charles Darwin's Origin of Species (1859).

What was true of Baptists can also be asserted about Anglicans and Methodists of the past. Writing about the Episcopalian church, Lindsell averred: "Among the doctrines inherited from the Roman Church was its view of the Bible as the infallible Word of God. It rejected some of Rome's teaching with respect to biblical infallibility. It followed this doctrinal teaching until, like so many denominations that sprang out of the Reformation period, discarded it in the late nineteenth and twentieth centuries" (p. 68).

Lindsell, as he states, could have furnished much more historical evidence in support of his contention that Biblical inerrancy and infallibility was the historic teachings of Roman Catholicism and of the various Protestant denominations. Since this *Christian News* is read by many Lutherans it might not be amiss to show briefly how this was also the doctrinal position of American Lutheranism before the adoption of negative higher criticism, which rests in turn upon the higher critical methodology. American Lutheranism before the 1930's represented by all the major Lutheran churches believed and taught the infallibility of the Bible. The first Lutheran Church to question Scriptural inerrancy was the United Lutheran Church in America (ULCA) formed in 1918. The American Lutheran Conference, later the American Lutheran Church, became infected with views opposing Biblical infallibility when its new young professors began to obtain degrees from institutions of higher learning that taught and supported a negative higher criticism. The two one-volume commentaries, the *Old Testament* and the *New Testament* published by the former Muhlenberg Press, reveal that what had been happening in that branch of American Lutheranism first affected by the critical methodology.

The Lutheran Church-Missouri Synod, at first known as the Evangelical Synod of Missouri, Ohio and other states, has held and defended Biblical infallibility and inerrancy throughout its 130 years existence. The writings of Walther, Pieper, Koehler, *The Abiding Word*, and Engelder's *The Scripture Cannot Be Broken, The Brief Statement* (adopted the Synodical Convention at River Forest, 1932), *A Statement of Confessional Principles*, (adopted New Orleans, 1973) reaffirmed at Anaheim (1975) and many other writings set forth the inerrancy of the Bible.

The Attack Upon Biblical Inerrancy in Current Protestantism

Lindsell devotes chapters four through seven to churches and parachurches which in recent years have rejected or abandoned Biblical infallibility and have adopted partial inerrancy or limited inerrancy.

In chapter four (pp. 72-88) Lindsell writes about "The Lutheran Church-Missouri Synod Battle." In years gone by The Lutheran Church—Missouri was the most orthodox of the three largest American Lutheran churches. Lindsell says that "across the years it has remained faithful to its tradition and part of that tradition had included a strong conviction that the Bible is the inerrant Word of God. But things have been changing in the Missouri Synod in recent years and the denomination is currently embroiled in a controversy that many have labelled a battle for ecclesiastical power. It is a war for the soul of the denomination and the control of it by parties of varying persuasions" (p. 72). Even though it is an ecclesiastical battle for control of the resources and control of the denomination, yet in the final analysis it is a theological struggle, "and the key doctrine in the struggle is biblical inerrancy, the historical-critical method, form and redaction criticism, etc., all have a role in the battle, but they are subsidiary. They simply express methodologies that are secondary to the primary question: is the Bible completely trustworthy in its entirety?" (p. 73).

Lindsell sets forth the position of The Lutheran Church-Missouri Synod as enunciated in *The Brief Statement of 1932*; a confessional statement which the 1947 Centennial Convention (held at Chicago) incorporated in the official proceedings. The first article of the *Brief Statement* reads:

1. We teach that Holy Scriptures differ from all other books in the world in that they are the Word of God. They are the Word of God because the holy men of God who wrote the Scriptures wrote only that which the Holy Ghost communicated to them by inspiration, 2 Tim. 3:16; 2 Pet. 1:21. We teach also that verbal inspiration of the Scriptures is not so-called "theological deduction," but that it is taught by direct statement of the Scriptures, 2 Tim. 3:16; John 10:35; Rom. 3:2; 1 Cor. 2:13. Since the Holy Scriptures are the Word of God it goes without saying that they contain no errors or contradictions, but that

363

they are in all their parts and words the infallible truth, also in those parts which treat of historical, geographical, and other secular matters. John 10:35.

Eventually in the 1950's and 1960's professors and pastors in the Lutheran Church-Missouri Synod began to attack this opening paragraph of the *Brief Statement.*

The Augsburg Confession, one of the primary symbols of all Lutheran Churches, does not have a statement dealing with the doctrines of Scripture. Many of the sections are not relevant today in the sense that they are in controversy as they were in the sixteenth century. There was no conflict between Luther and his followers and the Roman Catholic Church whether or not the Bible was inerrant and infallible. There was a serious difference however, about the Luther contention that **Scripture Alone (sola Scriptura)** was the source of religious authority. The Lutheran Church-Missouri Synod was following Luther and the authors of the Lutheran Confessions when it believed and taught and defended Scriptural inerrancy.

Lindsell examines the positions of a number of clergy of the Lutheran Church—Missouri Synod. He quotes Dr. Martin E. Marty of the Divinity School of the University of Chicago, editor of the liberal Christian Century, who wrote a pamphlet entitled "Lutheranism, a Restatement in Question and Answer Form." To the question: "Do not the Lutheran Confessions or creeds define Lutheranism?" he responded: "Indeed, they do, but they define it in a special way. In effect they say, "This we believe! and not 'This you must believe! It is true that some Lutherans use them to build fences, to rule heretics out and the orthodox in, to enforce loyalty." Where do Lutherans obtain their religious data?" He answered that this way:

Lutherans "yield to no other Christians in regard for its authority..." Lutherans believe that the Bible is divinely inspired, that in some special way God saw to it that the humans who wrote it, without stepping aside their own personality and style, imparted His own truth. They believe that it is "infallible" and unerring in its setting forth of all that one needs to be right with God; Scriptures will not mislead believers. Some Lutherans go a step further and speak of the Bible as being 'inerrant' in the sense that its details are unfailingly accurate even when they talk about matters of geography, of history, of 'science.' Most Lutherans do not begin with such statements, however, they adhere to the Bible because it brings them Jesus Christ and speaks with authority to them in matters of faith and hope (pp. 10-11).

Here the reader will find the new position in Missouri stated, namely, that the Bible cannot be trusted in all that it speaks about, but only in the area of Christology and soteriology. Marty has stated that he does not believe the Bible free from errors regarding history, geography or science.

Lindsell characterizes the Marty position as follows: "For if all other sources disagree with Scripture, then one must make the choice between belief in Scripture and belief in the sources that contradict it. It is here that Marty makes his neat distinction, one that is at the center of the

Missouri Synod's troubles" (p. 74). The Bible can be trusted for it will not mislead the reader relative to the plan of salvation. But at that point its reliability ceases (p. 74).

Lindsell claims, and correctly so, that for almost a century and a half the Missouri Synod has held the view of Biblical inerrancy and Scriptural infallibility. Another Missourian to challenge the historical position of his Synod is Paul G. Bretscher in his book *After the Purifying.*

Bretscher claims that the *Brief Statement* defines the Bible as the Word of God. That was the position of the majority in the Synod. However, he claims that there is a minority position, which holds "that the Word of God means the Spirit's proclamation of grace in Christ to sinners, and the Scriptures as the fountain and norm of that Word" (pp. 16-17).

The Missouri Synod's position that the Bible in its entirety is the Word of God and infallible is called by Bretscher "dross," which must be removed, which will be accomplished when the Synod will recognize that "the Word of God is Law and Gospel. Only that in the Bible that has to do with the Gospel and justification by faith is truly God's Word." Bretscher further claimed that Luther himself limited the concept of Word of God to Law and Gospel. Whatever, therefore, in the Bible does not have Christ in it, can and does contain error. Bretscher, as cited by Lindsell, represents a school of thought "which opposes inerrancy", understands "the inspiration, authority, and inerrancy of the Scriptures in terms of the Gospel. They found this understanding of the Word to be both Scriptural and Confessional." "The sum of it is this": says Lindsell, "Whatever has to do with the Gospel in the Bible is inspired and can be trusted; whatever does not have to do with the Gospel has error in it — it is not inerrant. This, of course, leaves it to those who hold this view to decide what parts of the Bible have to do with the Gospel and what parts do not. And it ends up assuming that whatever it is the individual wishes to disbelieve can be labelled as not part of the Gospel" (pp. 77-78 in *The Battle for the Bible*).

It is Lindsell's conviction that Bretscher does not understand Luther or has ignored many statements in which Luther has come out strongly for Biblical inerrancy. He also believes that if Bretscher, Marty and other Missourians cannot in conscience accept the historic position of the synod's doctrinal affirmation on inerrancy, they ought to be honest enough and withdraw from The Missouri Synod.

The position of Professor Walter E. Keller, of Valparaiso, on the historicity of Adam and Eve is cited, as expressed in *The Cresset*, which Keller rejects but claims it immaterial if a person denies that Adam and Eve were the parents of the human race, because such a view does not effect Law and Gospel. The historical data of the Bible may be challenged because Keller's theology "sees all the intention of Scripture in a Gospel understanding only, thereby making unimportant the historicity of the narrative described" (A quotation of Keller cited on page 80).

Tietjen at Concordia Seminary St. Louis
When President John Tietjen was president of Concordia Seminary,

St. Louis, he defended Professor Arlis Ehlen who adopted and taught that Exodus 14 contained the expansion account of what happened at the Red Sea (or the Sea of Reeds) and thereby questioned the historicity of the Mosaic account. In defending his position, when he denied the existence of angels, Ehlen wrote: "In this matter as in all others connected with Biblical exegesis, I am concerned to be totally faithful to the intention of the Divine Author. . . . I accept (in connection with the Red Sea crossing of the Israelites) what the Sacred writers evidently intended by their elaboration of the miraculous details; namely, to magnify the glory of God's great act of Salvation and to heighten its impact on those who hear in faith. In this case, too, my ultimate concern therefore, is to be faithful to the intended meaning of the Biblical text." This was accepted by Dr. Tietjen as acceptable, for he reported: "I have had a number of doctrinal discussions with Dr. Ehlen in recent months. In those discussions he has specifically affirmed the authority of Scripture in its entirety and in all its parts. He has stated that he affirms **the facticity of what Scripture intends to present as facts**" (Bold face supplied). The important item in this assertion is the word "intended." Lindsell asserted about Tietjen's acceptance of Ehlen's interpretation: "Both Ehlen and Tietjen knew and understood that by the use of this device they were saying they do not think 'that Scripture intends to present as fact what the clear sense of Scripture presents as a fact.' By this methodology, the historicity and facticity of anything in Scripture can be destroyed" (p. 81).

In Concordia Seminary, St. Louis, (prior to January 1974) dispute concerning the use of the historical-critical method was high on the agenda. Tietjen declared unabashedly that "it would be impossible to operate a Department of Exegetical Theology at a graduate school without the use of the historical-critical methodology." However, the same methodology was also used on the regular seminary level, prior to a student's beginning graduate study. Dr. Robert Preus, a professor for 17 years at the St. Louis, Concordia Seminary, before assuming the presidency of Concordia Theological Seminary, Springfield, IL (now Ft. Wayne) claimed that its use at St. Louis led to the rejection of many miracles, the temptation account, various details of the baptism of Jesus (including the descent of the dove and the voice of God from heaven.)

Some of the St. Louis Concordia exegetical professors (now with Seminex) claimed it was a neutral method. But this is not true. Professor Wenthe of Springfield stated that "the historical-critical method is not a neutral tool, but rather a very special instrument that is inseparable from its own presuppositions, procedures, and results. As one surveys the anti-supernaturalistic presuppositions, the secular procedures and the far-reaching results, it becomes obvious that a wedding between the bride and 'Lutheran presuppositions,' is as impossible as the marriage of light and darkness." This is also the verdict of Dr. Ladd of Fuller Seminary, who in an article published in **Interpretation** said: "The point we are stressing is that the historical-critical method denies the role of transcendence in the history of Jesus as well as in the Bible as a whole, not as a result of scientific study of the evidences, but because of its philosophical presuppositions about the nature of history... The historical-critical method excludes by definition that which I believe" (p. 82).

Lindsell also referred to the Walter Janzow Survey, the doctoral dissertation of the president of Concordia Teachers College, Seward, a dissertation accepted by the University of Nebraska toward a doctorate in sociology. Janzow made a study of Missouri's elite (professors, synodical officials and district presidents) the clergy and the laity. Eighty-nine percent of Missouri's laity fell within the upper range of theological orthodoxy; eighty-two per cent of Missouri's clergy were found there, but only sixty-nine percent of "elite," (including professors and teachers at the terminal schools) belonged there. Of the "elite" only fifty-one percent accepted the Bible as the inspired and inerrant Word of God as Missouri had defined inerrancy in *The Brief Statement*, whereas sixty-five percent of the parish clergy and eighty-three per cent of the laity. These statistics are indeed revealing!

The case in Missouri shows, what has been seen a number of times before that the defection from inerrancy begins at the theological seminaries. Professors do exercise a great influence on students. Lindsell claims that in the case of Missouri "it appears to have resulted from post graduate studies pursued by men trained in Missouri schools who secured doctorates in secular or liberal institutions. They were enamored of the historical-critical method, and numbers of them left their old moorings with respect to biblical infallibility. More frequently, than not, men with this kind of training did not go into the parish ministry, but headed for institutions where the possibility existed to disseminate this newfound learning among younger minds that could easily be influenced away from historic Missouri viewpoints" (p. 83).

Questions

1. The founding of Westminster Theological Seminary of Philadelphia was occasioned by ____.
2. Who wrote "Thy Word is Truth?"____
3. Why was the Regular Association of Regular Baptists formed? ____
4. Spurgeon was a staunch defender of ____.
5. The first Lutheran Church to question inerrancy was ____.
6. Who in the Lutheran Church-Missouri Synod affirmed the inerrancy of the Bible? ____
7. What does Lindsell write about the LCMS in more recent times? ____
8. There was no conflict between Luther and Rome about ____.
9. What did Martin Marty say about the inerrancy of the Bible? ____
10. What did Missourian Paul G. Bretscher challenge? ____
11. What did Walter Keller of Valparaiso University deny? ____
12. Arlis Ehlen questioned ____.
13. John Tietjen of Concordia Seminary, St. Louis ____ Ehlen's position.
14. Robert Preus claimed that the use of the historical-critical method in St. Louis led to ____.
15. What did the Walter Janzow survey show? ____
16. The defection from inerrancy begins at ____.

Part III

When President J. A. O. Preus became president of the Missouri Synod it seemed clear to him and many others that something would have to be done to stop this new type of indoctrination that was occurring at 801 De Mun Avenue, whose new president had been elected a few months before the Denver Convention of July 1969. A fact-finding committee found that false teaching was being propagated and the New Orleans Convention found the majority of the Concordia St. Louis faculty guilty of false teaching. Eventually Dr. Tietjen was found guilty by the Board of Control of having permitted the development of false teaching at St. Louis and he was legally removed. The majority of the faculty and the majority of the student body exiled itself from the campus and established a Seminary In Exile, known as Seminex.

In his battle with Dr. Preus and the conservatives in Missouri, he gained the support of the Association of Theological Schools on the excuse that academic liberty was at stake. Of this Lindsell writes: "This was a charade for even the Association has always agreed that every denomination has the right to decide what shall be taught at its institutions. To do this is theoretically an 'infringement of academic liberty, but it is the only safeguard that guarantee the integrity of a denomination.' Once the spurious claim of 'academic liberty' prevails, license then makes possible the propagation or viewpoints opposed to the denomination's standards. The result is suicidal" (p. 84).

Tietjen announced that the issue was not so much theological as ecclesiological. He claimed it was a struggle for the power of the denomination. Lindsell says that in a way this was the case. The Tietjen group planned on taking over the denomination but failed. Those who were trying to take Missouri down a road were halted by Preus and his supporters. But there was a great theological issue at stake. Two different theologies were being propounded and that group which controlled the Synod would have its theological stance to prevail.

In an article published in *Christianity Today* John Tietjen accused Dr. J.A.O. Preus of promoting the slogan: "They are taking your Bible away," as a smokescreen. However, he did admit that there were issues between his followers and those of Preus. Tietjen claimed the struggle was crucial for each soul was at stake. The former Concordia Seminary president (now president of Seminex) agrees with Bretscher when he writes: "The Word of God is the message of God's judgment and of his promise. Everything in the Bible is either a word of law that condemns or a word of promise that saves. In its proper sense the Word of God is good news about God in action to save. Preeminently the Word of God is good news about Jesus Christ himself." While Law and Gospel are the two central doctrines of the Bible, yet the Bible also includes everything else contained in the canonical Scriptures of the Old and New Testament.

In chapter 5 Lindsell takes up the situation in the Southern Baptist Convention, where he believes "probably 90 percent of the people in the pews believe in biblical infallibility. But in recent years the same thing has been happening at the Baptist seminaries in the Bible Belt and what had transpired at institutions of higher learning in the Lutheran Church — Missouri Synod. "Among faculty members of Southern Baptist colleges and seminaries where do you find articulate spokesmen coming out in favor of inerrancy. The silence is deafening!" (p. 208). Historically the Southern Baptists are supposed to be a creedless church. But they did take a definite stand on the Bible in the *New Hampshire Confession of Faith* in 1925. In this Confession of faith are articles on the Bible. It reads:

The Holy Bible was written by men divinely inspired and is the record of God's revelation of Himself to man. It is a perfect treasure of divine instruction. It has God for its author, salvation for its end, and truth, without any mixture of error, for its matter. It reveals the principles by which God judges us; and therefore is, and will remain to the end of the world, the true center of union, and the supreme standard by which all human conduct, creeds, and religious opinions should be tried. The criterion by which the Bible is to be interpreted is Jesus Christ.

Lindsell gives a number of examples of professors associated with various Southern Baptist seminaries who have questioned the inerrancy and infallibility of the Bible, because of the adoption of various forms of the higher critical method. Professors specifically cited and quoted from are Professors Robert S. Allen of the University of Richmond (p. 91), Dr. William, Hull, a long-time professor at Southern Baptist Seminary at Louisville (pp. 93-95), Dr. Howard P. Colson, editorial secretary of the Sunday School Board in *Outreach* questioned the inerrancy of the Bible. Lindsell also cites the case of the *Broadman Bible Commentary*, written by many men subscribing and promoting higher critical theories, which automatically requires rejection of the reliability and inerrancy of the Bible.

In chapter 6, "The Strange Case of Fuller Theological Seminary," Lindsell writes about a seminary in which he for a number of years was professor of missions. Fuller seminary was founded in 1947 through the efforts of Charles E. Fuller of the "Old Revival Hour." Harold John Ockenga was its first president. The following constituted the faculty: Wilbur M. Smith, Everett F. Harrison, Carl F. H. Henry, and Harold Lindsell. It did not begin with a statement of faith, which was left to the faculty to formulate. It took a number of years before this statement was finished and in time a number of new faculty were added. With the addition of Bela Vasady the first theological eruption took place in the history of Fuller. When the theological statement of the faculty was complete, this was its position on the Bible: "The books which form the canon of the Old and New Testaments as originally given are plenary inspired and free from all error in the whole and in the part. These books constitute the written Word of God, the only infallible rule of faith and practice" (p. 107). Lindsell believes this was a strong statement and would include freedom from error in matters of fact, science, history, and chronology as well as in matters having to do with salvation. Each year every faculty member was required to sign the statement on biblical inerrancy. Bela Vasady could not do this and left the faculty.

With 1962 there came a crisis when it became apparent that a number of board of control and faculty members did not subscribe to this position. C. David Weyehauser, a wealthy layman who underwrote the operating budget of Fuller, came out for Biblical fallibility and opposed total inerrancy (p. 108). When two faculty members indicated they did not subscribe to the seminary's original statement on inerrancy the board did nothing. Another contributing factor to the reversal on Biblical inerrancy which occurred at this conservative seminary was the appointment of Daniel Fuller, son of the Charles E. Fuller, as dean of the faculty. Young Fuller had studied at Basel under Karl Barth and has been influenced by him. Before going to Switzerland he had held to Biblical inerrancy but after his return he came with a changed position. He encouraged the hiring of a former graduate of Fuller, a friend of his who also had studied at Basel and did not accept Biblical inerrancy, and that man's name was Calvin Schoonhoven. Although he did not believe in total inerrancy, he was appointed to the faculty.

Another development in "the strange case of Fuller Seminary" was the appointment of David A. Hubbard, a member of Westmont College, Santa Barbara. At the time he was hired he was embroiled in a controversy over a syllabus for the Old Testament authored by Hubbard and Robert Laurin, setting forth teachings different from historic Christianity. They included matters like the non-historicity of Adam and Eve, and Wellhausen approach to the Pentateuch, the late dating of Daniel and other points. The offensive parts had been written by Laurin, but were defended by Hubbard.

In chapter 6, pp. 110-121, Lindsell gives a complete picture of the fact that the president, the dean of the seminary, George Ladd, outstanding New Testament scholar, Paul King Jewett have all given up complete and total infallibility. The influence of neo-orthodoxy is clear in the case of a number of faculty members.

In chapter 7, "Other Denominations and Parachurch Groups" Lindsell shows the same departure from traditional and historical Scriptural inerrancy taking place in North Park Theological Seminary, the only theological school of the Evangelical Covenant Church of America. From there the editor of *Christianity Today* traces the start of theological erosion in the Evangelical Theological Society, the American Scientific Affiliation, followed by the Wenham Conference on Scripture and finally the case of the Free University of Amsterdam.

Chapter 8 treats "Deviations that Follow When Inerrancy is Denied." It is Lindsell's contention that the doctrine of Scripture inerrancy was hardly noticed in church history because it was not attacked. "It was not seriously challenged since the New Testament was written, any more than the inerrancy of the Old Testament was challenged before and during Jesus' day" (p. 141). However in the United States the struggle began in the 1880's and the chief debaters were Warfield, Hodge, Briggs, and Smith. The next period in which this struggle was repeated was fought during the 1930's with the name of J. Gresham Machen prominent in this battle for the Bible's inerrancy. The third period is the one right now, during which a battle is going on in a number of denominations.

In chapter 8 Lindsell shows what has happened once the doctrine of the Bible's inerrancy is surrendered. The Unitarian Universalist denomination is the "grossest illustration" when this important teaching is given up, which occurred in New England in the last Century. This denomination came out of Trinitarian Congregationalism. Then the 1967 poll of NCC delegates found analyzed in an article entitled "The New-Time Religion." This poll gave convincing evidence as to what happens when the complete inerrancy of the Bible is surrendered.

Lindsell claims that "it is not unfair to allege that among denominations like Episcopal, United Methodist, United Presbyterian, United Church of Christ, The Lutheran Church in America there is not one single theological seminary that takes a stand in favor of biblical infallibility" (p. 145). He further cites the case of Bishop Pike, the action taken by the Episcopalian Lambeth Conference, the situation of Lutheranism in the U.S. as shown by the evidence in *A Study of Generations*, the New Confession of The United Presbyterian Church, the United Church of Christ, The United Methodist Church, the views of Scripture of William Barclay, Archbishop Temple, The Barclay-Bruce Commentary all of which show a new anti-biblical position over against the historical position on inerrancy of Lutheranism, and the various church bodies classified as Protestant.

Chapter 9 of Lindsell's book deals with "Discrepancies in Scripture." The alleged discrepancies of the Bible are the basis for rejecting Biblical inerrancy. The problem of Bible difficulties and seeming contradictions cannot be dismissed with a wave of the hand. However, Lindsell contends that he does not consider them a threat to Biblical infallibility nor does he hold that these constitute an insuperable problem. Concerning this he writes:

I can say, however, that a multitude of what formerly were difficulties have been solved, so that detractors have had to back water again and again. But as each apparent discrepancy is resolved, another objection is raised. Although in hundreds of cases criticisms of them have been shown to be unfounded, those who refuse to believe in inerrancy never seem to be satisfied. Why is this so? Does it not constitute a frame of mind that wants to disbelieve? (p. 161).

Lindsell discusses a number of alleged errors that have been cleared by archaeology or by a sound method of Biblical interpretation. He refers to men endeavoring to break down the reliability of the Scriptures especially Robert Mounce's "Clues to Understanding Biblical Accuracy," which he proceeds to answer.

Chapter 10 shows what happens when the Bible's inerrancy and reliability is challenged; ultimately it leads to the denial of other Biblical teachings. Lindsell begins this chapter with this assertion: "History affords notable examples of institutions and denominations that have gone astray. At times it is not easy to perceive how this happened. The trend away from orthodoxy may be slow in movement, gradual in its scope, and almost invisible to the naked eye. When people awaken to what has happened it is too late" (p. 185). "Theological aberrations, like cancer, begin as a small and seemingly insignificant blemish, but when it is left it grows and spreads. One of the classic cases of a theological disease that overtook an institution is that of the liberalism that took over Union Theological Seminary in New York" (p. 185).

Charles Augustus Briggs, famous Old Testament scholar, who obtained his doctorate from a German university in 1889, in a volume entitled. *Whither? A Theological Question for the Times*, went hammer and tongs against Biblical inerrancy. Briggs went after Hodge, Warfield and Patton over inerrancy, men who were members of the Princeton faculty. Briggs became the virulent proponent of a negative type of higher criticism. In this book Briggs wrote: "There can be no doubt that recent criticisms have considerably weakened the evidence for miracles and predictive prophecy. To many minds it would be easier to believe in the inspiration of the Scriptures and the divinity of Jesus Christ if there is no such thing as Miracles and Prediction in the sacred Scriptures" (p. 187).

To those individuals in Christendom today and in American Lutheranism who are willing to be permissive or allow anti-Scriptural views to be promoted, a statement of Briggs from this book might be quoted: "The more conflict the better. Battle for the truth is infinitely better than stagnation in error. Every error should be slain as soon as possible. If it be our error we should be most anxious to get rid of it. Error is our greatest foe ... Truth is the most precious possession."

Briggs stirred up a hornet's nest in the Presbyterian church and eventually he was tried for heresy with the New York Presbytery acquitting Briggs of the heresy charges, but the General Assembly of the Presbyterian Church in 1893 excommunicated Briggs for heresy.

Union Seminary separated from the Presbyterian Church in 1892 and embarked upon a path which was to see this seminary become the most radical seminary in the United States. The theological seminary is the place where usually the theology, beliefs and practice of a church body are determined. This has happened in so many cases and at different times in the United States.

The history of Union Seminary since the days of Briggs is interesting as to what it reveals. The theological position of Briggs as compared with the present theological stance of Union Seminary would be considered orthodox. This shows that once an institution has given up Scriptural infallibility and inerrancy, it goes from one theological aberration to another.

Throughout the years Union Seminary, a very heavily endowed seminary, has had a great influence on the churches in the world. In one respect it has failed miserably in terms of what Briggs claimed was essential, namely in its failure to evangelize the masses, something for which Briggs called. Tillich, Niebuhr and Bennett have exercised a great influence on many theological students who in turn have affected the theological views of thousands of people. Harry Emerson Fosdick, professor of homiletics at Union and pastor of the influential Riverside Church, denied every fundamental truth of the Apostles' Creed.

William Sloan Coffin, Jr., Robert McAfee Brown, both known for radical views and actions, were affiliated with Union Seminary. John Tietjen, the former president of Concordia Seminary, St. Louis, is a Th. D. graduate of Union.

The Conclusion of the Book

In chapter 11, Lindsell summarizes what has been given in the previous 199 pages of this controversial volume. The book purports to be a strong apologetic for the doctrine of Biblical inerrancy. It is the book author's conviction that "evangelical Christianity is engaged in the greatest battle of its history. The central issue at stake in this battle is epistemological: it has to do with the basis of our religious knowledge. Does the knowledge come from reason, the church, or from the Bible?" (p. 200).

After briefly recapitulating what has happened in conservative denomination, Lindsell makes his final appeal. He does not deny that individuals can be evangelical relatively speaking, but in a technical sense no person can lay claim to the evangelical badge who denies Biblical inerrancy, no more than a person can claim to be evangelical who denies the virgin birth of Christ, His deity, the vicarious atonement, or Christ's resurrection from the dead. Like the doctrines just enumerated, the doctrine of Biblical inerrancy guarantees these other doctrines.

Lindsell appeals to those evangelicals who have moved away from total Biblical inerrancy to partial inerrancy to rethink their position on this important Christian teaching. He does not doubt that a person can be a Christian if he does not accept complete reliability of the Word of God. But he contends that there are pitfalls down the road for those supporting partial inerrancy which eventually will have Christological implications.

The appeal to evangelicals still holding total Biblical inerrancy is to continue to adhere to it as well as to defend it. "I urge you to contend for the faith once delivered to the saints. I urge you to dialogue with evangelicals who sit on the fence or have capitulated. I urge you take whatever action is needed to secure a redress of this situation" (p. 210).

That a new day would dawn for the Christian Church if it were to return to this traditional understanding of this doctrine so largely given up by liberal and neo-orthodox churches, Lindsell does not doubt for a moment. "I can foresee, in that event, a new surge of spiritual power, a new advance in the task of evangelizing the world where Christ is honored, the true Gospel preached, and the kingdom of God manifested in holy power before the eyes of unconverted men. May the Lord speed that day!" (p. 211).

Questions
1. The LCMS's 1973 convention in New Orleans found ____.
2. Tietjen announced that the issue was really a struggle for ____.
3. What did Lindsell say about the Southern Baptist Convention? ____
4. What happened at Fuller Theological Seminary? ____

5. A young Fuller was influenced by ____.
6. What happened once inerrancy was surrendered? ____
7. How many seminaries in denominations like Episcopal, United Methodist, United Presbyterian, United Churches of Christ, and the Lutheran Church in America take a stand on biblical infallibility? ____
8. Briggs of Union Seminary became ____.
9. What happened at Union Seminary in New York? ____
10. Harry Emerson Fosdick denied ____.
11. Tietjen earned his Th.D. at ____.
12. Lindsell wrote that evangelical Christianity is engaged in ____.

Part IV

II. Reactions To Harold Lindsell's Book
The Battle For The Bible
Published by Zondervan Publishing House,
Grand Rapids, 1976. 218 pp.

That those individuals and institutions who have come under attack in Lindsell's book should respond was of course to be expected. Other individuals who are not mentioned in the book but who have surrendered Biblical inerrancy and Biblical trustworthiness, have also been attacking Lindsell's position and arguments. In the following the rebuttals of a number of theologians and scholars who have responded since the publication of *The Battle for the Bible* will be given together with an evaluation of their criticisms made against Biblical inerrancy and Biblical infallibility.

1. Dr. David Hubbard As Spokesman For
Himself And Fuller Theological Seminary
Dr. David Hubbard, president of Fuller Theological Seminary, whose views on the nature of the Bible were given and criticized by Lindsell (pp. 109, 121), reacted against Lindsell's book in a twofold manner. First, Hubbard addressed a letter on April 5, 1976 to the Fuller faculty in which he made suggestions for the defense of Fuller's stance on the Bible and also put forth counter arguments against those advanced by Lindsell. Secondly, in a convocation in behalf of Fuller's attitude toward the Bible, Hubbard responded before a large audience. *Christianity Today* has reported the essence of Hubbard's rebuttal.[1] One of the dangers of the editor of *Christianity Today*'s book according to Hubbard is that it destroys the unity among evangelicals.[2]

This assertion of Hubbard raises the question: How much unity is there among evangelicals, when the term "evangelical" covers a broad spectroscope of theological opinion, including adherents of Calvinism, Arminianism and Pentecostalism. If Lutherans are placed under this umbrella, then another set of theological differences is being added. Since

374

there are many theological differences among the various denominations and individuals who might be labelled "evangelical" and since there is only unity on a limited number of doctrines, one less would not radically change the situation. Except in the case of the rejection of Biblical inerrancy the whole structure of Christian doctrine is placed in jeopardy because of the alignment of the proponents of limited inerrancy and limited infallibility with the historical-critical method. If Lindsell's view on inspiration is inadequate then it must be also noted that the founder's view of Fuller, Charles E. Fuller, was also inadequate because Lindsell, one of the original faculty members of Fuller, held the same view advocated by Charles Fuller. This would be one of those numerous instances where theological seminaries departed from the theological stance of the founder or founders of their respective institutions. Unity at all costs is the principle now followed by Hubbard, even though a traditional doctrine of historic Christianity is being surrendered.

Hubbard stated in his convocation "that Fuller Seminary is committed to the uniqueness and full inspiration of the Bible," however, "with the realization that it is the Word of God given to us in the context of human language, human culture, and human history. It is the only infallible standard by which our Christian thinking and Christian living must be judged."[3] This sounds very good but as Hubbard continued his address he shows how he understands the words "in the context of human language, human culture, and human history." The purpose of the scholarship at Fuller has as its purpose "not to destroy but to build up. It is not to lay bare the humanity of the Bible, but to expose the way in which the Spirit of God used the humanity of the Scriptures in order to bring us his truth." Hubbard further asserted that his seminary needed to affirm more consistently and effectively what it is to believe and learn from responsible critics and be open to review and renewal.[4]

Lindsell in his chapter on Fuller Seminary and Hubbard's activity in it has shown precisely what Hubbard means by learning from "responsible critics." Lindsell claims that Hubbard supported the Documentary Hypothesis, the rejection of Adam and Eve, the second century date of Daniel and other critical issues held and advocated by Professor Laurin.[5] Hubbard's article on "The Pentateuch" in *The New Bible Dictionary* presents all the views held in the last 1900 years on the Pentateuch. He gave a good overview of the various critical theories but does not speak adversely about the Pentateuchal views that contradict the Old Testament assertions on Mosaic authorship or those of the New Testament. In fact, he wrote: "Whatever the origin of the Pentateuch, it now stands as a document possessing a rich inner unity." He gives the impression that the erroneous and anti-Scriptural positions of critical scholars are acceptable.

Hubbard attacks Lindsell's book as being "a rehash of the outdated nineteenth century issues."[7] The issues that were fought over in the nineteenth century were over the nature of the Bible as inspired and inerrant Word of God and over the adoption of higher critical views on Mosaic authorship, Isaianic authorship, Danielic authorship, the integrity of Biblical books, the nature of Biblical prophecy, miracles, inspiration, revelation, and accommodation to pagan Near Eastern literature. This assertion of Hubbard tells people precisely where the latter stands and why he cannot appreciate Lindsell's criticisms. Lindsell is correct when he claims that the denial of Biblical inerrancy goes hand in hand with the adoption of the historical-critical method.[8]

2. Pinnock's Criticism Of Lindsell

That Pinnock should disagree with Lindsell comes as a shock and disappointment, because he wrote books and journal articles in defense of Biblical inerrancy and Biblical infallibility. In recent years Pinnock has been a strong defender of Biblical inerrancy. In 1967 the Presbyterian and Reformed Publishing House issued his *A Defense of Biblical Infallibility*. In 1973 there was held a "Conference on the Inspiration and Authorship of Scripture," at Ligonier, Pennsylvania, at which the following scholars read papers: John Warwick Montgomery, J. I. Packer, John H. Gerstner, John M. Frame, Peter R. Jones and R. C. Sproul. Their essays were published as *God's Inerrant Word: An International Symposium on the Trustworthiness of Scripture*, edited by John Warwick Montgomery (Minneapolis: Bethany Fellowship, Inc., 1973, 288 pp.) These seven scholars signed the following statement, called "The Ligonier Statement," which read as follows:

We believe the Holy Scriptures of the Old and New Testament to be the inspired and inerrant Word of God: We hold the Bible, as originally given through human agents of revelation, to be infallible and see this as a crucial article of faith with implications for the entire life and practice of all Christian people. With the great fathers of Christian history we declare our confidence in the total trustworthiness of the Scriptures, urging that any view which imputes to them a lesser degree of inerrancy than total, is in conflict with the Bible's self-testimony in general and with the teaching of Jesus Christ in particular. Out of the obedience to the Lord of the Church we submit ourselves unreservedly to his authoritative view of Holy Writ.[9]

According to *Christianity Today*, Dr. Pinnock recently published his "Inspiration and Authority: A Truce Proposal for the Evangelicals," in which its author states that "in an attempt to heal the breach, which I have in the past myself have helped to create, I am setting forth an irenical position which could minister reconciliation."[10]

How does Pinnock propose to effect reconciliation? Answer: By making concessions and questioning whether or not the Bible teaches its own inerrancy. Now is that not a compromise that is tantamount to throwing the baby away with the bathwater! Such a stance amounts to repudiation of the Ligonier statement! In trying to act as would-be mediator and reconciler he refers to the fact that Harrison quoted Francis Patton to the effect that one need not believe that the Bible taught its own inerrancy and total reliability. He would permit freedom in this area; a person may hold inerrancy but if not persuaded of this fact, he may hold errancy. How can a theological teaching be true and not true at the same time? If the Bible is not errorless but errant then that person is wrong who holds Holy Scripture to be errorless. In that case, a man teaching and promoting facts about the Bible which are false would be sinning and misleading people. When scholars, following the historical-critical method, teach errancy they automatically repudiate inerrancy and vice versa, those scholars promoting inerrancy automatically reject errancy and the unreliability of the Scriptures in all areas where they have spoken and where they have been placed under a cloud.

The interpretation of the Holy Scriptures will be different depending on which of these positions is adhered to. How can the two be united, unless it matters not what a person teaches and what he sets forth on the teachings regarding salvation, eschatology, Christology, the relations of the testaments to each other, the authorship of canonical books, the Christocentricity of the Bible, fulfilled prophecy and other Biblical topics.

Pinnock claims that the use of the term "inerrancy" requires major modifications almost as soon as it is uttered, and we should shy away from terms with this "liability." There are many doctrines held traditionally by the church from which many people shy because they cause people to be offended. For example, the doctrine of original sin, the teaching that all men and women are guilty before God as sinners because of original sin. Why should people be considered guilty even before they have committed an actual sin? It does not appear fair, says the natural man, and so many people, pastors and theologians refuse to accept this Biblical teaching and especially that because of this sinful condition infants must be regenerated by the waters of baptism.

Or how about the Biblical doctrine of predestination? The Scriptures teach that if a person is saved it is because he has been predestined by grace in Christ before the foundation of the world and that man can do nothing toward saving himself. The same Bible also teaches that if people are lost, it is because of their having rejected God's offer of salvation. Many cannot harmonize these teachings and so reject them. Lutherans have held these clear assertions of the Bible, despite the difficulty of harmonizing them to the satisfaction of modern logic. Lutherans do not take the position that one can hold views different from those clearly enunciated in the Word of God.

Pinnock in his most recent article further argues against inerrancy as a viable and useful term because "there are several disadvantages with the term as well. First, inerrancy does not describe the Bible we actually use. It is so strict a term that it can refer only to the lost autographs. Second, just because it points to a text we do **not** have, it fails to assert forcibly the authority of the text we **do** have. Third, by its very nature inerrancy directs attention at once to the small difficulties in the text rather than to the infallible truth of its intended proclamation. Finally, it has become the slogan of the one of the parties in the discussion we have been reviewing, and serve to exacerbate the conflict and ill-feeling."[12]

Because those employing some form of the historical-critical method, by means of which they are forced to find contradictions in the Bible, the writer contends that this may account for the following position of Pinnock who claims:

It seems to me, in view of the serious disadvantages the term inerrancy presents, that we ought to suspend it from the lists of preferred terminology for stating the evangelical doctrine of Scripture, and let it appear only in the midst of working out details. It is sufficient for us in public statements to affirm the divine inspiration and final authority of the Bible.[12a]

In response to these criticisms of inerrancy it should be noted that conservatives who defend Biblical inerrancy and Biblical infallibility never have argued for the inerrancy of the text transmitted in the manuscripts copied by many different scribes. Since, we do not possess the autographs, how can the opponents of inerrancy argue that the original text was not errorless and not completely reliable in all of its statements, whether pertaining to doctrine, geography, history and science? If the autographic text of the Old and New Testament Scriptures contained errors and contradictions, what criterion in the Bible is indicated for distinguishing the chaff from the wheat in God's Word?

The prefatory statement of the editor of the series of which Pinnock's book, *A Defense of Biblical Infallibility*, is a part can be cited relative to the alleged difficulty of the non-existence of the autographic text in answering Pinnock's objection to inerrancy:

First, an inerrant, infallible autograph is the only view of the original Scriptures which accords with the nature of God of Christian theism. A holy God, in whom is no darkness and who cannot lie, could not inspire men to write less than a perfect account of the revelation received from Him. Nor would the writer's finiteness and sinfulness, all the modern sophisticated objections to the contrary notwithstanding, prove to be insurmountable obstacles to such a task, one must conclude that precisely that kind of revelation — an inerrant, infallible one — was given to man in the original words of the Bible.[13]

Reymond further contends that in the second place:

An inerrant, infallible autograph is the only sourcebook which can yield **incontestable truth**. Presumably, the entire theological enterprise in all of its investigations and research is pressing ultimately for incontestable truth. To arrive at this goal, the orthodox theologian, by utilizing the very best aids in textual criticism establishes a trustworthy text. Next by rigorously applying the most accurate rules of hermeneutics, he determines the meaning of the text. Now if the autograph underlying this scientifically established, correctly interpreted text itself is infallible the meaning derived by means of these two steps would be the objective truth. It would only remain for the pastor and teacher to convey this truth in a relevant way to needy men.[14]

However, at the same time Reymond claims:

The theologian who would deny the infallibility of the autographs, however, after moving through exactly similar steps and arriving at precisely the same meaning of the autographs, must press on to a

378

third step, namely, the effort to determine whether the meaning he has arrived at is true or not, an effort would obviously be controlled by alien presuppositions grounded in pure subjectivism.[15]

Why a scholar like Pinnock, who wrote so strongly and forcibly on Biblical inerrancy and who has written such an excellent book, *Biblical Revelation - The Foundation of Christian Theology* (Chicago; Moody Press, 256 pp.) has proceeded to undermine his own writings, is puzzling as to what kind of motives would be the cause for reversing himself on a critical theological issue!

Footnotes

1. *Christianity Today*, May 7. 1976
2. **Ibid.**
3. **Ibid.**
4. **Ibid.**
5. Harold Lindsell, *The Battle for the Bible* (Grand Rapids: Zondervan Publishing House, 1976). pp. 109-110.
6. D. A. Hubbard. "Pentateuch." in J.D. Douglas, *The New Bible Dictionary* (Grand Rapids: Wm. B. Eerdmans Publishing Company, 1962), p 964.
7. *Christianity Today*, **op. cit.**,
8. Lindsell, **op. cit.**, p. 204.
9. John Warwick Montgomery, editor. *God's Inerrant Word: An International Symposium on the Trustworthiness of Scripture* (Minneapolis: Bethany Fellowship, Inc., 1974), p. 7.
10. As reported in *Christian News*, May 10. 1976, p. 16.
11. As given in "Neo-Evangelical Dislike 'Inerrancy'," in *Christian News*, May 10, 1976.
12. **Ibid.**
12a. **Ibid.**
13. Robert L. Reymond, editor's preface in Clark H. Pinnock, *A Defense of Biblical Infallibility* (Philadelphia: Presbyterian and Reformed Publishing Company, 1967), p. v.
14. **Ibid.**, pp. v-vi.
15. **Ibid.**, p. vi.

Questions

1. Hubbard of Fuller Seminary supported ____.
2. "The Ligonier Statement" said ____.
3. What happened to Clark Pinnock? ____

Part V

3. Carl F. Henry's Attack On Lindsell's Book

One of the colleagues of Lindsell at Fuller Seminary, when it originally was organized, was Carl. F. H. Henry, who therefore, must have been one of the faculty members who was in favor of and in sympathy with the position as set forth in the earliest statement of belief of this seminary, founded by a man who believed in the verbal and plenary inspiration of the Bible and of its inerrancy and infallibility. It therefore, comes as a great surprise and disappointment that Henry has come out against the views of Lindsell. In a book review of Lindsell's *The Battle for the Bible*, written for Volume I, No. 1 of *The New Review of Books and Religion* (published by the Seabury Press and Book Service, 815 Second Avenue, New York, N.Y.) Henry is critical of Lindsell's book.

Henry finds fault with Lindsell's book on a number of counts. His first criticism is stated as follows:

What needs equally to be emphasized — and here Lindsell fails us — is the vast multitude of scholars, clergy, and laymen in all circles who still hold firmly to a fully authoritative and inerrant Bible. This remains indubitably the case in the National Association of Evangelicals, the American Council of Christian Churches, in large pockets of laymen, and among clergy in the ecumenically-related denominations than is sometimes thought.[16]

In retort to Henry one might legitimately ask why Lindsell should report the number of individuals and institutions adhering to Biblical inerrancy when that is not the main concern of Lindsell's book? The truth of the matter is that the main-line Protestant denominations' seminaries have given up Biblical infallibility. Among Lutheran seminaries only the two Concordias of the Lutheran Church — Missouri Synod still hold it, one small unofficial seminary of the ALC, Bethany Lutheran Seminary of The Evangelical Lutheran Synod and the seminary of The Wisconsin Evangelical Lutheran Synod at Mequon, Wisconsin. Among Protestant seminaries still holding to Biblical-inerrancy are Covenant Seminary of St. Louis, Dallas Theological Seminary of Dallas, Texas, Talbot of California, Trinity of Deerfield, Illinois and Westminster of Philadelphia. In France the Faculte Libre de Theologie Reformee; in Germany Bibelschule Bergstrasse are the relatively few institutions still holding Biblical inerrancy. But this represents a small percentage of Protestant seminaries and departments of theology still adhering to a stance once generally held. To this might also be added the change in Roman Catholicism where there has occurred a redefining of what is involved in Biblical inerrancy and Biblical infallibility, which is no longer the traditional Roman Catholic position on this theological issue. Lindsell's concern is legitimate when one considers what the churches once believed compared with the present situation and time now when Biblical inerrancy and Biblical infallibility are redefined as to amount to an abandonment and rejection of this once-believed teaching.

Henry further contends against Lindsell that the Bible does not expressly teach its own inerrancy. Henry complains about *The Battle for the Bible* as follows: "But he presents no relevant texts; in fact, scriptural documentation is conspicuously absent for many of his claims."[18]

Henry is correct that the Bible does not teach its inerrancy if the requirement would be a statement such as: "The Bible in all its parts is infallible and inerrant." However, doctrines are established in two ways: 1. by a direct and clear statement of the text; or 2. by inference from various passages. Lindsell devoted chapter 2 (pp. 28-40) to showing the inerrancy and infallibility of the Holy Scriptures. Everett F. Harrison, who together with Lindsell, Wilbur Smith and Carl Henry constituted the original Fuller faculty, in an article appearing in *Christianity Today* (C. F. Henry, editor), entitled "Criteria of Bible Inerrancy," began his contribution with this assertion: "Inerrancy is not a formally stated claim on their own behalf. It is rather an inference that devout students of the Word have made from the teaching of the Bible about its own inspiration. If the Spirit of God has really wrought in the production of this Book from start to finish, it is hard to conceive error, save such as may have crept into the text in the course of transmission."[19]

Lindsell cites the following Bible passages in support of his stand that the inspiration of the Scriptures by God is a doctrine and that a book that claims to be entirely God-given is not consonant with the claim that God inspired mistakes, errors and contradictions: 2 Timothy 3:16,17; 2 Peter 1:21; I Thess. 2:13; I Cor. 14:37; John 10:35.

Down throughout the Christian centuries, beginning with Jesus Himself, men have believed in the inerrancy and reliability of the Scriptures. Frederick C. Grant, a critical scholar, stated in *An Introduction to the New Testament*, about the scriptures as follows:

Everywhere it is taken for granted that what is written in scripture is the work of divine inspiration, and it is therefore trustworthy, infallible, and inerrant. The scripture must be "fulfilled" (Luke 22:37). What was written for our instruction (Rom. 15:4; I Cor. 10:11); what is described or related in the Old Testament is unquestionably true. No New Testament writer would dream of questioning a statement contained in the Old Testament, though then exact manner or mode of its inspiration is nowhere stated explicitly.[20]

This is the assertion of a critical scholar who does not believe himself bound by Scriptural teaching. But he does accurately enunciate the position of the Scriptures concerning its inerrancy and infallibility.

The 19th century theological giant Benjamin Warfield wrote concerning the Scripturalness of the church's historic position on inerrancy as follows:

We do not adopt the doctrine of the plenary inspiration of the Bible on sentimental grounds, nor even, as we have already had occasion to remark **on a priori** grounds of whatever kind. We adopt it specifically because it is taught us as truth by Christ and His apostles, in the Scriptural record of their teaching, and the evidence for its truth is, therefore, as we have already pointed out, precisely that evidence, in weight and amount, which vindicates for us the trustworthiness of Christ, and His apostles as teachers of doctrine.[21]

Father Burtschaell, a contemporary Roman Catholic scholar who does not espouse Scriptural inerrancy, has, however, stated in his monograph. *Catholic Theories of Biblical Inspiration Since 1810,* that Biblical inerrancy was the doctrine of the early Christians:

Christians early inherited from the Jews the belief that the biblical writers were somehow possessed by God, who was thus reckoned the

381

Bible's proper author. Since God could not conceivably be the agent of falsehood, the Bible must be guaranteed free from error. For centuries this doctrine lay dormant as doctrine will: accepted by all, pondered by few. Not until the 16th century did inspiration and its corollary. Inerrancy, come up for sustained review. The Reformers and Counter-Reformers were disputing whether all revealed truth was in Scripture alone, and whether it could dependably be interpreted by private or official scrutiny. Despite radical disagreement on these issues both groups persevered in receiving the Bible as a compendium of inerrant oracles dictated by the Spirit. Only in the 19th century did a succession of empirical disciplines newly come of age begin to put a succession of inconvenient queries to exegetes. First, geology and paleontology discredited the view of the cosmos and the cosmogony of Genesis. Next, archaeology suggested that there were serious historical discrepancies in the sacred narrative. Later, as parallel oriental literatures began to be recovered, much of Scripture lay under accusation of plagiarism from pagan sources. Literary criticism of the text itself disclosed that the writers had free tampered with their materials and often escalated myth and legend into historical event. After all this, considerable dexterity was required of any theologian who was willing to take account of the accumulation of challenging evidence, yet continued to defend the Bible as the classic and inerrant Word of God.[22]

Another change levelled against Linsell's book is that its author "repudiates historical-method and as irreconcilable with evangelical commitments; by implications he requires its expulsion from evangelical institutions. Happily, this view will be rejected by most evangelical scholars any unhistorical alternative will cripple rather than strengthen biblical faith."[23]

In defense of Lindsell we may say that the latter has shown what the results are when the historical-critical method is employed in preference to the historical-grammatical method. Any person who practices the historical-critical method the way it is commonly understood and utilized, is forced to reject many of the factual statements of the Bible. The practitioners of the historical-critical method, who use a radical type of literary criticism, form criticism, redaction criticism and content criticism, cannot possibly hold to the reliability, inerrancy and trustworthiness of Holy Writ. The practitioners of the historical-critical method question clear statements of the Scriptures, reject its assertions as untrue, depict the various books as having many contradictions (many created by the method being employed), conflicting theologies and as replete with errors and contradictions. If Henry is defending the historical-critical method as employed by liberal scholars, it is not difficult to see why he would oppose this book! Lindsell has shown the intimate relationship between the use of the historical-critical method and the surrender of Biblical inerrancy together with other devastating results for the doctrines of historic Christianity.

Henry is also disturbed by Lindsell's coupling "dire warning with strange contradictions and evangelistic overstatements that threaten Lindsell's good intention to be objective and irenic." This reviewer would see Lindsell's book as a contribution to the subject of Biblical apologetics, and considers it a defense of a vital doctrine against the attacks of its detractors and abandoners. It is difficult to see why this book needs to be irenical when so much is at stake, when errancy is defended as characterizing the Bible, which Lindsell's believes belittles the Word of God.

Toward the end of his critical review Henry makes the revealing concession of the importance of Lindsell's apologetic effort, when he states:

"In what the author affirms as the central issue, he is unquestionably right: the evangelical camp has been steadily infiltrated by an aberrant view of scripture. This process of erosion has not been arrested, although most evangelicals on the move from inerrancy have as yet not made concessions beyond the errant scripture.[24] (Bold face supplied)

Henry does not believe that Lindsell's book will appeal to non-evangelicals, and how persuasive it will be for evangelicals waits to be seen. He concludes his book review with these words: "A Bible unencumbered with some of his theories and standing on its own invulnerable supports may be far more powerful than one propped up by retaining wails engineered by resolute evangelicals."[25] In his book Lindsell has tried to show that inerrancy is the only view that does justice to the claims of the Bible and anything less is not true to the Bible's claim of being the Word of God, Who does not lie or deceive as men often do. If the Bible and the religion its sets forth needs no defense and explanation, then Henry's many excellent books in the field of Christian apologetics and doctrine were unnecessary, one can turn the argument against Lindsell's effort upon Henry's writings that the Bible needs no defense but is able to hold its own against all attacks and against all detractors.

Henry in one of his most recent books, *Evangelicals in Search of Identity* has given another reason,[26] not so clearly spelled out in the book review article to which has just been alluded. It had been Henry's hope in 1948 or even earlier that Protestantism might become a great force in America by its influence on society and culture. As Henry surveys the last thirty years of American evangelicalism he is disappointed that the dreams he had envisioned for American Protestantism or evangelicalism had not been realized. Twenty-five years ago the evangelical movement was supposedly like a caged lion ready to be loosed and exercise its power on the American scene, but lo, the lion did not know which way to go, and now supposedly is in great danger of losing his potential power. According to Henry American evangelicalism has squandered its heritage over questions of **social concern and Biblical inerrancy**.[26]

Chapter 5 of this book is entitled: "Conflict over Biblical Inerrancy." Henry began this chapter like this: "The issue of inerrancy is today dividing evangelicals into ever more rigidly competitive camps."[27] He believes that the Wenham (Gordon) Conference was a kind of turning point in the inerrancy controversy, where at a meeting of reputable theologians unanimity could not be reached, with evangelical scholars ranged on both sides of the inerrancy/errancy issue. This conference was held in 1966. The former editor of *Christianity Today* agrees with Lindsell about the situation concerning the rejection of inerrancy at Southern Baptist seminaries. Asbury and Fuller seminaries experienced internal faculty disagreement regarding inerrancy. Relative to Fuller Seminary he wrote: "As Fuller hedged on its original commitment concerning Scripture, the enthusiasm of such faculty members as Wilbur M. Smith, Gleason Archer, and Harold Lindsell waned; E. J. Carnell also resisted alteration.[28] Also the Christian Reformed church was affected by this controversy about the trustworthiness of the Bible so that this church body was forced to set forth in a synodical study and report decisions on Biblical infallibility in 1971 and 1972. According to Henry it was neo-orthodoxy which caused the erosion in the Southern Baptists seminaries. At Concordia Seminary St. Louis it was the employment of the historical-critical method which brought on a crisis at this Lutheran Seminary (Now Seminex) relative to the inerrancy of the Bible. Henry also claims that in the Evangelical Theological Society there is an unpublished struggle over the inerrancy statement required of all of its members. Members sign the yearly statement but in practice do not hold to it.

It is the conviction of Henry that more and more young graduates of evangelical colleges who have earned doctorates from non-evangelical divinity schools now question or disown Biblical inerrancy. "Scores of young evangelicals emphasize that scholars uncommitted to inerrancy are producing substantial evangelical works. They repudiate the 'domino theory' that a rejection of inerrancy involves giving up "one evangelical doctrine after another."[29] Scholars like G. C. Berkhouwer, George Ladd, Bruce Metzger, and possibly F. F. Bruce would be some who have given up inerrancy. F. F. Bruce has written an appreciative introduction to the book of Dewey Beegel, *Scripture, Tradition and Infallibility* (Eerdmans, 1973) in which Biblical inerrancy is attacked and rejected.

While Henry is in favor of Biblical inerrancy, yet he holds that non-acceptance of Biblical inerrancy or the support of errancy ought not to divide the evangelical camp! Henry, as the first editor of the influential fortnightly magazine *Christianity Today* states that this journal was committed to inerrancy, but as editor he never proceeded to divide evangelicals over this issue. Henry takes an ambivalent position; on the one hand he believes that surrendering Biblical inerrancy does not result in surrendering other Biblical doctrines and therefore should not divide the evangelical camp. At the same time he points out "that inerrancy and not errancy is the logical implication of the divine authority and inspiration of Scripture; that the champions of errancy have adduced no objective biblical, theological or philosophical criterion to distinguish supposedly errant from inerrant passages, that errancy introduces epistemic instability as evidenced by disagreements over biblical reliability even among its evangelical advocates, let alone among liberal advocates whose irreconcilable differences drove neo-orthodoxy to affirm that no part of the Bible is in itself God's Word."[30] Again in pointing out the weaknesses of the errancy stance Henry stated: "The real question is whether, once

384

scriptural errancy is affirmed, a consistent evangelical faith is maintained thereafter only by an act of will rather than by persuasive epistemological credentials. A volitional faith may also affirm that God can and does use poor grammar and may equally use errant statements and resort to a theology of paradox."[31]

The logic of Henry's position is difficult to grasp. He believes in Biblical inerrancy and yet conceding that those who reject it should be treated as if the matter were not of great consequence because their position should not be considered so significant that they should be avoided as false teachers.

4. Lutheran Attacks On Lindsell's Book
(1) Stauderman of the Lutheran Church in America

An editorial in *The Lutheran*, September 1, 1976, official organ of the Lutheran Church in America (LCA), has attacked Lindsell's book for defending and insisting on Biblical inerrancy. Stauderman implies in his editorial that those individuals who promulgate the truth that the Bible is completely reliable in all of its statements are guilty of "idolizing the Bible." Stauderman claims that person who claim the Bible is inerrant and truthful in all its assertions are guilty of committing idolatry by worshipping a book. This charge is ridiculous because those who prefer this charge have never seen a Christian stand before the Bible and praying to it as an idol made of paper. All Christian go to the Bible for their beliefs about Christ and salvation. There is no knowledge about the things that matter eternally, except as revealed in the Bible. Lutherans do not believe in extra Biblical revelation. Stauderman, if he is a Lutheran, gets his theology from the Bible. Since when, however, are those to be faulted with idolatry if they take all in the Bible seriously, including its infallibility on all subject spoken of, while those who limit what can be accepted from the Bible now are true worshippers of God and His Son?

The editor of the Lutheran does not inform his reading public why he **really** defends the errancy position. The true reason for his attack on Lindsell's book is that he is defending the use of the higher-critical approach to the Bible which has been practiced for over 30 years in the former ULCA and now in the LCA. Arguments advanced by Stauderman do not come to grips with the matter. The argument contained in the following Statement is irrelevant: "Parts of the Bible that do not relate to this central theme are less important, as Luther has wisely pointed out. To idolize the book rather than Christ. If King Pekah killed 120,000 valiant men in one day and took captive 200,000 women, sons, and daughters, that may be an interesting body count, but it certainly isn't of equal importance to the fact that on one day men crucified the Son of God as an atonement for us all."[32]

However, in reply to this criticism of inerrancy it should be stated that the fact that there are teachings that are necessary for salvation and facts not necessary cannot be employed to support the contention that on non-fundamental teachings and facts that Bible can be in error but in those assertions that pertain to salvation there are no mistakes. Such reasoning simply does not accord with the declarations of the Bible that in its entirety it is the inspired and infallible Word of God. II Timothy 3:15-17 which tells us that the purpose of the Bible is able to make men wise unto salvation by creation of faith in Christ Jesus also asserts that **all** Scripture is God-spirited or God-breathed.

Stauderman has really not told his readers why he is opposed to Scriptural inerrancy, and that is that the historical-critical method dominates not only in the LCA seminaries but also the curriculum writers of religious educational materials put out by this largest of the three major Lutheran churches in the United States and Canada.

The only reason Stauderman advanced against inerrancy is the following: "Lutheran traditionally have held a **sensible position** in regard to the Bible." (Boldface supplied) He, however, fails to explain wherein this so-called "sensible position" consists. Furthermore, he certainly is not speaking for Lutherans and certainly does not represent the attitude toward the Bible held by Martin Luther or of the Lutheran Confessions. In addition Stauderman misrepresents Luther's position as being in agreement with the LCA's stance of the nature and character of the Bible. Although he accuses Lindsell and those subscribing to the latter's position of the Bible's inerrancy as being idolaters, he himself is an idolater because of his bowing the knees before the golden calf of the historical-critical method.

(2) President (Bishop) David Preus' Attack on Inerrancy

The Lindsell volume specifically in chapter 4, entitled "The Lutheran Church-Missouri Synod Battle," takes up the issue of errancy/inerrancy as it has developed in a church body that has always held to Biblical Inerrancy and Biblical trustworthiness. Engelder's *The Scripture Cannot Be Broken*, William Arndt's *Does the Bible Contradict Itself?* and *Bible Difficulties* are just a few of the works which advocate and defend Biblical inerrancy.[34] The moderates within Missouri, embracing the historical-critical method, had to logically reject inerrancy as was done by Arthur C. Piepkorn in one of the issues of the *Concordia Theological Monthly* [35] and a booklet by John D. Frey, distributed by ELIM to clergy in the LCMS, a writing bearing the title, *Is the Bible Inerrant?* The clear and unequivocal answer of the latter is: it is errant, and not inerrant.[36]

Since the controversy has broken out in a dramatic way by the walk out of the majority of the St. Louis Concordia faculty, January, 1974 both The Lutheran Church in America and the American Lutheran Church have in many different ways indicated their support of the moderates In the LCMS. The titular heads of these two Lutheran Churches have come out against inerrancy and support of the higher-critical method.

The *Lutheran Witness Reporter*, vol. 2, No. 39 has brought the information that the president of the ALC, Dr. David Preus, claims that the debate about Biblical inerrancy is "one of the less important theological matters." "At a forum sponsored by The American Lutheran Publicity Bureau, Dr. David Preus, is reported as having said that inerrancy is "a slippery word that means many different things to different people."[38]

Because of this fact the ALC's president suggests it "ought not to be dominating" Lutheran theological debate and that it has "unnecessarily and damagingly been elevated" as a major issue, particularly in the Lutheran Church-Missouri Synod.[39]

It is not too difficult to see why David Preus would make such assertions and claims; he is simply defending the seminaries of his church that for a number of years have been using the historical-critical method, a method creating difficulties for inerrancy and one which also now controls curriculum writers of Lutheran educational materials. Under such circumstances, it is downright embarrassing to mention inerrancy, much less discuss it as a fact characterizing the Bible. Furthermore, inasmuch as the ALC practices altar and pulpit fellowship with the LCA, which also holds to Biblical fallibility, who wants to discuss, much less subscribe to a doctrine of inerrancy?

The ALC leader also claimed that the Lutheran Confessions make possible a variety of Lutheran views on inerrancy, that inerrancy is not "boundary material." In the 16th century both the Roman Catholic Church and the Lutheran Church held to the reliability and trustworthiness of Holy Writ and this is also the position reflected in the Lutheran Confessions. The belief in inerrancy underlies the doctrine of the Bible subscribed to by the confessional writers. The inroads produced by the higher-critical method were still about two centuries distant and thus could not have been used by them.

In a recent book published (1976), a clergyman of the ALC, the Reverend Ernst Karsten, has proposed to defend the view that some parts of the Bible are inspired and others are not. This distinction of course implies that those words of Scriptures that are not God's Word may be rejected if the reader so wishes. Karsten has expressed the erroneous view that a person living close to his Lord can determine which portions are inspired and which not. Such reasoning must be labelled pure enthusiasm and subjectivism, which becomes possible when Bible expositors adopt the historical-critical method.

At the recent convention of the ALC, Dr. J.A.O. Preus, president of the LCMS challenged the American Lutheran Church to uphold its constitutional position on Biblical inerrancy when he addressed the ALC delegates.[40] Dr. J.A.O. Preus said: "I must be frank to tell you that certain statements and positions taken in recent years cause us to wonder whether there are those in the ALC who have departed from the official position of their Church." LCMS's president said that the ALC's constitutional reference to inerrancy is "the most clear and outstanding statement in American Lutheranism." The fight to uphold the inerrancy of the Bible is the main reason for the "great conflict" in Missouri.

(3) Richard Neuhaus's Attack on Lindsell's Book

The doctrine of inerrancy has been not only attacked in the LCA, the ALC but also in the LCMS. The Reverend Richard Neuhaus in the 1976 *Forum Letter*, in the supplement to *Forum Letter*, June 1976, claims that official Missouri has aligned itself with Lindsell's book *The Battle of the*

387

Bible. Of this book the Brooklyn clergyman wrote: "In that book the *Christianity Today* editor excommunicates all but the most hard-core fundamentalists from 'the evangelical community.' Even such bastions of conservatism as Fuller Seminary in California attack Lindsell for his sectarianism. Yet the Preus camp now identifies with Lindsell, all along claiming it has not sold its Lutheran birth right for a pottage of fundamentalism."[44] Only the uninformed who have not read Lindsell's book and who are unacquainted with the history of Lutheranism will be persuaded by the language of Neuhaus. The LCMS has held Biblical inerrancy and Biblical infallibility for over a century before Lindsell's book was ever published. It also just so happens that Martin Luther held to and defended the inerrancy of the Holy Scriptures. Speaking about the charge of sectarianism, who pray is breaking off from the LCMS to form a rival body and who at the present is trying its level best to take as many congregations and people out of the LCMS? Neuhaus uses the term fundamentalism in a pejorative sense without first defining what he means by the word "fundamentalism."

The American Heritage Dictionary of the English Language defines fundamentalism: "Belief in the Bible as factual historical record and incontrovertible prophecy, including such doctrines as the Genesis, the Virgin Birth, the Second Advent and Armageddon."[42] Webster defines fundamentalism as: "Orthodox religious beliefs based on a literal interpretation of the Bible (e.g. complete acceptance of the story of creation as given in Genesis and rejection of the theory of evolution) and regarded as fundamental to the Christian faith."[43] Fundamentalism is also employed as a word indicating that a fundamentalist is a person who does not espouse theological liberalism.[44] If Neuhaus does not adhere to the fundamentals of the Christian faith, such as the inspiration of Holy Writ, the Virgin Birth of Christ, the inherent sinfulness of man, the need for the new birth, the deity of Christ, the vicarious atonement, the resurrection of Christ from the dead, Christ's bodily ascension and His second visible return for judgment (this is what the terms historically has meant) then where does Neuhaus stand theologically? Are not the moderates "fundamentalists," inasmuch as they reduce the teaching of Holy Writ to just a few teachings needed for membership in the Christian Church and for fellowship with each Other? True Lutherans do not merely subscribe to the fundamental doctrines of the Bible but accept and believe all given by God in His Word by revelation and inscripturated in the Biblical canon.

Footnotes

16. Carl F. H. Henry, "The War of the Word," *The New Review of Books and Religion,* Volume I. Number 1, September, 1976, p. 7.
17. John Warwick Montgomery, "Biblical Inerrancy: What is at Stake," in J.W. Montgomery, **op. cit.,** p. 20.
18. Henry, **op. cit.,** p. 7.
19. Everett F. Harrison, reprinted in Millard J. Erickson, *The Living God, Readings in Christian Theology* (Grand Rapids; Baker Book House, 1973), pp. 311-316.

20. Frederick C. Grant, *An Introduction to the New Testament Thought* (New York: Abingdon Press, 1950), p. 75.

21. B. B. Warfield, *The Inspiration and Authority of the Bible.* ed. Samuel G. Craig (Philadelphia; Presbyterian and Reformed Publishing Company, 1948), pp. 218-219.

22. James T. Burtchaell, Catholic Theories of Biblical Inspiration since 1810. A Review and Critique (Cambridge, Eng.; Cambridge University Press. 1969), pp. 1-2.

23. Henry, *The War of the Word*, **op. cit.**, p. 7.

24. **Ibid.**

25. **Ibid.**

26. Carl F. H. Henry, *Evangelicals in Search of Identity* (Waco, Texas; Word Books, Publisher, 1976), cf. chapter 5 and 6, pp. 48-64.

27. **Ibid.**, p. 48.

28. **Ibid.**, p. 49.

29. **Ibid.**, pp. 50-51.

30. **Ibid.**, pp 54-55.

31. **Ibid.**, p. 55.

32. Albert P. Stauderman, "Idolizing the Bible," *Lutheran*, September 1, 1976.

33. Lindsell, **op. cit.**, pp. 72-88.

34. Th. Engelder, *Scripture Cannot Be Broken. Six Objections to Verbal Inspiration* (St. Louis: Concordia Publishing House, 1944). 498 pp.: W. Arndt, *Does the Bible Contradict Itself?* (St. Louis: Concordia Publishing House, 1926), 142 pp.; W. Arndt, *Bible Difficulties* (St. Louis: Concordia Publishing House, 1932), 117 pp.

35. Arthur Carl Piepkorn, "What Does 'Inerrancy' Mean?" *Concordia Theological Monthly*, 36:577-593, February, 1965.

36. John D. Frey, *Is the Bible Inerrant?* (Prairie Village, Kansas 66208: 1976), 43 pp.

37. As quoted in "ALC leader: inerrancy overplayed." *Reporter*, 2: No. 39, October 4, 1976, p. 2.

38. **Ibid.**

39. **Ibid.** A

40. Reported by Religious News Service, October 11, 1976, Cf. "Synod Leader Challenges the ALC; Uphold Bible Inerrancy Position," *Christian News,* Vol. 9. No. 41, October 18,1976, pp. 1, 13.

41. Richard Neuhaus, "As Missouri Turns, Year Eleven, Episode Eleven, June, 1976." A Supplement to *Forum Letter*, June, 1976.

42. William Morris, editor, *The American Heritage Dictionary of the English Language* (Boston/New York/Atlanta/Geneva/Illinois; American Heritage Publishing Company and Houghton Mifflin Company, 1969). p. 533.

43. Webster's *New World Dictionary of the American Language* (Cleveland and New York: The Work. Publishing Company, 1964), p. 586.

44. William W. Sweet, "Fundamentalism." inVergilius Ferm *An Encyclopedia of Religion* (New York: The Philosophical Library, 1945), p. 291.

Questions

1. It comes as a great surprise and disappointment that Carl F. Henry ____.

2. Among Lutheran seminaries only ____ still held to Biblical inerrancy?

3. What did Father Burtschaell write about inerrancy? ____

4. Many who signed the statement of the Evangelical Theological Society on inerrancy do not ____.
5. What did *The Lutheran* say about Lindsell's book? ____
6. What did Arthur C. Piepkorn write about the inerrancy of the Bible? ____
7. ALC President David Preus defended the position of ____.
8. What did Richard John Neuhaus write about Lindsell's book? ____

Part VI

5. President Mccall's Reply To Lindsell's Book

One of the chapters in Harold Lindsell's *The Battle for the Bible* concerned itself with the Southern Baptist Convention. Lindsell mentioned a number of individuals, members of influential Southern Baptist schools, who had questioned and rejected Biblical inerrancy and Biblical trustworthiness. Southern Baptist Theological Seminary, located at Louisville, Kentucky had once been a seat of orthodoxy with such men as John R. Sampey and A.T. Robertson staunch adherent of the inerrancy of the Bible and also opponents of radical types of Biblical criticism. At the same seminary today there are faculty members who have taken positions in opposition to Biblical inerrancy and promote the higher-critical method of Biblical interpretation.

President Duke McCall in the June, 1976 *Southern Baptist Seminary* came to the defense of his seminary and its professors and others who came under attack in Lindsell's book.[45] In his critique of *The Battle for the Bible* McCall claims that the editor of *Christianity Today* "arouses too many snakes but kills none of them."

McCall does not come to real grips with the major issues raised by Lindsell but attempts to discredit the latter's book by claiming that Lindsell engages in "a silly game with words: human ideas, logic, or rhetoric do not make the Bible true. The Bible is true because of what the Holy Spirit has done, is doing, and will do with the Scriptures. When a 'fundamentalist' leaves the Holy Spirit out of the process by which God causes men to know the truth of his revelation, a basic fundamental has been lost."

The issue to which Lindsell has addressed himself is this: how much of the Bible as God's Word is truthful, reliable and free from error? Did the Holy Spirit inspire all or only parts of the books of the Old Testament and the New? Is the Bible errant or inerrant? Lindsell does not define what he means by fundamentalism.[46] Lindsell is accused of "fundamentalism" because of his effort, to quote McCall, "to aid the troops which fight under the flag of inerrancy, infallibility, and verbal inspiration." Because the editor of *Christianity Today* employs these words and insists that these are vocables which accurately and faithfully represent the characteristics of the Bible, he is said to be guilty of "stirring up snakes."

While McCall accuses Lindsell of engaging in a confusing war of words, the former himself does some word playing and confusing the facts. McCall understands perfectly what Lindsell means by the words "inerrancy," "infallibility," and trustworthiness, namely, that the Bible is free from error, a stance he does not accept as once understood even years ago at Southern Baptist Seminary.

However, since the autographs, which are said to be inerrant, are no longer in existence, it therefore according to the President of Southern Baptist Seminary, is inappropriate to speak of inerrancy, inasmuch as our transmitted manuscripts have errors in them. Since we have at length answered this same argument advanced by Pinnock it will not be answered here (Cf. *Christian News*, November 22, 1976, p. 9). In dealing with the assertion of Lindsell that there are copyists' mistakes which, therefore, logically cannot be attributed to the autographs, McCall engages in the following specious type of argumentation: "But he assures his readers that this kind of error does not keep the Scriptures from being inerrant. Come now, even a master of imaginative rhetoric must know that you cannot say there are mistakes but there are no mistakes, there are errors, but there are no errors, fallible men have been infallible scholars." Lindsell argues that errors and mistakes are attributed to the copied manuscripts, but not to the original books as they left the pens of the Holy writers, whose writings are called "God-spirited," "Spirit-produced" **(theopneustos)**. It appears that this essential difference McCall does not wish to recognize or even state that Lindsell is making it. How unfair therefore, McCall's statement: "That sort of statement only confuses the situation and proposes to divide Christendom in a battle over the meaning of words."

In opposition to President McCall one might cite the evaluation of another president, namely the remark of Dr. Harold J. Ockenga, president of Gordon-Conwell Theological Seminary of New England, who wrote: "There is a pressing need for Dr. Lindsell's book *The Battle for the Bible* in the burgeoning evangelical branch of Protestantism. If evangelicalism bids to take over the historic mainline leadership of nineteenth century Protestantism, as Dr. Marty suggests, this question of biblical inerrancy must be settled. It is a time for an evangelical historian to set forth the problem. Dr. Lindsell has done the church, and especially the evangelical cause a great service in writing this book."[47]

McCall seems to imply that the meaning of a Biblical text may change from time to time. He confuses the nature of the Bible as the Word of God and the fact that the Holy Spirit uses the Word to convict people of sin, righteousness and judgment. Does this conviction occur because the Holy Spirit convinces a sinner on the basis of clearly understood words that he needs to repent of his sins, confess them and believe on the Lord Jesus as His Savior or does the Holy Spirit do this apart from the Word? McCall wrote: "The Bible is true because God inspired holy men of old to reveal the truth, and it is the continuing work of the Holy Spirit to guide men into all truth (John 16:13). The Holy Spirit can and does use any translation of the Holy Scriptures, and, beyond the dictionary meaning of words, he makes men perceive the eternal truth." We ask Dr. McCall: Did the Holy Spirit inspire men to write error, mistakes and write down erroneous theological notions? If the advocates of limited inerrancy are correct, then this is precisely what happened. Then men must sit in judgment over what the Holy Spirit has caused holy men to write down! They need to distinguish error from truth. No person will quarrel with McCall that the Holy Spirit can and does convert men through translations, but just what is this sentence supposed to communicate, namely, that the Holy Spirit makes men perceive the eternal truth beyond the dictionary meaning? Surely, false renderings of God's Word in the original cannot be an instrument for doing what the correct God-intended words were designed to accomplish.

This writer wonders what the readers of McCall's article, "'Battle for the Bible' arouses too many snakes" understand when they read this sentence: "Incidentally, that business about 'words have specific meaning' is a very naive understanding of the nature of human language. The fact is that words are symbols with varied nuanced meaning." McCall seems to imply that the reader of the Bible cannot be certain as to the exact intended sense of a Biblical author. He claims that Lindsell attempts to state in other words what the quotations of different scholars given in his book really mean. In trying to comprehend what the Bible says and teaches, McCall claims "I prefer the Holy Spirit as a guide into what the Scriptures say rather than Dr. Lindsell or any other human being." McCall seems to imply that the Holy Spirit, the true Author of Holy Writ, used language which is susceptible of different meanings and that the Holy Spirit is needed for a special communication to understand correctly the message of the Bible. If this is true, then the Bible is an unclear book and is not perspicuous. If the message of the Bible, couched in human language, written by men whom the Holy Spirit employed, cannot be comprehended as written, then the whole theological enterprise is in jeopardy of sinking in a quagmire of uncertainty. It has always been the belief of Christian theologians and Christian believers that the Bible was clear and that its message could be understood. McCall's understanding of the purpose of the science of Biblical hermeneutics is extremely faulty.

In the last decade the various forms of Biblical criticism, such as literary, form, redaction and content, have been used by the professors at Southern Baptist Seminary and other Baptist seminaries. The people of the Southern Baptist Convention would be shocked if they really knew what was truly involved in the use of these various types of criticisms now generally employed at most Protestant seminaries. One of the principles followed by critical scholars has been stated by McCall when he criticized Lindsell when speaking about the relative size of the mustard seed "that Jesus was talking about the seeds commonly known to the people of that day...", asserting against Lindsell: "But that is precisely the logic of the argument used by Dr. Lindsell's foes in contending that statements in Scripture were accurate within the CONTEXT in which they were spoken or written but were not necessarily universally true. To put it simply, if Dr. Lindsell can use that form of logic, he cannot deny it to others. As a result, another handful of little snakes slipped through the grass."

Here McCall contends that the message of the New Testament is culturally conditioned. What was true at Christ's and Paul's time is not necessarily true today. This is the way those argue who hold to a changing ethics (known as situation ethics). This fits in precisely with process philosophy. Instead of holding to "a changeless Christ— for a changing world" we now have "a changing Christ for a changing world." In Paul's day women are not permitted to hold the pastoral office. Now Baptists, Methodists, Pentecostals, Episcopalians, Lutherans and other Protestant denominations permit woman's ordination. In Paul's day homosexuality was forbidden in the Scriptures, but now Protestant churches are condoning homosexuality and even ordaining homosexuals into the ministry. In Paul's time the government was said to have the power and right to punish murderers but now Protestant churches have gone on record as being opposed to Romans 13, condemning capital punishment. Instead of the Word of God determining religious beliefs and practices, the culture of humanism decides for Christians what they are to believe and what kind of ethical lives they may live.

Lindsell is also taken to task by McCall for solving "a whole set of problems by affirming that not all Scriptures has the same value" (p. 38). Who decides what parts of Scripture are of the first magnitude and what parts are of the second magnitude? Is not that precisely the same human editing process which lets one man interpret the Book of Jonah as a great tract on the missionary intention of God and another interprets it as a miraculous fish story? Here McCall has thrown together two different theological issues and by placing them on the same level has muddied the waters for people, who need to distinguish between fundamental and non-fundamental teachings and also what is the true nature of the Book of Jonah. There are certain doctrines that a person must know to be saved. The Biblical passages which set forth the fundamentals of salvation are the passages of the first magnitude; those not necessary, for salvation, yet clearly revealed, are of the second magnitude, using McCall's terminology. The purpose of the Book of Jonah has been stated by Jesus Christ in the New Testament. Jesus cites Jonah's experiences as a sign(miracle) of His own death and resurrection. Matthew 12:38-42 and Luke 11:30 show that Jesus believed Jonah was an historical personage, that he preached successfully in Nineveh; otherwise could not have declared: "The men of Nineveh will rise up in the Judgment with these people and condemn them, because they repented when Jonah preached; and here you see more than Jonah. The queen from the south will rise up in the Judgment with these people and condemn them, because she came from the ends of the earth to hear Solomon's wisdom; and here you see more than Solomon" (Beck's translation). Originally the historicity of the Jonah account was rejected because of its miracles, but now the new approach is to claim that the Book of Jonah was written as a missionary tract and that the historical facts are unimportant to the intent of the fifth-century author.

393

McCall in his critique is leaving the door wide open for the charismatic movement, many of whose proponents argue that they receive special revelations from the Holy Spirit. That surely is the case if McCall is correct that the Holy Spirit has privately to indicate to the Biblical reader what a given printed text of the Bible means. The problem is that He will suggest one interpretation to one reader and still another meaning to another!

McCall concluded his critique of Lindsell's book by asserting: "Fighting over words used to describe the Bible will serve the devil. Studying the Bible will open hearts to the miraculous workings of the Holy Spirit. Alas, some men would rather fight than become the children of God" (I John 4:1-11).

Does McCall imply that Lindsell is not a child of God because he has defended the reliability of God's Word? McCall is misleading his leaders by claiming that Lindsell's book is a war about needless words. Ideas and concepts are expressed in words. Paul wrote to Timothy: "Teach and urge them to do these things. If anyone teaches anything else and will not agree with the **sound words** of our Lord Jesus Christ and godly teaching, he is proud and doesn't know anything" (I Tim. 6:2-3). If according to McCall the Holy Spirit can perform miracles, why could God then not create a fish as stated in Jonah 1:17, an interpretation the users of the historical-critical method do not accept.

Since the devil is mentioned as being served when one challenges limited inerrancy and defends the inerrancy of Scripture and since Lindsell has supposedly caused many snakes to fill the theological grass, one might mention that the Devil, called Satan in the Old Testament, was the first one to question the reliability of God's Word when through the medium of the serpent, Satan said to Eve: "Yea, hath God really said?" The Devil, the propagator of false doctrine, false hermeneutics and anti-scriptural theology, was the first higher critic by his endeavoring to raise doubt in Eve's mind relative to the true meaning of God's Word as given to Adam. Another southern theological president gives an entirely different evaluation of Lindsell's book, when he wrote: "... I think this will be one of the most strategic books to be published for some time to come, it is a mine of information on the whole battle between fundamentalists and liberals with which our current generation of evangelicals are only partially aware."[48] With this assessment of Dr. John F. Walvoord of Dallas Theological Seminary many in Christendom will agree.

Footnotes

45. President McCalls "'Battle for the Bible' arouses too many snakes," in *Southern Baptist Seminary*, June 1976 has been reproduced in *The Christian News*. June 14, 1976. p. 12.
46. Compare the different definitions for fundamentalism in the following books: Johannes Knudsen. "Fundamentalism." *The Encyclopedia of the Lutheran Church* (Minneapolis Augsburg Publishing Company. 1965). II. p 895.: Gabriel Hebert, Fundamentalism and the word of God I London: SCM. 1957), p. 22, Alan Richardson. *A Dictionary of Christian Theology* (The Westminster Press, 1969) 132.

47. This statement of Dr. Ockenga is found in the Foreword of Lindsell's book.

48. This evaluation of Lindsell's book made by Dr. Walvoord is published on the jacket of Lindsell's book.

Questions

1. President Duke McCall of the Southern Baptist Seminary came to the defense of _____.
2. McCall's critique is leaving the door wide open for _____.
3. Who first questioned the reliability of God's Word? _____

Part VII

6. Donald W. Dayton's Attack On Lindsell's Book

One of the theological seminaries coming under attack in Lindsell's *The Battle for the Bible* was North Park Theological Seminary in Chicago. Donald W. Dayton, director of Mellander Library and assistant professor of theology at North Park Theological Seminary, has written a review article "'*The Battle for the Bible*': *Renewing the Inerrancy Debate*." This rebuttal was published in the liberal *Christian Century* Nov. 10, 1976.[49] To this writer's knowledge this is the most thorough review yet to appear in the theological journals and magazines since the book's publication in the earlier part of this year. The review is mostly negative and critical.

Dayton claims that even "this short summary will indicate the quality of Lindsell's case and its lack of theological and historical subtlety. Lindsell reveals little awareness of the exegetical difficulties of his position and no 'feel' at all for the critical problems and the 'phenomena of Scripture' forcing other evangelicals to qualify their doctrine of Scripture. His historical analysis is simplistic and dichotomous, for the most part ignoring contrary evidence and the scholarly debates surrounding the interpretations of the material he quotes." Toward the conclusion of his book review article he makes this judgment: "Ironically, Lindsell's book may very well prove to be a potent force for undermining the very position he defends. The superficiality of the book, combined with its timing in the midst of already swirling controversy, may provide the occasion for a wholesome repudiation of its stance. The rush of theologians and church leaders to dissociate themselves from *The Battle for the Bible* may indicate that this rejection is already taking place." Another judgment made in the course of the article states: "His book is actually a repristination (and often less subtle than earlier expressions) of a particular time-bound formulation of biblical authority that is being seen by increasing numbers of evangelicals not only to have outlived its usefulness but to have become a positive hindrance to the understanding of the fuller and deeper significance of the Scriptures."

In his repudiation of Lindsell's book, Dayton has marshalled four kinds of evidence against it. First, he endeavors to show that the doctrine of inerrancy as adopted by Protestant churches of a conservative stripe was influenced by the so called "Princeton theology," rooted in the earlier work of Charles Hodge and continued by such theological stalwarts as A. A. Hodge and B. B. Warfield. The theological stance of the nineteenth century Princeton men was eventually derived from the writings of Francois Turretin of Geneva, who is a representative of post-Reformation scholastic traditions. In support of this conclusion Dayton cites the work of Claude Welch, who in his *Protestant Thought in the Nineteenth Century*, Vol. 1 asserted about Turretin's theology that it "became a haven sought (properly or not) by all sorts of conservative revivalists and fundamentalists in the face of the threats of biology and biblical criticism." Dayton contends that the National Association of Evangelicals and the Evangelical Theological Society were influenced by the views of the Princeton theologians in their understanding and formulation of the doctrine of the Bible's inerrancy, reliability and trustworthiness. Actually all those individuals accepting and propagating Warfield's views about the nature of the Bible have adopted a position which allegedly goes back to a period of theological deterioration, which characterized the age of Protestant scholasticism. Those theologians, pastors, and laymen holding to total inerrancy supposedly are perpetuating a view which was not that of the Protestant Reformers. Dayton claims that denominations and scholars who once held Biblical inerrancy and total Biblical trustworthiness are now rethinking their positions and are having second thoughts about their former position which they are now in the process of changing.

Dayton admits that in The Lutheran Church — Missouri Synod a similar view about the inerrancy of the Bible has been held and that this is one of the major bones of contention that has caused disunity and polarization in this once influential church body in world Lutheranism, whose influence for good has been dulled by the polemic which has characterized much of its recent published literature. In rebuttal to Dayton's claim the defenders of Biblical inerrancy have mustered sufficient evidence from the writings of Luther and the Lutheran Confessions to show that the historic position of the Lutheran Church — Missouri Synod did not primarily derive its views about the inerrancy and total trustworthiness of the Bible from post-Reformation scholasticism, so a period allegedly responsible for religious and theological sterilization, a judgment that has been challenged as to its validity by scholars knowledgeable with the theology and hymnology of this period.

Calvin and Luther both held the identical view about the verbal and plenary inspiration of the Bible. The allegation that the view held and defended by Lindsell is not in harmony with true Reformation tradition is simply not borne out by the facts. It was only with the coming of negative Biblical criticism that the doctrine of the Bible's inerrancy and trustworthiness has been challenged. The sad fact is that so many professors went to liberal and neo-orthodox seminaries to get their doctoral degrees or to universities where anything but a sound Christian view of life was held and propagated, and where they were influenced by men who had become famous in the academic world for their views.

At the same time the adoption of positions contrary to those they once had held and which were the theological positions of the churches they belonged to, now gave them an opportunity to do something different from what they were expected to do by the church bodies they represented and also gave occasion for the publishing of journal articles and books that would influence the thinking of students, pastors, lay people, denominations and congregations in new directions.

The view of the Bible held by the so called Princeton school of the last century (and one might add by those who have defended Biblical inerrancy) is depicted by Dayton in the following descriptive statement: "The determinative feature of the view of Scripture conveyed in this tradition is found in a seldom articulated 'suppressed premise' grounded not so much in exegesis as in the rationalist and scholastic tendencies of post-Reformation orthodoxy.

"The syllogism goes like this: God is perfect; the Bible is the Word of God: therefore the Bible is perfect (inerrant). The 'suppressed premise' here is actually the focusing of a whole metaphysic emphasizing the 'perfection' and 'immutability' of God and a highly determinative view of God's working in the world more obviously at home in the 'high Calvinism' of the old Princeton theology."

The view advocated by Dayton and those "evangelical scholars" which he adduces to support his view all claim that the humanity of the Bible has not adequately been taken into account by Lindsell. When giving expression to Biblical truth the Biblical authors did it in language which was time-bound and expressed often erroneous views of reality. Modern science and modern human learning have shown the Bible to be in error. Thus it is important to distinguish theological truth from error.

While Dayton has accused Lindsell of superficiality, he has not shown that the Scripture texts discussed by Lindsell in his book supporting total inerrancy do not teach the doctrine. Dayton has not shown that the view held by Christians down through the ages, subscribed to by Lindsell, was not the view of the nature of Holy Writ held by Roman Catholicism, Lutheranism, Presbyterianism, and Arminianism, before the Age of the Enlightenment. It was only with the coming of Biblical criticism with its attack on the reliability of the Bible that the doctrine of the verbal and plenary inspiration of the Bible was given up and a view quite contrary to the historic doctrine promulgated.

Paul E. Kretzmann has correctly perceived the importance of the doctrine of the verbal and plenary inspiration of the Bible when in the preface to his book, *The Foundations Must Stand* he wrote: "Among all doctrines of the Bible there is none that occupies a more critical position than that of the inspiration of Holy Writ. We commonly refer to this doctrine of the Christian religion, the articulus stantis et cadentis ecclesiae (the doctrine of the standing or falling church). But even this fundamental truth of personal faith is not a matter of subjective certainty.

"It rather depends, as do all other articles of faith, on the objective certainty of the Word of God, as a whole and its parts. In this respect the doctrine of the inspiration of the Bible is fundamental for the entire corpus doctrinae (body of Christian doctrine). If Christians in general, and particularly Christian theologians, preachers, and teachers, cannot be sure of the matters which they present in their teaching, then the Bible will cease to be the norm of doctrine and rule of life, and Christianity will cease to be the one absolute religion."[52]

Dayton brings up the old warn out charge that Lindsell's views about the inerrancy of the Bible leads to a "dictation theory of inspiration." Thus the North Park theologian writes: "This position (though exegesis is brought to bear on the question) that the Bible must be inerrant and infallible if it is in any real sense the 'Word of God.' This is a priori leads rather directly to an immediacy and absoluteness of inspiration which, despite protests to the contrary results in a 'dictation' view of inspiration and ultimately to a 'docetic' view of Scripture in which the human element is present (supposedly) but never determinative.

"These assumptions are generally developed in the direction of viewing the Scriptures largely in the categories of divinely given propositions, doctrines and information. As Carl Henry has put it, the Bible is 'a book of divinely disclosed doctrinal truth . . .'"

This statement of Dayton is quite revealing as to why he cannot subscribe to verbal inspiration. How does the North Park librarian think the Bible is inspired? How did the prophets in the Old Testament state Yahweh's will except in propositional statements? When Jesus wanted to prove a point that He was making, He would quote from an Old Testament book and cite a specific Bible verse. When overcoming the Devil in the wilderness, Jesus three times rejected the Devil's offer by a quotation from the Mosaic Book of Deuteronomy. Let Dayton count the number of times Paul quotes from various Old Testament books in Romans in support of the doctrines which the apostle had written down under the inspiration of the Holy Spirit. The phrase: "It is written" followed by a Biblical Old Testament citation occurs with great frequency in various New Testament writings. In the Old Testament canonical books the phrase "Thus says the Lord," or "saying of Yahweh" occurs hundreds of times. Each time one of these kinds of phrases is employed there comes a doctrinal or ethical assertion.

Although Bible-believers have repeatedly rejected the claim and accusation that to hold to an inerrant Scripture is tantamount to espousing a mechanical or static view of revelation, this charge is repeated over and over. Concerning this charge, Dr. Edward Young asserted nearly twenty years ago as follows: "The Bible, therefore, whether we will or not, is constantly being thrust unto the forefront of discussion and one can only be amazed, to say nothing of being saddened, at the glibness with which many speak of the old-fashioned view of inspiration as being out of date and relevant for the present age.

"That most modern writers have not taken the trouble to state this doctrine correctly and consequently are erecting a man of straw to attack is a fact, sad but true. The real issue, at the present book will seek to make clear, is that modern man is not ready to listen to the voice of the one living and eternal God, but prefers rather the changing sands of human opinion for the foundation upon which to build his religious life."[53]

The fact that there are differences in style in the various books, the fact that in the Gospels the same account is reported in different words and one account reports details the parallel account does not is against the view that the Biblical writers were typewriters who were not permitted to exercise their gifts and talents. Koehler rejects the allegation that this all-inclusive control exercised by the Holy Spirit did not reduce the human writers to mere automats, when he wrote:

"They were not like mechanical instruments in the hand of God, not knowing what they were doing; but the act of writing was on their part a conscious, volitional and intelligent act; they knew what they were doing and writing. David knew that the Spirit of God spake by him (2 Sam. 23:2), and Paul was fully conscious when he wrote his letters to the churches (2 Thess. 3:17)."[54]

Those who hold to verbal and plenary inspiration are said to espouse a docetic view of the Bible according to Dayton. The heresy called "docetism" espoused the concept that Christ was only seemingly a human being, but not in reality. To claim that Lindsell and those who follow or hold the same concept about the nature of the Scriptures are holding to a docetic Scripture simply runs contrary to the facts as they are in evidence in the Bible. The proponents of total inerrancy are called docetists because they do not subscribe to the idea that the Bible as God's Word contains error. The advocates of limited infallibility claim that to be human is to err. This alleged that if the humanity of the Bible is really taken into account, then errors and mistakes are to be expected, because that simply is the nature of human beings. This position, however, contradicts the Biblical assertions that God's Word is true and reliable.

In writing about the Evangelical Covenant Church, Dayton claims that this body, mentioned by Lindsell as once supporting Biblical infallibility, which has its roots in pietism and revivalism, "carried an implicit critique (occasionally raised to the status of an explicit theological alternative) of the rationalism and intellectualism of the scholastic and confessional traditions." However, does Dayton think that by supporting the different types of criticism, all of which have rationalistic presupposition, that the negative higher criticism used in the Old and New Testament fields, that form, redaction and content criticism, now standard in all divinity schools of the liberal and neo-orthodox stripe, are free from intellectualism?

Higher criticism certainly operates with hostile presupposition as far as the Bible is concerned. In his article Dayton, in the second place, endeavors to discredit *The Battle for the Bible* by citing the fact that conservative groups which "took shelter in the Princeton theology" during the founding of the Evangelical Theological Society and the National Association of Evangelicals are now wondering whether they did not make a mistake by adopting the Princeton position. Dayton informs his readers that "this development is most clear among Wesleyan groups that have begun to wonder if they did not buy into too much of the Princeton legacy during the fundamentalist/modernist controversies." Dayton claims: "There is a discernible tendency among such groups to affirm a more developmental, historically conditioned and 'Arminian' doctrine of Scripture that avoids the characteristic vocabulary of the absolutistic and a historical 'inerrancy' formulation."

While this writer does not subscribe to the position of fundamentalism: "Let us have unity on the essentials and charity on non-essentials," he still would credit the fundamentalists with having fought a necessary battle against theological liberalism which was taking over many American Protestant churches in the first quarter of this century. Doctrines such as the following are fundamental and essential to a correct presentation of the Christian faith: 1. The verbal and plenary inspiration of the Bible; 2. The sinfulness of man and his need for conversion; 3. the Virgin Birth of Christ; 4. The deity of Christ; 5. The Vicarious and substitutionary death of Christ for man's salvation; 6. The Resurrection of Christ; 7. The Visible Return of Christ to judge the living and the dead. These are teachings that were defended over against theological liberalism by various Protestant and Lutheran writers in *The Fundamentals*, which appeared in twelve volumes. Anyone opposed to this worthy effort on behalf of the Christian faith clearly indicates where he stands and is not in a position properly to understand the Bible's teachings about its own unique character as God's Word.

The third argument adduced by Dayton to discredit Lindsell's book is to call attention to what is going on in so-called evangelical denominations today. Thus Dayton writes: "Lindsell has pointed to currents of great significance not only for the future of the evangelical world but also for the larger American church. There is undeniably a remarkable ferment in the evangelical world and a discernible movement toward a new paradigm of biblical authority. A number of factors seem to be giving impetus to these currents."

One of the factors in the movement to give new paradigms is the use of biblical criticism by evangelical scholars today. In his book Lindsell has shown that when scholars and pastors begin to espouse the kinds of Biblical criticisms which have come into vogue in the last two hundred years, they must change their ideas about the nature of the Bible and must argue against Biblical inerrancy and the total trustworthiness of the Bible.

Most of the cases Dayton cites are new interpretations and approaches by Fuller Seminary professors, like Ladd, Jewett and the "Church Growth Movement," now being sponsored at Fuller Seminary. Dayton admits that "there is a sense in which Lindsell has 'got the goods' on Fuller Theological Seminary and certain members of the ETS. These institutions were founded self-consciously to perpetuate a view of Scripture very close to Lindsell's. Their problem is whether modern questions (some of them also ancient) allow such a position to be maintained." The question of ethics is involved when presidents and professors set about deliberately to change the theological stance of an institution or organization which goes directly against the doctrinal formulation of the seminary's founder or a society's position on the nature of the Bible and replaces this with one quite different in character!

400

Lindsell is, however, credited by Dayton with correctly pointing out the situation which developed in The Lutheran Church — Missouri Synod when Tietjen and a majority of his faculty endeavored to lead the synod down a different theological path by refusing to abide by the historic position of the synod on the inerrancy and complete trustworthiness of the Bible. Dayton justifies the action of the "moderates" (as they like to call themselves) by claiming that the doctrine of Scripture adopted by the founding father of the LCMS came into existence as a result of a reaction to the emergence of the "Evangelical United Front — a reaction grounded in Lutheran scholasticism just as the Princeton theology was grounded in Reformed scholasticism."

However, the position held by the founding fathers of the LCMS goes back to Luther,[54] in whose writings Walther, Fuerbringer, Sihler, Cremer, Graebner and other leaders were well read. H. E. Jacobs wrote about Luther and scholasticism as follows: "Lutheranism began as a vigorous protest against scholasticism. Luther taught by expounding the various books of the Bible. To him St. Paul was the greatest of systematic theologians, and the Epistle to the Romans the text-book in dogmatics for all time.

"But the organizing mind of Melanchthon has scarcely made a beginning in lecturing on Romans, until he found it expedient to formulate and arrange the definitions of the common theological terms employed by St. Paul in his epistle; and from this proceeded the ampler treatment of Melanchthon and his followers. Chemnitz, Haffenreffer, and Hutter simply lectured upon these 'Common Places' of Melanchthon. In Chemnitz, however, a biblical method prevails. His tendency is constantly to illustrate from what we would now call biblical theology.

"He appreciates the gradual development of doctrine in Holy Scripture, and examines the proof-texts in their context and historical setting. The scholastic period is properly in the seventeenth-century."[55] The position of the LCMS on the inerrancy and infallibility of the Bible is based solidly upon the passages in the Old and New Testaments describing what the Bible is. It agrees with the position given in numerous writings of Luther and with many assertions supporting the total trustworthiness and complete infallibility of the Holy Scriptures as set forth in various of the Lutheran Confessions.

The present controversies in Protestantism and among so called evangelicals Dayton informs his readers do not so much involve doctrine as they do hermeneutical questions. That is true, but this has been the case for nearly two thousand years of church history. Depending on what kind of hermeneutics a Biblical interpreter employs will determine his understanding and exposition of the Bible. Doctrines are determined by the theologians' hermeneutics. Biblical hermeneutics is first of all determined by the interpreter's understanding of what the Bible is.

Is the Bible the Word of God? or does it only contain the Word of God? Some of the basic Biblical hermeneutical principles are derived from the Bible itself. There is a great difference between the historical-grammatical method and the historical-critical method. Each method of hermeneutics approaches the Bible with different presuppositions, which in turn determine how the Bible is understood. No system of hermeneutics is pre-suppositionless.

The higher-critical method has produced diametrically-opposed views compared to what the Protestant churches once held about many Biblical doctrines. The fact that in conservative churches significant changes are occurring is due specifically to the adoption of higher-critical views. That is precisely the contention of Lindsell when tying up the rejection of inerrancy and Biblical trustworthiness with the adoption of the higher-critical methodology.

Finally, Dayton endeavors to discredit the influence of Lindsell's book by referring to critical reviews by scholars who once did or still adhere to Biblical inerrancy. The refutations and criticisms of Clark Pinnock and Carl F. Henry are given; this writer has discussed in detail the criticism of these two Biblical scholars in *The Christian News* of November 22, 1976 and November 29, 1976.

Footnotes

49. Donald W. Dayton, *"The Battle for the Bible*: Renewing the Inerrancy Debate," *Christian Century,* November 10, 1976 has been photographed as evidence and is found in *The Christian News,* November 15, 1976, pp. 13-14.
50. Milton L. Rudnick, *Fundamentalism and the Missouri Synod* (St. Louis: Concordia Publishing House, 1966), chapters 8-9, in which the matter of the relationship of The Lutheran Church-Missouri Synod to fundamentalism is discussed.
51. Bernard Ramm, *Protestant Biblical Interpretation* (Grand Rapids: Baker Book House, 1970), pp. 56, 58.
52. P. E. Kretzmann, *The Foundations Must Stand* (St. Louis: Concordia Publishing House, 1936), p. 3.
53. Edward J. Young, *The Word is Truth* (Grand Rapids: Wm. B. Eerdmans Publishing Company, 1957), p. 15.
54. "Walther, Carl Ferdinand Wilhelm," Erwin C Lueker, Editor in Chief, *Lutheran Cyclopedia* (St. Louis: Concordia Publishing House, 1954). p. 1118b.
55. H. E. Jacobs, "Scholasticism in the Lutheran Church," Henry Ester Jacobs and John A. A. Haas, *The Lutheran Cyclopedia* (New York: Charles Scribner's Sons, 1899), pp. 434-435.

Questions

1. Donald Dayton's review of *"The Battle for the Bible"* was published in ____.
2. Calvin and Luther both held ____.
3. "Docetism" espoused the concept that ____.
4. What does Surburg say about "fundamentalism?" ____
5. The position held by the founding fathers of the LCMS goes back to ____.
6. The position of the LCMS on inerrancy is based solidly on ____.
7. There is a great difference between what two methods of Bible interpretation? ____

Why Should A Christian
Study the Old Testament?

Christian News, January 24, 1977

The Old Testament is today a much-disputed book, not only among those outside of the church, but also among those within it. At various times in the centuries following the ascension of Christ, the Old Testament has been attacked. In the second century Marcion wrote a book to show that the Gospel and the Old Testament contradicted each other. Marcion recommended the separation of Christianity from Judaism because; according to his interpretation the God of the Old Testament was different from the one of the New. The Creator God of the Old Testament was the author of evil works, who was also the author of law, a vengeful and bloodthirsty being; while the God of the New Testament was the author of the Gospel characterized by love, abrogating the law and the prophets.

According to Braaten, the rise of the historical method was responsible for placing a great gulf between the Old and New Testaments.[1] For Schleiermacher, the father of modern theology, the Old Testament did not possess the same degree of inspiration as the New, and consequently did not have the normative status of the New. He was in favor of allowing the New Testament to stand by itself because it alone expressed purely the pious self-consciousness of Christians; at best, the Old Testament might be added as an appendix to the New Testament books. Emil Brunner claimed that Schleiermacher was guilty of putting the Old Testament on a level with paganism.[2] Thus in *The Christian Faith* Schleiermacher wrote: "Christianity does indeed stand in special connection with Judaism; but as far as concerns its historical existence and its aim, its connection to Judaism and heathenism are the same."[3]

Adolf von Harnack (1851-1930) took a very hostile attitude toward the Old Testament and in his work Marcion: *Das Evangelium vom fremden Godt* wrote:

> The rejection of the Old Testament in the second century was an error which the great church rightly opposed; holding on to it in the sixteenth century was a destiny which the Reformation was not able to escape; but for Protestantism to preserve it since the nineteenth century as a canonical document is the result of a religious and ecclesiastical paralysis. To clear the table and to honor the truth of our confession and instruction, that is the great feat required of Protestantism today — almost too late.[4]

In the twentieth century the "German Christians," motivated by anti-Semitism, endeavored to persuade the Christians of Germany to get rid of the Old Testament. Alfred Rosenberg in his *Myth of the Twentieth Century* argued that a pure Aryan race should not use a book written by Jews, which presented a tyrannical God to the world. Although the Nazi threat of eliminating the Old Testament as a part of the Biblical canon was removed by the military defeat of Germany in 1945, still a low view of the relationship of the Old Testament to the New is currently held by the existentialist school of Biblical interpretation.

The Old Testament scholar Hans Wolff asserted in 1962 that for the average theologian in Europe the Old Testament is not normative nor canonical. In most pulpits in Europe the Old Testament is not used as the basis for preaching.[5] Concerning this matter Braaten wrote: "Modern existentialist theology, as relevant as its insights have been into the nature of human existence, has come to grief in its treatment of the Old Testament."[6] A debate by Gerhard von Rad and Hans Conzelmann had made it clear that the Old Testament is regarded with a deprecatory attitude.[7]

While it is true that no Old Testament theologian today is advocating the removal of the Old Testament from the canonical Scriptures, yet as Braaten has written: "Schleiermacher's view that the Old Testament is only historical background, to be studied as a literary aid in understanding the New, lingers on in current existentialist-hermeneutical theology."[8] It is generally conceded that Bultmann has exercised a great influence on theological thought in the last three decades.

Those New Testament scholars and theologians who have followed the views of Bultmann as expressed in his writings, have been led to adopt a low view of the Old Testament, unlike the New, the Old is not considered to be a vehicle of God's living Word to the church and mankind today.

Although primarily a New Testament scholar, Bultmann has expressed himself on the Old Testament and its relation to the New. His programmatic essay, "The Significance of the Old Testament for the Christian Faith," became the basis for theological discussion between Bultmann and a number of European and American theologians. It is available in a volume edited by Bernard W.Anderson, as *The Old Testament and the Christian Faith*.[9] Another essay valuable for ascertaining Bultmann's views on the Old Testament is his "Prophecy and Fulfillment."[10] A reading of Bultmann materials will indicate that he held a low view of the Old Testament. By claiming that the Old Testament has no relevance for Christians, Bultmann has denied canonicity to the Scriptures of the Old Covenant.[11]

In his Sprunt Lectures in 1963 Walther Zimmerli asserted: "The Old Testament is an alien factor in recent Protestant theology . . . The Old Testament is honored and its words are read from the pulpit, yet when the systematic theologian endeavors to unfold what the Christian faith is, and to describe it in essential parts, then the Old Testament is chiefly an embarrassment . . . The situation can arise in which a hermeneutic attempts seriously to grasp the real need for the word and proclamation of the Old."[12]

What has happened in the German church has had its parallel in America. In the United States the disappearance of the Old Testament from preaching and as a book to be read from in the worship services has taken place so quietly that many people have not been aware of how in practice the Old Testament has become obsolete or silent.[13] In Europe and in America the abandonment of the Old Testament, whether advocated in practice or theory, has been occasioned by a low view of the Bible, which considers the Holy Scriptures merely a record of God's revelations, and speaks of the Bible as a Raymond F. Surburg book replete with errors, mistakes, contradictions, outworn scientific and ethical conceptions.

Not all Christians in the United States and Europe share this low view of the Bible. Among many who believe the Bible to be the Word of God and the authoritative rule for life and living, there is still a tendency manifested to neglect the reading, study and promotion of the writings of the Old Testament.[14] There are various reasons for the neglect of three fourths of the Bible. An average Bible having 1300 pages will devote about one thousand pages to the thirty-nine books of the Old Testament.

Parts of the Old Testament are no longer in force. In Colossians 2:16, 17 Paul clearly stated: "Allow no one therefore, to be your judge in regard to eating and drinking or the observance of a festival or a new moon or a Sabbath. These are shadows of things to follow, but the body is Christ." This means that portions of Exodus, Leviticus, Numbers and Deuteronomy are no longer in force. The history of the Old Testament contains the history of the Jewish people, their wanderings, conquests, wars, defections, punishments and their relationships with other Near Eastern peoples.

To understand many of the historical books, and even in a book like the Psalms, a knowledge of historical geography is required for an intelligent comprehension of the messages of these books. The time periods dealt with are removed from our time by 2,500-3,000, or even 4,000 years. Much in the Old Testament does not appear to be relevant and have meaning for the twentieth century with its complex problems. Many Christians feel that their time and effort are far more profitably spent in the study of the New Testament books.

Yet despite the arguments that have been brought for not studying and neglecting the Old Testament, the question can profitably be asked: "WHY SHOULD A CHRISTIAN STUDY THE OLD TESTAMENT?"

Answer One: Because it was the Bible of Jesus Christ.[15]

Our Lord knew the Old Testament well, reading and memorizing them so that they became a part of Him. Through them Jesus learned the Father's will for His ministry and His eventual death. The whole pattern of his life and behavior was undergirded by the deep conviction that "the Scriptures must be fulfilled" (Mark 14:49). For what the Bible said, God said, that was the belief of Jesus Christ. The Old Testament was Holy Scripture for Jesus. The Master-Teacher grounded all His life and work upon it and in it. In the great temptations, in which Jesus was subjected by the archenemy of mankind He met all the onslaughts of Satan with three passages from the book of Deuteronomy (Matt. 4:4 is a quotation from Deut. 8:3; Matt. 4:7 is a quotation from Deut. 6:16). Often Jesus quoted from the Old Testament. "Have you not read what David did when he was hungry, also those with him," (Matt. 12:3, where Christ cited I Sam. 21:1-6 and Lev. 24:9.) In connection with the instruction on divorce,

Jesus said: "Have you not read that he who made them at the beginning made them male and female," Matt. 19:4, where the Lord is citing Gen. 1:27.

Jesus took the Pentateuch seriously. He chided his contemporaries for misinterpretation of the Scriptures. "What is written in the Law, how readest thou? (Luke 10:26)" To the leaders of the Hebrew nation He said: "You know not the Scriptures nor the power of God" (Matt. 22:29).

When Jesus visited Nazareth on His first Galilean ministry, our Lord attended as was His custom, the synagogue on the Sabbath day. The leader of the synagogue asked Him to speak and so Jesus read the first verses from the 61st chapter of Isaiah and then concluded: "Today is this Scripture fulfilled in your hearing." A clear instance of prophecy and fulfillment!

When Dives requested Abraham in heaven, that the latter should have some person sent from the dead to warn his brethren, Jesus stressed the validity and essentiality of the Old Testament: "They have Moses and the prophets, let them hear them . . . If they hear not Moses and the prophets, neither will they be convinced if someone should rise from the dead (Luke 16:29, 31)."

In speaking about His betrayal, Jesus quoted from Zechariah 13:7: "It is written — I will strike the shepherd, and the sheep will be scattered." On the cross Jesus quoted from three different psalms verses.

Not only did Jesus regard the Old Testament as the Word of God and therefore authoritative in matters of doctrine and ethics, but He also expected those who would be the children of God to use, read and search the Old Testament. "Search the Scriptures for in them you think that you have eternal life and they are they which testify of me" (John 5:39). "Search the Scriptures" is a command that still is pertinent for today's children: of God, because the Old Testament is the Word of God.

Answer 2: Because the inspired Apostles, Paul, Peter and other inspired New Testament authors considered the Old Testament as the Word of God.[16]

The Scriptures which were utilized in the Early Church between A.D. 30-60 was the Old Testament. The Book of Acts, the Pauline and Petrine Epistles, together with the writings of John show that the Old Testament was the source for establishing the pattern of the life of Jesus. In preaching at Thessalonica, Paul employed texts from the Old Testament (Acts 17:2), to support the message which he proclaimed. Earle wrote about Paul's attitude and use of the Old Testament:

"Paul's use of the Old Testament cannot be understood apart from his attitude towards it. To him the Scriptures are holy and prophetic; they constitute the very oracles of God (ta logia tou theou), and they 'were written. . . for our learning.' All his important doctrines are buttressed by an appeal to his Bible: to place the origin of Scripture in God. Paul's phrase 'Godbreathed' (theopneustos) could hardly be improved upon. In his view of the Old Testament the apostle is in agreement

not only with Christ and the other New Testament writers but also with the whole of Judaism and the early Church."[16]

While Paul sometimes refers to the "law," "the writings," or "the law and the prophets," the prevailing usage of Paul is to refer to the Old Testament by the term "the scripture" (he graphe). These expressions may be traced to the threefold division of the Hebrew canon prevalent in the first century A.D. Lightfoot regarded the singular graph in the New Testament as always a reference to one particular Scripture passage.[17] While this is generally true, Warfield is more accurate when he wrote: "Often the reference is to the Scripture as a whole, to that unitary written authority to which final appeal was made. In some of those passages it is no less than impossible to take it otherwise."[18]

Romans is largely built upon the Old Testament books; the great arguments of this great Pauline theological writing are proven by the Old Testament Bible.[19] The Romans epistle has 55 quotations and references, most of them are quotations. The word "Scriptures" is employed seven times; the phrase "it is written" is found sixteen times with twenty-five quotations. The Apostle to the Gentiles appealed to the Old Testament Scriptures as the final authority, by asking "What sayeth the Scriptures?" (Romans 4:3), "the Scripture saith" (9:17; 10:11; 11:2-4). Paul speaks of the "Prophets" as Scriptures (1:1; 16:26). For Paul "spoken" is the equivalent to "written" (4:18, 23).

First Corinthians contain two references to "the Scriptures" in general, embracing the basic facts of Christianity (1 Cor. 15:3,4). This Pauline letter contains fifteen quotations and twelve allusions. The phrase "gegraptai, it is written," is found no less than nine times. Just as is the case in Romans, the background for Paul's teaching in Corinthians is the Old Testament Scriptures. Galatians has twelve Old Testament quotations and references and several Old Testament allusions. The argumentation of Paul rests upon the authority of the Old Testament as the Word of God.

A number of times Paul asks the significant question: "What says the Scriptures?" (4:30). The word "Scriptures" occurs three times (3:6; 2:22; 4:30,) and "it is written" four times (3:10, 13; 4:22, 27). The Scriptures are personified in 3:8, also in 3:22. In 3:16 a doctrine hangs on a letter. In I Timothy there is the phrase: "The Scripture saith" (5:18). In II Timothy 3:16, there is the notable passage: "All Scripture is given by inspiration of God."

Paul held the same position, as did the Judaism of his day, namely, that the 24 books of the Hebrew Old Testament were the Word of God and consequently authoritative.

The stance of Simon Peter, primus among pares, was the same as that of Paul. In I Peter there are nine quotations, and at least sixteen references and allusions to the Old Testament. The word Scripture is employed once and is implied twice (2:6-8). "It is written" is found in 1:16. Second Peter has important references to "the Scriptures" as inspired (1:20, 21), two quotations (2:22; 3:13), and at least nine allusions.

H. S. Miller claims that "the value and importance of the Old Testament in the composition of the New, and the views of the New Testament writers concerning the inspiration and authority of the Old Testament writers concerning the inspiration and authority of the Old, are focalized, illustrated, and illuminated in this wonderful Epistle to the Hebrews."[20] According to Miller there are 35 quotations including 5 repetitions and 53 more allusions, making a total of at least 88. Nearly every one of the epistles' 13 chapters abounds in quotations and allusions, or both. The word "Scripture" does not occur and "it is written" occurs but once (10:7), but "He saith," and equivalent expressions, occur repeatedly: referring to God (20 quotations), to Christ (4 quotations, 2:11-13; 10:5-7), and to the Holy Spirit (2 quotations, 3:7-11; 10:15-17). Quotations are made from Genesis (chs. 2,22), Exodus (ch. 25), Deuteronomy (chs. 31, 32), Joshua (ch. 1) 2 Samuel (ch 7), 8 Psalms (2, 22, 40, 45, 95, 102, 104, 110), Isaiah (ch. 8), Jer. (ch. 31), Haggai (ch. 2). There are also quotations from and allusions to Leviticus, Numbers, Proverbs, Daniel, Hosea, Habakkuk, and Zachariah. Sixteen Old Testament books are used in the composition of Hebrews, and many of them are used several times. The Epistle contains abundant proof that the Old Testament is **God speaking** (1:1,- 2). It makes clear some of the Messianic Psalms. All books are placed on the same level. Human authors are not mentioned; Deity alone is seen. The entire picture of the person and work of Christ, from the Creation to the Second Coming is given and largely in Old Testament language. Practically all of the greater Old Testament characters are mentioned, and are treated as historical: "Cain, Abel, Noah, Abraham, Melchizedek, Sarah, Isaac, Jacob, Esau, Levi, Judah, Joseph, Moses, Aaron, Joshua, Rahab, Barak, Gideon, Jephthah, Samson, Samuel, David (23 in all)."[21]

Answer 3: Because the Old Testament is able to make wise unto salvation by creating faith in Jesus Christ.

The outstanding characteristic value of Old Testament reading and study is its ability to create faith in Christ Jesus and to maintain saving faith in Jesus Christ, the promised Messiah of the Old Testament. Not only the New Testament testifies to Jesus Christ, but the Old Testament as well.

In debate with the Jewish people, Jesus asserted: "Ye search the Scriptures for in them ye think ye have eternal life and they are they which testify of me" (John 5:39). On Easter afternoon and Easter evening Jesus unequivocally asserted to two different groups of disciples that His suffering, death and resurrection had been foretold. In speaking with Cleophas and his friend, Jesus, as Luke reports, began with Moses (the Pentateuch) and went through all the Prophets (the former and the latter) and in all the Scriptures what had been predicted about his life and mission (Luke 24:27). On Easter evening Jesus said to those who were present (behind locked doors) including those to whom he had spoken on Easter afternoon: "These are my teachings which I spoke to you while I was still with you, that everything written in the Law of Moses and in the Prophets and the Psalms about Me must come true. He then opened

408

their minds to understand the Scriptures." He said to them: "So it is written, that Christ must suffer and rise from the dead on the third day, and that repentance and remission of sins must be preached in His name" (Luke 24:44).

Paul begins his great classic letter, Romans, with the following assertion: "Paul, a servant of Christ Jesus, a called apostle, set apart for the Gospel of God, which in advance He promised through His prophets in the sacred Scriptures regarding His Son, who as to His human nature was descended from David and according to the Spirit of holiness was openly designated as the Son of God with power when he was raised as the Son of God with power when He was raised from the dead, even Jesus Christ our Lord" (1:1-3).

The great concern of Old Testament prophecy was Jesus Christ, for as Peter wrote to the congregations of Asia Minor: "About this salvation the prophets who prophesied of the blessing intended for you, made inquiry and research to find out to whom or to what time the Spirit of Christ within them pointed, when it predicted the sufferings that were destined for Christ, and the glories along with them. To them it was disclosed that they were rendering their ministries not for themselves, but for you, the announcements that are now made to you by those through the Holy Spirit sent from heaven have been bringing you the good news, such as angels long to stoop and look into" (I Peter 1:10-12).

In the early chapters of Acts, Luke provided us with samples of the preaching of Peter. The latter's sermon on Pentecost, the first apostolic Gospel sermon recorded, was based entirely on prophecies of the Old Testament; first, the outpouring of the Holy Spirit, as foretold by Joel; then the resurrection of Christ, from the sixteenth Psalm; and finally His exaltation to power at the right hand of God as prophesied by David in Psalm 110.

In the second sermon of Peter, Acts 3, the apostle made the appeal in a similar way, calling upon his hearers to accept Jesus as the Promised Christ of the Old Testament: "Those things which God before had showed by the mouth of all of his prophets, that the Christ should suffer. He hath so fulfilled" (v. 18).

When Peter and John were brought before the Sanhedrin for healing the lame man, Peter full of the Holy Spirit, said to the leaders and elders: "Then you should all know, that all the people of Israel should know, that this man stands here before you completely well by the power of the Name of Jesus Christ — whom you crucified and God raised from death . . . Jesus is the one from whom the Scriptures say, 'The stone that you builders despised, turned out to be the most important stone.' Salvation is to be found through him alone for there is no one else in all the world whose name God has given to men, by whom we can be saved" (Acts 4:10-12).

In his Pentecost sermon in the house of Cornelius, Peter said: "And he commanded us to preach the Gospel to the people, and to testify that he is the one whom God has appointed Judge of the living and the dead. All the prophets spoke about him, saying that everyone who believes in him, will have his sins forgiven through the power of his name" (Acts 10:42-43).

The apostle John wrote in Revelation 19:10 that "the witness of Jesus is the spirit of prophecy." The witness of Jesus by angels, apostles, and martyrs found in Revelation is the same witness as the witness of prophecy. In commenting on this verse Dr. Lenski wrote: "Some restrict this ('the prophecy') to the prophecy contained in these visions in Revelation, but the substance is that of all Scriptures."[22]

Philip the Evangelist found Christ in the Old Testament. No passage is more helpful in showing us how the New Testament Christians interpreted the Old Testament than the episode involving Philip, who was sent by the Holy Spirit to convert the Prime Minister of Candace, Queen of Abyssinia. He had attended one of the great festivals of Judaism in Jerusalem. The festival visitor had procured a copy of the Prophets, which he was reading on his way home to Africa, Philip the Evangelist, led by the Spirit of God, came near to Gaza as the eunuch was reading the 53rd chapter of Isaiah. When Philip had joined him and had heard the African Prime Minister reading the Isaianic passage, he asked the latter whether he understood what he had read. They reread chapter 53 and when they came to verses 7 and 8, Philip asked his pupil; "Of whom speaketh the prophet this?" These were the verses of the Great Servant passage which spoke of the atoning death of Jesus Christ. Luke then reported that Philip "starting from this passage, he told him the Good News about Jesus" (v. 35). If this was not truly speaking about Jesus' suffering and death, then Philip was guilty of reading a meaning into the chapter it was not intended to have.

Because of its many predictive prophecies about the person and work of Jesus Christ, the New Testament Christian will wish constantly to study and read the Old Testament because the Old Covenant Scripture sets forth the same plan of salvation as does the New Testament.

Answer 4: Because the Old Testament does not differ from the New Testament in the doctrine of salvation, the Means of Grace are the same in the Old Testament as they were in the New Testament. Francis Pieper pointed this out in Volume III of his Christian Dogmatics when he wrote:

> The Gospel of Christ, the divine message of the remission of sins by faith in Christ, was the means of grace for the whole era of the Old Testament. So the scriptures themselves inform us, declaring: "To Him give all the Prophets witness that through His name whosoever believeth in Him shall receive remission of sins" (Acts 10:43). Abraham believed in Christ; "Your father Abraham rejoiced to see my day; and he saw it and was glad" (John 8:56). Moses wrote of Christ (John 5; 46). The Christians of the New Testament have the same faith as Abraham, are called "the children of Abraham" (Gal. 3:7), and "Abraham's seed" (Gal. 3:29). The New Testament Scriptures state explicitly that the Christian doctrine of justification, justification by faith in Christ without the deeds of the Law, is witnessed in all the Scriptures

of the Old Testament martyroumena hup tou nomou kai ton propheton (Rom. 3;21).[23]

In both his Romans and Galatian Epistles the Apostle Paul argues that the doctrine of justification is not a new doctrine that he is advancing, but that it was the belief of Abraham and David, to mention two outstanding Old Testament characters who were justified by faith in Christ. Paul states that even under the Law Christ remained in force as means of grace. Gal. 3:17 asserts: "The covenant that was confirmed before of God in Christ, the Law, which was 430 years after, cannot disannul that it should make the promise of non-effect." When Christ came in the fullness of time, the Jews did not accept Him as the promised Messiah foretold in the Old Testament Scriptures. Unfortunately today in a large segment of European and American Lutheranism, Lutheran scholars cannot find the same plan of salvation in the Old Testament as they do in the New. Pieper wrote concerning this matter, a position already found in the first decades of this century, when he averred: "For the same reason, namely, disregard of the words of Scripture, some theologians past and present have been blind to the fact that ever since the Fall throughout the entire Old Testament era, the Gospel has been the divinely appointed means of communicating grace to men and that faith in the Gospel made men the children of God."[24]

Beginning with the Fall, Luther and the Lutheran theologians of the 16th and following centuries, accepted Genesis 3:15 as the first Gospel promise. Luther called the first promise after the Fall both "very lucid and clear," as also "very dark."[25] It was very dark as to its accompanying circumstances, since as yet nothing of Abraham's Seed, David's Branch, Mary's Son, was known. Clear, however, because Gen. 3:15 promises the Woman's Seed, in whom God Himself is the acting subject, who will make an end of the devil in his work of destroying mankind, that is He will abolish death itself as well as the death of men. Luther wrote about Gen. 3:15: "The Seed of the woman shall bruise thy head. This passage is the absolution whereby God acquitted Adam and Eve and all of us. For if the Seed is so strong that He crushes the head of the Serpent, then He also crushes all its power; then the devil is overcome and all the loss made good which Adam had incurred, and he is again placed in the state he was in formerly."[26] For this reason Luther does not grant that there was a difference between the faith of Adam and Eve and the faith of New Testament Christians as related to the plan of salvation.[27]

Quenstedt held the same view of Luther on the nature of the faith of Old Testament saints, when he wrote:

> Substantially the same Gospel which today is preached in the whole world stood in full vigor and freshness and was promulgated also in the Old Testament, and indeed from the earliest times of the fallen human family, through which the grace of God, the remission of sins, and one and the same salvation in Christ, the Redeemer of the world, was announced and offered to all; and all in the Old Testament, as many as were justified and saved, were justified and saved by faith in the merits of Christ, which benefited before it existed (quod profuit,

antequam fuit).[28]

The position of Luther, Quenstedt, and others was the understanding of Christ and the apostles. This did not mean that the Lutheran interpreters did not acknowledge a difference in the degree of the knowledge of the clarity of the Gospel as known by the Old Testament members of the Church of God.

The rites of circumcision and the Passover, instituted by Yahweh, were, ever since their institution means of grace for the time of the Old Testament. The promise in Genesis 17:7: "I will establish My covenant between Me and thee and thy seed after thee in their generations for an everlasting covenant, to be a God unto thee, and to thy seed after thee," was tantamount to asserting that the Israelites were being assured of the remission of sins by the rite of circumcision.[29] It was for this reason that Paul denominated circumcision "a seal of the righteousness of the faith."[30]

Exodus 12:21ff shows that the Children of Israel were saved from punishment and death because they were obedient and followed Moses' God-given directive to smear the blood of the pascal lamb on their doorposts. It was because of the typical act of pointing to the sacrificing of Christ, God's Pascal Lamb, that the Israelites were saved from destruction and death. Concerning this Luther wrote: "It is not true that the Sacraments of the New Testament differ from the Sacraments of the Old Testament as to their signification (namely, as God-appointed signs of the grace of God)..." "Both our and the father's signs or Sacraments have a word of promise attached which calls for faith and can be fulfilled by no other work. Therefore they are signs or Sacraments of justification."[31] With Luther Francis Pieper would agree, the latter correctly asserting: "Both through the Word about the coming Messiah and through circumcision and the Passover, the Sacraments of the Old Testament, the remission of sins was given and, by the believers appropriated."[32]

Answer 5: The Old Testament must be known properly to understand the New Testament.

The careful reader of the New Testament will observe many cross references to almost all books of the Bible. A look at footnotes of the Revised Standard Version will show that over 1,300 Old Testament passages are referred to, either as direct quotations or as allusions. The listing in the appendix of the Nestle *Novum Testamentum Graece* will graphically illustrate the great use of the Old Testament by New Testament authors.[33] Another list that shows the extensive use of the Old Testament by the New Testament writers is given in Henry Barclay Swete's *Introduction to the Old Testament in Greek* (Cambridge: At the University Press, 1900).[34]

(Swete lists the special passages quoted in each book of the New Testament as follows: Matthew has 40, Mark 19; Luke 17; John 12; Acts 12; Acts 23; Romans has 42; I and II Corinthians 19; Galatians 10. Of the imprisonment Letters (Colossians, Philippians, Ephesians, Philemon) only Ephesians has five direct quotations. Hebrews quotes 28 passages

412

from various Old Testament books. While the Book of Revelation does not have any direct quotations, it constantly alludes to events, personalities and passages of the Old Covenant's Scriptures; it has been estimated that there are about 450 references and allusions to Old Testament materials in the 22 chapters of the Apocalypse. Edward Reuss, in his *History of the Canon*, wrote: "There is hardly a page in the New Testament where Old Testament is not cited."[35]

The ideological milieu in which the New Testament operates is basically a Hebrew book, as may be seen from the many terms employed — words such as glory, peace, covenant, truth, spirit, life, the day of the Lord, sin, atonement, suffering servant, salvation, and many others. The New Testament theological terminology cannot be understood apart from the Hebrew Old Testament and its Greek translation, the Septuagint.

In addition to the above arguments. Professor Myers claims that the New Testament cannot stand alone and must be combined with the Old Testament. Thus he asserted: "It requires the weight of more than fifteen hundred years of Hebrew religion-historical experience to prevent its evaporation in speculative theology or erosion of the incarnational aspects of God's revelation by a subtle gnostic attitude toward history."[36]

The Hebraic background of a number of Old Testament books is very pronounced. The first book of the New Testament, the Gospel according to Matthew, surely cannot adequately be understood apart from a knowledge of the Old Testament.[37] Matthew desires that the Hebrew people, who have not yet accepted Jesus of Nazareth as the promised Messiah, to see that the many Old Testament prophecies accepted as Messianic by the Hebrew rabbis, were fulfilled in the person and life of Jesus Christ. A characteristic of his Gospel is the phrase, "this happened that it might be fulfilled which was spoken by the prophet," a phrase that occurs at least 45 times in the 28 chapters of this Gospel. Another New Testament book that requires a good knowledge of the Old Testament is the anonymous Epistle to the Hebrews. Written to Hebrew Christians who were being tempted by non-Christian Jews to apostatize and return to the type of Judaism they had given up in favor of Christianity, the author (possibly Paul, Barnabas, Apollos, Timothy) shows how the religion and teachings of Jesus Christ are superior to the religion and teachings of Judaism. "Better than" is the key of the Epistle. [38]

The Hebrew's author shows how Christ is superior to the angels and supports this with a list of Old Testament passages taken from various Old Testament writings. Chapter 1 of Hebrews shows the Christocentric character of a number of Old Testament passages and thus makes an important contribution to the subject of Biblical hermeneutics. In chapter 3 the author shows the superiority of Jesus to Moses; in chapter 4 to Joshua; and in chapters 5 to 10 the superiority of the priesthood of Melchizedek to that of Aaron. Jesus was not descended from Levi but from Judah. The Epistle of the Hebrews is replete with Old Testament quotations as well as with references to the Levitical cultus instituted in the days of Moses. No adequate interpretation is possible of the Hebrews Epistle apart from a thorough knowledge of the Old Testament.

413

Chapter 11 lists the heroes of faith of Old Testament history. In this chapter there are references to Abel, Enoch, Noah, Abraham, Sarah, Isaac, Jacob, Joseph, Moses, Rahab, Gideon, Barak, Samson, Jephthah, David, Samuel. The same chapter also refers to various historical events in connection with the just mentioned people, also to the miracles in Daniel of protecting the friends of Daniel in the fiery furnace, protecting Daniel from being eaten by lions. Also to the Old Testament miracles of resurrection, for we are told: "Women received back their dear ones alive from the dead" (1 Kings 17:23; 2 Kings 4:37). Hebrews 11 cannot be really understood apart from the allusion to events and personalities referred to in the Old Testament.

James is a thoroughly Jewish book, saturated with references and allusions to the Old Testament. The James Epistle is addressed to the Twelve Tribes of Israel, probably written before many Gentile congregations had been established. James has been called by one writer "the most Jewish book in the New Testament." The most Jewish books are said to be the Gospel according to Matthew, Hebrews, James and the Apocalypse. Matthew, Revelation and Hebrews have more of a Christian element than James.[39] In James there is no mention of the incarnation and resurrection of Christ, who is just mentioned twice in the epistle. There is no missionary message; there are no details about the Second Coming of Christ. There appear to be many parallels to ideas expressed in the Sermon on the Mount.

The following have been mentioned as constituting the Jewish features of James: 1. It is addressed to the 12 tribes of the Dispersion; 2. the meeting place is the synagogue; 3. Abraham is mentioned as "our Father" (2:21); 4. God is given the Old Testament name of "The Lord Sabbaoth" (5:4); 5. sins of the flesh are not inveighed against but by those to which the Jews were more conspicuously liable, 2:2-4; 4:4-6; 5:7-11; 3:1-12; 4:11, 12; 6. the law is not to be spoken against nor judged reverently and vaguely; 7. the illustrations of faithfulness and patience are founded in the Old Testament characters as: Abraham, 2:21; Rahab 2:25; Job 5:11; Elijah 5:17, 18; 8. many references to Old Testament books. There are allusions to Genesis, Exodus, Leviticus, Deuteronomy, Joshua, Job, Proverbs, and Isaiah.[40]

The one chapter Epistle to Jude contains a rather large number of references to Old Testament characters and happenings.[41] The author, Jude, wishes to warn his readers against apostasy; he warns them about the heretical agnostics who already seem to have led certain Christians astray. While there are no direct Biblical quotations, a knowledge of the Old Testament is presupposed. He lists a number of examples from Old Testament times, when sensualists were punished. In verses 5-6 he alluded to the miraculous deliverance of the children of Israel, many of whom perished in the wilderness because of unbelief. The great destruction of Sodom and Gomorrah, reported by Moses in chapter 19 of Genesis, is cited as an example of sensuality which was not left unpunished. In verse 9 Jude reports a fact not given in Deuteronomy, namely, that Michael and the Devil disputed about the body of Moses. Cain's way, Bal-

414

aam's error as well as Korah's rebellion are given as evidence of individuals who forsook the ways of God and thus were guilty of apostasy.

The last book of our presently arranged New Testament is the Apocalypse, a book which cannot be understood without a knowledge of the apocalyptical literature of the Old Testament. While there are no express quotations from the Old Testament, yet the book is a mosaic of Old Testament phrases,[42] taken especially from the apocalyptic portions, as may be seen when examining certain passages from Isaiah, Zephaniah, Zechariah, Ezekiel and Daniel. Examples of the use of Old Testament apocalyptical portions can be seen as follows: Compare Rev. 1:13ff with Ezek. 1:7; 43:2; Dan. 10:5; Rev. 4:1 with Ezek. 1:26ff.; Rev. 4:6ff., with Ezek. 1:26ff; Is. 6:2; Rev. 5 with Ezek. 2:2,9; Zech. 5:1-3; Rev. 6:14 with Is. 34:4; Rev. 7:3 with Ezek. 9:4; Rev. 10:5f., with Dan. 12:7; Rev. 10:9-11 with Ezek. 3:13; Rev. 11:1 with Zech. 2:1; Rev. 11:3f., with Zech. 4:2,11, 14; Rev. 12:7 with Dan. 7:2-8; Rev. 14:20 with Is. 63:3; Rev. 19:17 with Ezek. 39:17-20; Rev. 20:8 with Ezek. 38:2; Rev. 20:12 with Dan. 7:10; 12:1; Rev. 21:1 with Is. 55:17-19; 66:22; Rev. 21:10ff., with Ezek. 48:30ff.,; Rev. 22:1f., with Ezek. 47:1,12; Zech. 14:8. Chapters 17 and 18 are almost entirely from the Old Testament.

Answer 6: The Old Testament gives Christianity a Historical Setting.

Unlike the Buddhist faith and other Far Eastern religions, whose religious beliefs are not necessarily tied up with historical events that are essential to these faiths, Christianity has its center in events in history. Jesus Christ was born during the reign of Caesar Augustus, crucified under Pontius Pilate and died and was buried in a province of the Roman Empire during the reign of Tiberius. The birth of Christ in Bethlehem had many events leading up to it. As John B. Taylor wrote:

In this story there are three focal points: call and choice of Abraham to be the forefather of God's people, the divine deliverance of the exodus and the crossing of the Red Sea under Moses, and the restoration of the exiled Jews from the Babylonian captivity in the sixth century B.C. All these were historical incidents which stand out like mountain peaks on the canvas of the Jewish background to the rise of Christianity.

Unlike other religions which are mainly built around the views of one great man, the religion of the Bible looks back to actual historical events when God did something tremendous. The Old Testament tells the story of the great things God did before Christ was born, and the New Testament tells of God's greatest act in sending His Son to live and to die for mankind. [43]

The great historical events that constitute the heart of the Christian message have their antecedents in the Old Testament, which is also characterized by its historical character.

Answer 7: The Old Testament is a vital part of the Inspired

415

Revelation of God, described in the New Testament as having various uses and purposes.

The New Testament clearly shows in many different ways that the writings of the Old Testament are the Word of God. What could be clearer than Paul's assertion that the Old Testament, on which Timothy had been nourished since babyhood, was **theopneustos? Theopneustos** means "God-spirited" or "God breathed." Just as the breath comes out of a person, so the Scriptures came out from God. The term **theopneustos** indicates that in their entirety the Old Testament Scriptures are from God and by God.[44] Paul informed Timothy that "every Scripture is inspired by God and so useful for teaching, for reproof, for correction, and for instruction in right doing; so that the man of God may be complete, perfectly equipped for every good work."[45] In this passage Paul employs four terms which are a matter of key importance. What is the precise meaning of these four terms? If these four words, "doctrine," "reproof," "correction," and "instruction in righteousness" describe the value of the Christian use of the Old Testament, then we must examine their precise meaning as given in the Greek.

The first word used by Paul is **didaskalia**, rendered in the KJV "doctrine," in other translations "teaching." **Didaskalia is employed twenty-one times** in the Greek New Testament, nineteen times by Paul and twice by Christ in the Synoptic Gospels. Fifteen of the twenty-one occurrences are in Paul's last letters, Titus and 1 and II Timothy. The best translation is teaching, which comes very close to doctrine.[46]

The second of the four terms is **elegymos**, which the KJV renders "reproof." **Elegymos** occurs only in this passage in the New Testament, but it is used in the Septuagint in connection with "chastisement" or "punishment"[47] "Reproof" is a, fairly adequate translation for **elegymos** as the word carries with it the idea of correction or censure. Gaebelein believes that "conviction" would bring out the real meaning of this Greek word.[48]

The third word employed in this significant passage is **epanorthosis**, translated "correction" in the Authorized Version. Again this Greek word is the only occurrence in the New Testament. Literally the word **epanorthosis** signifies "restoration to an upright position or state; hence correction and improvement."[49] The word is, therefore, preferably translated "restoration."

The fourth word is **paideia**, used twice in the New Testament, rendered in the KJV as "instruction in righteousness." According to Thayer, **paideia** means first of all "the whole training and education of children in relation to the cultivation of mind and morals and employs for this purpose new commands and admonition and reproof and punishment."[50] As for other than children, Thayer defines it as "whatever in adults also cultivates the soul, especially by correcting mistakes and curbing passions; hence instruction which aims at the increase of virtue." In the light of this information, it might be better to translate **paideia** as "education in righteousness."[51]

While the Scriptures are declared by Paul to be profitable for a series of four definite and clearly differentiated uses, the Scriptures are to be productive of doing something beneficial for mankind. "All Scripture is God breathed, and is profitable for teaching, for conviction, for restoration, for education in righteousness: that the man of God may be perfect thoroughly furnished unto all good works." Philosophy may be satisfied with dealing with truth in the abstract, but the Bible, while interested in the truth, is also concerned with the consequences from the embracement of Biblical truth. In another of his epistles Paul put it this way: "By grace are ye' saved through faith, and that not of yourselves; it is the gift of God; not of works lest any man should boast. For we are his workmanship, created in Christ Jesus unto good works, which God has ordained that we should walk in them" (Eph. 2:8-10). The incarnate Word of God became flesh to save mankind from its sins and offer reconciliation and a new life with God and with this new life there was to be an accomplishment of good works.

In the light of this fourfold purpose of the Old Testament Scriptures (and also of the New Testament Scriptures), how can the various writings composing the Old Testament serve teaching, conviction, restoration and education in righteousness?

However, before embarking on a discussion of this fourfold use of the Old Testament, a word should be said about the order and the progression of the four words. Would it have made any difference if Paul had reversed the order and said: "Conviction, education in righteousness, restoration and teaching?" The answer is that it makes a great deal of difference, because Paul is definitely speaking about the Holy Scriptures. Correctly does Gaebelein contend: "There is nothing haphazard or accidental about the order of those four words; they set a logical progression of ideas which summarizes the way in which the Bible acts upon the human heart and life. Therefore, to change their order would be fatal to an accurate description of the way in which Scripture works. But Paul never makes a mistake like that."[52]

Didaskalia, "teaching" comes first. How can a person be saved and how can he live as a man of God if he does not know what is involved in being saved and what he is being saved for? The Bible teaches the facts of Christianity. True faith and responsible and God-pleasing living are not based upon feeling, upon mysticism or pragmatism. The human mind is so constituted that it requires something upon which to exercise faith. "Teaching" comes first, not second, third, or fourth.

Elegymos, "conviction" is portrayed as the second step in making wise unto salvation in Christ Jesus. It is through the word of God that the sinner is brought to a conviction of sins and also through the Word of God that he is convinced that Jesus died for his sins and that through the work of the suffering Servant he is saved.

Epanorthosis, "restoration" to an upright state is a part of the manner in which a person becomes wise unto salvation, and is involved in the process of making "the man of God." The Word of God is the teaching which, when applied to the individual, produces the conviction of sin and works repentance. However, if the man of God is to be formed according

417

to God's pattern, he will also need the work of restoration. The Bible teaches that man is a fallen creature, fallen to the extent of being spiritually speaking, dead. In order to have fellowship with God, man needs to be born again. It is through the teaching of Scripture, through which the Holy Spirit operates that the fallen sinner is brought to an upright position again. Renovation is not enough but there must be a new heart and a new life created. "And only the Bible message of redemption through the blood of Christ and justification guaranteed by His resurrection avails for this regeneration of fallen sinners."[53]

Paideia, "education in righteousness" logically follows the other three steps. Through the teaching of Scripture the new man in Christ has been created, but he needs to be taken in hand and educated. One of the great purposes of both the Old and New Testament Scriptures is to give "education in righteousness." In Christian education the Holy Scriptures are employed to bring about this type of education in righteousness. Although it is usual to translate **paideia** as "instruction" it means especially "training, discipline." Just as a child is trained and disciplined, so the Scriptures are of value in training and disciplining the believer in all righteous living. This same Greek word is translated "nurture" in Ephesians 6:4, "Chastening" in Hebrews 12:5, 7, 11 and "chastisement" in Hebrews 12:8. As the Word of God is studied and applied to an individual's life, it enables him to live righteously.

The results of such use of the Scripture eventuates in the man of God being made "perfect," in Greek **artios**, meaning "complete, capable, efficient." The Greek **artios** does not mean perfect in the sense that there are imperfections in the individual. This is the one and only time that the word occurs in the New Testament. It is derived from the word aro, meaning "to fit" or "to be specially adapted." Vincent says that the idea of **artios** is that of "mutual, symmetrical adjustment of all that goes to make the man, harmonious combination of different qualities and powers."[54]

The Old Testament is here described as especially equipping the believer to do God's Work, the work God wishes and wants the believer to do. The believer, who is so equipped by reading and heeding the Word of God as found in the Old Testament, is thoroughly furnished unto all good works. The words "thoroughly furnished" are translated from one Greek word, **exartizo**. This word is related to **artios**, but with the added preposition (ex), it has the sense of "altogether fit" or "fully fitted."

From this we see that the Old Testament has no lack of power to prepare the man of God to do "all good works." The Greek word is singular for "works," and thus more correctly should be rendered "all good work."

Answer 8: Because in the Old Testament there are forms of literary genre that are not found in the New Testament.

The New Testament has four types of distinctive literature: the Gospels, Acts, the church history of Luke, the twenty-one epistles (13 by Paul, 8 by Peter, James, Jude, John, Hebrews) and the apocalyptical book of Revelation. There are distinctive forms of inspired literary genre found in the Old Testament, not at all represented in the New Testament. The

Old Testament has types of literature not found in the New; appreciation of the former is a **sine qua non** for the reader of the New Testament.

It has previously been pointed out that there are over one thousand direct quotations and allusions from the Old Testament. Adequately to understand many of the Old Testament references and allusions in the Old Testament books from which these have been excerpted and drawn need to be read and understood. Three hundred and ninety pages out of a total of seven hundred and fifty in one edition of the *Revised Standard Version* contain the historical books Genesis to Joshua, Joshua to II Kings. 1 and II Chronicles, Esther, Ezra and Nehemiah, all of which can be classified, as they are in the Septuagint, as historical books. In these twelve books we have an inspired history beginning with creation and covering the primeval period, the patriarchal, the Mosaic, the era of the conquest under Joshua, followed by that of the Judges. With Samuel the transition from theocracy to the days of the united monarchy occurs with Saul, Ishbaal, David, and Solomon as rulers. This is followed by the division of the United Kingdom on Solomon's death with a northern kingdom and a southern kingdom thereafter existing side by side. The Books of Samuel, Kings, and Chronicles give Old Testament readers the information regarding the history of Israel's United Kingdom and Divided Kingdoms. Ezra, Esther and Nehemiah supply the Biblical reader with the history of Judaism after the return from the Captivity. Each of the twelve historical books has its own spiritual truths to teach and makes a specific contribution to the Old Testament. It is especially from a study of God's actions with his people as reflected in these historical books that the New Testament reader can truly appreciate the fact that the Old Testament contains **Heilsgeschichte** or the history of salvation. Even the genealogies found in Genesis, Exodus, Ezra, and Nehemiah and in the first nine chapters of I Chronicles have a specific contribution to make to an understanding of the plan of God for mankind. Only when the history of the Old Testament is truly grasped, can the New Testament reader comprehend the statement of St. Paul: "When the fullness of the time was come, God sent forth his son born of a woman, placed under the law that we might receive the adoption of sons" (Gal. 4:4).

St. Paul encourages New Testament Christians "to let the Word of Christ dwell in you richly as you teach and admonish one another in all wisdom and as you sing hymns and spiritual songs, with thankfulness in your hearts to God" (Col. 3:16). In this passage Paul encourages the Christians at Colosse to make use of the Psalms of the Old Testament. The Psalter is a unique book in the Old Testament canon of the Bible. The New Testament quotes more frequently from this Old Testament inspired book than any other in the Old Testament. The Psalms have come to be known as the prayer book of the Second Temple. The 150 poems of this collection reflect all the experiences to which the human soul and spirit can be exposed and in which man can become involved; in these poems is found the entire gamut of emotional experiences that characterize man's existence. The Psalter has been a favorite devotion book of both Jews and Christians down through the centuries. The Psalter is called the Word of God in the New Testament; further also the Holy Spirit is said to have spoken through David who authored 75 out of the 150 poems of the Psalms book.

Luther said that "a Christian ought to know the Psalms as well as he knows his five fingers; then also the four evangelists will be well understood" (St. L., 22:781). Again he declared: "Every Christian who would devoutly pray ought to use the Book of Psalms. In the Book of Psalms you will find yourself and the right kind of self-knowledge and also God Himself and all creatures" (14:24). "The Book of Psalms is the book for all saints; each will find psalms and words in it as though they were written to supply his own particular needs"(14:23). "The Book of Psalms might well be called a small Bible, for it very clearly prophesies Christ's death and resurrection and portrays His kingdom and the condition and true nature of entire Christendom" (14:20). "In the Book of Psalms the Holy Spirit supplies us with the words and thoughts for our prayers and petitions to our heavenly Father" (4:215).

In the Harvard Classics this assertion is made about the Psalms that we find "profundity of feeling, simplicity of expression, and variety of religious experiences. The religious moods to which they give utterance are manifold. Adoration and thanksgiving, prayer, and penitence and imprecation, history and prophecy, the general worship as a whole, people and the intimate impulses of an individual soul — all these and many more are represented in the supreme collection of sacred song" (44:146).

It is against the background of the Psalms that the New Testament hymns found in chapters 1 and 2 of the Lucan Gospel can be properly appreciated. The Benedictus of Zechariah, the Magnificat of Mary, Elizabeth's Hymn of praise, the Gloria in Excelsis of the Heavenly Angelic Chorus, and the Nunc Dimittis of Simeon have their background in the Old Testament psalmody.

In Colossians 3:16 Paul calls upon the followers of Christ to "teach and admonish one another with all wisdom." One of the distinctive literary forms in the Old Testament was the so-called **Chochmah** literature (wisdom Literature), found in Proverbs, Ecclesiastes, Job, and in certain psalms. Certain New Testament books utilize wisdom thoughts from this Old Testament literary genre. The Sermon on the Mount, verses in 1 Corinthians and James have passages pertaining to wisdom. The New Testament portions that could be classified as wisdom passages are few in number as compared with the material that specifically has been classified as belonging to the **Chochmah** literature of the Old Testament.

In the Old Testament we have the proverb as a unique literary genre. The greatest concentration of proverbial material is to be found in the book of Proverbs, which has been aptly described as containing "Laws from heaven for living on earth." Writing in the form of proverbs has the advantage of stating truth so briefly that it is easily remembered; hiding it in a figure of speech excited the mind:

"To Understand a proverb and a figure;
The words of the wise, and their dark sayings" (Prov. 1:6).

Francis Bacon has made the following assertion about the literary power of the aphoristic method of presenting truth:

The writing of aphorisms hath many excellent virtues, whereto the writing in method does not approach, for first it trieth the writer, whether he be superficial or solid, for aphorisms, except they be ridiculous, cannot be made but of the pith and heart of science; for discourse of illustration is cut off. So there remains nothing to fill the aphorisms but some good quantity of observation; and therefore no man can suffice, nor in reason will attempt to write aphorisms, but that he is sound and grounded.[56]

Jesus had in mind the words in chapter 25:6, 7 when He said it was better to take the lowest seat at the feast, and Paul found his forcible metaphor about heaping coals of fire upon the head of an enemy in the 21st and 22nd verses of the same chapter.

Another important contribution of the Old Testament to theological teaching is the Book of Ecclesiastes. There would have been a real gap in the Bible had it not been included. This book has been completely misunderstood by many of its students who have written monographs and commentaries on it. As literature the book has been recognized as outstanding. Stedman said this about Ecclesiastes: "Whether prose or verse, I know nothing grander than Ecclesiastes in its impassioned survey of mortal pain and pleasure, its estimate of failure and success; none of more noble sadness; no poem working more indomitable for spiritual illumination."[57] However, we are interested in Ecclesiastes as God's Word. In this book Solomon, writing probably from a lifetime of experiences came to realize that apart from the fear of Yahweh and the keeping of God's Commandments, there can be no lasting happiness. Many experiences and pursuits in themselves noble and necessary, cannot apart from God give lasting satisfaction. The quest for satisfaction ends with the conclusion: "Fear God and keep his commandments: for this is the whole duty of man" (12:14).

A type of literature which occupies many pages of the Old Testament is that written by the prophets. Not only the four major prophets (Isaiah, Jeremiah, Ezekiel, Daniel) but also the Twelve Minor Prophets (Hosea. Joel, Amos, Obadiah, Jonah, Micah, Nahum, Habakkuk, Zephaniah, Haggai, Zechariah and Malachi) will supply the Biblical student with material for religious education and instruction. The prophetic literature of the Old Testament is unique. Dinsmore is correct when he wrote: "No other nation, either before or since, has a literature quite like this — page following page representing the Most High as speaking directly to the people, arguing, pleading, exhorting; the Everlasting earnestly concerned in the welfare of a feeble and shifting people. In the Hebrew seers we have a unique group of men and a unique literature."[58]

Fritz has suggested that for a better appreciation of the Prophetic literature that the New Testament believer "should make a careful study of the time during which, and the conditions under which, the prophets made utterances, and the purpose for which the Lord sent His prophets; also a careful study of the prophetic language. When this background has been acquitted, the contents of the prophetic books will be better understood. In fact, such understanding is necessary for a clearer presentation of the prophetic writings and their application to present conditions and needs."[59]

Answer 9: Because the New Testament Christian and believer who happens to function as teacher and pastor will find material in the Old Testament that will contribute vital understanding of God's revelation to mankind.

The teacher and preacher will find treasures for purposes of religious instruction, whether in Sunday school, Bible class or the worship services that cannot be ignored without doing an injustice to those whom they have been called to serve as proclaimers of God's Word. Sunday school teachers, parochial school teachers and pastors in connection with religious education in the various agencies of the church should not neglect the inculcation of the Old Testament facts and truths. To be able to utilize the Old Testament effectively, a thorough knowledge of the Old Testament will be required of those who would instruct the various age groups found in a congregation.

Years ago already when in conflict with rationalistic churchmen the champions of Biblical orthodoxy stressed the fact that Christianity is based upon divine revelation and therefore came to regard the inclusion of the history of revelation as well as the genesis of Christianity as an integral part of the education of the young.[60] One of the positive contributions of Von Hofman, the great theologian of Erlangen, was to emphasize the desirability of connecting Bible stories in such a manner as to show a connected plan of salvation. In recent years the views of an unbiblical philosophy of education have resulted in affecting the instruction of Biblical history. The value of the Old Testament and also in part the New Testament as records of the history of redemption is denied; yes, often, in fact their historicity is rejected. Negative higher criticism, utilizing form and redaction criticism, has rejected the historicity of the first eleven chapters and has cast doubt upon the reliability of much of the historical narratives in Genesis 12-50, the contents of Exodus, Numbers, Joshua, Judges and 1 Samuel. In the New Testament even the narratives of Jesus' infancy and of His resurrection and ascension are dismissed as legendary.

Martin Reu, outstanding Luther scholar and Lutheran theologian, already forty-five years ago lamented the exclusion of Old Testament history from the program of religious education. The former famed Wartburg professor wrote:

And, indeed if modern criticism were right, according to which this part of the Bible is highly legendary and mythical or at best a mere "Jewish Chronicle," then instruction in Old Testament history would be less important than national history and certainly would deserve no place in the curriculum of the church school. But let us not forget that the Old Testament was the Bible of Jesus; that through its connection with the history of the New Testament it has become part and parcel of the history of salvation; that it is preparatory to the New

422

Testament history or revelation; that it is preparatory to the New Testament history of revelation to such an extent that many single facts of the New Testament simply cannot be understood without the Old; and even Jesus Christ and His life work cannot possibly be fully appreciated save as He is recognized as the goal toward which for more than a thousand years God directed the course of human history, and as the Savior who in the fullness of time should still the longing of the whole pre-Christian world (Gal. 4:4).These facts indicate the necessity for an introduction into Old Testament history, and, at the same time, the duty of relating everything with a view to Him as its goal.[61]

The many characters discussed in the course of Old Testament history are excellent models of individuals whose lives displayed an evangelical life of faith worthy to be held up for imitation. On the one hand they were men who had unshaken faith in Yahweh, who repeatedly turned their hope to the promises of God, and who manifested courage by persevering in their faith despite bitter adversity. The teacher who knows that one of the purposes of religious instruction is to train his pupil in godly living will not wish better examples. Solomon wrote by divine inspiration: "Righteousness exalteth a nation, but sin is a reproach to any people," thus implying that there are moral principles people must he acquainted with and according to which they must live.

"In order that this may be achieved the teacher should draw forth and impress upon children's hearts the holy divine thoughts of permanent value which are contained in the individual Bible story, whether they have reference to the life of faith in its God-ward or its man-ward aspects. A particular welcome opportunity to do this presents itself when the teacher joins a number of stories for the delineation of the character of such outstanding persons as Abraham. Moses, or David, and subsequently in a higher sense, even Christ Himself; he must carefully draw forth The typical traits that to this day continue to be essential to a truly evangelical life and must cast light upon God's relation to these persons and upon their attitude toward God and Their fellowmen."[62]

The pastor in the pulpit as proclaimer of God's message will also utilize the Old Testament. Some pastors neglect the Old Testament as a source for sermon texts and themes. Relative to this matter Reu wrote:

"In order to preach wisely and well upon the Old Testament texts, the preacher should always bear in mind two facts. On the one hand, that it is the same God of our salvation who has revealed Himself in the Old Testament, in deed and word, and who meets us in the New Testament as the Father of our Lord Jesus Christ. On the other hand, that His revelation in the Old Testament, while leading up to Christ, is of the merely preparatory character; so that it must be determined from the standpoint of Christ — both on the mount of beatitudes and on Mount Calvary — what in it is of value and what is not."[64]

To fail to use the Old Testament in preaching would entirely deprive the believers of a congregation of a rich treasure of edifying material, and to run counter to the position of Jesus as well as the stance of the apostles over against the Old Testament and those assertions of the New Testament that testify to the value of the Old Testament for Christians (Romans 15:4; 2 Tim. 3:16).

The Old Testament contains many pages of material which can properly be used in preaching. Since Christ is the heart of the Old Testament, the Messianic passages will of course be utilized for sermonizing. The more prominent ones are: Gen. 3:15; 9:25-27; 12:1-3; 22:18; 49:8-12; Numb. 24:18-24; Deut. 18:15-18; 2 Sam. 2:1-10; 2 Sam. 2:1-10; 2 Sam. 7:12-17; Is. 2:2-4; 4:2-4; 7:14; 9:2-7; 11:1-11; 32:1-8; 40:1-3; 42:1-9; 49:1-9; 50:4-9; 52:13; 53:12; 60:1-6; 61:1-3; Psalms 2, 8, 16, 22, 24, 45, 69, 89, 110, 118; Jer. 23:5-6; 33:13-15; 31:31-34; Ezek. 34:11-17; 23,24; Da. 7:13-14; 9:25-27; Zech. 9:9; Hag. 2:7-10; Joel 3:1-5 (Hebrew text).

In the following the reader will find a partial list of topics and themes from various Old Testament books that have been resorted to in the past history and pedagogical use of the Old Testament:

Genesis.

Chapters 1-11 deal with the origin of the universe, of sin, of redemption, of marriage, family life, of the corruption of society, of the beginning of nations (ch. 10) and the origin of different languages (ch. 9). Certainly the Universal Flood is employed by Jesus in the New Testament to compare it with conditions as they will obtain at the end of the world (chs.6-9). Chapters 12-50 give the selection of Israel as the chosen people of God, and the homiletician can make application to our own time. In Gen. 37-50 the outstanding features of the Life of Joseph can be stressed in setting forth the requirements of the Christian life.

Exodus.

Chapter 1-12 deal with the bondage and deliverance of Israel; chapter 20 with the giving of the Law. The Ten Commandments, with ceremonial and moral laws, will be an important chapter for preaching and instruction. The episode of the Golden Calf (ch. 32) can effectively be employed in preaching. In the history of Israel from Abraham to the Giving of the Law the following special topics are suggested by Dean Fritz: "Even the ungodly in this world are blessed because of God's children, Gen. 39:1-6, Joseph dealing kindly with his brothers, 50:15-21; the Lord's hardening of the heart of the sinner who continually despises the Lord's warnings and pleadings, Ex. 10:27 to 11:1; the Passover lamb, chapter 12, hindrances removed by the Lord (Red Sea), chapter 14; the pillar of cloud by day and pillar of fire by night, 14:19,20; the song of victory, 15:1-19; longing for the flesh-pots of Egypt, for the sensual pleasures of the old life, 16:3; the holding up of Moses' hands, or need of cooperation with our spiritual leaders, 17:10-12."

The Book of Numbers.

The Aaronic blessing, 6:22-27; the brazen serpent, 21:4-9.

The Book of Deuteronomy

The greatest commandment, 6:1-9; the song of Moses, 32:1-7; the blessing of Moses, 32:1-7; the death of Moses, 34:1-8.

The Book of Joshua

In this book we find encouragements to hold fast to the Word of the

Lord, 1:1-10; "As for me and my house, we will serve the Lord" 24:14,15.

The Book of Judges
Another generation which knew not the Lord, 2:8-15.

The Book of Ruth
Ruth's attachment to Naomi and the true religion, 1:15-17.

The First Book of Samuel
"Speak, for thy servant heareth," 3:1-10; Parental indulgence of the sins of their children invites the curse of the Lord, 3:11-19; Jonathan and David are an example of true personal friendship and love, 18:1-4.

Second Book of Samuel
David's prayer reflecting the innermost thoughts of his pious heart, 7:18-29; David's sins reproved by Nathan and David's repentance, 12:1-14.

The First Book of Kings
David, when about to die, charges his son to remain faithful to the Lord, 2:1-4; Solomon's prayer, 3:5-15; Elijah at the brook Charith and with the widow Zarephath, 17:1-16; Elijah at Mount Horeb, 19:1-18, Elijah pronounces God's judgments upon Ahab and Jezebel, 21:17-19.

The Second Book of Kings
The little maid of Israel confesses her God in the house of Naaman, the leper, 5:1-14; building a theological seminary (the iron that swam), 6:1-7.

The Second Book of Chronicles
Azariah promises God's help to King Asa, 15:1-8; the evil reign of Zedekiah and the Babylonian captivity, 36:11-21.

The Book of Ezra
Ezra's prayer of repentance, 9:6-15.

The Book of Nehemiah
Trowel and Sword, 4:7-21; reading and studying God's Word, 8:4-8.

The Book of Job
"Happy is the man whom God correcteth," 5:17-19 or v. 27; "I know that my Redeemer liveth," 19:25-27.

The historical books of the Old Testament contain a wealth of permanently valid truths, whose place cannot be taken by anything else, in their depiction of the leading people and individuals, which repeats itself, in modified and heightened form, on the pages of the New Testament. The pastor who desires to illustrate the nature of faith by living Biblical examples should go to the historical accounts of the Old Testament. If the truth is to be illustrated that righteousness exalteth a nation and sin is a reproach to a people, the history of Israel contains many examples to illustrate this oral truth. The value that Old Testament history can have for the Biblical pastor and teacher is well stated by Reu: "Here is seen the practical application of true religion in the various social relationships, whereas in the New Testament the underlying principles are fully stated but seldom developed and applied. Provided that the preacher takes his stand under the cross of Calvary, it is scarcely possible to overestimate the edifying value of the entire course of Old Testament history, with its constantly recurring factors of human sin and

425

divine grace, and with its continual forward trend toward Christ as its end and goal."[65]

In the prophetic books of the Old Testament there are many excellent texts that could serve as sermon topics or as materials for devotional addresses. The following are some of the texts in the Major and Minor Prophets the pastor would find useful and suggestive:

Isaiah
Religious formalism reproved, 1:1-20.
Salvation and victory for God's people, 25:1-9.
The Voice crying in the wilderness, 40:1-11.
The garments of salvation, 61:10,11.

Jeremiah:
My people have committed two evils, 2:9-13.
A wonderful and horrible thing committed in the land, 5:30-31.
Trust in man cursed, in God blessed, 17:5-8.

Ezekiel:
God hath no pleasure in the wicked, 18:19-23.
The watchman unto the house of Israel, 33:7-20.
The Great Shepherd, 34:11-16.

Daniel:
Daniel remains faithful to his God in a strange land, 1;3-21.
The resurrection, 12:1-4.

Hosea:
The divine Helper and Redeemer from sin and death, 13:9-14.

Joel:
The Pentecostal blessing, 2:28-32.

Obadiah:
God's special providential care for His people for His people against their persecutors, 1-21.

Jonah:
Neglect of duty when called to it by the Lord merits his displeasure.
A great city repents, 3:1-10.
God's great mercy upon sinners should fill our hearts with great joy, 4:1-11.

Micah:
O, My people, what have I done to thee? 6:3-8.

Nahum:
God delivers His people, 1:12-12-15.

Habakkuk:
The just shall live by faith, 2:4.
Habakkuk's prayer concerning God's deliverance and the prophet's faith, 3:1-10.

Zephaniah:
"Rejoice, the Lord has taken away thy judgments; He is mighty and will make you a name and praise among all the people of the earth," 3:14-20.

Haggai:
The people reproved for not building the Lord's house 1:2-14.

The glory of the New Testament Church, 2:6-9.
Zechariah:
Hypocrisy unmasked, 7:1-7.
The Coming of the King, 9:9.
Malachi:
Showers of blessing promised to liberal givers, 3:7-12.
The Son of Righteousness with healing in His wings, 4:1-3.
Dean Fritz also has suggested the following as texts suitable for sermons and for topical discussions:
Genesis:
Isaac's Marriage, 24:14, 12, 50-67.
Jacob's Wrestling with God at Peniel, 32:24-30.
The Christian's Life Pilgrimage, 47:7-9.
Exodus:
From Marah to Elim, Ex. 15:22-27.
Jehovah-Nissi, 17:8-16.
The Holy Name of God, 20:7.
Who Is on the Lord's Side? 32:26.
Numbers:
Discontent, A Common Evil, 14:1-4, 26-40.
Deuteronomy:
The Christian Training of Children, 5:39-6:9.
Thou Shalt Remember the Lord Thy God, 8:1-20.
The Feast of Weeks, or The Old Testament Harvest Home Festival a Pattern for a Right Observance of Our Day of Thanksgiving, 16:9-11.
Joshua:
The Accursed Thing Must Be Destroyed, 7:10-13.
Judges:
Another Generation Which Knew not the Lord, 2:10-23.
The Sword of the Lord and Gideon, 7:15-23.
A Man's religion Put to the Test, 10:10-16.^
I Samuel:
Hannah, A Godly Woman, 2:9-20.
Parents, How Are You Bringing Up Your Children? 3:11-14.
The Great Sin of Rejecting the Word of God, or To Obey is Better than Sacrifice, 15:10-23.
In the Name of the Lord We Conquer our Enemies, 17:45-54.
The Skirt of Thy Robe in My Hand, or Loving the Enemy, 24:1-22.
I Kings:
A Prayer Pleasing to God, 3:5-15.
The Half Was Not Told Me, 10:1-13.
The Truth Plainly Told, 18:17, 18.
The Seven Thousand In Israel, 19:1-18.
II Kings:
Follow Not After Strange Gods, I Kings 22:51-11 Kings 1:4.
The Healing of the Spring, 2:19-22.
Man's Extremity Is God's Opportunity, 3:16-20.
Healing Deadly Pottage, 4:38-41.

Set Thine House in Order, 20:1,
I Chronicles:
Who Is Willing to Consecrate His Service This Day unto the Lord? 29:1-9.
Psalms:
Loving the Habitation of God's House, 26b-28.
The Christian Training of Children, 78:1-8.
The Duty of the Christian Congregation to Enlarge Its Sphere of Influence, 96:1-13.
Serve the Lord with Gladness, 100.
Proverbs:
The Eyes of the Lord, 15:3.
A Word Spoken in Good Season, How Good Is It? 15:22, 23.
The Influence of the Christian Home, 22:6.
Ecclesiastes:
The Christian in the House of God, 5:1.
Isaiah:
A Vision of Self, 6:5-8.
The Faithfulness of God, 54:10.
Return unto the Lord for He Will Abundantly Pardon, 55:1-7.
Jeremiah:
It Is An Evil Thing and Bitter to Forsake God, 2:19-30.
The Everlasting Love of God, 3:1-7.
The Old Paths-the Good Way, 6:16a.
Present conditions and the Church's Opportunity, 6:6-17.

Conclusions:

The Old Testament is a part of the Canon of Holy Scriptures. Opinions have differed with regard to the relationship of the Old Testament to the New. The Reformed Churches as a rule in the past have placed more stress on the Old Testament than has been the case in Lutheranism. The rationalists of the eighteenth and nineteenth centuries together with the Socinians have considered the New Testament as the only source for revelation that is binding for today. The tendency of Higher Criticism has been to minimize the value of the Old Testament for theology and ethics. However, the connection between them is vital, for the New Testament has its roots in the Old Testament. There is but one Kingdom of God and the history and the development of God's kingdom is one coherent story as completely related in both Testaments.

While the New Testament is the climax of divine revelation and therefore logically has the preeminence, as a direct source for the teachings about Christ and salvation, yet the Old Testament is God's Word that makes a distinctive contribution to the entire understanding of the New Testament. The two Testaments constitute an inseparable unity. The reasons for the importance of the Old Testament for the interpretation of the New might be set forth as follows: First, the conception of the one God of the New Testament rests upon the concept of God in the Old, where the doctrine of monotheism is preeminent, however, with indications of the teaching of the Trinitarian character of God also indicated. Second, "the verbal peculiarities of the language and the modes of thought found in the Old Testament, furnish the only clue to the meaning of the New. No man can be a master of the New Testament without a deep acquaintance of the Old." Third, "the Old Testament is rich in matter, of inexpressible interest and value, a value, which grows rather than diminishes with time. It is rich in instruction, rich in all that edifies." If the world did not possess the New Testament, the Old Testament would stand out especially as a book without equal. Fourth, the Old and New Testaments stand together; they both stand or fall together. As Dr. Krauth asserted a century or so ago, "What is a key without a lock, and what is a lock without a key!"

Footnotes

1. Carl Braaten, *New Direction In Theology Today,* Vol. II. *History and Hermeneutics* (Philadelphia: The Westminster Press, 1968), p 105.
2. Emil Brunner, "The Significance of the Old Testament for our Faith," in Bernhard W. Anderson, ed. *The Old Testament and the Christian Faith* (New York: and Evanston: Harper & Row, Publishers, 1963), pp. 244-245.
3. Friedrich Schleiermacher, *The Christian Faith,* H R. Mackin and J. S. Stewart, eds. (Edinburgh: T. & T. Clark, 1928) (1963), p. 60.
4. Quoted from Hans Joachim Kraus, *Geschichte der historischen-kritischen Erforschung des Alten Testaments von der Reformation bis zur Gegenwart* (Neukirchen: Verlag der Buchhandlung des Erziehungsverein, 1956), p. 35.
5. Hans Waller Wolff, *Gesammelte Studien zum Alten Testament* (Munchen: Chr. Kaiser Verlag, 1964), p 325.
6. Braaten, **op. cit.**, pp. 103-104.
7. Exchange found in *Evangelische Theologie,* 24. 3 and 7, 1964.
8. Braaten, **op. cit.**, p. 107.
9. Rudolf Bultmann, "The Significance of the Old Testament for Christian Faith," in Anderson, **op. cit.**, p. 8-35.
10. Rudolf Bultmann, "Prophecy and Fulfillment," in Claus Westermann, ed. Essays in *Old Testament Hermeneutics,* English Translation by James Luther Mays (Richmond. Va.; John Knox Press. 1964). pp. 50-75.
11. James D. Smart, *The Strange Silence of the Bible in the Church* (Philadelphia: The Westminster Press. 1970). pp. 19-20.
12. Walther Zimmerli, *The Law and the Prophets: A Study of the Meaning of the Old Testament* (Harper & Row, Publishers, Inc., 19671, p. 2.
13. Smart, **op cit.**, p 21.
14. **Ibid.**, John B. Taylor, *A Christian's Guide to the Old Testament* (Chicago: Moody Press, 1966), pp. 5-6. Raymond F. Surburg. *How Dependable Is the Bible?* (Philadelphia: J. P. Lippencott Company, 1972), pp. 11-17.
15. Relative to the use of the Old Testament by Christ, cf. Robert P. Lightner, *The Savior and the Scriptures* (Philadelphia: Presbyterian and Reformed Publishing Company, 1966), pp. 1-57. Robert M. Grant, *The Bible in the Church* (New York: The Macmillan Company, 1948), pp 71-76.
16. **Ibid.**, pp 17-30; E. Earle, *Pauls Use of the Old Testament* (Grand Rapids: Wm. B. Eerdmans Publishing Company. 1957), 204 pp.
17. J.B. Lightfoot, *The Epistle to the Galatians* (London: Macmillan Company, 1884), p 147

18. B.B. Warfield, **Revelation and Inspiration** (New York: Oxford University Press. 1927), p. 140.

19. Miller, **op. cit.**, p.

20. **Ibid.**

21. Harold E. Monsor, *Cross-Reference Digest of Bible* References (New York and Chicago: Cross-Reference Bible Company, 1914), pp. 86-87.

22. Johann Andreas Quenstedt, *Didactico-Polemica sive Systema Theologicum,* **II.** p. 1013f. Cf. also p. 1014.

23. Francis Pieper, *Christian Dogmatics* (St. Louis: Concordia Publishing House. 1953), III, p. 211.

24. **Ibid.**, p. 212.

25. St. Louis Edition of the Works of Martin Luther, I, p. 296.

26. **Ibid..** III, p. 66.

27. **Ibid.**, III, p 661; XII, p. 499ff.

28. Cf. R.C.H. Lenski, *The Interpretation of St. John's Revelation* (Columbus: Wartburg Press, 1965) on chapter 19:3.

29. Pieper, **op. cit.,** III, p. 214.

30. Joh. Guiliemi Baieri. *Compendium Theologiae Positivae,* denuo edendum curavit Carol Ferd. Guil. Walther (St. Louis: Concordia Verlag, 1879), III, p. 426.

31. Luther in St. Louis Edition, V. p 62.

32. Pieper, **op. cit.,** III, p. 215.

33. Eberhard Nestle, *Novum Testamentum Grace* (Stuttgart: Priv. Wurtt. Bibleanstalt, 1953), pp. 658-671; cf. also Kurt Aland, Matthew Black and Bruce M. Metzger (London: Published by the United Bible Societies, 1966), 897-917.

34. Henry Barclay Swete. *Introduction to the Old Testament* (Cambridge: At the University Press, 1900), pp. 382-391.

35. Edward Reuss, *History of the Canon,* (New York: 1884), p. 5.

36. John M. Myers, *Invitation in the Old Testament* (Garden City, New York: Doubleday & Company, 1966), p. 2.

37. Donald G. Guthrie, *New Testament Introduction – The Gospels and Acts* (Chicago: The InterVarsity Press, 1965), pp. 19, 23.

38. Graham Scroggie, *Know Your Bible, Vol. II Analytical, New Testament* (London: Pickering & Inglis Ltd., no date), pp. 273-275. Merrill C. Tennery, *The New Testament, An Historical and Analytic Survey,* (Grand Rapids: Wm. B. Eerdmans Publishing Company, 1953), p. 375.

39. Scroggie, **op. cit.,** pp. 296-297.

40. **Ibid.**, pp. 296-297, 299.

41. **Ibid.**, p. 304.

42. H. B. Swete, *The Apocalypse of St. John* (New York: The Macmillan Company, 1906), p. cxl; Everett F. Harrison, Introduction to the New Testament Grand Rapids: Wm. B. Eerdmans Publishing Company, 1964), p. 434.

43. John B. Taylor, *A Christian's Guide to the Old Testament* (Chicago: Moody Press 1966), p. 8.

44. Cf. discussion in Raymond F. Surburg, *How Dependable Is the Bible?* (New York and Philadelphia: Lippencott Company, 1972), pp. 57-58.

45. Richard Francis Weymouth, *The New Testament in Modern Speech* (Boston: The Pilgrim Press, 1943), pp. 512-513.

46. J. B. Smith, *Greek-English Concordance to the New Testament* (Scottsdale, Pa.: Herald Press, 1955), p. 87.

47. **Ibid.**, p. 120.

48. Frank E. Gaebelein, *The Christian Use of the Bible* (Chicago: Moody Press, 9146), p. 31.
49. **Ibid.**
50. J. B. Thayer-Grimm, *A Greek-English Lexicon of the New Testament*, being Grimms-Wilke Clavis Novi Testamenti, tr. By Thayer (New York: 1897), p. 473.
51. **Ibid.**, p. 473.
52. Gaebelein, **op. cit.**, p. 44.
53. **Ibid.**, p. 46.
54. Marvin C. Vincent, *Word Studies in the New Testament* (Grand Rapids: Wm. B. Eerdmans Publishing Company, 1946), IV, p. 318.
55. Cf. footnote 33.
56. Francis Bacon, as quoted by Charles Allen Dinsmore, *The English Bible as Literature* (Boston: Houghton & Mifflin Co., 1931), p. 246.
57. E. C. Stedman, *Nature and Elements of Poetry*, as quoted by Dinsmore **op. cit.**, p. 211.
58. Dinsmore, **op. cit.**, p. 211.
59. John H, C Fritz, *The Preacher's Manuel* (St. Louis: CPH, 1941), p. 124.
60. M. Reu, *Catechetics* (Chicago: Wartburg Publishing House, 1931), p. 294.
61. **Ibid.**
62. **Ibid.**, p. 296.
63. M. Reu, *Homilelica* (Chicago: Wartburg Publishing House, 1927), pp. 271-288.
64. **Ibid.**, p. 274.
65. **Ibid.**, p. 273.

Questions

1. Marcion said the God of the Old Testament was different from the God of ____.
2. Schleiermacher was the father of ____.
3. In most pulpits in Europe, the Old Testament ____.
4. Bultmann has denied canonicity to ____.
5. Parts of the Old Testament are no longer in ____.
6. Jesus knew the Old Testament ____.
7. Inspired New Testament authors considered the Old Testament ____.
8. Paul speaks of the "Prophets" as ____.
9. First Corinthians contains two references to ____.
10. The Old Testament is able to make wise unto ____.
11. Philip found Christ in the ____.
12. Does the Old Testament differ from the New Testament in the plan of salvation? ____
13. What did Luther say about Genesis 3:15? ____
14. The ideological milieu in which the New Testament operates is basically a ____.
15. Hebrews 11 cannot be understood apart from____.
16. Christianity has its center of events in ____.
17. Theopneustos means ____.
18. "Teaching" comes ____.
19. In the New Testament there are more than one thousand ____.
20. The Bible of Jesus was ____.
21. The Old and New Testament both stand or fall ____.
22. What did Krauth say about a lock and a key? ____

Jesus and the Canon
Did Jesus and the New Testament Writers Recognize Apocryphal and Pseudepigraphical Books As Canonical?

Christian News, February 6, 1978

This article is in response to a letter appearing in *The Lutheran Witness*, January 1978, p. 21, in which the Rev. Robert M. Brueckner, Central Nyack, New York, states that the writer of this response was guilty of an overstatement in an article, "Introducing the Apocrypha," in the Nov. 27 issue of *The Lutheran Witness*. Pastor Brueckner takes issue with the following statement: "The Roman Catholic Church at the Council of Trent (A.D. 1545) declared that the Old Testament contained 45 books, thus adding to the number of the 39 books recognized by the Jewish synagogue and by Jesus Christ. These additional writings were never considered as God-inspired by Palestinian Jews."

Pastor Brueckner claims that "there is no proof that the Jews and Jesus recognized only 39 books in their Holy Scriptures in the early first century. It wasn't until 90 A.D. that a synod of rabbis met at Jamnia, a village in Judea near the Mediterranean Sea, and declared the Old Testament Canon completed and that it consisted of the 39 books of the Old Testament commonly found in the Protestant version of the Bible. The possibility of adding more books to this canon was thus ended."

Pastor Brueckner further contends that "until about 90 A.D., when the canon was made official by the rabbis at Jamnia, Jesus and His fellow Jews may have recognized even some of the apocryphal writings as being Holy Scripture. Indeed, the Letter of Jude would tend to confirm even a recognition of the pseudepigrapha as being Holy Scripture, while a study of the New Testament indicates that nowhere does it appear that the 'canonical' books of Ruth, Ezra, Ecclesiastes, and the Song of Solomon are in any way referred to. If these books are not in any way referred to in the New Testament, were they 'canonical' to Jesus?"

In responding to these assertions and positions, the writer will begin with answering the question, "What was the Old Testament canon like that was recognized by Jesus and the Apostles?"

When Jesus appeared to His disciples in the upper room in Jerusalem on the evening of the resurrection, He impressed upon those disciples who were present (Thomas was absent) that all which had happened to Him was in harmony with what had been predicted in the Old Testament Scripture. He reminded them that "all things must need be fulfilled, which are written in the law of Moses, and the prophets, and then psalms concerning me (Luke 24:44)." This statement indicates that our Lord Jesus was acquainted with the three sections into which the Hebrew Bible was divided — the Law, the Prophets, and the 'Writings.' The Psalms probably are mentioned because it is the first and longest book in this third section. Possibly also because the Book of Psalms contains more Messianic prophecies than any other book of the Writings.

The Hebrew Old Testament canon contained the following books: I. The Torah: the Five books of Moses. II. The Nebiim, the Prophets: divided into the Former Prophets (Joshua, Judges, 1 and 2 Samuel (counted as one book) and the Latter Prophets: Isaiah, Jeremiah, Ezekiel, and the 12 Minor Prophets (counted as one book). III. The Kethubim or Writings: They are divided into three divisions: 1. Poetical Writings: Psalms, Job, Proverbs; 2. The Megilloth or Scrolls: Song of Songs, Ruth, Lamentations, Ecclesiastes and Esther. III. The Kethubim or Writings: Historical Books: Ezra-Nehemiah (counted as one book), Daniel, and 1 and 2 Chronicles. The usual number given by both Jewish and Christian scholars was 24 books and constituted the Old Testament canon. Sometimes Lamentations was considered one with Jeremiah who was considered the author of Lamentations and Ruth, a story dealing with the period of the Judges was counted with Judges, thus arriving at the number of 22, instead of 24 as the number comprising the Old Testament canon.

Is there any pre-Christian witness on the extent of the Hebrew canon? Conservative Old Testament scholars believe that there is. The earliest extant reference to the three main divisions is to be found in The Prologue to the apocryphal book of Ecclesiasticus, a book composed about 190 B.C. in Hebrew by Jesus ben Sirach. The Prologue of this book was written in Greek by Sirach's grandson. In this Prologue, dated about 130 B.C., we read: "Whereas many and great things have been delivered to us by the Law and the Prophets and by others that have followed their steps - my grandfather, Jesus, when he had much given himself to the reading of the Law and the Prophets and other books of our fathers, and had gotten therein good judgment, was drawn on also himself to write something pertaining to learning and wisdom." The third part of the Hebrew canon, called the Kethubim or Hagiographa or Writings, are here referred to as (a) books by others who have followed in the footsteps of the prophets, (b) other books of our fathers. This statement indicates that in the second century B.C. already a threefold division was known. Archer also points out that I Maccabees alludes to two occurrences in Daniel (I Macc. 2:59,60) and quotes Ps. 79: 2,3 (I Macc. 7:17) and these two books were considered canonical; both Psalms and Daniel were part of the Kethubim.[2]

Josephus, a contemporary of St. Paul and many of the Apostles, refers to an Old Testament canon of twenty-two books in his apologetical book, *Contra Apionem* (Against Apio, a Roman hater of Jews). In I;8, Josephus wrote:

We have not tens of thousands of books, discordant and conflicting, but only twenty-two containing the record of all time, which have been justly believed to be divine.

After referring to the five books of Moses, thirteen books of the Prophets, and the remaining books (which "embrace hymns to God and counsels for men for the conduct of life"), Josephus makes this important assertion:

From Artaxerxes (the successor of Xerxes) until our time everything has been recorded, but has not been deemed worthy of like credit with what preceded, because the exact succession of the prophets ceased. But what faith we have placed in our own writings is evident by our conduct; for though so long a time has now passed, no one has dared to add anything to them, or to take anything from them, or to alter anything in them.[3]

This quotation of Josephus (A.D. 37-95) is interesting for it asserts that by the time of Malachi, the last prophet of the Old Testament, the three divisions of the Hebrew canon were known and that the Hebrew Old Testament was comprised of twenty-two books.

Floyd Filson in his book, *Which Books Belong in the Bible?* believes that Philo, an Alexandrian Jew (40 B.C. 20 A.D.) was thoroughly acquainted with both canonical and apocryphal books. Yet he writes: "But there is no evidence that he elevated to the rank of canonical Scripture any book not in the Hebrew canon."[4]

A number of critical scholars in the past have argued for the existence of two different canons: the Palestinian and the Alexandrinian, which was in Greek and supposedly accepted a number of the apocrypha as Scripture. To this Filson has responded:

Until someone brings forth definite evidence that Philo or some substantial group of ancient Jews specifically assigned full canonical authority to some of these other books, it would be to the credit of scholarship to stop making the unqualified statement that the Septuagint, which we know from Christian copies, proves that the Jews had an Alexandrinian canon much larger than the Palestinian. No one can prove that they did, and the available evidence, such as the usage of Philo, favors the conclusions that they did not.[5]

Filson further claims that while Jesus quotes from the writings of the Law, the Prophets and the Writings that He never quotes from the Apocrypha as Scriptures. "This ignoring of the Apocrypha is what we would expect," argues Filson, "and the other disciples followed the usage of Jesus."[6]

The argument of critical scholars is to the effect that the third part of the Hebrew Bible, the Writings was fluid and was not determined until the time of the Synod of Jamnia (A.D. 96 or 116). The reference in Luke 11:51 seems clearly to show that I and 2 Chronicles were the last books in the Writings. In summing up all the martyrs whose blood had been shed in Old Testament times, Jesus used the expression "from the blood of Abel unto the blood of Zechariah, who perished between the altar and the sanctuary." F.F. Bruce says that Abel is obviously the first martyr of the Bible but why should Zechariah be the last? Because in the order of books in the Hebrew Bible Zechariah is the last to be mentioned.[7] In 2 Chronicles 24:21 the Chronicler tells how Zechariah was stoned while he prophesies to the people "in the court of the Lord."

What about the argument that it was the Synod of Jamnia or Jabne which finally allegedly determined the books that belonged to the Kethubim, or Writings? While it is true that the rabbis at Jamnia were perplexed about books like Esther, Proverbs, Song of Songs, Ecclesiastes and Ezekiel, they discussed these books wondering why they "were books that

434

defiled the hands," but they did not discuss as the issue as to whether these should be admitted among the recognized God inspired books. F.F. Bruce has made the following judgment about the activity of the Jewish rabbis at Jamnia:

We should not exaggerate the importance of the Jamnia debates for the history of the canon. The books which they decided to acknowledge as canonical were already generally accepted, although questions had been raised about them. Those which they refused to admit had never been included. They did not expel from the canon any book which had previously been admitted.[8]

J.S. Wright had put it this way: "The Council of Jamnia was the confirming of public opinion, not the forming of it."[9] The Old Testament Danish scholar claims that the "discussions of Jamnia have not so much dealt with acceptance of certain writings into the Canon, but rather with their right to remain there."[10]

Did Jude quote Pseudepigraphical Books as canonical?

In his letter to *The Lutheran Witness* Pastor Brueckner claims: "Jesus and His fellows may have recognized even some of the apocryphal writings as being Holy Scripture. Indeed, the Letter of Jude would tend to confirm even a recognition of the pseudepigrapha as being Holy Scripture." In the one-chapter Jude book, in verses 9 and 14 there appears to be use of two different pseudepigrapha, which the Jews at no time held to be inspired Scripture. In verse 9 Jude refers to the fact of a personal contention for the body of Moses between the archangel Michael and the Devil, and in verse 14 Jude alludes to a prophecy attributed to Enoch. The first allusion can be found in *The Assumption of Moses*. The statement in verse 14, it is claimed, may be found on *The Book of Enoch*. There is no textual evidence that Jude is quoting from these two books as inspired Word of God and that in Jude we have evidence for the stance that a New Testament writer recognized two pseudepigrapha as canonical. Just as Paul quoted from the Greek poets Epimenedes, Aratus and Menander (Acts 17:28; I Cor. 15:33; 2 Tim. 3:8; Titus 1:12), so Jude refers in one instance to a fact that had happened to be true and happened to be recorded in a non-canonical book. In Jude 1:14-16 the Biblical reader finds the nearest approach to a formal citation, which is supposed to stem from Enoch 1:9. Concerning this usage of Enoch by Jude, Merrill F. Unger wrote: "If this is a formal quotation (which is dubious), it is unique. It is not the case of the citation of an apocryphal book at all, but strictly speaking, a pseudepigraphical work never recognized by anyone as canonical or laying any claim to canonicity..."[11] P.E. Kretzmann explained the assertion of Enoch in verse 14 as follows:

His (i.e. Jude's) quotation, ascribed by himself to Enoch, the seventh patriarch in line from Adam, may without hesitation be considered as having been taken from the apocryphal Book of Enoch: for the possibility of the Lord's having acknowledged a fact recorded in an apocryphal book is not excluded. Still it may also have been transmitted to the apostles in some other manner, very likely by the Lord Himself, in one of His discourses on the

end of the world. Matt. 24:3-26; Luke 21:5-36. At such a time Jude also was told what Enoch had prophesied concerning the Deluge and the Last Judgment.[12]

Footnotes

1. H.S. Miller, *General Biblical Introduction - From God to Us.* (Houghton, New York, 1944), p. 104.
2. Gleason L. Archer, *A Survey of Old Testament Introduction* (Chicago: Moody Press, 1964), p. 63.
3. **Ibid.**, p. 63.
4. Floyd V. Filson, *Which Books Belong in the Bible? A Study of the Canon.* (Philadelphia: Westminster Press, 1957), p. 83.
5. **Ibid.**
6. **Ibid.**, p. 84.
7. F. F. Bruce, *The Book and the Parchments* (London: Pickering and Inglis, 1950), p. 96.
8. **Ibid.**, p. 97.
9. J. S. Wright, *The Evangelical Quarterly*, April, 1947, p. 97.
10. Aage Bentzen, *Introduction to the Old Testament* (Copenhagen: G.E.C. Gad Publishers, 1948), I, p. 31.
11. Merrill F. Unger, *Introductory Guide to the Old Testament* (Grand Rapids: Zondervan Publishing House, 1951), p. 101.
12. Paul E. Kretzmann, *Popular Commentary of the Bible - New Testament* (St. Louis: (Concordia Publishing House, no date), II, p. 587.

Questions

1. Robert M. Brueckner wrote in the *Lutheran Witness* ____.
2. Josephus wrote that the Hebrew Old Testament was comprised of ____ books.
3. Jesus never quotes from the Apocrypha as ____.

Member Beck Revision Committee

August 5, 1978

Dear Pastor Otten:

I trust that the Beck revision committee had a profitable meeting at Camp Trinity and that some good improvements were adopted. Sorry to miss the meeting. I had surgery for two hernias and for the removal of a wire which had been used as a suture in one of my previous operations. This was my sixth stay and fifth operation since May 1965. I hope to be ready when the seminary opens its new school year in September.

I have responded to the letter of Rev. Cain of Phoenix, Arizona who has listed most of the standard arguments advanced by higher critics against the historicity of Daniel as well as its sixth century date.

My reply is quite thorough and I believe effectively answer all his arguments. I believe his letter and my response are worth publishing.

I am sorry that my type writer was constantly skipping spaces, know that I had to connect parts of words with =. If you should decide to publish it, I hope your workers do not have too much trouble reading the manuscript.

During the spring quarter I taught an elective in Biblical Aramaic to five students, two of whom are going on for graduate study, one to Harvard (W.A. Maier III) and Burge to M.S.T. study in St. Louis and Garwood ministry to the Philippines.

May you and your family have an enjoyable summer and may God then bless you in your fight and battle for the truth and reliability of God's word and for you stand to return to the historic Lutheran theology as it was once held in the LCMS.

Fraternally,

Raymond Surburg

Defending the Book of Daniel

Christian News, August 21, 1978

An Answer To Historical-Critical Objections
To The Sixth-Century Date of Daniel And To The Charges of
The Book of Daniel's Historical Blunders

In letter dated May 23, 1978, sent by a Pastor Marvin F. Cain to the editor of *Christian News*, the former expressed the view that a rather curious statement appeared in the May 15, 1978 issue of *Christian News*, on page 15, under XIV. The Old Testament item 5: "The Sixth Century B.C. Prophet Daniel wrote the Book of Daniel. It contains no errors." The Reverend Cain of Phoenix, Arizona then listed six items, which he believes show clearly that the Book of Daniel does contain errors and mis-

437

takes (Cain's entire letter follows). In what follows evidence will be presented to answer the allegations of error existing in the present Book of Daniel. After submitting six different points, Cain summarized his presentation in these words: "What, in effect we have in the historical data in Daniel is an incorrect account of the fall of Jerusalem, wrong people carried captive, non-existent rulers mentioned, anachronisms in rulers and contradictions in the status of Daniel in Babylon. So, what I would like to know is, what person, skilled in the Hebrew and late Aramaic of Daniel, knowledgeable in Biblical history, and the history of the ancient near east, and up to date in his reading of works on Daniel by Lutheran and other scholars around the world, ever made the statement which you cite: 'The Sixth Century B.C. Prophet Daniel, wrote the Book of Daniel. It contains no errors.'"

The interpretation of the Book of Daniel has differed considerably, depending on whether a scholar began with the assumptions that miracles and prophecy were impossible and were not to be accepted as historical realities, or whether a scholar believed in the supernatural. Including direct revelations from God to man, that God could reveal to man what the future course of his people and of world kingdoms would be. The interpretation and understanding of the Book of Daniel will also be determined by whether the reader of Daniel believes that this book is God-breathed (theopneustos) and one of the 39 books of the Old Testament that is the Word of God and not merely a book that was written by an anonymous author who made mistake after mistake. Daniel is not only the author of the Book, he was also its chief actor. Like other major and minor prophets, Daniel was the recipient of revelations from God, revelations pertaining to his time as well as to the future history of the kingdom of God and the coming of the Messiah. In Matthew 24:15 Jesus said; "When you see what the prophet Daniel told about the abomination laying waste the land and standing in the holy place (anyone who reads this should understand it), then if you're in Judea, flee to the hills" (Beck, *An American Translation, New Testament*, p. 34). This passage shows that the coming of the Roman armies against Jerusalem was predicted by the prophet Daniel. Our Lord's testimony was not simply that the book was named after Daniel, but that its prophecies were spoken by him.

Since the third century of the Christian era, the date and authorship of Daniel have been a battleground between those who accept what the Bible says about itself, and those who refuse to accept its clear assertions. Dr. Culver claims that "so far as is now known, every Jew and Christian of early antiquity accepted the book as having been written in the Babylonian and Persian periods of the sixth century, in and near the city of Babylon, as the book claims. The New Testament, as well as several non-Biblical works, unquestionably accepts the genuineness of the book." Robert Culver, "Daniel," in *The Wycliffe Bible Commentary*, edited by Charles F. Pfeiffer and Everett F. Harrison. Chicago; Moody Press, 1962, p. 769).

One of the first critics to deny that Daniel wrote the book bearing his name was Porphyry, a neo-Platonic philosopher of the third century A.D.

On a visit to Sicily Prophyry at the age of forty years, wrote a volume in fifteen books entitled *Against the Christians*. Most of this book has been lost, however, parts of the twelfth book in which Porphyry attacked Daniel, have been preserved in Jerome's commentary on Daniel. Jerome claims that Porphyry denied that Daniel in the sixth century B.C. was the author of this biblical book, and asserted that Daniel was written by somebody else than the prophet Daniel, by a person who lived in Judea during the times of Antiochus Epiphanes. The reason that Porphyry proposed the second century B.C. view was that the Book of Daniel speaks too accurately about the times of Antiochus Epiphanes. Therefore, reasoned the neo-Platonist philosopher, the book contains history and not prophecy. The author of Daniel lied for the sake of reviving the hopes of his Jewish compatriots of his 2nd century.

Concerning this criticism of Porphyry, Edward Young remarked: "Porphyry's criticism of Daniel, therefore, was based upon his anti-theistic philosophical presuppositions. He thought that predictive prophecy was impossible, hence he denied that Daniel could have uttered such prophecy" (Edward J. Young, *An Introduction to the Old Testament*; Grand Rapids: William B. Eerdmans Publishing Company, 1969, p. 362.) One thing, Young claims, must be said about Porphyry's views; "He clearly recognized that if an unknown person wrote under the guise of Daniel's name, this unknown person was a deceiver. In fact, this is the principal objection to holding the view that some unknown Jew wrote the book of Daniel and simply used Daniel's name as a guise. This is a deception, and there is no escaping the fact." (**Ibid.**, p. 362.)

What the 19th century scholar Pusey said, "The Book of Daniel is especially fitted to be the battle-ground between faith and unbelief, it admits no halfway measures. It is either Divine or an imposture," is true. (E.B. Pusey, *Daniel the Prophet*, New York: 1891, p. 75). Since the age of rationalism and the adoption of the higher critical approach, the arguments of the pagan philosopher Porphyry have been basically adopted. It is true that Pusey said a little over a century ago: "Human inventiveness in things spiritual or unspiritual is very limited. It would be difficult probably to invent a new heresy. Objectors of old were as acute or more acute than those now; so that the ground was well-nigh exhausted" (E. P. Pusey, *Daniel the Prophet*, p. iii.).

According to J.E.H. Thomson, Daniel in *Pulpit Commentary*, Chicago: Wilcox and Follett Company, 1900, p. xliii, the real reason why some scholars have not accepted the genuineness of Daniel is the fact that predictive prophecy is not possible. Robert Pfeiffer on page 755 of his 900 plus page *Introduction to the Old Testament,* New York: Harper & Brothers, 1941, p. 755 makes this assertion: "This traditional theory, by accepting the book at face value, necessarily presupposes the reality of the supernatural and the divine origin of the revelations it contains. Such miracles as the revelations to Daniel of the details of Nebuchadnezzar's dreams and their meaning (2:19,30, 31 ff.), the divine deliverance of the three confessors from the fiery furnace (3:24-28) and of Daniel in the lion's den (6:22-24 (H:23-25), and a hand without a body writing a message on the wall belongs to the realms of the supernatural. Historical research can deal only with authenticated facts which are within the sphere of natural possibilities and must refrain from vouching for the truth of supernatural events. The historicity of the Book of Daniel is an article of faith, not an objective scientific truth-no offense being intended for its learned and able advocates. In a historical study of the Bible, convictions based on faith must be deemed irrelevant, as belonging to subjective rather than objective knowledge" (p. 755).

The following are the various reasons why critical scholars have rejected the historicity of the events of the Book of Daniel and assigned it to the second century B.C. (1) The author makes historical mistakes and commits serious blunders. (2) The Hebrew and Aramaic of Daniel are of types much later than the sixth century. (3) Several terms used are Persian and Greek words that a Jewish author of the sixth century could not have known. (4) The position of the book in the third section (Writings or Hagiographa) of the Old Testament indicates late origin, after the prophetic canon was closed. (5) There is no external testimony to the existence of Daniel prior to the second century. (7) The stories are fanciful, unhistorical and unreal. (8) Apocalyptic literature, did not arise until well down in Hellenistic period. For the critical position, consult some of the following books; Curt Kuhl, *The Old Testament*. Richmond: John Knox Press, 1961, pp. 272-280; Carl G. Howie, *Ezekiel, Daniel*. Richmond: John Knox Press, 1961, pp. 89-98.; Bernard W. Anderson, *Understanding the Old Testament*, Third edition; Englewood Cliffs, New Jersey: Prentice-Hall, 1975, pp. 576-579.' Stanley Brice Frost, *Old Testament Apocalyptic*. London: The Epworth Press, 1952, pp. 180-209.; James A. Montgomery, *A Critical and Exegetical Commentary on the Book of Daniel*. New York; Charles Scribners' Sons, 1927, pp. 57-112.

A Listing of the Historical Blunders and Mistakes together with Answers Given for them by the Defenders of the Historicity of Daniel

1. Pastor Cain wrote: "Daniel 1:1 states, 'In the third year of Jehoiakim king of Judah came Nebuchadnezzar unto Jerusalem and besieged (sic) it' (KV). Yet, II Kings 24 states that Nebuchadnezzar laid siege (sic) to Jerusalem when Jehoiachin, not Jehoiakim, was the ruler. A second siege (sic) took place when Zedekiah was king (II Kings 25:1-7; Jeremiah 35: 1-10), at which time the city fell. There is no evidence from either archaeology or the Bible to support the idea that Nebuchadnezzar besieged (sic) Jerusalem at the time of Jehoiakim" (page 1 of letter).

"2). Daniel 1:2 states that The Lord gave Judah (and Jerusalem?) into Nebuchadnezzar's hand during the reign of Jehoiakim. But II Kings and Jeremiah indicate that happened when Zedekiah was king of Judah, not Jehoiakim" (Page 1 of Cain's Letter).

"3). Daniel 1:2 states that Jehoiakim was carried captive to Babylon but II Kings 24:15 indicates that it was Jehoiachin, not Jehoiakim, who was taken to Babylon. Jehoiakim died in Jerusalem (II Kings 24:6). However, II Chronicles 36:6 states, contrary to II Kings and history, that Je-

440

hoiakim was taken captive. Apparently the author of Daniel had read Chronicles, but Chronicles was not written for more than a century later, since the Chronicler's work also includes the stories of Ezra and Nehemiah" (page 2 of Cain Letter).

The texts cited by Cain as contradictory, it should be noted, are understood by many scholars in a different way than they are interpreted by Pastor Cain. A number of reputable scholars believe that the taking of Daniel and his three friends to Babylon occurred in 605 B.C. The discovery of four additional tablets of the Babylonian Chronicle in 1956 by D. J. Wiseman in the British Museum has furnished an account of the shattering defeat of the Egyptians by the Babylonians at Carchemish in 605 B.C. R.K. Harrison, of the University of Toronto, argues that "one result of this victory was that the Babylonians seem to have demanded hostages of Judah as evidence of good faith toward Babylonia, and it was this group which went into captivity in the third year of Jehoiakim (Dan. 1:1,-3), including the young man Daniel" (R. K . Harrison, "Daniel," *The Zondervan Pictorial Bible Encyclopedia*, Grand Rapids; Zondervan Publishing Company, 1975), 11, p. 22). Henry Snyder Gehman in *The New Westminster Dictionary of the Bible* in his article on "Jehoiakim," pp. 451-452 states: "He began to reign in 609 B.C., at the age of 25 years. He was obliged to collect heavy tribute from the people for Pharaoh Nebuchednezzar defeated Neco at Carchemich (605 B.C.) and advanced, probably afterward, against Jerusalem, and Jehoiakim became his servant (II Kings 24:1; Jer. 46:2; Dan. 1:1-2.). Three years later he rashly rebelled against Nebuchadnezzar. There were other troubles afflicting the kingdom. Syrians, Moabites, and Ammonites made predatory incursions into its territories, as did bands of the Chaldeans, whom Nebuchadnezzar probably dispatched on learning of the revolt (II Kings 24:2). The Babylonian king himself, or his army, eventually entered Jerusalem and bound the Jewish rebel with chains to carry him to Babylon (II Chron. 36;6). The purpose of carrying him to Babylon was apparently abandoned. He died or was murdered, and his body had the burial of an ass, being drawn and cast forth beyond the gates of Jerusalem (Jer. 22:19; 36:30; Jos. Antiq. x.6,3). He reigned 11 years and was succeeded by his son Jehoiachin (II Kings 23:36; 24:6).

Jehoiachin came to the throne in the year 598/597 B.C. According to II Kings 24:8, he was then 18 years old. However, his reign lasted only 3 months and 10 days. During this short period. Nebuchednezzar sent his generals to besiege Jerusalem, which surrendered after the 8th year of Nebuchadnezzar had begun (Cf. II Kings 24:12; Cf. Jer. 52:28). Jehoichin, his wives, mother, the palace servants with many skillful artisans were taken into captivity (II Kings 24:8-16; II Chron. 36:9-10).

Cain's assertion "There is no evidence from either archaeology or the Bible to support the idea that Nebuchadnezzar besieged (sic) Jerusalem at the time of Jehoiakim," is not true. *The Babylonian Chronicle* makes the taking of Daniel in 1:1 a likelihood. Since when, furthermore, must there be two statements of the same event in Scripture to make any Biblical assertion true?

Cain misreads Daniel 1:2 when he states "That Jehoiakim was carried to Babylon, but II Kings 24:15 indicates that it was Jehoiakim Daniel 1:2, rendering the Hebrew faithfully: "And the Lord gave Jehoiakim, king of Judah, into his hand and some of the vessels of the house of God; and he brought them to the land of Shinar, to the house of his god; and the vessels he brought to the treasure of his god." In dealing with the allegation that Jehoiakim was taken to Babylon, Leupold in his *Exposition of Daniel*, answers this misinterpretation as follows:

The question is raised, "Does **waybhi'em**, 'and he brought them,' refer to the deportation of the vessels only or to the deportation of the vessels and the captives?" We hold the solution to be very simple. Captives have not been mentioned, except the king, and he was not deported. Consequently the writer is disposing of the vessels first; the suffix "them" can refer grammatically only to the vessels. Of these it is said that they were taken "to the land of Shinar," the ancient name of the wicked land, which is first used in Gen. 10:10 and 11:2, and here comes into use again as the wicked spirit of olden limes is revived in the oppression of God's people, cf. Zech. 5:11 for a similar use. Shinar is, of course, Babylon.

(H.C. Leupold, *Exposition of Daniel*, Columbus: Wartburg Press, 1949, p. 57).

Other commentators who limit the taking of only the vessels are: Calvin, Maurer, Stuart, Rosenmueller, Keil, Haevernick and Driver.

Under his third listing of a contradictory problem relative to the reign of King Jehoiakim, Cain claims that II Kings 24:6 and II Chron. 36:6 are in contradiction. The Kings text informs us that Jehoiakim died in Jerusalem, while II Chronicles states that he was taken captive. Professor La Sor in commenting on II Kings 24:5-7 wrote: "**Slept with his fathers**, indicates a peaceful, death, but according to 2 Ch. 36:6 Nebuchadnezzar 'bound him in fetters to take him to Babylon,' and Jeremiah (22:19) says he was to have 'the burial of an ass' (i.e. none). One suggestion is that Jehoiakim revolted again and when Nebuchadnezzar attempted to take him to Babylon, he was wounded and died and his body was cast away." William Sonford La Sor, "I and II Kings," in D. Guthrie, J.A. Moyer, A.M. Tibbs, D. J. Wiseman, *The New Bible Commentary: Revised* Grand Rapids: Wm. B. Eerdmans Publishing Company, 1970, p. 367. Professor Jack P. Lewis in writing about the death of Jehoiachim said: "After three years' vassalage Jehoiachim revolted (II Kings 24:1) and brought down the wrath of Nebuchadnezzar upon himself, but before the fall of Jerusalem, he was succeeded on the throne by his son Jehoiachin. The circumstances of Jehoiachim's death are not clear to us. Josephus reports that Nebuchadnezzar slew him and cast his body unburied before the walls (Ant. x. 6.3 [97]). Jehoiachin, the new king capitulated (II Kings 24:10ff.). Not only the royal family and officials, but also ten thousand men of valor and the smiths and craftsmen, were exiled (II Kings 24:14; Cf. v. 16)." (Jack P. Lewis, *Historical Backgrounds of Bible History*. Grand Rapids: Baker Book House, 1971), pp. 77-78).

Cain's interpretation of the date in Daniel, II Kings and Chronicles is not subscribed to by Bible scholars that this writer has consulted and quoted. The passages cited as contradictory in nature can satisfactorily be explained as not conflicting with each other.

Cain has also put forth another objection to the historical reliability of Daniel, when he wrote: "6) According to Daniel 1:5, Daniel and his friends were not in a training school for three years, at the end of that time Nebuchadnezzar gave them special honors in his kingdom (Daniel 1:20). Yet in Daniel 2:1ff., in Nebuchadnezzar's second year, "the king made Daniel a great man" (Daniel 2:48) (page 2 of letter).

A consulting of Biblical commentaries dealing with the Book of Daniel will show that a number of possible solutions are possible for what appears as an apparent contradiction. Culver for instance gives this explanation as a possibility: "Most recent scholarship takes the apparent discrepancy as a simple matter growing out of Hebrew or Babylonian methods of counting regnal years. Among suggestions of this sort Driver's view (endorsed by Young) is good: "There is not, perhaps, necessarily a contradiction here with the 'three years' of 1,5,18. By Heb. usage, fractions of time were reckoned as full units. Thus Samaria, which was besieged from the fourth to the sixth year of Hezekiah, is said to have been taken 'at the end' of three years (I Kgs. xviii. 9, 10) and in Jer. xxxiv. 14 'at the end of seven years' means evidently when the seventh year had arrived (cf. also MK 8:31, etc.). If, now, the author, following a custom which was certainly adopted by Jewish writers, and which was general in Assyria and Babylonia, 'postdated the regnal years of a king, i.e. Counted as his first year not the year of his accession but the first full year afterwards, and if further Nebuchadnezzar gave orders for the education of the Jewish youths in his accession year, the end of the three years ... might be reckoned as falling within the king's second year (Driver, *Daniel, Cambridge Bible for Schools and Colleges*, p. 17). As with most difficulties of this sort, the solution will almost be resolved once the author's point of view and manner of using words have been ascertained" (Culver, "Daniel," **op. cit.**, pp. 777-778.).

For a still different solution, Cf. Leon Wood, *A Commentary on Daniel*. Grand Rapids: Zondervan Publishing House, 1973, pp. 48-49.

Belshazzar, son of Nebuchadnezzar, a Mistake?

Another objection to the historical reliability of Daniel is advanced by Cain in these words; "4) According to Daniel 5:2, Belshazzar was a son of Nabonidus instead and he did not even succeed Nebuchadnezzar but was the fifth ruler after Nebuchadnezzar" (Page 2 of Letter).

Not too many years ago the historical character of Belshazzar was questioned. (Raymond P. Dougherty, *Nabonidus and Belshazzar*. Yale Oriental Series, XV). Yale University Press, 1929 has shown the truthfulness of Chapter 5 of Daniel which depicted Belshazzar as the regent when the city of Babylon fell to the Medo-Persian conquerors. Various tablets from Babylonia have revealed that Belshazzar shared the throne as coregent or king with his father. From Ur, the traditional home of Abraham, there has come a tablet recording two dreams, a text in which the man referred to studies the stars in favor of an interpretation "favorable to my lord Belshazzar, the crown prince." Cf. Pritchard, *Ancient Near Eastern Texts*, p. 309, n. 5).

There also exist two legal documents dated to the 12 and 13th years of the Nabonidus that include oaths sworn by the life of Nabonidus, the king, and Belshazzar, the crown prince, a unique type of oath in Akkadian cuneiform literature. A translation of a cuneiform text in Ancient Near Eastern Pictures. Princeton: Princeton University Press, 1950, p. 306, a part of a series known as the Babylonian Chronicle, states that Nabonidus (556/555-539 B.C.) resided at Tema from the seventh through the eleventh years of his reign. While the crown prince, his officials and his army were in Akkad (i.e. Babylonia.), and that during those years the festival of the new year was omitted. In the so-called "Verse Account of Nabonidus" there is a complaint registered that Nabonidus, when his third year was about to begin; "entrusted the 'Camp' to his oldest son, the firstborn, the troops everywhere in the country he ordered under his command. He allowed all things to go, entrusted the kingship to him and, himself embarked upon a long journey. He invaded Arabia, capturing Tema, rebuilt the town, and made his residence there. (Pritchard, *Ancient Near Eastern Texts*, p. 313). An inscription from Harran states that Nabonidus was away ten years from Babylon. It has been suggested that Nabonidus felt that he had to remain at this outpost to keep down the Arab tribes who threatened Nabonidus' lucrative caravan route which passed through Tema. Another supposed reason for Nabonidus' ten year absence from Babylonia advocated by some scholars was the fact that Nabonidus favored the chief god of Ur, Sin, who was also the chief god of Harran, his home town, and thus Nabonidus found himself at odds with the Babylonian priesthood of Marduk, powerful in Babylon.

Therefore, Daniel was not writing about a fictitious king, named Belshazzar, as was once argued by critical scholars. Critics, however, claim that the author of Daniel was in error when he calls Belshazzar, the son of Nebuchadnezzar. (5:1,2; cf. vs. 11, 18, 22). In answer it should be stated that this was correct according to Semitic usage. In similar fashion, Jehu, the usurper, is called the "son of Omri" by the Assyrians as recorded on the Black Obelisk of Shalmaneser III, although without any blood relation at all, "son of" being used in connection with royalty in a broad sense of successor. It has also been suggested that Nabonidus may have married a daughter of Nebuchadnezzar in order to legitimize his usurpation of the throne in 556 B.C.

The Question of the Identity of Darius the Mede
Cain, like most critical scholars, claims there was no Darius the Mede, who succeeded Belshazzar. Thus Cain wrote: "Unfortunately there never was a Median named Darius. Darius was a Persian. If the Darius of Daniel 5;31ff is Darius the Great, he not only did not succeed Belshazzar, but he came after, not before, Cyrus, who was also a Persian. This is contrary to Daniel 6:28." (Page 2 of Letter).

In opposition to critical scholarship, conservative scholars hold that

Daniel did not confuse Darius the Mede with Darius Hystaspes, king of Persia, who was the third successor of Cyrus the Great, conqueror of Babylon. Archer claims that the critical position is impossible to defend in the light of the Book of Daniel itself, which makes no such confusing identification. No explanation can be found for calling Darius the son of Hystaspes a Mede, when he was known to be the descendant of an ancient royal line. Furthermore, the writer of Daniel says that Darius the Mede was sixty-two years old when he assumed the rule in Babylonia, yet it was well known to the ancients that Darius the Great was relatively young when he began his reign. It is also stated in Daniel 9:1 that Darius was made (homlak) king over the realms of the Chaldeans. The fact that he was made king would indicate that he was appointed by a higher authority, which agrees with the view advanced by conservatives that Cyrus appointed Darius the Mede as viceroy in Babylonia. Says Archer: "Since Chronological reckoning shows that he must have been only a sub-king who ruled under the authority of Cyrus, this established that Cyrus' policy to permit subordinate rulers to reign under him with the title of king" (Gleason L. Archer, *A Survey of Old Testament Introduction*. Chicago: Moody Pres, 1964, p. 372).

Assuming that Daniel did not make the mistake of confusing Darius the Mede with Darius Hystaspis, who then was Darius the Mede? So far ancient records do not mention a Darius the Mede. The publication of cuneiform texts, published in the early decades of the 20th century, have made it possible for Bible students to have a clearer understanding of the fall of Babylon in 539 B.C. It seems most likely that a man called Gubaru was none other than Cyrus the Mede, who was appointed by Cyrus to be governor of Babylon. It is known from the Nabonidus Chronicle that Cyrus appointed sub governors in Babylonia immediately after the fall of Babylon. (*Ancient Near Eastern Texts*, p. 306. John H. Whitcomb, in his book *Darius the Mede*. Grand Rapids: Wm. B. Eerdmans Publishing Company. 1959 has shown that Gubaru (not to be confused with Ugbaru, governor of Gutium, the general under Cyrus who conquered Babylon and died three weeks later, according to the Nabonidus Chronicle) is mentioned a number of times in the cuneiform documents as governor of Babylon and the Region-Beyond-the-River, that is the entire Fertile Crescent. Thus Gubaru ruled over the following countries: Babylonia, Syria, Phoenicia, and Palestine. (Cf. Whitcomb, *Darius the Mede*, pp. 10-24) The designation of Darius as "king" is not an inaccuracy, even though he was subordinate to Cyrus the Great. Belshazzar is called "king", even though he was second ruler in the kingdom next to Nabonidus in the Babylonian kingdom.

Whitcomb also cites W. F. Albright in The Date and Personality of the Chronicler" (*Journal of Biblical Literature*, XL, p. 11, n. 2) as follows: "It seems to me highly probable that Gobryas did actually assume the royal dignity along with the name 'Darius', perhaps an old Iranian royal title, while Cyrus was absent on a European campaign . . . After the cuneiform elucidation of the Belshazzar mystery, showing that the latter was long co-regent with his father, the vindication of Darius the Mede for history

445

was to be expected.... We may safely expect the Babylonian Jewish author to be acquainted with the main facts of Neo-Babylonian history." It is quite possible, as Albright suggests that the name Darius, Persian **Darayavahush**, was a title of honor just as "Caesar" or "Augustus" became in the Roman empire. In Medieval Persian (Zend) we find the word **dara**, meaning "king." Possibly **Darayavahush** would have meant "the royal one."

The Date of the Aramaic of Daniel

Pastor Cain in his letter has also raised the general critical claim that the Aramaic of Daniel is late Aramaic and thus could not be from the time of Daniel. Thus Cain wrote: "I would like to know the name of the first-rate Aramaic scholar, be he LCMS or other, who has studied the Aramaic of Daniel 2-7 and concluded that the book was written in the sixth century B.C" (Letter page 2).

R. K. Harrison, in his scholarly and comprehensive *Introduction to the Old Testament* (Grand Rapids: Wm. B. Eerdmans Publishing Company, 1969, p. 1124) asserted: "The linguistic evidence that critical scholars once advanced with such enthusiasm as proof of a Maccabean date for Daniel has undergone sobering modification of late as a result of archaeological discoveries in the Near East. In 1891 S.R. Driver could write quite confidently that the Persian words in Daniel presupposed a period of composition after the Persian empire had been well established; the Greek words demanded, the Hebrew supported, and the Aramaic permitted a date subsequent to the conquest of Palestine by Alexander the Great in 332 B.C. (Cf. S.R. Driver, *Introduction to the Literature of the Old Testament* (New York: Charles Scribner's Sons, 1891, p. 508). H. H. Rowley in a number of writings endeavored to support this aphorism of Driver's especially relative to the Aramaic. (Cf. H.H. Rowley, The Aramaic of the Old Testament. London: Humphrey Milford, 1929). as well as his articles in the *Zeitschrift fuer Alte Testament Wissenschaft*, L (1932), pp. 256ff.; and in the *Journal of the Royal Asiatic Society*, (1933), pp. 777ff.).

However, subsequent discoveries have shown that the appeal to the Aramaic elements is not reliable as means for determining late date of composition. Aramaic research and study have shown that the term "Aramaic" is a rather general term employed to describe a number Semitic dialects which are closely related to Hebrew and also related closely to each other. Semitic linguistic research has now come up with the following classification: Old Aramaic, Official Aramaic, Levantine Aramaic and Eastern Aramaic. The oldest form of Aramaic is found in the north-Syrian inscriptions, which are dated from the tenth to the eighth century B.C. This Old Aramaic was the basis for Official Aramaic employed in governmental offices during the Assyrian Period (Ca. 1100-605 B.C.) and in the succeeding Persian period. Imperial Aramaic, another name for Official Aramaic, became the international language of the Persian Empire. During Assyrian times, it became practice to attach "dockets" to cuneiform texts, the purpose of which was to give a brief indication of names and dates connected with the tablets, as well as to furnish a summary of its contents. Harrison states "that Official Aramaic was still in use on 'dockets' throughout the Hellenistic period (330-30 B.C.), as well as on coins, on papyri and ostraca from Egypt, on Mesopotamian and Egyptian inscriptions, and in some bilingual inscriptions from Asia Minor" (R.K. Harrison. *Introduction to the Old Testament*, p. 1124). Levantine Aramaic arose among the early Aramean nomads who occupied Syria and Palestine, and even during the Hellenistic period (330-30 B.C.) when Greek was the international language Levantine Aramaic was still the popularly spoken language in New Testament times.

Eastern Aramaic came with the Arameans who invaded the Tigris-Euphrates Valley, with some of its dialects surviving into Muslim times. From Genesis 31:47 it is evident that Laban was an Aramean who used Aramaic, as may be seen from the name Jegar-shadutha for the cairn Jacob called "Galeed," "a witness heap."

Before the discoveries at Ugarit and the discovery of a new Semitic language, now called Ugaritic, it was customary to claim that Aramaisms in a Biblical book were an indication of late authorship. But as Young has pointed out, certain Aramaisms that were formerly regarded as Aramaisms are found in the Rash Shamrah texts, dating from the Amarna Age, (1400-1360 B.C.) and contain certain Aramaisms found in Daniel. (E.J. Young, *The Prophecy of Daniel*, pp. 23, 247; *Introduction to the Old Testament*, p. 371).

The Aramaic authority Franz Rosenthal has shown that the kind of Aramaic used by Daniel is the type of Aramaic which came into existence in the courts and chancelleries from the seventh century on and subsequently became wide spread in the Near East. Harrison, therefore, claims that "Thus it cannot be employed as evidence for a late date of the book, and in fact it constitutes a strong argument for a sixth-century B.C. period of composition. The Aramaic sections of Daniel (2;4b-7:28) are by nature closely akin to the language of the fifth-century B.C. Elephantine papyri and that of Ezra (4:7-6:18; 7:11-26), while the Hebrew resembles that of Ezekiel, Haggai, Ezra, and Chronicles, and not the latter Hebrew of Ecclesiasticus, as some writers have maintained, arguing from Hebrew fragments preserved in rabbinic quotations and also from the Syriac of the Peshitta version." Harrison also claims that "more recent studies in Biblical Aramaic have cast grave doubts upon the advisability of distinguishing sharply between eastern and western branches of the linguistic group, as older scholars were wont to do, thus seriously weakening the force of the assertion by Driver" (Harrison, *Introduction to the Old Testament*, p. 11 25.)

Driver claimed that the Persian loan-words in Daniel support a date later than earlier relative to the time of composition of Daniel. K. A. Kitchen, in *Notes on Some Problems in the Book of Daniel*, pp. 35-44 has examined the newer data relevant to the arguments of Driver and others and has shown that Persian words were used or could be used of Babylonian institutions prior to the conquests of Cyrus, as Driver supposed, since the work was composed in the Persian rather than the neo-Babylonian period of Near Eastern history. Utilizing the arguments of Kitchen, Harrison asserts: "In the interests of objectivity it should be noted in passing that the Persian terms found in Daniel are specifically Old Persian words, that is to say, occurring within the history of the language to about 300 B.C. This would indicate that the Aramaic of Daniel in this respect at least is pre-Hellenistic, and that it did not draw upon any Persian expressions or terminology that might have become current after the fall of the empire" (R.K. Harrison, *Introduction to the Old Testament*, p. 1126).

The presence of Greek words in Daniel, formerly hailed as incontrovertible evidence against an earlier than Maccabean dating, has now been completely exploded as a valid objection to a sixth-century date for Daniel. The three words; Harp, sackbut, and psaltery now no longer constitute a barrier to an early date for Daniel's composition. Albright has shown that Greek culture had penetrated the Near East long before the Neo-Babylonian period. Edwin M. Yamauchi, in *Grace and Babylon: Early contacts Between the Aegean and the Near East* HAS SHOWN FROM ARCHAEOLOGY the untenability of higher critical arguments against the Book of Daniel. (This is one of the *Baker Studies in Biblical Archaeology*, Nr. 4).

Kitchen has examined the Aramaic of Daniel in the light of newer evidence as reflected in Aramaic studies and concluded: "The date of the book of Daniel, in short cannot be decided upon linguistic grounds alone. It is equally obscurantist to exclude dogmatically a sixth-century (or fourth) century date on the one hand, or to hold such a date as mechanically proven on the other, **as far as the Aramaic is concerned**" (K. A. Kitchen, "The Aramaic of Daniel" in D.J. Wiseman, T.C. Mitchell and R. Joyce, W. J. Martin and K. A. Kitchen, *Notes on the Book of Daniel*. London: The Tyndale Press, 1965, p. 79).

Professor Archer of Trinity Seminary, Deerfield, Illinois, an Aramaic specialist, has examined the Aramaic of the "Genesis Apocryphon", one of the remarkable discoveries from the First Cave of (Qumran, a midrash of Genesis written in Aramaic. In a contribution to the volume, *New Perspectives on the Old Testament* (Waco, Texas, Words Books, Publishers, 1970, pp. 160-169). Archer has shown that "the *Genesis Apocryphon* furnishes very powerful evidence that the Aramaic comes from a considerably earlier period than the second Century B.C. The fact that Targumic and Talmudic words abound in this first-century document indicates a considerable interval in time between its composition and that of Ezra and Daniel. Its use of normal Semitic word order in the clause as over against Daniel's tendency to follow a policy of placing the verb late in the clause points to a definite difference either in geographic origin (which would eliminate the possibility of Daniel's Maccabean Composition in Palestine) or in epoch. Either inference is fatal to the pseudepigraph theory, it is fair to say, therefore, that the overall testimony of this scroll leads to the abandonment of a long-cherished position of higher criticism, and makes the genuineness of Danielle authorship of Daniel an even more attractive option than it was before," p. 169.

Professor Edwin Yamauchi has examined the Greek words in Daniel and shown in the light of Greek influence in the Near East that they can be dated many centuries earlier than Driver did in famous statement earlier referred to in this essay. Cf. "The Greek Word in Daniel in the Light of Greek Influence in the Near East," in *New Perspectives on the Old Testament*, J. Barton Payne editor, pp. 170-200.

Earlier books worth looking at are the writings of Robert Dick Wilson, *Studies in the Rook of Daniel* Series 1 and 2, also articles in *The Princeton Theological Review and Charles Boulflower, In and Around the Book of Daniel* reprinted by Zondervan Publishing House, 1963.

* * *

Defending Book of Daniel

September 27, 1978
Dear Pastor Otten,
Enclosed please find the Rev. Marvin F. Cain's letter, written in reference to my article "Defending the Book of Daniel." I have answered his reply and endeavored to point out great differences in our respective theological positions.

I trust that the Lord is blessing you, your family, and ministry.
Fraternally,
Raymond Surburg

* * *

Liberal Lutheran Pastor Challenges Inerrancy and 6ᵗʰ Century B.C. Dating of Daniel

Errors in God's Word
Letter from Pastor Cain
Christian News, August 21, 1978

Thank you for sending copies of the May 15, 1978 issue of *Christian News* to me. I appreciate having the full text of the LCMS statement on the *Lutheran Book of Worship (LBW)*.

Since most of the objections to the *LBW* seem not to apply to the *Service Book and Hymnal (SBH)*, why don't you folks in the LCMS simply adopt the *SBH* and be done with it? In a few years there will be thousands of copies of the *SBH* available at little or no cost to LCMS congregations. That way you could still have a recent Lutheran hymnal to use, with no Albert Schweitzer festival to clutter up things.

In that same issue of *Christian News* you had a series of statements in parallel columns representing the LCMS position in opposition to that of the rest of American Lutheranism (and world Lutheranism). Apart from the fact that the statements were not documented, and I would like to know who made some of them, one statement struck me as most curious.

I refer to the statement on page 15, under IV. The Old Testament, item 5; "The Sixth century B.C. Prophet Daniel wrote the Book of Daniel. It contains no errors." I would like to know how you, or whoever made that statement, deal with the following:

1) Daniel 1:1 states, "In the third year of Jehoiakim king of Judah came Nebuchadnezzar unto Jerusalem and besieged it" (KJV). Yet, II Kings 24 states that Nebuchadnezzar laid siege to Jerusalem when Jehoiachin, not Jehoiakim, was the ruler. A second siege took place when Zedekiah was king (II Kings 25:1-7; Jeremiah 35:1-10), at which time the city fell. There is no evidence from either archeology or the Bible to support the idea that Nebuchadnezzar besieged Jerusalem at the time of Jehoiakim.

2) Daniel 1:2 states that The Lord gave Judah (and Jerusalem?) into Nebuchadnezzar's hand during the reign of Jehoiakim. But II Kings and Jeremiah indicate that happened when Zedekiah was king of Judah, not Jehoiakim. 3) Daniel 1:2 states that Jehoiakim was carried captive to Babylon, but II Kings 24:15 indicates that it was Jehoiachin, not Jehoiakim, who was taken to Babylon. Jehoiakim died in Jerusalem (II Kings 24:6). However, II Chronicles 36:6 states, contrary to II Kings and history, that Jehoiakim was taken captive. Apparently the author of Daniel had read Chronicles, but Chronicles was not written for more than a century later, since the Chronicler's work also includes the stories of Ezra and Nehemiah.

4) According to Daniel 5:2, Belshazzar was a son of Nebuchdnezzar. However, Belshazzar was a son of Nabonidus instead and he did not even succeed Nebuchadnezzar but was the fifth ruler after Nebuchadnezzar.

5) In Daniel 5:31, mention is made of "Darius the Median" who succeeded Belshazzar. Unfortunately, there never was a Median named Darius. Darius was a Persian. If the Darius of Daniel 5:31ff is Darius the Great, he not only did not succeed Balshazzar, but he came after, not before, Cyrus, who was also a Persian. This is contrary to Daniel 6:28.

6) According to Daniel 1:5, Daniel and his friends were put in a training school for three years, at the end of that time Nebuchadnezzar gave them special honors in his kingdom (Daniel 1:20). Yet in Daniel 2;1ff, in Nebuchadnezzar 's second year, "the king made Daniel a great man" (Daniel 2:48).

What, in effect, we have in the historical data in Daniel is an incorrect account of the fall of Jerusalem, wrong people carried captive, non-existent rulers mentioned, anachronisms in rulers and contradictions in the status of Daniel in Babylon. So, what I would like to know is, what person, skilled in the Hebrew and late Aramaic of Daniel, knowledgeable in Biblical history, and the history of the ancient near east, and up to date in his reading of works on Daniel by Lutheran and other scholars around the world, ever made the statement which you cite: "The Sixth Century B.C. Prophet Daniel wrote the Book of Daniel. It contains no errors."

I would also like to know the name of a first-rate Aramaic scholar, be he LCMS or other, who has studied the Aramaic of Daniel 2-7 and concluded that the book was written in the sixth century B.C.

If you do not wish to answer this letter yourself, perhaps you could send it to the author of the above mentioned quotation in *Christian News* of May 15, 1978, p. 15.

Sincerely yours,

(Rev.) Marvin F. Cain

Our Savior's Lutheran Church

Phoenix, Arizona

(Ed. The May 15 *CN* was sent to all LCA and ALC churches).

Questions

1. Pastor Marvin F. Cain challenged *Christian News* to show ____.
2. Daniel was the recipient of ____.
3. What did Jesus say in Matthew 24:15? ____
4. What did Porphyry say about Daniel? ____
5. The neo-Platonist philosopher said the Book of Daniel contains ___ and not ___.
6. The real reason why some scholars do not accept _____ is that for them ____ is not possible.
7. What are some reasons why critical scholars reject the historicity of the events recorded in the Book of Daniel? ____
8. Various tablets from Babylonia have revealed that Belshazzar shared the throne as ___ with his ____.
9. Was Daniel in error when he called Belshazzar the son of Nebuchadnezzar? ____
10. Cyrus permitted subordinate rulers to reign under him with the title ____.
11. It seems most likely that a man named ____ was none other than Cyrus the Mede.
12. The Rash Shamrah texts dating from ____ contain certain Aramaisms found in ____.
13. Does the presence of Greek words in Daniel prove that Daniel was not written in the Sixth Century B.C? ____
14. What has Professor Edwin Yamauchi shown? ____

The Sources of the Pentateuch

Christian News, September 18, 1978

Ed. Many of our readers, including Lutheran Church-Missouri Synod President Jacob Preus, have urged us not to publish material by such liberals as Rev. Robert Brueckner and Rev. Wayne Saffen. Although liberals seldom publish anything by conservatives, we want to be entirely fair to the liberals. We defend the freedom of the press. *Christian News* is absolutely certain the orthodox position is correct and maintains that it has nothing to fear by presenting the position of liberals. "All the facts should be laid on the table," as Dr. William Beck, the translator of An American Translation often told us. Truth will win out. Let the liberals expose themselves. We want our readers to know exactly what the liberals are saying and how they argue.

Pastor Brueckner is a clergyman of both The Lutheran Church-Missouri Synod and the Association of Evangelical Lutheran Churches. The LCMS's Atlantic District President Ronald Fink is defending Pastor Bruecker and other liberal New York clergymen who are members of both the LCMS and the AELC. President Fink claims that LCMS President Jacob Preus supports his policy of letting liberals like Pastor Bruecker remain in the LCMS.

We have asked Professor Raymond Surburg, Th.D., Ph.D., of Concordia Seminary, Ft. Wayne, Indiana to respond to Pastor Brueckner's "The Sources of the Pentateuch" (Following this article).

x x x x

The Sources of the Pentateuch
By Rev. Robert M. Brueckner

The material of the Pentateuch consists of stories and codes of laws that were transmitted orally from one generation to the next. Then, in the tenth century B.C. an editor compiled some of these narratives into a book. Because he used the name of **Jahweh** to refer to God, his work or source of the Pentateuch became known as "J". His work, which exhibits enthusiastic nationalism seems to have originated in southern Judah. His message is: "By you all the families of the earth shall bless themselves" (Gen. 12,3; 18:18).

In the ninth and eighth centuries B.C. an editor, apparently of the northern kingdom of Israel, gathered together his sources and placed them in a book in which he emphasized the message: "Fear God" (Cfr. Genesis 20:22-24; 31:34-35) This source has been called "E" because it uses the name Elohim as the Hebrew word for God.

The "D" source refers to the book of Deuteronomy which was apparently found in 621 B.C., and originated at about that time during the repairing of the temple at Jerusalem under King Josiah. II Kings 22:8f. There was a parallel between the reforms of Josiah and individual laws in the book of Deuteronomy: Deut. 12:13 ff. us II Kings 23:8a,9,19; Deut. 17:3 us II Kings 23:11f; Deut. 23:17 us II Kings 23:7; Deut. 18:10 us II Kings 23:10. "You will experience good in the land."

The "P" or priestly source is the last of the three sources from which the tetrateuch has been composed. It owes its name to its ever-apparent interest in the cultic and ritual rules of priestly observance. It is characterized by preciseness of definition and of a preference for chronology and genealogy. (Genesis 1:1-2:4a) It was probably composed during the exile in Babylon around the time of Ezra in the 5th century B.C. Its message is: "Be fruitful and multiply" (Genesis 1:28 - cfr. Genesis 5:1-28; 11:10-26; 48:3-6; 35:9-13).

The source of chapter 1 is obviously that known as "P" or the "Priestly document." This source is characterized by a preciseness of definition, a preference for chronology and genealogy, and an interest in the cultic and ritual rules of priestly observance. Since the "P" document is of late redaction, during the Babylonian exile, it would also be characterized by allusions to conditions in Babylonia at the time of redaction.

The latter is seen in certain items mentioned in this chapter and by means of certain words that are used. Genesis 1:1-2 give the impression that the world was a watery chaos, a description that would be filled with meaning in Mesopotamia, where the rivers overflow their banks and inundate the land.

The Hebrew word for "void" in verse 2 appears to be an allusion to the Phoenician nocturnal mother goddess, Baau. The Hebrew word for "deep" (which von Rad renders "primeval flood") may allude to the Babylonian dragon of chaos, Tiamat, who opposed the Babylonian creator-god, Marduk, Chaos signifies the threat to everything created.

The God Who enters and shapes history once and for all brings order out of chaos. Genesis 1:2 and the Spirit of God was moving over the face of the waters. (Cfr. Deut. 32:11) According to the Sumerians, IM DUGUD, a giant bird, causes the wind by flapping its wings. Thus, in Genesis 1:2 the "wind" or Spirit of God is demythologized from the Sumerian, and God is the Creator of wind. In Genesis 1:3 the Hebrew word used for "light," appears to have the same root in Hebrew and Babylonian-Assyrian as the Hebrew word for Ur, the city of Chaldea from which Abraham departed to Mesopotamia and ultimately Canaan.

Ur was the seat of moon-god worship. Here we may have a subtle allusion to God's calling of Abram from Ur of the Chaldees, and as he sojourned temporarily in Mesopotamia, so the exile of the Jews in Babylon is only temporary. Israel, the land of Canaan, is their home. (Genesis 12:1) "Light" in verse 4 is contrasted to "darkness," a word that can also be used as symbolic of judgment, terror, dread, mourning, confusion—this indicating that Israel's God, through Abram, delivers and blesses. (Genesis 12:1-3) Verse 5 tells us that God is the Author of time. A day is described according to the Hebrew formula—it begins at sunset. A day is composed of darkness and light.

In verse 6 God speaks and there is created the solid "vault of heaven," the "firmament," a metal expanse to separate the waters above the earth, the rain, from the waters on the earth (v.7). And God called the firmament Heaven (or sky) (v. 8).

In verse 9 God says: Let the waters under the heavens be gathered together in one place, and let the dry land appear. Here we have terminology that is reminiscent of the older story of the Exodus, as it is recorded in Exodus 14. Exodus 14:16,22,29 show the waters of the sea divided so that the people of Israel walked on dry ground. Here we have a subtle confession of faith in the Creator Who has delivered His people.

In verse 10 God calls the dry land "Earth," and the waters that were gathered together he called Seas. The word here used for seas is the same as that used for the Babylonian god, Tiama, the dragon of chaos, the sea god who was feared by land-loving peoples. Thus, Israel's God has bound the god of chaos, and in this work He looks and upon examination, like a craftsman, saw that it was good. Here we are reminded of those who saw the works of Jesus and said: Who is this, that even wind and sea obey Him? (Mark 4,41) In fact, the following story of the Gerasene demoniac may even allude to these verses of Genesis, for the herd of swine which the unclean spirits entered rushed down the steep bank into the sea, and were drowned in the sea. (Mark 5:13) In Genesis 1:11,12 God speaks to the earth (land?) and it brings forth the plants that are to be used by man and beast (1:29,30) for food. God's creative word of command is behind the seedtime and harvest, the fruitfulness of the earth. (Cfr. 8:22)

Another allusion to conditions in Babylonia is seen in the section of verses 14-19. Here "the stars are considered as creatures and as dependent upon God's ordering creative will. The expression 'lights' or 'lamps' is meant to be prosaic and degrading. These created objects are expressly not named 'sun' and 'moon' so that every tempting association may be evaded; for the common Semitic word for 'sun' was also a divine name." The sun and the moon are not gods who wield authority. They are, together with the stars, lights controlled by their Creator and subject to Him. The "lights" which God has created shall determine the seasons and shall rule the day and the night as part of God's once and for all creation. The statement mentioned in passing, He made the stars also, may refer to the stars in such a way as to discount all regard for Mesopotamian astrology. (Cfr. Romans 8:38-39) "Man's world, down to each individual destiny, was determined by the working of the powers of the stars." "Signs" are perhaps occurrences such as eclipses of the sun and moon. Implicitly, worship of the heavenly host is nonsense!

Now the world is ready as a dwelling place for living creatures. "Let birds fly above the earth" may be a phrase to show that flying is their purpose and they are not meant for augury. The verb **bara** is used here for "create" instead of creating by word, an indication that there is a direct relationship between creature and Creator. Even the "sea monsters," those personifications of chaos, are created by God, have a personal relationship to Him, and God looks at His creation, and God saw that it was good. In keeping with the Priestly theme God blessed them, saying, "Be fruitful and multiply and fill the waters in the seas, and let birds multiply on the earth." – A fitting answer of faith and trust in the face of fears of the "sea monsters" and the practice of augury of the birds!

The creation of the land animals (verses 24-25) the first work of the sixth day concludes the work of the fifth day. Here we find the introducing of animals into the world according to their kinds. And God saw that it was good. The animals were created by God. But they were not created to be worshipped. They are the handiwork of Him Whom Israel worships.

In verses 26 and 27 the solemn divine decision emphasizes man's supreme place at the climax of God's creative work. The plural "us, our" (3:22; 11:7) probably refers to the divine beings who surround God in His heavenly court (I Kg. 22:19; Job 1:6; Is. 6:8; Ps. 29:1) and in whose image man was made. And yet, the divine image may more fittingly be the fact that man is to have "dominion" over so much of God's creation, thus giving man the obligation and opportunity to treat it and care for it with respect and deep concern. Fittingly, the Hebrew word **ha Adam** is here translated "man," and not Adam. Luther, too, translates it **menschen** mankind. The Septuagint uses the word ANTHROPOS and the Vulgate uses **hominis**, both in the accusative case, of course. The proper name, Adam, does not occur until well into chapter two. According to a number of ancient Oriental myths, a god makes a man or another god in his likeness. In ancient Egypt the Pharaoh was regarded as "the image of God living on earth." Male and female are created in the image of God, and therefore, as divine-like beings they are not to take part in the base cult prostitute worship of the heathen — another indication to the Israelites that their inheritance is much better than that of succumbing to the religious practices around them. Verses 29-30 suggest the paradisiac peace of the primeval age (compare Hosea 2:18; Isaiah 11:6-8). The very good of verse 31 indicates that Israel's faithful Creator-God has done everything perfectly and, unlike the heathen gods, does not have to renew or improve His work on every New Year.

Chapter 2 verse 1 reads in the R.S.V.: Thus, the heavens and the earth were finished and all the host of them: The word used for finished can also have the meaning of "crown" in Aramaic. Thus, this word could indicate that mankind was the crown of God's creation of the heavens and the earth; mankind was the purpose for which all was created. The creation is there to serve man, not man the creation. It took six days to complete God's work. Ancient Near East literature indicates that an action goes on for six days and the climax is always on the seventh day. Thus, we read in the Gilgamesh Epic that the flood lasted six days. (Cfr. Exodus 24:15-18 and Joshua 6:12-21) Genesis 2:2-3 are a fitting close to this Priestly document, since these verses give a reason for observing the Sabbath. The Babylonian creation epic also contains a concluding act following the work of creation— it is the public glorification of the god Marduk in the assembly of the gods as the chief god's name his fifty names and praise him. "How different, how much more profound, is the impressive rest of Israel's God!" A rest existed before man and still exists without man perceiving it. The world is no longer in the process of being created — not even at New Year's! The word "host" in 2:1 is somewhat puzzling. But, perhaps this word, in fact, comes from the Assyrian and Aramaic word Zabah which means "desire" and ultimately, "beauty." And so, the verse would read: as the heavens and the earth were finished, and all their beauty! God hallowed, that is, set apart or consecrated the seventh day because on it God rested from all his work which He had done in creation. "This is the account of heaven and earth and that which proceeded from them" (BDB). The seventh day is a reminder of Israel's Creator-God Who entered history and authored time and calls His people to Himself in the heathen surrounding in which they live. But even this day is superseded by God Himself in Christ, Who is "the Lord of the Sabbath day," which "was made for man, not man for the Sabbath."

The Theological Dilemma

Israel is in exile in Babylon during the fifth century. The people appear to have become quite complacent in this land. They may even be experiencing much of the Babylonian "good life." Intermarriage between Jew and Gentile may be a possibility, too, thus causing this people to lose their identity as a nation. The adopting of and abiding by superstitions, the Worships of false gods, the accepting of a false view of the world order and cosmos — all may play a part in the theological dilemma. There exists a distinct possibility that the exiles will forget God and His promise to Abraham to make of him a great nation, to bless him, so that he will be a blessing. And so, the Priestly writer brings to mind the God of Israel, Who entered history by creating a completed world, and rested in order that mankind might enjoy His creation.

The "P" document of Primeval History is probably placed at this point in the Pentateuch because it begins with the creation of the world, culminates with man and the Sabbath day, and thus leads into the more detailed "J" document, thus preserving two important Israelite traditions. And, it brings to the fore and emphasizes to the exile reader the importance of a disdain for Babylonian and other heathen cults and the working of the God of Israel in the shaping and creating of the world, a work which reached its climax on the Sabbath. "The Babylonian Sabbath is an unlucky day, a day on which the demons have power. The biblical Sabbath, however, is the day of the creator God, who has produced the universe. In this universe there is no room for gods apart from him" (Claus Schedl, History of the Old Testament, Vol. I, P. 231).

The Traditions

In the "Memphite Theology of Creation," which dates from the beginning of Egyptian history (about 3 000 B.C.) we read: "All the divine order really came into being through what the heart thought and the tongue commanded .... Thus life was given to him who has peace and death was given to him who has sin." The Mesopotamian Creation Epic relates: When Marduk hears the words of the gods His heart prompts (him to fashion artful works ... 'Blood' I will mass and cause bones to be ... Verily, savage-man I will create. He shall be charged with the service of the gods that they might be at ease.'" A tower is built for Marduk to dwell in. Marduk ("Son of the Storm") is a fertility god. For the religions around Israel

456

New Year's Day is always the beginning of life. They held to a seasonal pattern. But Israel testifies to a God Who is active in history. Everything in the Old Testament is found elsewhere in ancient history. But the Old Testament bears witness to the God of History. In the Incarnation God became a party of history. "In the beginning was the Word and the Word was God" (John 1:1). The Old Testament is the history of the Word of God as it affects Israel and other peoples.

Psalm 8, "a Psalm of David," is in accord with Genesis 1:26 and indicates that God has given man a share in His own dignity by conferring on man dominion over the rest of creation. Psalm 33 is "a hymn to God as creator and lord of history." The emphasis upon the divine word in verses 6 and 9 reflects Genesis 1:1-31. The content of this Psalm indicates that it could have been composed during the exile. Or, it may also be a Psalm of David. The tradition behind the "P" source evidently presents man as the crown of God's creation and thus leads up to man's creation. The "J" source, on the other hand, begins with the crown and works backward.

Bibliography

Brown, Driver, Briggs - *Hebrew and English Lexicon of the Old Testament* - Oxford, 1957

Gaster, Theodor H. - *Myth, Legend, and Custom in the Old Testament*- Vol. I - Harper and Row, 1975

Fretheim, Terence E. - *Creation, Fall, and Flood* - Augsburg, 1969

Kaiser, Otto - *Introduction to the Old Testament* - Augsburg, 1975

Pritchard, James B., editor - *The Ancient Near East*, Vol. I - Princeton University Press, 1973

Schedl, Claus - *History of the Old Testament*, Vol. I - Alba House, Staten Island, N.Y., 1973

von Rad, Gerhard - *Genesis* - The Westminster Press, Philadelphia, 1974

Weiser, Arthur - *The Old Testament: Its Formation and Development* - Association Press, New York, 1961?

The Oxford Annotated Bible - Revised Standard Version - New York, Oxford University Press, 1962

Questions

1. Lutheran Church-Missouri Synod President Jacob Preus urged *Christian News* not to publish ____.
2. *Christian News* defended the freedom of ____.
3. William Beck said put all the facts on ____.
4. Jacob Preus defended the policy of not letting liberals like Brueckner ____.
5. Robert Brueckner said the Pentateuch consists of ____.
6. According to Brueckner, the "J", "E", "D", and "P" sources come from ____.

An Evaluation of Genesis 1:1-2:4a As Interpreted from an Historic Historical-Critical Framework

Raymond F. Surburg's Response to Brueckner
Christian News, September 18, 1978

The materials which Pastor Brueckner has sent in to *Christian News* (p. 8) for publication sets forth what he believes is the correct interpretation of Genesis 1:1-2: 4a, which is considered by historical-critical scholars as the introduction to the document known as the Priestly Code (P). He is of the opinion that Lutheranism has only really recently begun to understand the interpretation of the Bible as proposed by scholars who are devotees of the higher-critical methodology. For over a hundred years the Lutheran Church-Missouri Synod has not correctly interpreted the Book of Genesis. He believes that the LCMS's two seminaries at St. Louis and Ft. Wayne are wrongly interpreting the Bible. True hermeneutical practice and proper exegesis are found at Christ Seminary (formerly Concordia Seminary-in-Exile) and in the seminaries of the ALC and LCA, where the historical-critical method rules supreme. In what is published in this issue of *Christian News* is the correct understanding of Genesis 1:1-2:4a, a pericope which traditionally was understood as giving Biblical readers the truth about the creation of the cosmos, the origin of the earth, the beginning of time and space, the manner in which heaven and earth, the heavenly bodies, animals and mankind were created.

At the outset let it be said that Brueckner's presentation is quite different from what the Bible teaches and what historical Lutheranism understood what was being taught by the first thirty-four verses of Genesis. In this exegetical presentation Brueckner is setting forth ideas and views which have been propounded and advocated for decades by liberal Lutheran Old Testament scholars of Europe and also by Protestant scholars of the modernistic stripe. For substantiation the reader need merely consult the books suggested to the reader as sources and as support for the positions advocated in his exegetical paper.

In the introduction he briefly defines the essentials of the Four-Source Documentary Hypothesis, namely, that the Tetrateuch (i.e. Gen-Numbers) is an historical work that utilized three sources — the yahwistic document (J), the Elohistic document (E) and the Priestly Code (P). However by contrast, von Rad, on whose *Commentary on Genesis* he leans, advocated a Hexateuch, namely, that the first six Old Testament books, Genesis through Joshua, constitute the first major historical corpus. Another school of thought however claims that Genesis through Deuteronomy constitutes the first historical corpus. Now who is correct?

In harmony with the critical approach to the Pentateuch, Brueckner does repeat the general position that the Book of Deuteronomy (D) is a fourth source, separate from J, E, and P and D is a source originating in the 7th century B.C.

Since his paper was designed to enlighten the readers of *Christian News* why his interpretation is correct, it would have been proper for him to show why this hypothesis of the Four Documents is true and valid. Brueckner does not seem to be aware that the Documentary Hypothesis has been in trouble for many years. Already in the early fifties of this century Professor Flack of the Hamma Divinity School admitted in an article on the Pentateuch that it was in great difficulty and that all facets of the theory were being and had been challenged by historical-critical scholars themselves! Dr. Cyrus Gordon, world-renowned archaeologist, specialist in Near Eastern languages, in an article that appeared in *Christianity Today*, November 23, 1959 has shown how the various criteria for separating the four sources, J,E,D and P are wrong and in this article he refutes them.[2] Gordon claims that archaeology has shown the fallacies in the four-source Documentary Hypothesis. He claims that JEDP are artificial sources. In rejecting the JEDP hypothesis Gordon wrote: "No two higher critics seem to agree on where J, E, D, or P begins or ends. The attempt to state such matters precisely in the Polychrome Bible discredited the use of colors but not the continuance of less precise verbal formulations. The 'history' of Israel is still being written on the premise that we can only do so scientifically according to hypothetical documents to which exact dates are blandly assigned. While most critics place P last chronologically, some of the most erudite now insist that P is early, antedating D in any case. Any system (whether P is earlier or later than D in such a system makes no difference) that prevents us from going where the facts may lead is not for me. I prefer to deal with the large array of authentic materials from the Bible world and be unimpeded by any hypothetical system."[3]

By assuming that no material in the Pentateuch comes from before the tenth century B. C. and that the Priestly Code is from the fifth century B. C., Brueckner of necessity denies the Mosaic authorship of the First five Books of the Old Testament. This is contradicting the teaching of Holy Writ. The Mosaic authorship is taught in both the Old Testament and in the New. For Brueckner the Pentateuch is a mosaic, which was put together by what has been called the "scissor and paste method." Professor C. R. North, a supporter of the Documentary Hypothesis, in his article on the "Pentateuch" in Hasting's *Dictionary of the Bible* asserted: "There is little doubt that the words 'the book of the law of Moses,' were by the beginning of the Christian era, understood to imply that he did. Similarly, the NT takes Moses' authorship for granted and it can hardly be denied that our Lord shared the common view."[4]

North admits that Jesus Christ did hold to the Mosaic authorship, but is forced to conclude "that our Lord's knowledge of questions of this kind was that of his contemporaries, and that the acceptance of such limitations was one condition of a true incarnation."[5] The critical Lutheran scholar Curt Kuhl admits that the New Testament taught the Mosaic authorship of the Pentateuch (Luke 2:22; 24:44; John 7:23 and others) as do various passages of the Old Testament (Joshua 1:7-8; I Kings 3:2; II

Kings 21:8; Malachi 4:4), but he brushes this Scriptural evidence aside with the assertion: "The witness of the New Testament is of little value for evidence that Moses wrote as are the few passages in the Old Testament where reference is made to the Law of Moses." Appealing to the doctrine of the Kenosis, namely, that in the state of humiliation Jesus humbled Himself and according to His human nature did not know, for example, the time of the day of judgment, scholars are now trying to justify questioning many assertion the Lord made about Biblical books. While it is not necessary to support that during His state of humiliation Christ was conscious of all truth at every moment of time, it is essential to hold to the conviction that every given pronouncement of our Lord is free from the contamination of error, unless we are to undermine completely the confidence in Christ as a reliable teacher of doctrine. If Christ is not to be trusted completely in all his assertions, how is the reader of Christ's sayings going to know where to draw the line between matters of eternal import and those of purely parochial interest? In this connection one may quote the searching question from the lips of Jesus Himself: "If I have told you earthly things and ye believe not how shall ye believe if I tell you heavenly things?"

Brueckner in his exegetical paper assumes that behind the final writing of the various documents, J, E, D, and P there is a long history of oral traditions, traditions which were utilized by the final editors of the Tetrateuch, Pentateuch or Hexateuch. These traditions came from different centers in the Northern and Southern Kingdoms. Critical scholars contend that these traditions often are contradictory, in fact, this supposedly was one of the clues that alerted scholars that contradictory account of the same historical events are found in the Pentateuch, and that there are contradictions in Joshua, Judges and I and II Samuel.

Such a view has serious implications for the Old Testament as the inspired Word of God. Concerning this serious issue Unger wrote:

If one maintains that the contents of the Pentateuch...were not first transmitted as a book but as a tradition and not reduced to writing till centuries after Moses, and then only as two often divergent traditions (J and E) were united with still later Deuteronomic and Priestly traditions, the admission is inevitable that the account of the "Mosaic age" set forth in the Pentateuch is fundamentally unreliable. No theory that the later redactors who combined the documents J, E, D and P were "inspired'" can alleviate the suspicion of historical unreliability, as such a theory is at variance with the internal evidence of the documents themselves, which ascribe at least two of the three legal codes and considerable narrative directly to Moses' pen.[7]

During the second half of the 19th century many scholars took the view that the authors of J, E, D, P reflected in them their own views as to how the history of Israel is supposed to have developed. These documents were more important for shedding light on the time of the authors or editors of these documents than on the earlier periods with which they were purporting to deal. This interpretation, the reader of Brueckner's exegetical effort will find he has implicitly adopted. In Brueckner's presentation Genesis 1:1-24a deals not with events which occurred at creation but these 35 verses are an apologetic attempt to counteract a serious theological situation of Judaism of the 5th century B.C.

Brueckner also appears to have consulted and used the book by Terrence E. Fretheim, *Creation, Fall and the Flood*, one of a ALC professor at Luther Seminary, St. Paul, Minnesota, which deals with the interpretation of chapters 1-11 of Genesis. In this volume, the reader will find an amalgam of the Documentary Hypothesis together with an infusion of form criticism.[8]

Herman Gunkel was dissatisfied with Wellhausen's conclusions, one of the great popularizers of the Documentary hypothesis, believing that J, E, D, and P had much older material in them then Wellhausen's views would allow. Gunkel argued that there was a long tradition behind these written documents, namely, an oral tradition which had changed considerably in the course of the transmission. He predicted that the oral tradition behind these written sources was composed of an amalgamation of different types of literary genre (literary type). For Gunkel it was necessary to try to determine the situation in life (German: Sitz-im-Leben) that gave birth to the various kinds of literary genre that he isolated. Furthermore, in the century-long transmission of the oral traditions new Sitz-im-Lebens resulted in the reshaping of the oral tradition. Before the Old Testament interpreter deals with a given text, it will be necessary to practice geology of the text and try to establish how the transmission has changed and what the situation was which gave birth to the original material. Form criticism as developed by Gunkel, Gressmann and other adherents of this school of form criticism has continued anew in another form the attack upon the historicity and reliability of many Biblical books, portions of books and individual chapters under the guise of such literary genres as "myth," "saga," "folktale," and "legend." As far as Gunkel was concerned the Book of Genesis contained no reliable history but was a collection of different types of legends. The results of the use of form criticism as applied to various Old Testament books opposes and rejects the New Testament's understanding of Genesis and other Biblical books as belonging to the category of history. The insistence on a long period of oral transmission before the main stream traditions were written and later combined is a naturalistic device to explain the miraculous as popular legend and folklore. Supernatural facts, which stand irrefutable and unshaken in the Mosaic documents, impregnable to all other methods of attack, are dissolved like wax in the crucible of the critics because of a method purposely invented to reject them.[9]

An Evaluation of the Exegesis of Genesis 1:1-2:4a.

According to Brueckner the Sitz-im-Leben for the opening pericope of the P account was the situation in Babylonia, in a section of his essay he describes a supposed theological dilemma for the priests, who believe the exiles were enjoying the good Babylonian life too much. Through intermarriage the possibility had arisen that the Jews would be tempted to adopt heathen customs, also worship the Babylonian gods and also accept a false view of world order and cosmos and thus forget the God who had promised Abraham that he would make the Hebrews a great nation.

That the P Source is the latest of all the four sources of which the Pentateuch has been made from, as has been shown, is a faulty assumption. There is nothing in Genesis 1:1-2:4a to suggest this situation depicted by Brueckner and which constitutes for him the foil for the interpretation of what really is the definitive account of the cosmos' and worlds creation, with all that is in them. The Creation Account, the most complete and detailed in the Bible, has nothing to do with the life and times of the Hebrews during the Babylonian Exile, but all other creation statements found in Holy Writ, and there are more than seventy-five in the Old Testament, go back and derive from this opening chapter of the Bible, where the Biblical reader finds a definitive, authoritative and reliable account of what happened at the beginning of the world's history. The account in 1:1-2:4a is not a polemic against Babylonian gods and religion.

In Brueckner's exposition the reader will find strange interpretations occurring. Instead of **exegesis** (i.e. setting forth what is in the text) the reader will find **eisegesis** (reading in to the text materials and ideas extraneous to the text), in the interest of supporting his fifth century origin of P and Genesis 1:1-2: 4a, he finds the creation account characterized by allusions to conditions at the time of the redaction. "The latter is seen in certain items mentioned in this chapter and by means of certain words that are used" — says Brueckner. As evidence he cites verse 2 of Chapter 1 which states that the world was a watery chaos, which he claims can be appreciated when it is realized that "in Mesopotamia, where rivers overflow their banks and inundate the land." What relationship is there between the original creation of the earth, which Moses described as being in a condition in which earth and water were still not separated and which will be separated in the following verses and the Tigris and Euphrates rivers or the many canals that were created by the inhabitants of the Mesopotamian valley? As evidence for the Babylonian origin of the P creation account Brueckner claims that the Hebrew word for "void" in verse 2 appears to be an allusion to the Phoenecian nocturnal goddess, Baau. The Hebrew word for "void" is **bohu**, which has no relationship whatever to the name, Baau. Furthermore, it might be asked how does a Phoenecian goddess suggest a Babylonian origin of Genesis 1? Another telltale giveaway for the Babylonian origin of Genesis 1 is supposed to *be* the word "deep", which is the English rendering for the Hebrew **tehom**. The word **tehom** may, says the pastor of Central Nyack, allude to the Babylonian dragon of chaos, **Tiamat** who was defeated by Marduk. Here the suggestion is being made that the priests of Babylonia were utilizing the **Enuma Elish** Epic of the Babylonians, a literary production which originated a number of centuries before the P document. Here we have repeated a view made many decades ago by the Babylonian school which held that the writers of the Old Testament were greatly influenced by Babylonian theology and literature. There are a number of Assyriologists like Kinnier Wilson and Donald Wiseman, British Assyriologists, who reject this view and claim there is absolutely no relationship between

the Babylonian word **Tiamat** and the word **tehom.** They reject this identification on philological and linguistic grounds. Dr. William Foxwell Albright asserted: "It is a little difficult to see how this mythological
structure can be connected in any direct way whatsoever with the Biblical
story, though many scholars have tried to establish such a connection."
Brueckner claims that the chaos signified a threat to everything created.
This certainly is a complete misreading of Genesis 1, where this mixture
of land and water, which was unformed and uninhabited, was simply the
beginning stage for a series of creative activities described in Genesis 1,
beginning with verse 3. Why should God be threatened by his own creation? Everything in Genesis 1 is said to have been good. This is an assertion which occurs seven times in the Bible's first chapter.

Another word which supposedly suggests the Babylonian origin of P's
creation account is the Hebrew word **or,** "light." Asserts Brueckner: "Or
appears to have the same root in Hebrew and Babylonian-Assyrian as
the Hebrew word for Ur, the city of Chaldea from which Abraham departed from Mesopotamia and ultimately Canaan. Ur was the seat of the
moon-god worship. Here we have a subtle allusion to God's calling of
Abraham from Ur of the Chaldees, and as he sojourned temporarily in
Mesopotamia, so the exile of the Jews in Babylonia is only temporary. Israel, the land of Canaan, is their home (Genesis 12,1)." Koehler-Baumgartner in their *Hebrew Dictionary* do not suggest that the city of Ur is
related to the root **'wr,** the Hebrew root from which the Hebrew word **or**
comes.[12] Even if the Hebrew word for "light" and the Hebrew proper noun
"Ur" came from the same Hebrew root, how can any sound interpreter
bring them into relationship in Genesis 1? Instead of practicing sound
exegesis Brueckner allegorizes and reads ideas into the text ideas that
are not there. The following is some more allegorizing when he writes:
"'Light' in verse 4 is contrasted to 'darkness,' a word that can also be used
as symbolic of judgment, terror, dread, mourning, confusion-thus indicating that Israel's God, through Abram, delivers and blesses (Genesis
12:1-3)." Still another alleged indication indicative of Babylonian influence is the statement in Genesis 1,2 and the Spirit of God was moving
over the face of the waters (Cfr. Deut. 32,11). Brueckner suggests that
this idea was probably derived from the Sumerians, who believed that
IN DUGUD a giant bird causes the wind by flapping its wings. "Thus in
Genesis 1:2 the 'wind' or Spirit of God is demythologized from the Sumerian and God is the Creator of wind. Traditional Lutheran and Protestant
theology understood Genesis 1:2 as speaking of the creative activity of
the Holy Spirit, and that 1:2 says absolutely nothing that God is the creator of the wind!

In his interpretation of verse 6 Brueckner espouses a mistranslation
of the Hebrew word **rakiah**, which if it were accurately translated,
should be rendered "expanse." The idea that the Hebrews believed in a
three-story universe, in which the first story supposedly was "the vault
of heaven," a metal expanse to separate the waters is sheer nonsense.
For information as to what lies behind this metal vault, consult the article by Dr. Gaenssle in the *Concordia Theological Monthly* October,

1952.[13] There the reader will find a complete rebuttal of the arguments of historical-critical scholars that the three-story universe was adopted by the Hebrews from the Babylonians and is to be found in various passages of the Old and New Testament. It was Rudolf Bultmann who claimed that the concepts of the Bible, found in both Old and New Testaments, concerning the nature of the cosmos needed to be demythologized. This means that the reader has no reliable information about how the universe came into being and all Bible assertions of a cosmological nature are hopelessly outdated and useless. This would then permit the acceptance of the so-called scientific speculations about the origin of the universe and the earth, speculations which are constantly changing.

In his interpretation of verse 10 Brueckner claims that "the Word used for 'seas' in the Hebrew (which is **mayim**) is the same as that used for the Babylonian God, **Tiamat**, the dragon of chaos, the sea god who was feared by land-loving people." In reading the *Gilgamesh Epic* any reader will find that **Tiamat** is not the same as **mayim**. According to tablet IV of this epic, after Marduk has defeated **Tiamat**, "He (i.e. Marduk) split her like a shellfish into two parts: half of her he set up and ceiled it as sky, pulled down the bar and posted guards, he bade them to allow not her waters to escape." (Lines 137-139 in the translation of Speiser, in Pritchard, *Ancient Near Eastern Texts Relating to the Old Testament.* Princeton: Princeton University Press, p. 67; the Acadian text may be found in S. Langdon, *The Babylonian Epic of Creation.* Oxford: At the Clarendon Press, 1933), p. 146; English translation, p. 147). There is no evidence for what Brueckner offers as responsible interpretation. Genesis 1 does not present a conflict between Elohim (God) and the god of chaos, whom Brueckner would have us believe was bound by Yahweh. In order to give his pagan interpretation some religious respectability, he then brings in unrelated New Testament data. He engages in imaginary homiletizing instead of setting forth what the text teaches.

Another allusion to conditions in Babylonia to support the 5th century origin of the P version of creation is alleged to be found in verses 14-19, verses which give an account of God's creative activity on the fourth day. On this day God created the sun, moon and the stars. Brueckner, following his higher-critical sources, argues that the purpose is apologetic, the names given the sun, moon (called the larger and smaller lights) are purposely not mentioned in order to deprecate them. It is argued by some of the critical scholars that the words "lights" and "lamps" are prosaic and degrading. The Central Nyack, N.Y. pastor writes: "These created objects are expressly not names 'sun' and 'moon' so that every tempting association may be evaded; for the common Semitic word for 'sun' was also a divine name" (In the essay this is a part of a quotation, whose source he does not give). It would seem to this reader that if this assumption were true that the P writer could have very effectively rejected the supposed worship of the sun and moon by directly using "shemesh" (Hebrew: sun) and "yareach" (Hebrew: moon) and stating that God made them! Here again something is being read into the text which is not in any way indicated. The way the Genesis text refers to the stars is also supposed "to

464

discount all regard for Mesopotamian astrology!" It is marvelous what a person can find in a text when he wishes to do so.

On the fifth day of creation God gave the first command: "Let there be swarms of living things swimming in the water, and let birds fly above the earth in the firmament of heaven." The word "firmament" which Brueckner called a solid vault of metal in his exegetical paper makes no sense whatsoever, for how can the birds fly in something which is solid? In verse 14 God said "let there be light in the firmament of heaven." How could the heavenly bodies move in solid metal? Relative to the birds who are to fly around in the air he claims that the fact that the birds were supposed to fly above the earth "may be a phrase that flying is their purpose and they are not meant for augury." What proof for such a supposition that this is against is augury? In interpreting verse 21 Brueckner believes that the "sea monsters" (Hebrew tamamo), were the personifications of chaos. The so-called word "sea monsters" is simply a term for whales, sharks and other large marine animals which God brought into being on the fifth day. Note again the attempt to read unrelated notions into a Biblical account! This is eisegesis, not **exegesis**. For Brueckner the real purpose of verses 20-21 is: "A fitting answer of faith and trust in the face of fears of the 'sea monsters' and practice of augury of the birds!"

Concerning verses 24-25, which describe the creation of the land animals (verses24-25), Brueckner states that "the first work of the sixth day, concludes the work of the fifth day." In normal English usage there is a difference between the concept "ending" and the concept of "beginning." He claims that the animals made on the sixth day were not to be worshipped. Where in the text is there any hint of such a suggestion? Again Brueckner tries to support his claim of the primary purpose of Genesis 1:1-2:4a is apologetic.

In verse 26 Moses informs us that God said: "Let us make man in our image, after our likeness." Concerning this plural "us" and "our" Brueckner writes: "The plural"us, our' (3.22; 11,7) probably refers to the divine beings who surround God in His heavenly court (1 Kg. 22.19; Job 1.6; Is. 6.8; Ps. 29.1) and in whose image man was made." Here the Central Nyack pastor adopts the higher-critical view that the Hebrews adopted from pagan mythology the concept that there was a chief God who presided over others gods. In Ugaritic literature we know that El was the head god who presided at meetings of the divine council of the gods (which is polytheistic). The Old Testament writers are supposed to have adopted this pagan idea, making Elohim preside over the heavenly court consisting of God and the angelic beings. According to Brueckner mankind, not Adam, was made in the image of the divine beings who surrounded God, for his sentence reads 'man', not Adam, was created in the image and likeness of the angels. But the angels were spirits! However, James asserts that men were made after the similitude of God, and not of the angels (3:9).

We agree that the creation of man is the summit of God's divine work. The "us, our" of Genesis 1:26 should be interpreted as a deliberation of the Holy Trinity, not of a divine consultation with the angels. Brueckner is not consistent, for in one sentence he claims that the Hebrew **Ha adham** (man) was created in the image of the divine court (a plural concept) and then he writes as follows: "According to a number of ancient Oriental myths, a god makes a man or another god in his likeness. In ancient Egypt the Pharaoh was regarded as "the image of god living on earth." "Male and female are created *in the image of God* (italics supplied), and therefore, as divine-like beings they are not to take part in the base cult prostitute worship of the heathen-another indication to the Israelites that their inheritance is much better than that of succumbing to the religious practices around them." Note here again the attempt to make everything in Genesis 1:1-31 to be of an apologetical nature, endeavoring to support the Sitz-im-Leben for the writing of the Creation Narrative, as coming from the 5th century B.C., which actually gives the true facts about the beginnings of the cosmos, the planet earth, life, the heavens and the earth and all that is in them.

The essayist whose exegetical effort we are evaluating is following the traditional higher-critical position when he claims that verse 26 is not in harmony with Genesis 2, where Adam appears. However, after Genesis 1:1-2:4a, the beginning of the P document, the next material ascribed to P is Genesis 5, which reads: "This is the book of the generations of Adam, in the day that God created man, in the likeness of God made he him. Male and female created he them." So P tells us that 1:26 is to be understood of one man and one woman. According to the Word of God found in 1 Chronicles 1:1 and Luke 3:38, where Adam is called "the son of god," we have references to the Biblical truth that Adam was created not in the image of the angels but of God, and the true God is the Triune God.

In dealing with the conclusion of the Creation Account, Brueckner states that the heavens were finished and that the verb "finish" can also have the meaning of "crown in Aramaic." The Hebrew word **kalah**, used in 2:1 for "finished" has other meanings in the Old Testament, it is the context that determines the meaning for a given verb or noun, it is unscientific **exegesis** to read a meaning which the same verb may have in a different context or in another Semitic language into a given passage in the Old Testament, especially when in 2:1 there is no problem with the establishment of the fact that 2:1 informs us that God was finished with his creative activity in the six days, described in chapter 1:1-31.

Relative to the Biblical teaching that God created the world in six days, Brueckner endeavors to give the impression that the P writer was using a literary device of describing the creation in *six* days because this was a characteristic literary device employed in Near Eastern literature. Thus he writes: "It took six days to complete God's work. Ancient Near Eastern literature indicates that an action goes on for six days and the climax is always on the seventh day. Thus, we read in the *Gilgamesh Epic* that the flood lasted six days (Cfr. Exodus 24:15-18 and Joshua 6.12-21)." How does Brueckner know that the author of the *Gilgamesh Epic* did not believe the flood lasted six literal days? Who says that the use of six is merely a literary construct?

Exodus 20, the chapter that gives the Ten Commandments, in the sabbath commandment states that the Hebrews are to work for six days and rest on the seventh, "for in six days Jehovah made heaven and earth, the sea, and all that is in them is, and rested on the seventh day." In the exegetical essay under discussion, the essayist says: "Genesis 2.2-3 are a fitting close to this Priestly document, since these verses give a reason for observing the Sabbath." Genesis 2:3 only teaches that God blessed the seventh day, and hallowed it. What reason is stated for keeping the Sabbath? The reason is given in Exodus 20:11 and 31:14-17.

Brueckner claims that he finds the word "hosts" of Genesis 2:1 somewhat puzzling. His suggestion is: "But, perhaps this word, in fact, comes from the Assyrian and Aramaic word **aba'** which means "desire" and ultimately "beauty." And so, the verse would read: "Thus the heavens and the earth were finished, and all their beauty!" Koehler-Baumgartner in their *Hebrew Dictionary* derive the word hosts **Tsebaoth** (feminine plural in Hebrew) from a root **tsaba**, which in Akkadian, South Arabic, Ugaritic, Egyptian and Ethiopic "wage war."[11] The Hebrew **Tsebaoth** in the Old Testament is used of the armies of Israel, the angelic hosts and the heavenly bodies.[14] This "beauty" interpretation has no warrant in comparative Semitics nor in the usage of the Old Testament. One of the often used names for God in writings after the days of Samuel is "Yahweh of hosts."

The Ebla and the P Source

Dr. Clifford Wilson, an Australian archeologist, in his book *Ebla Tablete: Secrets of A Forgotten City*, Master Books: San Diego. California, 1977, claims that he attended a public lecture given by professor Pettinato of Rome, to whom the academic world is indebted for its information about the remarkable discoveries at Tell Mardik, ancient Ebla, in which he stated that there are three copies of a poem from Ebla, which give a version of creation quite different from those found in the *Enuma Elish Epic* and the *Atrahasis Epic* of the Babylonians.[15] This tablet says Wilson does not have "gross absurdities as gods fighting, cutting each other in half, making the earth from one half of a monster goddess and the heaven from the other, with the Tigris river flowing from one eye and the Euphrates from the other."[16]

The poem of which Pettinato spoke has ten lines, all of which he claims he has not been able to decipher. When Pettinato was pressed as to what it stated, Wilson reports that he said "that the creation tablet was closer to Genesis Chapter 1 than anything yet discovered, it said that there was no heaven, and Lugal ('the great one'), formed it out of nothing; there was no earth, and Lugal made it; there was no light, and he made it. It must be stressed that the Professor was talking in answer to questions, and was not giving an exact translation." He also elaborated on this poem by stating that the "light" was associated with the sun and the moon, and that the concept of creation was to make something out of nothing. The word "Lugal" originally meant "the great one," and it came to mean king. This tablet comes from the period 2400-2250 B.C. and not from between 500-450 B.C.

In the light of the Ebla evidence no longer can the Genesis creation account be considered a demythologized version of the Babylonian version, because at Ebla we have, if what Pettinato has stated a "purified" version coming from the third millennium before Christ, and therefore, centuries older than the Babylonian account.

Wilson claims in the light of the Tell-Mardkh Ebla evidence: "Clearly it is the Babylonian story that has become distorted and corrupted. The Bible record of creation is seen for what it is. The original record is a writing of ancient times, uncorrupted and majestically acceptable to those who will believe in the Creator God."[17]

Brueckner follows the critical position when he assigns the P creation story to Genesis 1:1-2:4a. However, the Genesis creation account properly terminates with verse 3 and not in the middle of verse 4a.

At Genesis 2:4 a new pericope begins which bridges the creation account (1:1-2:3) and the 3rd chapter, the record of the fall. In 2:4 we meet with the first of a series of ten or eleven "these are the toledoth". **Elleh toledoth** (these are the generations) is the phrase around which the material of Genesis is organized, in 2:4 this phrase can be rendered: "These are the begettings of the heaven and earth." Chapter 2:7 shows how Adam was taken from the earth and his wife Eve is taken from him, so that in the final analysis they both are the begettings of the earth.

The claim of Bruckner "that the tradition behind the 'P' source evidently presents man as the crown of God's creation and thus leads up to man's creation. The 'J' source, on the other hand, begins with the crown and works backward," is simply not factual and furthermore rests on the assumption that the Book of Genesis has two different and contradictory creation accounts. Chapter 2:4-25 tells about the garden of Eden, its two important trees and the circumstances under which Adam and Eve, those creation is given in more detail, may remain there, it concludes with the divine institution of marriage.

Psalm 8 Brueckner believes to be in accord with Genesis 1:26. But the Holy Spirit through the author of Hebrew applies that verses of Psalm 8:6-9 to Christ and so the verses interpreted as speaking about man are actually a prediction about Christ's dominion, over creation.

Genesis 12:3; 18:18 are alleged to be the central message of the J source. This verse Brueckner renders according to the Revised Standard Version: "By you all the families of the earth shall bless themselves." However, the Hebrew form, translated in the RSV and other liberal translations, as a reflexive is a niphal, a passive and should be rendered "by you all the nations of the earth shall be blessed." Paul in Galatians 3 cites the passage: "Through you all the nations of the earth shall be blessed" as having a Messianic meaning. These passages are paralleled by those in Genesis which state: "Through thy seed all nations shall be blessed" (22:18; 28:14). In Galatians 3:16 Paul states: "Now to Abraham were the promises spoken, and to his seed. He said not. And to seeds, as of many; but as of one, and to thy seed, which is Christ." This is also the understanding of the Formula of Concord in the discussion of Law and Gospel (cf. Tappert, *The Book of Concord*. Philadelphia: Fortress Press,

1959), p. 562.

This writer can envision Brueckner responding to what has been written in this critique of his interpretation, that the views he has set forth are those held by many Old Testament and Biblical scholars. He might even respond and say that he has the weight of scholarly opinion on his side. To this the present writer would respond, that the truth of the Bible is not determined by the counting of heads. In fact, in various writings of Brueckner's which have appeared in *Christian News* over the last years, he expressed the view that only those who follow the historical-critical method in dealing with Holy Scripture are truly scholarly.

But Old Testament knowledge and scholarship in the Near East is not limited only to critical scholars. There have been and still are a large number of conservative scholars who have doctorates either in Near Eastern Languages or Semitics and Old Testament interpretation who can read the ancient documents written in Egyptian, Hittite, Sumerian, Accadian (Babylonian-Assyrian), Aramaic, Phoenecian, Hurrian, Moabite, Hebrew, Ugaritic, the languages of Asia Minor, Urartian, Ethiopic, Arabic, South Arabic and Elamite and can assess what the ancient believed and evaluate that has and is being produced by historical-critical scholars.

Here are the names and works of some of these scholars: Gleason Archer, *A Survey of Old Testament Introduction.* Chicago: Moody Press, 1970, pp. 73-169. Merrill Unger, *An Introductory Guide to the Old Testament.* Grand Rapids: Zondervan Publishing House, 1951, pp. 213-279; Edward J. Young, *An Introduction to the Old Testament.* Grand Rapids: Wm. B. Eerdmans publishing Company, Revised edition, 1960, pp. 107-156; Roland Kenneth Harrison, *Introduction to the Old Testament.* Grand Rapids: Wm. B. Eerdmans Publishing Company, 1969, pp. 3-82.

The four authors just cited have Ph.D's from Harvard, Johns Hopkins, Dropsie College for Graduate Hebrew and Semitic Studies, and the University of London, respectively. No critical scholar can question these degrees.

Other conservative scholars, who have written books and monographs against the Documentary Hypothesis, are Allis, W. A. Maier, Yamauchi, Youngblood, Kline, Robert Dick Wilson, William Green, Kitchen, Charles Pfeiffer, G. H. Livingston, G.A. Aalders, Alexander Heidel, G. T. Manley, Cyrus Gordon, Walter C. Kaiser, James Kelso, Melvin Kyle, Waltke, J.B. Payne, Gerhardud Vos, Joseph Free, I. R. Thiele, Howard V. Voss, MaCrae, Roehrs and H. Hummel and others. All these scholars have earned doctorates from so called prestige institutions, so they can hardly be classified as not knowing what it is all about.

Finally, we would mention three Hebrew professors of the University of Jerusalem who have either totally rejected the Documentary Hypothesis as Cassuto and Segal have done and Yehezkal Kaufmann who has questioned basic assumptions, one being the theory advocated by Brueckner that P is late, Kaufmann says it is quite early. Cassuto has published a book in which he has taken up the basic criteria for the JEDP and rejected them in eight chapters. Cf. U Cassuto, *The Documentary Hypoth-*

esis. Jerusalem: Magnes Press, 1961. M. H. Segal, *The Pentateuch-Its Composition and Its Authorship*, Jerusalem: The Magnes Press, 1967 has demolished the argument of the *Documentary Hypothesis*. Yehezkel Kaufmann, *The Religion of Israel*. Chicago: University of Chicago Press, 1960 has challenged a number of the higher critical views and rejected them.

Footnotes

1. Elmer E. Flack, "Pentateuch" in Lefferts A. Loetscherr *Twentieth Century Encyclopedia of Religious Knowledge* (Grand Rapids: Baker Book House, 1955), II, 862-63.
2. This article was also reprinted in *Christianity Today Reader* (Westwood, J.J.: Fleming H. Revell, 1966), pp. 91-99.
3 **Ibid.**, p. 97.
4. C.R. North, "Pentateuch" James Hastings, *Dictionary of the Bible*, revised by Frederick C. Grant and H. H. Rowley (New York: Charles Scribner's Sons, 1963),k p. 744.
5. **Ibid.**
6. Curt Kuhl, *The Old Testament, Its Origins and Composition* (Richmond: John Knox Press, 91961), p. 48.
7. Merrill F. Unger, *Introductory Guide to the Old Testament*, (Grand Rapids: Zondervan Publishing House, 1951), p. 232.
8. Terrence E. Fretheim, *Creation, Fall and the Flood*. (Minneapolis: Augsburg Publishing House, 1969). In this volume the accuracy and historicity of the facts of Genesis 1-11 are questioned.
9. Cf. Raymond F. Surburg, "Form Criticism and its Implications for the Interpretation of the Old Testament", in J. Jungkuntz, editor. *A Project in Biblical Hermeneutics*. Published by the Commission on Theology and Church Relations of The Lutheran Church-Missouri Synod, 1969.
10. Donald Wiseman, *Illustration from Biblical Archeology* (Grand Rapids: Wm. B. Eerdmans Publishing Company, 1958), p. 8. J. V. Kinnier Wilson, "The Epic of Creation," in D. Winton Tomas, editor, *Documents from Old Testament Times* (New York: Harper & Brothers, 1961), p. 14.
11. William Codwell Albright, *Recent Discoveries in Bible Lands* (Pittsburgh: The Biblical Colloquium, 1951), p. 61.
12. Ludwig Koehler and Walter Baumgartner, *Lexicon in Veteris Testament Libros* (Leinden: E. J. Brill ,1958), p. 23.
13. Ludwig Koehler and Walter Baumgartner, *Lexicon in Veteris Testament Libros* (Leiden: E. J. Brill, 1958), p. 23.
13. C. Gaenssle, "A Look at Current Biblical Cosmologies," *Concordia Theological Monthly*, 23: 739-749, October, 1952.
14. Koehler Baumgartner, **op. cit.** pp. 790-91.
15. Clifford Wilson, *Ebla Tablets: Secrets of a Forgotten City* (San Diego: Master Books, Division of CLP, 1977), pp. 47-49.
16. **Ibid.**, p. 49.
17. **Ibid.**, p. 53.

Questions

1. Robert Brueckner does not seem to be aware that the Documentary

Hypothesis has ____.

2. The Mosaic authorship of the Pentateuch is ____.
3. What is exegesis? ____
4. What is eisegesis? ____
5. What did Rudolf Bultmann claim? ____
6. In the light of the Ebla evidence no longer can the Genesis creation account be considered ____.
7. The Holy Spirit through the author of Hebrews applies Psalm 8:6-9 to ____.
8. Does the RSV correctly translate Genesis 12:3 and 18:18? ____
9. In his writings Brueckner shows that he accepts ____ method.
10. Who are some Bible believing scholars who reject historical criticism? ____
11. What have the Hebrew scholars Cassuto and Segal written about the Documentary Hypothesis? ____
12. Does the Book of Genesis have two different creation accounts? ____
13. Genesis 12:3 and18:18 are alleged to be the ____ message of the J source.
14. How does the Revised Standard Version translate Genesis 12:3 and 18:18? ____
15. The truth of the Bible is not determined by ____.
16. Who are some of the conservative scholars who have written books against the documentary hypothesis? ____
17. Who are some Hebrew professors who have written books against the J-E-D-P sourse hypothesis? ____

Lindsell's Bible in the Balance

October 20, 1979
Dear brother Otten:
Enclosed please find a partial review of Dr. Lindsell's book, *The Bible in the Balance*, the sequel to his 1976 volume, *The Battle for the Bible*. His new volume contains interesting information about the situation in Protestantism and in Lutheranism. Back in 1976 you ran my rather lengthy book review over seven issues of *Christian News*. If you are interested and you consider it worthwhile, I will complete the rest of the book. Many of readers of *Christian News* will not buy or read Dr. Lindsell's book, but they might read a summarization with an evaluative comment by the writer of the review.

You weekly fill a gap and keep people informed as to what is going on and also have over the years published devotional materials. God bless your continued efforts.

Fraternally,
Raymond Surburg

Lindsell and Henry Hamman from Australia

November 20, 1979
Dear friend and Brother Otten:
Thank you for publishing the first part of Lindsell's book review and the book review of Nichol's and Gordon Clark.

The last three weeks I have had a low-degree temperature which has made me feel lethargic and sick. Today I am going into Parkview hospital in Ft. Wayne for perforated hernia surgery, which the surgeon believes was the cause for my temperature and sick feeling.

I have not yet completed my review of Lindsell's book, but will do so when I am released from the hospital. I had a hernia operation in the same spot where the hernia was perforated 16 months ago.

I am supposed to deliver by the end of February a manuscript, *The Principal of Biblical Interpretation* to Concordia Publishing House. It is supposed to be a text book on hermeneutics for colleges and seminaries. I have been working on this for about 15 months and the MS is in the process of being typed, although I am still referring and trying to improve the contents of each chapter. I hope Concordia will accept it; it may be too orthodox and apologetical.

Dr. Robert Preus brought Hamman over here without consulting any of us. He is far from orthodox. The Australian seminary of which he will serve as head, has professors which use the historical critical method.

472

Recently I blocked an essay on the Gospel from being published by the *CTQ*, which Hamman submitted, to which a number of us in the Exegetical Department objected. Augsburg Publishing House is going to publish a book by Hamman, which I understand deals with the same ideas as those delivered at Valporaiso. When that book is published next year, I will be glad to review and possibly write an article taking issue with his views.

It was too bad that Dr. Preus had him here for a whole school year. Dr. Hamman is leaving this week for Australia. I think that Dr. Preus thought he was thoroughly conservative and in learning to his chagrin that he was not and is not. I believe you have pointed out the weakness in his position and later, next year, we can take up his perineum views when the Augsburg book comes out.

May your family have a happy and blessed Thanksgiving.

Yours in Christ,

Raymond Surburg

Ed. The December 1, 1980 *Christian News* reviewed Hamman's "The Bible Between Fundamentalism and Philosophy." The same issue published "The Battle for Inerrancy Continues Within LCMS – Valparaiso and an UnGodly God." *CN* noted that most of the professors at Valparaiso University where Hamman lectured denied the inerrancy of the Bible and supported Bretscher's position. Volume VIII *Marquart's Works - Bible and Historical Criticism* comments on Bretscher's position, pp. 88-90, 138, 145, 147, 148. In 1992 Bretscher sent a 13 page pamphlet titled *"Christian News* and Me" to every congregation in the LCMS. In 2001 Bretscher published *Christianity's Unknown Gospel* in which he denied the Trinity and deity of Christ. The *CN* editor filed formal charges of false doctrine vs. Bretscher. Bretscher then left the LCMS and was removed from the LCMS clergy roster before the *CN* editor had a chance to face him in an open public heresy trial which the LCMS wanted to avoid (*CN*, November 26, 2001).

Foundations of Biblical Inerrancy

Review by Raymond Surburg

Christian News, November 19, 1979

Foundations of Biblical Inerrancy. By David R. Nichols. BHM Books, Winona Lake, Indiana, 46509. 50 pages. Paper. $1.95.
The Concept of Biblical Authority. By Gordon H. Clark. The Presbyterian and Reformed Publishing Co., Phillipsburg, New Jersey, 08865. 24 pages. 75 cents.

Both of these monographs were written in response to the volume by Rogers, and a number of other professors and pastors, who disagree with Harold Lindsell's *The Battle for the Bible*. The volume edited by Jack Rogers, *Biblical Authority*, published by Word Books of Waco, Texas, endeavored to refute Lindsell's attack on Fuller Seminary, and certain Baptist seminaries, in which the inerrancy and factual reliability have been and still are being attacked. Lindsell's book has elicited a considerable response from a number of the so-called neo-evangelicals. The Roger's volume had contributions by Paul Rees, Clark Pinnock, Berkeley Mickelsen, Bernard Ramm, Earl Palmer, Rogers and David Hubbard, president of Fuller Theological Seminary. The studies by Nichols and Clark were written as rebuttals to the arguments advanced by the seven contributors of Roger's *Biblical Authority*.

The neo-evangelical movement during the last twenty years has been attacking and surrendering the concept of Biblical inerrancy, at least as it was conceived by conservative evangelicals and fundamentalists. The opponents of Biblical inerrancy contend that Lindsell and those who share this position are actually out of step with classical Christian tradition. The proponents of Biblical errancy hold, to quote Nichols, "the Biblical inerrancy as commonly understood today, is linked rather with post-Reformation scholastic orthodoxy typified by B. B. Warfield and Charles Hodge. This particular brand of orthodoxy is said to have widely influenced the ecclesiastical associations and organizations which were born in the wake of the Fundamentalist/Modernist controversy. The opponents of inerrancy contend that Biblical authority is best understood in terms of 'faith and practice,' and should not be equated with 'error-free statements' in relation to history, science, geography and chronology. The word 'inerrancy' is viewed as anachronistic, and is viewed by many of the 'errancy' advocates as 'not a very helpful word since it is a modern standard of precision and scientific accuracy. As seen today, it is not seen as descriptive of classical Christian thought on Biblical errancy'" (p. 7).

It is to these arguments set forth in a number of books and journal articles, that Nichols and Clark have set forth their objections. Nichols in Chapter 1, deals with "The Foundations of Semantic consistency," outlining the objections to inerrancy and then discussing the proper understanding of inerrancy. In Chapter 2 Nichols shows how Origen, Ireneus,

Justin Martyr, Polycarp and Clement, Josephus, Chrysostom and Augustine teach Biblical inerrancy. He further shows from the writings of Luther and Calvin that these two great reformers held the classical view that the Bible was inerrant. In Chapter 3, Nichols takes up John 10:34-36, II Timothy 3:16 and II Peter 1:20-21, biblical passages Hubbard had suggested might be understood differently than has been the case in past centuries and decades, when they were adduced in support of inerrancy.

Professor Clark in his *The Concept of Biblical Authority* deals particularly with the arguments advanced by Rees, Rogers, Ramm, and Hubbard. Clark, professor of philosophy, an orthodox Presbyterian, shows from the official documents of evangelical churches that Rees-Ramm-Rogers-Hubbard contributions are contrary to the historic confessional writings of Protestant churches and therefore are to be condemned. In his analysis Clark states (1) contrasts between the two theologies, and (2) the explication of the fallacious reasoning of the four writers of the seven found in the Roger's symposium.

The misuse of language and errors in reasoning are brought out very effectively by Clark, who shows how these men have misused the English language and have been wrong in positions which they have ascribed to the reformers and the faulty conclusions which they have drawn. Although the booklet of Clark is only 24 pages, he has conclusively shown the errors in the theological positions of the neo-evangelicals who have undertaken to undermine the very foundations of the Christian faith.

Clark makes his penetrating assertion: "In view of this book's lack of forthrightness, its pervasive propaganda device, its begging and dodging the question, its twisting the meaning of words, the question of its morality cannot be evaded" (p. 24).

On the back cover of Biblical Authority the claim is made that "*The Battle for the Bible* today threatens evangelicalism with schism." In a sense that is true! But the question is: Who is doing the dividing? Those who defend what the Bible says about itself or those who attack the Bible's inerrancy, truthfulness and reliability? This reminds a person of I Kings 18:17, "When Ahab saw Elijah, Ahab said unto him, Art thou he that troubleth Israel?"

Questions
1. The neo-evangelical movement has been attacking ____.
2. Nichols shows how ____ teach Biblical inerrancy ____.
3. Clark has shown the errors in ____.
4. Who is doing the dividing of evangelicalism? ____

A Book Review Article of Harold Lindsell's
"The Bible in the Balance"
(Zondervan, 1979)

Christian News, November 17, 1980

On April 26, 1976, Harold Lindsell published his now famous volume, *The Battle for the Bible*, and by June, 1976, 20,000 copies were in print. A number of evangelical leaders at that time asserted that Lindsell's book was one of the most important to be published in a long time, because it dealt with an issue that is central to the survival of biblical Christianity. In a review article of *The Battle for the Bible* this writer wrote: "For a number of years this book will occupy the attention of Christian scholars because the doctrine of the inerrancy of Holy Scriptures is the bedrock on which a sound Scriptural theology rests and one which does justice to the claims of Christ, who said of the Old Testament: 'The Scriptures cannot be broken.' (John 10:35) This book contains a mine of information on the whole battle between fundamentalism and liberals which many of this current generation of evangelicals are only partially aware." This prediction was fulfilled as a flurry of books and journal articles has given evidence.

In his new book, *The Bible in the Balance* (Zondervan Publishing House, Summer, 1979) Dr. Lindsell writes: "*The Battle for the Bible* appeared in the spring of 1976. *Time* magazine featured it in the religion section shortly thereafter. In a few months time the book elicited national and international responses which ranged from enthusiastic approval to intense opposition" (p. 9). The major journals of such theological seminaries like Southern Baptist Seminary in Louisville, and Southwestern Seminary in Fort Worth, Texas, carried critical articles. Disagreement with the Lindsell position was registered also in other periodicals.

The Bible in the Balance is intended to be a further look at what *The Battle for the Bible* was about and what the reactions to it were, and what the literature of the past three years has revealed about Protestant Christianity, especially that branch which now goes by the name of Neo-evangelicalism.

The 1976 volume was an eleven chapter book totaling 218 pages. The new volume has nine chapters and 384 pages.

The Effect of *The Battle for the Bible*
Dr. Lindsell reports in his new book: "A number of interesting chain reactions occurred following the release of the book. Some denominations and institutions changed their doctrinal statements because they were imprecise with regard to inerrancy. They strengthened them considerably to offset the possibility of misunderstanding as to their institutional posture and image. The National Association of Evangelicals made biblical trustworthiness the theme of its annual meeting of 1977. *The Wall Street Journal*, a business daily newspaper, which normally limits its

coverage to financial and business matters, ran a feature story on its editorial page relative to the question" (pp. 9-10).

The International Council of Biblical Inerrancy was organized and its stated purpose is "to take a united stand in elucidating, vindicating and applying the truth of Biblical inerrancy as an integral element in the authority of Scripture." Many outstanding conservative scholars belong to this organization, an organization Lindsell claims he had nothing to do to bring into being, but now serves on its Advisory Board. A number of Lutheran scholars and pastors from the Lutheran Church-Missouri Synod were at its organizational meeting, among them Dr. Robert D. Preus.

In chapter 5 of *The Battle for the Bible* (pp. 89-105) Lindsell discussed the situation in the Southern Baptist Convention, focusing among others on The *Southern Baptist Seminary* at Louisville, Kentucky, headed by its president McCall. Lindsell gave a number of examples of professors associated with various Baptist seminaries and universities who had questioned the inerrancy and infallibility of the Bible, because of the adoption of various forms of the higher critical methodology. Professors specifically cited and quoted from were Robert S. Allen of the University of Richmond (p. 91), Dr. William Hull, a long-time professor at *Southern Baptist Seminary* at Louisville (pp. 93-95), and Dr. Howard P. Colson, editorial secretary of the Sunday School Board, who in *Outreach* questioned the inerrancy of the Bible. *Broadmann Bible Commentary*, written by many men subscribing and promoting higher critical theories, which automatically requires rejection of the reliability and inerrancy of the Bible, was mentioned in evidence for the surrender of Biblical inerrancy at a seminary which years ago held and taught Biblical inerrancy.

President McCall responded in the June, 1976, *Southern Baptist Seminary*, in an article in which he reviewed *The Battle for the Bible*, claiming that Lindsell's book "aroused many snakes but kills none of them."

In chapter 6 of *The Battle for the Bible* Lindsell had presented "the strange case of Fuller Theological Seminary."(pp. 106-121). Fuller Seminary responded in a number of different ways. One issue of the seminary's *Theology, News and Notes* was given over to the inerrancy issue. In 1977 Word Publishing House of Waco, Texas published a volume titled, *Biblical Authority*, edited by Jack Rogers of the Fuller faculty. It contained essays by President Hubbard, Paul Rees, Bernard Ramm, Berkely Mickelsen, Clark Pinnock and others. This book was answered by *The Foundations of Biblical Authority*, edited by James Montgomery Boice. Contributors to it were John Gerstner, James I. Packer, Gleason Archer, R. C. Sproul, Kenneth Kantzer, James Boice and Francis Schaeffer (Zondervan, 1978).

The Christian Century published an article by Donald Dayton of North Park Theological Seminary which was extremely critical of Lindsell's book. Union Theological Seminary, liberal standard-bearer of liberal theology, devoted the Winter 1977 issue of its *Union Seminary Quarterly Review* to the matter of the issues that were dividing the evangelicals. One contribution is of special significance in this Winter number. It is the article titled, "Biblical Hermeneutics: The Academic Language of Evangelical Identity." Its author, Gerald T. Sheppard, a graduate of Fuller Seminary, has set forth interesting facts about those who follow the hermeneutics now espoused by Fuller and those seminaries agreeing with it against Biblical inerrancy.

Another book spawned by the controversy over the nature of the Bible was the Westminster book, *The Debate About the Bible* by Stephen T. Davis, associate professor of philosophy and religion at Claremont (California) Men's College. Davis especially took issue with Francis Schaeffer and Harold Lindsell. Toward the end of his book Davis claimed that, "it should be the aim of theologians to convince the people that the Bible was the only infallible rule of faith and practice, but not that it was inerrant."

While influential scholars came out against Lindsell's stance as reflected in *The Battle for the Bible*, there were also scholars who defended Lindsell's view on the inerrancy and infallibility of the Bible. Within a few months there were responses to the rebuttals of Presidents Hubbard and McCall; answers to the allegations of Carl F. Henry and rebuttals to the criticism of Pinnock, Barnard, Ramm, Dayton, Davis and others. *Christian News* carried a series of articles on *The Battle for the Bible* by the present writer (Cf. issues of Nov. 1, 8, 15, 22, 29, Dec. 20, '66, Jan. 3, '67) in which there was set forth the basic contents of Lindsell's book, followed by the view of Hubbard, Henry, Pinnock, and a number of Lutherans who had criticized Lindsell's inerrancy position. Gleason Archer came out in defense of Lindsell when he responded to the article of Dr. Fred Thompson entitled "The Wrong War," (Winter, 176 of *Action*). This is now reprinted as Appendix 2 of *The Bible in the Balance*. Professor Gordon Clark criticized a number of the opponents of Lindsell's *The Battle for the Bible* in a 24-page monograph, entitled *The Concept of Biblical Authority* (The Presbyterian and Reformed Publishing Company) and David R. Nichols has also defended Lindsell by taking up the arguments of Jack Rogers, *Biblical Authority*. Two incisive book reviews of Jack Rogers' *Biblical Authority* were written by Norman Geissler and by Robert Preus, both reviews are reprinted in *The Bible in the Balance* as Appendix 3 and Appendix 4, pp. 359-366.

The Purpose of *The Battle for the Bible*
The major thrust of the 1976 volume of Lindsell was directed toward two questions: "(1) What is the source of our religious knowledge; i.e. from where do we get answers to life's important questions such as: Where did I come from? Who am I? What is the purpose of life? and What happens to me when I die? (2) Is the source from which I get the answers to my basic questions reliable? i.e. - Does the source tell me the truth?" (p. 11).

Lindsell answered these questions by claiming that the source of the Christian faith was to be obtained from Christ the Living Word, and from the Word of God as given in the Bible. Our knowledge of Christ as Savior can only be found in the Word of God Written. Without the Word of God Written there could be no foundation for the Christian faith. The Christ of the Christian faith is the God-Man as set forth in the Chalcedonian Creed.

Is the source from which a Christian obtains his answers reliable? Lindsell defended the historic Christian position that the Bible is trustworthy in all of its parts. He states unequivocally: "The Bible is authoritative, and as the authoritative Word of God it is revelatory. God has made known to men that which they could not discover any other way." While God has made Himself known in nature, natural revelation cannot really make God known as Savior and Redeemer. Therefore, God has given mankind a special revelation, to be found in His Incarnate Son and in the revelations in the Written Word. The Bible was inspired by the Holy Spirit and is inerrant in the autographs. The Holy Scriptures are the Word of God and the word of men, but as the New Hampshire Confession of Faith says, "It has God for its author."

In the 1976 book Lindsell claimed that the doctrine of the Bible's inerrancy is a doctrine deduced from the Bible just as are the doctrines of justification by faith, the vicarious atonement of Christ, the deity of Christ and many other doctrines. Inerrancy and infallibility involve matters of faith as well as practice. Inerrancy is concerned with all phenomena of the Bible, not just with teachings pertaining to doctrine and ethics. If the Bible contains errors, then Paul's statement that all Scripture is profitable would not be true, because error cannot be profitable.

In *The Battle for the Bible* it was claimed that inerrancy was the position not only of the New Testament but of the subsequent history of the Christian Church until the time of rationalism, when the Bible came under attack. It was a major thesis of the 1976 book that "Biblical inerrancy has become the focal point for defection in the modern church. Just as the Christological controversies stirred up the early church, and as justification alone lay at the heart of the Protestant Reformation, so the trustworthiness of the Bible lies at the center of the theological struggle today. This is not to say there were no opponents for the first eighteen centuries of the Christian era. But it does mean that opponents of inerrancy constituted small minority and the issue itself was not the centerpiece of any great controversy" (*The Bible in the Balance*, pp. 13-14).

In *The Battle for the Bible* Lindsell furnished concrete evidence for the charge that Christian churches have been infiltrated by theologians who assert that the Bible is errant. In Protestantism this was a part of the liberalism and neo-orthodoxy which infected, and in some cases controlled entire church bodies. The new development that has occurred is that theologians once opposed to liberalism and neo-orthodoxy now have adopted the latter's erroneous views about the nature of the Bible. Lindsell did not claim, nor does he now, that a person who denied infallibility and inerrancy cannot remain faithful to the corpus of Christian doctrine.

In his first book Lindsell contended that those who denied the inerrancy of the Bible had no right to the term "evangelical." In his 1979 volume, Lindsell writes: "Perhaps the most complex and perplexing question I addressed deals with the definition of who is and who is not an evangelical. This particular discussion brought forth loud dissent and raised the hackles of some who wished to be called evangelical despite the denial of inerrancy." In chapter 8 of the current book this matter is taken up for debate (pp. 303-321).

One of the reasons for Lindsell's *The Bible in the Balance* was to evaluate and answer the objections and charges that were made since the publication of *The Battle for the Bible*. The author of the latter volume has thoroughly digested all criticisms, classified them, and has listed them on pages 16-18. *The Battle for the Bible* has caused fallout about which Lindsell says he is not unhappy. He says he was surprised by the attention given his book and its arguments. This shows there is great interest in the inerrancy question. The International Council on Inerrancy is one of its results and this new organization plans to spend about ten years in adequately coming to grips with issues involved in accepting Biblical inerrancy.

Lindsell Answers Critics and Refutes Them

Chapter 2, (pp. 22-69) takes note of all writers who reacted in print to *The Battle for the Bible*. The former editor of *Christianity Today* states the objections of his opponents and then answers them. One of the results of the publication of Lindsell's book was to reveal the disappointing fact that the influence of a faulty view on the nature of Scripture was more widespread than believers' in inerrancy would have expected. In a number of instances Lindsell showed that statements made by his critics fell far short of the truth. He answered Donald Dayton's article that appeared in the *Christian Century*, November 10, 1976, and the letter of Professor Smith, a Nazarene minister teaching at John Hopkins University. Smith took issue with a statement of Dayton, who had written "that evangelicals who reject verbal inerrancy of the Scripture on matters of history and cosmology are taking their cues from modern Biblical scholarship." Smith also claimed that "those coming out of the Wesleyan, Lutheran, or Calvinistic traditions have drawn their views about the nature of Holy Scripture from the writings of the Reformers, who taught that not ... the words but the meaning require close and critical examination of texts, rather than incantation of supposedly inerrant words."

Both Smith and Dayton agree however, in this that modern critical scholarship is at the heart of the disbelief in Biblical inerrancy. That is the point which Lindsell made in his first book, namely, that the historical critical method is the reason for the switch from an inerrant Bible to one that is errant. (*The Battle for the Bible*, pp. 81, 204). Nothing, of course, could be farther from the facts for Luther, Calvin and the other Reformers clearly in their writings have defended the inerrancy of the Word of God. Another false position was made by Smith when he claimed that evangelicalism of the nineteenth century was committed "on all sides to the authority of the Bible in matters of faith and doctrine, not history and cosmology." Lindsell devotes about seven pages of chapter 2 to show how erroneous were the claims of Smith relative to his assertion that nineteenth century evangelical Christians did not hold to an inerrant and completely trustworthy Bible.

Carl F. Henry, a believer in Biblical inerrancy, a former editor of *Christianity Today*, took the strange position that this foundational doctrine, should not be used to break up the unity and cooperation among Evangelicals which Henry has fought for over a period of many years. Lindsell answered all his criticisms and clarified certain statements which Henry may have misunderstood.

On pages 36-43 he responds to the criticisms of Clark Pinnock, who in his book *Biblical Revelation, The Foundation of Christian Theology* (Moody Press, 1971) and in other published writings had come out very strongly for Biblical inerrancy and the trustworthiness of the Bible in all its statements. Pinnock appears to be on a theological journey that is heading for a less and less orthodox position.

Bernard Ramm, a prestigious Christian scholar, author of many volumes, wrote a severe critique of Lindsell's book for *The Reformed Journal*, published by Eerdmans Publishing Company. It is a theological journal which stands to the left of The Christian Reformed Church's *Banner*. Two of its editors are James Daane and Lewis B. Smedes, two Fuller Seminary professors. Ramm does not agree with Lindsell that the doctrine of the inerrancy of the Bible is a watershed for evangelicals. From Ramm's previously published books this would be a natural conclusion. Ramm's *The Christian View of Science and Scripture*, a widely read book, would not permit the inerrancy of Holy Writ on all subjects discussed. Chapter VIII, "The Problem of Inerrancy and Secular Science in Relation to Hermeneutics;" in *Protestant Biblical Interpretation* (1970) would not allow the position that the Bible is inerrant in all of its scientific statements. Ramm claimed that Lindsell was fighting the wrong war. The real problem according to Ramm, as he sized up the current situation, was:

The contemporary battle for the Bible asks whether most of the Biblical history is credible, or whether all we have of the true words and deeds of Jesus is a demitasse full of shreds, or whether the Prison Epistles and the Pastoral Epistles are Pauline, or whether the Revelation is anything more than a weird book of apocalypticism.

Here Ramm seems to be recognizing the validity of the use of the historical critical method with its utilization of a radical literary criticism, a destroying of the reliability of Biblical content by means of form criticism. This illustrates Lindsell's claim that those scholars calling themselves evangelicals, who now are using and defending the historical-critical method, logically must surrender the inerrancy of the Bible. Nearly ten pages are devoted to Stephen T. Davis' *The Debate About the Bible*. This book written by a former student of Fuller Seminary was designed to support the arguments of Fuller against Lindsell. Davis claims that he is a believer in infallibility but not in inerrancy. Dr. Davis asserts that the Bible is the Word of God. Further, he avers "that the Bible teaches that it in inspired, authoritative, and trustworthy." However, this does not mean for Davis that it is inerrant. Lindsell characterizes this position as having an Alice-in-Wonderland quality about it. Lindsell effectively points out that if the whole Bible is God's Word and if there are errors in the Bible then God is responsible for the errors

481

in the Bible. Either God is directly responsible for their existence or He permitted them to slip in. This means the Bible is a book full of truth and error. What criteria are to be employed in sifting the truth from the error? How is the reader to distinguish between matters pertaining to faith and morals and those dealing with historical, geographical and scientific matters? The only logical answer would have to be: man using his reason and utilizing the historical-critical method.

Chapter 2 in which Lindsell answered questions raised by his opponents concludes with the Mennonite Brethren, who have denominational schools at: Manitoba, Canada; Hillsboro, Kansas; and the Pacific College and Mennonite Brethren Biblical Seminary, Fresno, California. These schools publish a quarterly known as *Direction*. The April, 1977 issue was devoted to a critique of *The Battle for the Bible*. Lindsell's reaction to this April number is: "The quarterly makes it apparent that the infiltration of an aberrant view of the Bible is to be found in the depth of that denomination's institution" (p. 60).

Dr. Loewen criticized Lindsell claiming that inerrancy is not taught in 2 Timothy 3:16,17 and 2 Peter 1: 21. Lindsell responds to this criticism by saying that he did not base his case for inerrancy alone on these two passages. Loewen also tried to show that Luther did not believe in Biblical inerrancy, because of the latter's distinction between the "incarnate Word," "the written Word," and the "spoken Word." But this argumentation does contradict the fact that Luther did hold to an inerrant Word of God, the Bible. Loewen did admit that Luther explicitly asserted that the Scriptures are true and that God did not lie in His Word. Many quotations could be given from *Luther's Works* conclusively showing that Luther cannot be called upon to support the modern "evangelical" stance that the Bible was not free from error. Loewen has espoused an erroneous position on how the inerrancy and inspiration of the Bible are established. Thus he wrote: "For the real infallibility of the Word of God can never be established unless the message of Scripture has in fact transformed the heart and mind, thought and deed." Luther would have opposed such a view totally. The inerrancy of the Bible, in fact, the doctrine of bibliology is objectively established from the word of Holy Writ and not by pious experience. In the same issue of *Direction*, Dr. Devon Wiens contributed an essay, entitled "Hearing the Word: To understand what I read — the Pilgrimage of a Bible Scholar." Beginning with a rejection of "some old myths that had never worn very well anyway, such as evangelical methods of fundamentalism and dispensationalism" he came to know critical modes of interpretation and also the need to engage these critically. In his doctoral program he became acquainted with Bultmann's theology and hermeneutics. At first Wiens was impressed by it, but later reacted against it. Wiens is not sympathetic to the "traditional hamstringing of the Word with its carefully structured, predictable ways and with 'old-fashioned' ethical mores and doctrinal stances remaining inviolate," but he now is inclined to follow: "the Reformation Anabaptist stress upon allowing the Spirit to break forth new meanings from His Word has taken on significantly new dimensions for me. The contemporary charismatic renewal has also spoken effectively to this point." Wiens' approach to interpretation would totally be rejected by Luther, whom the Mennonite endeavored to use in his attempt to attack Lindsell's inerrancy view.

The Updating of the Situation Relative to Biblical Inerrancy in Smaller Groups and Para Groups

In *The Battle for the Bible* Lindsell in chapter 7 (pp. 122-140) reported on the situation of North Park Theological Seminary, the seminary of the Evangelical Covenant Church of America. After that Lindsell traced the beginning of the erosion of inerrancy in the Evangelical Theological Society and The American Scientific Affiliation, and then the Free University of Amsterdam.

Chapter 3 of the follow-up volume deals with the history of the smaller groups as currently known with special reference to Biblical inerrancy. Lindsell devotes pages 72-78 to the erosion in evidence in the ranks of The National Association of Evangelicals. The NAE was founded in 1942 as a counterpart to the Federal Council of Churches in Christ in the United States, now known as the National Council of Churches. The NAE's statement of faith has as its first article: "We believe the Bible to be the inspired, the only infallible, authoritative Word of God." Back in 1942 the word "infallible" meant the same as "inerrant." Those who refuse to go along with the Standard Dictionary's definition of infallible, like Hubbard and the new anti-inerrantists, are trying to capitalize on the fact that the NAE statement does not employ inerrant but only infallible. But in 1942 the term "infallible" meant without error. There is evidence that the NEA has been infiltrated by people who believe the Bible does have errors. As an example, Lindsell cites the contributions of Dr. Fred P. Thompson, the president of Emmanuel School of Religion, Johnson City, Tennessee, to *United Evangelical Action*, the official NAE magazine, in which he criticized Lindsell's book. According to Thompson, Lindsell was fighting "The Wrong War." In the article Thompson claimed that the Bible was the "infallible rule of faith and practice for the People of God." This does not agree with the NAE statement on Scripture, according to which no limitation is given as to how much of Scripture is infallible. Thompson endorsed the use of the historical-critical method, which he claimed Lindsell rejected. Dr. Gleason Archer responded to Thompson's article which appeared in the Spring 1977 issue of *United Evangelical Action*. (This has been reprinted in Appendix 2, pp. 356-359 of *The Bible in the Balance*). The NAE has members that do not agree with the NAE's statement on the Bible. If they were honest they would disassociate themselves from the NAE. Contributors to *United Evangelical Action* ought not to be allowed to publish attacks on the inerrancy of Holy Writ as they have in the last three years.

The Christian Reformed Church and the Inerrancy Question

The Battle for the Bible also caused a fall-out in The Christian Reformed Church. Three publications which in some way were related to

483

the Christian Reformed Church got involved, namely, *The Banner*, *The Outlook* and *The Reformed Journal*. The second of these supported inerrancy, the first and third were anti-inerrancy.

Dr. Lester De Koster, editor of *The Banner*, came out in print with a number of articles against *The Battle for the Bible* and ran a series of articles about inerrancy. The issue about inerrancy had been a matter of debate before the appearance of Lindsell's book. The synod had dealt with this issue in connection with the case of the Reverend Doctors Edwin Walhout and Allen Verhey. De Koster termed Lindsell's first book as "a highly incompetent work, at most a reservoir of unseemly gossip."

De Koster began his articles with the Belgic Confession, (1561) the theological cornerstone of the Christian Reformed Church's Confession. On the Bible it states: "We receive all these books, and these only, as holy and canonical, for the regulation, foundation, and confirmation of our faith; **believing without any doubt all things contained in them** ... because the Holy Spirit witnesses in our hearts that they are from God." De Koster also gave quotations from Calvin which supported the inerrancy teaching of the Bible itself. Some of these were: "God opens His own most hallowed lips"; "The Scriptures are the very school of God's children"; They "obtain full authority among believers only when we regard them as having sprung from heaven, as if there the living Word of God were heard." Lindsell had supported all these positions. So why De Koster's caustic criticism?

De Koster made much of the argument that the Christian becomes certain of the Bible's inspiration and inerrancy when the Holy Spirit gives the person these convictions. Lindsell has correctly pointed out that there are believers to whom the Spirit does not give that conviction! How can the Holy Spirit talk out of both sides of His mouth? The truth is that the nature and character of the Bible are determined objectively by what the text of Holy Writ says about itself. It is not dependent upon some subjective experience of the person reading the Bible.

The Outlook, a conservative journal among Christian Reformed people, came out against De Koster and defended Lindsell's views about the inerrancy. Edwin H. Palmer, the executive secretary of the New International Version, defended the stance of Lindsell on inerrancy and reminded DeKoster that there was no contradiction to the Bible's claim to inerrancy and the witness of the Holy Spirit. Dr. Palmer concluded his rebuttal of De Koster by writing: "Once we begin to fiddle-faddle with the inspiration and inerrancy of all the Bible, we will begin to question Adam and Eve, Paradise and the fall (Kuitert), Jericho (Koole), or the resurrection of the saints at the crucifixion of Jesus (Baarda), or Paul's instruction about women (Prof. Jewett of Fuller) .. . and so on ...Yes, inerrancy-partial or total-is the crucial question."

The Reformed Journal and Inerrancy

Eerdmans Publishing Company, once a bastion of Calvinistic orthodoxy, but now the publishers of neo-orthodox and neoliberal books, is also the publisher of *The Reformed Journal*, which is committed to take the

Christian Reformed Church from its traditional doctrinal stance. James Daane has attacked *The Battle for the Bible* and has argued that it can still be true that God has not lied even though the Spirit has inspired errors in the Bible. James Daane, a professor at Fuller, is the editor of *The Reformed Journal*. Daane has advanced the strange argument that the existence of errors in Holy Writ does not mean that God has told men that which is not true. To this argument Lindsell responds: · "An untrue statement is perhaps a lie of ignorance although it is not less untrue because the one who told the untruth was unaware of any error. But God can hardly be unaware of any error. And for God to allow error in Scripture when He knows all the truth would be a matter of self-contradiction on His part" (p. 83, *The Bible in the Balance*).

Dr. Cornelius Van Til of Westminster Seminary published a book about Daane's theology (cf. his *The Theology of James Daane*). In his book Van Til shows how Daane has espoused neo-orthodoxy and has forsaken the historic theology of the Reformed Confessions and has encouraged the Christian Reformed Church to espouse the new hermeneutic, which rejects the view that in the Bible man has a finished revelation of God in history through Christ and the Scriptures, and instead to adopt a philosophy based on such men as Immanuel Kant.

The Reformed Journal has been used by Harry Boer to promote the concept of errors in the Scriptures. Boer's articles were put together and published as a volume by Eerdmans. In his discussion of the rejection of the term "inerrancy" Boer begins from the basis of higher criticism, which he claim makes impossible the inerrancy of the Bible and therefore proposes to substitute "trustworthy." "An infallible message is, of course," says Boer, "a reliable and trustworthy message. But a reliable and trustworthy message is not necessarily an infallible one."

Dr. Boer is opposed to an infallible and inerrant Bible because he is committed to the historical-critical method, a hermeneutical methodology which by 1970 has permeated the Christian Reformed Church in America. A controversy raged about inerrancy at the Synod of the Christian Reformed Church. The 1971 and 1972 meetings saw reports brought in on "The Nature and Extent of *Biblical Authority*." Boer insisted that the claims of higher criticism are to sit in judgment over the assertions of the Bible. What the critics come up with is more reliable for Boer than what the Bible proclaims. In line with this presupposition, Dr. Boer asked: "Should we not rather understand the infallibility of the Scripture in such a way that it does not include the assumption (sic) that all data in Scripture are necessarily harmonizable?" But Dr. Boer fails to appreciate the truth that inerrancy is a teaching of the Bible and not an assumption made by those who teach and defend the Bible's inerrancy. To give up inerrancy according to Dr. Boer will help the church in its missionary endeavors because it will relieve tensions which Christians face when trying to harmonize the difficulties and contradictions of Scripture.

According to Lindsell the Christian Reformed Church is facing a frontal attack on its historic doctrine of Holy Scripture as the inspired, infallible and totally trustworthy Word of God. This spells grave danger and theological trouble in the immediate years ahead.

In *The Battle for the Bible* Kiutert was mentioned for sponsoring theological teachings that were a departure from those as set forth in the Calvinistic Confessions. A further development relative to Kuitert's theological odyssey to the left is to be found in interviews of Kuitert and P. Jongeling by Godfried Bomans, published in *Gesprekken* met *Bekende Nederlanders*. Relative to Kuitert's belief about a life after death, the Dutch theologian said he did not believe that on judgment day that the graves will open and all dead arise. This he says he cannot believe. Somehow people will return to God from whom they came.

Another case of erosion is represented by Herman Dooyeweerd, a famous Dutch philosopher, recently connected with the Toronto Institute. A 1977 book, which contains interviews published by Tjeenk Willink of Zwolle (Holland), Dooyeweerd in a question put to him, made a distinction between the Word of God and the Bible. The Dutch philosopher responded: "... you certainly cannot say that everything in the Bible is inspired ... If the apostle Paul writes to his fellow worker Timothy that he has forgotten his travel-cast somewhere and asks if he will bring it when he comes, would one have to regard that text inspired because it's in the Bible... ? Wouldn't that be an absurdity?"

Dooyeweerd also denies the doctrine of the Trinity and espoused a form of Sabellian modalism. Logically Lindsell concludes that the Christian Reformed Church on both sides of the Atlantic is in deep trouble, because at the Free University of Amsterdam, Berkouwer is pushing Barth as a conservative theologian and a goodly number of European and American Calvinistic scholars have been infected by the virus of the new hermeneutic.

The Young Life Institute of Colorado

The Young Life Institute was established to prepare leaders for campus work. Dr. Paul King Jewett who rejects Paul's view on the subordination of woman to man according to a number of New Testament passages, has exercised a great influence over the staff members of Young Life. William S. Starr, the former president of Young Life, wrote a booklet, *Focus: Security* in which he took issue with *The Battle for the Bible* claiming that there was something wrong with Lindsell's demand for inerrancy because it was dividing the church. Starr wrote: "To me Lindsell loses his perspective on Christ in his cause to protect the Bible. In his eagerness to be guardian of the Scriptures he forgets that the Lord has already provided a guardian in the Holy Spirit." While some members of Young Life believe in Biblical inerrancy, Starr endeavors to build a bridge between those supporters that do not. He also wrote: "Nowhere in the Bible do we find the term 'Authority of Scripture.' That is a human invention," Lindsell reminds Starr that the word Trinity is not found in the Bible, but that does not mean the Christian doctrine of the Trinity is not a Biblical teaching. Starr claims that, "What we do have in Scripture is the Authority of Christ only, which is always expressed in terms of power, power to do something, power to accomplish something in His name."

However, if a person follows the authority of Jesus he will accept His teachings and also Christ's position on the inerrancy of the Bible. In answer to the allegation that the doctrine of inerrancy divided the church, Lindsell correctly retorts that those who propound teachings contrary to the Bible are the dividers of the church.

The 1977 catalogue of Fuller Seminary reveals the interesting and significant fact that "the Institute of Youth Ministries was established in 1977 to combine the theological resources of the School of Theology with the field expertise of the Young Life Campaign, a leading national evangelical Christian outreach to high school youth . . . Although the institute is designed primarily for persons preparing to serve on the staff of Young Life, other persons preparing for ministry with youth may pursue this concentration." Fuller which no longer supports Biblical inerrancy has established control on this important youth agency.

Dr. Harold Lindsell devoted chapter 5 of *The Battle for the Bible* to The Southern Baptist Convention (pp. 89-105), and in *The Bible in the Balance* he devoted chapter 4 to The Southern Baptist Convention, concerning which he claimed that it was heading and moving toward a crisis (p. 113). Pages 113-182 deal with the situation of the Southern Baptist Convention. In his 1976 book Lindsell, himself a member of the Southern Baptist Convention, had stated that a number of people did not believe in Biblical inerrancy. Those members of the Southern Baptist Convention who had surrendered the belief in Biblical inerrancy were evaluated against the backdrop of the New Hampshire Confession of Faith, a confession generally accepted by the churches of the Convention.

The New Hampshire Confession of Faith speaks about the Bible and reads as follows:

The Holy Bible was written by men divinely inspired and is the record of God's revelation of Himself to man. It is a perfect treasure of divine instruction. It has God for its author, salvation for its end, and truth without any mixture of error, for its matter. It reveals the principles by which God judges us; and therefore is, and will remain to the end of the world, the true center of Christian union, and the supreme standard by which all human conduct, creeds, and religious opinions should be tried. The criterion by which the Bible is to be interpreted is Jesus Christ.

Concerning this statement about the Bible Lindsell wrote: "It is important to note immediately that the confession does not rule out creeds. It simply states that creeds as well as religious opinions are to be judged by the Bible, not the Bible by man-made creeds. It also notes that the Bible needs to be understood. In doing this, Jesus Christ is the criterion. And he is the One who said the 'scripture cannot be broken' (John 10:35). He also told us: 'Think not that I am come to abolish the law and the prophets: I have come not to abolish them but to fulfill them. For truly, I say to you till heaven and earth pass away, not one iota, not a dot, will pass from the law until all is accomplished' (Matt. 5:17,18)" (pp. 113-114).

Lindsell further pointed out that Jesus Christ believed in the complete trustworthiness of the Old Testament. But as far as the New Testament was concerned Jesus promised the evangelists and apostles, the N.T. authors, that the Holy Spirit would guide them into all truth. And that they would declare things the Spirit wanted them to speak and record (John 16: 13).

According to Lindsell the Southern Baptist Convention "makes no claim to speak for local churches or for the people who are members of local congregations. Baptists accept the principle of soul liberty which is nothing less than the right of all people to believe as they choose" (p. 114). But the former editor of *Christianity Today* asserts that this "soul liberty" does not mean that a Baptist may hold views that are not Baptist views or that Baptists do not have a general consensus of doctrines that would constitute Baptist beliefs. In a number of ways Baptists show that there is a consensus about basic Christian doctrine.

Baptist Ideals

In 1964 the Southern Baptist Convention published a booklet titled Baptist Ideals. It was the Sunday School Board that distributed the booklet in the denomination. Two segments of this booklet are important. The first deals with the Bible. Page 2 describes the Bible as the Word of God, which is inspired and trustworthy. The booklet was prepared for the one hundred and fiftieth anniversary of the first Baptist national organization of America. The author was Ralph A. Herring, chairman, and eighteen other Southern Baptist Convention leaders and scholars. At the end of Baptist Ideals, point 9 speaks about self-criticism. If the Baptist denomination was to remain healthy, both the local congregation and the denomination must accept the responsibility of constructive self-criticism.

In harmony with point 9, Lindsell as a member of a cooperating congregation, availed himself of this right to offer constructive criticism as to what has been transpiring theologically in the Southern Baptist Convention, where certain influential individuals have departed from the Baptist stance on the inerrancy and infallibility of the Bible.

Herschel H. Hobbs

A former president of the Southern Baptist Convention is Dr. H. Hobbs, who now is pastor emeritus of the First Baptist Church, Oklahoma City, Oklahoma. At one time he was the speaker on the "Baptist Hour." He published some time ago *A Layman's Handbook of Christian Doctrine* (Broadman Press), in which he stated that the Bible was the Word of God, truth without any mixture of error for its substance. Thus Hobbs agrees with the scripture statement of the New Hampshire Confession.

Theological Seminaries

The fact that Southern Baptists have spelled out their confessional position is seen by looking at a number of theological seminaries in the Convention. Southwestern Baptist Theological Seminary employs the New Hampshire Confession of Faith and requires its faculty members to give assent to this confession. Thus it would appear that doctrinal orthodoxy is a requirement for professors of Southwestern. Likewise The Southern Baptist Seminary of Louisville has a doctrinal statement similar to the one contained in The New Hampshire Confession. Faculty members are required to assent to this "creed" when assuming a professorship. However, Lindsell points out, there is no provision as to what happens to a professor who changes his doctrinal views after teaching there for some time. The most famous case in *Southern Baptist Seminary* history was the case of Professor Toy who changed his mind, but had the integrity to leave and taught subsequently at college.

The Baptist Hymnal

This hymnal published by the Broadman Press contains an introduction which states that the hymns selected for *The Baptist Hymnal* were evaluated by a subcommittee who evaluated the hymns to determine whether or not they were in harmony with Baptist beliefs. It says: "Hymn texts were critically examined for theological accuracy and doctrinal soundness." The implication of such an assertion means that Southern Baptists are concerned about orthodoxy of doctrine. This means that Southern Baptists have gone beyond the stance that they only hold to the Bible and to no creedal statements.

Critiques of *The Battle for the Bible*

According to Lindsell two points stand out immediately. The first is that The Southern Baptist Convention has a generally accepted theological position, stated in books, pamphlets, convention confessions, confessional statements adopted by certain seminaries and the whole thrust of *The Baptist Hymnal*. The second point is that the theological commitment of Southern Baptists has been breached. This is evident from many letters received by Lindsell from Southern Baptist people who claimed that the Southern Baptist denomination is being influenced from without to give up its commitment to the inerrancy and infallibility of the Bible. It is also apparent from those theologians who have sharply disagreed with Lindell's book, *The Battle for the Bible*.

The Southwestern Journal of Theology

Professor William L. Hendricks of the Southwestern Seminary reviewed Lindsell's *The Battle for the Bible* in a very negative manner. Although Southwestern Seminary has a statement on the Bible that it is inerrant, Hendricks accused Lindsell as speaking from a very small base. Hendricks claimed that Lindsell was in error, because the Bible says nothing about its infallibility and inerrancy. Hendricks averred that classical Christianity did not hold the views which Lindsell advocated. "Truth, Hendricks claims was Jesus Christ, and not to believe in Christ was error. Error is not to allow the witness to Christ as set forth in John's Gospel. However, if the text of John's Gospel contains errors and wrong information, how then can a person really believe in Christ," Lindsell responds.

The Southern Baptist Seminary Review and Expositor

Lindsell claims that the treatment Hendricks accorded his first book was mild compared to the criticism that appeared in *The Review and Expositor*, the theological journal of the *Southern Baptist Seminary* at Louisville. The book review was authored by Bill Blackburn of Shelbyville, Kentucky, a graduate of Southern. Blackburn labelled the book as atrocious. He claimed *The Battle for the Bible* relied on atom bombing. Further that it was a book written in a non-irenic spirit. "The book was filled with half-truths, guilt by association, non sequiturs, quotations taken out of context, conclusions drawn from statements by others that one has no right to assume would be concluded by the author of the statement, sweeping generalizations, and misuse of Scriptures." Blackburn advised his readers to ignore Lindsell's book and read and accept the views concerning the nature of Scripture as found in Smart's *The Strange Silence of the Bible in the Church* or Beegle's *Scripture, Tradition and Infallibility*. By his advocacy of these two books Blackburn has totally disassociated himself from Biblical inerrancy and opted for and defended the errancy of the Bible. By using Blackburn's book review *Southern Baptist Seminary* substantiated Lindsell's charge that this seminary has departed from the seminary's original doctrinal position.

Duke McCall of Southern Seminary at Louisville

The Southern Baptist Theological Seminary of Louisville is the oldest theological seminary of the Southern Baptist Convention and therefore has always occupied a prestigious place in Southern Baptist circles. Dr. McCall, the president of the seminary, attempted to refute Lindsell's charges in the seminary's publication called *The Tie*. In its June, 1976 issue he claimed that *The Battle for the Bible* would not "destroy the heresy he opposes nor divide the Southern Baptist Convention by his silly games of words." In concluding his attack on Lindsell McCall said that "some men would rather fight than become the children of God." The president of Southern Seminary at Louisville claims that more snakes have been stirred up than can be killed. These snakes have arisen because Lindsell fought under the flag of inerrancy, infallibility, and verbal inspiration. McCall claimed that these were the slogans of the new Fighting Fundamentalism. McCall argued that because there are copyist's errors in the transmitted manuscripts, it followed that the original autographs must have had errors, a conclusion which is a non sequitur. This argument for the inerrancy of the Bible has frequently been answered because many anti-inerrantists have raised this objection before. It was his contention also that fallible men, like the Biblical authors, could not write inerrancy writings. Lindsell correctly pointed out that if the Bible is not trustworthy in all of its statements, then it must be untrustworthy in its theological assertions! What becomes of the Baptist teachings by such a standard?

A year after the article by McCall had appeared in *The Tie*, he reported that he had received a letter by an unnamed brother who asked the questions: Do you believe that God inspired every Word of the original manuscripts? (2) Do you believe that there were errors in the original manuscripts? (3)

Do you believe that Adam and Eve were the first two human beings and that they gave birth to Cain, Abel, Seth, and other sons and daughters? McCall labelled the letter a piece of vicious crank mail. (Lindsell, *The Bible in the Balance*, p. 124) He never answered the three questions but put three counter questions: (1) Do you believe that God lost control of the Scriptures after the disappearance of the original manuscripts? (2) Do you believe the original manuscripts are the only reliable, trustworthy Scriptures? (3) Where did Cain get his wife? The letter was only answered in this unsatisfactory manner because Southern students wanted to know how their president had responded to the three questions, "written by some illiterate moron." (Lindsell, p. 124)

Lindsell Answers His Critics in
The Southern Baptist Convention

In Appendix i of *The Bible in the Balance* (pp. 353-356) here printed from "A Book Review Article of *'The Battle for the Bible,'*" by Raymond F. Surburg who answered President McCall's Reply to Lindsell's first, Book. Further Lindsell wrote: "Basically the question has surfaced whether I provided sufficient documentation for my thesis that Southern Baptists have been infiltrated by an aberrant view of the Bible." If he is wrong, Lindsell says he owes an apology to all whom he attacked in his first book. On pages 126-182 of his new book he gives first hand evidence to substantiate the charges made in *The Battle for the Bible* in 1976.

It is a fact of church history that the theological position of seminaries determines the theological tenor of the denominations they were established to serve. The Southern Baptist Convention has six seminaries, of which The Southern Baptist Seminary at Louisville, KY and the Southwestern Theological Seminary at Fort Worth, Texas, are the most influential. The Louisville institution has exercised a great influence in the life of Baptists, furnishing multitudes of pastors for the parishes; its graduates serve as professors on college and seminary faculties. Lindsell claims that Southeastern Baptist Theological Seminary in Wake Forest, North Carolina is a lengthened shadow of Southern. Most of its founding faculty were graduates of Southern.

There is evidence that numbers of Southern Baptists are unhappy with the products of the official seminaries. Lindsell claims that he only disclosed what was obvious to many in the Southern Convention in chapter 5 of *The Battle for the Bible*. Dr. W. A. Criswell, former president of the Convention and the pastor of the First Baptist in Dallas, Texas, the largest congregation of the Convention, is dissatisfied with the college and seminary training being offered Baptists. The result is that First Baptist Church houses a new institution on its grounds designed to prepare men and women for the ministry.

In Memphis, Tennessee Dr. B. Gray Allison and others began the Mid-America Baptist Theological Seminary. Dr. Gray Allison was a member of the faculty of New Orleans Baptist Theological Seminary. Dr. Allison has had experience in various Southern Baptist institutions, so his testimony ought be valuable in determining whether or not the Bible is still held to be trustworthy in all its teachings or not. The new institution in Memphis was started to make possible for Baptists to have an option relative to theological education. Mid-America Baptist Theological Seminary is staffed by individuals who hold to the inerrancy and infallibility of the Bible as traditionally understood. The fact that this seminary has grown is evidence for the fact that there are Southern Baptist peoples who want Baptist orthodoxy taught.

Still another institution established at Jacksonville, Florida, was Luther Rice Seminary by Dr. Robert Witty almost two decades ago, for the same reason that Dr. Witty and others felt that Baptists seminaries were not teaching Baptist orthodoxy. This institution by resident courses and extension courses is endeavoring to prepare Baptist ministers who are grounded in the teaching of an inerrant Bible. Of it Lindsell says: "This school has an ecumenical ministry that embraces virtually every mainline denomination and reaches out across the globe" (p. 127).

The Original Theological Positions of Southern and Southwestern Seminaries

Since Dr. McCall claims that Lindsell is in error, in fact he called the latter's charges as "poppycock," which a simple telephone call to Southern could have settled. Lindsell first showed what the original doctrinal platform of Louisville was and what is now being taught by some of its more famous professors. Before taking up Southern, Lindsell takes up the position of the founders of Southwestern, Dallas, Texas. Southwestern was established in 1901, an outgrowth of the theological department of Baylor University and was known as Baylor Theological Seminary, but in 1907 The Baptist General Convention gave it its present name. Till 1910 it existed on the Waco campus. In 1910 Fort Worth citizens provided a campus. In 1925 the control passed from the Texas convention to The Southern Baptist Convention. In its 71 year history it has had five presidents. The first was B.H. Carroll. Carroll wrote a book titled *Inspiration of the Bible*, published posthumously in 1930. From this book Lindsell quotes on pages 129-137 the position of Carroll on: inspiration, the Holy Spirit and Scripture, the goal of inspiration, the Genesis account of creation, the infallibility of Scripture, right understanding about inspiration, answers to objections, plenary and verbal inspiration, science and the Bible, Joshua and the sun that stood still and supposed contradictions in the Bible.

After reading these portions of Carroll's book any fair reader must agree with Lindsell's evaluation: "No one can doubt where B.H. Carroll, the founder of Southwestern Theological Seminary, stood on the issue of the Scriptures. He held to verbal, plenary or full inerrancy. This was the platform on which the seminary was built. This was the heartthrob of a great man whose views were the views of Southern Baptists generally. Carroll's position was that also of his successor Dr. Lee Scarborough, as may be seen from the latter's *Gospel Messages*. The new president Russel A. Dilday assured Dr. Lindsell, that Southwestern faculty and adminis-

492

trative staff have made the following commitment that the Holy Bible was written by men divinely inspired and is the record of God's revelation of Himself to man. It is a perfect treasure of divine instruction. It has God for its author, salvation for its end, and truth, without admixture, for its matter" (p. 138). While the statement is not reproduced here in its entirety, it is from the New Hampshire Confession of Faith. Lindsell observes that there are faculty members of Southwestern, the largest seminary in the world, including Dr. Hendrichs, who do not hold Carroll's positions on the nature of the Bible.

The Southern Baptist Theological Seminary
What was the theological position of the founding fathers of *Southern Baptist Seminary*? Two of its oldest founders were Basil Manly and James Petigru Boyce. Both held to Biblical inerrancy. John Sampey, Old Testament professor and president, followed in the train of Manley and Boyce and held the line on the trustworthiness of the Bible.

Basil Manly on Scripture
In 1891 Basil Manly wrote *The Bible Doctrine of Inspiration* Explained. The title indicated that Manly believed that the Biblical doctrine was being attacked, and it was by people coming from Germany who had been infected with German higher criticism. Dr. Manly rejected the presuppositions of the historical-critical method which distinguished between the Word of God and the Bible, claiming that the two were not synonymous. Manly agreed with F.L. Patton of Princeton, who in his book *Inspiration* said:

The books of the Bible... were composed by men who acted under the influence of the Holy Ghost to such an extent that they were preserved from every error of fact, of doctrine, of judgment; and these were so influenced in the choice of language that the very words they used were the words of God.

It was Dr. Manly's contention that this statement represented the view of the Bible held by the church through the post-Christian centuries. Manly became involved in a debate with Professor George T. Ladd, the author of *The Doctrine of Sacred Scriptures*, who insisted on the distinction that the Bible and the Word of God are not synonymous terms. Manly vigorously rejected the view that the Bible only contained the Word of God but was not in its entirety the Word of God. The latter view goes back to Le Clerc and Grotius. It was also the stance of Semler. Manly in his book, *The Bible Doctrine of Inspiration Explained and Vindicated* wrote: "The doctrine we hold is that commonly styled PLENARY INSPIRATION or FULL INSPIRATION. It is that the Bible as a whole is the Word of God, so that every part of Scripture is both infallible truth and divine authority" (p. 59). Quoted by Lindsell on page 140.

Manly did not want to sit in judgment over the Bible, but that the Bible judged men. Inerrancy according to Manly was predicted by the autographs and not of the copied manuscripts which contain copyist errors. It is the purpose of the science of textual criticism to remove these various types of errors made by copyists which textual criticism has classified and can spot. Manly also realized what the implications were that flowed from adopting the higher criticism brought over to America especially from Germany. Whenever and wherever negative Biblical criticism has been adopted, the first doctrine to be attacked and surrendered was the inerrancy of the Bible.

James Petigru Boyce, Systematic Theologian at Southern Seminary

Boyce was one of the most distinguished scholars and educators at *Southern Baptist Seminary* and the author of *Abstract of Theology*. His successor, Professor Kerfoot, did not differ in his views from those of Boyce and Manly. In *Abstract of Theology*, as revised by Kerfoot, Boyce asserted: ...

No other book has ever been found more reliable whenever its statements could be tested. It carries upon its face everywhere the verisimilitude of truth. Its own testimony is with most persons who read an all sufficient evidence of its truthfulness.

We may argue **a priori** as to the character of this revelation as follows: a. It must come from God... b. It must be suited to our present condition... c. It must be secured from all possibility of error so that its teachings may be relied on with equal, if not greater, confidence than those of reason (pp. 35,36,37) Cited by Lindsell, *The Bible in the Balance*, p. 146.

John R. Sampey, Old Testament Scholar and President of Southern Seminary.

Sampey taught for many years at Southern Seminary. Among books authored by him was *Syllabus for Old Testament Study* (1903). The position taken by Sampey shows that he agreed with Carroll, Manly, Boyce, Kerfoot on the doctrine of the Bible. Thus he wrote:

As to the inspiration of the Bible. Conservatives hold that the writers were preserved from all errors by the inbreathed Spirit. Radicals reject such a theory with scorn. Some liberals believe in a sort of inspiration which heightened the spiritual perceptions of the Scriptural writers, but did not preserve them from error.

Dr. Sampey claimed that the authority of Jesus and His statements about the Bible was enough to show the error of radical criticism. Thus he wrote:

Whereas Radicals set aside His authority, and moderate liberals point to the limitations of His knowledge as a man, Jesus has Himself said that the Scriptures cannot be broken (John 10:35). If Radical critics break the Scriptures, they will also break the authority of Jesus as our Divine Teacher, *Syllabus for Old Testament Study*, pp. 58-59.

In the early days of Southern's history there was the case of Dr. Toy, who had been influenced by higher criticism and brought his case before the administration and the trustees. The result was that Toy departed; the administration and trustees upheld the historical doctrinal position of the seminary. Toy became professor at Harvard College, where in the course of time his views became even more radical than they had been at Louisville.

Is McCall Correct That There Have not Occurred Significant Doctrinal Changes at Southern Baptist Seminary?

Dr. McCall claimed that Lindsell's charge of aberrant doctrinal views was "poppycock." On pages 148-177 Lindsell proceeded to prove that a radical change has occurred, that professors at Southern no longer hold to the original position of the Seminary, that they believe the Bible contains errors and mistakes. **The Bible is errant.**

Broadman Press's *Is the Bible a Human Book?*

Is the Bible a Human Book? was published in 1970, and was put together by Joseph H. Green and Wayne Ward of Southern Seminary. A number of its contributors had associations with Southern. A reading of the volume shows that a number of contributors rejected the infallibility and inerrancy of the Bible. The coeditors informed their readers that there are those who cannot accept the inerrancy of Scripture; presumably they must be talking about themselves. This deduction would be supported by the tenor of the articles comprising *Is the Bible a Human Book?* Their answer would be, yes! Because it is a human book, one should naturally expect to find mistakes in it. They cannot appreciate the fact that because the Holy Spirit was the ultimate Author that the Holy Spirit could prevent those whom He inspired from making mistakes.

Various contributors of this volume have given expression to the standard objections advanced against the total trustworthiness of the Bible. Thus Dr. Flamming, author of the chapter "Could God Trust Human Hands?," claims Mark begins his Gospel with a number of mistakes. These mistakes do not affect the redemptive work of Christ, so Flamming argues. He comforts himself on this wise: "If God could use Mark with sixth grade grammar, and an occasional misquote from the Old Testament maybe he can use me too." Again: "If God is as obsessed with perfection as we are, God could hardly trust man to write the Bible, for nothing man touches ever comes close to perfection (Rom. 3:23)" (p. 5).

Another contributor to *Is the Bible a Human Book?* was John R. Claypool, former pastor of the Crescent Hill Baptist Church in Louisville. He said he rejected the "dictation theory and all its claims to literal infallibility and inerrancy. I join them in this rejection, but for reasons deeper than errors in the Bible" (pp. 27-29). He contended that is heresy to speak of the Bible as the final authority in all matters religious. He believes that new revelations are made possible by encounters through the Bible! This means Claypool believes in an ongoing revelation.

His anti-Biblical handling of Scriptures is seen in Claypool's doctoral dissertation, *The Problem of Hell in Contemporary Theology* (May, 1959, 284 pages). He rejects the idea of eternal punishment, even though Christ taught it clearly. He employed speculation to reject a doctrine he disliked.

Another writer John M. Lewis, pastor of the First Baptist Church of

Raleigh, N.C., wrote about "The Bible and Human Science." He rejects the Genesis account of creation and prefers the views of atheistic Charles Darwin. He repeats the outworn allegation that Genesis 1 and 2 contain two contradictory creation accounts, of which Genesis 2:4a-25 contains supposedly the most primitive. He says that "if one takes these (creation) accounts as literal scientific truth he does violence to the real intent of the Bible itself."

The volume, *Is the Bible a Human Book?* , shows how an erroneous view about the Bible and its teachings has permeated the Southern Baptist Convention. Brooks Hays, one-time president of the Southern Baptist Convention, in his contribution, entitled "What the Bible Means to Me," went so far as to state that "inerrancy is an irrational and unhistorical position of a few literalists who claim 'verbal inerrancy of the writings.'" Hays by background, according to Lindsell, is a politician and a layman who has written nonsense.

Lindsell showed how a number of the professors on the faculty of *Southern Baptist Seminary* advocated theological views contrary to Baptist orthodox teachings. Professor Frank Stagg, who previously taught at New Orleans Baptist Seminary, has given evidence of espousing a quasi-orthodox view of the Trinity as well as opposing the substitutionary atonement of Jesus Christ. In a review of Barclay Newman's book, *The Meaning of the New Testament* Stagg praised the author because he used the historical-critical approach in his discussion of New Testament teachings. Furthermore, Dr. Stagg wrote a chapter titled "Glossolalia in New Testament" in which he used and supported source criticism, which involved the use of historical-critical methodology. In his *New Testament Theology* he revealed his anti-Trinitarian bias when he wrote: "Thus the Spirit is the continuing presence of Jesus Christ (John 20:22), Paul could write of the risen Christ and the Holy Spirit in such a way as to make the terms almost interchangeable (Rom. 8:9f.)" (p. 39), (quoted by Lindsell, p. 155). The page 39 clearly espoused the ancient heretical view of modalism. "The New Testament knows God as Father, Son and Holy Spirit, yet it knows God as one alone. One may suggest that in his transcendence he is known as Father, in his immanence as Holy Spirit, and in his ultimate presence and self-disclosure as Son.... It is the uniqueness of the New Testament that the Father and the Spirit are understood in terms of Jesus Christ." Nowhere does Stagg say that there are three distinct persons in the Godhead, Father, Son and Holy Ghost.

On page 145 on his *New Testament Theology* Stagg comes out against the vicarious and substitutionary atonement. Thus he wrote: "Jesus **paid** to liberate us from our sin. Of course he paid no one, neither the Father nor the Devil. He simply paid ..." (Neither propitiation and expiation) is satisfactory. Because propitiation is so linked to pagan ideas of the appeasement of God, it is not suitable for translating New Testament ideas. On pages 140-145 the reader will find a repudiation of the vicarious and substitutionary death of Christ, a doctrine taught in a number of Biblical passages. Lindsell in evaluating Stagg's doctrinal position wrote: "If his views are orthodox then millions of Southern Baptists are unorthodox.

If the death of Christ was not vicarious and did not render satisfaction to offended deity, then the *Baptist Hymnal*, as well as the writings of men like A.T. Robertson, Basil Manly, B.H. Carroll, and literally thousands of Baptists pastors, must be removed from Southern Baptist literature. Scores of Sunday schools lessons have told millions of students what is not true." Lindsell correctly claimed that modalism or Unitarianism is not viable alternative to historic trinitarianism without such an erroneous doctrinal view affecting other Christian teachings. "And since trinitarianism has always been one of the Baptist distinctive, to change to modalism or straight Unitarianism is to forsake the faith of our fathers" (p. 157).

The Case of William E. Hull

In *The Battle for the Bible* Lindsell devoted pp. 93-95 to the case of William E. Hull of Louisville, who until 1975 had been a long-time professor at *Southern Baptist Seminary*, Louisville. *The Baptist Program* published an article entitled "Shall We Call the Bible Infallible?" This lecture was first delivered as a sermon at the Crescent Hill Baptist Church in Louisville. At the time of the delivery Hull was the Dean of the School of Theology of Southern Seminary. Dr. Hull had received his B.D. and Th.D. degrees from Louisville and he had also pursued post-doctoral studies at the University of Goettingen in Germany (1962-63). In his inaugural address as Dean of the School of Religion, Hull praised Rudolf Bultmann whose program of demythologization resulted virtually in a denial of every cardinal Christian doctrine. He also acknowledged his indebtedness to C.H. Dodd, Emil Brunner, Soren Kierkegaard and Dietrich Bonhoeffer. As a result of being influenced by these unorthodox thinkers he agreed with Kyle Haselden's assertion: "God is now to be seen Lord of the 'Flux' as well as of 'fidelity'." This is a position that holds that Christian doctrine is not fixed and subject to the whims of fallible theologians. In an address delivered February 23, 1968 to the Association of Baptist Professors he enunciated the view that the younger men are impatient and wish to move on, being dissatisfied with past theological formulations.

In yet another address Dr. Hull proceeded to belittle the King James Version and to praise "Today's English Version," also known as - *The Good News for Modern Man*, published by the American Bible Society. This translation was the work of Robert Bratcher, a graduate of *Southern Baptist Seminary*. Of this non-literal and periphrastic rendering Hull asserted: "What are the implications of widespread ABS acceptance of the TEV (Today's English Version)? To begin with, we have here the employment of a much more daring translation theory than that adopted by the RSV . . . . Of course, Southern Baptists do not realize all of this . . . Shout it not from the housetops, but the TEV is clearly incompatible with traditional notions of verbal inspiration, and the theologians built thereon. It could be that Southern Baptists will embrace the TEV with their hearts before they grasp the implications with their heads." William E. Hull, *Southern Baptist Theological Scholarship: Harbingers of Hope* (typescript of address presented to Southern Baptist Theological Seminary by President Duke McCall, 1968), p. 2. (Quoted by Lindsell, *The Bible in the Balance*, p. 160).

In the Summer 1967 issue of *Review and Expositor* Hull published an article on "The New Quest for the Historical Jesus." In this contribution he agreed that all former quests had failed. Scholars are now engaged in the so-called "third quest" which is also going to fail. Those who did not accept the material in the Gospels as dependable are the people guilty of seeking for a so-called "historical Jesus" they will never find. What does this place, Dr. Hull? This article of Hull's is as about devastating to the trustworthiness of the Bible as can be imagined. Here is liberalism at its worst. President McCall has defended this theological liberal!

The Case of Dr. Dale Moody

In the *Review and Expositor* Dr. Moody had an article titled "Tabletalk on Theology" in which he attacked the Biblical doctrine of creation and defended evolution. He rejected the historicity of Adam and Eve. Lindsell showed how Moody has attacked a number of doctrines held by orthodox Baptists, among them the doctrine of predestination.

Like others at the Southern Baptist Theological Seminary he opts for theological change and development. He believes the teachings of the Bible must be related to "the pressing and social problems that beset the church in an age of revolution. No evasive and oppressive conservatism will be adequate for the theological task of the future" (p. 356 of *Tabletalk in Theology*). Moody reviewed favorably John Macquarries' book, *Principles of Christian Theology*, in which the latter presents a Unitarian form of the doctrine of Trinity.

Higher Criticism Practiced at Southern Baptist Seminary

Dr. Lindsell alluded to a number of Southern staff members and contributors to the seminary's theological journal, *The Review and Expositor*, such as Page H. Kelly, Donald Williams, Marvin E. Tate, and Clyde Francisco who in books and articles have adopted the standard higher critical views on the Old Testament. The non-acceptance of the Mosaic authorship of the Pentateuch, a Deutero-Isaiah is promoted. An examination of *The Broadman Commentary* reveals that all the higher critical views once rejected by Dr. J. Wash Watts in *A Survey of Old Testament Teaching* are now advocated. Lindsell could also have referred to the revised edition of Clyde T. Francisco's *Introduction to the Old Testament*,1977 and ask readers to compare it with the first edition, to see what changes in Old Testament studies have occurred at Southern.

Professor G.R. Beasley-Murray wrote a commentary on James, 1 Peter, Jude and 2 Peter for the series edited by William Barclay and F.F. Bruce. He places 2 Peter in the second century and thus makes 2 Peter a pseudepigraphon, a false and spurious writing!

In *The Battle for the Bible* Lindsell adduced the case of Robert S. Alley of the University of Richmond, who denied the deity of Christ. No Christian with even an elementary knowledge of Scriptures knows how dev-

498

astating and soul destroying such a view is. And yet to this day Dr. Alley is in good standing in the Southern Baptist Convention.

The Character of the Louisville Student Body

A study of the Louisville student body was made by a graduate of Southern, Noel Wesley Hollyfield. The latter's Master of Theology dissertation was entitled: "A Sociological Analysis of the Degrees of 'Christian Orthodoxy' among Selected Students in the *Southern Baptist Seminary*." The thesis committee of Southern approved it. Of this thesis Lindsell wrote: "The thesis committee of Southern approved it." Of this thesis Lindsell wrote: "The thesis is the best available evidence to further confirm the allegation that Louisville has been deeply infiltrated by non-evangelical belief" (p. 172). Only 55% of the student body believed in the virgin conception and birth of Christ. Only 38% held that it was absolutely necessary to hold the Bible was God's truth. Only 58% believed that the Devil actually existed was absolutely necessary. Hollyfield concluded that "a trend toward doctrinal liberalism was discovered in the Th.M.-Ph.D. students." It seems that as students progressed up the educational ladder at Southern, the more liberal they became.

The Theological Situation in the Southern Baptist Convention

Many in the Southern Baptist Convention hold to the traditional doctrinal position; they hold to the inerrancy and trustworthiness of the Bible. At the 1978 convention the messengers reiterated their stand that God is the author of the Bible and that Scriptures is free from error, but many members do not realize that in their seminaries and theological literature the Bible is under attack. Before the 1978 convention, Professor E. Glenn Hinson, a professor at Louisville, wrote an article for the *Christian Century*, in which he characterized Southern Baptists as taking in "conservative to liberal theology ... John Birch to Norman Thomas politics, laissez-faire to Marxist economic, pragmatism to idealism" (quoted by Lindsell, p. 175).

At present the Southern Baptists present an ambivalent stance to the world. Questions that need to be answered, according to Lindsell, are: "What is it Baptists believe that remains forever unchangeable? What is it we believe can never be negotiable? Does it include the doctrine that the Bible is the Word of God written in its entirety and is inerrant in all its parts?"

April 7, 1980

In chapter 6 of *The Battle for the Bible* Dr. Harold Lindsell discussed what he called "The Strange Case of Fuller Theological Seminary," (pp. 106-121). Fuller had been founded in 1947 by Charles D. Fuller, who also had established the "Old Fashioned Revival Hour." Its first president was Harold John Ockenga, minister of the Park Street Church in Boston. The seminary began with thirty-seven Students and four professors: Wilbur M. Smith, Everett F. Harrison, Carl F. H. Henry and Harold Lindsell. In a short time its student body numbered three hundred. As time passed

499

on new faculty members were added, building erected and endowment secured. Fuller has become a very influential seminary in the last thirty years.

One of the chief purposes for the establishment of Fuller was that it was to be apologetic and set forth a conservative theology, counteracting the liberalism and neo-orthodoxy which were very popular in America in the late forties and in the early fifties.

At Princeton Theological Seminary, where Fuller's son, Daniel Payton Fuller had studied for a while, the position on Biblical inerrancy held by Charles Hodge and Benjamin Warfield had been surrendered. Charles Fuller wanted to have a theological institution where his son could obtain an orthodox theological education.

Lindsell wrote about the beginnings of Fuller and its stand on inerrancy as follows in *The Battle for the Bible*: "It was agreed from the inception of the school that through the seminary curriculum the faculty would provide the finest theological defense of biblical inerrancy. It was agreed in addition that the faculty would publish joint works that would present to the world the best of evangelical scholarship on inerrancy at a time when there was a dearth of such scholarship and when there were few learned works promoting biblical inerrancy" (p. 107).

At first Fuller Seminary had no statement of faith. It took a number of years before the faculty composed a doctrinal statement in which were set forth Fuller's position in major Christian doctrines. The following was its statement on Scripture: "The books which form the canon of the Old and New Testaments as originally given are plenarily inspired and free from all error in the whole and in the part. These books constitute the written Word of God, the only infallible, rule of faith and practice."

The catalog stated in its preface to the doctrinal statement that each year each faculty member signed this statement without reservation. Bela Vasady who joined the faculty prior to the formulation of the doctrinal statement refused to sign the statement on Scripture and being a man of integrity, left the seminary faculty.

In or about 1962 Lindsell claimed it became apparent that there were members on the seminary board and on the faculty who believed that there were errors in the Bible. One of the key board members was C. Davis Weyerhaeuser, a wealthy layman who helped to underwrite the annual operating budget. Later on he became chairman of the board. At this time also two professors openly came out for errors in the Scriptures. It also developed that the son for whom Charles Fuller had partly founded the seminary experienced a change of mind relative to Biblical inerrancy. Daniel Payton Fuller. with a Th. D. from Northern Baptist Theological Seminary and with study time at Basel, Switzerland under Karl Barth, returned to become academic dean of Fuller. But he no longer espoused Biblical infallibility or Biblical inerrancy.

Other developments listed by Dr. Lindsell were the hiring of Calvin Schoovenhoven to the faculty: first as librarian and then as a New Testament appointment. At his examination he stated that he did not believe in Biblical inerrancy. Although some faculty members protested, nevertheless, he was hired. Schoovenhoven was a friend of dean Fuller and also had studied at Basel.

Dr. David Hubbard became the successor of Edward John Carnell as president of Fuller, being the choice of Charles Fuller and also of his son. At the time he was considered for the presidency of fuller, Hubbard was on the faculty of Westmont College, Santa Barbara, California. He had co-authored a syllabus on the Old Testament with Robert Laurin, then on the faculty of American Baptist Seminary in West Covina, California. This syllabus contained views that were inimical to orthodox Christianity. Lindsell wrote about this syllabus: "The syllabus contained teachings that were opposed to historical evangelical understandings. They included matters like the non-historicity of Adam and Eve, the Wellhausen approach to the Pentateuch, the late dating of Daniel, and other points. The offensive parts had been written by Laurin who, in turn, was defended by Hubbard as an outstanding evangelical" (p. 109).

In December, 1962, a faculty-trustee meeting was held at Huntington Hotel in Pasadena, California, which Lindsell claims (p. 110, *The Battle for the Bible*) some have called "Black Saturday." The issue at this meeting was the matter of whether or not the Bible was infallible. Lindsell claims that it became apparent that a number of board members and professors did not hold to Biblical infallibility or inerrancy. Edward Johnson, president of Financial Federation resigned from the Fuller Board claiming that the doctrine of Biblical infallibility was a benchmark and if that was changed, Fuller would lose its bearings. After the stenographers had typed up the proceedings, Charles Fuller decided that the transcribed records be turned over to him, lest copies of the "Black Saturday" meeting fall into the wrong hands and could hurt the school. The records, therefore, never became available to those interested in determining what happened at the Huntington Hotel.

Further Developments at Fuller

With the 1965-66 seminary catalog there no longer appeared the statements which has been found in earlier catalogues, namely, that every faculty member without reservation subscribed to the original statement of the infallibility of the Bible. In view of the new attitude, a number of faculty resigned. Among those eventually resigning were Wilbur Smith, Harold Lindsell, Gleason Archer and board member Charles Woodbridge. There were board members and faculty members who had subscribed to Biblical inerrancy who decided to remain.

When Fuller opened its new School of Psychology and its School of World Missions and thus began to make it possible for students to earn professional and academic degrees, more faculty members were added, among them James Daane. At this time Fuller, whose founder was a premillennialist, no longer made it a part of the seminary doctrinal statement that its faculty had to be adherents of premillennialism. The allowance of amillennialism was a development that occurred under the presidency of Dr. Carnell, a graduate of Westminster, who was an amillennialist. Charles Fuller himself was a dispensationalist and a premillennialist.

501

Daniel Fuller Repudiates Inerrancy

At the December, 1967 meeting in Toronto, Daniel Fuller delivered a paper entitled: "Benjamin B. Warfield's View of Faith and of History." Here at Toronto, Fuller openly came out and asserted that the Bible was not free from errors. Fuller presumed to be able to correct Warfield and held that the Bible was inerrant in revelational matters but errant in non-revelational matters. Because the Bible does contain errors, Fuller contended that the Bible, therefore did not teach a doctrine of Scriptural infallibility.

Lindsell asked the very pertinent question on page 114 of *The Battle for the Bible*, how the distinction is arrived at as to what data are revelational and what are non-revelational. One could argue that the virgin birth was a matter of biology and not a part of the doctrine that makes a person wise unto salvation. One could argue for two or more Isaiahs on the ground that the authorship of the Book of Isaiah does not contribute anything to the doctrine of salvation. One could deny the historicity of Adam and Eve and claim that one could be saved without a knowledge as to whether they were or were not the first human beings.

Dr. Ladd and Inerrancy

Dr. George Ladd in his book, *The New Testament and Criticism*, came out for the errancy of Scripture relative to the areas of history and fact. On pages 16f, he stated: "It is the author's hope that the reader may be helped to understand that the authority of the Word of God is not dependent upon infallible certainty in all matters of history and certainty."

Hubbard and the Fuller Alumni

In 1970 President Hubbard sent out a letter in which he claimed that there were those who were going beyond Benjamin Warfield and demanding that Biblical inerrancy also applied to every scientific, historical, geographical factual and theological assertion of the Bible. Hubbard was misrepresenting the Warfield position for Briggs of Union Seminary in Warfield's day argued that one error in the Bible would totally demolish Warfield's stance on Biblical inerrancy: Daniel Fuller also understood this to be the position of Warfield.

President Hubbard in his unpublished letter wanted to do away with the word inerrancy, which he claimed was "too precise, too mathematical" a term to describe appropriately the way in which God's revelation has come to us in a Book. Lindsell remarks that this was strange for Daniel Fuller in the Seminary Bulletin Vol. XVIII, No. 1, March, 1968 had written: "We assert the Bible's authority by the use of such words as infallible, inerrant, true and trustworthy. There is no basic difference between these words. To say the Bible is true is to assert its infallibility."

Fuller's New Doctrinal Statement

Ten years after the inerrancy controversy began at Fuller, the seminary issued a new statement of faith. Two changes were made: the one pertained to premillennialism which was dropped and the other which dealt with the statement on Scripture. The new Fuller statement on the Bible reads: "Scripture is an essential part of the trustworthy record of this divine disclosure. All the books of the Old and New Testaments, given by divine inspiration, are the written word of God, the only infallible rule of faith and practice." If all faculty members subscribe to it, then Lindsell contends that "it does not mean free from all error in the whole or in part," which is found in Fuller's original statement on Scripture!

In documenting his original case against Fuller Seminary Lindsell cited the case of Paul King Jewett, a colleague of Ladd and Fuller. In 1954 Jewett published a book, Emil Brunner's *Concept of Revelation*, in which he defended the belief in an infallible Bible. The book was dedicated to Gordon Haddon Clark, one of Jewett's former teachers, and a staunch advocate of Biblical inerrancy and infallibility. However, that Jewett has changed his mind as is evident from his book, *Man As Male and Female* (Grand Rapids: Wm. B. Eerdmans, 1975) in which he claimed that Paul erred in advocating the subordination of the wife to her husband. He asserted that Paul in I Corinthians and Ephesians had erred; he pitted Galatians 3:28 against Paul's other statements. Lindsell concludes: "I simply am pointing out that Professor Jewett's conclusion that Paul is wrong in his teaching about subordination shows that he has attributed error to the apostle in a matter having to do with faith and practice and thus invalidated the new Fuller Seminary statement of faith" (p. 119, *The Battle for the Bible*). Chapter 5 of *The Bible in the Balance* is titled: "Fuller Theological Seminary at Bay" (pp. 183-243).

Since the publication of *The Battle for the Bible* the situation at Fuller has gotten worse. Lindsell believes that his first book had three effects on Fuller. 1. They took the charge seriously; 2. They endeavored to blunt the criticism; and 3.They tried to forge a coalition of scholars and friends to support Fuller theologically and promotionally. Lindsell had claimed that those who denied the inerrancy and infallibility of the Bible were no longer evangelical and that is a charge they wished thoroughly to refute.

Dr. Hubbard's Convocation Address

On April 8, 1976 Hubbard called the seminary community together to counteract Lindsell's book. Dr. Hubbard delivered an address: "Reflections of Fuller's Theological Position and Role in the Church." Fuller's president claimed that Lindsell's volume was built on the following thesis: "The Bible itself and the history of the Christian church support an interpretation of inerrancy that includes not only the intent of the biblical authors and their theological teachings but also every detail of geography, history, and science; second, the conviction that only those churches, institutions, and individuals who adhere to that definition of inerrancy can remain true to the evangelical faith."

Hubbard charged that Lindsell had threatened evangelical unity by his narrow definitions and by his wrong definition of "evangelical." Hubbard claimed that he was especially concerned about Lindsell's book, because it set forth an unbiblical view of the Bible.

In evaluating Hubbard's address and rebuttal, Lindsell gives a history of Hubbard's views on Biblical inspiration and Biblical infallibility. In 1962 Dr. Hubbard was on the faculty of Westmont College, and while there he had introduced syllabus for Old Testament co-authored with Professor Robert Laurin. The Board of Trustees was disturbed by this syllabus, for in it positions rejected by orthodox scholars were adopted. Under date of December 13, 1962 Dr. Hubbard wrote Roger Voskuyl, president of Westmont College, that he voluntarily had signed the Westmont Statement of Faith and that he affirmed his belief in the plenary, verbal inspiration of the Bible. Among other assertions, Hubbard wrote: "I believe that the Bible is exactly what God wanted it to be the very word, that it is infallible in its teachings, completely accurate in its historical statements, and fully·authoritative in matters of faith and practice . . ." (*The Bible in the Balance*, p. 186).

While making this statement Hubbard at the same time did not refrain from using a syllabus that showed that there were contradictory accounts in the Bible and which stated that God did not give men through the Bible scientific history or cosmology, or that inspiration did not guarantee the accuracy of the sources used by Biblical writers. While Laurin wrote the objectionable parts of the syllabus, Hubbard did not refrain from using the syllabus. Despite Laurin's higher critical views in the syllabus Hubbard claimed there was no liberalism or neo-orthodoxy in the syllabus.

It would seem, so Lindsell correctly argued, that if the late date of Daniel, the non-historicity of Adam and Eve, the use of the Documentary Hypothesis and mistakes in the Bible are correct, then orthodoxy has assumed a completely new meaning. In view of the understanding of inerrancy already held in1962, it was no surprise to Lindsell that in 1976 Hubbard should label Lindsell's position in *The Battle for the Bible* as "unbiblical."

Theology, News and Notes

Hubbard followed up the convocation address with a special thirty-two page issue of *Theology, News and Notes*. This special 1976 issue claimed that it was going to treat: "The Authority of Scripture at Fuller." Clark Pinnock, author of *Biblical Revelation* (Moody, 1971) attacked *The Battle for the Bible* in which he gave his objections to the book. In his critique, Dr. Pinnock did not hesitate to state that there were errors in the Bible, that Stephen confused the facts of the Abraham story of Genesis. Thus Pinnock was retreating from the position he took in *Biblical Revelation* in 1971.

In addition to Pinnock, Dr. Paul Rees of World Vision and former president of The National Association of Evangelicals wrote an article, entitled "Are We Trying to Outdo the Reformers?" As Lindsell pointed out, Dr. Rees' remarks completely missed the point of the debate because *The Battle for the Bible* was concerned with the results of inspiration and not with the mode of inspiration in the Bible.

Theology, News and Notes had a book review by Donald Payton of North Park Seminary, reprinted from *The Other Side*, a magazine which does not believe in Biblical inerrancy. Dr. LaSor, outstanding Biblical scholar, wrote a contribution for *Theology, News and Notes*, called "Life under Tension-Fuller Seminary and '*The Battle for the Bible*.'" According to Lindsell LaSor made a rather odd observation about the seminary's original statement of faith. Although Bela Vasady refused to sign the original seminary doctrinal statement because he did not believe in Biblical inerrancy, LaSor signed it because he said: "I felt there was nothing to be gained by refusing to sign the Statement." LaSor claims that Bela Vasady Was "disappointed" with him for signing the Statement. It thus appears that LaSor originally signed the inerrancy statement, although he did not believe it.

The last contribution to *Theology, News and Notes* was by President Hubbard, called by him "What We Believe and Teach." Some of the arguments in this article are irrelevant to the charge of the fact that Fuller has abandoned verbal inerrancy and infallibility. In discussing the word "inerrancy," Hubbard wrote: "When inerrancy refers to what the Holy Spirit is saying to the churches through Biblical writers, we support its use. Where the focus switches to an undue emphasis on matters like the chronological details, the precise sequence of events, the numerical allusions, we would consider the term misleading and inappropriate."

Lindsell correctly points out that Hubbard's definition of inerrancy is unsatisfactory and that Hubbard does not believe the Bible is without mistakes in all of its parts.

The Case of Paul King Jewett

Dr. Jewett in Male as Male and Female has charged that Paul was in error in what he taught about women in the church and in the home. He said that Ephesians 5 disagreed with Galatians 3: 28. Measured by Galatians 3: 28 Paul's teachings in Corinthians and Timothy are wrong! A committee examined Jewett's views and found them deficient: in fact, the committee sharply disagreed with him and said so in plain language, yet the same committee recommended to the Seminary not to take any action against one of their professors who claimed that God's inspired apostle erred. Dr. Lindsell contends that the case of Dr. Jewett supports his second allegation against Fuller Seminary, namely, that "It has breached its new statement in the case of Paul King Jewett who denied the infallibility of Scripture in regard to a matter of faith and practice ..."

The Third Barrage against *The Battle for the Bible*

Fuller Seminary published *Biblical Authority*, edited by Jack Rogers of the Fuller faculty, a book which Word Books of Waco, Texas issued.

Biblical Authority accused Lindsell of threatening evangelicalism with his divisive book. It reminds one of Ahab accusing Elijah that he was responsible it had not rained for three and a half years! Who was dividing the evangelical movement, asked Lindsell, those who claim that the Bible is not reliable in all that it teaches or those who defend the utter dependability of Holy Writ in all its statements? Besides Hubbard and Rogers, the following men wrote chapters for *Biblical Authority*: Paul Rees, Clark

505

Pinnock, Berkeley Michelsen, Bernard Ramm and Earl Palmer. Some chapters had nothing to do with the controversy, namely, that present Fuller had forsaken the stand once held by Charles E. Fuller, when he was chairman of the Board of Trustees of the Bible Institute of Los Angeles and preacher on "the Old Fashioned Revival Hour." Some of the contributors claimed they held to Biblical inerrancy, yet President Hubbard had claimed Biblical infallibility and inerrancy was unbiblical. To account for this inconsistency Lindsell wrote: "Why the seminary would use such men to help their cause can be explained only on the basis of the incipient inclusiveness of the Fuller approach, or a willingness to go along with inerrantists who support Fuller because they also are latitudinarian at this point" (p. 196).

Geoffrey Bromiley, teaching at Fuller, according to Lindsell holds to Biblical inerrancy. Thus Hubbard has on his faculty, one who according to his position holds to an unbiblical view, and that would make such a wrong view on the nature of the Bible heretical! And yet Hubbard does not get rid of professors who hold and teach what is allegedly unscriptural!

A Response to Biblical Authority

A number of inerrantists responded to Fuller's attack on the doctrine of Biblical inerrancy. In 1978 there appeared *The Foundations of Biblical Authority* (Zondervan), published in the fall of 1978. The following theologians responded to the Fuller book: Francis Schaeffer, John Gerstner, J.I. Packer, Gleason L. Archer, R.C. Sproul, James Boice, and Kenneth Kantzer. Dr. Norman Geissler reviewed the Fuller book in *Christianity Today*. Dr. Robert Preus reviewed *The Foundations of Biblical Authority* in the *Concordia Theological Quarterly* and this is reprinted in Appendix 4 of *The Battle for the Bible*, pp. 365-366.

Jack Rogers and Biblical Inerrancy

Professor Rogers' chapter shows clearly that he rejects Scriptural infallibility. He claimed that Augustine, Calvin, Rutherford and Bavinck did not consider the Bible an authority when it spoke about matters of science. To claim that what the Bible teaches about scientific matters is correct, Rogers claimed, would result in the trivialization of the central concern of the Bible, whose objective is to bring men to faith in Christ and thus be saved. Lindsell correctly asserts that such argumentation is "deceptive and misleading" (p. 197). No evangelical believes that the Bible was given to be a textbook on science or denies that the object of Holy Writ is to bring man to salvation, only found in Christ Jesus. But the question is: does the Bible give erroneous information on scientific matters when it accidently refers to them? If it does, then the Bible is errant. If there are scientific errors, then according to the position of Messrs. Rogers and Hubbard we have in the Bible both an errant and inerrant Word of God. Such being the case, each Bible reader will need to decide what portions are correct and what parts contain error. This would mean that the Holy Spirit has inspired error and that the Word of God contains falsehood and truth. If so, the Bible cannot be a trustworthy revelation of divine truth (p. 199).

Dr. Rogers claimed that "it is historically irresponsible to claim that for two thousand years Christians have believed that the authority of the Bible entails a modern concept of inerrancy in scientific and historical details" (*Biblical Authority*, p. 44). Then Rogers cited Augustine, Calvin, Rutherford and Bavinck.

By means of two lengthy quotations, Lindsell proved that Augustine regarded the Bible as being free from errors in all its parts. In a letter to Jerome, Augustine averred that to admit one single mistake or error in the Bible would open the door to a floodtide of unbelief (*The Bible in the Balance*, pp.199-200).

In order to prove that John Calvin did not advocate Biblical inerrancy, Rogers used statements from Calvin's writings selectively. He ignored Edward A. Dowey's *The Knowledge of God in Calvin's Theology*, a Columbia University doctoral dissertation, in which Dr. Dowey, no supporter of Biblical inerrancy, has shown that Calvin believed in an inerrant Bible. Dr. Dowey was one of the prime movers of the Revised Confession of 1967 of the Presbyterian Church UPUSA. While Calvin never referred to the Bible as a scientific textbook, he never asserted that the Bible contained scientific errors.

Samuel Rutherford and Inerrancy

Samuel Rutherford (1600-1661) in 1643 took prominent part in the preparation of the *Westminster Confession* and is credited with having written the *Shorter Catechism*. Rogers claims that Rutherford taught that the Bible should not be looked upon as an authority in matters of science. Rogers concluded from this that the *Westminster Confession* of Faith did not hold to the Bible's inerrancy. But the fact that Rutherford did not consider the Bible an authority in the area of science does not warrant the claim of Rogers that Rutherford believed that there were errors in the Bible.

It seems that Rogers is only repeating the arguments of higher critic Charles Augustus Briggs who opposed the inerrancy stand of B. B. Warfield and Charles Hodge of Princeton Seminary. Briggs in his book *Whither* tried to show that the framers of the *Westminster Confession* did not hold to Scriptural inerrancy. Warfield responded to Briggs in "The Doctrine of Inspiration of the Westminster Divines," an essay included along with five others in *The Westminster Assembly and Its Work*. On pages 270-271 Warfield furnished evidence that Rutherford, while not holding that the Bible was a textbook in science, nevertheless believed and advocated the inerrancy of the Bible.

Herman Bavinck and Inerrancy

Herman Bavinck (1854-1921), Dutch theologian, who in theology adhered to the *Heidelberg Catechism* and the canons of the Synod of Dort, was cited by Rogers as supporting an errant Bible. In support of his contention Rogers quoted:

"The writers of Holy Scripture probably knew no more than their contemporaries in all these sciences, geology, zoology, physiology, medicine etc. And it was not necessary either. For Holy Scripture uses the language of daily experience which is always true and remains so. If the Scripture has in place of it used the language of the school and had spoken with scientific exactness, it would have stood in the way of its own authority."

Again Rogers quoted Bavick as declaring: "The real object to which the Holy Spirit gives witness in the hearts of the believers is no other than the divinitas of the truth, poured out on us in Christ. Historical, chronological and geographical data are never in themselves, the object of the witness of the Holy Spirit."

On the basis of these, Rogers concluded that Bavinck did not believe in inerrancy as applying to all of the Bible. Dr. Jerome De Jong of Faith Reformed Church of South Holland, Illinois, called Lindsell's attention to the following statement of Bavinck's as found in his Dogmatics, where the latter wrote: "But like the human in Christ, no matter how weak and lowly, yet free from sin, so also is the Scripture 'conceived without error.' Human in all parts yet also totally divine" (*Gereformeerde Dogmatik* (Kampen: J.H. Kok, 1928), Vol. I, p. 406.

In marshalling evidence for his errancy position Rogers conveniently ignored the theological position of The Wisconsin Evangelical Lutheran Synod, The Lutheran Church-Missouri Synod and the American Lutheran Church, the New Hampshire Confession of Faith and the research of a scholar like George Duncan Barry, who in *The Inspiration and Authority of Holy Scripture*, showed that it was the teaching of the Christian Church during the first five hundred years of its existence that the latter adhered to the inerrancy and infallibility of the Bible.

Fuller and the Reformed Tradition

Biblical Authority, according to Lindsell, gives the impression that "Fuller's approach to the inerrancy of the Bible is thought of almost without exception in terms of the Reformed tradition, the *Westminster Confession* of Faith, and the Princeton theology" (p. 206, *The Bible in the Balance*). The same approach is followed by Stephen T. Davis, a Presbyterian, in his *The Debate about the Bible*.

Rogers made the claim that "the false equation of the theory of inerrancy with the position of the *Westminster Confession* was never repudiated" (p. 41 of *Biblical Authority*; Waco; Word, 1977). Rogers limited his arguments to the Reformed tradition, as represented by *The Westminster Confession* and the Princeton theology.

Both Rogers and Hubbard, so Lindsell contends, imply the stance on Biblical inerrancy should be traced to Princeton, to Hodge and Warfield. But such conclusions of the Fuller professors are not in harmony with historical facts, because Charles Hodge wrote his Systematic Theology to replace the work on dogmatics by Francois Turretin, which had been used at Princeton Seminary. Charles Briggs, whose arguments Rogers utilized, had faulted Turretin's *Institution* for disagreeing with the *Westminster Confession* which allegedly did not teach Biblical inerrancy.

Warfield, however, allowed that Briggs' evaluation was wrong. John Rogers simply, according to Lindsell, was rehashing Briggs' wrong views about inerrancy.

Other Protestant denominations, including Lutherans, taught Biblical infallibility and they knew nothing or very little of the dogmatics of Princeton. The fact is that it was only with the coming of the historical-critical method that the concept of Biblical inerrancy had to go because it was one of the presuppositions of this method that the Bible was contradictory and replete with errors.

Lindsell Answers Dr. Hubbard

On pages 208-219 Lindsell in *The Bible in the Balance* answered the charges and views relative to the nature of Bible as expressed by Hubbard in the final chapter of *Biblical Authority*. Hubbard's chapter was entitled: "The Current Tension: Is There A Way Out?" Lindsell summarized the character of Hubbard's presentation as follows: "In Dr. Hubbard's chapter we find a potpourri of conflicting data, an **ad hominem** appeal for peace rather than purity and an attempt to identify himself and his institution with evangelicalism (p. 208)." The way out of the present tensions would be to give up the idea that inerrancy and infallibility apply to "every detail of every kind of statement of Scripture" (*Biblical Authority*, p. 156). Hubbard also argued that the type of mentality that suggests that the existence of a proved error places one on a slide that insures further diminution of Biblical authority was not true.

Hubbard believes that terms like **error, inerrancy**, and infallibility are not to be defined by secular, twentieth-century criteria as they are reflected in our standard dictionaries. He assumes that ancient stands of accuracy were different from those that obtain today. But this distinction is assumption on Hubbard's part. Hubbard defined error in the Bible as follows: "Error theologically must mean that which leads us astray from the will of God or the knowledge of the truth." This definition leaves the whole area of geography, chronology, history and the non-theological open to error and misinformation. How can errors found in many chapters of the Bible be "profitable," a truth Paul claims about the Old Testament? Hubbard also tried to bolster his case by claiming that The National Association of Evangelicals did not insist on inerrancy because their statement of belief states: "We believe the Bible to be the inspired, the only infallible, authoritative word of God." Because the NAE does not employ "inerrant," but "infallible" Hubbard argued they did not hold to inerrancy of the Bible. But according to standard dictionaries "infallible" means "without error!" The president of Fuller also cited Moody Bible Institute as an example of an organization which did not hold to inerrancy, but this is to fly into the face of facts because Moody Bible Institute definitely teaches the inerrancy of the Scriptures and insists its Professors believe and teach it.

The Views of Daniel P. Fuller on Inerrancy

Dr. Daniel P. Fuller is the president of "The Old Fashioned Revival

Hour," founded by Charles E. Fuller, father of Daniel, and he is also director of its radio broadcast "The Joyful Sound." *In Today's* Christian, published by the radio program, Daniel Fuller published an article titled "I Was Just Thinking." The intent of this article was to allay the fears of listeners of the radio broadcast that he, Fuller, did not hold to the inerrancy of the Bible, a charge made against him by Lindsell. Fuller wrote: "I have always affirmed the complete inerrancy of the Bible." The Fuller Evangelistic Association has a doctrinal statement on the Bible, which is not different from their early statement. Lindsell claims that "this statement explicitly affirms that the Bible is free from error in the whole or in its parts." Now Drs. Hubbard and Fuller are members of the association. This means that both have signed two different statements, the one of the Fuller Evangelistic Association and Fuller's most recent one, different from Fuller Seminary's original statement about the Bible. One affirms an inerrant, an errorless Scripture, the other does not!

According to Fuller, even though Jesus made a mistake when he stated that the mustard seed was the smallest of seeds, Jesus was not guilty of error, because he had no intention of teaching botany. Thus Fuller claimed he always taught the Bible is inerrant. Incidentally, Jesus when he spoke this parable was claiming that the mustard was the smallest seed among those known to his hearers in Palestine, not in the whole world.

At Fuller there is this strange paradox to be found that the seminary president claims the Bible is errant, but the academic dean says it is inerrant (based on the distinction of revelational and non-revelational data).

James Daane and Inerrancy

Dr. James Daane is a professor at Fuller and hails from the Christian Reformed Church, whose headquarters are in Grand Rapids, Michigan. He is also one of the editors of *The Reformed Journal*, associated with the **avant garde** wing of the denomination, in which an aberrant view about the Bible has been taught due to the influence of Drs. Berkouwer and Kuitert. In May 1977 a group of so-called young evangelicals met at Chicago and drew up a document called: "The Chicago Call: An Appeal to Evangelicals." Forty-six professors, pastors, editors and lay leaders attended. Daane tried to prevail upon this group to adopt a statement on the nature of the Bible which would repudiate the position of Dr. Harold Lindsell.

But Daane failed. Instead the group adopted the following: "We affirm the Scriptures as the infallible Word of God." Since Daane does not believe in the inerrancy of Scripture, Lindsell observed "One wonders why he even permitted his name to be attached to the Call, since it included an important doctrinal statement he does not accept" (p. 223).

The Case of Ray Sherman Anderson

Dr. Anderson is a graduate of Fuller Theological Seminary. He earned a doctorate under T.F. Torrance of Edinburgh. He was engaged to teach at Westmont College. When the time arrived for him to be granted tenure

510

at Westmont College, this was not given him. Dr. Anderson's doctoral dissertation was published under the title *Historical Transcendence and the Reality of God*. This was done under Torrance, who had taught at Fuller, and who went beyond Karl Barth's idea of transcendence. According to James D. Spiceland of the faculty of Western Kentucky University, Barth held that "we are not capable of conceiving God, going on to say that God is not only invisible to the physical eye of man, he is also invisible to the spiritual eye." T.F. Torrance goes even beyond Barth. Anderson was influenced by Torrance and his doctoral dissertation departs from the historical understanding of Christianity about God. Professor Demarest in a review of Anderson's book claimed that the latter has departed from the thought world of the Bible. After Westmont College refused to give Anderson tenure, he was hired by Fuller and is now a professor on its faculty.

The Missionary Views of Charles Kraft

Dr. Kraft is professor of the School of World Mission at Fuller Seminary. By lengthy quotations Lindsell showed how Dr. Kraft has drifted away from Scriptural teachings in his "mission views". Kraft has been involved in anthropological and sociological studies as they pertain to missions. Dr. J. Robertson McQuilken, President of Columbia Bible College and former missionary to Japan, showed how Kraft has advocated views that approve of a Mohammedan's erroneous ideas as taught in the Quran about God and the deity of Christ as usable in missionary work among Muslims. (Cf. *The Bible in the Balance*, pp. 226-227). According to Dr. Kraft a Muslim does not need to be convinced of the death of Jesus for man's sins in order to be saved, but that the Mohammedan person need simply pledge allegiance and faith to God who worked out the details to make it possible for his faith response to take the place of a righteousness requirement. Kraft, as cited by McQuilken, claimed that a Muslim need not be told about the Trinity; also the deity of Christ need not be proclaimed to a Mohammedan nor must it be accepted by the latter. McQuilken also further asserted that Kraft is one of a number of "evangelical" scholars who hold that people can be saved without knowledge of Christ. At the Pan African Leadership Assembly held at Kenya, December, 1976 Kraft advanced the idea that polygamy need not to be abandoned by African Christians.

Here is a professor, affiliated with Fuller Seminary, who has and is promulgating views that flatly contradict the New Testament. At the PALC Conference Kraft made statements that disagreed with the Bible.

The Teaching of Ralph P. Martin of Fuller Seminary

Dr. Ralph P. Martin is Professor of New Testament at Fuller. He wrote a commentary on *Ephesians* for *The Broadman Bible Commentary* series. Eerdmans of Grand Rapids has also published Martin's *New Testament Foundations*, vol. II. Here we have two volumes that clearly show that Dr. Martin is a proponent of the higher-critical method. Although the Ephesian epistle asserts that its author is Paul, Martin denied this and ascribes the authorship to Luke. He also follows the higher-critical views on the authorship of the Pastorals, 1 and 2 Timothy and Titus by denying that Paul is their author. For Luke to have written Ephesians and by claiming the Pastorals are in error when they ascribe the Pastorals to Paul, this is tantamount to saying that Paul is being credited with something he did not write. To claim that Luke is the writer of Ephesians is to state that Paul made a false claim or that Holy Spirit erred when allowing such false statements to appear in canonical books. We agree with Dr. Lindsell's assertion who calls such action as deception. Lindsell wrote: "But for him (i.e. Luke) or anyone else to artfully lead the readers to think it was a genuine letter from Paul when it actually was not would bring the canonicity of the book seriously into question. To speak of biblical inspiration and then to suppose that the Holy Spirit was a party to such deception is utterly beyond imagination" (p. 230).

Martin has cast doubt on the authorship of 1 and 2 Peter. He believes that there might be a possibility that Peter wrote 1 Peter, but the latter did not write 2 Peter. Jude and 2 Peter was assigned by Martin to A.D. the second century. Martin delivered a speech at London Bible College, where he once was a professor, a speech in which the papers reported him as asserting that the attempt to make inerrancy of the Bible the touchstone of evangelical orthodoxy is a retrograde and divisive movement in American Church life. Lindsell has shown on pages 228-236 that Dr. Martin was waging a battle against the original doctrinal statement on inerrancy held by Fuller when it first was founded and organized. The evidence is very clear: Fuller once believed, held and taught inerrancy, but has given up this view of Scripture. Lindsell claims that this is the belief of Dr. Ockenga, the co-founder of Fuller Seminary. The same position regarding Fuller's defection is held by Drs. C.F. Henry, Charles Woodbridge and Gleason Archer.

Fuller Seminary Graduates Reflect the Errancy Position

Graduates often give evidence in their writings and teachings what they were taught by their theological mentors. This is true of Fuller's graduates. According to Lindsell, LaSor observed that the leaven of the errancy view was early apparent when David Hubbard, Daniel Fuller and Ray Anderson were students. They went aboard for graduate study, where they were converted to neo-orthodoxy and liberalism: When these men returned to teach at Fuller, they were farther to the left than their teachers had been. The students of Hubbard, Daniel Fuller and others now teach their erroneous views about the nature of the Bible to their students.

Gerald T. Sheppard

Gerald T. Sheppard, a graduate of Fuller with a Ph.D. from Yale, is now Assistant Professor at Union Theological Seminary, New York City. He published in *Union Seminary Quarterly Review* an article titled: "Biblical Hermeneutics: The Academic Language of Evangelical Identity." Lindsell urges all readers of his book to secure or read this article, because Dr. Sheppard places the Fuller theology in a correct perspective and also shows how liberalism has penetrated evangelical thinking. Correctly Sheppard sees that the problem of Fuller and other evangelical seminaries is a hermeneutical one. Shepard claims that President Hubbard has endeavored to place Fuller between neo-orthodoxy and liberalism. "But anachronistically setting Fuller in opposition to movements no longer robustly definitive of theology currently in vogue at the so-called 'liberal' seminaries, Hubbard hopes to reassert the older, sharper identity of being evangelical . . . Despite these strident affirmations of Biblical infallibility, responses from Fuller indicate a serious inconsistency in distinguishing evangelicalism from neo-orthodoxy." Gerald T. Sheppard, "Biblical Hermeneutics: The Academic Language of Evangelical Identity" in, Volume XXXII, Number 2, Winter 1977, p. 89 as cited by Lindsell, *The Bible in the Balance*, p. 237. Hubbard has been attempting to give Fuller the image of being an evangelical seminary, but Sheppard wrote about this attempt as follows:

"By defining evangelical over against the purported 'neo-orthodoxy' of other seminaries, Hubbard has sought, likewise, to protect Fuller's uniquely marketable 'evangelical' status- without forfeiting her new ecumenical -spirit. Nevertheless, the obscurity is a distinction between the terms 'inerrancy' and 'infallibility,' coupled with the uncertainty over whether scholars like Karl Barth are 'evangelical' or 'neo-orthodox,' suggests that many of the differences between Fuller and the so-called non-evangelical seminaries have already seriously broke down." *Sheppard, Biblical Hermeneutics*, **op. cit.**, p. 89 as quoted by Lindsell, *The Bible in the Balance*, p. 237.

Sheppard has also pointed out the important fact that while neo-orthodoxy is to be distinguished from liberalism, still the re-discovery of Reformation theology is to be distinguished from Earlier Protestant orthodoxy, because neo-orthodoxy uses the historical-critical methodology which the sixteenth century did not employ. The result of utilizing the historical criticism is to produce views that often are in agreement with "liberalism."

Whither Fuller Seminary?

Lindsell claims that if Fuller were to return to its early stand on the Bible and abide by it, this would require the dismissal of a large number of the current faculty. It would also necessitate the reorganization of the school of theology, the school of mission, and the school of psychology. The former editor of *Christianity Today* agrees with the conclusions of Dr. Richard Quebedeaux, (*The Worldly Evangelicals*, New York: Harper Row, 1978, p. 85) that all three schools of the seminary have departed from orthodox.

Lindsell seriously doubts that the Board of Control of Fuller will attempt any such reorganization and make the necessary changes, in view of the fact that they would not dismiss Jewett and allow such men as Kraft and Martin to teach their erroneous views.

Questions

1. Gleason Archer came out in defense of ____.
2. Who else defended Lindsell and the inerrancy of the Bible? ____
3. What is at the center of the theological struggle today? ____
4. The historical critical method is the reason for ____.
5. Ramm does not agree with Lindsell that the doctrine of inerrancy is ____.
6. Luther cannot be called upon to support ____.
7. Is the truth of the Bible dependent upon some subjective experience of a person reading the Bible? ____
8. What did Edwin Palmer, executive secretary of the NIV, say? ____
9. What happened to Eerdmans Publishing Company? ____
10. What did Herman Dooyeweerd say about inerrancy? ____
11. To change to modalism or straight Unitarianism is to forsake ____.
12. William Hull acknowledged his gratitude to ____.
13. What did Robert S. Alley, in good standing in the Southern Baptist Convention, deny? ____
14. As students progressed at Southern Baptist Seminary, the more ____ they became.

Does the Lutheran Church-Missouri Synod's Doctrine on the Nature of the Bible Promote Fundamentalism?

Christian News, December 7, 1981

In recent months two prominent theologians (Drs. Bohlmann and Scharlemann) warned members of the Lutheran Church-Missouri Synod (LCMS) against the dangers of fundamentalism. These warnings seem to have the approval of *Lutheran Perspective* (formerly *Missouri In Perspective*), as may be seen from the article appearing in the November 2, 1981 issue, entitled: "Fundamentalism: Combating it with Greater Biblical Appreciation."[1] The article referred to Scharlemann's article in *Affirm* in which he was concerned about the fact that members of the LCMS have become victims of the type of fundamentalism promulgated by the electronic church with its emphasis on being born again and on its millennialism.

Lutheran Perspective contends that the stance of the LCMS on the nature of the Bible, namely, that the entire Bible from Genesis 1:1 to Revelation 22:21 is the infallible and inerrant Word of God, is conducive to the promotion of fundamentalism. The following statement in the *Brief Statement* of the LCMS is erroneous and unacceptable to *Lutheran Perspective*:

> Since the Holy Scriptures are the Word of God, it goes without saying that they are in all their parts and words the infallible truth, also in those parts which treat of historical, geographical, and other secular matters.[2]

and then proceeds to compare this with the following belief of Dr. Jerry Falwell:

> ....the Bible is absolutely infallible, without error in all matters pertaining to faith and practice, as well as in areas such as geography, science, history, etcs.[3]

These theological positions of the LCMS and Falwell are described by *Lutheran Perspective* as "only logical extension of a view of the inspiration of Scripture that sees God having a direct hand in the writing of every word." *Lutheran Perspective* objects to the following assertion of John Drickamer, as quoted by the writer of the article: "God taught the writers the exact words they were to use ... God is the real author of the Bible."[4]

When pastors, teachers and lay people in the LCMS believe and teach that the entire Bible is God's infallible and inerrant Word, *Lutheran Perspective* claims that "this literalistic fundamentalism" allows people to isolate portions of phrases, and to treat them "on an equal footing with the totality of Scripture." By taking individual passages, *Lutheran Perspective* avers that "a whole new theology equal in authority to the saving Gospel, can be constructed out of a handful of random verses."

The author of "Fundamentalism: Combating it with Greater Biblical Appreciation" is utilizing arguments and advocating positions which or-

515

thodox Lutheranism in the past has rejected as untenable. Here the argument is implicitly being advocated that one may reject clear Biblical teaching if the latter does not agree with other passages of the Bible. To object to individual verses as the basis for Christian doctrine and for instruction in Christian ethics is to oppose the method by Christ, Paul, Peter and other New Testament authors. Over fifty years ago Franz Pieper warned against the argument that "the whole of Scripture takes precedence over individual passages."[5] The "totality of Scripture" as a determining principle of interpretation makes no sense whatever. The fact is, that it was the Reformer of the 19th century, Schleiermacher, who promoted this concept. In his *Glaubenslehre* he wrote: "Quoting individual Bible passages in dogmatics is a very precarious, yes, in and by itself unsatisfactory procedure."[6] Pieper observed that this senseless phrase has been adopted by practically all the chief representatives of modern theology, from the extreme left to the extreme right. It was von Hofmann, who in his *Schriftbewels* put forth this idea to counteract the traditional view of Christian writers that Scriptural doctrine is to be based on specific passages, called by the scholars "sedes doctrine," "seats of the doctrine."[7] The 19th century Lutheran scholar Kliefoth was right when he called the contrast between the whole of Scripture and the individual passages "an inconceivable concept."[8]

The whole corpus of Scriptural doctrine can only be obtained by taking each doctrine from those passages which treat of the doctrine. Individual passages of course dare not be interpreted out of context. Pieper claimed that this concept "of the whole of Scripture" or "the whole of Christian doctrine" is an invention of man and this placing of "the totality of Scripture" over against the *sedes doctrinae* is an invention to block the authority of Scriptures.[9] If a person can reject the clear statements of the Bible in favor of an explanation that denies what these passages teach and simultaneously claim that the whole of Scripture allows giving the clear passages of the Bible a different meaning than that which they set forth, then the perspicuity and reliability of the Bible have been surrendered to the whims of those who reinterpret the Bible to satisfy the speculations of some name theologians or to the Spirit of the times. The doctrine of the nature of the Bible is based upon a series of clear passages which cannot be surrendered.

Lutheran theology has always distinguished between fundamental and non-fundamental doctrines.[10] The doctrine of justification by faith, the heart of the Christian Gospel, is the central doctrine of God's inscripturated revelation. This writer fails to see how holding to the reliability and inerrancy of the entire Bible in any way denigrates the Gospel. In fact, because all Scripture is God-breathed (2 Tim. 3:15-17), it gives the Biblical reader the conviction that the wonderful plan of salvation is God's plan and is not merely the speculation of a Paul, Peter or John. To claim that the use of the proof-text method when properly employed hinders the Gospel is simply a non-sequitur.

While the LCMS and the electronic church hold certain theological beliefs in common, there are great differences which separate the LCMS from the electronic evangelists, who usually are dispensationalists and millennialists. The past literature of the LCMS has characterized these erroneous systems of Biblical interpretation and rejected them. If members of the LCMS listen to the electronic evangelists and accept their interpretations, then this is due to the fact of their lack of knowledge or that the sermons that they hear and the literature they are given by their churches fail to indoctrinate and warn them against the aberrations of these electronic sensationalists who reject infant baptism, the possession of faith by small children, emphasize man's part in his conversion and have a view of prophecy which is literalistic in the extreme. The people of the LCMS need to read literature and take courses that come to grips with the erroneous theological views of the electronic church.

A New Doctrine of Inspiration

The article in *Lutheran Perspective* in order to support its views about the nature of the Bible has come up with a view of inspiration which has no resemblance to the doctrine of inspiration which was held by Melanchthon, Luther and the authors responsible for the writing of *Formula of Concord.*

Thus *Lutheran Perspective* recommends to the LCMS that in order to foster a greater appreciation of the Bible it needs to adopt a better view of "inspiration." Thus the members of the LCMS are told:

> The place to begin may well be with an understanding of "inspiration," that squares with what the word normally means: "to motivate and encourage." That is what God did, when he motivated and encouraged Scriptural writers to share His mighty acts of deliverance, along with their own words of praise and good counsel (I Cor. 7:12), with future generations.[11]

Those knowledgeable with the theological developments in the last thirty years will instantly recognize the erroneous view of G. E. Wright of Harvard (now deceased) and B. W. Anderson who taught that revelation took place primarily through five mighty acts of God. While it is true that the mighty acts of God are one of the nine different ways in which God gave revelations of himself during the Old Testament, it is not the main method. In fact, Wright and those who accepted his views as expressed in *God Who Acts*[12] and *The Book of The Acts of God*[13], coauthored with Reginald Fuller, argue for limiting the concept of Biblical revelation to mighty acts of God, whose meaning was differently understood by those who witnessed them. Thus revelation was said to be comprised of the mighty act plus its interpretation. The latter must be examined according to historical critical principles.[14] Thus the mighty act of God's delivering Israel from Egypt has two different interpretations in the Bible, one in the J-account and the other in the P-account. The P-account contains the version that the waters of the Red Sea were divided by Moses and the people walked between two walls of water through the Red Sea. This is called the expansion account, which differs considerably from the J-account, according to which allegedly a wind happened to blow up when the Israelites came to a muddy place at the Sea of Reeds and made it dry

517

enough so the people could walk through. For some reason there grew on the Israelites the conviction that at the Sea of Reeds God had acted mighty. The J-story grew and grew as generation after generation retold the story and added material not true to the situation, resulting in what was finally in P. It is the human interpretations given the five major five mighty acts that the scholar must evaluate and thus the Biblical statements can be challenged and rejected as not being entirely factual. The five mighty acts of God were: "(1) The Israelite patriarchs, whose stories are preserved in the book of Genesis, had received certain promises and the history of the nation **was interpreted** as a fulfillment of these promises. (2) The exodus from Egypt **was interpreted** as God's freeing of a people from slavery. It was a setting free and it was interpreted by the historian as a fulfillment of the promise. (3) A special and unique experience had taken place in the wilderness after the people had left Egypt. It took place at Mount Sinai, where the understanding of society and of community obligation was somehow obtained in a law or teaching regarding community duty. (4) The conquest of Canaan whereby Israel secured a land for itself, **was interpreted** as God's gift or an inheritance..... (5) The conquests of David were regarded as the final fulfillment of the promise of land, the promise of security from enemies and from slavery."[15] (Boldface supplied). Wright claims that these five basic elements have a high probability that they are factual and rest on a real historical footage.

However, this limiting the Old Testament to five basic facts fails to account for the wisdom books, the poetry of the psalms and the prophetic Old Testament books! Further, the interpretation often preceded the event, so that Wright's theory of revelation mainly through mighty acts of God is seriously deficient. The same analysis and criticism might be made about Fuller's mighty acts for the New Testament. The Bible cannot be accounted for adequately by speaking of Scripture as a response to God's acts.

Webster's *New World Dictionary of the American Language* listed six different shades of meaning for the word "inspiration", the third of which is: "to inspire," defined: "an inspiring influence; any stimulus to creative thought."[16] But the sixth meaning reads: "In theology, a divine influence upon human beings resulting in writings, as of Scripture, or in action as of a saint."[17] The Christian Church has received its understanding of "inspiration" from the Scriptures and did not come up with a meaning which contradicts what various books of the Bible teach about the nature of the God-breathed Book. Christian have always regarded the Bible as God's Word in all its chapters and verses. In the 1954 edition of the *Lutheran Cyclopedia*, Dr. E. L. Lueker set forth the historical position of Lutheranism when he began his article on the doctrine of inspiration this way:

By confessing the doctrine of inspiration, we declare our belief-based on the words of the Bible itself-that the Holy Spirit exercised a special influence by which he guided His chosen instruments to speak the things he desired them to speak, and to write the things he desired them to write in the precise manner and in the very words in which He desired these things to be spoken or written.[18]

This article further pointed out that there is a difference between revelation and inspiration. Lueker stated that "a Scripture based upon, or sprung from illumination would not be simply and in the Scriptural sense the 'Word of God.'"[19] It was further also asserted in the same article: "The fact of inspiration is taught in various passages of Holy Writ, both of the Old and of the New Testament. What is written in the Bible is at one time attributed to 'the Holy Spirit' or to 'God' without mention of the divine person, at other times to the human being, the instrument which God employed for the purpose of utterance."[20] Scripture given in support of this position are: Matt. 19:4,5 and Gen. 2:4; 2 Sam. 23:1,2; Matt. 22:43; 15:4 and Mark 7:10; Acts 28: 25 and John 12:14; Acts 1:16.

The same presentation also asserted:

That the Holy Spirit suggested to the sacred penmen both thoughts and the words (verbal and plenary inspiration) they uttered as they wrote, is a truth established by such texts as the following: 2 Tim. 3:16; Jer. 30:2; 1 Thess. 2:13; 2 Pet. 1:19-21; John 10:34,35; Matt. 22:43,44; Gal. 3:16; Heb. 12:27; 4:11.[21]

The Functional View of Scripture Advocated

Lutheran Perspective made as a further suggestion for a better appreciation of the Bible the need to emphasize what the Scriptures accomplishes rather than what they are. The reason the Scriptures have been kept by the Church through the ages has not been because they are a "talisman, or sacred artifact, but because they achieve their marvelous purpose of bringing people into a confrontation and ultimately through His Spirit, a trusting relationship with the God who sent His Son to save them."[22] That the Bible created faith in Christ and also prompts Christians to live a life rich in good works is surely the purpose of the Bible. That is what Paul told Pastor Timothy in his second letter to him (3: 17). However, the purpose of the Bible is one matter, the nature of the Bible is yet a different one. Both are found in the Bible and it is wrong to use one to negate the other or to claim that as long as one holds correctly to the function of the Bible one need not hold the doctrine of the Bible's inerrancy and reliability. The Bible contains what the theologians have called fundamental and non-fundamental doctrines. While it is true that a person can be saved without a knowledge of non-fundamental doctrines, this does not permit the rejection of doctrines not essential for salvation, because Christ instructed His church: "Teaching them to observe all things whatsoever I have commanded you" (Matt. 28:20).[23] Furthermore, the doctrine of Scripture is the basis for all we know about Jesus Christ, mankind's only Redeemer. If the Bible is errant and unreliable in many of its assertions and teachings, then how can a Bible reader know of a certainty that the doctrines which are fundamental are trustworthy? Historic Lutheranism has always taught both the material and formal principles of theology.

Need for the Understanding of Literary Genre

Another suggestion for greater appreciation of the Bible made by the author of the article in *Lutheran Perspective* is to understand the variety of literature that comprises the Bible, "none of which conforms to the modern standards for writing history (for correspondence, for that matter) that have been in existence only for only a relatively short period of time." The modern LCMS Christian must be made to realize that the Biblical writers worked with what they had. This is another way of saying that the Biblical writers did not have the advanced sophisticated knowledge that our century has, and that statements that appear to say one thing when they are read, are really to be understood in quite a different way.

Actually what is being advocated here is the acceptance and practice of the historical-critical method, a method which over the last two hundred years has developed a number of different types of criticism, such as a radical form of literary, form, redaction and content criticisms.[24] When these are applied either singly or a number of them conjunctively in the interpretation of the Scriptures, the result is either the rejection of the reinterpretation of many of the literal and factual assertions of God's Word. Chapters 1-11 of Genesis, formerly held to record factual history, now are understood to be saga or myth, and thus these important chapters do not report historical happenings of the direct communications of God with Adam, Eve, Cain and Noah.

If the LCMS were to follow the recommendations of *Lutheran Perspective* relative to Biblical interpretation, it would necessitate the jettisoning of much of its past exegetical, dogmatical and homiletical literature. It would also mean that the interpretation of the Bible would become the preserve of those who have mastered the complicated techniques of the variants types of criticism comprising the historical-critical method. Thus the Bible would be taken out of the hands of the common man and become the domain of the experts for they alone would be abreast of the latest developments in the science of Biblical criticism which is constantly on the move and never bas arrived at a final position. The average Christian reader would never know when a text, a paragraph, chapter or Biblical book would be God's Word or simply the outmoded expressions and teaching of a bygone age, whose views were determined by their limes just as ours allegedly are.

Footnotes

1. *Lutheran Perspective*, Vol. 9, No. 2, November 2, 1981, p. 6. Photographed in the December 7, 1981 *Christian News*.
2. *Brief Statement of the Doctrinal Position of the Missouri Synod* (St. Louis: Concordia Publishing House, 1932), p. 4.
3. As quoted by *Lutheran Perspective*, **op. cit.**, p. 6
4. **Ibid.**, p. 6.
5. F. Pieper, *Christian Dogmatics* (St. Louis: Concordia Publishing House, 1950), I, p. 201.
6. Friedrich Schleiermacher, *The Christian Faith*, trans. H. R. Mackintosh and J. S. Stewart (Edinburgh: T. & T. Clark, 1948), par. 30.
7. Johann Christian Konrad von Hofmann, *Der Schriftbewels*, 2d edition, I, p. 671ff.
8. Theodore Kliefoth, *Der Schriftbeweis* des Dr. J. Ch. K. V. Hofmann, p. 32 as cited by Pieper, **op. cit.**, p. 201.

9. Pieper, **op. cit.**, p. 202.

10. John Theodore Mueller, *Christian Dogmatics* (St. Louis: Concordia Publishing House, 1953), p. 47-48.

11. *Lutheran Perspective*, **op. cit.**, p. 6.

12. G. Ernst Wright, *God Who Acts, Biblical Theology in Recital* (London: SM Press, 1952), p. 2

13. G. Ernst Wright and Reginald Fuller, *The Book of the Acts of God* (New York: Doubleday & Company, 1957).

14. Langdon Gilkey, "Cosmology, Ontology and the Travail of Biblical Language," reprinted in *The Concordia Theological Monthly*, 33: 143-154, March 1962 has pointed out the weakness of Wright's views and that of Bernard Anderson's, *Understanding the Old Testament*. Also James Barr, "Revelation through History in the Old Testament and Modern Theology, Interpretations, 56:4-14," 1963 and in *Old and New In Interpretation*, chapter 3, "Concepts of History and Revelation," pp. 65-102 has greatly challenged Wright's views on Biblical revelation.

15. Wright and Fuller, **op. cit.**, pp. 19-20.

16. *Webster's New World Dictionary of the American Language*, College Edition (Cleveland and New York: The Publishing Company, 1964), p. 757.

17. **Ibid.**

18. E.L. Luecker, "Inspiration, Doctrine of," *Lutheran Cyclopedia* (St. Louis: Concordia Publishing House, 1954), p. 511.

19. **Ibid.**

20. **Ibid.**

21. **Ibid.**

22. *Lutheran Perspective*, **op. cit.** page 6, column 3.

23. Mueller, **op. cit., op. cit.**, p. 47-57.

24. Cf. Edgar Krentz, *The Historical-Critical Method* (Philadelphia: Fortress Press, 1975), 88 pp. and the whole series of the Fortress Press: *Guides to Biblical Scholarship* which deals with all the known types of Biblical criticism.

Questions

1. Who warned members of the LCMS against the dangers of fundamentalism? ____

2. What did *Lutheran Perspective* say about Fundamentalism? ____

3. The "totality of Scripture" as a determining principle of interpretation is ____.

4. What is "sedes doctrine?" ____

5. The electronic evangelists usually are ____.

6. Christians have always regarded the Bible as ____.

7. The Bible contains what theologians have called ____.

8. Historic Lutheranism has taught both the ____ and ____ principles of the Bible.

9. *Lutheran Perspective* is promoting the ____ method.

10. Should the Bible only become the domain of experts? ____

The Theology of the
Apocalypse or Revelation

Christian News, October 7, 1985

A. Introduction

In dealing with the Book of Revelation we are studying a book of the Scriptures which is not easy to interpret. This will consequently also present problems to the person endeavoring to set forth a theology of this apocalyptic book. Stevens says: "The obscurity of the book is partly due to the nature of its theme, the program of the future which God has not clearly revealed, and partly to the nature of its language and materials. It is purposely obscure in its references to the dread power of Rome. It deals in visions and symbols. It is a book of enigmas. The interpretation of its language must always be, in considerable part, conjectural."[1] Dr. Weidner concurs when he writes: "The prophetic character of the Apocalypse renders it difficult to estimate its biblical theological value, but it does not lessen that value. In conformity with the whole plan of the book, many views, full of significance, are presented only in images, whose interpretation is not easy, and often it is difficult to draw the distinction between literal fact and the prophetic coloring. Nevertheless, we are able to examine the objective contents of the book—its doctrine, its direct and indirect statements—in their theological significance."[2]

The theology of the book of Revelation can be presented in different ways. Authors and theologians organize their presentations in different ways. Weiss, Feine, Stevens, Weidner and others treat the theology of Revelation separately, while Zahn, Karl Miller, Schmid and others treat the teachings of the Apocalypse as a part of Johannine theology, and discuss it together with the Gospel and Epistles of John.

Again those who treat the teachings of the Revelation separately organize their material variously. Dr. Bernhard Weiss deals with the theology of the Johannean Apocalypse under two chapters: The Apocalyptic Picture of the Future and the Conflict of the Present.[3] Thomas Bernard in his Bampton Lecture in 1864 dealt with the teachings under six headings, namely, that revelation is 1) a doctrine of the cause of the consummation; 2) a doctrine of the history of the consummation; 3) a doctrine of the coming of the Lord; 4) a doctrine of victory; 5) a doctrine of judgment, and 6) a doctrine of restoration.[4] Professor Stevens organized it as follows: the Lamb of God, the Christian community, the anti-Christian world power, and conflict and victory.[5] Feine treats it under the captions of: The Christology, the doctrine of salvation (die Heilslehre) and the eschatology (Die Endvollendung).[6]

The great topic of the Book of Revelation is the Second Coming of Christ and the things related to this. It also sets forth the conflict between good and evil in the world. The purpose of the book is to give comfort, faith, and courage to the people of God. It is no wonder that this book has been used in time of difficulties and trial by Christian people since its writing. Rightly understood the book can be a tremendous blessing.

B. The Theology or Revelation

1. The Doctrine or God.
a. The Name and Nature or God.

The name of God is feared by the devout (11:18), blasphemed by the beast (13:6), as well as by men when they suffer from the plagues (16:9). It is probably the name of Jehovah which Christ will write upon those who overcome (3:13) and which he will place on the 144,000 who are with the Lamb (14:1), and which the servants of God bear upon their foreheads.

The name of God is expressed in many ways: "He which is and which was and which is to come" (1:8; 4:8; 11:17;16:15) (King James), is revised "who is and who was and who is to come;" God is "the Alpha and Omega, the beginning and the end" (21:6; 1:8), or the one that "liveth forever and ever" (4:9; 10:6; 15:7).

The Apocalypse emphasizes that He is the "only Holy One," whom all must fear and adore; that He created the whole world by His will (4:11; 10:6). John represents God in opposition to the false gods of the Gentiles, "which can neither see, nor hear, nor walk."

Both the titles of "our Lord" (4:11; 11:15); and "the Lord God" (1:8; 4:8; 11:17) are found in the book. Concerning this latter title Weidner writes: "This latter name is synonymous with the Old Testament Adonai Jehovah, or Jehovah Elohim, and is more solemn and emphatic than the simple term of 'God.' There can scarcely be any doubt that John, in his formula expressing the living and energetic eternity of God 1:4,8; 4:8; 11:17; 16:5), intends to represent and interpret the sacred and incommunicable named of Jehovah" (Ex. 3:13-15).[7]

The following are some of the attributes descriptive of God in Revelation: holy, just and true (6:10; 15:4; 16:5). Throughout the book stress is placed upon the ethical perfection and absolute goodness of God (4:8). His ways are righteous and true (15:3), his judgments true and righteous. In 13:10; 14:9-11; 18:6-8 and 22:12 we have John's understanding of the justice of God.

b. The Doctrine of the Holy Spirit

John distinguishes the Spirit as a Being distinct from God the Father, from Christ, and the Church. In ch. 1:4,5 John writes: "Grace to you and peace, from him who is and who was and who is to come; and from the seven Spirits that are before his throne, and from Jesus Christ." The Holy Spirit is at times designated as the Seven Spirits (1:4), and seven Spirits of God (3:1; 4:5; 5:6); at other times the Spirit (2:7,11,17,29 and other places), or "the spirit of prophecy" (19:10). The expression "the seven Spirits of God" is used to denote the whole fullness of the Spirit's nature. When in 22:17 the Spirit and the Bride say to Christ, "Come" we need no further proof that the writer conceives the Spirit as independent of the Son and the Church. Although the Spirit is expressly distinguished from the Bride, the Church (22:17), and speaks to the churches (2:7,11 etc.), the Spirit does not stand outside the Christian, "for the testimony of Jesus is the spirit of prophecy which testimony is possessed by the believers" (19:10). The Spirit does not stand outside of Christ, but Jesus has the seven Spirits (3:11), the Lamb has seven eyes, which are the seven spirits of God (5:6) and the testimony of Jesus in the Spirit of prophecy (19:10). In 1:4,5 John undoubtedly is thinking and writing in a Trinitarian sense.

c. The Works of God.

God is represented as the Creator of the world. The twenty four elders sing: "Worthy art thou, our Lord and our God, to receive the glory and the honor and the power; for thou didst create all things and because of thy will they were created" (4:11). The angel standing upon the sea and upon the earth swore by "him that liveth forever and ever, who created the heaven and the things that are therein, and the earth and the sea and the things that are therein" (10:6). The angel flying in mid heaven with the eternal good tidings calls upon the inhabitants of the earth to "worship him that made heaven and the earth and the sea and the fountains of waters" (14:7).

God is a King who governs the world: He sits on a throne (4:2). While God is truly King of the world and everything He has made, still His rule is being opposed by the forces of evil, headed by the Devil, the deceiver of the divine government of God, the deceiver of the whole world (12:9).

What is the aim of the divine government of God? In the great song of chapter 12 we have the answer: "Now is come the salvation, the power, and the kingdom of our God and the authority of the Christ." The purpose of God is achieved when men are delivered from Satan and brought to God. The realization of this goal of men being brought to God is synonymous with the completion of the Kingdom of God. At various stages in the progress of the book of Revelation this is celebrated by way of anticipation (11:15,17; 12:10; 19:1,6).

2. The Person and Work of Christ

Most commonly Christ is called by His historical personal name, Jesus (1:9; 12:17; 17:6; 19:10; 20:4; 22:16); twice the Lord Jesus (22:20, 21), three times Jesus Christ (1:1,2,5); twice the Christ (20:4,6), and twice the Christ of God (11:15; 12:10).

In regard to Christ's person we find the union of the human with the Divine clearly indicated. He is the Lion of the tribe of Judah, the Root of David (5: 5; 22:16), and therefore of human descent, of the lineage and race of Israel, to whom the Messianic promise was given. But likewise the Book of Revelation ascribes Divine acts and Divine names, Divine attributes and Divine worship to Christ. He is "the first and last" (1:17; 2:8), "the Alpha and the Omega" (22:13), the "holy and true"

(3:7), "the Word of God" (19:13). As God alone in the Old Testament tries the heart and reins (Psalm 7:9), so is this attribute ascribed to Christ (2:23), and this heart-searching glance is described in this way, that His eyes are like flames of fire (1:14; 2:18; 19:12). The angels of God are represented as Christ's (1:1; 22:16); the four living creatures and the twenty-four elders fall down before Him as before God Himself (5:8,14). Ch. 19:10 makes worship a prerogative of God; and in Revelation we find repeated doxologies are ascribed to Christ (1:6; 7:10). Throughout the book reverence is paid Christ which is divine and consequently the Book of Revelation teaches clearly the divinity and deity of Jesus Christ.

The Work of Christ

It is love from which the work of Christ proceeds (1:5). According to Revelation the teachings on the work of Christ can be organized under the following heads:

a) In His testifying to the Word of God, Christ is called "the faithful witness" (1:5), "the Amen, the faithful and true witness" (3:14), and believers are depicted as holding "the testimony of Jesus" (19:10).

b) Christ overcame the Devil. In 12:3-9 we have a representation of this conflict. In 12:3-4 the Dragon is depicted as standing before the woman, ready to devour her child as soon as it is born. That the Devil really attacked Christ, and that Jesus entered into conflict with him, is expressed in the statement that Jesus overcame (3:21; 5:5).

c) The Apocalypse continually sets forth Jesus as the crucified One, under the figure of the Lamb that was slain (5:6,12; 13:8; 7; 14; 12:11). The use of the "little lamb" Arnion, twenty-nine times, may serve to sharpen the contrast between the Lamb, as though it had been slain and the announced Lion of the tribe of Judah (5:5). "Lamb of God" is the most characteristic designation of the Savior. "The figure of the lamb in this book, as well as in 1 Peter 1:19," says Dr. Weidner, "evidently is derived from the paschal Lamb, while the passage in Isaiah 53:7 was also at the same time uppermost in the Apostle's mind. It is implied that the death of Jesus on the Cross was an atoning and sacrificial character."[8] It is "in the blood of the Lamb" that the saints have "washed their robes and made them clean," (7:14; 22:14) that is, the death of Christ is redemptive; it is a means of purification from sin. The same truth is expressed under the figure of purchase (agoratzo) when it is said: "Thou wast slain, and didst purchase unto God with thy blood of every tribe, and tongue, and people, and nation, and madest them to be unto our God a kingdom of priests" (5:9). Professor Stevens says of the person and work of Christ in Revelation as follows:

> Although no formulated doctrine of the person and work of Christ should be sought in the Apocalypse, it will be found that the book is peculiarly rich in its descriptions of the dignity and glory of his person and of the surpassing greatness of his redeeming work.[9]

d) Great stress is also laid on the **resurrection** of Christ (1:8; 2:8). He is "the first-born of the dead." (1:5) He is now alive forevermore, and has

525

the keys of death and Hades (1:18). He now sitteth with the Father in His throne (3:21), which is the throne of God and of the Lamb (22:1,3).

We have also a description of the work of the exalted Christ. As God's Anointed, Jesus shares with God the lordship over His kingdom (11:15; 12:10). He is the Ruler of the kings of the earth (1:5) "the Lord of lords, and the King of kings" (17:14). He also is the possessor of the key of David and thus has complete power over the Messianic Kingdom (3:7, after Isaiah 22:20). He is the Lord of believers (11:8; 14:30; 22:20,21) and they are His servants (1:1; 2:20) and bear his name (14:1; 3:12). Christ is represented as "in the midst of the throne" (5:6; 7:17). This probably refers to the efficacy of the sacrificial death of Christ and His priestly intercession for the people. John also sees "one like unto the Son of man" in the midst of the seven golden candlesticks (1:12,13). This represents that He is ever present with His Church on earth and always active among believers. It is He who searcheth the reins and hearts and giveth unto each one according to his works (2:23).

The exalted Christ will come again (1:7), (20:22) in great glory, accompanied by an army of saints (19:11-19).

3. The Angelology of Revelation

Angels play a prominent part in the Book of Revelation. In Chapters two and three we have the angel of the various churches addressed by which designation the pastors of these congregations is meant. Each chapter of Revelation, save the fourth, sixth and thirteenth mentions an angel or angels. The revelation of Jesus Christ was sent by God to his servant John by an angel (1:1). It is an angel who asks the question: "Who is worthy to open the book and loose the seals thereof?" (5:2).

John saw and heard the voice of many angels round about the throne (5:11). In chapter four angels are represented as holding the four winds of the earth (7:1). In chapter 8-11 we have portrayed the sounding of the seven trumpets of judgement by seven angels. Chapters 16 and 17 describe to us how the seven angels pour out the seven bowls of the wrath of God into the earth. In the chapters adduced and in other places of the book, it is clear that God used angels to announce his judgments against the wicked of the world and that they were used by God as His servants.

In connection with the doctrine of the angels it is best to discuss the doctrine of Satan for it is evident that the Devil must once have belonged to the good angels. Concerning this Weiss writes: "To these angels (namely the good) must once have belonged (XV. 2, ho diabalos hai ho satanas) , who xii 3, 13, appears as the five-colored angels (i.e. according to 2 Kings iii, 22 lxx., the blood-colored great dragon) or with allusion to Gen. iii as the old serpent (vv 9, 15, xx. 2); for he was also as indeed indirectly follows from xii 8f., originally an inhabitant of heaven."[10]

In the Apocalypse the personal principle of evil is called "the devil" (2:10; 12:9; 20:2,10) and "Satan" (2:9,13,24; 3:9; 12:9; 20:3,7), "the Old Serpent" (12:9; 20:2)," the Serpent (12:14,15), "the Great Red Dragon" (12:3; cf. 12:4,7,9; 20:2,7), "the Old Serpent." The name kategon denotes the enemy of men, because he is the disturber of their union with God.

He is the antagonist of men, their accuser before God (12:10), the deceiver of the whole world (12:9; 20:10). The word Satan refers to him as the adversary and antagonist of men and of God. The two words (Devil and Satan) mean about the same thing, the first being from the Greek and the second being from the Hebrew.

As Satan, the old Serpent, seduced our first parents, so does he still seduce and deceive the whole world (12:9; 20:8). The nations of the earth who worship Satan and his angels are his special sphere of activity. He appears as the ruler of the world with seven crowned heads (12:3). Satan is the old enemy of God, who hinders the realization of the Kingdom of God on earth. When Christ was born Satan attempted to devour Him (12:4,5). In this the old serpent was foiled. By Christ's exaltation the victory over Satan was achieved, and the Kingdom of God and His Messiah shall be established (12:10). Christ by His death and His ascension into heaven has robbed Satan of the right to accuse the followers of the Lamb (12:10). But this does not mean that Satan' s power has been destroyed. "A short time" is given him to lose his wrath upon men (12:12).

A very difficult and mysterious question is that of Satan's relation to heaven. Although Satan and his angels had been cast out of heaven at some time previous to the fall of man (2 Peter 2:4; Jude 6), yet it seems that he was still permitted, in the counsel of God to enter His presence (Job 1:6-12; 2:1-7; 1 Kings 22:21; Zechariah 3:1,2). Dr. Weidner asserts: "No matter how mysterious the passage in Rev. 12:7-12 may seem, it is evident that the casting down of Satan from his office of accuser in heaven is connected with the great justifying work of redemption. John here gives us such a glimpse into the world of spirits which can be compared with what Christ reveals to us, in Luke 10:17,18; John 12:31 with what Peter unfolds in 1 Peter 3:19,20 and with the revelations of Paul in Col. 2:15; Ephesians 4:8-10. We have a right to infer that Satan, when he found himself unable to overcome Christ here on earth by subtlety carried war into heaven itself, returning thither with his angels, with the vain hope of supplanting Christ on the throne of heaven - God permitting it, in His eternal counsels, for the sake of the glory of His Son. "But Michael and his angels were cast down with him" (12:7-9). Henceforth Satan no longer returns to heaven. Satan is now confined to the earth and to Hades. He persecutes the Church through unbelieving Jews, called Satan's synagogue (2:9); by them he throws the believers in prison (2:10), and where such persecution exists there has been established his throne. Satan manifests himself as the special enemy of the Church of God, in that he equips the two beasts against her. Power is given by Satan to the first beast, represented by ten horns (12:3; 13:1) and to the second beast he will give the power of working miracles, through which Satan misleads the inhabitants of the earth.

4. Wickedness and the Victory over the World's Wickedness

Even the person who reads Revelation hastily gets the impression that something is described here that is very wicked. A portion of mankind who are punished by the plagues released by the four angels loosed by the sounding of the sixth angel in chapter nine are represented as repenting not of the works of their hands and as being guilty of idolatry and out of it grew such sins as murders, sorceries, fornications and thefts. In chapter 21:8 we have the wicked described as "the fearful, the unbelieving, and abominable, murderers, fornicators, sorcerers, idolaters and liars." That is a sad list of wickedness and is reminiscent of the one Paul gives in Galatians 5:19-21. Here we have the sins of the world with its underlying wickedness toward Christ and the church. This wickedness is depicted as widespread. In chapter 20:8 the number of those opposed to Christ is as the sand of the sea. The opposition toward Christ and His church is stubborn and intense.

The wickedness of the world has as its promoter and author the Devil. In chapter 12 the Dragon was ready to devour the child of the woman. Chapter two of Matthew is only properly understood when we read Revelation 12 where the Devil attempts to kill the Christ Child.[12]

The devil works in two ways. He works through men as agents and also in the hearts of people. It is only by working in their hearts that Satan works through men as agents. Revelation answers the question as to how the Devil works in human hearts. He deceives the whole world. The task of Satan is to get people to believe what is false.

Despite the prevalence of wickedness the Book of Revelation brings the assurance of victory. This is close to the theme of Revelation which is a book of victory.

The vision, following the opening of the seals, was that of the white horse and the rider, who rode forth to conquer (6:2). The Apocalypse deals with the victory of Christ and the Church. The wickedness surrounding the Christian is a temptation to him. In the seven letters to the churches (chs 2 and 3) we have the statement: "He that overcometh." In the seven letters to the churches the thought is stressed that the wickedness of the world was a temptation to the Christian. Those are going to enter the new heaven and the new earth who have overcome (21:7).

It is through faith in the blood of the Lamb that the Christians achieve the victory over the enemies. Not only the victory of the Christian is foretold but also the victory of Christ and his Church.

5. The Wrath and the Grace of God.

The Book of Revelation emphasizes the reality of the wrath of God. Orge and thymos are the two words for wrath used in the book 14:19; 6:16, 17; 15:1-7.

Orge is a settled attitude of opposition and indignation and thymos is the breaking out of that attitude in a special form. Nothing demonstrates the wrath of God more than the fate of the wicked. The Beast, the Devil and every man's name not found in the book of life will be cast into the lake of fire. But before the final scene we have a number of examples of God's wrath being manifested upon the earth. When the sixth seal was opened, the kings of the earth, and the princes, the chief captains and the rich hid themselves and said to the rocks: "Fall on us, and hide us from the face of him that sitteth on the throne, and from the wrath of the

Lamb, for the great day of their wrath is come; and who is able to stand? (6:16-17).

The seven trumpets announce various judgments (ch 9 and 11:18). In chapter 14 the second angel with the sharp sickle is described as casting his sickle into the earth, and gathering the vintage of the earth and cast it into the winepress, the great winepress of the wrath of God. Chapter 15 opens with John seeing another sign in heaven, "great and marvelous, seven angels having seven plagues, which are the last, for in them is finished the wrath of God" (15:1). The following chapter shows how the seven angels pour out the seven bowls of wrath of God into the earth. Chapter 17 and 18 give the judgment of God against the great harlot.

It has been said that the book of Revelation is a book of contrasts. The grace and kindness of God are just as prominent as the wrath of God. The greeting of John to the churches is: "Grace to you and peace" (1:4). The promise is given in the seven letters to the churches of Asia Minor to those who are faithful is the crown of life (2: 10), or "to him will I give to eat of the tree of life, which is in the Paradise of God" (2:7). The promise to the church of Pergamum is: "To him that overcometh, to him will I give of the hidden manna, and I will give him a white stone, and a new name written" (2:17). In all of the seven letters we have a great and glorious promise given to those who are faithful.

At the end of Chapter seven where there is a description of the status of those before the throne, we are told that " God shall wipe away every tear from their eyes" (v. 17). In the new earth there shall be no curse anymore; and they need no light of lamp, neither light or sun, for the Lord God shall give them light and they shall reign forever" (22:5). The severity and goodness of God are found throughout the book.

6. Ecclesiology (The Doctrine of the Church).

Chapters two and three are the chief source for the teachings of the Apocalypse on this subject. According to the description of the churches of Ephesus, Smyrna, Perganum, Thyatira, Sardis, Philadelphia and Laodicea we find them having both excellency and defects. In the letters addressed to these churches there are to be found the commendations as well as the rebukes of Jesus. The Lord commends the toil and patience of the Ephesian church, the tribulation and poverty the church of Smyrna was suffering, the fidelity of the church of Pergamum, in holding fast to Christ's name and for not denying the Christian faith, the love and faith of the church of Thyatira, and the missionary spirit of the Philadelphian church.

But the church has also defects. The Lord rebukes Ephesus for having forsaken its first love, Pergamum for permitting false doctrine, Thyatira for allowing false teaching and immorality to be taught in its midst, Sardis for being stagnant and dead, and Laodicea for its lukewarm and satisfied spirit. The seven letters to the churches are valuable doctrine and will help churches in every age to see themselves as they are and also help them to realize what God demands of a perfect life-instilling and growing church. Persecution, false teaching and worldliness are en-

529

emies which Christian churches are constantly called upon to fight and avoid them as dangerous to sound growth and healthy spiritual church life.

7. The Christian
a. As He is Here and Now
Christians are members of God's kingdom. John in the greeting tells the readers that Christ by His blood made them to be "a kingdom and priests to his God and Father" (1:6). As priests Christians have direct access to God, and present to Him their praise and thanksgiving. Christ speaks of the Christian as "my servants." (2:20). Even now they are washed white in the blood of the Lamb" (7:14). The names of the Christians have been written into the book of life (13:8) from the foundation of the world (17:8). The Christians are also called "saints" and as such they keep the commandments of God and the faith of Jesus (14:12). In the Greek we have the term hagios for 'saint.' Here the word means separated to God's service (5:8) or in the moral sense of sharing God's purity (3:7).[13] In chapter 22:11 we have the holy or righteous in opposition to the adikol or filthy. God is also called holy in Revelation, but He is holy in a sense that He is separate from everything that is sinful. The believers are called holy not because they are pure but because their sins are washed away in the blood of the Lamb. With the believer holiness is a matter of growth. According to 14:13 the hagiol are blessed because they die in the Lord.

Revelation presents a beautiful picture of the life and destiny of the Christian.

b. The Christian as He Shall Be Hereafter.
In the seven letters to the churches of Asia Minor Christ tells those congregations something of life of the Christian in the hereafter. The Ephesian Christians are told that if they overcome they shall "eat of the tree of life, which is in the Paradise of God" (2:7). The Christians of Smyrna are encouraged to remain faithful unto death for then the second death will not hurt them (2:11) The Pergamese Christians receive the assurance that they will be given of the hidden manna, and receive a white stone, arid upon the stone a new name written (2:17). Chapter 22 pictures the future life of the Christian. In it we have a description of the glory and privileges of the Christian.

8. The Eschatology of the Apocalypse.
Paul Feine asserts concerning the doctrine of the last things in Revelation: "Die Apokalypse handelt von allen Buchern des Neuen Testaments am ausfuhrlichsten uber die letzten Dinge (Kapitel 19ff)."[14]

a. Concerning Death in General
John distinguishes between spiritual death (3:1), natural death 2:10,23; 9:6; 12:11; 13:3; 18:8; 21:4) and eternal death (2:11; 20:6; 14; 21:8). Spiritual death is the opposite of life as blessing and salvation.

Natural death, the end of earthly life, overtakes all men, but for the believers the power of death has been overcome by Christ, because He was
dead, and behold now He is alive for evermore, and has the keys of death
and Hades (1:18) i.e., He has the power of death Hades. In this passage,
as well as in Rev. 6:8;20:13,14 Hades appears in close connection with
death — in fact, as a consequence of death. But in these passages a distinction must be made between them. In 1:18 death is personified and
regarded as a possessor of gates. The place of death, which appears closed
in with gates is Hades. In Rev. 20:13,14 death and Hades appear personified as demonical powers, and for believers are abolished (1 Cor.15:26).
They are cast into the lake of fire, and become identical with it — into
which also all unbelievers, whose names shall not be found written in
the Book of Life will be case (20:14,15). Death shall find no place in the
new heaven and new earth (21:4). Natural death, in contradistinction to
eternal death, which is the second death (20:4) is the end of earthly life.

b. The State of the Soul After Death.

John conceives of the universe as consisting of three great regions —
heaven, earth, and Hades (5:3, 13). Heaven is above the earth, and is
thought of as the ideal sphere of existence; earth is the sphere of the development of the struggle between heaven and hell; and the lower world,
or Hades, is the antithesis to heaven, the home and center of the power
of death and of the Devil.

Hades is the place of death, conquered by Christ (1:18). The souls of
the unbelievers (20:13-15) are delivered into Hades.

John also speaks of the lower world as "abyss" (9:1,2,11; 11:7; 17:7;
20:1,3). It seems to be the same place as Hades, but is regarded as the
present abode of the Devil and his angels as distinguished from "the lake
of fire," which shall become their abode after the judgment (20:10). The
abyss out of which comes the beast (11:7; 17:8) and the locusts (9:1-3) is
the seat of Satan. This abyss, which is the home of Satan and his kingdom, is identical with Hades, and is the invisible but real world where
the souls of the ungodly and the evil angels abide. Here Satan wields his
power, and into his kingdom passes the soul of every unbeliever at his
death.

The believers enter heaven at death, but they do not immediately receive their full and final glory, which they will first attain after the resurrection. Rev. 6:9 reads: "And when he opened the fifth seal I saw
underneath the altar the souls of them that had been slain for the word
of God." In heaven are to be found the martyrs, those who have surrendered their lives for the Gospel and all believers who have died in the
Lord.

The matter of eschatology is differently understood, conceived and presented by Christian denominations. Many Christian people believe in two
comings of Christ at the end of time. A part of their scheme calls for a
general conversion of the Jewish people, a reign of Christ on earth for a
thousand years followed by the great judgment. We have the premil-
lenialists and post millenialists. Chapter 20 of Revelation has been the

bone of contention in this matter of the interpretation of the millennium In our understanding of this chapter we follow Dr. Lenski of Capital University of Ohio. Who is the opinion that the thousand years began at the incarnation and the enthronement of the Son (12:5) and continues until Satan's final plunge into hell (20:10), which is the entire New Testament period.[15]

c. The Second Coming of Christ.

The Second Coming of Christ in glory is the great theme of the Apocalypse. Chapter 20:11-15 describes the judgment scene when "the dead great and small, standing before the throne; and books were opened, which is the book of life; and the dead were judged out of the things which were written in the books according to their works. And the sea gave up the dead that were in it; and death and Hades gave up the dead that were in them and they were judged every man according to their word. And death and Hades were cast into the lake of fire.... And if any was not found written in the book of life, he was cast into the lake of fire."

The Christians enter into a new life in the new heaven and new earth of which we have such a superb and beautiful description in chapter 21.

James Orr in his article on the Revelation of John summarizes the theology of the book as follows: "On this it is hardly necessary to dwell for expositors are now well agreed that in its great doctrines of God, Christ, man, sin, redemption, the teaching of the Apocalypse does not vary essentially from the great types in the Epistles. It is granted by all writers that the Christology is as high as anywhere in the New Testament. The point in which its eschatology differs from the rest of the New Testament is in its introduction of the millennium before the final resurrection and judgment. This enlarges, but does not necessarily contradict, the earlier stage of thought."[16]

Footnotes

1. G. B. Stevens, *The Theology of the New Testament*, Charles Scribner's Sons, New York, 1917, p. 525.
2. R. F. Weidner, *Biblical Theology of the New Testament*, Lutheran Literary Board, Burlington, Iowa, 1891, II, p. 256.
3. B. Weiss, *Biblical Theology of the New Testament*, translated by J.E. Duguld, Edinburgh, T. & T. Clark, 1893, II, pp. 248-283.
4. T. D. Bernard, *The Progress of Doctrine in the New Testament*. American Tract Society, New York, 1896, pp. 200-227.
5. G. S. Stevens, *The Theology of the New Testament*. Charles Scribners, p. 523-563.
6. P. Feine, Theologie des Neuen Testaments, Heimriche Buchhandlung, pp. 389-394.
7. Weidner, **op. cit.**, p. 257.
8. Weidner, **op. cit.**, p. 269.
9. Stevens, **op. cit.**, p. 537.
10. B. Weiss, *Biblical Theology of the New Testament*. Edinburgh, T. & T. Clark, 1891, II, p. 270.
11. Weidner, **op. cit.**, p. 265.
12. R.C.H. Lenski. *The Interpretation of St. John's Revelation, Lutheran Book Concern*,

Columbus, Ohio, 1935, p. 359.

13. G. Abbott-Smith, *A Manual Greek Lexicon of the New Testament*. Charles Scribner's Sons, 1929, p. 5.

14. Paul Feine, *Theologie des Neuen Testaments*, J. C. Heinrichsche Buchhandlung, Leipzig. 1922, p. 393.

15. R. C. H. Lenski, *The Interpretation of St. John's Revelation*, **op. cit.**, pp. 568, 569.

16. *The International Standard Bible Encyclopedia*. Wm. B. Eerdmans Publishing Company, Grand Rapids, 1939, IV. p. 25 87.

Questions

1. Is the book of Revelation easy to interpret? ____
2. The great topic of Revelation is ____.
3. The purpose of the book is to ____.
4. John is thinking and writing in a ____ sense.
5. The Book of Revelation clearly teaches the ____ of Jesus Christ.
6. Christ overcame ____.
7. ____ is the most characteristic designation of the Savior.
8. Great stress is laid on the ____.
9. ____ play a prominent part in Revelation.
10. Devil and Satan mean about the ____.
11. Satan is now confined to ____.
12. Satan persecutes the Church through ____.
13. The task of Satan is to get ____.
14. The ____ horse rode through to conquer.
15. The seven trumpets announce various ____.
16. The Book of Revelation is a book of ____.
17. The Church of Pergamum was rebuked for permitting ____.
18. The Church of Thyratira was rebuked for ____.
19. The Church of Sardis was rebuked for ____.
20. The Church of Sardis was rebuked for ____.
20. The Church of Laodocia was rebuked for ____.
21. Christ speaks of the Christians as ____.
22. Revelation presents a beautiful picture of ____.
23. The souls of unbelievers are delivered into ____.
24. At death the believers enter ____.
25. Lenski is of the opinion that the thousand years began at the ____ and continue until ____.
26. Christians enter into a new life in the ____.

The Sermon on the Mount

Christian News, May 12, 1986

The Sermon on the Mount with special reference to the Beatitudes (Past and current misconceptions, including that of Robert Schuller)

The ministry of Christ was characterized by preaching, teaching and the doing of good works, many of which involved the performance of miracles.

The Four Gospels contain all we know about the life, activities of Jesus and the instructions Christ gave his disciples (except a few of the Pauline Epistles). About fifty per cent of John's Gospel consists of the sayings and sermons of Jesus.[1]

Matthew has organized his Gospel around five major discourses of Jesus. Thus Burke wrote: "The body of Matthew is organized around five discourses, each ending with the translational formula, 'When Jesus was finished...'" The Sermon on the Mount is the first of these discourses, and coupled with the narrative section which follows in chs. 8-9, forms a characterization of Jesus' early Galilean ministry.[2]

Scroggie has listed no less than forty-five distinct sermons or discourses in the Four Gospels, the longest of which is the Sermon on the Mount.[3] Biblical commentators have been high in their praise of this discourse of Jesus. Burke claimed that no other block of Jesus' teaching has enjoyed such wide influence and intensive examination. Its uniqueness derives from the fact that some of its parts have attained classical status on their own.[4]

William Arndt has this evaluation of the Sermon: "Christians have always regarded the Sermon on the Mount as particularly valuable and instructive. Many expositions of it have been written, and in the Gospel commentaries a good deal of space is devoted to it."[5]

Since the second century no block of Scripture of comparable size has exercised as great an influence. In the pre-Nicene period passages from this sermon were cited or referred to more than from any other Portion of Holy Writ. To this day, both Christian and non-Christians are being challenged by this early sermon of Jesus. The sayings of the Sermon on the Mount changed Tolstoy's social theory and also influenced Ghandi's program of non-resistance as a device to unsettle the British in India. Even Nietzsche, who disliked the Sermon, could not ignore it.[6]

Martin Luther penned a large treatise on Matthew chapters 5-7, which may be found in the *Concordia Revidierte Walsh Luther Edition*, Vol. VII, 350-677.[7] Augustine wrote a famous treatise on the Sermon on the Mount while still a bishop at Hippo (A.D. 393-396) and labelled it the "perfect rule or pattern of the Christian life" "— a new law in contrast to the old." Monastic orders interpreted it "as a counselor perfection," designed not for the common people. Richard Davis claimed: "The Sermon on the

Mount has achieved the pinnacle status in the West as an expression of the highest moral idealism. It has been understood as the premier amplification of the 'love thy neighbor' ethic and the Golden Rule."[8]

The Sermon on the Mount has been the most popular sermon with readers of the Gospels. Why? Probably because students of the church's literature have found in the Sermon's fresh message, up-to-date, timely and relevant instructions for living.[9] The Sermon contains important lessons for every generation, especially if the Bible is considered God's reliable Word and therefore inspired. The Sermon on the Mount has implications for today's Christians.

Divergent Views Held about Many Aspect of the Sermon

Divergent views have been advocated throughout the centuries about this early sermon of Christ. Was it delivered at one time, at one sitting or is it a composite of different sayings of Jesus uttered over a longer period of time? Again at what juncture of Christ's ministry was it uttered? For whom was the Sermon intended? For His disciples or for the general public? What is the relationship of Matthew chapters 5-7, which contains the complete Sermon on the Mount and Luke 6:20-49? Are the two Discourses the same?[10]

The Position of Critical Scholarship on the Unity of the Sermon on Mount

Critical scholarship, which has espoused form and redaction criticism in Gospel interpretation, contend that Matthew's Sermon on the Mount was not delivered at one time, but a composite discourse created out of various sayings of Jesus uttered at different times. In fact, the Roman Catholic scholar Grassi holds that it was the needs of the early Christian Church which caused the writer of the First Gospel to select those sayings that he chose to incorporate in Christ's first alleged sermon. Wrote Grassi: "Literary analysis reveals that the Evangelist has given us a compilation of sayings of Jesus, some of which were originally uttered on other occasions."[11] The following demonstrates the existence of other sayings of the Sermon on the Mount in other parts of Matthew, Mark and Luke.[12]

Sermon on Mount - 5:13, 5:15, 5:17-18, 5:21-28, 6:29, 5:31-32; Luke- 14:34-35, 11:33, 18:17, 12:57-59, 18:18; Mark- 9:49, 11:21, 10:11-12; Matthew - 18:8-9, 19:3-9.

Dibelius, one of the earliest New Testament scholars to adopt form criticism, held that Jesus did not deliver the sermon as a connected discourse, but that the sermon is a composite of different sayings gathered into a sermon.[13] However, the impression that Matthew gives his readers is that Jesus sat Himself down on a mountain side and delivered a sermon especially to His disciples, which was also heard by a large multitude that hath gathered to hear Jesus.

It is not necessary to hold that material set forth in the Sermon on the Mount could not have also been delivered on other occasions. Arndt believed that "on general principle a person will have to hold that our Lord in His ministry of more than three years must have frequently repeated the same truth in order that the people of the various sections might become acquainted with them. In fact, there is a passage in Luke 12:22-34, not reported by Him as belonging to the Sermon on the Mount, which is very similar to what Matthew hands down as a part of this stirring discourse, 6:19-31."[14] The context of the account of the Sermon on the Mount states that people came from various places to hear Jesus, and would He in view of this merely have spoken a few sentences? It has even been suggested that what we have in Matthew 5-7 is an epitome of a longer address delivered on this occasion. For the Biblical test to say that Jesus delivered this Sermon and He did not would belie the accuracy of the Word of God.

Are Matthew 5-7 the Same as Luke 6:20-49?

Some claim that the Sermon on the Mount, as given in Matthew chapters 5-7, is not the same Sermon reported in Luke 6:20-49, named by some as the Sermon on the Plain.[15] Here again scholarly opinion differs. Many scholars believe that the Sermon on the Mount and The Sermon on the Plain are the same, except that the Lucan version is much shorter. The two discourses are not altogether alike. However, Arndt believed: "But when we look at the contents, especially when we think of it that both begin with the Beatitudes and that they set forth the Christian life and that they stress the same virtues largely, we arrive at the conclusion that the two evangelists report the same discourse; Luke merely giving it in briefer form than Matthew."[16]

The Sermon given in Luke was recorded after Christ appointed the twelve apostles; while in Matthew it is given as delivered at about the middle of Christ's Galilean ministry. However, Arndt, who believes Matthew 5-7 and Luke 6:20-49 are the same sermon states: "But the difficulty vanishes when we are told that Matthew does not report chronologically but topically."[16a]

Time of Deliverance of the Sermon on Mount

If the view is correct that Matthew 5-7 and Luke 6:20-49 give the same sermon, a stance with which Mark agrees, the time the sermon was delivered was the summer of A.D. 28. Jesus had been active in Galilee for about a year. A brief trip to Jerusalem had interrupted the Galilean ministry, probably at the time of the Passover of the year A.D. 28. In Arndt's view Jesus had not stayed in Jerusalem very long. John 5 Arndt averred reported this Passover. Sometime after the Jerusalem visit Jesus went to a place where there was a mountain and after praying all night on that mountain, Jesus came down and appointed the twelve apostles and then before a large audience delivered the Sermon on the Mount.[17]

Place Where Sermon Was Delivered

Neither Matthew nor Luke mention the name of the mountain. A thirteenth century tradition located this mountain on the "horns of Hattin."[18] This is not a mountain but a hill sixty feet high. Some have felt that there is a contradiction between Matthew and Luke, for Matthew says Jesus delivered it on a mountain and Luke says that Jesus uttered it on a plain. Averred Arndt, "The two statements can be well harmonized. Where Jesus met the multitudes was a place in the mountain or hill country on a plateau, where a number of people could easily gather."[19]

A Comparison of Matthew's and Luke's Versions
Luke's version was about two thirds shorter than that of Matthew. The Matthean version omitted some statements given by Luke, particularly the section, called "the woes." Also the Lord's Prayer found as an integral part of Matthew is found in another place in Luke, in chapter 11 and the exhortations about riches and worry are given in Luke chapter 12.

The General Contents of Matthew's Sermon
An outline of the Matthean version of the Sermon on Mount, one which is useable would be the following:
1) The Beatitudes, chapter 5:1-12.
2) Mission of the disciples here on earth, 5:13-16.
3) The spiritual meaning of the Law of Moses, 5:17-48.
4) The rejection of the ex-opere-operato view of Christian deeds like almsgiving and fasting, 8:1-18.
5) The proper attitude with respect to needs of the body, food and clothing, 8:19·34.
6) The course of Christians toward an erring brother, his attitude toward prayer and toward men in general, 7:1-12.
7) Closing exhortations (straight gate, false prophets, no mere lip service, of correct hearing of the Word), 7:13,23.[20]

The True Nature of the Sermon on the Mount
What is the position of the Sermon on the Mount in New Testament and especially in the teachings of Jesus? What is the purpose of the Sermon of the Mount? There has grown up a large exegetical literature treating this first of all of Jesus's sermons or discourses. Not only do all commentaries logically discuss its contents, but special monographs and books have been issued dealing with all aspects of the Sermon. Not only theologians but even social workers, ethicists have manifested an intense interest in these unique sayings and instructions of Jesus of Nazareth. One of the most recent attempts has been that by Schuller of California's Crystal Palace Church, who has issued what some claim is a best seller dealing with the Beatitudes.[21]

Robert Schuller has utilized the various Beatitudes to foster his psychological version of helpful Christianity to foster healthy and happy living. There are those who have claimed that the Sermon on the Mount represents the essence of Christianity. In Matthew 5-7 we are said to have the "the Creed of Christianity." The literature of the twentieth century, as well as that of earlier centuries, has given many divergent interpretations. Thus Richard Davis wrote: "Within Christendom, its status no less high, has been understood in quite different ways."[22]

In an early part of this century, when mankind thought it was heading for a millennial age, a number of writers claim that the world has in the Sermon directives for a new social order. Thus Kent wrote: "His primary aim was to deliver men from the effects of wrong beliefs, motives and habits of living and to restore them to complete physical, mental, moral and spiritual health. He endeavored to unite them in the universal fraternity, which he describes as the kingdom or reign of God, and thus to develop a perfect social order."[23]

Hillis wrote many years ago: "Tomorrow education will reread the Sermon on the Mount and seek to make rich the teachings of the Christian religion ... Today all political economy is being rewritten in the length of the Sermon on the Mount ... A most impressive political document."[24] Clow asserted: "When the will of God is done on earth as in heaven, the kingdom of God and of heaven shall fitly have come. Every social problem shall be solved, and all social unrest shall be stilled." These were predictions which were nullified by two major world wars and a host of smaller wars since 1914.

Christ — Not a New Law Giver

There are still visionaries who believe that mankind will by dint of reasonableness achieve millenarian and utopian conditions. When that is achieved, then the Sermon on the Mount will serve or can serve as the "Contribution for the Kingdom of God." The Beatitudes are said constitute "The Preamble of this New Constitution." For many the Sermon on the Mount constitutes the real teaching of Christ, even though the Sermon on the Mount is only the first of a number of Sermons and other discourses of Jesus.

Many scholars and expositors of the Sermon on the Mount fail to realize that most of the Sermon is LAW, if not all of it.[25] It is an erroneous view to assert that the teachings of the Sermon on the Mount is the heart and essence of Christ's teaching. If that were the case, what are we to do with the rest of his teachings and especially with the reason for Christ's suffering and death? That does not mean that, as certain Roman Catholic scholars say, that Christ is the New Lawgiver setting forth more laws. Moses was the first lawgiver, Christ, the second and higher.[26] Christ is not enunciating new laws, but stating the correct interpretation of those already given by Moses.

Arndt claimed that it is a mistake to hold that the Sermon contains a sweet message. "Just the opposite is true. The greater part of it is Law, in its sterner form. If anywhere, we see how much the LAW demands, how all-embracing, all comprehensive it is. The Savior penetrates to the hidden recesses of the heart and show how even God's will must be obeyed."[27]

Francis Pieper held that the Sermon on the Mount was Law and not Gospel. The Beatitudes set forth the truth that the "promise of remission of sins is connected to good works not because He means that good works are a propitiation, but they follow reconciliation, but for two reasons."[28]

In the interpretation of the Sermon on the Mount many show that they

538

do not distinguish between Law and Gospel. Explained Arndt: "The sermon is not a proclamation of good news, of joyous tidings, but rather sets forth stern truths that Christianity is not easy going, indulgent religion, permitting the service of sin, but demands of us the best service we can render God. To understand it, we must bear in mind that it was preached to the disciples, to people who had become believers of the Gospel of forgiveness which He powerfully taught. The acceptance of this Gospel is pre-supposed in those to whom the sermon is addressed."[29] Arndt continued: "This Sermon is designed to show the followers how they were to live in this world and be in harmony with God and their fellowmen.

To lead God-pleasing lives as an outgrowth of saving faith in Christ Jesus is the real purpose of Jesus' first extended discourse." So Arndt contended that "every one of us should diligently study the Sermon on the Mount, not indeed to be made acquainted with the way of salvation, for that is not intended to set forth—but to see how our life must be ordered, if our faith in Jesus and His redemption is sincere. That is forcefully convinces us of our sinfulness and thereby makes us realize our need of God's pardon is another important feature."[30]

The Relationship of the Sermon to the Rest of Christ's Teachings

The history of the interpretation of Matthew 5-7 and Luke 6:20-49 reveals that the Sermon on the Mount has been wrongly interpreted because it was not understood in the light of Christ's other teachings as well as the theology of other New Testament writings. If the Bible has one ultimate author, and if the Bible presents one consistent system of theology, then the Sermon on the Mount cannot be pitted against the Pauline doctrine of justification by faith, apart from works. It is wrong to isolate the Sermon on the Mount from other teachings of Christ. Here Burke expresses a view we reject. The latter asserted: "An unfortunate feature of much post-Reformation Christianity has been the interpretation of Jesus in the light of Paul rather than the converse."[31] Mark stated the purpose of Christ's mission as being: "The Son of Man came to seek, and to save that which was lost and to give his life a ransom for many." What was the purpose of the crucifixion of Christ, if not to pay for the sins of the world? John the Baptist announced the purpose of Christ's ministry as being "take away the sins of the world" (John 1:29). Jesus insisted that men first believe on Him. If Jews and Gentiles in Christ's time could acquire salvation by keeping the Law including the Sermon on the Mount, why did Christ have to die? Furthermore, Jesus promised his disciples the Holy Spirit, Who would guide them into all truth, and also to bring all truth back to their remembrance. Paul claimed to be an apostle of Jesus Christ and to proclaim Christ's teachings and not his own. The Sermon on the Mount must be understood in the light of the whole teachings of Christ and of his most important Apostle, Paul.

Serious Problems in the Interpretation
of the Sermon on the Mount

There are commands in the Sermon on the Mount that have struck the readers forcefully, namely, its insistence on conduct which runs counter to what normally is done by people such as avoiding vengeance, readiness to suffer wrong, the willingness to forgive and love our enemies. These commandments are so exceptional and unusual that most people find it difficult or impossible to keep them. How to interpret these extraordinary commandments has produced much ingenuity as to how to make these palatable to the average Christian. Here are some of the attempts, in both the past and in the present to deal with these extraordinary commandments of the Sermon on the Mount:

In the past Roman Catholic theologians have taught that many of the hard-to-keep commandments were meant for those who desired to achieve a special degree of perfection. This was the view at Luther's time. These hard-to-keep directives were understood to be evangelical counsels and were meant for those who wished to attain special eminence in serving God. Here are the following evangelical counsels: 1. not to retaliate evil treatment; 2. not to practice vengeance; 3. to turn the other cheek ; 4. not to resist evil; 5. to let the cloak be taken together with the coat; 6. to go two miles when compelled to go one; 7. to give everyone that which he asks; 8. to lend to every borrower; 9. to pray for the persecutor; 10. to love the enemies ; 11. to do good to those who hate us; 12. to pray for those that despitefully use us.[32]

This reformation-period Roman Catholic interpretation meant that portions of the Sermon of the Mount only applied to a special class of people. However, when one reads Christ's Sermon there is no hint that only certain individuals are meant, and that others need not take Christ's commandments seriously.

2. There have been those who have interpreted the commandments in a super-literal or literalistic sense. There have been those who have thought that the Sermon on the Mount was given to direct all human relations which exist between members of a family, people's relationship to the state, and the relationship of governments to each other. There have been individuals who did put out their eye and cut off their hand because with these human members sins were committed. According to this view, Jesus here lays down laws for governments in the treatment of criminals, for the federation of peoples, the course they are to take when war threatens or arises.[33] To adopt this understanding of the teachings of the Sermon on the Mount would be following a line of reasoning beyond the intent of that Christ wished to teach. For one, it would forbid other Scriptural teachings. Romans 12:1-7 would be impossible to carry out. It would result in a chaotic society. View No. 2 has led to pacifism and erroneous sociological and penological theories and views.

3. A third view was sponsored by the former famous scholar and missionary Albert Schweitzer. The latter held that the Sermon on the Mount was not meant for all time, but for the brief interval between the time when the Sermon was spoken and the imminent coming of the day of

judgment, which was considered as coming very soon. Thus the super human tasks given the disciples were but for a few years. Jesus was mistaken about the proximity of the coming of the Parousia, the coming Judgment. So this was at best an "Interim Ethics."[34] This view denigrates the deity of Christ and there is nothing in the Sermon on the Mount to suggest or support the view of Schweitzer.

4. The View of the Dispensationalists

Dispensationalism divides the whole history of the world from Creation until the Final Judgment into seven distinct time dispensations. They are: 1. the dispensation of Innocence; 2. the dispensation of conscience; 3. the dispensation of government; 4. dispensation of grace; 5. the dispensation of the law; 6. the dispensation of the church or of grace; and 7. the dispensation of the kingdom.[35] The fifth dispensation of the law began with Israel's choosing the law for grace and concluded with the death of Christ on Calvary. This means that most of the Gospels, excluding Mark 16, Matthew 28; Luke 24 and John 20-21, are meant for the Jews and do not concern the church, which was only founded after Easter, especially on Pentecost.[36]

C. I. Scofield is his hermeneutical manual, "Rightly Dividing the Word of Truth," claims in one of his major studies that "the Jew, the Gentile and the Church of God must be separated." The entire Old Testament deals with Israel; there are no prophecies in the Old Testament that pertain to the future church. Israel and the church must be separated, there is no lineal descent between them. Christ offered Himself to the Jews between 27-30 A.D. His sermons in the Gospels were directed to them. Since Christ was rejected by His Jewish contemporaries, the method of living prescribed in the Sermon on the Mount will be filled in the Kingdom Age, which will begin after the church age dispensation. Lewis Chafer claims that there were three different systems of divine government in the world: (1) the teachings of the Law of Moses; (2) the teachings of grace, and (3) the teachings of the kingdom. The teachings of the Law were accepted as a rule by Israel at Mount Sinai "and was at no time addressed to the nations of the world."[37] It was a peculiar form of government for a peculiar people, and accomplished a peculiar purpose in condemning the failure of man and leading him to Christ. Its full detail is revealed in the writings of Moses; but the history of Israel under the law occupies the rest of the Old Testament, and the major part of the Gospels up to the record of the death of Christ. In the doctrinal teachings of the New Testament, very much additional light is given on the character and purposes of the Law of Moses. There the law is held in contrast with the teachings of grace. There, also will be seen more fully in the latter discussion, the law is represented as having passed out of force through the death of Christ; and it may be observed that the death of Christ, the law is in no wise treated as being directly in force.[38]

5. A fifth view was sponsored by Ritschl, who proposed a set of generalized moral principles, which sometimes included a program for societal renovation.[39] Those who believe that the Sermon on the Mount contains

sound psychological advice for happy living and existence and claim that in this discourse mankind possesses the real constitution for a real utopia or millennium on earth are interpreting the kingdom referred to in the Sermon on the Mount with being an earthly kingdom.

Thus Lord Acton defined the Sermon as a revelation for a morally new society. He claimed that Jesus contrasts the spiritual idea is underlying moral conduct with the mere external requirements of the law.

Looking for a warless world and a world where all men's needs are met as they are required — this being the nature of the kingdom of God — is a utopian dream which fails to take into account the evil heart of man and man's basic sinfulness and the need for a new heart and mind. Jesus told Pilate "that His kingdom was not of this world (John 18:36)," The Savior told the Pharisees that the "kingdom does not come with observation, neither shall men say 'Lo here, lo there,' for the kingdom of God is among you or within you" (Luke 17:20). Jesus gently rebuked his disciples when on the day of the Ascension, they asked Jesus whether at this time he would restore the kingdom of Israel. Acts 1:6.

The purpose of Christ's mission was briefly but comprehensively stated by Christ: "The Son of Man is come to seek and to save that which was lost" (Matt. 18:11). John 3:16 sets forth the true mission of Christians. Paul enunciated the same truth when he wrote: "Jesus first came into the world to save sinners." (1 Tim. 1:15), St. John declared: "The blood of Jesus Christ, His Son, cleanseth us from all sin" (1 John 1:7). (Concerning the just quoted passages, P. E. Kretzmann wrote: "These passages represent the distinctive characteristic, fundamental, essential doctrine of Christianity, without which the Christian religion would sink to the level of paganism. The free salvation of all men through the atoning power of Christ's blood is the one wonderful ray of light in the Bible which distinguishes this sacred Book of the East from all other religion of works and a final half-spiritual, half-temporal kingdom is set before men as the goal of their earthly ambition."[40]

The Time of Sermon's Deliverance Sheds Light on Nature and Purpose of the Sermon on the Mount

It is the conviction of Arndt, one time professor at Concordia Seminary, St. Louis, that it is important to determine the time when the Sermon on the Mount was delivered. According to this New Testament scholar the Sermon was not given at the beginning of Christ's Galilean ministry but at about the middle of it. Before delivering this discourse Jesus had been preaching and teaching about a year according to Arndt's calculations. Jesus arrived in Galilee late spring or early summer of A.D. 27, and "then entered upon His Galilean ministry". There may have been several interruptions before Jesus attended a feast in Jerusalem. The summer of A.D. 28 soon came. In this season Jesus met the people in the hill country not far from Capernaum. Arndt claimed: "All this sheds light on the situation. The Sermon on the Mount is addressed to the disciples of Jesus. After He had been teaching in Galilee for a year the result was there were many who regarded Him as their guide in religious matters.

Jesus had many followers. That is implied in Luke 6:1,13ff., where Jesus is said to have called His disciples to Himself and to have selected twelve of them to become His special apostles or ambassadors. In Luke 6:17 a great crowd of disciples is mentioned. Significant is the introduction of the Matthean report of the Sermon: Seeing the multitudes, He went up into a mountain, and when He was set, His disciples came unto Him, and He opened His mouth and taught them (5:1). The labors of Jesus had borne fruit; His message had been widely accepted."[41] Fahling in his *Harmony of the Gospels* has the same time table as does Arndt.[42]

Arndt contends that it makes a big difference whether Jesus delivered the sermon to people who believed on Him or to such which did not accept His teaching. If He addressed them as disciples who knew why He had come into the world, it is easy to understand how He would give them instructions about conduct as a child of God. On the other hand, if these people were not His followers one would expect that he would set forth the necessity of repentance, the method of obtaining forgiveness of sins on the basis of the work of the Messiah. But this essential message of discipleship is not contained in this Sermon on the Mount. It seems that the hearers are regarded as disciples and familiar with the plan of salvation. Before the utterance of the Sermon on the Mount, Jesus had been preaching and it may be presumed that the central truth of Christianity had been enunciated a number of times.[43]

The Purpose of the Sermon

P.E. Kretzmann, one time Professor of New Testament Interpretation at Concordia Seminary and a colleague of Arndt, believed that the Sermon on the Mount had two major purposes in view.

1. By His sharp comparisons Jesus wanted to arouse his hearers, especially those to whom the epithet "hypocrite" would apply, out of their lethargy of their slovenly righteousness. "He wanted to point out to them the utter inadequacy of a literal keeping of the externals of the law. He wanted to show all men, in fact, how far their best efforts are from a proper and adequate fulfillment of the will of God."[44] Any person who measures himself by the standard of ethics set forth in the discourse must realize, if he is honest, that he cannot keep the Law and is guilty.

2. The second purpose was to give a lesson in true sanctification to those who by God's grace had entered into the kingdom of God and are anxious to live in harmony with the highest will of God.[45] Individuals can use the Sermon on the Mount both as a mirror to reveal sin and as a guide to godly living.

Did Rabbinic Teaching Influence
Christ's Sermon on the Mount?

Christian and Jewish scholars have pointed out similarities between Christ's teaching in the Sermon on the Mount and Rabbinical teachings. Thus Emil Ludwig[46] and J. Klausner[47] have claimed that there is nothing new in the Sermon on the Mount, that all the significant teachings were already uttered by the Rabbis and Jewish teachers. It is claimed that every item of our Lord's teaching can be paralleled in either the Old Testament, the Apocrypha, or in the Talmudic and Midrashic literature of the period near to the time of Jesus. Dean Farrar did not put too much stock in this claim and said that bright sayings of the Talmud are as few as the grains of wheat in an almost "unmeasurable rubbish-heap in which they are imbedded."[48] The Jewish scholar Montefiore asserted about the Beatitudes: "The Beatitudes as a whole are not entirely Rabbinic, though we may find parallels to each statement taken individually. They may fairly be considered as new in spite of parallels."[49]

The Appeal of the Sermon on the Mount

The Sermon on the Mount has elicited much interest, not only in the commentaries on Matthew and Luke, which discuss it in detail, but also in individual studies, monographs and books. What is the appeal of the Sermon? What constitutes its greatness? A number of answers, all valid, can be advanced. First, it is a sermon coming from the mouth of Jesus who because He was the Son of God and the Savior of the world makes anything He had ever uttered , significant and attention-worthy. While all Scripture is God breathed (theopneustos), people are especially attracted to anything Jesus did or said during His earthly existence. All sayings of Jesus have been the subject of special study by the sons and daughters of men. The Sermon on the Mount because of its length has had a special fascination for students the Gospels.

In addition to having the very words of the Son of God, the Sermon on the Mount is dealing with questions of a practical nature whose doing or not doing affect people's daily lives. Here the God-fearing person can find a description of the kind of life God expects Christians to live and how to deal with their fellowmen .[50]

The form which the Sermon has, also has contributed to its appeal and popularity. The Sermon is characterized by simplicity, directness, avoidance of superfluous verbiage, concreteness, picturesque, vivid expressions and gripping illustrations.

The Interpretation of the Beatitudes (Matthew 5:1-10)

The Sermon on the Mount, both in its Matthean and Lucan versions, begins with a series of assertions which promise blessings to the children of God. Each assertion begins with the Greek word "makarios." In the Septuagint "makarios" translates the Hebrew word "Ashre," which means "the blessings of".[51] "Ashre" and "makarios" mean more than simply "happy" as the word is often rendered. To interpret the opening words of each of the Beatitudes as merely "happy" which reflects an attitude of mind, does not do complete justice to the word **makarios**, because blessedness is bestowed on those who practice what Jesus sets forth in each of his assertions, beginning in the Greek with the word "makarios." The word "beatitude" comes from the Latin beatitudo. Another English term for beatitude is "macarism." Since the days of Ambrose the word "beatitude" has been limited to these sayings which open the Sermon on the Mount.[52]

How Many Beatitudes Are There?

Bible students have differed in their enumeration of the number of macarisms contained in the Sermon's introduction. Some scholars stop at verse 10, and count 7, others include verse 11 and thus count eight. The former believe that with verse 11 a new subject is begun and should therefore not be counted as a part of the Beatitudes proper. Arndt holds that verse 11 and 12 belonged to the Beatitudes and thus gave eight macarisms.[53]

The Source of the Beatitudes

Critical scholars claim that the sayings found in Matthew and in Luke were derived from a source called Q (German word Quelle for Source) which the writers of the Gospel of Matthew and Mark are alleged to have consulted and appropriated materials from this Q document.[54] The Sermon on the Mount, and consequently the Beatitudes, were allegedly composed as a sermon for post baptismal instruction. The Roman Catholic Grassi wrote: "Since the collection of Jesus's sayings was made by the early Jewish-Christian church in view of their own needs, it was especially directed to those clearly committed themselves to the good news."[55] According to Grassi, the Beatitudes concern the kingdom blessings not only now, but also have an eschatological note which will be fulfilled when Christ comes which was considered imminent.[56]

That the Q source and that the Sermon and its Beatitudes were written for the post-Easter time of the Church, does violence to the fact that Matthew chapters 5-7 and Luke 6:20-49 report a sermon preached at least a year and a half before Christ's death and resurrection. This kind of interpretation does violence to what the Gospels actually report that this was an actual event of Christ's life.

The Nature of the Beatitudes

Are the Beatitudes Law or are they Gospel? If they are taken separately from the Sermon, the Beatitudes could be either Law or Gospel. If the Macarisms are considered as spoken to lay people as a rule for a way of life, they are LAW. However, averred Arndt, "if the Savior's intention in these words was to give strength and encouragement to His disciples to console them in their sorrows, to dry their tears and make their distressed hearts rejoice, then the section is GOSPEL. While the Sermon for the most part is LAW, this does not prevent the opening part to be Gospel."[57] Kretzmann is of the opinion that the entire Sermon on the Mount is law, and this would include the Beatitudes.[58] Fahling claimed that "the Sermon on the Mount is essentially a proclamation of the Law, but not in the fiery manner of Sinai, where thunder, lightning, and voice of the trumpet shook the hearts with terror and agitation."[59] Fahling does not state whether the Beatitudes are Law or Gospel. Ylvisaker, in his decision of "The Purpose and Aim of the Sermon on the Mount" contrasts the giving of the Law on Mt. Sinai and the teaching of Christ on Mount Tabor. He concludes his section with these words: "On Sinai we are confronted throughout by the rigor of the Law, while in the Sermon on the

545

Mount our ears are attuned to the melodious music of the Gospel."[60]

There are a number of quotations in the *Christian Dogmatics* of Francis Pieper which appear to identify the entire Sermon on the Mount with the Law. He rejects the Roman Catholic idea that Christ was a new Lawgiver. In his discussion of the distinction of Law and Gospel, he seems to classify the Sermon under the Law category. [61]

In opposition to other Lutheran Church-Missouri Synod theologian Arndt is convinced that the Beatitudes, which set forth great Christian virtues, do not of necessity have to be classified as Law.[62] Arndt believes that in the Beatitudes we have descriptions of Christians. He argued thus: "If the Senior had said, 'Blessed are people if they are poor in spirit,' one could agree that one has a statement fitting the Law category. But the emphasis lies on 'blessing.' The meaning may be paraphrased thus: 'Other people may despise you and treat you with contempt, but I say to you that you are blessed.' The blessedness of which Jesus speaks of is the possession of great spiritual treasures, God's favor, and His aid in all the vicissitudes of life."[63]

Matthew introduces his account of Jesus' preaching or teaching with these words: "Now when he saw the crowds, he went up a mountainside and sat down. His disciples came to Him and He began to teach them saying." Jesus was sitting at a place which was high enough to serve as a pulpit. The great crowd stood or sat about Him. According to the custom of the Rabbis Jesus gave His instruction in a sitting position.

In the following discussion of the Beatitudes the correct interpretation will be set forth, together with past and current misunderstandings. One of the most recent inadequate interpretations of the Beatitudes may be found in a book by the radio and TV preacher Robert Schuller, who recently authored a book, entitled: "Be (Happy) Attitudes," published by Word Books of Waco, Texas. Darrell Sifforth, writer for Knight-Ridder Newspapers, has called the book a blockbuster and in an article has summarized Schuller's understanding of the true meaning of the Eight Beatitudes.[64] The book is designed to help people psychologically to have proper attitudes of mind by creating Happy attitudes about various situations.

Matthew and Luke's Beatitudes Compared

In Luke's version of the Sermon of the Plain, believed by many scholars to be the same as the Sermon on the Mount, there are only four beatitudes and four woes.[65] In Luke's version the Beatitudes are given in the second person. If Jesus spoke the Sermon on different occasions He would have used both forms. It would not be unreasonable to assume that Jesus paused and spoke at more length on each Beatitude. Every Beatitude had such far-reaching consequences that Jesus expatiated on each to help his hearers to reflect on them and thus understand the import of each macarism.

Kretzmann contends that the first Beatitude strikes the keynote of the entire Discourse.[66] "Blessed are the poor in spirit, for theirs is the kingdom of heaven." Luke reads: "Blessed are the poor for yours is the king-

546

dom of God" (NIV). Some wished to interpret the Lucan macarism as saying that if one is poor he has an advantage over the rich, to the poor belongs the Kingdom. Such is interpretation does not fit Matthew's version of the rest of the Scriptures. This Beatitude does not favor the economically disadvantaged. Schuller has summarized what he thinks is the essence of this blessedness of Jesus: "I need help; I cannot do it alone."[67] This does not really come to grips with the real teaching of this Beatitude. Jesus was not giving a special message for the economically poor, although many, if not most of Christ's disciples were poor; in fact, many were slaves. The Bible has words for the poor, the rich are to help them; the latter are not to take advantage of the poor. But here he is speaking of the spiritually poor. They are the poor in spirit. Those to be blessed are those who are aware of their moral deficiencies. Those who are rich but spiritually poor are not to be blessed. Those who abase themselves and possess humility are those who can enter the kingdom of God. The subjects of Christ's kingdom should not expect the blessing-bestowing king to shower them with jewels or with money. The blessings of King Jesus reverse the world's standard of blessing in secular matters. This Beatitude does not support revolution finding blessing in secular matters. This Beatitude does not support revolution theology.

Why does Jesus call the "poor in spirit" as happy and as receiving blessing? Fahling answers this question like this: "True, most of them have not much of this world's goods nor do they have their affection set upon them. In addition, they do not boast of good works and saintly virtues, but rather deplore their spiritual poverty in the sight of God.[68] However, seeking, and through faith in Christ being partakers of the imperishable riches of the kingdom of God, they are truly to be accounted happy."[69]

In the second half of the first Beatitude the Savior gives the reason for the "poor in spirit" being called "blessed," for theirs in the kingdom of heaven. Jesus did not say that they would become future possessors of the kingdom of heaven, but that they possess it right now. They are now members of a kingdom, a present entity which outshines anything the world can offer. The following Scripture passages: Luke 16:16; 17:21; John 18:36 support the now nature of the kingdom of God or of heaven. Dispensationalists would have us believe that there is a great distinction between the kingdom of God and the kingdom of heaven.[70] A comparison of passages employing both designations will reveal that they are interchangeable concepts. The dispensationalists contend that one refers to the church and the other to the kingdom to be established in the Kingdom dispensation. When in the Lord's prayer we pray "Thy kingdom come" we are praying for the same kingdom of which Christ speaks in Beatitude one.

What Precisely is Meant by "the Kingdom of God?"

The concept "kingdom of God" or "kingdom of heaven" has been the subject of great discussion on the part of New Testament scholarship. Many commentators hold that the kingdom of God must be understood as being the rule or reign of God. Still others have held that the kingdom of God covers the sum total of those who are God's children, the believers. The term, therefore, would be the equivalent of the term: the holy Christian Church. The latter view is round in the older theological literature of Lutheranism. A third view of more recent origin holds that the term "kingdom of God" signifies "rule" or "reign," while at other times it must mean kingdom, realm, the sum total of subjects ruled over by a king. Arndt believes that all three views are permissible from a doctrinal stance. In interpreting the first Beatitude, the question is: which of the three did Christ have in mind? Arndt is persuaded that in Matthew 5:3 it means kingdom or realm.[71] Christians, who are poor in spirit, are said to be subjects of the realm over which God has placed them. On the other hand, Kretzmann defined the term this way: "For the kingdom of heaven is the sum total of all gifts in Christ Jesus as they are enjoyed here on earth in the Christian Church and finally above in the kingdom of glory. Inasmuch as the riches of the kingdom are in their possession, the disciples of Christ strive more diligently to cultivate the poverty which Jesus praises and to exercise it daily."[72]

The Second Beatitude

"Blessed are they that mourn, because they will be comforted" v. 4.

This verse has often been used to comfort people who have experienced a great tragedy or lost some loved one by death. The literal meaning would seem to support this idea, namely, any person who mourns will be comforted. According to Schuller's interpretation, it means: "I'm really hurting — but I'm going to bounce back."[73] The latter's understanding claims that a person suffering a tragedy can bounce back by his grit and determination. That interpretation states that a person can accomplish overcoming sorrow by his own strength; while the second Beatitude asserts that God will comfort those who mourn. This Beatitude has a spiritual meaning and does not simply mean that when a person mourns he automatically will be comforted by God. The disciples of Jesus are subject to the conditions and circumstances that bring about mourning (cf. Luke 6:21-22; John 12:20; Acts 14:22). Mere grace is not a virtue and a sign that a grieving individual is a child of God. This Beatitude, like all others, refers to something that distinguishes God's people from those who are not. True Christians feel sorry for their sins. They mourn their loss of spiritual possession. Sinning is to the true believer a cause for deep mourning. Those who repent and in faith look to Christ will be comforted by Jesus. "Be of good cheer, thy sins are forgiven thee."

The Christians in the world will suffer discrimination, abuse and imprisonment.[74] Christ will comfort those who suffer for His name sake. Whoever mourns because of Christ will be comforted (Rom. 14:17).

The Third Beatitude

"Blessed are the meek because they shall inherit the earth." V. 7. The word in Greek translated "meek" is **prau** and means "gentle" or "tenderhearted." Leivestad has shown that the adjective refers to the gentle and

548

humble attitude that expresses itself in a patient submissiveness to offense, free from malice and the desire to revenge.[75] Schuller has interpreted this assertion of Christ to mean: "I am going to remain cool, calm and corrected."[76] But there is much more contained in this Beatitude.

Psalm 37:1 teaches: "The meek shall inherit the earth and enjoy great peace." Jesus is speaking of those who are kindly disposed, the gentle, the forgiving people. The Savior is addressing Christians and encouraging them to cultivate this quality.

These words were addressed to the regeneration and not to the unregenerate. Jesus is not speaking merely of people in general who may be meek, but rather of such as are not filled with self-righteousness, pride and conceit. They are bowed down with grief, and are willing to suffer with a meek spirit. Christians must be kind, willing to forgive and be ready to suffer and when ill-treated not seeking revenge.

Those Christians who practice tenderheartedness are considered weak in the eyes of the world. Those who are gruff, stern unforgiving looking for vengeance are considered strong. Christians are considered weak and despised. Still despite what the world thinks, the gentle child of God is blessed indeed. The Christian remembers that he is weak and imperfect and he constantly must remind himself that he is in need of God's help. Although the Christian falls short of this ideal, he knows that he must persist in his endeavor to strive to possess this Christian quality. Jesus must be the great Exemplar he will follow (I Peter 2:21-23).

Those who are tenderhearted will inherit the earth. Does that mean that the Christians will be wealthy here on earth by and by, or does Christ speak of the kingdom of glory? What kind of blessing does Christ promise? Luther believed that our Lord was speaking of outward, earthly blessings. Gentleness of spirit will be blessed by God. While spiritual gifts are included in this third Beatitude, though paradoxical, Luther contends it refers to this life.[77] The forgiving Christian often wins out in this life, a truth shown many times in human experience, while those who insist on their rights, ever-ready-to-fight persons come to grief. Those expositors who take Luther's view point to Luke 18:29,30; I Peter 3:18-21 and Psalm 37:11. However, if Christians are not blessed in this life for some reason, known only to God, it will be realized for certainty in the life to come, in the kingdom of glory.

The Fourth Beatitude

"Blessed are those who hunger and thirst after righteousness, for they will be filled" v. 6.

Schuller has summarized this Beatitude as: "I really want to do the right things."[78] This can hardly be said to really express what Jesus was teaching. In this macarism Jesus is speaking of a spiritual quality. Those Christians who hunger and thirst after righteousness realize that their lives are very imperfect and they desire to fulfill all the commandments of God more fully.

There appears to be a divergence of opinion among commentators exactly as to what kind of righteousness Christ refers. Here is Luther's understanding: "Therefore understand here the external righteousness before the world, as we comport ourselves one to another. That this, briefly is the meaning of these words: that is a truly blessed person that always continues and with all might strives after this, that all things everywhere be in proper order and every person do right, and help to hold and further such as a condition with words and deeds, with counsel and action."[79]

"Righteousness" is a concept that appears a number of times in the Sermon on the Mount. Jesus declared "Unless your righteousness exceeds the righteousness of the scribes and Pharisees you cannot enter into the kingdom of God;" at another time the Savior declared: "Seek you first the kingdom of God and its righteousness." This writer favors the view of Drumwright that "righteousness probably did not in this instance mean goodness as much as it meant right standing with God."[80] In Isaiah, "righteousness" was used to define "salvation." Such men are characterized by the most intense craving for the gift of God's grace. Without this righteousness, for which Christians hunger and thirst, people would die. God will give them this righteousness. Jesus is that righteousness in His person, the fulfillment of Jeremiah's promise that "the Lord is our righteousness" (Jer. 23:5-6). In Matthew 5:10-11 Jesus indicated that suffering for righteousness, for His sake, and suffering for Him are the same thing. God will supply those desiring righteousness with it.

The Fifth Beatitude

"Blessed are the merciful, for they shall be treated mercifully." v. 7 Schuller summarized this Beatitude like this: "I am going to treat others the way I want them to treat me."[81] Again the California preacher has not set forth the real meaning of the fifth Beatitude. His suggestion gives a selfish motivation, while the Christian begins with the willingness and desire to show mercy to others. Here Christians are encouraged to feel compassion for those suffering and in need of help. Jesus is teaching that those who are merciful practice compassion for others are blessed people. A heart full of compassion for physical and spiritual needs of people will be blessed. Even here on earth their charitable deeds will bring good returns. It is certain, however, that in heaven God will richly reward them. Their sins will be forgiven. It is of course not their mercy which provided for their forgiveness. God's love and Christ's substitutionary death on Calvary have provided that. However, by their good works Christians show in this world that they have the true justifying faith, which must manifest itself in good works.

Those who show mercy often have the experience in this life that when they are in need of acts of mercy, that they themselves are the recipients of needed acts of mercy and kindness.

The Sixth Beatitude

"Blessed are the pure in heart for they shall see God." Schuller summarized this macarism: "I've got to let faith flow free through me."[82] That interpretation seems to miss the intention of Christ considerably. This Beatitude shows that mere outward purity in keeping the Law is insufficient in God's economy. Ylvisaker claimed that there is a logical relationship between the fifth and the sixth macarisms. "The fifth macarism has reference to the activity and the sixth to the spirit of simplicity, the genuineness and the uprightness, which is to characterize this cheerful activity."[83]

"Heart" in this Beatitude refers to the center of the mind and soul. "When Jesus speaks of the heart that is pure, He has in mind the contrast to hypocrisy, lies, and deceit. It is the honest and integrity of the mind and heart, which is a stranger to every false way (Psalm 119:104)."

Here Jesus speaks of the aversion to sin and the desire to cultivate "whatever things are true, whatsoever things are honest, whatsoever things are just, whatsoever things are pure, whatsoever things are lovely, whatsoever things are good report, if there be any virtue, and if there be any praise think on these things (Phil 4:8)." "Purity of heart" is the opposite of "love of the flesh, the opposite of the love of the world, the opposite of love of the eyes, and the pride of life (I John 2:15-16)."

Luther wrote: "There is a pure heart which sees and considers what God has said and values the Word of God ever and above its own conceits. In the Old Testament there are frequent references to 'pure' hearts, with the emphasis on pure (Ps. 73:1; 32:2; 51:12; 24:3,4). This purity is a fruit of the cleansing of the spirit through regeneration and sanctification. They that are pure in heart 'shall see' God."[84]

What does that mean "shall see God?" Does it refer to seeing God, having a knowledge of our Maker and Savior, which is obtained from the Scriptures? That was Luther's understanding of this phrase. In contrast, Arndt contends that inasmuch as the future is used by Christ, ("they will see God"), it seems preferable to refer this to the blessed eternity which a Christian will see after death and after the Day of Judgment. God is pure and only the pure will see God.[85] St. John wrote that "when he appears we shall see Him as He is. And every man who has this hope in Him purifies himself even as he is pure" (I John 3:24; Cf. also Rev. 22:4; Heb. 12:4) Franzmann remarked on this Beatitude: "They shall see God at the end of days. The vision of God is for Biblical thought not a mystical experience— but an eschatological one. In this age men hear God's Word; they shall see Him face to face in the world to come (I Cor. 13:12; Rev. 22:4)."[86]

The Seventh Beatitude

"Blessed are the peacemakers, for they shall be called the sons of God." v. 9.

Schuller has summarized this macarism as follows: "I am going to be a bridge builder."[87] Again the question must be asked: Does this adequately set forth Jesus' teaching in verse 9?

The expression "peacemakers" is the equivalent of those who promote peace. Luther said: "It is they who would make peace, not only for themselves, but also for others. The word suggests that peace is a work of God, for He ultimately establishes peace." The angel's message was: "Peace on earth, and good will to men" (Luke 2:14). Jesus is called by Isaiah "the Prince of Peace" (Is. 9:6). Those who establish peace on the basis of truth,

551

with love as the impelling love, do this work of God. And the children of God must love peace, must follow peace (Heb. 12:14); they must live peaceably with all men as much as lieth in them. (Rom. 12:18), thus wrote Ylvisaker.[88]

How do Christian peacemakers act? Christians use their influence to squelch quarrels, jealousies, rivalries, wars, conflicts between neighbors, communities and nations. It is the obligation of every Christian to work for peace.

The Christian peacemakers will be called the sons of God. God has established peace between God and man through the sacrifice of His Son. Whoever works for peace and trusts in Christ, thereby manifests that he is a Child of God. People may call such a person a weak individual, they may despise such a person, but his actions and course of life will have God's approval. If a Christian as peacemaker is exiled or imprisoned for such activity, he nevertheless knows that he is a member of God's family, which in the final analysis is all that counts.

The Eighth Beatitude

"Blessed are they who are persecuted on account of righteousness, for the kingdom of God is theirs." v. 10. Schuller summarized this beatitude: "I can choose to be happy."[89] This epitomization seems to miss the entire point of Christ's promise. If a Christian is faithful to Christ's teachings, lives them, he is likely to suffer persecution. If a Christian follows the path of righteousness and in the fear of God and love of God does what God has commanded, the Christian must expect opposition. In past times and also in the present (in Communist countries) Christians have been imprisoned and killed because of their faith. Christians have died among tortures because of their pursuit of righteousness. While in America people are no longer imprisoned or tortured, still there is a more subtle kind of persecution in the form of job discrimination, mockery and ridicule heaped on Christians because of their Christian convictions.

Jesus congratulates all these followers who are persecuted on account of devotion to righteousness. He promises them that the kingdom of heaven belongs to them. It should be noted that Christ uses the present tense. Even now they are members of the kingdom of heaven; they are members of the Christian Church. This is an honor of which no persecution can rob them.

The Ninth Beatitude

Blessed are you when you on my account people revile you and persecute you and say all manner of evil against you by way of lying. In this verse Jesus elaborates on verse 10. Jesus speaks of the same kind of persecution Christians will suffer. They will be reviled; they will be charged falsely by the enemies of Christ. The followers of Christ will suffer because of their Master... Because a Christian practices righteousness, he will suffer. History records how time and again Christians have been made to suffer because of their Christian beliefs and principles. It is a distinctive honor to suffer in Christ's interest, because they bear His name.

In speaking of persecutions Jesus emphasized a thought, on which Peter in his First Epistle dwells considerably (cf. 1 Peter 1:18-23; 3:16ff; 4:14-16), namely, that the persecution should not be the result of wrong doing, but the Christian must suffer innocently, because of Christ. If persecution is due to wrong doing, then the persecution should be endured patiently, because it was deserved.

Luke's Woes

Luke has only four Beatitudes. These are followed by four woes. These woes are not contained in Matthew's version of the Sermon. The thought has been expressed by Lagarde that Matthew does not include these woes because he intends to bring solemn warnings more definitely later on. One may think of the impressive woes of chapter 23.[90]

Footnotes

1. This may be easily ascertained by looking at a Bible in which the sayings of Jesus are printed in red.
2. G.T. Burke, "The Sermon on the Mount," Walter A. Elwell, editor, *Evangelical Dictionary of Theology* (Grand Rapids: Baker Book House, 1984), p. 1005a. George Eldon Ladd, "Matthew," C.F. Henry, editor, *The Biblical Expositor* (Philadelphia, A.J. Holman Company, 1960, III, p. 29.
3. W. Graham Scroggie, *The Unfolding Drama of Redemption. The Bible As A Whole, Part I* (London: Pickering & Ingalls, 1953), p. 556.
4. Burke, **op. cit.**, p. 1105.
5. William F. Arndt, *The Sermon on the Mount* (St. Louis: Concordia Mimeo Company, 1944), p. 1.
6. Burke, **op. cit.**, 1005b.
7. St. Louis Edition of *Luther's Works*, 7, pp. 350-677, in the Weimar Edition of *Luther's Works*, 32, 302ff.
8. Richard Davis, "Sermon on the Mount," Carl F. Henry, *Baker's Dictionary of Christian Ethics* (Grand Rapids: Baker Book House, 1973), p. 616.
9. Arndt, **op. cit.**, p. 1.
10. For the critical answers to these questions, cf. K. Grayston, "Sermon on the Mount," George Arthur Buttrick, editor. *The Interpreter's Dictionary of the Bible* (New York and Nashville: Abingdon Press, 19621, IV, pp. 279-289.
11. J.A. Grassi. "Sermon on the Mount," *New Catholic Encyclopedia*, 23 p. 119.
12. **Ibid.**, p. 119: cf. also "Sermon on the Mount" in L.F. Hartmann, *Encyclopedic Dictionary of the Bible*, translated from the Dutch (New York: McGraw-Hill Book Company 1963) p. 2173.
13. Arndt, **op. cit.**, p2.
14. **Ibid.**, p. 2.
15. Cf. Russet Benjamin Miller, "The Sermon on the Mount," and "The Sermon on the Plain," in James Orr, General Editor, *The International Standard Bible Encyclopedia* (Grand Rapids: Wm. B. Eerdmans Publishing Company, 1939), iv. pp. 2732-2736 and p. 2736.
16. Arndt, **op. cit.**, p.2.
16a. **Ibid.**

17. William Arndt, *New Testament History* (St. Louis: Concordia Publishing House, 1940), p. 48.

18. Charles P. Roney, *Commentary on the Harmony of the Gospels* (Grand Rapids: W. B. Eerdmans Publishing Company, 1948), pp. 130-131.

19. William F. Arndt, *Bible Commentary - The Gospel According to St. Luke* (St. Louis: Concordia Publishing House, 1956), p. 182.

20. Arndt, *New Testament History*, **op. cit.**, p. 49.

21. Darrell Sifford, "Minister's best seller a celebration of Jesus," "Be (Happy) Attitudes," *Fort Wayne News Sentinel*, Saturday, Jan. 11, 1986 Section 40.

22. Davis, **op. cit.**, p. 616.

23. Kent, *Life and Teachings of Christ*, p.p. 127-128.

24. Hillis, *Influence of Christ*, p. 10, 47, 48, 75.

25. G. Stoeckhardt, *Die biblische Geschichte des Neuen Testament* (St. Louis: Concordia Publishing House, 1906), p. 88.

26. J. A. Grassi, "The Sermon on the Mount," **op. cit.**, 23, p. 119.

27. Arndt, *The Sermon on the Mount*, **op. cit.**, pp. 3-4.; *Luke, The Gospel of Luke*, **op. cit.**, p. 183.

28. Francis Pieper, *Christian Dogmatics* (St. Louis: Concordia Publishing House, 1951), II, p. 542.

29. Arndt, *New Testament History*, **op. cit.**, p. 48.

30. Arndt, *New Testament History*, **op. cit.**, p. 49.

31. Burke, **op. cit.**, p. 1006a.

32. Cf. Arndt, *The Sermon on the Mount*, **op. cit.**, pp. 4-5.

33. P.E. Kretzmann, "The Sermon on the Mount," *Biblical Commentary – New Testament* (St. Louis: Concordia Publishing House, 1924), p. 41.

34. Donald Guthrie, "Albert Schweitzer," *Baker's Dictionary of Christian Ethics*, **op. cit.**, p. 604; George Ladd, "Interim Ethics," *Baker's Dictionary of Ethics*, **op. cit.**, p. 332.

35. Theodore H. Epp, *Rightly Dividing the Word of Truth* (Lincoln, Nebraska: Back to the Bible Publishers, 1954), 96 pp; Dr. C.I. Scofield, *Rightly Dividing the Word of Truth*, 2 Timothy 2:15 (Westwood, New Jersey; Fleming H. Revell Company), reprint of 1896 edition, pp. 12-15.

36. Scofield, **op. cit.**, p. 5.

37. L. S. Chafer, *Systematic Theology* (Dallas Texas: Dallas Seminary Press, 1948), IV, p. 205.

38. **Ibid.**, p. 205.

39. Burke, **op. cit.**, p. 1005.

40. P. E. Kretzmann, *Biblical Commentary, New Testament* (St. Louis: Concordia Publishing House. 1924), 1, p. 42.

41. Arndt, *Sermon on the Mount*, **op. cit.**, p. 6.

42. Adam Fahling, *A Harmony of the Gospels* (Grand Rapids: Zondervan Publishing House, no date), p.p. 56-57.

43. Arndt, *Sermon on the Mount*, **op. cit.**, p. 6.

44. Kretzmann, **op. cit.**, I, p. 42.

45. **Ibid.**

46. Emil Ludwig, *The Son of Man*, p. 130.

47. J. Klausner, *Jesus of Nazareth* (New York: The Macmillan Company, 1925), p. 384.

48. Dean Farrar as quoted as Adam Fahling. *The Life of Christ* (St. Louis: Concordia Publishing House, 1936), p. 263.

49. C.C. Montefiore, *Rabbinic Literature and Gospel Teachings* (London: Macmillan Company, 1930), p. 1.

50. Arndt, *The Sermon on the Mount*, **op. cit.**, p. 1.

51. G. Abbott-Smith, *A Manual Greek Lexicon to the New Testament* (New York: Charles Scribner's Sons, 1929) p. 275.

52. J. C. Lambert, "Beatitudes," *The New International Standard Bible Encyclopedia*, **op. cit.** 1, p. 419a.

53. Arndt, *The Sermon on the Mount*, **op. cit.**, p. 6.

54. Frederick C. Grant, "Sermon on the Mount," *Americana Encyclopedia*, 1985 Edition, 24, p. 581.

55. J. A. Grassi, "Sermon on the Mount," *New Catholic Encyclopedia*, 23, p. 119.

56. **Ibid.**, p. 119b.

57. Arndt, *The Sermon on the Mount*, **op. cit.**, p. 7.

58. Kretzmann, *The New Testament*, **op. cit.**, 1, p. 22.

59. Fahling, *The Life Christ*, **op. cit.**, p. 263.

60. U. Ylvisaker, *The Gospels - A Synoptic Presentation of the Texts, Matthew, Mark, Luke and John* (Minneapolis: Augsburg Publishing House, 1932), p. 252.

61. Pieper, *Christian Dogmatics*, **op. cit.**, I, 559; II, p. 338. III, 494, 526.

62. Arndt, *The Sermon on the Mount*, **op. cit.**, p. 7.

63. **Ibid.**

64. Darrell Sifford, "Minister's Best Seller, a celebration of Jesus' Be (Happy) Attitudes", *Fort Wayne News Sentinel*, Jan. 11, 1986, 40.

65. Arndt, *Commentary on Luke*, **op. cit.**. p. 184.

66. Kretzmann, *Popular Commentary, New Testament*, 1, p 23.

67. Sifford, **op. cit.**, C.

68. Fahling, *The Life of Christ*, **op. cit.**, p. 264.

69. **Ibid.**

70. Lewis Sperry Chafer, *Systematic Theology*, **op. cit.**, VII, pp 223-224.

71. Arndt, *The Sermon on the Mount*, **op. cit.** pp. 8-9.

72. Kretzmann, *The New Testament Commentary*, 1, p 23.

73. Sifford, **op. cit.** 4D.

74. Charles R. Erdman, *The Gospel of Matthew - An Exposition* (Philadelphia: The Westminster Press, 1946), p. 54.

75. P. Leivestad, "The Meekness and Gentleness of Christ, II Cor. X. 1." *New Testament Studies*, 12. Jan. 1966,159.

76. As quoted by Sifford, **op. cit.** 4D.

77. *St. Louis Edition of Luther's Works*. 7,369.

78. Schuller as quoted by Sifford, **op. cit.**, 4D.

79. *St. Louis Edition of Luther's Works*, **op. cit.**, 7, p. 373.

80. H. L. Drumwright, "Sermon on the Mount," *Zondervan Pictorial Bible Encyclopedia*. Merrill C. Tenney, Editor, (Grand Rapids: Zondervan Publishing House, 1975), V(Q-Z), p. 353.

81. As quoted by Sifford, **op. cit.** 4D.

82. Sifford, p. 4D.

83. Ylvisaker, **op. cit.**, p. 256.

84. As cited by Ylvisaker, **op. cit.**, p. 257.

85. Arndt, *The Sermon on the Mount,* **op. cit.,** 11.
86. Martin Franzmann, *Concordia Self-Study Commentary* (St. Louis: Concordia Publishing House, 1979), p. 19. (N.T.)
87. As quoted by Sifford, **op. cit.,** 4D.
88. Ylvisaker, **op. cit.** p. 257.
89. As quoted by Sifford, **op. cit.,** 4D.
90. Arndt, *Commentary on Luke,* **op. cit.** p. 188.

Questions

1. Was the Sermon on the Mount delivered at one time? ____
2. Robert Schuller utilized the various Beatitudes to foster ____.
3. Most of the Sermon on the Mount is ____.
4. Is the Sermon on the Mount the heart and essence of the teachings of Jesus? ____
5. Is the Sermon on the Mount intended to set forth the way of salvation? ____
6. What did Albert Schweitzer teach about the Sermon on the Mount? ____
7. Jesus told Pilate that His kingdom was not ___.
8. It seems that the hearers of the Sermon on the Mount were ____.
9. Are the Beatitudes Law or Gospel? ____
10. Is there a distinction between the Kingdom of God and the Kingdom of heaven? ____
11. Righteousness means ____.
12. Christian peacemakers will be called ____.
13. It is a distinctive honor to ____ in Christ's interest.

Is the Bible Inerrant?

Christian News, July 28, 1986

Is The Bible Inerrant? is the title of a booklet of 43-pages, published in 1978 by the Reverend John D. Frey, then of Prairie Village, Kansas. This attack upon the historic position of The Lutheran Church-Missouri Synod was distributed ten years ago throughout the length and breadth of the Synod by the ELIM organization. It is the contention of this booklet that the Bible is indeed errant, that the Holy Scriptures contains inaccuracies, mistakes and contradictions. That the Bible is inerrant and not inerrant Frey claims is the only possible conclusion which can honestly be drawn from an impartial reading of the Bible. (Ed. Frey left the LCMS and joined the AELC. Elim's Lutheran Perspective continues to promote Frey's booklet.)

The Bible is said to contain inaccuracies and mistakes when Biblical statements about the nature of the world are compared with the conclusions of 20th century science. It is also claimed that a study of the Old Testament quotations in the New Testament shows that they are not in agreement with the Old Testament texts that are supposedly being quoted.

A number of times in both Testaments where the reader finds parallel accounts of the same events and references to the same personalities, it will be discovered that the accounts disagree and significantly vary and thus the conclusions must be drawn that there are statistical and historical inaccuracies and mistakes. While Frey does admit that some of the errors, contradictions and inaccuracies may not have been in the original writings (called autographs), still he claims that many accounts cannot be explained on this assumption, but clearly show that there are errors in the autographic accounts (cf. p. 25).

The 1976 pastor from Kansas further contends that the Bible's inspiration does not guarantee absolute correctness in the original writings nor that the Bible's authority as God's Word is affected by the presence of numerous inaccuracies, mistakes and contradictions. He further argues that the Word of God does not teach the infallibility and reliability and truthfulness of all that has been recorded by "the holy men of God who spake as they were moved by the Holy Ghost." Questioning the inerrancy and reliability of the total Scriptures was a new development in the history of The Lutheran Church-Missouri Synod and historically speaking may be traced to the late fifties and sixties of this century. Sixty years ago (1926) Dr. William Arndt, professor of New Testament exegesis and hermeneutics at Concordia Seminary, St. Louis, authored a book, *Does the Bible Contradict Itself?* This volume considered the following types of passages: 1. Passages of a historical nature from the Old Testament; 2. Passages of a historical nature from the New Testament; 3. Passages of a doctrinal nature from the Old Testament; 4. Passages of a doctrinal nature from the New Testament Concerning this book and the texts discussed, Arndt said: "I can honestly say that my aim was not to fasten merely upon such apparent discrepancies as can be shown easily, but to treat those that are most baffling and paraded most frequently in support of the view that the Bible is a book of errors" (p. iv). Six years later Arndt continued his discussions of problem passages in the Bible in the follow-up book, *Bible Difficulties An Examination of Passages of the Bible Alleged to Be Irreconcilable with Its Inspiration*. In the latter book Arndt discussed the miracles in the Bible, moral difficulties, historical difficulties from the view of science and finally a group of miscellaneous passages. It is interesting to note that a number of instances cited in Frey's book were answered by Arndt over five decades ago. In the nineteen seventies both of these books were reprinted by its original publisher, Concordia Publishing House of St. Louis. In 1985, the Concordia Seminary Press of Fort Wayne reissued both of Dr. Arndt's volumes.

Some of the readers now being exposed to Frey's attack on the accuracy and reliability of the Bible will probably think that here are some new discoveries. Many of the alleged discrepancies have been recognized for centuries, dating to the time of the Early Church. Over a century ago Professor Haley published a 473 page book, in which he listed and discussed practically all known and suggested discrepancies, errors, inaccuracies and mistakes which agnostics, atheists, rationalists and Bible-doubters advanced throughout the centuries.

The attack upon the inerrancy of the Bible is tied up with a denial of the verbal and plenary inspiration and accuracy of the Bible, which was sponsored during the age of rationalism. It was during this period of church history that a type of criticism was spawned which would only accept those teachings and happenings that could be justified before the bar of reason and were consonant with current scholarly views. Critics rejected the Biblical canon, questioned the authority of the Bible as the Word of God, and rejected the supernatural elements of the Bible.

The major Lutheran Churches in America in the last three decades were taken over by a group of young scholars who were trained at seminaries and universities by advocates of the higher critical method. To be able to practice the various kinds of criticism in vogue, the inerrancy, historical truthfulness and reliability of the Scriptures had not only to be questioned but out rightly rejected.

The LCMS also was affected as a new crop of younger scholars took over at our seminaries, terminal schools and junior colleges between 1958·1975. To make viable the conclusions of the higher-critical·method the traditional Lutheran stance of the inerrancy of the Bible was attacked. The first such written attack is to be found in *The Concordia Theological Monthly*, Vol. XXXVI (Sept. 1965). pp. 577-593.

The booklet under discussion contends that the Bible itself does not use that term "inerrancy," but that its coinage is a construct made to support a position which is not Scriptural. The Bible is only inerrant (i.e. truthful and reliable) when it speaks about Christ and the way of salvation and those doctrines associated with it.

Passages like John 5:39, John 20:30-31, Romans 15:4 and 2 Timothy

3:16-17 set forth the real purpose of the Scriptures and the various purposes as given in these passages tell men in what areas the Bible is true and infallible. But concerning peripheral areas these passages "do not teach that every last fact recorded in the Bible has been accurately given and in such fields as anthropology, psychology, history, geography, education of any other discipline which does not directly impinge on the plan of salvation, consequently Biblical information and assertion can be wrong and do not need be accepted."

In his monograph Pastor Frey has cited anywhere between 30 and 40 examples of inaccuracies, mistakes and contradictions in both Testaments, which on the face of it seem to support the contention that the Bible is not inerrant. Some readers may believe they are unanswerable. This writer believes they can be answered. The theological works of men like Keil, Delitzsch, Reider, Young, Arndt, Torrey, Engelder, Haley, Montgomery and others have offered reasonable solutions which therefore would not necessitate accepting the thesis of Frey's book: "The Bible contains errors and mistakes."

To answer in detail all the examples given by Frey would require as many pages as his book has devoted to this issue. But it will be worthwhile and necessary to deal with his basic approach to the Bible.

Frey does not believe that we cannot know whether we actually possess the entire Word of God. The matter of what books actually belong to the cannot has not yet been solved. Thus he wrote: "The possibility exists that there are some differences in the books that make up the Old Testament canon, as well as the New, remains an open question to this day" (p. 26). Again he wrote: "The passages that teach inspiration of all apostolic writings, and testimony from history and the ancient church tell us that our New Testament is a collection of these writings. "Of course history is fallible, and for that reason we cannot be absolutely certain and rigid in equating our New Testament with apostolic writings. As mentioned before, the canon remains an open question'" (p. 29).

Uncertainly thus surrounds the amount of God-inspired texts and books that are authoritative and how much of the Bible's sixty-six books is inerrant.

It is also Frey's belief that passages like John 17:17, Titus 1:1-2, Hebrews 6:18 and 2 Samuel 22:31, all of which speak about God's Word being either truthful, or the fact that God does not lie, do not apply to the entire Bible, but only to those portions that deal with Christ and our salvation. They cannot, it is claimed, be used to ascribe inerrancy to all of the Word of God. By employing human beings, God placed limitations upon Himself, for it is human to err and since God employed human writers one normally expects them to make mistakes, which Frey claimed they did. But is that doing justice to these Scriptural passages? Where in any of these passages does the reader find a restriction that God only spoke the truth when he had His holy writers write about the work of redemption or the plan of salvation?

The opponents of Biblical inerrancy have claimed that the insistence of orthodox teachers in various Protestant churches about the errorlessness of the original Scriptures is irrelevant since no living person has them or has seen them. In reply to this claim we retort that an inerrant, infallible group of autographs is the only view which comports with the nature of God Who is utter holiness, in Whom there is no darkness and who cannot lie or deceive, that he cannot inspire men to write less than a perfect account of His revelation. Because ultimately God the Holy Spirit is the ultimate Author of all of Holy Writ the writers' finiteness and sinfulness did not prevent the prophets and people chosen in the Old Testament and the evangelists and apostles, authors of the New Testament, from setting forth an errorless account of what transpired and what were the teachings regarding life and doctrine which the Triune God desired all men to know.

Only an errorless, infallible original group of Biblical writings could make available the real and whole truth. What Reymond has written is true:

> To arrive at this goal, the orthodox theologian, by utilizing the very best aids in textual criticism, establishes a trustworthy text. Next, by rigorously applying the most accurate rules of hermeneutics, he determines the meaning of the text. Now if the autograph underlying this scientifically established, correctly interpreted text was itself infallible, the meaning derived by means of these two steps would be objective truth. It would only remain for the pastor and teacher to convey this truth in a relevant way to needy men. The theologian who would deny the infallibility of the autographs, however, after moving through exactly similar steps and arriving at precisely the same meaning of the autographs, must press on to a third step, namely, the effort to determine whether the meaning he has arrived at is true or not, an effort which would obviously be controlled by alien presuppositions grounded in pure subjectivism.

Editors preface to Clark H. Pinnock, *A Defense of Biblical Infallibility* (Philadelphia, 1967), (p. 1-11).

The claim that the Scriptures as they left the writers contained errors and mistakes is tantamount to making the Bible composed of two different levels of data, those given by men (which may be rejected) and those given by God. This thus presupposes that man sits in judgment over the Holy Scriptures and by the employment of man-made criteria decides what can be accepted and what cannot. This results in a separation between the Bible and the Word of God. By this procedure only that is binding which man decides is truly the Word of God. This limits the authority of the Bible and restricts what can truly be accepted as limited to the area of the Christological and soteriological teachings of Holy Writ.

Luther asserted against this position: "It cannot be otherwise for the Scriptures are divine; in them God speaks and they are His Word." Calvin held the identical position. Historical Protestantism in the past advocated the identical stance on the Bible, that all of the Bible, not merely portions of the Bible are the Word of God. It is presumptuous for any person to claim that what God has had recorded may be rejected in parts because it does not agree with modern science, modern psychology, modern psychiatry, modern historiography, modern literary Biblical criticism, and the modern spirit of the times.

Questions

1. Who distributed John Frey's *Is the Bible Inerrant?* ____
2. Questioning the inerrancy of the Bible was a new development in ____.
3. Dr. William Arndt authored a book called ____.
4. Who took over the major Lutheran denominations? ____
5. What appeared in the September 1965 *Concordia Theological Monthly?* ____
6. Frey's thesis was ____.
7. It is presumptuous for any person to claim ____.

125th Anniversary of Walther's Birth
The Influence of Luther's Principles of Interpretation on C.F.W. Walther's Hermeneutics

Christian News, September 29, 1986

The existence of many different Christian sects and denominations, although all purport to base their theological tenets on the Bible, has been a source of perplexity to Christian and non-Christians alike of both the past and the present alike. While a number of reasons have been advanced for this situation one of the underlying causes bas been correctly stated by former Yale Divinity professor Burrows, when he wrote: "Wrong methods of interpretation have prevented Christians hitherto from arriving at any unity in their understanding of the Scriptures."[1]

There is no error of the human mind which has not claimed support for itself on the basis of some Scripture passage. Polygamy, slavery, racial discrimination and a host of abnormal and absurd religious developments have all used the Bible as the basis for their position.[2] The conclusions which religionists have deduced from Scripture have been determined by the manner in which they have handled Scripture. Even such anti-Christian cults as Christian Science, Mormonism, Spiritualism, Jehovah Witnesses and the newer cults of recent decades have adduced Scriptural warrant for their religious systems.

The differences that distinguish Lutheranism and historic Roman Catholicism, as well as various Protestant bodies from Tridentine theology, are traceable to different hermeneutical approaches to the Bible. The Protestant Reformation was made possible by Luther's rejection of certain hermeneutical principles and the adoption of others not used by Rome.[3] There are a number of different hermeneutical principles that control Roman exegesis and doctrinal teachings when compared with basic principles of hermeneutics as used by Lutherans and Protestants.

Luther is usually considered the father of the various Lutheran churches that sprung up in Germany, Norway, Sweden, Denmark, Iceland, Finland and other European countries, from which lands Lutheranism spread eventually to North America, Central America, South America, Asia, Australia, Africa, certain islands in the various oceans of the world. Those wishing to know the basic principles of Lutheranism can find them in the Book of Concord of 1580.[4] The writings constituting the Book of Concord also contain the hermeneutical principles used by Luther, Melanchthon and the various authors of the *Formula of Concord*. The Lutheran Age of Orthodoxy of the sixteenth and seventeenth centuries basically followed the theology and therefore also the hermeneutics of the Lutheran Confessions. However the Age of Rationalism which followed the Age of Orthodoxy witnessed the challenging as well as the rejection of the teachings and hermeneutics of the

Lutheran Confessions.[5] The Age of Rationalism had a devastating effect on true Lutheran teaching and church practice. It was during this age that C.F.W. Walther was born, lived and received his theological education.[6] The type of theology to which Walther was exposed was far removed from what Luther taught and believed.

On October 25 of this year it will mark one hundred and seventy five years ago that Walther was born in Langenschursdorf, Saxony. His father and grandfather had been Lutheran pastors. C. F. W. Walther was educated in his home town and in Hohenstein, and in the Gymnasium at Schneeburg, from which he graduated in 1829. He studied theology at the University of Leipzig. There he rejected a group of student who read Pietistic books and discussed spiritual experiences. To this group belonged Walther's brother Otto Herman Walther and individuals who later joined and emigrated to America, led by Pastor Stephan, who later made himself bishop. C. F. W. Walther completed his studies at the University of Leipzig and from 1834 till 1836 he served as tutor. In 1837 he became the pastor at Braensdorf, Saxony.[7]

Since on May 11, 1987 it will also be the centennial of the death of C. F. W. Walther, a great deal of attention will be given to the theology and thinking of the man who under God determined the theological direction of "Die Evangelisch-Lutherische Synode vom Missouri, Ohio and Anderen Staaten," later renamed the Lutheran Church-Missouri Synod. As pastor of Trinity Church in St. Louis, as professor and president of Concordia Seminary, St. Louis, as synodical president, as editor and writer Walther has exercised a great influence in molding the direction not only of The Lutheran Church-Missouri Synod, but also of nineteenth century conservative Lutheranism.[8] Not only during his lifetime, but for many years after his death, Walther influenced the teaching and practice of American Lutheranism.

Walther's principles of interpretation greatly influenced the exegetical practice as well as the homiletics of Lutheran pastors. Walther's influence can be seen from the perusal of the writings of Stoeckhardt, A. L. Graebner, L. Fuerbringer, Arndt, P.E. Kretzmann and also by reading the article in *The Abiding Word* in 1947, dealing with Biblical Interpretation.[9] In that presentation the reader will find the hermeneutics of Luther and the Lutheran Confessions as well as that of Walther. In 1947 The Lutheran Church-Missouri Synod celebrated its centennial and the various articles in *The Abiding Word* (2 volumes) reveal the stance of the Synod relative to its theology and the hermeneutics that determined its Scriptural doctrines. Since 1947 there were serious departures from the historic position of the Synod and in attempt has made to introduce the historical critical method in interpretation. Ultimately, this led to a split with about 100,000 people leaving the Synod and forming a new church governed by critical methods of hermeneutics. Others in the Synod may be tempted to adopt newer method, of interpretation, especially when the majority of Lutheran professors in seminaries of the LCA, ALC and the recent offspring group, known as AELC, are using every new method that comes along. Membership in organizations, like the Society of Biblical Literature and other learned societies, represents a temptation for certain scholars to fall in line, claiming that one can use the historical-critical method, and the new hermeneutic provided one begins with Lutheran presuppositions.

The two anniversaries of Walther are a good time for the LCMS to examine her hermeneutical principles and the theological doctrines developed by the use of that hermeneutical methodology.

It will be the purpose of this essay to show the influence which Luther had upon C.F.W. Walther. In Walther the Lutheran Church in America has one of the best interpreters of Luther's hermeneutics and theology. Luther has set forth his hermeneutics in many statements and assertions in his voluminous writings. His commentaries, sermons and writings dealing with texts from the Old and New Testaments are replete with various hermeneutical rules and assertions as to how Holy Writ is properly to be understood.[10] The observant student, who compares Walther's writings with those of Luther, will find a great deal of similarity between these two German theologians. It will be seen that they both followed similar hermeneutical principles in their interpretation of the Scriptures. Luther became the model for Walther who lived three hundred years later.

In the winter semester 1831-1832 Walther spent the semester recuperating it home from an illness and during that time he read copiously in the writings of Luther.[11] From that time on Walther became a life-long student of the Wittenberg Reformer's writings. The use of Luther by Walther has great influence upon the latter's thinking and understanding of Holy Writ in his lectures and books Walther frequently quoted from his great Lutheran forbear and popularized Luther with the Lutheran clergy as well as making the laity of the Synod, he so well served, appreciative of Luther's theology and doctrinal practice.

Walther imbibed the hermeneutical rules of Luther as they are set forth and explicated in his numerous writings and also as they are used in the Book of Concord, toward which Luther contributed the two Catechisms, the Smalcald Articles. Luther's hermeneutical contributions are also evident in the Augsburg Confessions written and composed by Melanchthon. The *Formula of Concord*, written after Luther's death, also reflects the use of Luther's hermeneutics by the various authors of the *Formula of Concord*.

While Luther never wrote a book of Biblical hermeneutics neither did Walther. But the latter listed and discussed the major basic Lutheran hermeneutics in his book, *The Lutheran Church - The True Visible Church of God of Earth*.[12] In Theses XIII-XXI the fundamental rules are given, supported with statements from Holy Writ, the writings of Luther according to the St. Louis edition, and the writings of Lutheran theologians of Lutheran orthodoxy.

The Bible the Source of Doctrine Alone

Luther and Walther recognized the writings of the prophets and evangelists and apostles as the only source and norm for the establishment of doctrine. All teachings of any church were to be judged by these apostolic Scriptures. Both Luther and Walther rejected reason, human tradition and new revelations.[13] Luther did not accept the teachings of the Roman Magisterium. Reason, which played such an important role in the formulation of doctrines and dogmas in Roman theology was repudiated. Thus Luther wrote in the Smalcald Articles: "The Word of God alone shall establish articles of faith and no one else, not even an angel from heaven" (II:2).[13]

Tradition is not allowed according to Luther as asserted by him in the Smalcald Articles (II: 2) and also in a number of his writings (St. L. 15:1926; 1670). In the Smalcald Articles Luther also rules out new revelations as a source for religious knowledge (III: 8:11:2).[14]

Walther followed his spiritual father in rejecting reason used magisterially as a method for arriving at doctrines and for determining ethical directives. Walther was adamant in his rejection of the consensus of the rationalistic professors of Germany who controlled the thinking of universities in Saxony. In Thesis XIII Walther declared: "The Ev. Lutheran Church recognizes the written Word of the apostles and prophets as the only source and perfect source, norm, and judge of all teaching - a. not reason, b. not tradition, c. not new revelations."[15] Walther cited the following Bible passages as setting forth this hermeneutical principle: Deut. 4:2; Josh. 23:6; Is. 8: 20; Luke 16:29; 2 Tim. 3:15-17; I Cor. 1:21; 2:4-5,15: Col. 2:8; Matt. 15:9."

The Infallibility of the Word of God

Both Luther and Walther refused to believe the allegation that Holy Writ had errors and mistakes in the text as it left the pens of the inspired writers. Luther wrote: "The Scriptures has never erred."[17] or "It's impossible that Scripture should err."[18] C. F. W. Walther appears to have been of the same opinion. In *Lehre und Wehre*, vol. 21:35, he averred" "Whosoever believes with all his heart that the Bible is the Word of God cannot believe anything else but that it is inerrant."

When Luther lived the historical-critical method had not yet been developed and its conclusions applied to the exegesis of the Bible. But by Walther's time a higher criticism of a negative type had been developed in Germany and other European countries.[19] Lutheran theologians in Germany have the dubious honor of developing and promoting a type of Biblical Criticism that undermined the reliability and infallibility of the Old and the New Testaments. Walther, as has already been stated, was reared in rationalistic surroundings. One of the rationalism's tenets was that the books of both the Old and New Testaments contained errors, contradictions and mistakes. Such a presupposition clearly undermined the reliability of God's Word and made dubious its teachings.

The infallibility of the inerrancy of Holy Writ become a burning issue in the nineteenth century in Germany.[20] Nineteenth- century Germany produced an unbroken phalanx of theologians who attacked the claims which the Word of God made about itself. In the January issue of 1886 of *Lehre und Wehre,* Walther took issue with professors, Volk and Muehlau, who rejected the inerrancy of the Bible. When these two professors made this claim, there was no protest from any theological faculty in Germany, for they all generally agreed with them and repudiated the inerrancy of God's Word.[21]

According to Walther's position such a stance was entirely wrong, because the readers of the Bible would be able to decide as to what is true and what is false, erroneous and deceptive. The act of distinguishing as to what belonged to the plan of salvation and what was not essential to it, amounted to the reader sitting in judgment on how God had expressed Himself in HIS Word, and, therefore was tantamount to refusing to submit to God's authority as expressed by His writers in His Word.

The Clearness and Perspicuity of the Bible

Both Luther and Walther believed in the perspicuity or clarity of God's inscripturated Revelation. Both of these Lutheran exegetes understood Psalm 119:105: "Thy Word is a lamp unto my feet and a light unto my path," as teaching the perspicuity and clarity of the Bible. They further were convinced that II Peter 1:19, where the Word of God is called "a more sure word of prophecy," showed and taught clearly the clarity of God's Word. In various writings of the Reformer this truth was enunciated.[22] In his exposition of Psalm 37 Luther stated: If any one of them (the papists) should trouble you and say: "You must have the interpretations of the Fathers since Scripture is obscure," then reply: "It is not true there is no clearer book upon earth than the Bible, which in comparison to all other books is like the sun in relation to all other lights. They say such things because they want to lead us away from Scripture and elevate themselves over us in order that we might believe their sermons based upon their own dreams do not permit yourselves to be led out and away from Scriptures, no matter how hard they (the papists) may try, because if you get away from Scripture, you are lost: then they will mislead you as they please. But if you stay in the Bible you have the victory. . . Be absolutely certain that there is nothing else than the clear sun behind. So if you find an obscure passage in Scripture, do not be alarmed, for certainly the same truth is set forth in it which is in another place taught plainly. If you cannot understand the obscure, then adhere to the clear."[23] Walther in Thesis XIV wrote: "The Ev. Lutheran Church holds to the clearness of Scripture" (There are no "views" and "open questions").[24]

The Bible Interprets Itself

Both Luther and Walther followed the Biblical hermeneutical principle that Scripture interprets Scripture. The only authentic interpreter of the Bible, is the Bible itself. Human reason, under the direction of the Holy Spirit, is the instrument through which interpretation and exposition take place. In his writings Luther has written clearly on this principle. Thus he said: "No clearer book has been written than the Holy Bible... It is a horrible crime against Scripture and all Christendom to say that the Bible is dark and not so clear that everybody may understand it in order to teach and proclaim his faith."[25] With this position Walther agreed when he wrote in Thesis XVI: "The Ev. Lutheran Church accepts God's Word as it interprets itself."[26] In a number of passages in the New Testament the Holy Spirit tells us that David Isaiah, and Moses spoke about Jesus many centuries prior to Jesus' birth. Jesus says that Abraham saw Christ's day (John 8:56). John 12:41 states that Isaiah in Chapter 6 saw the glory of Christ. The New Testament tell us clearly that in Old Testament times the coming of Christ, the establishment of the Messianic Age and its blessings were foretold. Modern critical scholarship rejects the clear assertions of the New Testament about the Old Testament, thus rejecting the principle that Scripture interprets Scripture. In this respect, there is a great cleavage between Biblical Lutheran hermeneutics and higher critical hermeneutics.

The Literal Sense is the True Sense of a Passage

Both Luther and Walther held that the literal sense of the text was the true sense and that the text had only one intended sense. By Luther's time it was customary to find four different senses in a text Luther rejected the fourfold meaning ascribed to a Biblical text. During the Middle Ages, in fact, lasting till the time of the Reformation, the Roman Church sponsored the theory that the fourfold sense of a Biblical passage was permissible with regard to individual texts.[28] This meant that the reader or interpreter could give a text a meaning which was not at all suggested by the text's literal meaning and intent. To follow such a hermeneutical procedure means injecting a highly subjective element into the understanding of God's Word. The same text cannot have one meaning in one place, in the Old Testament and another in the New Testament. Thus in Psalm 110, the most frequently cited Messianic text in the New Testament, it is said by critical scholars to refer to David or some other king and is a psalm used at the coronation of the king.[29] Yet the New Testament portrays Christ as claiming that in Psalm 110:1 and 110:4 David was speaking about the future Messiah with whom Jesus identified Himself. The writer of Hebrews also treats Psalm 110 as speaking about Christ. So here one has the situation where critical scholars claim that Jesus was giving the Old Testament text a completely different meaning than the writer of Psalm 110 had in mind.

Against allegorization in interpretation, Luther in commenting on Isaiah 36:6, asserted:

The Christian reader should devote his first effort to searching what is called the literal sense. It alone is the entire substance of faith and Christian theology it holds its own in tribulation and temptations and gains the victory over the gates of hell and triumphs to the praise and glory of God. But allegory is often uncertain and unreliable and very unsafe as a prop of faith, since it frequently depends upon human conjectures and opinions. If anyone leans on it, he is leaning on the reed of Egypt.[30]

Walther subscribed to these views of the Reformer. He says in Thesis XVI: "The Ev. Lutheran Church accepts God's Word as it interprets itself." Walther further has nine corollaries under Thesis XVI. Corollaries C and D say as follows: "The Ev. Lutheran Church acknowledges only the literal sense as the true sense." (C), and corollary D say: "The Ev. Lutheran Church holds the literal sense has but one sense."[31] He quotes Pfeiffer to the effect that a person can never be certain of any sense, if he ignores the common sense rule: "A text has only one intended sense." He also referred to Luther's statements in the St. Louis edition of Luther's writings, vol. 18:1307 and 4:1304f.[32]

Luther insisted that the Scriptures be interpreted in their literal sense because they had been given by God. Averred the Wittenberg Reformer: "The Holy Spirit is the plainest writer and speaker in heaven or earth. His words can therefore have no more than one sense, and it is the most obvious sense. This we call the literal or natural sense . . . It is surer and safer to abide by the words in the simple sense."[33]

Thus for Luther the meaning of Genesis 2:7: "And the LORD God formed man from the dust of the ground and breathed into man the breath of life and man became a living being," could not be interpreted as now, that out of some apelike creature there evolved a man. Walther would argue the same way. When a text was to be understood to a literal sense, the reformer was convinced that it should not be dealt with figuratively.

Treating a text figuratively when its intention is literal concerning such interpretative procedure Luther declared:

It is the manner of all who evade arguments by means of figurative language, arrogantly holding the text itself in contempt and having for their aim merely to pick out a certain term and twisting and crucifying it on the cross of their own opinion with utter disregard of the circumstances, of the preceding and following context, and of the intent and purpose of the writer.[34]

Luther insisted:

Whoever is so bold as to give the words of Scripture a meaning that differs from the sense that their simple sound confers is obliged to prove his explanation from the text before him or from the article of faith.[35]

On another occasion he declared:

Neither a conclusion or a figure of speech should be admitted in any place of the Bible, unless evident contextual circumstances or the absurdity of anything militating against an article of faith requires it. On the contrary, we must everywhere adhere to the simple, pure and natural meaning of the words. This accords with the rules of grammar and the usage of speech which God gave men.[36]

Walther in thesis XVI, corollary B reads: "The Ev. Lutheran Church, in the interpretation of the words and sentences, holds to the usage of language."[37] Under F he opined: "The Ev. Lutheran Church acknowledges the literal sense may be the improper sense as well as the proper; but it does not depart from the proper sense unless forced by Scripture itself — either the circumstances of the text itself or a parallel passage or analogy of faith."[38]

The Context Determines Meaning

Both Luther and Walther agreed that in the interpretation of Holy Writ the interpreter must be guided by the context and intention of the writer. Thus Luther wrote: "Neither the God elusion or a figure of speech should be admitted in any place of the Bible unless evident contextual circumstances or the absurdity of anything obviously militating against an article of faith requires it. On the contrary we must everywhere adhere to the simple, pure and natural meaning of the words. This accords with the rules of grammar and the usage of speech which God has given men."[39]

Walther shared the same principle when he asserted in Thesis XVI E: "The Ev. Lutheran Church, in interpreting, is guided by the context and the intention. Otherwise the Scripture is garbled.[40] Walther cited the Apology as setting forth this principle: "Passages, when produced in their entirety very frequently brought the interpretation with them." Article III, Paragraph 159.[41]

The Original Text Determines the Meaning of a Text

One of the revolutionary hermeneutical principles adopted by Luther was the insistence that the Vulgate, a translation, did not determine the meaning of a Biblical passage. Thus Luther in his letter to the councilmen of Germany declared:

Let us then, foster the languages as zealously as we love the Gospel. For it is not meaningless that God caused His Scripture to be written in these two languages only: the Old Testament in Hebrew the New in Greek. The languages, therefore, which God did not despise but chose above all others we, too, ought to honor above all others.[42]

By rejecting the Vulgate as the original text, mistranslations were automatically eliminated. Thus the Vulgate's translation of Genesis 3:15, where Jerome mistranslated the third masculine personal hu by "she," is thus taken care of and an important Roman Catholic text in Mariology removed.[43]

Walther under Thesis XVI, agreed with Luther when writing: "The Ev. Lutheran Church lets the original text alone decide."[44] He quoted Pfeiffer to the effect: "This must be maintained over against the papists, who ascribe canonical authority to their Latin version, the Vulgate."[45]

Dark Passages Must Be Interpreted in the Light of the Clear Ones

Peter in his second letter to the congregations of Asia Minor called attention to the fact that in the letters of Paul there were somethings that were difficult to understand (3:16). With this Luther agreed, as did also Walther. In his commentary on Deuteronomy the Reformer asserted: "It is the nature of Holy Writ that it interprets itself on the basis of passages and places and by means of the rule of faith. That is above all the most certain way to establish the meaning of Scripture, namely by comparison and by taking into consideration of many passages that you must contrive to obtain understanding."[46] In a sermon delivered on the Gospel for St.

James Day Luther declared that dark passages are not to be enlightened by human wisdom but by a comparison with other Bible passages."[47]

In Thesis XVI, G Walther wrote: "The Ev Lutheran Church interprets dark passages by the clear ones."[48] In support of this hermeneutical rule Walther cited the writings of Luther (St. L. 3:2042; 11: 3108 f). He also concluded a quotation from Quenstedt who averred. "For above all there exist Biblical assertions which are like the sun in relationship to others which in comparison shine like stars."[49]

Doctrines Only to Be Established from
Seats of Doctrine (Sedes doctrinae) Passages

Both Luther and Walther held to the rule that articles of faith were to be deduced from passages which specifically taught them. Here are Luther's words setting forth this principle "It is not enough to cite a different passage without the slightest regard to whether it proves the same point or something else. No mistake as more easily and commonly made in dealing with the Bible than bringing together Scripture passages that are different, as though they were identical."[50]

Walther followed the father of Lutheranism in using this same hermeneutical rule in his exegesis. Thesis XVI, he asserts: "The Ev. Lutheran Church takes articles of faith from the text constituting the seat or doctrine and judges all ober dicta accordingly."[51] The St. Louis professor referred to Luther's view as the latter expresses it in his treatise. "On the Heavenly Prophets" (St. L. xx285f.) and a statement from Gerhard's **de interpretation**, S.S. Par 212.[52]

The Entire Bible Is God's Word

Both Luther and Walther accepted the entire Bible as the Word of God. Both of these Lutheran theologians considered nothing in the Bible as superfluous or of little worth but everything needful and important, and they accepted all teaching deduced or necessary from the word of Scripture. Luther spoke about the matter in St. Louis ed., vol. 20:775. Walther enunciated Luther's position in Thesis XVII, which stated. "The Ev. Lutheran Church accepts the whole written Word of God as God's Word, deems nothing in it superfluous or of little worth but everything needful and important, and also accepts the teaching deduced of necessary from the word of Scripture."[51a] The St. Louis divine adduced the following Scripture as setting forth this position: Matt. 5:18,19; Rev. 22:18,19 and Matt. 22:29-32.[53]

In the Bible or God's Word Luther did not include the books of the Apocrypha, many of which were only available to the Greek and Latin languages. Relative to the Old Testament this meant a smaller canon than the one followed by Rome, from which certain doctrines were adduced that disagreed with those in other parts of the Old and New Testament. Both the Council of Trent (1545-67) and Vatican I (1870) had declared the Latin Vulgate as the text to which ultimate appeal had to be when the finality for certain doctrines was to be determined. Walther followed Luther in declaring, as he does in Thesis XVI,A: "The Ev.

Lutheran Church lets the original text alone decide."[54] He cited Pfeiffer: "This must be maintained over against the papists, who ascribe canonical authority to their Laun version, the Vulgate."[55]

The Importance and Necessity of
Giving Each Doctrine Its Proper Place

Both Luther and Walther contended that it is necessary to give each doctrine its proper place, as assigned by the Scripture. Outstanding in Luther's theology was the belief that the heart of Holy Writ was Christ.[56] One of the chief hermeneutical principles of Luther was his Christological principle. That for him was a hermeneutical rule. Thus Luther wrote: "The whole Scripture exists for the Son of God."[57] The reason the Reformer emphasized Christ was that with him the doctrine of justification by faith was intimately bound with Christ. Luther made Christ the center of the whole Bible because Christ Himself said that the Old Testament testified to Him (John 5:39) and Paul declared that all Scripture, given by inspiration was able to make its readers believe in Christ (2 Tim. 3:15-17). Christ was the main thrust of the Old Testament and the heart of the New Testament because as the Lamb of God he took away the sins of the world. (John 1:29). Through Christ the world has reconciled to the Father.

Walther again followed Luther in his Christological approach, when he wrote in the Thesis XVIII; "The Ev. Lutheran Church gives to each teaching of God's Word the place and importance it has in God's Word itself."[58] Under A of this thesis Walther declared: "It makes the teaching concerning Christ of justification, the foundation and marrow and guiding star of all teaching."[59] Biblical support he found in the following Scriptures: 1 Cor. 3:11; 2:2; 15:3 and Rev. 19:10. He also showed that this was the theological stance of the Lutheran Confessions, listing Articles XXVI and XXVII of the Augsburg Confession.[60] Walther completely agreed with Luther when the latter asserted: "Scripture as to be understood as testifying for Christ, not against Him; it must therefore be considered as a referring to Him; or not to be considered true Scripture."[61] In affirming that Scripture is God's Word insofar as it impels toward Christ, Luther was laying down a hermeneutical principle of interpretation, not of selection. There is no part of Scripture which does not impel toward Christ.[62]

The Distinction Between Law & Gospel

A central concern for Luther when dealing with the contents of Holy Writ was properly to distinguish between Law and Gospel. Plass said about the making of this distinction on Luther's part: "Few, if any, theologians have insisted more emphatically than did Martin Luther on the indispensable necessity of sharply defining the areas within which the Law and Gospel were designed to apply. And probably no statement of the Doctor on this point is better known than his words in the New Year's Sermon of 1532, on Gal. 3:23-24 which was devoted to this subject."[63]

571

In this sermon Luther made this illuminating assertion: "The difference between Law and Gospel is the height of knowledge in Christendom. Every person and all persons who assume or glory in the name of Christian should know and be able to state this difference. If this ability is lacking one can not tell a Christian from a heathen or a Jew, or such supreme importance is the differentiation."[64]

"That is why Paul so strongly insists on a clean-cut and proper differentiation among Christians of these two doctrines. To be sure both are God's Word, the Law or the Ten Commandments, and the Gospel, the latter first given by God in Paradise, the former on Mt. Sanai. But everything depends on not mixing them together, otherwise one will know and retain the proper understanding of neither the one or the other; nay, while under the impression of having both, one will have neither."[64]

"Therefore place the man who is able to divorce the Law from the Gospel at the head of the list and call him a Doctor of Holy Scriptures, for without the Holy Spirit the attainment of this differentiation is impossible."[64]

Walther was greatly impressed with the need to differentiate between Law and Gospel. One of the greatest books written by this follower of Luther was the volume considered a classic by many *The Proper Distinction between Law and Gospel*, a volume replete with quotations from Luther's writings.[65] In Thesis XVIII B Walther averred: "The Ev. Lutheran Church distinguishes sharply between Law and Gospel."[66] As Scriptural support he referred to John 1:17, Rom. 10:4; 2 Tim. 2:15. The *Formula of Concord*, Epitome V is listed as teaching the same principle. From the St. L edition of *Luther's Works* Walther cited vol. 8, p. 806.[67]

The Distinction between Fundamental and Non-Fundamental Doctrine.

Luther emphasized especially those doctrines as central that dealt with Christ and the plan for salvation. But this distinction did not permit or allow the rejection of teachings not essential to salvation. Luther wrote: "We should not be master of ourselves according to our mad heads, setting ourselves above Scripture."[68] In thesis XVIII, C Walther claimed that "the Ev. Lutheran Church distinguishes sharply between fundamental and non-fundamental articles of doctrine contained in Scripture."[69] Walther gave 1 Cor. 3:11-15 as a passage that enunciates this hermeneutical principle.[70]

The Distinction between the Old Testament and the New Testament

Not all commandments, ethical directives and injunctions given in the Old Testament are applicable to all times of human history. The Hebrews were Yahweh's chosen people. God gave them ceremonial laws, cultic directives, laws relative to food which had a preparatory function. The Sabbath commandment was not to be binding till Christ returns. The military program enjoined upon Joshua and Israel was not meant for all periods of human history. As Paul informed the Colossians, many of the ceremonials and Old Testament feast days were preparatory for Christ's coming, but when Christ came they were abolished. Luther, therefore distinguished between the revelation of God given to the Israel according to the flesh and the New Israel of God, which came into existence with the Messiah's coming. Luther considered the Old Testament as the twilight and midday of revelation. He wrote that "an Old Testament times the precious metal still lies half-buried in the pit." Again "The Old Testament contains the articles of faith only in a general way and in the manner points to Christ. Aside from this, it is not different from the New Testament."[72]

In a Sermon on I Peter 1:10-12 Luther has given an excellent discourse on the value of the Old Testament. He rejects the position of those who did not esteem the Old Testament highly and who were in favor of not using it much. He showed how the New Testament faith as based upon the Old but also pointed out that they are not the same in every respect.[73]

Walther held the same view about the difference between the two testaments, distinguishing between what was binding on present day Christians and what was not. Thus in Thesis XVIIIE, he declared: "The Ev. Lutheran Church distinguishes sharply and cautiously between the Old Testament and the New Testament."[74] Two New Testament passages given as teaching this distinction are given as being Gal. 4:1-5,7 and Col. 2:16-17.[75]

Only Those Doctrines Are To Be Accepted That Are In The Bible

Luther rejected many teachings and dogmas either taught by the Apocrypha by the Tradition of the Roman Church. Teachings and dogmas not contained in the Bible were not recognized or even rejected because they contradicted clearly revealed teachings of God's Word.[76] Walther followed his spiritual forbear by insisting on the acceptance and promulgation of those teachings found only in the canonical Scriptures. In Thesis XIX the former president of the old LCMS declared: "The Ev. Lutheran Church accepts no testimony as an article of faith which is not contained in the Word of God and therefore not absolutely sure and certain."[77] Hebrews 11:1; Titus 1:9; 2 Peter 1:19 are Bible passages given as proving this principle of hermeneutics.[78] Walther also quoted the Apology as follows: "There are many good men to whom this doubt is made more bitter than death. You do not consider sufficiently how great a subject religion is if you think that good men are in anguish for a slight cause whenever they begin to doubt concerning any dogma," Article IV, par. 31."[71] From the St. Louis edition of Luther's writings he cited passages from Volume 8, 1003 and Volume 48, 1678.[80]

Interpretation Must Agree with the Analogy of Faith

According to both Luther and Walther all doctrinal formulations must agree with the analogy of faith. What is meant by the analogy of faith? Arndt defined it "as the true norm of Scripture doctrine which no interpreter must offend; It is the sum total of all clear passages of Scripture

573

which set forth a doctrine of doctrines."[81]

In a sermon on John 6:27, Luther contended that because of the emphatic words of Christ that he alone gives salvation to men, all passages of Scripture must be understood in harmony with this basic teaching.[82]

Again a Sermon of February 11, 1531 Luther asserted:

We are, then, to ascribe our salvation in the Son alone and to give the honor to the Father who speaks of the Son through the Son. My good works are not to give me eternal life, but before I do anything good, I am to have eternal life and the Holy Spirit, and be a child of God. We must interpret Scripture according to this article. Whoever has this article will not err, but whoever lacks it will accomplish nothing.[83]

Walther took the same stand relative to the use of the analogy of faith when in Thesis XVI, he asserted: "The Ev. Lutheran Church rejects out of hand every interpretation not in harmony with the analogy of faith. (Rom. 12:7)."[84] His position Walther supported from the Apology, Article XX- VIII, par. 60, as follows: "Examples ought to be interpreted according to the rule. i.e. according to certain and clear passages."[85]

The Lutheran Confessions as A Hermeneutical Guide

In Thesis XXI Walther claimed that "The Ev. Lutheran Church is sure that the teaching contained in its Symbols is the pure God's truth because it agrees with the written Word of God in all points."[86] This position was found already in the statements found in the Augsburg Confession and the Smalcald Articles, all the product of Luther's lifetime.[87] Walther quotes from the Lutheran Confessions to establish and support this hermeneutical principle. No Biblical interpretation can stand which rejects the fundamental articles of faith as they have been set forth in the ecumenical creeds or in the confessional writings constituting the Book of Concord.[88]

Footnote

1. Millar Burrows, *An Outline of Biblical Theology* (Philadelphia: The Westminster Press, 1946), p. 51.
2. W.R. Harper, *Religion and the Higher Life* (Chicago: The University of Chicago Press, 1904), p. 171.
3. Raymond F. Surburg, "The Significance of Luther's Hermeneutics for the Protestant Reformation," *Concordia Theological Monthly*, 34:241-261, April 1953.
4. Cf. Ralph A. Bohlmann, *Principles of Biblical Interpretation in the Lutheran Confessions* (Revised Edition: St. Louis: Concordia Publishing House, 1983), pp. 1-111.
5. Lewis W. S pitz, "Lutheran Theology, After 1580," E. L. Lueker, Editor, *Lutheran Cyclopedia* (St. Louis: Concordia Publishing House, 1975), p. 506.
6. W .G. Polack, *The Story of Walther's Life* (St. Louis: Concordia Publishing House, 1935), John M. Drickamer, "C.F.W. Walther," Evangelium, 13:2, April 1981, p. 55-58.
7. Lewis W. Spitz, "Milestones in Walther's Life," *Concordia Theological Monthly*, 32:664, October, 1961.
8. Otto W. Heick, *A History of Christian Thought* (Philadelphia: Fortress Press, 1966), ii, P. 458-461.
9. Victor E. Mennicke, "Bible Interpretation," in Theodore Laetsch, Editor, *The Abiding Word* (St. Louis: Concordia Publishing House, 1947), II, pp. 35-58.
10. Cf. the series of articles by P. Hoppe, "Graundzuege Lutherischer Hermeneutik" *Lehre*

und Wehre, 28:57-71, February 1882: 108-111. Maerz, 1882; 148-156, April, 1882.

11. Lewis W. Spitz, "Walther's Contribution to Lutheranism," *Concordia Theological Monthly*, 32:583, October, 1961.

12. C.F.W. Walther, Do Evangelische-Lutherische Kirche die wahre sichtbare Kirche Gottes auf Erden (St. Louis: Lutherischer Concordia Verlag, 1891), pp. 58-138. This portion has been summarized by Wm. Dallmann, W. H. T. Dau and Th. Engelder, *Walther and the Church* (St. Louis: Concordia Publishing House, 1938), pp. 123-128. The translation in this book will be used in giving Walther's hermeneutical principles.

13. Concordia Triglotta, *The Symbolical Books of the Lutheran Church* (St. Louis: Concordia Publishing House, p. 467)

14. Triglotta, **op. cit.**, p. 482.

15. D. Martin Luther's *Saemtlichen Schriften*, 23 volumes in 25 vol. Edited by Johann G. Walch (St. Louis: Concordia Publishing House, 1880-1910), vol. 15. 1916; vol. 19, p. 858.

16. Walther, Die wehre sichtbare Kirche, **op. cit.** 60.

17. D. Martin Luther Werke, Kritische Gesamtausgabe (Weimar, 1883-), 15:1481.

18. *Luther's Works*, Weimar Ausgabe, 9:351.

19. Spitz, "Walther's Contribution to Lutheranism," *Concordia Theological Monthly*, **op. cit.**, p. 583.

20. Robert D. Preus, "Walther and the Scriptures," *Concordia Theological Monthly*, 32:670, November 1961.

21. **Ibid.**

22. *Luther's Werke*, St. L., 5:334, 18:166ff.

23. **Ibid.**, 5:334ff. Cf. also John Theodore Mueller, *Christian Dogmatics* (St .Louis: Concordia Publishing House, 1955), pp. 139-141.

24. Walther, Die wahre sichtbare, Kirche, **op. cit.**, p. 66.

25. *Luther's Werke*, Weimar, 8:236.

26. Walther, Die wahre sichtbare Kirche, **op. cit.**, p. 77.

27. Claus Westermann Editor, *Essays in Old Testament Hermeneutics* (Richmond: John Knox Press, 1964). Cf. the essay by Rudolf Bultmann "Prophecy and Fulfillment, pp. 50-75.

28. Robert M. Grant, *A Short History of the Interpretation of the Bible* (New York and London: The Macmillan Company, 1972), pp. 119-120.

29. Arthur Weiser, *The Psalms, The Old Testament Library*. (Philadelphia: Westminster Press, 1962), pp. 692-697.

30. *Luther's Werke*,Weimar Ausgabe, 14:560.

31. Walther, *Die wahre sichtbare Kirche*, **op. cit.**, p. 85.

32. **Ibid.**, p. 89.

33. *Luther's Werke*, Weimar Ausgabe, 23:92.

34. Weimar Ausgabe, 18:713.

35. **Ibid.**, 23:92.

36. **Ibid.**, 18:700.

37. Walther, *Die wahre sichtbare Kirche*, **op. cit.**, p. 81.

38. **Ibid.**, p. 92.

39. Weimar Ausgabe, 18:700.

40. Walther, *Die wahre sichtbare Kirche*, **op. cit.**, p. 92.

41. **Ibid.**, p. 91.

42. Weimar Ausgabe 15:36f.

43. *Biblia Sacra Juxta Vulgatam Clementinam* (Romae-Tornaci-Parisis: Typis Societatis S. Joannis Evang. Desclee et Socii, 1956), p. 3.

44. Walther, *Die wahre sichtbare Kirche*, **op. cit.**, p. 79.
45. **Ibid.**, p. 81.
46. *Luther's Works*, St. L. 3: 2042.
47. **Ibid.**, 11:3108.
48. Walther, *Die wahre sichtbare Kirche*, **op. cit.**, p. 69.
49. Theol. Didactico-pol. Th. I, Ch. 41, Sec. 2 Question 14, fol. 199.
50. Weimar Ausgabe, 18;728.
51. Walther, *Die wahre sichtbare Kirche*, **op. cit.**, p. 99.
52. **Ibid.**, p. 100.
52a. **Ibid.**, p. 104.
53. **Ibid.**, pp. 104-105.
54. **Ibid.**, p. 79.
55. **Ibid.**, p. 31.
56. A .S. Wood, *Luther's Principles of Interpretation* (London: Tyndale Press, 1960), p. 33.
57. *Luther's Works*, Weimar Ausgabe, Tr. 5, 5585.
58. Walther, *Die wahre sichtbare Kirche* ,**op. cit.**, p. 108.
59. **Ibid.**
60. **Ibid.**, pp. 109-110.
61. *Luther's Works*, Weimar Ausgabe, 39:1,47.
62. Cf. Raymond F. Surburg , "Luther's Attitude toward Scripture," Part II of *A Summary of Lutheran Hermeneutical Principles* (Springfield: IL: Concordia Seminary Printshop, 1975), p. 6.
63. Ewald M. Plass, *What Luther Says, An Anthology* (St. Louis: Concordia Publishing House, 1959), II, p. 732.
64. *Luther's Works*, Weimar Ausgabe, 34: 25,29.
65. C.F.W. Walther, *The Proper Distinction between Law and Gospel*. Reproduced from the German edition of 1897 by W. H. T. Dau (St. Louis: Concordia Publishing House, 1929), 426 pp. for a condensation, C.F.W. Walther, Walther C. Pieper (condenser) *God's No and God's Yes. The Proper Distinction between Law and Gospel* (St. Louis: Concordia Publishing House, 1973), 118 pp.
66. Walther, Die wahre sichtbare Kirche, **op. cit.**, p. 111.
67. **Ibid.**, pp. 112-113.
68. *Luther's Works*, Weimar Ausgabe, 47:367.
69. Walther, *Die wahre sichtbare Kirche*, **op. cit.**, p. 114.
70. **Ibid.**
71. *Luther's Works*, Weimar Ausgabe, p. 10, II 186.
72. **Ibid.**, W-T 4, No. 5105.
73. **Ibid.**, 12:275.
74. Walther, *Die wahre sichtbare Kirche*, **op. cit.**, p. 127.
75. **Ibid.**, p. 128.
76. *Luther's Works*, St. L., 17:1680-86; 8:1032-1034; 19:1604f.
77. Walther, *Die wahre sichtbare Kirche*, **op. cit.**, 130.
78. **Ibid.**, pp. 130-131.
79. **Ibid.**, p. 131.
80. **Ibid.**
81. W. Arndt, "Hermeneutics," *Lutheran Cyclopedia* (St. Louis: Concordia Publishing House, 1954), p. 463.
82. *Luther's Works*, Weimar Ausgabe, 33:20f).
83. **Ibid.**, 33; 165f.
84. Walther, *Die wahre sichtbare Kirche*, **op. cit.**, p. 100.

85. Apology, Article XXVII, Paragraph 60.
86. Walther, *Die wahre sichtbare Kirche*, o. cit., p. 138.
87. Augsburg Confession XXI. Smalcald Articles. Preface.
88. Walther, *Die wahre sichtbare Kirche*, **op. cit.**, Thesis XXI, B., P. 124 of also Arthur Carl Piepkorn, "Walther and the Lutheran Symbiosis," *Concordia Theological Monthly*. 32:606-620, October 1961.

Questions

1. What has been a source of perplexity to Christian and non-Christians alike? ____
2. Yale University professor Burrows wrote ___.
3. The basic principles of Lutheranism can be found in ____.
4. C.F.W. Walther was born in the age of ____.
5. Walther was born in ____.
6. He studied theology at the University of ____.
7. In 1837 Walther became the pastor at ____.
8. Walther served as ____.
9. What led to a split of some 100,000 leaving the LCMS? ____
10. The majority of the professors of the LCA, ALC, and AELC used ____.
11. Membership in or organizations like the Society of Biblical Literature represents a temptation for some scholars to ____.
12. ____ became the model for ____.
13. When he was ill in the winter semester 1831-1832 Walther read copiously ____.
14. Luther and Walther recognized the writings of the prophets and evangelists as ____.
15. Luther wrote "The Scriptures has never ____."
16. The ____ of Holy Writ became a burning issue in the nineteenth century.
17. Both Luther and Walther affirmed the ____ of Scripture.
18. Luther and Walther maintain that Scripture ____.
19. Modern critical scholarship rejects the clear assertions of the Old Testament about ____.
20. The literal sense is the one ____.
21. The New Testament teaches that David in Psalm 110 was speaking about ____.
22. For Luther the meaning of Genesis 2:7 could not be interpreted to refer to ___.
23. The papists ascribe canonical authority to ____.
24. Dark passages of Scripture are to be enlightened by ____.
25. Luther did not include ___ in the Bible.
26. Luther made ___ the center of the whole Bible.
27. Luther said the height of knowledge in Christendom is ____.
28. Who should be called a Doctor of Holy Scripture? ____
29. The ____ was not to be binding until Christ returns.
30. Luther distinguished between the revelation given to the Israel according to the flesh and to the ____.
31. What is the analogy of faith? ____

The Relationship of Genesis 3:15
To The Incarnation of God's Son

Christian News, December 15, 1986

Genesis 3:15 has been variously understood. Before the age of rationalism and the coming of the use of the historical critical method in Biblical interpretation, Genesis 3:15 was considered by Christians of different schools of theological persuasion to be a promise of a coming Redeemer, who would ultimately save the world from the curse of all forms of death (physical, spiritual and eternal), to which Eve and Adam had become subject to because of their disobedience of God's command. The first parents of the human race had received instruction that they could eat of all the trees in the garden of Eden, except the tree of the knowledge of good and evil, of which they were not to eat. After the fall of the woman and the man, God called all three participants to account: the serpent, Eve and Adam. A curse was pronounced on each of the three.

The words addressed by the LORD God to the serpent, contained a curse for the serpent and a future blessing for man. To the devil or Satan, who had employed the serpent as the instrument of temptation, God said: "I will set enmity between thee and the woman and between thy seed and her seed, he shall bruise thee in regard to the head and thou shall bruise him in regard to the heel."[1]

For the last one hundred years or so, the traditional Christian interpretation has been challenged and repudiated by higher critical scholars. A comparison of a number of modern Bible translations reveals a significant difference as to how the Hebrew of Genesis 3:15 is understood and translated. Already the Septuagint (LXX) in the third or second pre-Christian centuries did not correctly render the Hebrew text. The LXX test translated: Kai exthran theso ana meson sou kai, ana meson ths gynaikos, kai ana meson tou spermatos sou, kai ana meson tou spermatos autes. Autos sou teresei kephalen, kai su tereseis autou pternan."[2] "And I will put enmity between thee and the woman and between thy seed and her seed, he shall watch against thy head, and thou shall watch against his heel."[3]

The Vulgate has not translated the Hebrew text correctly. In Latin Genesis 3:15 reads: "Inimicitias ponam inter te et mulierem, et semen illius; ipsa conteret caput tuum, et tuinsidiaberis calcaneo ejus."[4]

"And I will establish a feud between thee and the woman, between thy offspring and hers, she is to crush your head, whilst thou dost ambush at her heel." Thus does Bishop Knox translate this Vulgate verse.[5]

Only the Peshitta of the three ancient versions has rendered the Hebrew of Genesis 3:15 correctly. This version has the following rendering for the verse, called the Protevangel: "I will set enmity between you and the woman between your seed and her seed; he will dash your head and you will bruise his heel."[6]

The Nature of the Literary Genre of Genesis 3

An examination of different translations now existing will reveal the fact that the respective translations will be determined as to whether their translators considered Genesis 3 as recording historical events that occurred in calendar time, or whether Genesis can be classified as myth, saga, allegory, poetry or containing non-literal depth language.[7]

How a scholar or translator understands the type of literature in Genesis will determine how he renders the Hebrew noun "tzera" and also the Hebrew verb "shuph." Does the word "tserah" have a plural or collective meaning or a singular connotation? Both meanings are found in the literature of the Old Testament.[8] Another important matter that is answered differently and this will also determine the translation of Genesis 3:15 is the question who was the tempter of Eve and Adam? Was it merely a snake or was it the devil or Satan who employed the serpent as his instrument of temptation?

The Serpent as an Instrument of Satan

The Bible teaches us that there existed an evil power and principle working in and through this snake, namely, the devil. It was this power that used the organs of the serpent to speak, just as the evil spirits usurped the powers of the human voice and entered into the swine in Mark 8. While there are scholars who claim that in the Old Testament Satan is a helpful angel;[9] the New Testament belies such an interpretation. The evil principle, spirit, and power is identified and described in the following Bible passages:

Revelation 12:9 where Christ, in his revelation to John, speaks of "that old serpent, called the devil, and Satan, which deceived the whole world." In the same book, chapter 12:2 the text speaks of "that old serpent which is the devil and Satan." Paul in 2 Corinthians 11:3 mentions the serpent that beguiled Eve as the same agency that corrupts Christians, i.e. the devil. In John 8:44 Christ says of the Jews that they are of their father, the devil, and that he is a murderer and that he is a liar and the father of it", i.e. the one who originated lies, the one guilty of the first lie, spoken in Eden. Romans 16:20 brings the greeting of St. Paul which is a plain illusion to this passage: "And the Gog of peace shall bruise Satan under your feet shortly."

To interpret Genesis 3 as a record of only a snake speaking and the word "tzera" as referring to the descendants of the snake and the descendants of woman as members of mankind completely eliminated the Messianic meaning of a verse that the Christian world for nearly two thousand years considered a prophecy of both the Incarnation and the Death of Christ, God's Son.

Recent Translation that Eliminate the Messianicity of Genesis 3:15

The Jewish Publication Society's Holy Scriptures according to the Massoretic Text of 1917 renders like this: I will put enmity between thee and the woman, and between thy seed and her seed, they shall attack you in the head, and you shall attack them in the heel."[10] The University of Chicago's An American Translation has this as its rendering: "And I will put enmity between thee and the woman, and between your posterity and hers. They shall attack you in the head, and you shall attack them in the heel."[11] The Roman Catholic's Confraternity's New American Translation has:

"I will put enmity between you and the woman, and be while you strike at its heel."[12]Moffatt, former professor of Union Theological Seminary, New York City, translated Genesis 3:15: "And I will set a feud between you and the woman between your brood and hers, they shall strike at your head, and you shall strike at their heel."[13]

The Jewish scholar Speiser in his Genesis, and in Anchor Bible has this rendering for Genesis 3:15: "I will put enmity between you and the woman, and between your offspring and hers; they shall strike at your head and you will strike at their heel."[14]

The Jerusalem Bible gives this translation for Genesis 3:15: "I will make you enemies of each other, you and the woman, your offspring and her offspring; It will crush your head and you will strike at his heel."[15]

The New English Bible of 1970 renders the First Gospel promise like this: "I will put enmity between you and the woman, between your brood and hers, they shall strike at your head, and you shall strike at their heel."[16]

The new Jewish Publication Society of America's translation of the Torah, for Genesis 3:15 has: "I will put enmity between your offspring and hers, they shall strike at your head, and you shall strike at their heel."[17] In all previous translations cited the Hebrew word "tzera" has been interpreted in the second occurrence as collective, thus eliminating any possible prophecy to the messiah, as is done in the Targum Pseudo-Jonathan and the Jerusalem Targum (Cf. Alfred Edersheim, *The Life and Times of Jesus the Messiah*, II, p. 711).

Translations and Versions which render the Second "Tzera" as an individual and "Shuph" as "Crush" or "wound."

The Kings James translates Genesis 3:15: "I will put enmity between thee and the woman and between thy seed and her seed; it shall bruise thy head, and thou shall bruise his heel." The British Revised Version has the same rendering, except for "it," referring back to the seed of the woman, it has "he."[18]

The American Revised Version of 1901 translates Genesis 3:15: "And I will put enmity between thee and the woman and between thy seed and her seed, he shall bruise thy head, and thou Shalt bruise his heel."[19]

For "bruise" the margin unfortunately has "Lie in wait." The New American Standard of A.D. 1963 translated Genesis 3:15: "And 1 will put enmity between you and the woman and between your seed and her seed, and he shall bruise you in the head, and you shall bruise him in the heel."[20]

The Holy Bible
Beck, in his American Translation correctly has rendered Genesis 3:15:

"And I will put enmity between you and the woman and between your descendants and her Descendant; He will crush your head and you will bruise his heel."[21] The Berkeley Version, sometimes called the Twentieth Century Translation, has this rendering for Genesis 3:15: "I will put enmity between you and the woman, and also between your offspring and her offspring, and he will crush your head and you will crush his heel."[22] The New Berkeley Bible has a footnote which states that this is the first Messianic prophecy in the Bible.

Martin Luther translated Genesis 3:15 in German like this: "Ich will Feidschaft setzen zwischen dir und dem Weibe, zwischen deinen Samen und ihren Samen und er wird dir den Kopf zertreten und du wirst ihn in die Ferse stechen."[23] In English this would be: "I will place enmity between thee and the woman, between thy seed and her seed, and he will crush your head, and you will sting his heel."

The New International Version has translated Genesis 3:15 like this; "I will put enmity between you and the woman and between your offspring and hers, he will crush your head and you will strike at the heel."[24] (Latter part of translation to be rejected).

The French translation of Louis, Segond has: "Je mettrai inimitie' entre toi, et la femme, entre a posterite et sa posterite: celle-ci t'ecrasera la tete and lui blesseras le talon."[25] In English this would read: "I will place enmity between you and the woman, between your offspring and her offspring. This one (F.) shall crush or tread down your head, and you will wound him in the heel."

The Norse Bible, Bibelen eller Den Heilige Skrifte (1930) has rendered Genesis 3:15 like this: "Og jeg vil sette fiendskap mellem dig og kvinnen og mellem din aett og hennes aett; den skal knuse ditt bode, men du skal knuse dens hael."[26] In English: "I will set enmity between you and the woman, between your seed and her seed, he shall crush your head, and you shall crush his heel."

A version of the Dutch Bible renders Genesis 3:15 like this:" En lk zal vijansschap zetten tusschen u en tusschen deze vrouw, en tusschen uw zaad en tusschen haar zaad; datzelve zal u den kop vermorzelen, en gij zult hel de verzenen vermorzelen. "[27] English translation: "I will set enmity between you and the woman, between her seed and your seed, the same shall crush or smash your head and you shall crush his heel."

A Swedish Bible translation has this: "Och jag skall saetta fiendskap emellen dig och qwinnona och mellem dina saed och henner sad. Den samme skall sondertrampa ditt bufwud; och du skall stinga honom hana hael."[28] English translation would be: "I will place enmity between you and the woman and between your seed and her seed, The same shall trample your head and you shall sting him in the heel."

A Spanish Version reads like this: "Y pondre enemistad entre ti y la mujer, y entre tu simiente y la simiente suya; esta te herira en la cabeza, y tu le heriras en calcanar."[29] English translation: "I will place enmity between you and the woman, between your seed and her seed, he will wound your head and you will wound him in the heel."

The Correct Translation of Genesis 3:15

Genesis 3; 15, the protevangel, is a prediction of what would occur in the future. Prophecy, of course, is a concept unacceptable to higher critical scholars and exegetes. The words of Genesis 3:15 were directed to the devil, the evil personality, which had utilized the serpent. Although, as has already been shown from the New Testament (Rev. 12:9; 20:2; 2 Cor. 11:3; Rom. 16:20; John 8:44) that Satan was behind this temptation, he is not mentioned by name. Boehl, in commenting on this passage, wrote: "God did not do the Devil the honor, who has hidden behind the serpent, to smite him down with lofty words, with the tongue of angels.

"God remained by the hull which Satan himself had selected, and knows how to capture him in this shell and place him in bonds."[30]

Neither is this promise directed to fallen man. The salvation which God promised did not require man's cooperation to make it effectual; nor is there any hope that man now dead in trespasses, could himself wish for, or accomplish this salvation.

The first Messianic prophecy contains two distinct but related predictions:

1) "And 1 will set enmity between thee and the woman." Prior to the fall the relationship between the serpent and the woman was cordial, which from then onward was to be turned into loathing and hatred. Furthermore, Yahweh himself establishes this hostility between the woman and the serpent.

The feud and hatred is to be between "the seed of the woman" and the "seed of the serpent." What is embraced by the expression "seed of the serpent?" It embraces all those who may come into the service of Satan, the evil angels, and human beings, who serve the devil's purpose. In Matthew 21:33 the Pharisees are called by Jesus "serpents" and "generation of vipers" and in John 8:44 Jesus called the unbelieving Jews "children of the devil."

When God said that there would be enmity between woman's descendants, i.e. human beings and the descendants of the serpent, it was not directed against the serpentine world.[31] The hatred and repulsion exhibited by men and women against snakes may be a natural and inveterate reminiscence of this event. However, it has been questioned that an hostility exists between men and snakes. Clark, in his *Commentary* has pointed out:

> It is not yet discovered that the serpentine race have any peculiar enmity against mankind, nor is there any proof that men hate serpents more than they do other noxious animals. Men have much more enmity to the common rat and magpie than they have to all the serpents in general, because the former-destroy the grain, etc., and serpents in general, for seeking to do men mischief flee his approach and generally avoid his dwelling.[32]

But the "seed of the serpent" has a far deeper meaning, and that is this: It refers both to the evil principle and power that utilized the serpent in that temptation, to all human and super-human agencies connected with Satan.

582

Critical interpretation of Genesis 3:15, relative to "the seed of the woman," has proposed different views. One view holds that the expression refers to all mankind and others takes it specifically to refer to one individual. The second is to be preferred to the first and for the following reasons.

The Hebrew word "tzera," "seed," is often used in the Scriptures of a single person. Consult, for instance. Genesis 4:25, where it is stated: "God has appointed me another seed, instead of Abel," namely, the individual Seth. In addition also compare 1 Samuel 1:11; 2 Samuel 7:12.[33]

That "tzera" refers to an individual is required by the context. Verse 15 speaks of an individual action which is usually interpreted of an individual person. "Bruising thy head" and "bruising thy heel" refers to an individual, if we understand this as a singular action. The view that "tzera," rendered as "offspring" as a collective representation of all seems very unnatural and unusual. It is also interesting that when Eve, according to Genesis 4:1 (according to the Hebrew text), exclaimed: "I have gotten a man — the LORD,[34] she was indicating that with the birth of Cain that the promise of Genesis 3:15 was already being fulfilled. Thus the word "tzera" was understood in an individualistic sense by Eve.

2) The second part of Genesis 3:15 states: "He shall bruise thy head and you shall bruise his heel." The second half of Genesis 3:15 begins with the pronoun "hu," which means "he." In the King James Version the word "it" is used to translate this third personal pronoun. The antecedent of "hu" is "tzera," "one individual seed." The Septuagint translated "tzera" by the Greek "sperma" (a neuter noun), but uses the pronoun "autos," not "auto" to refer back to "sperma."[35]

God announced to Satan that this one individual would bruise his head. The word for bruise is "shuph," which only occurs in Psalm 139:11 and Job 9:17. There appears some degree of uncertainty attached to the exact interpretation of this verb "shuph." Those favoring the idea that Genesis 3:15 speaks of snakes, derive the verb "shuph " as being the equivalent of "sha'aph," which is said to have the meaning "strike after," "to try to secure."[36]

Walter A. Maier, Sr., claims that "there is not a Biblical or post-Biblical example which entitles us to believe that 'shuph' is equivalent in meaning to 'strike after.'[37] The verb 'shuph' only occurs in the Aramaic in the sense of "snap after." Furthermore, Delitzsch in his *Genesis Commentary* has pointed out that no verb of hostile endeavor (as "snap after") is construed with double accusative, the accusative of the person and the accusative of the part or member of the body.[38] "To snap after," i.e. to try to reach, seems quite inadmissible for the first part of verse 15, "he shall bruise thy head." This "snap after" translation contained no comfort for our first parents nor did it contain little punishment for the serpent and the evil influences behind it. The purpose of Genesis 3:15 was to pronounce a curse upon Satan or the devil and give the human race hope. The liberal translation fails completely in this respect.

The translation of "shuph," "to bruise," "to injure" is substantiated in a number of ways. In Job 9:17, the other passages employing "shuph"

583

reads: "He breaketh me with the wind and multiplieth my wounds without cause." The verb "he breaketh me" is the Hebrew verb "Jeshuphoni" is explained by the parallelism "to multiply wounds." This clearly proves that "shuph" means "bruise" or "hurt" but not "snap after."[39]

The New Testament in Romans 16:20 refers to this verse, when Paul says that Satan may be crushed, or utterly destroyed. In the Greek Paul used the word "syntribein" which means to "rub," or "to crush," "utterly destroy."[40] The Peshitta and some versions derived from the Septuagint (the LXX itself misinterprets the force of "shuph") interpret "shuph" as "bruise" or "crush."

In Genesis 3:15 the verb "shuph" is used twice, namely, "he will bruise you," and "you shall bruise him in the heel." The Seed of the woman, i.e. Christ, would bruise or crush the Serpents' head. Crushing a serpent's head meant killing the snake, it meant administering a death blow. Hebrews says that the Son of God was manifested that he might destroy the works of the devil (Heb. 2:14). The head was the vital part of the serpent.

What is meant by the latter part of Genesis 3:15: "Thou Shalt bruise his heel?" In the contest in which the devil will be defeated, he in turn will inflict a wound. The picture is perhaps this. When "the Seed of the woman" crushes the serpent's head with his heel and thus completely destroys the serpent, the teeth of the serpent at the same time wound his heel. The two injuries cannot be compared in their finality, even though Christ dies, on the third day God raised Jesus from the dead.

The Interpretation of Genesis 3:15 in Luther's Writings

In 1523 Luther expounded on Genesis 3:15 and this exposition was later published in 1527.[41] In it the Reformer contended that there is no essential difference between the saving faith of the Old Testament and that of the New.[42] Luther found the divine design clearly stated in the protevangelium as he wrote: "I will put enmity between thy seed and her seed." God says: This amounts to saying: "You Satan, have attacked and deceived man through the woman through sin you might pose as their head and lord. I, in turn, shall lie in wait for you with the same weapon. I will take the woman and raise up a Descendant (semen) from her, and the Descendant will crush your head. Through sin you have corrupted and made guilty the nature of mankind, but out of this very flesh I will produce such a Man as shall crush your head. Through sin you have corrupted and made guilty the nature of mankind, but out of this very flesh I will produce such a Man as shall crush and lay low both you and all your powers."[43]

The oldest true human religion began in the garden of Eden, so asserted Luther in one of his last sermons, (January 31, 1546). In fact, he claimed that the Lutheran faith went back to Adam and Eve. Thus Luther declared: "We can prove that our faith is not new and of unknown origin but that it is the oldest faith of all, which began and continued from the beginning of the world. For when Adam and Eve, our first parents, came to grace again after this miserable fall in Paradise, they began to have faith in the Savior, the Son of God. For the promise which was given them ran thus: 'The woman's Seed will crush the serpent's head Gen. 3:15). From the first Gospel our faith has come and flowed.'"[44]

The *Formula of Concord* of 1577 interpreted Genesis 3:15 as Luther did. Thus in article V "Law and Gospel" it is asserted:

Since the beginning of the world these two proclamations have continually been set forth side by side in the church of God with the proper distinction. The descendants of the holy patriarchs like the patriarchs themselves, constantly reminded themselves not only how man in the beginning was created righteous and holy by God and through deceit of the serpent transgressed God's laws, became a sinner, corrupted himself and all his descendants, and plunged them into death and eternal damnation, but also revived their courage and comforted themselves with the proclamation of the woman's seed, who would crush the serpent's head; likewise, of David's son who should restore the kingdom of Israel and be a light to the nations (Ps. 110:1; Is. 40;10; 49:6) "who was wounded for our transgressions and bruised for our iniquities and with those stripes are healed."[45]

The *Hirschberger Bible* of the 18th century which employs Luther's German translation and furnished each verse with interpretative comments, considers the teaching of Genesis 3:15 as being a prediction of the coming of the Messiah and His conflict with Satan and the Messiah's ultimate victory over Satan.[46]

The Understanding of Genesis 3:15 in the Exegetical Literature of the Lutheran Church-Missouri Synod The Understanding of C.F.W. Walther

C.F.W. Walther in his lectures treating of *The Proper Distinction Between Law and Gospel*, in his ninth lecture asserted among other things:

Reverting to the Old Testament, we see even there what the character of the teaching of Christ is. We read in Gen. 3,15: "It (the Woman's Seed) shall bruise thy head". What is the importance of these words? The Messiah, the Redeemer, the Savior is not to come for the purpose of telling us what we are to do, what works we are to perform in order to escape from the terrible dominion of darkness, sin and death. These feats the Messiah not going to leave for us to accomplish, but He will do all Himself. "He shall bruise the serpent's head," that means nothing else than this, that he shall destroy the kingdom of the devil.

This Protevangelium, this First Gospel in Genesis, was the foundation from which the believers in the Old Testament drew their comfort. It was important for them to know: "There is One coming who will not only tell us what we must do to get to heaven. No, the Messiah will do all Himself to bring us there."[47]

Francis Pieper in his *Christian Dogmatics* asks the question: How old is the Gospel religion? He answered: "It was revealed immediately after the fall in the promise that the Seed of the woman would crush the head of the serpent (Gen. 3:15). (cf. Luther, I, St. L, 230ff; III, 650ff.)[48] All the Old Testament Prophets taught it **unisono** and all the children of God

585

in the days of the Old Testament believed it **unanimiter**, as Peter testifies: "To Him give all the prophets witness through His name whosoever believeth in Him shall receive the remission of sins" Acts 10:43). Paul too declares that the righteousness which is obtained **choris nomou** "without the law," by faith in Christ, was witnessed "by the Law and the Prophets" (Romans3:21). And he brings the historical proof for this in Romans.[49] Again Pieper wrote: "The Word spoken in the very beginning about the Seed of the woman who would crush the head of the Serpent (Gen. 31:15), what is it but doctrine?[50]

P. E. Kretzmann in his *Popular Commentary* makes this assertion about Geneis 3:15:

> What was a curse for the serpent and for the devil, who had used the serpent for his disguise was a glorious promise for fallen mankind, the first great Gospel proclamation; and enmity I shall set between thy seed and her seed. This is not a mere reference to the aversion which most men feel for snakes of every kind, as some liberal commentators have it, but sets forth the cardinal truth of the ages. This would be everlasting and uncompromising enmity between the descendants of woman on the one hand, and the devil and all satanic powers, on the other. And this enmity would show itself in continual warfare, would finally have its culmination in the event that the One great Seed of the Woman, He to whom the Old Testament looks forward, would utterly crush the heel of the Victor. To overcome the devil, to annihilate his power, that is a feat beyond the ability of any mere man: only God is able to do this. Christ the promised Seed of the woman, born of the descendants of Eve, and yet God almighty God, is the strong Champion of mankind, who delivered all men from the power of Satan and all his mighty allies. True, indeed, in doing so His heel was bruised. He was obligated to die, according to his human nature. But deliverance was effected, salvation was gained by the death of Jesus Christ on the cross, as the representative of all mankind.[51]

The eminent exegete George Stoeckhardt claimed that in Genesis 3:15 we have the first Gospel promise. He wrote: "What was a curse for Satan that was a comfort and promise for men. There we see what is truly grace. Grace, as Luther has remarked, is meant for the undeserving. The promise is directed toward Christ."[52]

The *Concordia-Self Study Commentary* asserted about Genesis 3:15 as follows:

> "Although no offspring of the woman had been able to overcome him by crushing his head, One born of woman (G 1 4:4) would come 'to destroy the works of the devil (Jn 3:8).' Mortally wounded, in the conflict. He nevertheless inflicted a deathblow on the demonic power. Jesus Christ, Executor of God's curse on Satan and man's Champion, enables man to look forward to a victorious end of the strife with his enemy because the "God of peace will soon crush Satan under your feet" (Rom. 16:20).[53]

The Concordia Self-Study Bible comments on Genesis 3:15: "The curse on the serpent constitutes the first Gospel, the Protevangel (Jn 12:31;

Acts 26:18; Ro 5:18-19; Heb 2:14; Rev. 12:1-9).[54]

Dr. Walter A. Maier, Sr., of *Lutheran Hour* fame, in his *Notes of Genesis,* when he taught this course at the St. Louis Seminary over fifty years ago, asserted:

In the Christian Church the interpretation has prevalently been directly Messianic in the Lutheran Church and rather typically Messianic in the Reformed Churches. According to this latter mode of interpretation, the seed of the woman is humanity in general, which with the help of the Messiah, overcomes the devil. The objection to this mode of interpretation will be shown in the following section. However, under the influence of rationalism and unbelief, the Messianic element of this Protevangelium has been entirely eliminated.[55]

Maier refers to the interpretation of Calvin who explained the essence of this verse as being " a promise of victory over the devil to mankind, united to Christ, its divine head."[56] Maier contended that this interpretation was in direct opposition to the New Testament and that it was too general and also minimized the Messianic element in Genesis 3:15 and at the same time weakened the direct connection between the Old Testament and the New Testament.[57]

The Roman Catholic Interpretation of Genesis 3:15

The Vulgate erroneously translated the Hebrew of Genesis 3:15, previously quoted in this article.[58] The Vulgate ascribes to a female Mary, what is ascribed to her son, Christ, by its mistranslation of "ipsa" for masculine "hu" and the Roman Catholic Church has used the Latin to support Mariolatry.

This rendering of "ipsa" assigning to Mary the work which Christ would perform is contradicted by other ancient versions, the Septuagint and the Peshitta. The Samaritan Pentateuch, another form of the Hebrew Pentateuch text, is also against the Vulgate's mistranslation.[59] It is further hostile to the entire New Testament which has no room for Mary as the one who would crush the serpent's head. A number of recent Roman Catholic translations, like the Jerusalem Bible, The Confraternity Translation, render "he" instead of "she" for the Hebrew "hu." Bishop Knox in his English translation of the Vulgate renders Genesis 3:15: "And I will establish a feud between thee and the woman, between thy offspring and hers, she is to crush thy head, whilst thou does lie in ambush at her heels." In a footnote Knox states that both the Hebrew and Septuagint have "he." However, he then asserts: "But most manuscripts of the Latin have "she," which plainly gives a better balance to the sentence. That the reference of this passage, in any case, is to the Incarnation is the general opinion of the Fathers."[60]

In the opinion of conservative Roman Catholic exegesis, Genesis 3:15 is the announcement made to Adam and Eve of a Coming Redeemer. The Vatican's "Katholischer Klein Katechismus" called Genesis 3:15 "die erste Frohbotschaft vom Erloeser," and then quotes Genesis 3:15 correctly according to the Hebrew text and not according to the Vulgate.

Rationalistic Translations of Genesis 3:15

The thrust of all rationalistic renderings is that these words do not contain a prophecy of the coming of the Messiah and the defeat of Satan. Both nineteenth century and twentieth century higher critical scholars have attacked this passage as not being Messianic and have interpreted it as having something to do with snakes or a warning against snake worship.[62]

Dillmann found in Gen. 3:15 "the idea of man's vocation to ceaseless moral warfare and the serpent's brood of sinful thoughts and an implicit promise of the ultimate destruction of the evil powers."[63]

The English scholar Skinner goes so far as to suggest the possibility "that it is the primary intention of the oracle (Gen. 3:15) is the protest of ethical religion against the unnatural fascination of snake worship."[64] The unbelieving "Lutheran" scholar Gunkel holds that originally "the seed of the woman" and "the seed of the serpent" were mythological characters that were engaged in a mythical combat.[65] Another Lutheran scholar claims that Genesis 3:15 cannot contain a blessing because it is a curse, and in a curse there cannot be a blessing.[66] But the fact of the matter is that there is! Westermann's literary and form critical views do not determine the meaning of Scripture, but only the text does.

Hanson in his book, *The Serpent Was Wiser*, which treats the first eleven chapters of Genesis, in his discussion of Chapter 3 ignores Genesis 3:15 because according to his strange and anti-biblical interpretation chapter 3 does not deal with man's fall into sin, but actually states something worthwhile happened to man. On page 41 Hanson wrote:

> For many centuries now, the adventure has been called the story of the fall of man. But why the "fall?" It is the story of something quite the reverse — the story of a creature rising up in self-assertion against his creator. Call it the rebellion of man, the rise of man, or, better still the story of man's discovery of himself. But let us not call it a fall.[67]

The idea that Genesis 3 speaks about a fall, claims Hanson, was taken over from the Orphic world of thought.[68] Since man did not fall but actually was making upward progress in maturity, no Savior is needed. Furthermore, Christianity and the New Testament have the wrong idea about Satan. Averred Hason:

> A more productive question with which to understand our traditional notion of original sin is to ask (as we have) after the identity of the serpent. An early sect of gnostic Christians, the Ophites, revered the serpent as the one who showed man the **gnosis** that makes him God, and they may have been the first and were not the only ones to see the wisest of all of God's creatures as a hero rather than a villain.[69]

The Birth of Christ a Fulfillment of Genesis 3:15

The prophecy of God to Satan was realized when as St. Paul stated in Galatians 4:4 "When the fullness of the time came God sent His son born of a woman, placed under the law, to redeem those under the law, that we might receive the adoptions of sons." The incarnation was the beginning of that journey which led the Son of God to the cross, where he died for the sins of the world, fulfilling the second part of Genesis 3:15, "and thou wilt bruise Him in the heel."

Footnotes

1 H. C. Leupold, *Exposition of Genesis* (Grand Rapids: Baker Book House, 1976), p. 163.

2 *The Septuagint Version of the Old Testament* (London: Samuel Bagster and Sons. Limited, no date), p. 4.

3. **Ibid.**

4. *Biblia Sacra. Juxta Vulgatam Clementinam* (Romae-Tomaci-Parisiis: Desclee et Socii, 1956), p. 3.

5. Knox, *The Holy Bible, A Translation from the Latin Vulgate in the Light of the Hebrew and Greek Originals* (New York: Sheed & Ward. 1956) p. 3.

6. Ketiba Kedisha (London: Trinitarian Bible Society, 1913), p. 2b.

7. Herman Gunkel, *The Legends of Genesis* (New York: Schocken Books, 1964), reprint of 1901 edition, p. 1; Alan Richardson, Genesis I-XI. London: SCM Press, 1953), p 27; Terrence Fretheim, Creation, Fall and Flood (Minneapolis: Augsburg Publishing House, 1969). Ralph Elliott, The Message of Genesis (St. Louis: The Bethany Press, 1962), p. 13; Julian Morgenstern, The Book of Genesis (New York: Schocken Books, 1965), p. 21. Dieterich Bonhoeffer, Creation and Fall, A Theological Interpretation of Genesis 1-3 (London: SCM Press, 1959)! Robert Graves and Raphael Patai. *Hebrew Myths The Book of Genesis* (New York, 1963).

8. William Holloday, *A Concise Hebrew and Aramaic Lexicon of the Old Testament* (Grand Rapids: Wm. B. Eerdmans Publishing Company, 1971), p. 93a.

9. James Kallas, *The Real Satan* (Minneapolis: Augsburg Publishing House, 1975), p. 15. Cf. also Richard S. Hanson, *The Serpent Was Wiser, A New Look at Genesis 1-11* (Minneapolis: Augsburg Publishing House, 1972), pp. 46-47.

10. *The Holy Scriptures According to the Massoretic Text. A New Translation* (Philadelphia: The Jewish Publication Society of America, 5677-1907), pp. 5-6.

11. *The Bible. An American Translation. The Old Testament.* J.M. Powis Smith. The New Testament. Edgar J. Goodspeed (Chicago: University of Chicago Press, 1931), p 7.

12. *The New American Bible. The Confraternity Edition* (New York: Catholic Book Publishing Company, 1970), p. 6.

13. James Moffatt, *A New Translation. The Bible* (New York: Harper & Sons, 1922), p 3.

14. Ephraim Speiser, *The Anchor Bible, Genesis* (Garden City, New York: Doubleday & Company, Inc., 1966), p. 22,24.

15. *The Jerusalem Bible. Reader's Edition* (Garden City, New York: Doubleday & Company, Inc., p. 7.

16. *The New English Bible With Apocrypha* (New York; Oxford and Cambridge University Presses, 1970), p. 4.

17. The Torch. The Five Books of Moses (Philadelphia: The Jewish Publication Societ of America, 1962), p. 7.

18. *The Holy Bible Containing the Old and New Testaments* (Oxford: At the University Press, 1892), p. 5.

19. *The Holy Bible Containing Old and New Testaments*. Revised and edited by the American Revision Committee, A.D. 1901 (N.Y. Thomas Nelson, 1901) p. 3.

20. *New American Standard Bible* (Philadelphia: Holman Company, 1973), p 2.

21. William F. Beck, *The Holy Bible, An American Translation* (New Haven; Leader Publishing Company, 1976), p. 4.

22. Gerril Verkuyl, *The Holy Bible. The New Berkeley Version in Modern English* (Grand Rapids: Zondervan Publishing House, 1969), p. 3.

23. Martin Luther, *Die Bibel oder die game Heilige Schrift des alten und neuen Testaments* (New York: Amerikanische Bibelgesellschafl, 1906) Seite 3.

24. *The New International Version* (New York).

25. Louis Segon, *La Sainte Bible* (Paris: 20 Rue De Tournon, 1911), p. 4.

26. *Bibelen Eller Den Heilige Skrift* (New York: Del Amerikanske Bibelselskap, 1943), p 4.

27. *Bijbel Dat Is De Gansche Heilige Schrift* (London: Britische En Buitenlandsche Bijbelgenootschap, 1921), p. 4.

28. *Bibelen eller den Heliga Skrift* (New York: Amerikanske Bible + Sallskapet, 1900), p. 7.

29. *La Santa Biblia, Antiguo Y Nueveo Testamento.* Revision de 1960 (Guatemala and other Latin cities of the Americas: Sociedades Unkias, 1960), p 3.ff.

30. Boehl. *Die Christologie des Alten Testaments*, p. 83 as quoted by Walter A. Maier, Sr. Notes on Genesis (St. Louis: Concordia Seminary Mimeo Company, 1929). p. 65.

31. **Ibid.**, p. 66.

32. Dom Clark, *Commentary of the Bible*, p 51.

33. Ludwig Koehler and Walter Baumgartner, *Lexicon in Veteris Testamenti Libros* (Leiden: E J. Brill, 1958), p 268.

34. Edward Mack, *The Christ of the Old Testament* (Richmond: Presbyterian Committee of Publications, 1926), p 45.

35. *The Septuagint Version of the Old Testament*, **op. cit.**, p. 5.

36. Maier, *Notes on Genesis*, **op. cit.**, p. 68.

37. **Ibid.**, p. 68.

38. Franz Delitzsch, *New Commentary on Genesis,* I, p 162 as cited by Maier, Notes on Genesis, op, cit., p. 68.

39. **Ibid.**

40. G. Abbott-Smith, *A Manual Greek Lexicon of the New Testament* (New York: Charles Scribners Sons, 1929), p. 434.

41. Ewald W. Plass, *What Luther Says, An Anthology* (St. Louis: Concordia Publishing House, 1959), 1, p. 257.

42. *D. Martin Luthers Werke.* Kritische Gesamtuasgabe (Weimar: 1883— 42, 144

43. **Ibid.**

44 **Ibid.**, 51, 152

45. Theodore G. Tappert, *The Book of Concord* (Philadelphia: Fortress Press, 1959), p. 562.

46. *Die Hirschberger Bibel*, notes written by E. Liebich, *Die Bibel Oder die game Heilige Schrift* (Konstanz Buchhandlung und Kunstgewerbe, 1844 reprinted 1926, Seite 4.

47. C.F.W. Walther, *The Proper Distinction Between Law and Gospel* (St. Louis: Concordia Publishing House, 1929. p. 70. The English was translated by W.H.T. Dau from the German edition of 1897.

48. Francis Pieper, *Christian Dogmatics* (St. Louis: Concordia Publishing House, 1950)

m 1, p. 21

49. **Ibid.**

50. **Ibid.**, I, p 70.

51. P. E. Kretzmann. *Popular Commentar, Old Testament* (St. Louis: Concordia Publishing House, 1923), I, p. 9.

52. G. Stoeckhardt, *Die biblische Geschichte des Alten Testaments* (St. Louis: Concordia Publishing House, 1906), p. 6.

53. Waller R. Roehrs and Martin Franzmann, *Concordia Self-Study Commentary* (St. Louis: Concordia Publishing House, 1971), p. 20.

54. Hoerber, Hummel, Roehrs, and Wenthe, *Concordia Self-Study Bible* (St. Louis: Concordia Publishing House, 1986), p. 10.

55. Maier, *Notes on Genesis*, op, cit., p. 72.

56. **Ibid.**, p. 73

57. **Ibid.**, p. 73.

58. F. Pieper, *Christian Dogmatics*, **op. cit.**, I, p. 347.

59. Brian Walton, *Biblia Sacra Polyglotta* (Graz-Austria: Akademisher Druck und Verlagsanstaltt, 19631, 1, p. 13.

60. Knox, *The Holy Bible*, op cit., p. 3.

61. *Katholischer Kurz-Katechismus* (Koenigstein: Albertus-Magnus Kolleg/Haus der Begegnung, 1982), Question and Answer 34, P. 10.

62. John Skinner. *A Critical and Exegetical Commentary on Genesis* (Edinburgh T. & T. Clark 1910), P. 81.

63. August Dillmann, as cited by Skinner, **op. cit.**, p. 81.

64. Skinner, **op. cit.**, p. 81.

65. Skinner, **op. cit.**, p. 82.

66. Glaus Westermann, *The Genesis Account of Creation* (Philadelphia: Fortress Press, 1960), p. 33,

67. Richard S. Hanson, *The Serpent Was Wiser. A New Look at Genesis I-XI* Minneapolis: Augsburg Press, 1972). p. 41.

68. **Ibid.**, p. 42.

69. **Ibid.**, pp. 46-47.

Questions

1. Before the coming of historical criticism Genesis 3:15 was considered by Christians of different schools to be a promise of ____.
2. Beck, in his American Translation of the Bible, correctly rendered Genesis 3:15 as ____.
3. In John 8:44 Jesus called the unbelieving Jews ____.
4. That "tzera" refers to an individual required by ____.
5. Walter A. Maier Sr. claims that ____.
6. The oldest human religion began in ____.
7. The Lutheran faith went back to ____.
8. How old is the Gospel religion? ____
9. What did Walter A. Maier teach about messianic prophecy? ____
10. What did the "Lutheran" scholar Gunkel maintain? ____

The Resurrection of Christ from a Historical-Critical Lutheran Perspective As Compared with a Biblical and Confessional Lutheran Stance

Christian News, April 20 and 27, 1987

Perhaps nothing in the Bible to which unbelievers in their attempts to prove that the Sacred Book of Christianity contains contradictions, point with greater frequency than to the four accounts of the resurrection of Christ. The respective passages are: Matthew 28:1-10, Mark 16:1-11, Luke 24:1-12, and John 20:1-18.[1] The charge is brought that in these four accounts there are many variations and contradictions especially when these are compared with Paul's resurrection account in I Corinthians 15:1-10 which is said to be the oldest account we possess relative to Christ's resurrection. Because of these alleged discrepancies the reliability and even the historicity of Jesus resurrection have been attacked.

The historicity and credibility of Christ's resurrection have been the subject of attacks by unbelievers over the Christian centuries. In centuries past it was the outspoken enemies of the Church which have engaged in trying to discredit this important event in Christ's state of exaltation, but now, sad to say, the same attacks have emerged within the bosom of the church by people who claim that they are Christians and a number of them are Lutherans. Traditionally, Christ's resurrection was rejected because those who could not believe the facticity of the resurrection did not believe in miracles and that God could act within history. The resurrection might be called: "the miracle of all miracles." Unbelievers have concluded that the resurrection is a hoax and was not a real historical event that occurred in or around Jerusalem in the first century A.D. If Christ's resurrection is not a reliable historical fact, what precisely do Christians around the world celebrate on Easter which is observed either toward the end of March or on one of the first three Sundays of April! In I Corinthians 10:11-19 Paul definitely has answered what the importance for every Christian is of the resurrection of Christ.

Theodosius Harnack wrote: "Where you stand with regard to the fact of the resurrection is in my eyes no longer Christian theology. To me Christianity stands or falls with the Resurrection."[2]

Other Major Religions Do Not Have A Resurrection of Their Founders

A number of Christian scholars have pointed out that of all major religions of the world are based on mere philosophical propositions. Of the four that are based on personalities rather than a philosophical system, only Christianity claims an empty tomb for its founder. Abraham, the father of Judaism, died about 1900 B.C. but no resurrection account has ever been claimed for him. In 1925 Wilbur Smith wrote: "The original accounts of Buddha never ascribed to him any such thing as a resurrection;

in fact, in the earliest account of his death, namely, the Mahaparinibbana Sutta we read that when Buddha died it was 'with that utter passing away in which nothing whatever remains behind.'"[3]

Professor Childress said:

There is no trace in the Pali scriptures or commentaries (or so far as I know in any Pali book) of Sakya Muni having existed after his death or appearing to his disciples. Mohammed died June 8, 632 A.D. at the age of 61, at Medina, where his tomb is annually visited by thousands of devout Mohammedans. All the millions and millions of Jews, Buddhists and Mohammedans agree that their founders have never come up out of the dust of the earth in resurrection.[4]

The Corporeal Resurrection of Christ Found in All Creeds

All the major creeds of Christendom have this statement: "And the third day he arose from the dead."[5] All traditional Christian Churches, such as the Roman Catholic, the Eastern Orthodox, Lutheran, Episcopalian, Presbyterian, Baptist, Congregational, Mennonite, the various Reformed Churches those classified as Arminian and other churches have statements in their confessional writings asserting their belief in Christ's bodily resurrection. With the coming of deism and rationalism in the seventeenth century the miraculous was challenged and the concept of revelation.[6] Out of rationalism grew the various types of criticism spawned by the historical critical method. A hostile type of literary criticism, form criticism, redaction criticism, content criticism, structural criticism have all led to the complete repudiation of the bodily or corporeal resurrection of Christ.

Lutheran Deniers of the Historical
Corporeal Resurrection of Christ

From the very beginning Lutheran scholars were involved in the creation and adoption of methods of hermeneutics that resulted in questioning the reliability of the Bible and challenging truth after truth of the doctrines of the Apostles' Creed and the two other Creeds of the Universal Christian Church.

One of the saddest developments of Lutheran ecclesiastical history since the days of the Reformation has been the rejection of the true account of Christ's resurrection by socalled Lutheran divines and professors and pastors. Bultmann, greatly honored by certain American Lutherans today, and who before his death was recognized as one of the world's greatest theologians, and whose views were tolerated by and in the Lutheran World Federation wrote: "Christ's death and resurrection are cosmic occurrences, not incidents that took place once upon a time in the past."[7] Again in another book he wrote: "Belief in the resurrection is simply and exactly the same as belief in the cross as 'salvation event.'"[8] In yet another work he declared: "And although it presents the Cross and Resurrection of Jesus in mythological terms the preaching of the Cross is nevertheless a decisive summons to repentance."[9]

The fact that Bultmann denies the bodily resurrection of Christ is that he does not believe in the intervention by God in the order of the universe. Further, He also declared: "I do indeed think that we can now know nothing concerning the life and personality of Jesus, since the early Christian sources show no interest in either, are moreover fragmentary and often legendary; and other sources about Jesus do not exist."[10]

Bornkamm and the Bodily Resurrection of Christ

Guenther Bornkamm contributed the essay on "Christ's Resurrection" in Augsburg's A New Look at the Apostles' Creed, where the reader will find the results of the historical-critical method's employment in the manner Bornkamm has explained away the bodily resurrection from the dead.[11]

He admits at the beginning of the presentation of his essay: "In primitive Christianity the confession of Christ's resurrection from the dead was not just an article of faith among many others but the basic content of the whole faith and of all confessions."[12] Bornkamm also cited Paul's arguments in I Corinthians. "If Christ was not raised, there is nothing in our message, there is nothing in our faith either." The German professor claims that Paul "declares that it is not our faith in the risen one that is illusion and fantasy but that, on the contrary, we would be victims of illusion and fantasy if we did not believe in and proclaim his resurrection."[13]

Again he said: "Whoever reads these two texts not only for edification but with the historical-critical attitude demanded by the New Testament taken as historical testimony can easily see that various texts differ greatly in style and time of composition."[14]

Dr. Gloege and the Resurrection of Christ

Dr. Gerhard Gloege, a European Lutheran scholar, usually referred to as a "post-Bultmannian," wrote in a volume published by the Lutheran Church in America:

> The ground of faith in the biblical view is not isolated and objectified matters of fact, not facts like what was falsely presented and passed-off as the objective fact of the resurrection of Jesus. Thus neither can any "picture" (not even a picture of Jesus), any "idea," nor any proposition or group of propositions either, serve as a ground of faith. Rather, the sole ground of faith is Jesus as the witness to faith in the pregnant sense of the "author and finisher of faith."[15]

Gloege, who was one of the chief essayists at the Fourth Assembly of the Lutheran World Federation, wrote in yet another book of "contradictions and improbabilities" in the Easter narrative recorded in the New Testament.[16] In his book The Day of His Coming Gloege averred: "What happened at Easter is not concerned with the revival of a corpse but a new heavenly form of existence,"[17] as far as this Lutheran scholar is concerned.

> Only in the legendary narratives of the Gospels is it possible to trace a line which seeks to make the empty tomb the first place of evidence to prove the resurrection. But here, too, the reserve is notice-

able; the empty tomb is not made into the object of faith. The message of the angels expressly forbids treating the tomb independently: 'Why do you seek the living among the dead? He is not here but has arisen' (Luke 24:5-6).[18]

Another very revealing assertion in the same volume was made by Gloege, when he wrote:

> Living by Easter faith we take up the stone anew each morning 'with joy,' as the hymn says. This Easter faith does not mean believing in the correctness of certain narratives and assertions or in the reality of certain events. In fact, strictly speaking it does not mean believing in the resurrection, but in the Risen One-personally.[19]

When Bultmann and Gloege claim that Christ did not corporeally rise from the dead, and still contend that one must believe in the person of Jesus that He lives, what kind of irrationality are they asking us to believe? How can that which is dead simultaneously be alive? The idea or thought that Christ lives has no basis in reality. How can one put confidence in something that does not exist. Uttering the words with no facts to base the idea on is nonsense. If when Christ was buried and He remained there and saw corruption, then certainly by the twentieth century Jesus must be completely gone, so in what do those put their faith relative to Christ when He obviously from their perspective does not exist?

A Process Theologian Dismisses the Resurrection of Christ

Process theology, better a philosophy, has dismissed the resurrection of Christ as unimportant. Thus wrote one such proponent as given by David Griffin: "Christian faith (as I understand it) is possible apart from belief in Jesus' resurrection in particular and life beyond bodily death in general, and because of the widespread skepticism regarding these, traditional beliefs should be presented an optional."[20] The cross is the historical fact; the Resurrection is its symbolic meaning.

In contrast to the Bultmannians and post-Bultmannians, Pannenberg contended that the resurrection is an historical event and that it must be proved by historical reasons. Thus Pannenberg wrote:

> There is no justification for affirming Jesus' resurrection as an event that really happened, if it is not to be affirmed as a historical event as such. Whether or not a particular event happened two thousand years ago is not made certain by faith but only by historical research, to the extent that certainty can be attained at all about questions of this kind.[21]

Later in this essay we shall adduce the testimony of lawyers and historians who do believe that we have documentary evidence for the historicity of the resurrection of Christ from the dead.

Althaus' Stance on the Resurrection of Christ

Althaus, in Braaten's opinion, has taken a mediating position between Bultmann and Pannenberg,[22] contending with Pannenberg that the resurrection was truly an event of history, empty tomb and all but also agreed that it cannot be verified by the critical methods of the historian.

In his dogmatics Althaus wrote:

> That Jesus was raised from the dead and appeared to his disciples as the Risen One is something we can only know for sure by faith under the impact of all the witnesses to Jesus, his life and message and death, as well as resurrection.[23] Christ's resurrection is an historic faith whether or not one believes it.

Regin Prenter and the Resurrection of Christ

Regin Prenter, Swedish theologian, in his discussion of Christ's resurrection is guilty of strange reasoning. He admitted that "on a particular day, the third day after the crucifixion Jesus Christ arose from the dead. And this event occurred at a particular place. He arose from the tomb in Joseph of Arimethea's garden, 'the place where they laid him (Mark 16:16).'"[24] In this sense Prenter contends the resurrection of Christ is proclaimed as an historical reality in contradistinction to the mystery religions well-known mythical stories about dying and rising deities.[25] Nevertheless, Prenter then proceeded to say that Christ's resurrection is not historical in the sense that other events are, because the resurrection of Jesus is an eschatological event and this cannot be substantiated. It cannot be proved by any person, but it can only be proclaimed.[26] Even though the New Testament informs the world that the tomb was empty, because no person saw Christ revivified, the resurrection event cannot be proved. Here the Scandinavian dogmatician engages in strange reasoning. The records tell the New Testament reader that Jesus' dead body was taken down from the cross, placed in the tomb of Joseph of Arimathea, a heavy stone was placed before the grave, a Roman guard was placed there so that no person could come and remove the body. On the third day after Christ's death early in the morning women who came to the tomb found the grave empty and the great stone rolled away, the guard gone and there were angelic visitors in the tomb, who declared: "Why seek you the living among the dead? He is risen." If a person were to walk into a hospital room where a person was very sick, and sometime later would return and find that person dead, would that person not be dead, even though no person was present when he breathed out his last breath and died? The logic of some theologians is difficult to comprehend when going against all evidence of Scripture.

Braaten in Lutheranism's Most Recent Christian Dogmatics

Carl Braaten of the Lutheran School of Theology, one of a number of contributors to the two volume Christian Dogmatics, discussed the resurrection of Christ on about three pages. Thus the Resurrection of Christ is depicted as an historical event and yet an historical event that is only true if one believes it. Thus the Chicago theologian wrote:

> However, no matter how positive the results of historical research may ever be in verifying the earlier testimonies to the resurrection of Jesus, we can never dispense with the role of faith in responding to the message of Easter.[27]

Further, he asserted: "The preaching and the faith it generates cannot take the place of the historical-critical examination of the text."[28] Again Braaten remarked: "The judgment of the historical is likely to lean in favor of the historical reliability of the resurrection reports only if they already approach the reports with the bias of belief that Christ is risen indeed."[29]

Still reason is important according to Braaten relative to the historicity of the resurrection, for:

> Faith does not close the eyes of reason: it may open them to see things that seem to contradict all analogies from ordinary human experience. Whether beyond death there is another kind of story to tell in language of myth and symbol or legend and metaphor does not lie within the purview of natural sciences to prove or disprove.[30]

Mythological symbolism, in Braaten's opinion, contributed to the understanding of the resurrection narratives of the New Testament. The same scholar claims that whether or not the accounts of Christ's resurrection can be classified as myth or as a truly historical event is today a burning question in current theology.[31]

Gustav Aulen and Christ's Resurrection

In 1948 the well-known Scandinavian scholar Aulen published his Faith of the Christian Faith. Christ's resurrection does not receive a special section but is treated as a part of "The Act of Exaltation."[32] Actually the reader who wishes to discover Aulen's stance on the Resurrection of Christ will not find much material. Here are some of this Swedish scholar's views on Christ's resurrection. Thus he wrote:

> In regard to how the exaltation takes place, theology cannot make any statement beyond the assertion that it is an act of God. This is true in regard to the resurrection as well as to the other formulas: ascended into heaven and sitting on the right hand of God. Theology cannot, without exceeding its function in either case make any statements which are not organically connected with the relation of faith to the continuous work of Christ. . . It is, therefore, entirely outside the sphere of systematic theology to make decisions in regard to those historical and exegetical questions which are connected with the resurrection of faith of the first disciples, or with the empty tomb, or with the manner in which Christ made himself known to his own.[33]

Aulen then claims that the New Testament presents different views as to how Jesus made himself known to his disciples and that there were different conceptions in primitive Christianity about Christ's resurrection and post-resurrection appearances. He claims the important thing is that God exalted Jesus, and that the resurrection, the ascension and session at "the right hand of God" is one act of God' s exalting Jesus."[34] Actually the resurrection, the ascension and session are three separate acts in time and follow each other.

Modern Lutheran Critical Theologians Do Not Accept the Reliability of the Resurrection Narratives

One wonders about the credibility of the New Testament, especially of the Gospels and of Paul, if in what they stated they are contradictory in what they have reported as actually as having occurred. Are we to believe that the Holy Spirit, who was to guide the disciples and apostles into all truth, permitted them to report events that did not happen?

Prenter, whom we have already discussed, reproduced the (oft-repeated -but unproven) allegation that "the tradition may also contain discrepancies in the witness concerning the earthly life of Christ, yet it would not be impossible to formulate an idea about the historical reality of the ministry and passion of Jesus. Yet the work and preaching of the miracle worker from Galilee and his death at Jerusalem are recorded with sufficient clarity to enable students to view them as historical, however, debatable the details might be. But regarding the resurrection of Christ the testimonies cannot be fitted together into a coherent picture of what actually transpired. Thus Prenter wrote: "The Gospel writers give different accounts so different[35] that it is not possible to bring them into a unified picture without resorting to arbitrariness and ingeniousness."[36] Prenter uses over three pages to show how the New Testament narratives contradict themselves.[37]

The Evaluation of the Resurrection
Narratives by Lawyers and Famous Persons.

Liberal critical Lutheran scholars were not the first persons to attack the reliability of the resurrection of Christ. The outspoken enemies of Christianity have done it periodically over the nearly two thousand years that the New Testament books have been read. There have been many who have defended the historicity, the miracle of the resurrection Bible and the trustworthiness of the Biblical records. Simon Greenleaf (1783-1853) was a famous Royal Professor of law at Harvard University and succeeded Justice Joseph Story as the Dana Professor of Law at Harvard University upon Story's death. It has been said by K. W. H. Knott that it was through the efforts of Justin Joseph Story and Greenleaf that the rise of the Harvard Law School to an eminent position among law schools was occasioned.[39]

Greenleaf wrote a treatise on law acclaimed to be still considered the greatest single authority on evidence in the entire literature of legal procedure.[40] In 1846, while professor of Law at Harvard, Greenleaf wrote a volume entitled: **An Examination of the Testimony of the Four Evangelists by the Rules of Evidence Administered in the Courts of Justice** (reprinted by Baker Book House, 1965 from the 1847 edition) in which the author examines the value of the testimony of the apostles to the resurrection of Christ. From every possible angle all the objections are answered and the utter credibility of the New Testament evidence is substantiated.

John Locke the famous British philosopher, said concerning Christ's resurrection in his book, A Second Vindication of the Reasonableness of Christianity (11th edition London, 1912, Vol. VII, pp. 339-442) as follows:

"Our Savior's resurrection . . . is truly of great importance in Christianity; so great that His being or not being the Messiah stands or falls with it; so that the two important articles are inseparable and in effect make one. For since that times, believe one and you believe both deny one of them, and you can believe neither."

Professor Ambrose Fleming, Professor of Electrical Engineering in the University of London, honorary Fellow of St. John's College, receiver of the Faculty medial 1928, one of England's outstanding scientists, declares in *Miracles and Science-The Resurrection of Christ*:

We must take this evidence of experts as to the age and authenticity of this writing, just as we take the facts of astronomy on the evidence of astronomers who do not contradict each other. This being so, we can ask ourselves whether it is probable that such a book, describing events that occurred about thirty or forty years previously, could have been accepted and cherished if the stories of abnormal events in it were false or mythical. It is impossible, because the memory of all elderly persons regarding events of thirty or forty years before, is perfectly clear.

No one could now issue a biography of Queen Victoria, who died thirty-one years ago, full of anecdotes which were quite untrue. They would be contradicted at once. They would certainly not be generally accepted and passed on as true. Hence, there is a great improbability that the account of the resurrection given by Mark, which agrees substantially that given in the other Gospels, is a pure invention. This mythical theory has had to be abandoned because it will not bear close scrutiny.[41]

Frank Morison, a lawyer, set out some years ago to discredit the resurrection of Christ. He had been raised in a rationalistic environment and was convinced that the Resurrection of Christ was nothing but a fairy tale and that it was intended to provide a happy ending for the life of a man which had ended in tragic failure. He set out to write a book of the matchless life of this man from Nazareth but leaving out the happenings the Gospels give after his burial. Morison studied the documents with care and instead of penning the kind of volume he intended, wrote a best seller, entitled **"Who moved the Stone?"** The book turned out to be one of the most powerful defenses of the miracle of Christ's resurrection from the dead ever written.[43]

An Examination of the Biblical Records Relative to the Resurrection and the Post-Appearances of Christ

No fairminded reader of the Four Gospel accounts of Christ's resurrection and His Christophanies during the forty glorious Easter days will contend that the accounts in Matthew, Mark, Luke and St. John and I Corinthian 15:1-10 purport to give a complete account of all the details of the resurrection day itself or of the various appearances Jesus gave over a forty-day period. No account gives a complete account of everything that transpired between the becoming alive of Jesus, the God-man according to both the divine and human natures and the day He visibly was taken from the physical presence of the disciples. Each of the five accounts reports some but not all that happened to Jesus after His bodily resurrection. If four different newspapers report on some political or sporting events and one paper reports this fact and another other facts and a third still some other aspects and a fourth newspaper still other facts, it does not follow because there are found different aspects of reality described in the four newspapers that they are contradicting each other.

To assume that Paul's account of Christ's resurrection is the oldest and that it can be the criterion for judging supposedly later written resurrection narratives does not follow. For one thing, Matthew and John were present on Easter, met and saw Jesus. Peter was a friend of Mark and could have told Mark what he knew about the events of the resurrection morning, noon, afternoon and night and also what happened on different occasions when Jesus appeared to His disciples. In addition, Luke claimed about his Gospel that he made careful research before writing his Gospel. Then there is also the matter of the fact that the Holy Spirit guided the Biblical writers as they penned their respective books. To pit one writer against another, Paul against the Evangelists, is to discredit the trustworthiness of the Holy Scriptures.

An Attempted Harmonization of the Events of Easter Sunday.

Matthew reports that Mary Magdalene and the other Mary came to the sepulcher early on Easter morning. Mark mentions Mary Magdalene, Mary, the mother of James and Salome. Luke gives the names of Mary Magdalene, Joanna and Mary, the mother of Jesus. John only mentions Mary Magdalene as coming to the tomb on Easter morning. Critics claim that we have contradictions here relative to who actually went early to the tomb of Christ. But is that true? William Arndt responded to this charge as follows:

All four accounts have the name of Mary Magdalene. Mark and Luke name Mary, the mother of James, as belonging to that company. It is she to whom Matthew refers in the term "the other Mary" (Cf. Matt. 27:56). Thus this Mary appears in the narrative of the three gospels. Hence, after all, there is a remarkable agreement between the accounts so far as the women are concerned. It is true, Mark is the only one to state that Salome belonged to this group on Easter morning, while Luke is the only one who mentions Joanna in the account. But that does not mean that Mark and Luke contradict each other. Their reports are supplementary. Salome was among these women, so was Joanna.[44]

While John mentions only Mary Magdalene in his account, he mentions that she had companions when she went to the grave. "They have taken away the Lord out of the sepulcher," said Mary to Jesus," and we know not where they have laid him (John 20:2)."

The Time When the Women Went to the Tomb

It is claimed that John and Mark contradict each other on the time the women came to the tomb on Easter morning. Mark reports that the women came to the grave as the sun was going up. John says that Mary

Magdalene came to the tomb while it was yet dark. This, we are told, is contradictory. But Arndt claims that this is easily resolvable, if one assumes that it took some time for the women to make their way to the grave, irrespective whether they stayed in Jerusalem or in Bethany. When the women group left where they were staying, it was still dark, but when they arrived at the tomb, located outside the city walls, the sun was probably appearing on the horizon. John was thinking of the time of departure, while Mark mentions the time when they got near the tomb.[45]

The Number of Angels in the Tomb

How many angels were in the tomb and how many announced the glad Easter tidings to the women? Matthew and Mark state that an angel spoke to the women, while Luke and John claim that there were two angels present at the tomb. Critics put their case this way for a contradiction: "The first two gospels say that only one angel was present at the grave on Easter morning. The last two gospels inform us that two were there. This is an evident disagreement."[46] However, the careful reader of the Easter accounts will see that this charge does not read the accounts fairly or accurately. Did Matthew and Mark state that only one angel was present? The little word "only" is missing. The fact that they do not specifically state that a number of angels were present and merely speak of one angel, they do not thereby deny that more than one angel was seen by the first visitors to the tomb. The fact that Matthew only mentions one is due to the fact that an angel of the Lord descended from heaven and came and rolled back the stone (Matt. 28:2). This angel was the one who spoke to the women. Because of his important role, the first evangelist limits himself to just mentioning this one angel and did not dwell on the other one who was present. This same observation might be made about Mark's only angel, who conveyed the message of Christ's resurrection and like Matthew disregarded to mention the presence of the second angel. Thus Arndt reasoned: "The vital feature for him evidently is that the women received the news of the resurrection not from a human being, not from a disciple, but from an angel, whether one or more angels appeared that was a matter of secondary importance."[47]

As an example how one author tells one fact and another author a different one without being contradictory, Arndt cited the following example to illustrate this possibility: "Walking the streets of Washington you might meet the president and his secretary. Let us assume that the President speaks to you and gives you some interesting information on a pending question in Congress. Upon meeting a friend of yours you would likely say: 'I saw the President, and this is what he said.' A few minutes later you might meet another friend, and you tell him: 'I saw the President and his secretary, and this is what the President said.' To a third person you might say: 'I met the President and his secretary and this is the information I received from them (It will be observed that in the latter case the plural of the pronoun is used). No person would claim that in speaking to his friends, this man contradicted himself."[48]

This illustration shows how in the matter of the angels present in the tomb, a number of options is possible. One may argue that one angel did the talking, the other nodding assent. Or the second may have confirmed the message by repeating the words uttered by the first. Whatever the case may be, the evangelists were justified in using the singular or the plural in the report. Only by disregarding the laws of language and the manner in which the human mind works can a person find a discrepancy here.

When Did Jesus Appear to Mary Magdalene?

Another alleged contradiction put forward by the critics against the reliability of the resurrection narratives is the fact that John reports the fact that Mary Magdalene was standing at the tomb when Jesus appeared to her in the garden, while Matthew states that Jesus appeared to the women after they had been to the tomb and been told the news by the angel: "He is not here but risen!" and were on their way to Jerusalem or Bethany to tell the disciples. What happened was that when Mary Magdalene was on the way with the other women and as they came near saw that the stone was removed, Mary Magdalene left the women and headed to where the disciples were to tell them that the stone was rolled away. When Peter and John heard this, they left and came running to the tomb. In the meantime while the women were returning to tell the disciples, they met Jesus and thus saw that He was alive. Later Mary Magdalene came back to the garden and then met Jesus in the garden. Matthew 28:9 should have read: "And as they went to tell his disciples, behold Jesus met them, excepting - Mary Magdalene." But that would have been an example of extreme literalism.

Another pair of passages held to be contradictory are supposedly Matthew 28:8 which says that the women "did run to bring His disciples word," while Mark 16:8 has "neither said they anything to any man, for they were afraid." The Matthean passage obviously implies that the women brought the good news to the disciples given them by the angel. The statement of Mark simply asserts that while the women were returning from the empty tomb they said nothing to any person they met on their way back to the city, either to Jerusalem or Bethany. In fact, the angel had told the women: "Go your way, tell his disciples and Peter that he goeth before you into Galilee." If they had not told the disciples they would have been disobedient to the angel's command.

Where Did the Appearances of Christ Occur?

Matthew 28:10,16,17 have been placed over against John 20:21. Did the Risen Lord appear to His disciples in Jerusalem? Matthew 28:10,16,17 read: "Then said Jesus unto them; be not afraid: go tell my brethren that I go before you into Galilee and there shall you see me . . . Then the eleven disciples went away into Galilee, into a mountain where Jesus had appointed them. And when they saw Him, they worshiped Him; but some doubted."

In John 20:19 John reports that Jesus appeared to the disciples behind locked doors. Matthew it is said knows nothing of Christ appearing to

His disciples in Jerusalem. But does Matthew say that Jesus never appeared to His disciples in Jerusalem? No Gospel writer mentions all the appearances of Christ after His resurrection. Why Matthew does not mention any appearance of Jesus in Jerusalem is not indicated. There is no conflict between Matthew and John. Matthew's is only more fragmentary.[49]

In this connection attention should be drawn to a book by John Wenhain entitled, Easter Enigma (Grand Rapids: Zondervan Publishing House, 1984), 162 pages. Wenham has been Vice Principal of Tyndale Hall, Bristol and Warden of Latimer House; Oxford. This British scholar does not agree with historical-critical scholars that the resurrection accounts are in conflict. In this volume he takes these narratives and shows that it is possible to harmonize the accounts into a comprehensive historical sequence. He does show that with a measure of reasoned conjecture and historical imagination that it is possible to defend the resurrection narratives against the charge of being contradictory and replete with inaccuracies and thus cast a doubt over the historicity of Christ's glorious resurrection.

A Comparison of Lutheran Critical Scholars and Scholars not Affected by Rationalism.

Before the adoption of the historical method by modern Lutheran scholars, the standard dogmatics used in all Lutheran denominations had no problems with the resurrection of Jesus Christ. They never questioned its historicity and did not claim that these various resurrection appearances had not occurred.

Here is a listing of a few Lutheran Dogmatics which believe in the resurrection of Christ as an event that occurred in space/time and accept the various Scriptural accounts as true and also defend the resurrection of Christ against its detractors:

Joseph Stump, *The Christian Faith* (New York: The Macmillan Company, 1932), pp. 173-178. Stump was President of Northwestern Lutheran Theological Seminary when he wrote this volume. Conrad Emil Lindberg, *Christian Dogmatics*. Swedish edition translated into English by Rev. C. E. Hoffstein (Rock Island, IL: Augustana Book Concern). Lindberg was a professor of theology and would represent the Swedish Augustana Synod before its merger with the ULCA (pp. 242-243). Martin Reu, *Lutheran Dogmatics*, (Dubuque, Iowa: Wartburg Theological Seminary, 1951. Revised edition, pp. 229-233). Reu was one of the great Lutheran scholars of the twentieth century, professor at Wartburg Theological Seminary and would represent the old Iowa Synod and later the American Lutheran Church. Heinrich Schmid, *Doctrinal Theology of the Evangelical Lutheran Church*. Translated from the German and Latin by Charles A. Hay and Henry E. Jacobs (Minneapolis: Augsburg Publishing House, 1961) Reprint edition, pp. 379-380. This work which originally was published in 1843 in Germany presents a compilation of theological statements drawn from fourteen Lutheran theologians who lived during the sixteenth and seventeenth centuries. There is no doubt to be found in Lutheran Orthodoxy relative to the historicity of Christ's resurrection or the reliability of the appearances of Christ after His resurrection or the reliability of the appearances of Christ after His resurrection. Henry E. Jacobs, *A Summary of the Christian Faith* (Philadelphia, 1905), defends the resurrection of Christ on pages 153-156. Jacobs was professor · at the Lutheran Theological Seminary, Mt. Airy, Philadelphia. John Schaller, *Biblical Christology. A Study in Lutheran Dogmatics* (Milwaukee: Northwestern Publishing House, 1981), defends the resurrection of Christ, pp. 105-108. Francis Pieper, *Christian Dogmatics* (St. Louis: Concordia Publishing House, 1951), II, pp. 320-323 defends Christ's resurrection. The literature of the Lutheran Church-Missouri Synod contains much material explicating and defending Christ's resurrection. E. Hove, *Christian Doctrine* (Minneapolis: Augsburg Publishing House, 1930), gives an excellent presentation relative to Christ's resurrection on pages 202-203. Hove was professor at Luther Theological Seminary, St. Paul, Minnesota in 1920's and 1930's.

The Lutheran Confessions and the Resurrection of Christ.

Lutheran theology prior to the adoption of the higher-critical methodology and its application to the Gospel narratives of the resurrection and to I Corinthians 15:1-10 followed the stance of the Lutheran Confessions. There can be no doubt that the authors of the various Lutheran Confessions believed in the historicity of Christ's resurrection from the dead.[50] Furthermore, the Lutheran Confessions did not believe the Holy Scriptures were replete with errors, contradictions, discrepancies and differing resurrection accounts that were contradictory.[51]

Footnotes

1. Adam Fahling, *A Harmony of the Gospels. The Fourfold Gospel* (Grand Rapids: Zondervan Publishing House, no date), pp. 216-217; Adam Fahling, *The Life of Christ* (St. Louis; Concordia Publishing House 1936), pp. 687-705.
2. As quoted by Wilbur Smith, *Therefore Stand. Christian Apologetics* (Baker Book House, 1965), p. 437.
3. **Ibid.**, p. 385.
4. Quoted in Samuel H. Kellogg, *The Light of Asia and the Light of the World*, as given by Smith, **op. cit.**, p. 385.
5. *The Book of Concord* (Philadelphia; Fortress Press, 1959), pp. 11, 19.
6. J. Haas, "Rationalism," H. E. Jacobs and J.A.W. Haas, *The Lutheran Cyclopedia* (New York Charles Scribner's Sons, 1899), p. 401.
7. Rudolf Bultmann, *Theology of the New Testament* translated by Kendrick Grobel (New York: Scribner and Sons, 1955), II, p. 299.
8. Rudolf Bultmann, *Primitive Christianity* (New York: Meridian Books, 1956), pp. 201-202.
10. Rudolf Bultmann, *Jesus and the Word* (New York: Charles Scribners, 1958).
11. Guenther Bornkamm, "The third day He arose from the dead," *A New Look at the Apostles' Creed*, edited by Gerhard Rein (Minneapolis: Augsburg Publishing House, 1969), pp. 45-50.
12. **Ibid.**, p. 45.

13. **Ibid.**
14. **Ibid.**, p. 46.
15. As cited by Herman Otten, *Baal or God* (New Haven Leader Publishing Co., 1965), p. 107.
16. Gerhard Gloege, *The Day of His Coming* (Philadelphia: Fortress Press, 1963), p. 279.
17. **Ibid.**, p. 281.
11. **Ibid.**, p. 284.
19. **Ibid.**, p. 294.
20. David Griffin, *Process Theology* (Philadelphia: Westminster Press, 1973), p. 12.
21. Wolfart Pannenberg, *Jesus-God and Man*, translated Lewis Wilkens and Duane Priebe (Philadelphia: Westminster Press, 1961), p. 149.
22. Carl E. Braaten, "The Humiliation and the Exaltation of Jesus Christ," in *Christian Dogmatics* (Philadelphia: Fortress Press, 1984), I, p. 549.
23. Paul Althaus, *Der Christliche Glaube* (Guetersloh: Bertelmann, 1948), p. 219.
24. Regin Prenter, **Creation and Redeemer**, translated by Theodore I. Jenson (Philadelphia: Fortress Press, 1916), p. 424.
25. **Ibid.**, p. 424.
26. **Ibid.**
27. Carl E. Braaten and Robert W. Jenson, editors with the following as contributors: Gerhard O. Forde, Philip J. Hefner, Hans Schwarz, and Paul R. Sponheim, *Christian Dogmatics* (Philadelphia: Fortress Press, 1984), p. 550.
28. **Ibid.**, p. 551.
29. **Ibid.**
30. **Ibid.**, pp. 550-551.
31. **Ibid.**, p. 551.
32. Gustav Aulen, *The Faith of the Christian Church*, translated by Eric Wahlstrom and G. Everett Arden (Philadelphia: The Muhlenberg Press, 1948), pp. 246-249.
33. **Ibid.**, pp. 247-248.
34. **Ibid.**, p. 234.
35. Prenter, **op. cit.**, pp. 424-427.
36. **Ibid.**, p. 425.
37. **Ibid.**, pp. 427-429.
38. Many books on Christian apologetics have taken up the cudgel's for Christ's resurrection against the enemies of the Bible. Cf. Leander S. Keyser, *A System of Christian Evidence* (Burlington, Iowa: The Lutheran Literary Boars, 1930), pp. 49-60; 110-118.
39. Cf. McDowell, *Evidence that Demands A Verdict* (Campus Crusade for Christ, 1972), I, p. 199.
40. Wilbur M. Smith, **op. cit.**, p. 423.
41. As cited by Smith, **op. cit.**, pp. 427,428.
43. Frank Morison, *Who Moved the Stone?* (London: Faber and Faber, 1987).
44. W. Arndt, *Does the Bible Contradict Itself?* (St. Louis: Concordia Publishing House, 1926), p. 70.
45: **Ibid.**, p. 71.
46. **Ibid.**, pp. 71-72.
47. **Ibid.**, p. 72.

48. **Ibid.**, pp. 72-73.

49. **Ibid.**, p. 75.

50. Cf. the article on "The Person of Christ" in *The Formula of Concord*. Theodore G. Tappert, *The Book of Concord* (Philadelphia Fortress Press, 1959), p. 596. The Three Ecumenical Creeds are also given as a part of the *Book of Concord*, pp. 18-19, where the Apostles' Creed, the Athanasian Creed and the Nicene Creed are given with their assertions of Christ's resurrection.

51. **Ibid.**, pp. 464-465.

Questions

1. Unbelievers maintain that the Biblical accounts of the Resurrection of Jesus contain ____.
2. Now some who claim to be Christians and Lutherans ____ the resurrection of Christ.
3. The resurrection might be called the ____ of all ____.
4. Theodosius Harnack wrote that Christianity stands or falls with ____.
5. Only Christianity claims an empty tomb for its ____.
6. All traditional Christian Churches have statements in their creeds asserting the ____ of Christ.
7. What has led to a repudiation of the resurrection of Christ? ____
8. What did Rudolph Bultmann say about the resurrection? ____
9. Guenther Bronkamm explained away the ____.
10. What did Gerhard Gloege write in a book published by the Lutheran Church in America about the Resurrection? ____
11. Process theology has dismissed the resurrection as ____.
12. Pannenberg contended that____.
13. Regin Prenter is guilty of ____.
14. Carl Braaten contends that the resurrection is only true if one ____.
15. Braaten maintains that mythological symbolism contributes to ____.
16. Who was Simon Greenleaf? ____
17. What did Greenleaf write in 1846? ____
18. *Who Moved the Stone* by Frank Morrison turned out to be ____.
19. Who guided the Biblical writers? ____
20. What illustration does Arndt cite in response to those who claim there are contradictions in the Bible about the resurrection of Christ? ____
21. John Wenain in his Easter Enigma shows ____.
22. What are some *Lutheran Dogmatics* which defend the historicity of the Resurrection? ____
23. What do the Lutheran Confessions teach about the resurrection of Christ? ____

The Meaning of 'Fullness of Time' in Galatians 4:4 and Its Relationship to - Christ's Incarnation

Christian News, December 21, 1987

Both the Old and New Testament predicted the incarnation of God's Son. In the Old Testament the prophet Isaiah foretold in chapter 7:14 the Virginal Conception of the Messiah, in chapter 9:5-6 His birth and the prophet Micah stated in 5:2 that Jesus would be born in Bethlehem. The angel Gabriel announced to Mary in Nazareth that the Holy Spirit would come over her and that she would conceive a child and that she would call him Jesus (Luke 1:31). Matthew states that before Mary and Joseph came together to live as man and wife that Mary was found pregnant by the Holy Spirit (1:18).

These predictions of Isaiah, Micah and Gabriel were fulfilled. Both Luke and Matthew record the historical event of Christ as having assumed human nature and being born as an infant. In addition to Matthew's and Luke's versions of Christ's birth, the Gospel of John has still another account of Christ's becoming man. John describes the important truth that Jesus was the Logos, who was with God from all eternity and that He created the universe and all in it. In chapter 1:14 the clear fact of Christ's birth is asserted in the words: "And the Logos became flesh and dwelt or tabernacled among us."

Besides the three Gospels, other books of the New Testament contain passages that speak about the incarnation of Jesus, the foster son of Joseph and his real mother Mary. The Apostle John in two of his three epistles denounced the heresy of a Gnostic sect, the Docetists who denied that Jesus had actually come permanently into the flesh. [2] In chapter 4:3 the Apostle declared: "This is how you can recognize God's Spirit; every spirit who confesses that Jesus Christ has come into the flesh is from God. And any spirit who doesn't confess this Jesus isn't from God" (Beck's An American Translation, New Testament, p. 301).

Paul, in a number of his epistles, has passages that teach the incarnation of Christ. In Romans Paul declared: "What the Law could not do, God has done in sending His Son to be like sinful flesh (8:3, Beck translation)." In his Philippian epistle there is this reference to the incarnation: "Although He was God, He decided not to take advantage of His being equal with God, as though it were stolen goods, but He emptied Himself, as a slave, became like other human beings and was seen to have the ways of a man" (Beck's translation). In writing to his associate Timothy, Paul, in an ancient hymn, declared: "It must be admitted that deep is the mystery of our faith: He appeared in the flesh, became righteous in spirit, was seen by angels, was preached among the nations, was believed in the world, was taken up in glory" (3:16). Also in his instruction to Titus, Paul taught: "For the grace of God hath appeared for the salvation of all men" (2:13). (Beck translation.)

The author of Hebrews also emphasized the fact of the incarnation of Christ. In this Christological epistle, the author stresses the necessity and importance of Christ's birth. Thus he wrote: "Now since all these children have flesh and blood, He in the same way took on flesh and blood in order to die and so take away all the powers of him who had the power of death, that is the devil, and so free those, who terrified by death, had to be slaves all their lives. It is clear He didn't come to help angels but Abraham's descendants" (2:14-17). (Beck translation.)

It is instructive to analyze the different incarnation texts of the New Testament. Each scripture asserts a different fact about the birth of Christ. From Luke's account (2:14) one learns that Jesus was born during the reign of Caesar Augustus (27 B.C.-14 A.D.).[3] From Matthew's account (Ch. 2) it becomes clear that Jesus was born during the reign of Herod the Great (37 B.C.-4 B.C.). Paul in Galatians 4:4 gives a very significant statement about the proper time for Christ to assume man's nature, when he informed the Galatians, namely, that Christ came "when the fullness of time had come." Certain conditions had to exist to make the coming of God's Son humanly speaking more propitious than at any other time in history. The spiritual needs of mankind were especially demanding a Savior. In this essay the writer purports to show what was involved in the expression "the fullness of time," which had come so that God did send forth His Son (John 3:16).

The Beginning of the Realization of the Plan of Salvation
The first preparation for the incarnation took place in eternity, before the world and the universe were brought into existence by the Triune God.[4] Relative to the decree of redemption Peter wrote: "Who (namely Jesus) verily was foreordained in these last times for you (1 Peter 1:20)." The same apostle declared on the day of Pentecost: "Him, being delivered by wicked hands have you crucified and slain (Acts 2:23)." John in the Apocalypse speaks of "the Lamb slain from the fountain of the world" (13:8).

After Eve and Adam had sinned, God immediately began to put into operation the plan of salvation. In the word of the Protoevangelium, Genesis 3:15, God promised mankind's first parents that from the seed of the woman a Person would come who would crush the Serpent's head. According to the New Testament the Serpent of Genesis 3:15 is identified with the Devil or Satan. Paul and John both make this identification. For at least four thousand years God prepared mankind for "the fullness of time." He chose one Semitic people, the descendants of Terah and Abraham and their offspring, Isaac and Jacob to be the carriers of the Messianic promise. Beginning with Genesis 12 until chapter 4 of the book of Malachi, Yahweh prepared a people for the coming of the Redeemer. After Genesis 12 the remainder of the Old Testament is mainly the record of the founding and development of the Theocratic people, Israel, from whom eventually God's Son would be born.

With Abraham there began a division of mankind into two groups, Israel, or the Jewish people, and the pagan or non-Jewish world.[5] As a result of this clear-cut division the history of Israel from Abraham to Christ had a twofold aspect in the pagan world man developed his natural ability apart from the influence of a direct divine revelation. For Israel it was essentially "an approach of God to man," in paganism man endeavored by his thinking to approach God on terms of work righteousness. The position of Judaism, that is, the kind that followed the precepts of Moses and the Prophets and the Writings' center in the redemptive work of the Christ to come, while paganism tried to develop ways of salvation which were unacceptable to the God of the Old Testament.

It is the purpose of the record of the Gospels and the Book of Acts to show how these two worlds, the Jewish and non-Jewish were united in Peter's vision on the housetop of Simon the tanner. Peter's subsequent visit to the house of Cornelius, the Roman centurion, shows how two antithetical worlds were united.

The nations which played the most prominent role in this process of unification are all represented on the superscription of Christ's cross on Calvary. The alleged cause for Christ crucifixion was stated in Hebrew, Greek and Latin. These three nation's contributions constitute the cornerstone of Western civilization. It was into the Graeco-Roman world that Christ was born and where Christianity had its origin and spread.

A. External Preparation for Christ's Coming
The Contribution of the Roman Empire to
"the Fullness of Time"

The Roman Empire was an important agency in preparing the world for the birth of Christ.[6] Christianity's origin and the birth of the Roman Empire were not far a part in time. Christ was born somewhere between 8 and 4 B.C., while the Roman Empire came into existence in 31 B.C.[7] Geographically the Roman Empire in which Christ was born enjoyed an extension from the Euphrates to the Atlantic, from the Danube and Rhine, and the fertile lands of Scotland to the African deserts. The vast territory of the Mediterranean Sea, north and south of it was divided into two general divisions: the Orient and the Occident or the West. Egypt, Arabia and the land around the Adriatic Sea constituted the East, while all dominions west of Asia belonged to the Roman West.[8]

Before Rome appeared on the world scene great empires had existed which had been built to be world empires, such as: the Assyrian, Babylonian, Persian and the Macedonian and each of these endeavored politically not only to incorporate different peoples but also to hold them together. But as one surveys the history of the aforementioned empires , their peoples were forcefully held together. Each in its turn helped in some way to prepare the way for the appropriate time for Christ to come, described by Paul as "the fullness of time." All great empires before the appearance of the Roman were united by force, by the use of deportations and uprooting of native populations from their original homes, but they did not win over the nations welded and consequently never became an organic unity. In neither the Assyrian, Babylonian, or even the Persian, which was an improvement over the two located in the Mesopotamian

Valley, or the Macedonian, which also attempted to bring West and East together through intermarriage was true unity achieved. In these pre-Roman empires the conquered and tributary people were never assimilated into a uniform culture and civilization. In fact in these empires the individual was not given much respect.[9]

The Macedonian Empire which followed the Medo-Persian reached its pinnacle with the rule of and conquests of Alexander the Great.[10] It is true that in the Macedonian Empire there was progress in fostering certain conditions which would be favorable to the spread of Christianity. As Qualben stated: "Through the conquests of Alexander the Great the sympathies of men hitherto so narrow and local, were widened; the distribution between Greek and Barbarian was gradually obliterated. Greek civilization with its matchless language, literature, art, philosophy and science, spread over Egypt and Western Asia. The civilized world was given a universal language. The rediscovery of the sea route from India to Europe greatly stimulated trade and commerce. Several famous universities and libraries were founded."[11]

The Empire of Alexander the Great at his death was divided among his four generals. Thus after a relatively short time Alexander's Empire disintegrated as it was fought over and its unity was destroyed.[12] The two empires that had significance for the Jewish people were those of the Ptolemais of Egypt and the Seleucids of Syria. Not too many years after the breakup of Alexander's vast dominion there came the Romans along and they succeeded in, uniting many civilizations and cultures and races into a unity not seen before. But the Macedonian conquests had made possible the intellectual conquest of the Romans by the Greeks, which turned out to be an important factor in the preparation of mankind for Christianity.

It is one of the significant and important developments of history that in the five hundred year history of the Roman Empire, from 31 B.C. to A.D. 476 that Rome was able to unite in itself all civilized nations of Europe, North Africa and the Near East. Although Rome conquered Greece in 46 B.C., eventually Greece conquered Rome through its culture religion, art and philosophy. Before the Roman Empire appeared upon the scene in European and Near Asian countries there were many different nations, laws and languages. Rome changed all this by fusing the various people into one heterogeneous mass, living under one emperor, under one government, and under one military organization. All these united people had one body of law, a common coinage, a central mail, one transportation system, one alphabet and one common culture.[13] In these respects the Roman Empire was unique, a world empire the like of which had not been seen before, but representing conditions ideally suited for the propagation and spread of Christianity.

The Roman Empire an Amalgam of Diverse Nationalities

The amalgamation of peoples using different languages and representing different cultures showed them the desirability of the one to the many. It became apparent to people that they could not war against each other as had been the practice for thousands of years and at the same time have their best interests served. Being isolated from each other and frequently going to war against each other were not able to foster the people's welfare and wellbeing. It happened in the unique Roman Empire that the barriers between Roman and Barbarian, Greek and Jews, were broken down, a concept which was in line with the teachings of Christ and St. Paul as expressed in Galatians 3:28.

The concept of unity as exhibited in the Roman Empire had also an educative value in that it could show that above all the many gods and goddesses worshipped by the Romans, the Greeks, the Egyptians and other peoples that there was One God above the many deities revered and served by their devotees. People in the Roman Empire could not help responding to the idea that there must be a higher spiritual unity, a universal God. Again, just as the unity of the Roman Empire promoted the idea of a supreme and universal God, so also the concept of a higher unity for mankind was fostered by the unity that characterized the empire that was established by Caesar Augustus.[14]

Rome's Treatment of Conquered Peoples

In contrast to the governing policy of the treatment of conquered peoples by the Assyrians, the Babylonians, the Greeks under Alexander and under the Diadochi, in the Roman Empire a policy of tolerance, reconciliation and assimilation was practiced.[15] Conquered people were not treated as enemies but as friends of Rome. Roman citizenship was given to provincials, who were permitted to take part in local government according to their traditions, governors, and officials. With Caesar Augustus the practice was initiated of bestowing Roman citizenship upon a limited number of provincials. Subsequent emperors extended this practice. In A.D. 212 all free born people, living in all Roman provinces enjoyed Roman citizenship.[16] Thus universal citizenship helped prepare the way for Christianity, where all believers enjoyed the citizenship of heaven and were equal members in God's kingdom. To the Galatian congregations Paul wrote: "You are all sons of God through faith in Christ Jesus; for all of you who have been baptized into Christ have clothed yourselves with Christ. There cannot be Jew and Greek, slave and free man, male or female; you are all one in Christ Jesus" (3:26-28).

The Unifying Influence of Roman Law

The unity of the Roman Empire was also fostered by one system of jurisprudence. Wherever there were Roman citizens in the vast Roman Empire the same law functioned and was practiced.[17] As Roman citizens increased in the empire, so did the number of people who benefited from it. The Apostle Paul fell back upon his Roman citizenship in connection with his missionary journeys and on occasion it saved his life.

Peace in the Roman Empire

At the time Christ was born and during the time Christianity spread in the Roman Empire peace was the order of the day.[18] The many bloody campaigns and conquests of the two centuries before the establishment of the Roman Empire had at least for a century or more come to an end. This situation was of course favorable for the missionary program of the spiritual kingdom which Christ's Apostles had the injunction from their Lord to establish. The missionaries and evangelists were free to move throughout the Roman realms. The existence of universal peace also helped Paul as he embarked on his three missionary journeys. According to Church tradition the Twelve Apostles were active in carrying out the Great Commission given them by Jesus (Matthew 28:20; Acts 1:8).

Universal Language

Bilingualism characterized the Roman Empire in the first century A.D. Latin was the official language of the Roman courts as well of the Roman army. Latin was not only the language of the courts, but especially the speech in the empire west of the Adriatic and in North Africa.[19] However, Koine Greek was the language of the Roman provinces in the East. In addition to that, Greek was the language of culture throughout the Roman Empire. Greek was the language of culture and was understood practically anywhere where Roman rule was in power.[20] It was because of this fact that the New Testament writers, all but one Jewish, who spoke Palestinian Aramaic, nevertheless, wrote their inspired books in Greek. It is as Qualben phrased it: "The Gospel of 'peace and good will toward men' was to use as its first medium of expression the most perfect instrument for the embodiment and conveyance of thought the world has ever known."[21]

The Contribution of the Roman Army to "The Fullness of Time"

Unbeknown to themselves the soldiers of the Roman army served to prepare the world of that day for the coming of Christ. The Roman army had been used in the conquering of many lands which became part and parcel of Rome's Empire. The imperial government did not keep auxiliary troops in their native districts. Soldiers were separated from their native homes and countries. They were stationed in parts of the Roman Empire strange to them. The personnel was recruited from the provinces. Troops were surrounded by strong Romanizing influences in their military stations. The result of this procedure was that service in the army amounted to attending a school of civilization. The various legions scattered throughout the Roman Empire became important agents for the spread of Graeco-Roman culture. Observed Qualben: "The army helped to shake the heap of meal (Mt. 13:33) into a more uniform body."[22] Thus the Roman army played a role and was a factor in bringing about those conditions that made possible what Paul termed "the fullness of time."

Strategic Centers of Trade and Commerce

A number of cities in the Roman Empire became centers for trade and commerce, culture and religion.[23] Paul and the Apostles used these flourishing cities of humanity for missionary purposes. On his missionary journeys Paul especially visited and often stayed for long lengths of time in them. Thus Paul visited Antioch, Athens, Corinth, Ephesus, various cities of Macedonia, and Rome and established congregations in these populous centers, from which then the Gospel was taken to adjacent communities. It is possible that a number of congregations in Asia Minor were founded by evangelists operating out of Ephesus. On this third missionary journey Paul spent three years in Ephesus; 18 months in Corinth during his second journey.

The Splendid Roman Highway System and Good Sea Lanes, Aids in the Spread of the Gospel

Between Rome and Italy there existed in the first Christian century a splendid highway system for travel from Rome and the more remote provinces of the empire.[24] There were also well-arranged sea routes that afforded transportation and travel to various ports of the Roman world by means of excellent ports located on the Mediterrean Sea.[25]

Caesar Augustus had built a golden milestone in Rome. From this unique milestone, five main highways enabled people to travel to all parts of the Roman Empire. These roads served the Apostle Paul well in his missionary travels, as well as the Apostles Peter, John and other of the Twelve, in speedily going with the Gospel of peace to many different provinces of Europe and Asia.

Along these highways the traveler could find stations where he or she could lodge and change horses. The traveler on the Roman highways received help by the markings of milestones along the way; yes, even from maps the traveler could ascertain the miles from one place to another. While these splendid highways served the Roman government, they also were of assistance to the missionaries and evangelists of the Christian Good News.[26]

The Contribution of the Postal System

Under Caesar Augustus' direction the Roman government established a postal system by land which was utilized by government agents and officials. Because of the effective of this postal system private citizens developed a similar kind for the public. Observed Qualben: "The comparative ease, swiftness and safety of travel gave a strong impetus to commercial intercourse and to travel in general, promoting a cosmopolitan atmosphere hitherto unknown. Nations came closer together. Sympathies and interests were broadened. The provincials became absorbed in the Roman race. Dress, manners, political, and legal institutions, language, and religion became more uniform-a unity in diversity."[27] We know that Paul sent a number of his epistles to congregations by couriers or persons who must have availed themselves of this postal system. Epaphras was the bearer of the letter to the Colossians and the Epistle to Philemon.

Secret Societies and Fraternal Orders

Because of the unequal distribution of wealth among the common people, there arose among them a desire to protect themselves against economic and social pressure by forming or joining fraternal orders, secret societies, or secret cults. These societies flourished during Rome's classical age, during the three centuries prior and after Christ's birth.[28] Some of these organizations were totally secular, others had a specific religious purpose. All of these societies, whether secular or religious, had a subordinate purpose to provide a burial place and provide a decent burial for its members.[29] However, the religious views of these organization were not those of the Christian faith and were in diametrical opposition to those of the New Testament.

It is held that the Golden Age of the Roman Empire lasted up to the year 100 of the Christian Era and provided benefits not known before to the average person, yet it failed to give its citizens the strength to live happy and soul-satisfying lives.[30]

B. Internal Preparation through Religion and Philosophy

As one surveys the world prior to the coming of Christ, historians of religion have noted that besides the outward conditions that prepared the Roman world for "the fullness of time," there were further internal conditions that probably even played a more important role. To appreciate Paul's assertion of Galatians 4:4, it is necessary to appreciate the transformation in the Roman world of its thoughts and emotions. To evaluate the thought world into which Christ was born, it is vital to understand the developments in Greek, Roman and Jewish thought that had occurred by the time the Virgin Mary gave birth to her first-born son.[31]

The Greek Preparation for the "Fullness of Time"

The non-Jewish world was greatly influenced by Greek philosophy. Earlier in their history the Greeks had developed by themselves a pantheon of gods headed by Zeus.[32] The gods and goddesses of the Greek people were actually a deification of the forces of nature. To the Greek deities were ascribed male and female sex. They were depicted as powerful human beings who had the manifest virtues and vices ascribed to men. The Greek gods and goddesses were jealous of their superiority over mankind. Because of this they denied unto mankind perfect happiness. Because of the type and character traits exhibited by the Greek gods they were unable to inspire their devotees to rise to a higher moral level than that which they themselves did not demonstrate. Early Greek religion did not postulate a devil, although evil design and evil suggestions were made by the gods. Greek religion did not truly have a conception of sin. In Greek religious thinking the moral consciousness was identical with the beautiful. Therefore, beauty, not holiness, was that for which men and women were to strive.[33]

The History of Greek Thought

Scholars have distinguished three distinct stages in the development of Greek thought and philosophy: 1. After 500 B.C., as a result of rational inquiry, philosophy freed itself from the theology found in Hesiod and Homer. Now man became the measure of all things. 2. With the fall of

Athens (400 B.C. and during the Macedonian supremacy) philosophy and religion freed themselves from political or state interests. 3. By the time of Christ Greek religion and philosophy further divorced themselves from scientific, thought and from universal philosophy. The result was that Greek thinking resulted in a narrow individualism.[34]

When the Romans came into contact with the Greeks, whom they had politically conquered, such were the philosophical views with which they were confronted. Earlier certain Roman leaders like Cato the Elder (232-147 B.C.) warned against Greek customs, Greek ideas and Greek innovations.

There were Roman men who believed that the adoption of Greek views would be the moral ruin of Rome society.

Roman Civilization before "the Fullness of Time"

Early in Roman history the Romans were controlled by the same institution, the city-state upon which Greek civilization was built. Speaking of the influence of Greece upon Rome, Qualben wrote: "From the Greeks they borrowed the idea of a confederate government; and developed by a firm belief that they were so-called upon to govern the world. The genius of the Romans expressed itself along concrete lines. They were deficient in imaginative and aesthetic power, as compared with the Greek, but they possessed a sobriety, a dignity and moral sense that the Greeks looked at"[35] While Greece, as has already been noted, furnished life's ideals, the Romans created the institution which made the realization of the Greek ideals possible.

Roman and Greek Religions Compared

The Roman gods and goddesses did not possess the same vividness exhibited by the Greek deities. Unlike the Greeks, the Roman had no home for the gods and goddesses located on Mt. Olympus.[36] The Roman deities, although they were perceived as having sex, being male or female, the Roman gods did not propagate children. Roman religion on the whole was abstract, formal and legalistic. The Roman deities did not promise their devotees rewards of a future life. The Roman gods were looked upon as really interfering with the lives of men and women and were considered as oppressing people because of their watchfulness directed to the people. Romans considered the gods necessary in order to secure their favors and as a means of getting along on life's way. Roman religion prescribed very elaborate and exceedingly scrupulous regulations as Romans carried out their worship service.[37]

For the average Roman originally religion was unconcerned about the state nor was it concerned with the condition of his soul. Personal morality, so important in the Judaeo-Christian religion, was unimportant for the Romans. A good Roman was expected to be careful in his observance of religious rites and conformity to the religious ceremonies was looked upon as evidence of truthfulness, sincerity and a dependable character. In this respect Roman religion was superior to Greek. Religion was considered a contract between the gods and the Roman citizen. The inner aspect of religion did not exist, but it was all external.[38] If the Romans performed the rituals exactly, then the gods were expected to keep their bargain by giving victory and favoring the Romans over their enemies. The Roman hated excess in religion, but also hated a lack of piety.

The State and Religion

Rome took the stance that it never made peace with a nation, except as a victor. However, victory over its enemies for Rome could only be achieved through the help of the gods. The result was that religion became interwoven with the affairs of government; this in turn led to a religious patriotism.

Interestingly enough, not priests, but government officials functioned as leaders at the state religious ceremonies. The head of religious affairs was known as Pontifex Maximus, and the latter was the head of the state.[39] Before 31 B.C. the Capitoline Jupiter and the "Dean Roma" headed the state religiously. However, after the Roman Empire came into being, the Emperor took the place of Capitoline Jupiter, and then there developed a worship of the emperor, one of the bad developments which would be the cause for the imprisonment, being cast to the lions or killed in some other way.'[40] Christians refused to call the Roman Emperor "deus," or LORD, the title they would only accept for Christ.

After 250 B. C. Rome was not dedicated to the ideals that had guided Rome for centuries. However, as the Empire grew and its citizens came in touch with other cultures, these traditional ideals suffered and were given up. The first negative influence causing the deterioration of Roman religion came from Greece, which although conquered by Rome, in turn affected the religious views of the Romans.[41] The latter considered their religious beliefs and practices outmoded, but the irony in this situation was that the Romans took over from the Greeks only the shell of what once had been taught and held in Greece. Roman men of culture adopted a skeptical, hollow and the unbelieving spirit of the Greeks, although many Romans would not acknowledge this openly and publicly.[42]

Other factors also contributed to the religious deterioration of Roman society. Because of their Greek and Oriental conquests, Romans came into contact and entered into close relationships with the degenerate life of Greece and the Orient. Wealth, luxury and slavery from the provinces had a debilitating and demoralizing effect on Rome's religious views. Divorce became common, there was a breakdown of the family, religious belief declined and morality suffered seriously.[43]

While this was occurring the common people lost faith in the Roman gods and goddesses. So the people turned to new cults which promised them assurance and certitude. When Rome conquered other nations it did not insist that they give up belief in their deities and permitted the propagation of the religions of conquered people. The number of deities that were officially allowed to exist and be propagated was many so that the Romans had a choice of many gods from whom to choose. In fact, conquered people were invited to have their gods represented in Rome, but in turn the provincials must recognize the Roman gods. The result was religious syncretism. In the midst of this confusion, people began to ask the question, what was the relationship of the one to the many?[44] Religious condition were therefore propitious for "the fullness of time" for a new religion and a world-Savior to be proclaimed. A new religion was needed to satisfy the soul-cravings of millions of people inhabiting the large Roman Empire. There developed a whole constellation of factors which made the time right for the birth of Christ and His atoning death for mankind and for this message to be proclaimed in the first Christian century.[45]

C. The Part Played by Jews and Judaism in Preparation for the "Fullness of Time"

Jesus told the Samaritan woman: "Salvation is from the Jews" (John 4:22). To the Syro-Phoenician woman Jesus asserted "that He was sent to the lost sheep of the house of Israel" The coming of Christ was predicted in the Old Testament Scriptures in numerous passages. God gave them the land of Canaan. Paul in speaking of the great advantages the Jews had over the Gentiles said to the Roman congregation: "They are the people of Israel. They were made God's family. They have the glory, the covenant, the Law, the worship and the promises. They have the ancestors and from them according to His Body came Christ, who is God over everything, blessed forever" (Ch. 9:4-5).[46] By the time Christ was born the three major portions of the Old Testament were in existence and recognized as the very Word of God, as shown by the reference to the Law, and Prophets and the Writings in Josephus and Ecclesiasticus.[47]

Unfortunately, using the Old Testament was the source, one sees that the descendants of Abraham according to the flesh did not live up to the covenant God established with Israel at Mt. Sinai, nor did they keep the covenant they made with Yahweh as recorded in Joshua 24. Frequently they went whoring after false and pagan gods and rejected the meaning of the Shemah: "Hear, O Israel, the LORD your God is one LORD." Because of breaking the Sinaitic and Joshua covenants, the Northern Kingdom was punished in that the Assyrians took the Ten Tribes into the Assyrian Captivity.[48] The same fate befell the Southern Kingdom, which fell in 587 B.C. when Nebuchadnezzar took thousands of Jews into the Babylonian captivity.[49] The temple was destroyed, its precious vessels became objects of booty, the ark of the covenant disappeared and the walls of Jerusalem were broken down. Read the Lamentations of Jeremiah to see how sad the years were after 587 B.C.

With the downfall of the Babylonian Kingdom under Nabonidus a change began in the history of the People of Israel or Jews. Under Zerubbabel and Joshua nearly 50,000 Jews returned to war-torn and desolate Judah, a part of the province of the Persian Trans-Euphrates satrapy. "The Second Temple was built between 520-516 B.C., with Haggai and Zechariah spurring the returned exiles on. The prophecies of Isaiah and Jeremiah about the return of a remnant were fulfilled. The scribe Ezra especially in the post-exilic period built up the religious and political theocracy which was to hold the people together for centuries.[50]

Palestine was brought under the domination of Alexander the Great (336-323 B.C.). This marked the beginning of Hellenism and its influence on Jewish religion and thought.[51] From 323-203 B.C. Palestine, after Alexander's death, came under the influence of the Ptolemais of Egypt.[52] The Seleucids took over control of Palestine in 198 B.C. and during the rule of Antiochus IV (175-164 B.C.) the Seleucids attempted to Hellenize the Jews, who inspired by Mattathias and his sons, resisted the Hellenization program of the Greek Seleucids. The descendants of Mattathias were called the Maccabees and between 167-141 B.C. under Simon Maccabeus an independent Jewish government was established.[54]

In 63 B.C. Pompey the Great made a Roman province of Syria and with it Palestine became an integral part of the Roman Empire. Herod the Great (37 B.C.- 4 B.C.) was the governor of Palestine. It was during the last years of Herod the Great's reign that Jesus was born in Bethlehem of Judea,[55] as predicted by the prophet Micah in 5:4.[55]

Great Historic Changes in Judaism After 587 B.C.

The two great captives, the ones of 722 B.C. and 587 B.C., resulted in great changes in Judaism. After 587 B.C. the Jews were living in three great centers of the ancient Roman world, namely, Egypt, Babylonia and Palestine.[56] Before the fall of Jerusalem the Jews had been farmers and shepherds, but in the Dispersion (Diaspora) the Jews changed occupations and became traders, merchants and sellers of goods. They consequently settled in the large cities of Babylonia, Egypt, and Persia. In time, it is believed, that the Jewish colonists in Egypt and Babylonia secured control of a considerable part of the trade of the ancient world.[57]

It was especially during the Babylonian and Greek periods that the Jews in the Dispersion began to lay the foundation for the "Golden Internationalism," during which the Jewish control of the world's monies begins.

Alexander the Great founded a number of cities named after him, the only one of the seventy established that survived was Alexandria in Egypt Many Jews were settled there and came to occupy a position of prominence. Probably one-eighth of Alexandria's population was Jewish.[58] Only a minority of Jews lived in Palestine in the three centuries prior to the birth of Jesus. There was a large population in the East and a large dispersion in the West. The Jewish worshippers present at Pentecost in the year A.D. 30 show, according to Acts 2:9-11, that the Jewish population had spread throughout a great part of the Roman Empire with Jerusalem its religious center.

Need of a Greek Old Testament Translation

The Jews in Alexandria and in the West needed the Old Testament rendered from Hebrew and Aramaic (half of Daniel, one-fourth of Ezra) into Greek, the language of learning and culture.[59] It is believed that the Hebrew Pentateuch was translated into Greek in Alexandria. Other parts of the Hebrew Old Testament were translated by probably the year 120 B.C.[60] The Septuagint (LXX) was important for the spread of Christianity. Most of the Old Testament quotations in the Greek New Testament

618

were from the Septuagint.[61] The early Christians used it in their missionary endeavors.

The Contribution of the Synagogue to the "Fullness of Time."

Wherever the Jews went and settled they established synagogues, where worship and instruction took place." The Apostle Paul on his missionary journeys, although appointed by Jesus to be the apostle to the Gentiles, would always seek out a synagogue and there present the Gospel of Christ to his fellow countrymen. Luke is the Book of Acts mentioned this a number of times.[64]

The Influence of the Pagan Environment on the Jews

As a result of their selling and merchandizing activities. Jewish merchants and traders met and dealt with divergent cultures and peoples in the Diaspora. The Jews of the Western Dispersion found certain features of Greek and Egyptian worship worth adopting. On the other hand, the Jews of the Eastern Dispersion found aspects of Chaldean astrology, fatalism and magic appealing. Persian dualism and Oriental mysticism influenced them.[65] It appears that some of the just mentioned religious views the Jews began to consider as supplementing the divine revelation found in the Old Testament Scriptures. That such was the case becomes clear when the Apocrypha and Pseudepigrapha are read, or when examining the writings of Philo and other Hellenistic writers, or perusing the Kabbalistic speculations that began to appear.[66]

Sources for the Studying of Liberal and Conservative Judaism

Considerable theological differences arose in Jewry in the two centuries prior to Christ's birth.[67] The views that were propounded may be classified as liberal and conservative. These are especially apparent in the theology of the Sadducees and the Pharisees. They are further evident by reading the works of Philo[68] and those of contemporary Judaism and in the Old Testament Apocrypha and the very large Epipseudical literature, particularly when they are compared with the canonical Old Testament books. How great the theological differences were may be seen by studying the events of the Maccabean uprising, 174-141 B.C.

The Four Major Sects of Judaism

By "the fullness of time" had come, there were four different sects in Judaism, namely, the Sadducees, the Pharisees, the Essenes of Qumranites, and the Zealots.[69] In addition, one must consider the Scribes, who did not form a separate class or sect. A number of writers, like Josephus have left posterity an account of the beliefs of the Essenes.[70] Since 1948, caves near Khirbet Qumran have produced new information on the Essenes, or the sect which lived at Qumran in caves.[71] The Essenes were formalists, skeptics with regard to standard Jerusalem Judaism; the former were also mystics. The Zealots were committed to freeing the Jewish people from Roman control.

The two prominent sects at Christ's time were the Sadducees and the

Pharisees.[72] The Sadducees were the nucleus of the priestly class and of the aristocracy. They denied the resurrection from the dead. For them the grave ended all. They rejected the belief in angels and spirits. For the Sadducees God did not exercise any influence on the choices people made. They only accepted the books of the Old Testament as the authoritative source for their religious beliefs and rejected all traditions. The Sadducees placed Hellenistic culture side by side with that of Judaism. They were the rationalists of Judaism, only permitting reason to determine their beliefs. The Sadducees lived only for this life and for them there was no hereafter.[73] Their activity centered in the Temple and the high priests came from their sect.

The Pharisees by contrast limited their activity to the synagogue. They believed in the immortality of the soul and taught a resurrection of the body. According to the Pharisees angels were either bad or good. Even though they were predestinarians, they still taught that man had a free will and that he was morally responsible. The Pharisees were the developers of the Oral Law, that is Tradition, which allegedly began with Ezra and was further developed by Jewish scholars during the four hundred years before the coming of the "fullness of time."[74] In the course of these centuries they worked out minute laws which were designed to rule every phase of Jewish life, later embedded in the Talmud, whose objective was to attain salvation by works.[75] Jesus came into conflict with Jews over these traditions which Jesus rejected.

Educational System of Palestine

Between 75 B.C.-70 A.D. the school system of Palestine attained its greatest development in 64 B.C. Rabbi Simon ben Shetach began a primary school system, which appears to have insisted on compulsory attendance. Later on another rabbi, Joshua ben Gamala advocated that children in every town and village be educated. This development also contribute to making conditions favorable for the coming of the Messiah and the spread of Christianity.[76]

The Messianic Expectation of the Jews

The Jewish people for a number of centuries were expecting the coming of the Messiah. This is evident especially from the Qumran texts which show that the people there were expecting two Messiahs, a priestly one and a kingly one.[77] Certain intertestamental Jewish books also expressed this hope. However, the Jewish Messianic hope was not centered on a suffering, redeeming Messiah, as predicted by Isaiah 52:13-53:12. They were expecting a Messiah who would do what David did in Old Testament times, free them from their enemies. When Jesus emphasized the fact that His Kingdom was not of this world, they rejected Him. Sadly John wrote many years after Christ's ascension: "He came into his own, but his own received him not (John 1:11)."

The Decree of Caesar Augustus

According to God's timetable, the factors existed which were of such a nature that it was a propitious time for mankind especially in that the promise given Adam and Eve and their descendants should be carried out To bring about the fulfillment of Micah's prophecy that the Messiah was to be born in Bethlehem in Judaea (5:2), God caused Caesar Augustus to issue a decree for a census of the whole Empire. Luke stated that this was the first census made during the governorship of Quirinius in Syria.[78] "So Joseph went up from Galilee, from the town of Nazareth, to Judaea, to David's town of Bethlehem, because he was of the house and lineage of David, to have himself registered together with Mary, who was betrothed to him and was with child."[79] In Bethlehem Mary gave birth to the Wonder Child of the ages. The uniqueness of Mary's child that he was God and man in one Person.

Paul's Teaching about Christ's Birth

The purpose of Christ's Incarnation is set forth in these words: "But when the right time came, God sent His Son, born of a woman, born under the Law, to free those under the Law and make us his sons. And because you are sons, God sent into our hearts the Spirit of His Son, who cries 'Abba! Father!' So you are no longer a slave but a son. And if you are His son, God has made you an heir."[80]

Footnotes

1. Revere Franklin Weidner, *Christology or the Doctrine of the Person of Christ* (Chicago: Wartburg Publishing House, 1913), p. 46.

2. **Ibid.**, p. 46.

3. Adam Fahling, *The Life of Christ* (St. Louis: Concordia Publishing House, 1936), p. 45.

4. On the decree of redemption cf., A.L. Graebner, *Doctrinal Theology* (St. Louis: Concordia Publishing House, 1910), pp. 43-44.

5. J. W. Shephard, *The Christ of the Gospels - An Exegetical Study* (Grand Rapids: Wm. B. Eerdmans Publishing Company, 1946), pp. iv-viii.

6. Theodor Zahn, *Grundriss der Geschichte des Leben Jesu* (Leppzig: A. Deichertsche Verlagshandlung D. Werner School, 1928), p. 9.

7. Cf. "A Chronological History of Rome," H. Wayne House Chronological and Background Charts of the New Testament (Grand Rapids: Zondervan Publishing House, 1981), pp. 48-49.

8. Cf. map of Roman Empire H. F. Vos, "Rome, Rome Empire," *Wycliffe Bible Encyclopedia* (Chicago: Moody Press 1976) II p. 1480.

9. Lars P. Qualben, *A History of the Christian Church* (New York: Thomas Nelson and Sons, 1940), p. 10.

10. Robert H. Pfeiffer, *History of New Testament Times With An Introduction to the Apocrypha* (New York: Harper & Brothers, 1949), p. 8.

11. Qualben, **op. cit.**, p. 9.

12. Cf. Victor Tcherikover, *Hellenistic Civilization of the Jews* (Philadelphia: The Jewish Publication Society of America, 1959), pp. 10-19.

13. Qualben, **op. cit.**, p. 10.

14. Vos, **op. cit.**, p. 1483.

15. Morton S. Enslin, "New Testament Times," in *The Interpreter's Bible* (Nashville:

Abingdon Cokesbury Press, 1951), Vii, p. 102.

16. Qualben, **op. cit.**, p. 11.

17. Madeleine Miller and J. Lane Miller, *Encyclopedia of the Bible Life* (New York and London: 1944), pp. 366-367.

18. Kenneth Scott Latourette, *A History of Christianity* (New York: Harper & Brothers Publishers, 1953), p. 21.

19. Merrill C. Tenney, *The New Testament - Its Historical and Analytical Survey* (Grand Rapids: Wm. B. Eermans Publishing Company, 1953), pp. 84-85.

20. Cf. Bruce M. Metger, "The Language of the New Testament," *The Interpreter's Bible*, **op. cit.**, VII, pp. 43-59.

21. Qualben, **op. cit.**, p. 12.

22. **Ibid.**, p. 13.

23. Madeleine Miller and Jane Lane Miller, *Encyclopedia of Bible Life* (New York: Harper & Brothers, Publishers, 1944), pp. 366-367.

24. "Transportation," in J. I. Packer, Merrill C. Tenney, William White, *The Bible Almanac* (Nashville; Thomas Nelson Publishers, 1980), p. 297. Bo Reicke, *The New Testament Era* (Philadelphia: Fortress Press, 1968), p. 12.

25. J. A. Thompson, *Handbook of Life in Bible Times* (Leicester, England: Inter-Varsity Press, 1986), p. 199.

26. "Trade and Commerce," William Neil (editor), *The Bible Companion* (New York: McGraw-Hill Book Company, 1961), p. 398.

27. Qualben, **op. cit.**, p. 13.

28. Kenneth Scott Latourette, *A History of Christianity* (New York: Harper and Brothers, Publishers, 1953), pp. 23-26.

29. Qualben, **op. cit.**

30. For the major events of this period, df. House, **op. cit.**, p. 49.

31. Merrill C. Tenney, *The New Testament - An Historical and Analytic Study* (Grand Rapids: Wm. B. Eerdmans Publishing Company, 1953), pp. 97-146.

32. P.E. Kretzmann, "Ancient Pagan Religions," in *The God of the Bible and Other "Gods"* (St Louis: Concordia Publishing House, 1943), pp. 22-23.

33. Qualben, **op. cit.**

34. **Ibid.**, p. 17.

35. **Ibid.**

36. Kretzmann, **op. cit.**, pp. 25-27.

37. Alan Hus, *Greek and Roman Religion* (New York: Hawthorn Books, Publishers, 1962), p. 119.

38. "Roman Religion," *Encyclopedia Britannica, Makropedia*, 15, p. 1058.

39. "Pontifex Maximus," *The Oxford Classical Dictionary*, Edited by N.G.L. Hammond and H.H. Scullard (Oxford: At the Carendon Press, 1970), p. 860.

40. Tenney, *New Testament Times*, **op. cit.**, pp. 112-117.

41. "Greek Religion," *Encyclopedia Britannica, Makropedia*, 8,406.

42. Qualben, **op. cit.**, p. 19.

43. **Ibid.**

44. **Ibid.**

45. Charles P. Roney, *Commentary on the Harmony of the Gospels* (Grand Rapids: Wm. B. Eerdmans Publishing Company, 1948), p. 25.

46. William Beck, **The Holy Bible - An American Translation** (New Haven: Missouri: Leader Publishing Company, 1976), New Testament, p. 199.

47. This represents the view of Josephus, cf. E. J. Young, *An Introduction to the Old Testament* (Grand Rapids: Wm. B. Eerdmans Publishing Co., 1964), p. 42.

48. D.D. Luckenbill, Ancient Records of Assyria and Babylonia (Chicago: The University of Chicago Press, 1926), II, sec. 55, which gives the Assyrian record of Israel going into captivity.

49. Jeremiah 39; Also chapter 52, which is the same as 2 Kings 25. R. K. Harrison, *A History of Old Testament Times* (Grand Rapids: Zondervan Publishing House, 1957), pp. 195-196.

50. Harrison, **op. cit.**, 220.

51. Bo Reicke, *The New Testament Era - The World of the Bible from 500 B.C. to A.D. 100* (Philadelphia: Fortress Press, 1968), p. 37.

52. Raymond F. Surburg, *Introduction to the Intertestamental Period* (St Louis: Concordia Publishing House, 1975), pp. 21-25.

53. H. L. Ellison, *From Babylon to Bethlehem - The People of God from the Exile to the Messiah* (Atlanta; John Knox Press, 1976), pp. 75-89.

54. Merrill C. Tenney, *New Testament Times* (Grand Rapids; Wm. B. Eerdmans Publishing Company, 1963), pp. 34-44.

55. H.W. Hoehner, *Chronological Aspects of the Life of Christ* (Grand Rapids; Zondervan Publishing House, 1973), p. 27.

55. **Ibid.**, p. 164.

56. Ellison, **op. cit.**, pp. 55-56.

57. Qualben, **op. cit.**, p. 23.

58. Cambden M. Cobern, "Alexandria," *The International Standard Bible Encyclopedia*, James Orr, General Editor (Grand Rapids; Wm. B. Eerdmans Publishing Company, 1939), I, pp. 93-94.

59. Surburg, **op. cit.**, pp. 72-79. J. W. Wevers, "Septuagint" *The Interpreter's Dictionary of the Bible*, George R. Buttrick, Dictionary Editor (Nashville; Abingdon Press, 1962), IV, R-Z, pp. 273-275.

60. Sir Frederick Kenyon, *The Text of the Greek Bible* (London: Ducworth 1937), p. 25.

61. Cf. the Index locorum of Old Testament texts from LXX quoted in the *New Testament Eberhardt Nestele, Novum Testamentum Graece* (Stuttgart; Privilege. Wuert, Bibelanstallt, no date), II, 658-671.

62. B.J. Roberts, The Old Testament and Versions (Cardif: University of Wales Press.

63. Merrill F. Tenney, *The New Testament An Historical and Analytical Survey* (Grand Rapids; Wm. B. Eerdmans Publishing Company, 1953), pp. 123-125.

64. Acts: 20; 13:5; 15:21.

65. Qualben, **op. cit.**, p. 25., C. Guignebert, *The Jewish World in the Time of Jesus* (London: Routledge and Keagan Paul Ltd., 1939), pp. 238-241.

66. Qualben, **op. cit.**, p. 25.

67. Reicke, **op. cit.**, pp. 153-173.

68. Cf. "Philo and His Writings," in Surburg, **op. cit.**, pp. 153-160.

69. **Ibid.**, pp. 124-127.

70. Josephus, Jewish Antiquities, XIII, 5.9.

71. Millar Burrows, *The Dead Sea Scrolls* (New York; The Viking Press, 1956), pp. 3-72.

72. Marcal Simon, *Jewish Sects at the Time of Jesus* (Philadelphia; Fortress Press, 1967), pp. 17-46.

73. F.F. Bruce, *New Testament History* (Garden City, New York, Doubleday and Company, 1971), pp. 69-73.

74. Cf. the comparative chart of the two sects compared in Qualben, **op. cit.**, p. 27.

75. Cf. Ernst R. Trattner, *Understanding the Talmud* (New York; Thomas Nelson & Sons, 1955), ph. 1-97.

76. Qualben, **op. cit.**, p. 27.

77. Charles F. Pfeiffer, *The Dead Sea Scrolls* (Grand Rapids; Baker Book House, 1962), pp. 53-54.

78. Ct Adam Fahling, *The Life of Christ* (St Louis; Concordia Publishing House, 1936), pp. 94-97; William F. Arndt, *Bible Commentary - The Gospel According to St. Luke* (St. Louis; Concordia Publishing House, 1956), p. 71-74.

79. Richard Francis Weymouth, *The New Testament in Modern Speech* (Boston: The Pilgrim Press, 1943), p. 137.

80. William F. Beck, **The Holy Bible - An American Translation** (New Haven; Leader Publishing Company, 1976), New Testament, p. 38.

Questions

1. Both the Old and New Testaments predicted ____.
2. John describes the important truth ____.
3. The Docetists denied ____.
4. What is the Protoevanglium? ____
5. Who did God choose to be the carrier of the Messianic promise? ____
6. In paganism man endeavors to approach God on terms of ____.
7. Christ was born into the ____ world.
8. The Roman Empire came into existence in ____.
9. What happened to the Empires of Alexander the Great at his death? ____
10. Rome was able to unite in itself ____.
11. Eventually Greece conquered Rome through its ____.
12. The unity of the Roman Empire promoted the idea of ____.
13. Universal citizenship helps prepare the way for ____.
14. The existence of universal peace helped Paul ____.
15. ____ was the language of culture throughout the Roman Empire.
16. How did the Roman army contribute to the fullness of time?____
17. The Roman ____ and good Sea Lanes aided in the spread of ____.
18. Christians refused to call the Roman Emperor ____.
19. What contributed to the religious deterioration of Roman society? ____
20. What were some factors which made the time right for the coming of Christ? ____
21. Most of the Old Testament quotations from the Greek New Testament were from the ____.
22. The Jewish people for a number of centuries were expecting the coming of ____.
23. The uniqueness of Mary's child was that he was ____.

An Evaluation of the Divergent Interpretations of the Lord's Mount Olive Discourse

Christian News, November 21, 1988

The liturgical calendar of the Lutheran Church has incorporated and emphasized texts taken from the Olivet Discourse for the last two Sundays of the church year[1] and also for the second Sunday in Advent.[2] The reason for these selections is that the Olivet Discourse deals with the subject of exchatology, the locus of Christian theology which is concerned with the last things.[3] This discourse is found in the three first Gospels, known as the Synoptics. It is not found, however in John's Gospel. Matthew devotes two chapters to it, Mark one and Luke nearly one. The Olivet Discourse is the last of the five around which Matthew has organized his life of Christ. It was a sermon addressed privately to the disciples, just as was His farewell address found in John 14-17, delivered as he walked on His way to the Garden of Gethsemane. In Mark's Gospel the Olivet Discourse is the only sermon found in it; scholars usually refer to it as "The Little Apocalypse."

Portions of the Olivet Discourse have already been fulfilled, while others are in the process of fulfillment. But the Second Coming of Christ and the end of the world as well as the end of the age are still futuristic. This address of Jesus is altogether prophetic; it has also been termed "apocalyptic," because in Matthew, chapters 24 and 25, Luke chapter 21:5-33 and in Mark chapter 13 the New Testament reader will find the unveiling of the concluding events of world and of church history.[4] The Olivet Discourse may be said to present a panoramic view of the great earth-shattering events which will transpire between the Lord's Ascension and His Return for the final judgment of the living and the dead.

A survey of the theological literature of the past and present reveals the fact that the Olivet Discourse is interpreted differently by scholars who are critically-oriented in their approach to Scripture,[5] as compared with the interpretations of dispensationalists,[5a] of premillennialists,[6] of postmillennialists,[7] and of amillennialists.[8] This confusing situation is determined by different and contradictory systems of hermeneutics. The differences between these opposing schools of interpretation of the Olivet Discourse, as recorded in Matthew's, Mark's and Luke's accounts, will be set forth in this essay.

The Occasion for the Olivet Discourse

When Jesus delivered this address He was sitting on the Mount of Olives addressing His disciples. He had just left the Temple for the last time, and as they are passing through its courts, the disciples draw attention to the superb beauty and splendor of its buildings. At the time Jesus spoke the discourse, the Temple was not yet complete.[9] The Jews and the disciples were proud of the structure Herod the Great was constructing. How surprised the disciples must have been when Jesus shocked them with His reply, "There shall not be left here one stone upon another, which shall not be thrown down."[11] Somewhat later, as they paused to rest on the western slope of the mountain, on their way to Bethany, four of the disciples came to Jesus with the request, "Tell us, when shall these things be? and what shall be the sign when these things are about to be accomplished?" (Mark 13:3-4).

Jesus took the occasion to predict not only the destruction of Jerusalem, but His own personal return, of which the former event was to be a "sign" and a symbol. In addition to the prediction of the destruction of Jerusalem, the Second Coming of Christ, Jesus also foretold the end of the world, the end of the age. P. E. Kretzmann claimed that the question of Peter, James, John and Andrew (Mark 13:3) was concerned above all with Christ's return and the signs which would precede and foretell His coming to judgment upon the city and the world.

Averred Kretzmann:

Note the three questions: When will the destruction of the Temple, city and the Jewish state take place? What special sign will indicate Christ's coming? When will the end of the world be?, the judgment of the living and the dead take place? There is no trace of an idea of a millennium in this question. The belief which the Jews held and which Christ here supports is that the present age of sin and death, will end with the Last Judgment, without any intervening time of millennial Glory.[10]

The Olivet Discourse Presents A Panorama of World History

In the Olivet Discourse the New Testament reader is presented with a panorama of events which will transpire between the Ascension and Christ's final coming for the last judgment. Many events will occur, historical and catastrophic in nature. During this long period of time, the glory of God's kingdom will be hidden by a veil of suffering, during this time period the Church will need to live by faith and not by sight (cf. 2 Cor. 5:71).[11] One event predicted forty years before it was fulfilled was the destruction of Jerusalem, brought about by the rejection of Christ, the promised Messiah of the Old Testament prophecy, by the Jewish nation. The great Temple, being built by Herod was not even finished when the Romans completely demolished this magnificent structure.[12] Jesus announced that both religious and secular conditions would occur and these were outlined by Jesus. The destruction of Jerusalem was so complete that Josephus reported that Jerusalem looked like a site which had never been occupied.[13]

The destruction of Jerusalem, Christ's Last Coming, and the end of the world and the end of the age are so intertwined that at times it is difficult to know which event is being referred to.[14] It is apparent that Jesus had two major events in mind in Matthew 24:34, and "that day" in 24:1 which are separated by a lapse of time. The view has been advocated that one looking at two distant mountain peaks, one being behind the other, the one farther away appears to be close while in reality they are far from each other in actuality.[15] Thus in Jesus' perspective, these two events, in one way, the destruction of Jerusalem is typical of the destruction of the world at the time when the Son of Man will come with His holy angels. Thus events far removed from each other timewise are depicted as close. Halley remarked: "What he said in a sentence may be an age." What happened in one case may be a "begun fulfillment of what will happen in another."[16]

The Olivet Discourse in the Three Sypotics

Jesus' prophetic Discourse is more concise in Mark and Luke than in Matthew. Mark and Luke include certain details which are not found in Matthew. Let the reader compare Matthew 24:8-9 with Mark 13:9ff. and Luke 21:12-16,18ff. However, Mark's and Luke's details, generally speaking, are less inclusive. Matthew has not embodied every detail. Thus the student of the Olivet Discourse will not find in Mark and Luke the description of the great tribulation (Matt. 24; 22-27), nor the exhortations in Matthew 24:37-51, the parables of ten virgins (Matt. 25:14-30), the portrayal of the Last Judgment (Matt. 25:31-40). But Ylvisaker contended that "but the larger compass in Matthew is not due to the fact that he has coordinated two or several discourses of Jesus, but the difference is explained by the plan of the Gospels."[17]

Eerdman, former professor of practical theology at Princeton Theological Seminary, in commenting on the Olivet Discourse claimed that we probably do not have a complete account of the Olivet Discourse.[18] There is no indication, however, that we do not have all that Jesus said in its entirety.

If we do not have, Christians can rest assured, that the Holy Spirit had the Gospel writers record for us all that Jesus wanted His followers to know about the events that will happen before His last appearance before the eyes of the world, both believers and unbelievers.

The contents of the Olivet Discourse given in Matthew 24-25 may be summarized as follows:

I. Prophecies as to the end of things: 24:1-51

1. Signs of the end of the world in general: 24:1-24.
2. Signs of the end of the world in particular: 24:15-22.
3. The period between the destruction of Jerusalem and the end of the world: 24:23-28.
4. Actual end of the world: 24:29-31
5. The suddenness of the catastrophe: 24:32-33.
6. Judgment on the rulers: 24:45-51.

II. Parable of Preparation for the end: 25:1-46

1. Parable of the ten virgins-about watchmen: 25:1-13.
2. Parable of the talent-about faithfulness: 25:14-30.
3. The coming of the Son of Man for World Judgment: 25:31-46.[19]

For a more detailed discussion of the relationship of Matthew 24-25 to Mark 13 and Luke 21:5-36, the reader may consult W. Graham Scroggie's *A Guide to the Gospels.*[20]

Divergent Interpretations Relative to the
Historicity of the Utterances on Tuesday of Passion Week

According to the Greek text of the three Synoptical writers, the Olivet Discourse was actually spoken by Jesus at the conclusion of a very busy day on Tuesday of Holy Week, which also was Christ's last public appearance in the Jerusalem Temple. There are scholars who hesitate to ascribe all or parts of the Olivet Discourse to Jesus.[21] Some have argued that the apocalyptical teachings of the discourse are different from the apocalyptical teachings of Jesus elsewhere. Colani's famous *Little Apocalypse Theory*, propounded in 1864 and taken up with modification by many since, was to the effect that verses 5-31 were a Jewish-Christian apocalyptic tract which was incorporated into the Gospel by the Evangelist. The problem with this theory was that it assumed that Jesus only spoke on ethical truths and not on eschatological issues.[22] Other scholars have questioned the genuineness of the Olivet Discourse on the grounds that what is said about "signs" does not agree with the teachings of Jesus as given in Luke 17:20ff. on the unexpectedness of Christ's coming. Wenham responds to this by asserting: "The view fails to take seriously the fact that in biblical apocalyptical teaching about the suddenness and signs is regularly found together."[23] Other objections to regarding the teachings as deriving from Jesus is that the Old Testament quotations are based on the Septuagint rather than on the Hebrew text are indecisive.[24]

The Anchor Bible's commentary on Matthew, authored by Albright and Mann, rejects the genuineness of the Olivet Discourse as being delivered by Jesus on the last day of His public ministry. These two scholars claim the discourse has been misunderstood by "ultra-conservatives." Thus they asserted:

> On the other hand, there are those who take an ultraconservative view of the recorded words of Jesus as inerrant, or who force considerations of creedal and conciliar orthodoxy as to the person and/or divinity of Jesus on the NT materials. The result has been unhappy. In both cases there has been a failure to do justice to first-century Jewish milieu in which Jesus spoke, taught, and acted. Allied with this failure has been a tendency to invest each word of the apocalyptic language of Jesus with a predictive meaning which would have been alien to orthodox and sectarian Judaism alike.[25]

Again, the same authors, Albright and Mann, asserted:

> Similarly, both for those committed to a view of verbal inspiration (in the last analysis depending on the possibility of discovering a "definitive" Greek text) and also for those committed to the Nicene and Chalcedonian orthodoxy, there has often been a failure to deal adequately (if at all) with the human nature and human thinking of Jesus. As a result, a good many presuppositions have unconsciously gone into the work of commentators of the material before us.[26]

This quotation is very revealing as to how critical scholars view the Bible as an error-prone book and also how they question the deity and the reliability of Jesus' teachings and utterances and rejected the historical doctrine of the verbal and plenary inspiration of Holy Writ which they have jettisoned. Their basic approach to the Bible is treating it as any other piece of world literature and denying the unique knowledge of Christ. Not acceptance of God's only-begotten Son, and also rejection of the reliable question of the Holy Spirit, the Third Person of the Godhead, are the reasons why critically oriented scholars refuse to accept the explicit teachings and assertions of Matthew, Mark and Luke relative to the important predictions about the future of the Jews and conditions as they will obtain between A.D. 30 and the unknown day when Christ will return.

Other scholars claim that the Olivet Discourse was not really delivered by our Lord, but in the Gospels the New Testament readers will find the apocalyptic expectations of the early church, which the Gospel authors have supposedly placed into the mouth of Jesus.[27] The Olivet Discourse may contain genuine sayings of Jesus critics claim, but by its emphasis upon premonitory signs (Mark 13:8,14,21) they were adaptions of Jewish apocalypse, which gave a wrong impression of the eschatological teachings of Jesus.[28]

In writing about the Olivet Discourse Vincent Taylor asserted: There can be little doubt that its basis is an apocalyptic forecast of the Parousia largely expected by the first Christians which includes genuine sayings of Jesus but by its emphasis upon premonitory signs, sayings (Mark 13:8, 14, 21) after the manner of a Jewish apocalypse, gives a wrong impression of the eschatological teaching of Jesus.[28]

Bultmann claimed: "Jesus then rejects the whole content of apocalyptic speculation, as he rejects the whole content of the time and the watching of signs."[29a] However, the text of the discourse clearly does point to different signs prior to the destruction of Jerusalem and also signs prior to the end of the age.[29]

According to Barrels, Matthew used Mark's "Little Apocalypse" (i.e. chapter 13) and added a number of parables pointing to the duty of being watchful and ready for the judgment. (Matthew 24:33-51, Ch. 25)[30] Barrels further asserts that there is no knowing whether or not the parables of watching were spoken on the Mount of Olives.[31]

Since Matthew, who was one of the disciples and apostles of the Lord, in fact, the only apostle among the three Synoptical writers, why would Matthew need Mark or Q. or any other source for obtaining information about what Jesus had spoken as the Olivet Discourse when he was on Olivet?

The Form-Critical Approach to the Olivet Discourse

According to form-criticism the Olivet Discourse contains material relative to the last week of Christ's life ending in His crucifixion, and was based on oral tradition which was handed down for decades and finally in the days after Jerusalem's destruction was put together by a group known as the Matthean School. The form-critical approach is even too much for the Anchor Bible's Matthew. Albright and Mann wrote: "Form criticism has distributed all utterances of evolutionary development, from a reconstructed 'primitive' preaching through an assumed 'Hellenistic' recording of the material (on good Hegelian lines), down to the systematic teaching of the Church of the second century A.D. has been very one-sided." The evaluation given by Soulen in his discussion of "form criticism" was that form criticism "weakens the Gospels as historical sources for the biography of Jesus.... Finally, FC's fragmentary approach to the Gospels ignored the thought and setting of the Gospel writers themselves."[32]

The Denial of A Future Coming of Jesus for the Final Assize
Traditional Lutheran theology has distinguished a threefold kingdom of Christ: the kingdom of power, the kingdom of grace and the kingdom of glory. Much of modern theology fails to take cognizance of this threefold existence of the kingdom of God, which eventually will end in the kingdom of glory, when Christ shall offer up the kingdom to His Father.[33]

Realized Eschatology and the Olivet Discourse
J.A.T. Robinson interpreted Christ's Parousia not as a final event of the future but as a symbolical or mythological presentation of what happens whenever Christ comes in love and power,[34] displaying the signs of his presence and the marks of his cross. Judgment day is a dramatic picture of every day. Robinson rejects as not true that Jesus employed language implying his return to earth from heaven. According to Robinson the sayings about return must be understood as expressing the twin themes of vindication and visitation. The English Bishop substituted for "realized eschatology" the concept of "inaugural eschatology," an eschatology inaugurated by Jesus' death and resurrection, which released and inaugurated a new phase of the kingdom in which "hereafter" (Matt. 26:64), the kingdom of God would achieve its fulfillment. The ministry before his death and resurrection Robinson described as "prophetic eschatology," because the signs of the coming kingdom were visible in anticipation.[35]

Realized eschatology, not followed by Robinson, was originally propounded by Albert Schweitzer.[36] Over against nineteenth-century liberalism, Schweitzer held that the teaching of Jesus was eschatological in character. Jesus believed himself to be the Messiah but when He found that the consummation did not come as he expected it (Matt. 10:23), He embraced death so that the Parousia as the Son of Man might forcibly be brought to come.[37] Bruce described Jesus' actions according to the German theologian as follows:

"Since the wheel of history would not respond to his hand and turn around to complete his last revolution, he threw himself on it and was broken by it, only to dominate history more decisively by his failure that he could have attained by attaining his misconceived ambition."[38]

Schweitzer believed that Jesus' message was eschatological in the sense of the crudest contemporary apocalypticism. Jesus set forth an ethic that was intended between the time of the beginning of his ministry and the consummation of his ministry ending in glory. However, Jesus' death was the destruction of his eschatological dream and so instead of

630

Christ's work being successful in his proclamation of the kingdom message. His kingdom proclamation was superseded by the teaching of the Church.[38a] Any person acquainted with his New Testament will see that Schweitzer's message was extremely one-sided and distorted and a complete rejection of the coming events as described in the Olivet Discourse.

After Schweitzer, Rudolf Otto and C. H. Dodd came forward with a version of eschatological thinking, now called "realized eschatology."[39] Dodd expressed his particular views in his work dealing with the parables of Jesus. Jesus had much to say about the kingdom of God. The entire 13th chapter of Matthew spoke about the kingdom of God. According to Dodd the Jewish hearers were challenged to make a decision and accept the fact that the kingdom had arrived. The British New Testament scholar contended that the kingdom had come in Christ's life, death and resurrection. The future coming of the kingdom did not enter in the beginning in the Lord's proclamation of the kingdom. Jesus' redeeming work constituted the decisive or eschatological manifestation of the power of God working to bring about man's salvation. When Jesus later concentrated on a future coming of the kingdom, this Dodd claimed, was tantamount to relapsing into Jewish apocalypticism, which further relegated to the beginning those elements of the Gospel which were distinctive of Christ's message. In the *Parables of the Kingdom* Dodd claimed that in the ministry of Jesus the Eschaton has moved from the future to the present, from the sphere of expectation into that of realized experience, Dodd further reasoned that in the unprecedented and unrepeatable events of Jesus' life "the powers of the world to come are present and made real."[40]

Joachim Jeremias, who acknowledged his indebtedness to Dodd, found that the *Parables of Jesus* gave expression to an eschatology "in the process of realization." Jesus' parables announce that the hour of fulfillment has struck and compelled the hearers to make up their minds about Jesus' person and mission.[41]

Robinson also spoke of "proleptic eschatology" because in the ministry of Christ there were also visible in an anticipatory manner the signs of Christ's future coming. In contrast to all the New Testament scholars so far cited, there is a difference between membership in the kingdom of grace and between the kingdom of grace which exists within the kingdom of power.[42] The end of this age and the end of the world is the high point toward which world history and the history of the church is heading.

To Whom Is the Olivet Discourse Directed?

Dispensationalists, who divide the whole history of mankind, beginning with the Creation and the last act of Christ, casting unbelievers into the lake of fire (Rev. 21),[43] into seven different time dispensations. They postulate the dispensation of innocency, the dispensation of conscience, the dispensation of government, the dispensation of grace, the dispensation of the law, the dispensation of the Church or grace, and the dispensation of the Kingdom.[44]

The Christian Church was not in view at all in the Old Testament. There is no connection between Israel and the Church. The kingship of the Messiah, Jesus, was to be fulfilled when Jesus would establish a Jewish kingdom in Palestine with Jerusalem as the capital. When Jesus said that the kingdom of God was at hand and asked the Hebrew people to accept Him as their King, the Jews refused and so the whole program was postponed to the future and unknowingly before, now the Church Age began with the Ascension, and Outpouring of the Holy Spirit. Most of the 89 chapters of the Four Gospels belongs to the Jewish Age, the Law dispensation, so that the Olivet Discourse was not at all intended for the Christian Church.[45]

Louis Sperry Chafer contended that the Olivet Discourse was intended primarily for Israel. He believed this discourse was Jesus' farewell to the Israel. In its fullest form it is recorded in Matthew 24-25. Sperry wrote:

The dominant themes in this discourse are the great tribulation and Israel's warnings concerning it (Matt. 24:9-28); the glorious appearing of Messiah in relation to Israel (24:29-25:30), including exhortations to "watch" (24:36-25:13), judgments upon Israel (24:45-25:30), and judgments upon nations because of their treatment of Israel (25:31-46). No reference is made in this discourse to the Church—her beginning, her ministries, her departure from this cosmos world. Similarly, no reference is made to salvation by grace or the security of those saved (cf. 24:50-51; 25:30). In like manner, no reference is made to the Person and work of the Holy Spirit. [46]

Merrill F. Unger, once a professor at Dallas Theological Seminary, where Chafer was the leading light, takes the same stance as Chafer. In Unger's Bible Handbook, the former professor of Semitic Languages and Old Testament Interpretation, asserted: "The rejected King as Prophet predicted in this discourse, the events of that still future time when we will resume dealing with Israel (cf. 23:39) and before His return to earth."[47] Relative to Matthew 24:4-26 Unger wrote: "These prophecies deal with Israel in the period of Tribulation just prior to the return of Messiah-King to establish His earthly kingdom, although the end of the present age will be characterized by the general conditions mentioned in 24:4-8. A comparison of 4-8 with Rev. 6 gives evidence that these verses have particular reference to the first half of the tribulation period when Israel will dwell in relative safety because of the covenant made 'with the prince that shall come,' Antichrist (Dan. 9:27a)."[48]

Unger's Handbook on the Matthean version of the Olivet Discourse shows what a completely different understanding of the eschatological teachings are held by dispensationalists. Matthew 24:9-26 are interpreted as follows: "Verses 9-26 describe the events of the last half of the Tribulation, after the world leader (Antichrist) has broken his covenant with Israel and forces idolatrous worship of himself (Dan. 9:27b); 2 Thess. 2:4; Rev. 13:15-18). This period will be characterized by great persecution, 9-10, 17f (Rev. 12:12:17), desolation of the temple and its worship, 15 (Dan. 9:27), unbelieving Israel being deceived by false prophets, 11-12 (Rev. 13:11-18), and believing Israel witnessing to the good news of the Messiah's kingdom, 14. The advent of messiah will terminate these events, 27."[49]

632

Unger does not hold that the "coming of the Son of Man" in 24:17 refers to Christ's final coming, but that Christ's Coming is followed by the national regathering of Israel's elect through special angelic ministries.[50] In 24:37-51 Israel is exhorted to be prepared for His return. The Judgment described in 25:1-30 of it Unger averred: "Then, prepare for the next event following Israel's regathering, her judgment, just prior to the establishment of Christ's kingdom. The judgment is illustrated in the parables of the ten virgins, 1-13, and the talents, 14-30. The ten virgins represent Israel at the end of the tribulation. The five wise symbolize the believing remnant, the five foolish, the unbelieving segment who only profess to look for Messiah's advent, 1-5. They will be without oil (a symbol of the Holy Spirit) and will be shut out of the messianic kingdom which is about to be set up, 6-10."[51]

The parable of the talents in 14-30 depicting a man traveling into a far country, Unger claims is Christ and represents Christ, during His absence from the earth. Christ entrusted his gifts to servants (Israel) during the Tribulation. The five and two talent servants will enter "into the joy of the Lord" (kingdom blessing), 21, 23. The man with one talent, a mere professor, is cast from the kingdom, swept away in judgment with the ungodly.[52]

The Judgment of the Nations According to Unger

Jesus, whom the Jews rejected as their King, announced in his prophetic discourse that event toward which Israel has been waiting, namely, the coming of Messiah, who will sit upon the throne of David. He will come in glory, this according to Unger makes the time definite. The occasion is for his Second Coming but not the final one, but is for the judgment of the nations, consisting of sheep and goats. The sheep are said to be those who accept the Gospel of the kingdom (Mt. 24:14) and who treat kindly Christ's brethren according to the flesh, the believing Jewish remnant (34-36). "Those who reject the Gospel of the kingdom and persecute the Jewish remnant are the goats" (41-46). By this action the goats show their league with Satan. "Those who thus align themselves against the 144,000 preachers of the coming kingdom (Rev. 7:18; 14:1-5) will share Satan's fate (41) (Rev. 20:10)."[53]

Ryrie, professor at Dallas Theological Seminary, in *The Ryrie Study Bible*, gives evidence of advocating the views of Chafer, Unger and other proponents of the *Scofield Reference* Bible. While the notes on the text are brief, there are enough statements showing advocacy of the dispensational system of Biblical interpretation.[54] To understand what today is a system of interpretation radically different, that of Calvin and Luther, one needs only to read C.I. Scofield's *Rightly Dividing the Word of Truth*, a booklet on Biblical interpretation that has gone through many editions since first promulgated. Scofield has worked out a system of eschatology which rests on a misinterpretation of Revelation 20, Romans 11:26, the Book of Daniel and other eschatological passages, and then proceeded to foist this upon Scriptural passages which in no way support this proposed system of the eschatological teachings of the Bible. There is certainly nothing in the Olivet Discourse that limits the address to the Jewish nation. While the Olivet Discourse does speak of great tribulation, what is said on the subject differs radically from the complicated views on the "tribulation" held by dispensationalists. Dividing the history of the world from creation to the last judgment into seven dispensations, with each dispensation having its own requirements for meeting God's standards, is completely foreign to the Bible.

While there is a valid use of the principle of hermeneutics that the same teaching may be found in parallel passages, the interpreter must be certain that passages adduced as parallel passages are really discussing the same theological issue. The truth of the matter is that both Jew and Gentile have the same word of God. There is no difference since the death and resurrection of Christ, between unbelieving Jews and unbelieving Gentiles, all are sinners and are under the wrath of God.[56] The same salvation which Christ earned by His vicarious suffering and death is available to both Jew and Gentile. Those Jews and those Gentiles who rejected Jesus Christ as their personal Savior will be found among the goats, and those Jews and Gentiles who were justified by faith and live a fruitful life will stand among the sheep, to whom Jesus, the Judge, will say: "Come, My Father's blessed ones, inherit the kingdom prepared for you from the foundation of the world" (Matt. 25:34).

The Final Judgment (Matthew 25:31-46), Parable or History?

The Matthean version of the Olivet Discourse climaxes in the World's Final Judgment. Crissey in her commentary on Matthew labelled Matthew 25:31-46 as a parable.[57] There is a great difference between designating Scriptural verses a parable or considering them as an historical event. Sherman Johnson in *The Interpreter's Bible* also calls Matthew 25's last sixteen verses a parable.[58] By contrast, conservative Biblical scholarship considers the action and words recorded in Matthew 25:31-36 as describing the last great act of the Son of God before believers and unbelievers will go to their final destinies.[59]

That same Jesus who was born in the manger of Bethlehem, and who took upon Himself the form of a servant - who was despised and rejected of men, and often had not where to lay His head - who was condemned by the princes of this world, beaten, scourged, and nailed to the cross - that same Jesus shall Himself judge the world when He comes in His glory. To Him the Father hath committed all judgment (John 5:22). To Him at last every knee shall bow, and every tongue confess that He is Lord (Philip 2:10,11). Jesus who will sit upon His throne on that great and dreadful day will be the believers' Savior, their Shepherd, their High Priest, their Elder Brother, their Friend. When Christians see Christ they will have no reason to be alarmed.

The Second Coming an Integral Part of Christ's Preaching

Those who claim that the teaching of Christ's Second Coming was not taught by Jesus prior to Tuesday of Holy Week or not at all, Jesus in the course of His ministry spoke about that event which represents the climax of the Olivet Discourse. Thus in Matthew 16:27 the Lord said: "The Son of Man shall come in great glory of His Father with his angels." In Luke 17:28-30 Jesus declared: "As it was in the days of Lot. . .so shall it be in the day that the Son of Man is revealed." In Mark 8:38 the Savior taught: "Whosoever shall be ashamed of me . . . of him shall the Son of Man be ashamed when He comes in the glory with His holy angels."[60] In the beginning of His Farewell Discourse to His disciples Jesus promised his disciples: "Behold, I go to prepare a place for you" (John 14:2-3).

Alleged Exegetical Problems in the Olivet Discourse
The "Abomination of Desolation"
In Matthew 24:15: "When you see what the prophet Daniel told about the abomination laying waste the land and standing in the holy place (anyone who reads this should understand it), then if you're in Judea, flee to the hills,"[61] here Jesus was citing Daniel 11:31; 12:11. This does not refer to Antiochus Epiphanes who erected a heathen altar in the Temple in 168 B.C. as Wenham claimed.[62] That this warning of Jesus refers to A.D. 69 or 70 is shown by the Lord's directive to flee to the hills as the Roman armies approached for the capture and destruction of the Holy City forty years after Jesus' Ascension. If it is supposed to refer to the end of the world, what would be the point in telling His followers to flee to escape hostile armies by leaving Jerusalem and head for the hills?

Wenham claimed that the phrase "abomination of desolation" to be cryptic. Kretzmann,[63] Fahling,[64] Ylvisaker[65] and others hold that "the abomination of desolation" refers to the Roman armies defiling Yahweh's Temple.[66]

The Disturbances in the Heavens
Matthew 24:29-31 informs Christians and the unbelieving world:
"Right after the misery of that time the sun will turn dark, the moon will stop shining, the stars will be falling from the sky, and the powers of heaven will be shaken. Then the sign announcing the Son of Man will appear in the sky, and then all the people on earth will mourn when they see the Son of Man coming on the clouds of heaven in the sky with power and great glory. And with a loud trumpet He will send out His angels, and they will gather His elect ones from the north, south, east and west, from one end of the sky to the other."[67]

Should these great disturbances in nature be understood literally? There are scholars who contend that these expressions and this description of Christ's Last Coming are given in figurative language.[68] The language is taken from Old Testament apocalyptical literature. Wenham, for example, claimed that in these verses we "have a historical reference to the fall of Jerusalem, the coming of the Son of man is a victory, not his return to earth and the gathering of the elect by God's messengers, which is the missionary outreach of the church."[69] By contrast there is to be found a host of interpreters who believe that the verses 29-32 of Matthew refer to the Second Coming of Christ accompanied by great astronomical events occurring in the heavens and in nature.[70] Other Old Testament

635

passages teach the same truths, which undoubtedly refer to the Parousia. Compare also the passages and verses in Matthew 13:4ff, I Thessalonians 4:14 and Revelation 1:8.[71]

The Meaning of the Expression:
"This Generation Shall Not Pass Away"

A statement of the Olivet Discourse which has occasioned considerable comment and also a divergence of opinion was our Lord's assertion: "I tell you truly that the present generation shall not pass away until all these begin to happen." Beck has rendered verse 30: "I tell you the truth, these people will not pass away till all this happens."[72] Does this verse mean that "this generation shall not pass away till all events predicted in the Olivet Discourse will be fulfilled?" If this is the meaning, then it appears that the Second Coming could not have occurred, because the generation of Christ's life time is all gone, dead and buried. It would further mean that Jesus was mistaken or else the authors of the Synoptic Gospels were portraying the beliefs of the early church relative to Christ's Parousia.[73] A comparison of various exegetes will show that they interpret this phrase either as referring to the time of Christ or to the end of time.

Kretzmann preferred the interpretation which stated that the Jewish race would be living at the time when Christ would appear. Thus he wrote:

> He referred to the race of the Jews. This people, this nation that had rejected Him, should not cease to exist to be a distinct people, separate from all the rest, until Christ's coming in glory would take place. They should remain as a standing testimony and proof of the truthfulness of Christ's words.[74]

In the constant existence of the Jewish nation the Christian believers have constant proof for the reliability and truthfulness of Holy Scriptures, also of the Olivet Discourse. Yes, "heaven and earth shall pass away, but My words shall not pass away," thus Jesus the coming Judge has assured His own.

Jesus' Ignorance About the Time of the Second Coming

One of the most puzzling statements made by our Lord in the Olivet Discourse was His assertion: "But concerning that day or hour no one knows, but only the Father (Mark 13:31)." During His state of humiliation Jesus frequently abstained from the full use of His divine nature, which was omniscient and omnipotent and omnipresent, attributes communicated to his human nature by virtue of the unity of the theanthropic union.[75] With so much information given by Jesus concerning His Second Coming, the disciples probably felt they ought to know the exact time of His coming, for that would greatly simplify matters. However Jesus rejected this idea. When that great day will burst on the world suddenly, no person knows, not even the angels, who know many secrets and mysteries of God. And what is more, even Jesus according to His human nature was ignorant of the exact time of the Parousia. Concerning this ignorance Kretzmann asserted:

> The Son of God, in His capacity as Savior of men and specifically according to His human nature, has renounced His right to this knowledge, chiefly for the sake of men, lest they be tempted to make inquiries and bother Him with importunate pleadings concerning the day and hour. Here is a secret which is hidden in the omniscience of the Father.[76]

Because Christians do not know the exact date of the Lord's coming, they should be constantly on their guard and be watchful.

J.C. Ryle, former bishop of Liverpool, over one hundred years ago had this interesting observation on Mark 13:32 and Matthew 24:36:

> There is deep wisdom and mercy in this intention, silence. We have reason to thank God that the thing has been hidden from us. Uncertainty about the date of the Lord's return is calculated to keep believers in an attitude of constant expectation, and to preserve them from despondency. What a dreary prospect the early church would have had before it, if it had known for certain that Christ would not return to earth for at least fifteen hundred years! The hearts of men like Athanasius, Chrysostom, and Augustine, might well have sunk within them, if they had been aware of the centuries of darkness through which the world would pass, before their Master came back to take the kingdom. — What a quickening motive, on the other hand, true Christians have perpetually had, for a close walk with God! They have never known in any age, that their Master might come suddenly to take account of his servants. This very uncertainty has supplied them with a reason for living always ready to meet Him.[77]

All attempts to set the day of the Second Coming, all chronological computations, based on arbitrary interpretation of Scripture numbers and data, such as have been put forth by the Adventists, Russelites, and others, are not only futile but also wicked; they spring from idle curiosity and are destructive of the watchfulness and constant preparedness required of the Christians. Recently Edgar C. Whisenant predicted that the Rapture would occur in 1988, sometime between September 11 and 13. Well, September and October are gone and no rapture![79]

Parables in the Olivet Discourse

The Olivet Discourse has ninety-one verses in Matthew's Gospel and forty-one of these are parables. In Matthew 24:32-35 contains the parable of the fig tree putting forth leaves, indicating that summer is near, so when people witness the astronomical events described in verse 29, then they will know the advent of Christ is near. Matthew 24:45-53 has the parable of the "faithful slave." Just like a slave will be faithful; and perform his assigned duties when his Lord is absent, so Christians are to be faithful in carrying out the various tasks Christ assigned His church on the day of the Ascension. Chapter 25:1-30 has two parables, namely, that of the ten virgins, the parable of the talents, each stressing the idea of watchfulness, faithfulness and final destiny. Matthew 25:31-46, considered by some a parable,[80] is not. Mark, it should be noted, gives a parable.

Matthew does not report, namely, the parable of the Porter (Mark 13:34-37).

The Olivet Discourse and the Old Testament

There are at least two important teachings about the Old Testament which deserve mentioning. Jesus compared conditions before the end of the world like the conditions in the days of Noah before the Flood was sent by God to wipe out mankind and all living creatures, except those people who were with Noah in the ark. The animals with Noah also escaped destruction. This means that Jesus Christ did not consider the universal deluge a saga or myth, but that the events described in Genesis 6-8 were actual historical occurrences. The analogy of Noah's time with its unconcern for God's warnings about its wickedness breaks down and the last times, when men will live similarly as was done in the days of Noah. Both the deluge and the coming of Christ are two historical happenings that Jesus believed them to be . . . the one having taken place, the other still in the future.

Jesus also taught that the coming of the Roman armies for the destruction of Jerusalem had been foretold by the prophet Daniel. Jesus called statesman Daniel, a contemporary of Jeremiah and Ezekiel, a prophet also, who in the prophetical and apocalyptical portions of his inspired book announced the historical fact of the "abomination of desolation" standing in the holy place. In the Olivet Discourse Jesus, the Lord of history, took a stance opposed by higher-critical scholars. The latter do not believe there even was such a person as Daniel, mentioned twice by Ezekiel. Furthermore, critical Old Testament scholars do not believe that Daniel was the author of the book that bears his name in the Old Testament canon, but was the product of an anonymous author of the second century B.C. Critical scholars deny that the Book of Daniel contains prophecies about the Babylonian, Medo-Persian kingdoms and that it predicts the coming of the Greeks, followed in turn by the Romans and that the Messiah will ultimately conquer the latter. Unbelieving scholars hold that what the reader finds in Daniel is completed history written up as if it were prophecy.[81] Such interpretations are contradicted by Matthew 24:25.

The Importance of the Olivet Discourse

Bishop Ryle of Liverpool in 1857 wrote:

"No history ought to receive so much of our attention as the past and future history of the Church of Christ. The rise and fall of worldly empires are events of small importance in the sight of God. Babylon, and Greece and Rome, and France, and England are as nothing in His eyes by the side of the mystical body of Christ. The march of armies and the victories of conquerors are mere trifles in comparison with the progress of The Gospel, and the final triumph of the prince of Peace."

Footnotes

1. *The Lessons - The appointed First Lesson, Second Lesson and Gospel readings for Series A of the three-year lectionary* prepared by the Inter-Lutheran Commission on Worship (Minneapolis, Augsburg Publishing House, no date), pp. 85-87. For Series B, pp. 79-80.

2. *Lutheran Worship*, Prepared by the Commission on Worship of the Lutheran Church-Missouri Synod (St. Louis, Concordia Publishing House, 1982), pp. 11-12 (for the First and also Second Sunday in Advent).

3. Heinrich Schmidt, *Doctrinal Theology of the Evangelical Lutheran Church*: translated by Charles A. Hay and Henry Jacobs (Minneapolis, Augsburg Publishing House, 1899), p. 624.

4. J. B. Torrance, "Olivet Discourse," in J.D. Douglas, Organizing Editor, *The New Bible Dictionary* (Grand Rapids: Wm. B. Eerdmans Publishing Company, 1962), pp. 908-909.

5. Sherman E. Johnson, "The Gospel According to St. Matthew," *The Interpreter's Bible* (Nashville, Abingdon-Cokebury Press, 1951), VII, pp. 853-854.

5a. Charles Caldwell Ryrie, *Dispensationalism Today* (Chicago, Moody Press, 1965), pp. 86-109.

6. J. Edwin Hartill, *Biblical Hermeneutics* (Grand Rapids,: Zondervan Publishing House, 1947), pp. 13-19; A. C. Gaebelein, *The Annotated Bible* (New York, Publication Office of "Our Hope," 1913), Vol. 1, The Gospels and the Book of Acts, pp. 50-53; 90-99; 165-166.

7. Lorraine Boettner, *The Millennium* (Grand Rapids, Baker Book House, 1958), pp. 3-108. Cf. Boettner's definition on p. 4. It contradicts the teachings of the Olivet Discourse.

8. John Theodore Mueller, *Christian Dogmatics* (St. Louis, Concordia Publishing House, 1935), pp. 621-623.

9. Adam Fahling, *The Life of Christ* (St. Louis: Concordia Publishing House, 1936), pp. 558-559.

10. Paul E. Kretzmann, *Popular Commentary of the Bible* (St. Louis, Concordia Publishing House, 1921), New Testament, I, p. 133.

11. Torrance, "Olivet Discourse," **op. cit.**, pp. 908-909.

12. Ralph Earle, "Mark," in Carl F. Henry, *The Biblical Expositor* (Philadelphia, A. J. Holman, III), p. 100.

13. Henry Alford, *The New Testament for English Readers* (Chicago, Moody Press, no date), p. 161.

14. Rt. Rev. J. C. Ryle, *Expository Thoughts on the Gospels, St. Matthew* (New York and Chicago, Fleming H. Revell, 1859), pp. 312-313.

15. Joh. Ylvisaker. *The Gospels* (Minneapolis: Augsburg Publishing House, 1932), p. 602.

16. Henry H. Halley, *Halley's Bible Handbook*. New Revised Edition (Grand Rapids: Zondervan Publishing House, 1965. 24th Edition, p. 446.

17. Ylvisaker, **op. cit.**, p. 606.

18. Charles R. Eerdman, *The Gospel of Matthew* (Philadelphia: The Westminster. 1956), p. 215.

19. Olaf Morgan Norlie, *The Outlined Bible* (Burlington: Iowa: Lutheran Literary Board, 1928), p. 241.

20. Graham Scroggie, *A Guide to the Gospels* (London: Pickering & Inglis, 1948), pp.

306-307.

21. Alfred Edersheim, *The Life and Times of Jesus the Messiah* (Grand Rapids: Wm. B. Eerdmans Publishing Company, 1971, One volume edition Volume 2), p. 431.

22. J.B. Torrance, **op. cit.**, p. 900.

23. D. Wenham, "Olivet Discourse," *New Bible Dictionary,* Edited by J.D. Douglas, and N. Hillyer (Leicester, England: Varsity Press, 1982) Second Edition, p. 857.

24. **Ibid.**

25. W. Albright and C. S. Mann, *The Anchor Bible, Matthew* (Garden City, New York; Doubleday & Company, 1971), p. 288.

26. **Ibid.**

27. Edersheim, **op. cit.**, II, p. 431.

28. Torrance, **op. cit.**, p. 900.

29. Vincent Taylor, "The Life and Ministry of Jesus," *The Interpreter's Bible*, op cit., Vol. 7, p. 125.

29a. Rudolf Bultmann, *Jesus and the Word,* Translated by Louis Pettibone Smith (New York: Scribner and Sons, 1930.

30. G. Barrois, "Olivet, Mount of," *The Interpreter's Bible Dictionary* (New York: Abingdon-Cokesbury, 1952), *K-q,* p. 598.

31. **Ibid.**

32. Albright and Mann, **op. cit.**, p. 288.

33. Joseph Stump, *The Christian Faith* (New York: Macmillan Company, 1932) pp. 200-203.

34. J.A. Robinson, *In the End, God* (London, James H. Clarke, 1950). J.A. Robinson, Jesus and His Cuming (SCM Press, 1957).

35. Albert Schweitzer, *The Quest of the Historical Jesus,* with a new introduction by James M. Robinson (New York, The Macmillan and Company, 1968.)

36. F.F. Bruce, "Eschatology," in Walter A. Elwell, Editor, *Evangelical Dictionary of Theology* (Grand Rapids: Baker Book House, 1984), p. 164.

37. **Ibid.**, p 366.

38. **Ibid.**, p. 364.

38a. "Schweitzer, Albert," in Richard Soulen, *Handbook of Biblical Criticism* (Revised Edition, Atlanta; John Knox Press), pp. 173-174.

39. Bruce, "Eschatology," **op. cit.**, p. 364.

40. C.H. Dodd, *The Parables of the Kingdom* (London, Nisbet and Co., 1936), p. 50.

41. J. Jermias, *Rediscovering the Parables,* (New York Scribners, 1966). 191 pp.

42. Mueller, *Christian Dogmatics*, op cit., p. 316.

43. C.I. Scofield, *Rightly Dividing the Word of Trinity* (2 Timothy 2:15) (Westwood, New Jersey; Fleming H. Revell Company), First Edition, 1896), 12-16. Sidlow Baxter, *The Strategic Grasp of the Bible* (Grand Rapids, Zondervan Publishing House, 1968), pp. 189-190.

44. Ryrie, *Dispensationalism Today*, **op. cit.**, pp. 48-64. Scofield, **op. cit.**, pp. 12-15.

45. Gaebelein, **op. cit.**, pp. 50-52.

46. Louis Sperry Chafer, *Systematic Theology* (Dallas, Dallas Theological Seminary, 1948), pp. 189-190.

47. Merrill F. Unger, *Unger's Bible Handbook* (Chicago, Moody Press, 1964), p. 485.

48. **Ibid.**, pp. 485-486.

49. **Ibid.**, p. 486

50. **Ibid.**

51. **Ibid.**

52. **Ibid.**

53. **Ibid.**

54. Charles Ryrie Caldwell Ryrie, *The Ryrie Study Bible* (Chicago, Moody Press, 1976), pp. 51-52.

55. Floyd E. Hamilton, *The Basis of Millennial Faith* (Grand Rapids, Wm. B. Eerdmans Publishing Company, 1942), pp. 35-37.

56. Charles R. Eerdman, *The Epistle of Paul to the Romans* (Philadelphia: Westminster Press, 1946), pp. 53-56.

57. Claire M. Crissey, *Layman's Bible Commentary- Matthew* (Nashville, Broadman Press, 1981), vol. 15, p 129.

58. Sherman E. Johnson, "The Gospel According to Matthew," *The Interpreters' Bible*, **op. cit.**, p. 562.

59. Matthew Henry's *Commentary on the Whole Bible* (New York, Fleming H. Revell, reprint of 1721 edition, V, pp. 379-380; Kretzmann, **op. cit.**), pp. 142-143.

60. William F. Beck, *The Holy Bible - An American Translation* (New Haven, Leader Publishing Company, 1976), New Testament, p. 34.

61. **Ibid.**

62. Wenham, **op. cit.**, p. 856.

63. Kretzmann, **op. cit.**, New Testament, p. 134.

64. Fahling, **op. cit.**, p. 562.

65. Ylvisaker, **op. cit.**, pp. 610-611.

66. Charles Patrick Ronig, *Commentary on the Harmony of the Gospels* (Grand Rapids, Wm. B. Eerdmans Publishing Company, 1948), p. 399. J.W. Shepherd, *The Christ of The Gospels* (Grand Rapids; Wm. B. Eerdmans Publishing Company, 1946), p. 517.

67. Beck, **op. cit.**, p. 34.

68. Eerdmann, *The Gospel of Matthew*, **op. cit.**, p. 215.

69. Wenham. **op. cit.**, p. 857.

70. G. Stoeckhardt, *Die biblische Geschichte des Neuen Testaments* (St. Louis: Concordia Publishing House, 1906), p. 259.

71. Halley, **op. cit.**, p. 447.

72. Beck, **op. cit.**, New Testament, p. 64.

73. Wenham, **op. cit.**, p. 857.

74. Kretzmann, New Testament, **op. cit.**, p. 238.

75. Edward W. A. Koehler, *A Summary of Christian Doctrine* (Detroit and Oakland; The Rev. Louis H. Koehler and Alfred W. Koehler 1939), pp. 91-92.

76. Kretzmann, New Testament, **op. cit.**, p. 239.

77. Rt. Rev. J.C. Ryle, *Expository Thoughts on the Gospels* (Chicago and New York; Fleming H. Revell, St. Mark) p. 292.

78. The Engelder, W. Arndt, Th. Graebner and F.E. Mayer, *Popular Symbolics* (St. Louis, Concordia Publishing House, 1943), p. 132.

79. Cf. editorial, "The Rapture Will Take Place This Week," *Christian News*, Vol. 29, September 12. 1988, p. 4.

80. Helen Barrett Montgomery, *The New Testament in Modern English*, (Philadelphia, Judson Press, 1924), gives the heading "Three Parables of Final Judgment for Matthew 25," listing the Parable of Ten Virgins, the Parable of the Talents and the Final Judgment.

81. Louis E. Hartman and Alexander A. De Leila, *The Anchor Bible - The Book of Dane!* (Garden City, New York: Doubleday & Doran, 1977), pp. 10-16.

82. Rt. Rev. J.C. Ryle, *Expository Thoughts on the Gospels - St. Mark* (Chicago and New York, Fleming H. Revell and Company, 1857), p. 273.

Questions

1. The Olivet discourse deals with the subject of ____.
2. The first three Gospels are known as the ____.
3. The Olivet discourse may be said to present ____.
4. Peter, James, John and Andrew were concerned above all with ____.
5. There is no trace of the idea of a ____ in the question of apostles.
6. The destruction of Jerusalem and Christ's Last Coming are ____.
7. What is the threefold kingdom of Christ? ____
8. Albert Schweitzer's message was ____.
9. What is "realized eschatology?" ____
10. What do Dispensationalists do? ____
11. Scofield has worked out a system of eschatology which rests on ____.
12. What is completely foreign to the Bible? ____
13. The same salvation which Christ earned by His vicarious suffering and death is available to both ____ and ___.
14. When Christians see Christ they will have no reason to ____.
15. The warning of Jesus in Matthew 24:15 refers to ____.
16. The "abomination of desolation" refers to ____.
17. In the constant existence of the Jewish nation of the Christian believers have ____.
18. During His state of humiliation, Christ frequently abstained from ____.
19. Why should Christians constantly be on their guard and watchful? ____
20. All attempts to set the date for the Second Coming are ____.
21. Who predicted the rapture would occur in 1988? ____
22. Both the deluge and the coming of Christ are two ____.
23. No history ought to receive as much of our attention as ____.

The Relationship of Isogogics to Effective Communication of God's Word

Christian News, May 1, 1989

In February 1989 the new *Lutheran Hour* speaker, Dr. Dale Meyer, sent a letter to the ministerium of the Lutheran Church-Missouri Synod, in which he set forth what he hoped with God's help to do and accomplish as Dr. Oswald Hoffmann's replacement. We wish both *Lutheran Hour* speakers God's richest blessings as they in the sermons they proclaim, the anthems rendered by the different choirs and the prayers offered may be instrumental in the conversion of many lost souls and we pray that many individuals may permanently be enrolled in the army of Jesus Christ. May also the faith of those who believe and are *Lutheran Hour* listeners have their faith strengthened. Let us pray that the *Lutheran Hour* will truly bring "Christ to the Nations."

What now follows is not to be considered a criticism of Dr. Meyer or to be construed as derogatory of the task he has embarked upon. However, in the February letter there is one sentence that disturbed and perplexed the writer, namely his attitude toward the discipline of "isagogics." On the middle of page 2 the new *Lutheran Hour* speaker wrote as follows: "How we go about making a difference is critical. My own view is that we, as the ministerium of our church, need to be far more insightful Bible students and teachers. **Teaching isagogics at the seminary never excited me. Not that it's unimportant, it is important, but I was far more excited by studying what God says through specific Biblical texts to individuals and society**" (Bold face is by author.)

That teaching isagogics never excited the new speaker is strange, when he himself stated that isagogics is not unimportant, yet even important. If a course is important in a theological curriculum should not a professor or instructor teach that course with excitement, that is, if he understands the contribution that it makes to the student's theological education and preparation for an effective career of communication, not of man's word but God's Word? The writer of this essay taught both Old and New Testament isagogics for the last thirty-five years; six years at Concordia Teachers College, Seward, Nebraska (1954-1960), and for twenty-nine years at Concordia Theological Seminary, Springfield, Illinois (1960-1976) and at its relocated site in Ft. Wayne, Indiana (1976-1989).

Because he believed that all the disciplines included in isagogics (in the wider sense) were extremely important for the effective communication of God's Word in Bible classes, in sermons, in counselling sessions, in the presentation of evangelistic messages, the writer was excited about isagogics.

The author of this essay wonders whether all in the ministerium of the LCMS are aware of the relationship to each other of all the disciplines that constitute the study of theology. He hopes that they do. What follows, nevertheless should be of interest to lay people who read *Christian*

News. It will show the latter what is involved in preparing a candidate for the ministerium of the Lutheran Church.

Years ago it was a requirement of all students entering our two seminaries to take a course, called "Theological Propaedeutics" or "Theological Encyclopedia." This course was designed to acquaint the theological novice with an overview of the whole field of theology and furnish the student with a bibliography pertinent to the whole field of theology, once called "the queen of the sciences." Traditionally theology was divided into four major fields: the exegetical, the historical, the systematic and the practical. However, in the course of time this course was dropped as the theological curriculum was changed, courses were dropped or added according to the prevailing philosophy of theological education popular at a given decade of the twentieth century. It was hoped that by taking courses in the four fields the student would by himself acquire, either by osmosis, or by having attention called from time to time to the interrelationships that exist between the four major fields, have obtained the same information he once received in that regular course.

Current Interest in Theological Propaedeutics

A survey of recent theological literature will reveal that the disciplines formerly discussed in "Theological Propaedeutics" or "Theological Encyclopedia" are still very much the concern of theologians in the second half of the twentieth century. Relative to theological method the interested person has volumes by: Lonergan, *Method in Theology,*[1] Hartt, *Theological Method and Imagination,*[2] Kaufman, *An Essay on Theological Methodology,*[3] the volume by Fabella and Torres, *Doing Theology in a Divided World,*[4] Ebeling has penned a book covering the whole field of theology, *The Study of Theology,*[5] Maddox was concerned with ecumenical theology, *Toward Ecumenical Fundamental Theology,*[6] or Adams, *Cross Cultural Theology.*[7]

It may not be out of place to show the relationship of isagogics (in the broader sense) to effective Bible class teaching and to effective sound Biblical preaching. Today, because of a claimed shortage of pastors for the congregations of the LCMS, proposals are being put forward to place lay people into congregations with considerable less training required normally of pastors who are admitted into the LCMS's ministerium. This means the elimination of a number of important courses.

In this essay the writer purports to show the importance of isagogics (in the broader sense) to the whole theological enterprise. How correct doctrine, correct liturgies, sound catechetical instruction, sound evangelism and stewardship and the effective communication of the Word of God are greatly dependent on the disciplines of the exegetical subdivision of theology. There is not a single discipline of isagogics (in the broader sense) which should not be taught with excitement and enthusiasm.

Every division, however, it should be stressed is only relative. In every department of theology, exegetical theology involves historical elements (introduction, archaeology, history of Israelite religion, history of Near Eastern religions) as well as doctrinal (criticism, hermeneutics, biblical theology) and practical (exposition). The same is true of other departments; in fact, it would not be difficult to distinguish 1) exegetical, 2) historical, 3) systematic, and 4) practical in each of the four main departments. Each takes the hand of the other and affords an outlook into the other.[8]

The Dutch scholar Kuyper in his *Encyclopedia of Sacred Theology* divided the area of theology into the following departments: 1) Bibliological, 2) Ecclesiological, 3) Dogmatological and 4) Diaconiological. Kuyper placed the following disciplines under the department of Bibliology: 1) the languages of the Bible and their cognates, 2) Biblical exegesis, 3) Biblical history, 4) Biblical theology, 5) Biblical hermeneutics, 6) Biblical antiquities, i.e. the study of ancient civilizations and archaeological research in relation to the Bible.[9]

Dr. Payne in his Theology of the Old Testament has given the following listing of disciplines as constituting the exegetical branch of theological study.[10]

1) Background — Historical appreciation of the Bible, Biblical geography, Biblical archaeology, Ancient Near Eastern History, Religions of the Near East.
2) Content — the textual appreciation of the Bible — Hebrew, Aramaic and Greek Grammar, Related Languages, Hermeneutics (principles of the Biblical interpretation), Exegesis (surveys, book studies, special passages).
3) Publication — the literary appreciation of the Bible. General introduction: textual criticism (lower criticism, canonics). Special introduction: higher criticism.
4) Truth — the revelational appreciation of the Bible. Biblical apologetics. Biblical theology.

Exegetical theology embraces all that relates to the exposition and elucidation of the Holy Scriptures. It consequently embraces exegesis as an art, and all branches of knowledge auxiliary to that art. Exegetical theology includes all those sciences which in any way deal directly with the Scriptures and sets forth the facts presented by the Bible. The objective of the exegetical disciplines is to study, investigate and appropriate the contents of the Bible.

According to Schaff the exegetical branch of theological study, both is first in the order of time and importance, and furnishes the foundation for all other branches.[11]

Hagenbach has stated that the objectives of "Theological Encyclopedia" are "to secure a proper appreciation of the Holy Scriptures by the student who enters upon its study, and to point out the scientific methods appropriate for his work. Sound views respecting the Bible must first of all be secured. It is of the highest importance that both the religious character and the historical nature of the Scriptures should be examined with holy zeal and unbiased judgment, in order that the reverence due to the Bible may not cause its human side to be overlooked, or that the many and diverse subjects discovered from the human point of observation may not lead to the rejection of its divine character of the Bible which constitutes the ground of its importance to religion and theology."[12]

Isagogics: Their Wider and Narrow Senses

The word "Isagogics" means "introduction," coming from the Greek "isagoge." Modern textbooks usually called "isagogics" by the name "introduction."[13] Asserted Young of Westminster Theological Seminary: "In its widest sense the term 'Biblical Introduction' refers to all those studies and disciplines which are preliminary to the study and contents of the Bible."[14] However, the word has come to be employed in a far more restricted sense. The German term is Einleitung or Einfuehrung. This is an area where German scholarship has especially been prominent. In recent times, the term borrowed from Germany, is considered a technical term for the designation of certain studies preliminary to the interpretation of the Bible.[15] If the assumptions and conclusions relative to these preliminary studies are wrong, then the interpretation of Biblical passages and chapters and books will be erroneous and in the case of the Bible promote false doctrines and soul-destroying heresies. Of what good is preaching and teaching that is wrong and misleads human beings?

Prior to centering attention on the disciplines now classified under "isagogics" in the narrow sense, this essay will first discuss the disciplines on which isagogics or introduction rests. Exegetical theology includes a number of disciplines necessary to practice exegesis, that is, to interpret the Bible correctly. The following disciplines belong to Exegetical Theology: Biblical Philology or the study of the original languages. Students at our Concordia Seminaries are required to possess a knowledge of Koine Greek, since the New Testament is written in this type of Greek. The Septuagint, one of the primary versions of the Hebrew Old Testament, is also written in Greek. This involves a knowledge of the grammar, syntax of this Indo-European language. The method of interpretation followed in the Lutheran Church since the days of the reformation is called the historical-grammatical method. The study of Greek grammar and syntax may for some people not be exciting, but how important they are for sound Biblical interpretation and putting into practice 2 Timothy 2:15.

Three fourths of the Bible is written in a Semitic language, namely Hebrew. A knowledge of Hebrew is indispensable for the genuine study of the Old Testament. There probably is no language of equal importance whose contents are more imperfectly reached in translation than the Hebrew.[16] Hebrew is necessary as a means for the genuine study of New Testament exegesis. The Greek of the Septuagint has been influenced by the Hebrew which it attempted to translate. The citations from the Old Testament in the New Testament can only properly be understood when they are compared with the Hebrew Old Testament.

Fifty percent of the Book of Daniel is not in Hebrew but in an Aramaic dialect, called Biblical-Aramaic. Also in Aramaic are portions of Ezra (4:8-6:18; 7:12-26) and one word in Genesis 31:47 and one verse in Jeremiah 10:11.[17] One of the languages which our Lord used was an Aramaic dialect, spoken also by His apostles. Of Jesus it is expressly stated that on four occasions He made use of the native Palestinian Aramaic dialect: when He raised the daughter of Jairus (Mark 5:4); when He opened the ears of the deaf man (Mark 7:34); when upon the cross (Mark 15:34) He uttered the "My God, My God, why hast Thou forsaken Me" and when He manifested Himself to Paul near Damascus (Acts 26:14). We are also informed that St. Paul on a number of occasions spoke in the Hebrew language (Acts 21:40; 22:2), which scholars believe means in Aramaic.[18] In New Testament studies a number of scholars have made much of their belief that the Gospels and a portion of Acts were written Aramaic;[19] spurred on by the reference of Papias that he wrote the Gospel in Aramaic. Students at our seminaries have the opportunity to study and use all three Biblical languages.

If a theologian should master Hebrew and Aramaic, there is still a greater reason why a pastor should daily read his New Testament in Greek. All translations are at best often interpretations. The pastor who stands before his congregation and proclaims God's Word must be sure he is reading what the Holy Spirit caused the holy writers to record and not merely give them sometimes a misinterpretation, depending on which translations was used. Of the study of the New Testament Weidner wrote many years ago as follows: "If the words of the Greek New Testament be divinely inspired, then surely it is the pastor's noblest occupation, patiently and lovingly to note every turn of language, every variety of inflection, to analyze and to investigate, to contrast and compare, until some accurate knowledge of those outward elements, which are permeated by the inward influence and the power of the Holy Spirit. If the New Testament Greek text is the inspired Word of God as it was written down by the evangelists and apostles, then no effort should be spared to understand the original language of the oracles of God." Weidner warned "that a pastor will have to answer before the tribunal of God for failure to attempt to explain the everlasting words of life with haste and precipitation. Every particle and preposition has a distinctive meaning and we should pause before we presume to hurry through the New Testament Scriptures with haste and irreverent speed."[20]

Biblical Introduction
This is one of the divisions of the exegetical branch of theology! At the Fort Wayne Seminary, three courses cover the sixty books of the Bible. Two courses treat the thirty-nine books of the Old Testament, and one course deals with the twenty-seven books of the New Testament. However, before the student or pastor can study the individual books about authorship, place of origin, time of writings, purpose of composition, and general content, it is necessary to ask which books constitute the books thus to be studied and how reliable is the text of these books.

Specific topics of General Introduction
The Text of the Biblical Books
In general isagogics it is customary to treat of the text and canon of

both Testaments of the Bible. Old Testament introductions logically deal with the text and canon of the Old Testament,[21] while New Testament introductions do the same for the New Testament.[22]

The Text of the Old Testament

Determining the correct text of Scripture is known as textual criticism. Since the original Holy Spirit-inspired books of Scripture no longer exist for examination, Jews and Christians are dependent on copies that have been made from the original text, known as the autographs.[23] Ever since the completion of the body of literature called the Bible, its various books have been copied by individuals interested in them. For the Old Testament this means that since about 400 B.C., the time when the Old Testament canon was complete, copies have been made of the twenty-four books of the Hebrew Old Testament (thirty-nine in European versions). The people who copied the Old Testament books were the scribes, the official students of the Old Testament.[24] The Jews manifested great awe and respect for the transmitted text. Because the Scribes were human they made copying mistakes, which subsequent copyists noticed and recorded.[25] Between 400 B.C. and 135 A.D. the text was zealously guarded. Especially in the days of the Masoretes great efforts were expended by students of the Law, the Prophets and the Writings, the three major divisions of the Old Testament Bible to preserve the text[26] from error.

Scribal errors and explanatory marginal notes doubtless resulted in slight alterations from the original, but the fidelity of Ezra and his school, the Great Synagogue and subsequent rabbinical schools and priests worked diligently to perpetuate the original Scriptures. It was the Masoretic scholars who devised the present vowel system and accents marks found in Hebrew Bibles.[27]

Until 1947 the oldest complete manuscript of the Old Testament was a codex written A.D. 1008. There were codices of the law from 825 and for the prophets from A.D. 875.[28] But since 1947 one complete MSS and parts of every Biblical book, except Esther, was found in caves located at Qumran, in the Judean desert, near the Dead Sea. These Dead Sea Scrolls are of great value from the viewpoint of antiquity and authenticity. Old Testament textual critics have a complete book of Isaiah, two chapters of Habakkuk, many Psalms, and portions of every Old Testament book, except Esther. Scholars have fragments of Exodus and Samuel, dated around 250 B.C. and 225 B.C. respectively. Thus copies of the Hebrew text between 250 B.C. and A.D. 66 are available for textual study and also for evaluating the character of the transmission between 400 B.C. and 250 B.C.[29]

Between 400 B.C. and the complete Hebrew Bible of the Middle Ages there also exist translations of the Hebrew Old Testament in Greek, Syriac and Latin. By studying these translations the Old Testament critic can obtain an idea of the kind of Hebrew text the Jewish and Christian translators had at their disposal.[30] In addition there is also the Samaritan Pentateuch of the Samaritan community, a mixed Hebrew sect that only accepted the Pentateuch or Torah.[31]

The Text of the New Testament

Old Testament textual criticism is separate from New Testament textual criticism. Here the word "critical" is employed in a good sense. Both types of textual criticism have as their objective to establish as far as possible the true text of the Bible.

The text of the New Testament came into existence between c. 45 and A.D. 100.[32] No other ancient writing approaches it in number of copies which were made from it and the time of printing. The existing MSS of the New Testament approach the date of origin far more closely than do the MSS of almost any other ancient writing and the New Testament stands alone virtually in the literature of antiquity as a work, which was translated into many other languages. There is a fragment of chapter 18 of St. John's Gospel which paleographers have dated as written in A.D. 135, about thirty-five years removed from the original text.[33] There are papyri uncials of entire New Testament books dated around A.D. 200.

The sources for the New Testament are voluminous, found in papyri, vellum codices and lectionaries used in the church services of all Christian churches. Furthermore, the New Testament was translated into Latin, Syriac Captic, Armenian, Georgian, Arabic and Nubian.[34]

The text of the New Testament has been the subject of intense study since the days of Erasmus till the present. The science of textual criticism has been refined to a point that New Testament scholarship is certain that only a half of a page of the entire New Testament text would be in doubt, and those variants affect no doctrine whatsoever. One New Testament scholar wrote concerning the existing variants in the New Testament text as follows: "The vast majority, however, make no difference in meaning, and the application of accepted principles of textual criticism make it possible to determine the original form of the text for all practical purposes although not to verbal perfection. No fundamental Christian doctrine is left in doubt by any textual variant."[35]

Biblical Canonics

Biblical canonics deals with the origin of the canon, which is different relative to each of the two Testaments. Biblical canonics also pursues the history of the collection and transmission of the separate books and the various facts connected with them.[36] The criteria of canonicity are both external and internal. The external criteria are the testimonies of traditions and Church authority; the internal criteria are the purity and power by which the several books authenticate themselves as inspired productions. The Roman Church emphasizes the first,[37] the Protestant Churches the second class of criteria.[38]

All books which constitute the Word of God are basic to all doctrinal teachings, used in preaching and teaching. The canon is concerned with the matter or seat of authority in religion. Lutherans (at least those faithful to Luther and the Lutheran Confessions) and many Protestants (who have not been victims of negative higher criticism) do not accept the inspired character of the Apocrypha, which according to Protestant counting has fourteen books, of which ten are recognized as deutero-canonical by the Roman Church. The Greek orthodox Church at times has accepted them and now even recognizes a number of them as God's Word. There are also liberal Protestants which recognize the Apocrypha, as the source for New Testament teachings.

Biblical canonics, which has as its purpose the consideration of the idea, historical formation, extent, character, authority and historical influence of the Canon of Scripture, by the very nature of the case requires a separate treatment, one dealing with the Old[39] and the other with the New Testament.[40] But inasmuch as the Holy Spirit is the author of the thirty-nine books of the Old Testament and the twenty-seven of the New, ultimately there is one Biblical canon. The New Testament books are used by the authors to interpret and relate by means of prophecy and fulfillment messages of the Old Testament to the New. The Bible rejects the claim that the Old Testament stands completely on its own, and an interpreter should never use the New Testament to interpret the Old Testament. This is a Jewish claim as well as the assertion of liberal Biblical scholars who are willing to accept the Apocrypha as source for theological beliefs.

The Place of Higher Criticism

In distinction from lower or textual criticism, there is higher criticism, or literary criticism which deals with individual writings and group of writings (as the Pentateuch) and endeavors to determine their authenticity, establish their historical origins, the design and character of the books under consideration, their authorship and the relationship to other writings of the same group.[41] Dealing with these questions should be exciting because of their implications for a correct interpretation of these writings, as well as texts taken from them for teaching and preaching. The term "higher criticism" is a neutral term and need not connote anything negative. The term "higher criticism," however, has been used to designate a type of literary criticism that has been hostile to the supernatural character of Holy Scriptures.[42] Miracles, prophecy as predicting future events, direct revelations of God to man in historical Biblical times are rejected. It has been well stated that good "higher criticism" follows the inductive method, like every other true science. It ascertains, collects and classifies the facts and phenomena, and then draws conclusions as the facts justify. It has no apologetic or dogmatic purpose, but aims at simply setting forth the truth concerning the origin, history and structure of the Biblical writings. It may result in the overthrow or in the confirmation of traditional theories.

Biblical criticism has often been used to inject doubt and infidelity, and rarely has any book been subjected to the abuse the Bible has in the last two hundred fifty years by critical Old and New Testament scholarship. The Old Testament has been approached from various ways in the nineteen and twentieth centuries. 1) There have been those who have held an extremely low view of Scripture. They have considered it nothing but the national literature of the Jewish people. 2) There are those who in dealing with the Bible wish to limit themselves to the human element.

They believe that it is possible to neglect the question of the inspiration of the Bible and still do justice to the Old Testament data. 3) Then there are those who approach the Bible with a neutral attitude. However, as Young has so aptly written: "The so-called neutral attitude toward the Bible is in reality not neutral at all, for it begins by rejecting the lofty claims of Divinity which the Bible makes against and it assumes that the human mind of itself can act as judge of Divine revelation. This is, in effect to substitute the mind of man as ultimate judge and reference point in place of God Himself."[43]

Similar positions have been taken by members of the school of comparative religions, which places the Judaeo-Christian Scriptures on a par with Near Eastern religions, and assumes that much of Biblical religion and theology has been borrowed from the religions of antiquity and those of New Testament and post-apostolic times from the mystery cults and religions.[44]

Higher criticism falls naturally into two divisions, that of the Old Testament and that of the New Testament. Attacks on the historic Jewish and Christian understanding of the literature of the Old Testament centers around the Pentateuch, Isaiah, Daniel, and Zechariah especially, but it should be noted that nearly every Old Testament book has felt the attacks of critical scholarship.[45] In the New Testament the areas of attack have been the Synoptic Gospels, the Johannine books, the writings of Luke, the epistles of Paul, the Petrine letters, Revelation of the Apocalypse. In addition, the coming of form, tradition and redaction criticisms have introduced new problems and attacks upon the veracity and reliability of the Bible.[46]

Basic to the whole theological enterprise and necessary for effective teaching and reliable preaching is a knowledge of Biblical hermeneutics. Hermeneutics teaches the theological student and future proclaimers of God's Word how to apprehend the written text of Holy Writ, it is related closely to the laws of thought, for its thoughts are clearly expressed in logical order, there is not much need of explanation, to grammar, or the science of the laws of language, and to rhetoric, or the science of the laws of speech.

Biblical hermeneutics treats of the laws and principles to be employed in the interpretation of Scriptures. These principles are the same as those utilized in the interpretation of secular writings.[47] In addition, Biblical hermeneutics accepts interpretative principles set forth in the Bible and uses principles that flow from the fact that the Bible is a divine book in which God has spoken and still speaks through it as a Means of Grace. Principles found in Scripture take precedent over the hermeneutics of secular hermeneutics especially when the latter contradict the interpretative principles of the Holy Spirit. To have sound Christian doctrine and Biblical ethical precepts, it is essential to have a knowledge of the correct rules of interpretation and also in interpretation or exegesis to set forth what the Scriptures teach. Otherwise the result will be often not only misconception of God's message but a changing of it, thus making it man's teaching instead of God's.

Martin Luther brought about a revolution in Biblical interpretation; if this revolution had not occurred the Reformation would have been impossible.[48] The following are at least eighteen principles or axioms followed by Luther and utilized in the Lutheran Confessions. The great leader in the early history of the LCMS was Dr. C.F.W. Walther, who in his classic. *The Lutheran Church the True Visible Church*, has summarized the hermeneutical principles of Lutheranism in Theses XIII-XXI.[49]

1. The Bible must be interpreted according to its own claims that it is the inspired Word of God.
2. The Bible canon is a unit as a whole and in all of its parts and therefore cannot contradict itself.
3. Since the Bible is God's Word in human language, it must be interpreted according to its human side.
4. The interpretation of Scripture is never an end in itself, but its purpose is the glorification of God and the salvation of sinful men.
5. The true interpreter of Scripture is a Christian who possesses the gift of the Spirit and believes that all his abilities come from God.
6. Biblical hermeneutics presupposes that God's Word is in the original languages of the Bible and that this text has been preserved in the extant manuscripts. Therefore, the interpreter operates with the best text available and closest to the original.
7. In determining the meaning of a word of Scripture, one must assume that the author used the word in its common meaning (usus loquendi) until it is obvious that he is using a different meaning.
8. The interpretation of every word and passage of Holy Scripture must be in agreement with its context.
9. No interpretation is correct unless it is grammatically correct, that is, according to the grammar and syntax of the language in which it originally was written.
10. Every interpretation of Scripture must be historically correct, that is, the Bible must be understood as a historical book, and be interpreted according to its historical circumstances both of the Bible itself and the world in which it was written.
11. The Bible should be interpreted with the assumption that the author had only one intended sense in mind when he wrote the given Word or passage. (**Sensus literalis unus est**)
12. **Scriptura Scripturam interpretatur. Scriptura sua luce radiat.**
13. All formulation of Christian doctrine must agree with the analogy of faith and must never contradict the analogy of faith.
14. All Biblical interpretation must have Christ as its center, teach Christ, and glorify Him as Lord and Savior.
15. In the interpretation of figurative language the interpreter seeks the point of comparison and does not go beyond it. (Ne tropus ultra tertium)
16. In interpreting types, the interpreter designates as typical those portions of Scripture which the Scripture itself indicates as typical.

17. In interpreting prophecy, one seeks the interpretation in the fulfillment, but all Biblical hermeneutics must be employed to make certain the fulfillment matches the prophecy.

18. To the doctrine of Scripture belongs also the valid and the necessary deduction from Scripture; not all doctrines of Scripture are taught in expressed words.[50]

The ability and skill to interpret the Scriptures correctly is foundational for courses in Christian doctrine, for courses in dogmatics; it is essential for writing Biblically sound sermons and to present the Bible correctly in Bible classes. To be able to recognize false doctrine and the misapplication of Biblical doctrine, is contingent upon an acquaintance of what constitutes correct and proper Biblical interpretation. A Biblically-sound-liturgics is also dependent upon a correct interpretation of the scriptures as used in liturgical prayers and in the selection of texts for the Sundays of the Church Year. Pastoral counseling will also be affected by whether the student and pastor knows what the true teachings of Holy Writ are. All departments of the seminary have a stake in this matter of providing students with a knowledge and skill in hermeneutics.

All courses in the exegetical department, with isagogics in the center, are important and any professor or instructor teaching any one of the disciplines belonging to the exegetical department should teach them with excitement and enthusiasm.

Special Isagogics or Introduction

Edward Young describes the difference between general and special isagogics as follows: General introduction is concerned with topics which relate to the Bible as a whole, such as the Canon and text. Special Introduction, on the other hand, deals with subjects which refer to the separate parts of individual books as unity, authorship, date, genuineness, and literary character. With the exception of a few introductory remarks this present work will limit itself to the subject of Special Introduction.[51] Guthrie in over one thousand page Introduction limits himself to Special Introduction.[52] Since at our two theological seminaries students only deal with a few books in each testament in depth, most of the future pastor's knowledge of the Bible is derived from the courses that are devoted to Special Introduction, so that most knowledge of Scripture as a whole depends on these important and essential courses. The topics discussed in Special Introduction, treating of unity, authorship, time of composition, general contents of each Biblical book, reliability of that recorded in the Bible's sixty-six books are important in determining how a Biblical book is understood and pericopes and passages in these books. Any person who thinks that isagogics as well as other disciplines in the exegetical department are not important, is not really aware of what is involved in presenting to people in the church what the Bible really teaches. Some of these disciplines may be of a technical nature, but they are important to the effective communication of the Word of God.

Footnotes

1. Bernard J. F. Lonergan, *Method in Theology* (New York: Herder and Herder 1972).
2. Julian Hartt, *Theological Method and Imagination* (New York, The Seabury Press, 1977).
3. Gordon D. Kaufman, *An Essay on Theological Method* (Chicago: Scholars Press, published for The American Academy of Scholarship).
4. Virginia Fabella and Sergio Torres, *Doing Theology* (New York Marknol 1982).
5. Gerhard Ebeling, *The Study of Theology*. Translated by A. Priebe (Philadelphia: The Fortress Press, 1978).
6. Randy Maddox, *Toward Ecumental Ecumenical Theology*. No. 47 of the series: Toward and Ecumenical Theology (Chico: The Scholars Press).
7. Daniel J. Adams, *Cross Cultural Theology - Western Reflections* (Atlanta: John Knox Press, 1977).
8. Revere Weidner, *Theological Encyclopedia and Methodology* (Chicago: Fleming H. Revell Company, 1898). Vol. I dealing with introduction and exegetical theology. Vol. II dealing with historical, systematic theology, practical theology. Second edition (Chicago): The Wartburg Publishing House, 1910), 307 pages.
9. Abraham Kuyper, *Encyclopedia of Sacred Theology - Its Principles*. (New York: Charles Scriber's Sons, 1989), pp. 627-336.
10. Barton Payne, *The Theology of the Old Testament* (Grand Rapids: Zondervan Publishing House. 1952), p. 20.
11. Philip Schaff. *Theological Propaedeutic, A General Introduction to the Study of Theology* (New York: Charles Scribner's Sons), p. 93.
12. K. R. Hagenbach, *Encyclopedia und Methologie der theologischen Wissenschaften* (Leipzig, 1884), Paragraph 36.
13. Edward J. Young, *An Introduction to the Old Testament* (Grand Rapids: William B. Eerdans Publishing Company, 1964), p. 15.
14. **Ibid.**
15. **Ibid.**
16. Weidner, **Op. cit.**, i, p. 123.
17. Hans Bauer and Pontus Leander, *Grammatich des Biblisch- Aramaeischen* (Halle/Saale: Max Niemeyer Verlag, 1927), p. 1.
18. Gustav Dalman, *Jesus-Jeshua - Studies in the Gospels*. Authorized translation by the Rev. Paul P. Levertoff (New York: The Macmillan Company, 1929), pp. 11-15,
19. Matthew Black, *An Aramaic Approach to the Gospels and Acts* (Oxford: At the Clarendon Press, 1962), Third revised edition.
20. Weidner, **op. cit.**, 1, p. 138.
21. Arthur Weiser, *The Old Testament: Its Formation and Development* (New York: The Association Press, 1961), pp. 331-385; John E. Steinmueller, *A Companion to Scripture Studies* (New York: Joseph F. Wagner, Inc., 1941), i, pp. 44-224: Brevard Childs, *Introduction to the Old Testament* (Philadelphia: Fortress Press, 1979), pp. 84-108.
22. Everett F. Harrison, *Introduction to the New Testament* (Grand Rapids: Wm. B. Eerdmans Publishing Company, 1964), pp. 59-130; Merrill C. Tenney, *The New Testament - An Historical and Analytical Survey* (Grand Rapids: William B. Eerdmans Publishing Company, 1953), pp. 417-430. Does not treat text, only the canon.
23. Bruce K. Waltke, "The Textual Criticism of the Old Testament," in Harrison, Waltke, Guthrie and Fee, *Biblical Criticism - Historical, Literary, and Textual*

(Grand Rapids: Zondervan Publishing Company, 1979), p. 48.

24. Enst Wuerthwein, *The Text of the Old Testament*. Translated by Erroll F. Rhodes (Grand Rapids: William B. Eerdmans Publishing Company, pp. 12,14.

25. "Scribe," in Pfeiffer, Vos and Rea, *The Wycliffe Bible Encyclopedia* (Chicago: Moody Press, 1975), II, pp. 1535-1536.

26. J. Weingreen, *Introduction to the Critical Study of the Text of the Hebrew Bible* (Oxford: At the Clarendon Press, 1982), p. 16.

27. Guy E. Funderbuck, "Texts and Versions (Old Testament)," Merrill F. Tenney, editor Zondervan *Pictorial Bible Dictionary* (Grand Rapids: Zondervan Publishing House, 1963), p. 84.

28. Wuerthwein, **op. cit.**, p. 12.

29. Charles F. Pfeiffer, *The Dead Sea Scrolls* (Grand Rapids: Baker Book House (1962), pp. 91, 105-106.

30. Wuerthwein, **op. cit.**, pp. 47-48; 80-82; 91-95.

31. **Ibid.**, pp. 42-46.

32. H. Wayne House, *Chronological and Background Charts of the New Testament* (Grand Rapids: Zondervan Publishing House, 1981), pp. 127-128.

33. Gordon Fee, "The Textual Criticism of the New Testament," in Harrison, Waltke, Guthrie and Fee, **op. cit.**, p. 130.

34. Fee, **op. cit.**, pp. 129-130. Bruce Metzger, *The Early Versions of the New Testament. Their Origin, Transmission and Limitations* (Oxford: At The Clarendon Press, 1977), 460 pages.

35. Guy E. Funderbuck, "Texts and Versions, (New Testament)," *Zondervan Pictorial Dictionary of the Bible*, **op. cit.**, pp. 843-844.

36. J.R. Mcrae, "Bible, Canon of," Walter A. Elwell, editor, *Evangelical Dictionary of Theology* (Grand Rapids: Baker Book House, 1984), pp. 140-141.

37. Schaff, **op. cit.**, p. 169.

38. Erwin Lueker, "The Apocrypha," *The Lutheran Cyclopedia* (St. Louis; Concordia Publishing House, 1975), pp. 38-39.

39. R.K. Harrison, *Introduction to the Old Testament* (Grand Rapids: William B. Eerdmans Publishing Company, 1966), pp. 260-287.

40. Harrison, *Introduction to the New Testament*, **op. cit.** pp. 91-114.

41. W. R. Roehrs, "Higher Criticism," *The Concordia Cyclopedia*, **op. cit.** p. 379.

42. Wick Broomall, *Biblical Criticism* (Grand Rapids: Zondervan Publishing House), 143-180.

43. Young, **op. cit.**, pp. 26-27.

44. Cf. the influence of the Panbabylonian School early in twentieth century; or the Egyptian school headed by Erman or the Ugaritic school sponsored by Gray, Pope and others; Cf. Gresham Machen,
The Origin of Paul's Religion (New York: The Macmillan Company, 1928), pp 211-293.

45. Robert H. Pfeiffer, *Introduction to the Old Testament* (New York Harper & Brothers, 1941), pp 129-292; 415-480; 748-472; 604-611.

46. Feine-Behm-Kuemmel, *Introduction to the New Testament*. Translated by A. Mattill (New York and Nashville: Abingdon Press, 1966), 400 pages.

47. Victor E. Menicke, "Bible Interpretation," in Theodore Laetsch, editor, *The Abiding Word* (St. Louis: Concordia Publishing House, 1947), I, pp 36-37.

48. Raymond F. Surburg, "The Significance of Luther's Hermeneutics for the Protes-

tant Reformation," *Concordia Theological Monthly*, 24:241-261, April, 1953.

49. C.F.W. Walther, *Die evangelische — Lutherische Kirche die wahre sichtbare Kirche Gottes auf Erden* (St. Louis: Lutherischer Concordia Verlag, 1891), pp. 54-166; Summary in Dallmann, Dau and Engelder, *Walther and the Church* (St. Louis; Concordia Publishing House, 1938), pp. 122-127. Raymond F. Surburg, "Walther's Hermeneutical Principles." In Arthur Drevlow, editor, *C.F.W. Walther: The American Luther* (Mankato, Minnesota; Walther Press, 1987), pp. 149-160.

50. These Hermeneutical Principles are based upon the following books: F. Fuerbringer, *Theological Hermeneutics* (St. Louis: Concordia Publishing House, 1924); George F. Schodde, *Outlines of Biblical Hermeneutics* (Columbus: Lutheran Book Concern, 1917); Victor Mennicke, "Biblical Interpretation," In Laetsch, *The Abiding Word*, **op. cit.**, pp. 35-58; Raymond F. Surburg, *The Principles of Biblical Hermeneutics* (Fort Wayne: Concordia Theological Seminary Press, 1980), 581 pages. Ralph Bohlmann, *The Hermeneutics of the Lutheran Confessions* (St. Louis Concordia Publishing House, 1978). Revised edition.

51. Young, **op. cit.**, pp. 15-16.

52. Guthrie, **op. cit.**, 1054 pages.

Questions

1. What disturbed Dr. Surburg about a letter written by *Lutheran Hour* speaker Dr. Dale Meyer? ____
2. Theology was once called ____ of the sciences.
3. Traditionally theology was divided into the four major fields ____.
4. There is not a single discipline of isagogics which should be taught with ____.
5. "Isagogics" means ____.
6. The method of interpretation followed in the Lutheran Church since the Reformation is ____.
7. Three fourths of the Bible is written in ____.
8. Fifty percent of the Book of Daniel is in ____.
9. One of the languages used by our Lord was ____.
10. The pastor should daily read his New Testament in ____.
11. Determining the correct text of Scripture is known as ____.
12. Great efforts were made especially in the days of the Massorettes to preserve the ____.
13. What was found in Qumran? ____
14. The science of textual criticism has been refined to a point that New Testament scholarship is certain that only ____.
15. No fundamental Christian doctrine is left in doubt by ____.
16. What do some liberal Protestants teach about the Apocrypha? ____
17. The term "higher criticism" need not connote anything ____.
18. Biblical criticism has often been used to inject ____.
19. Biblical hermeneutics treats of ____.
20. Martin Luther brought about a revolution in ____.
21. Who summarized the hermeneutical principles of Lutheranism? ____

The Presuppositions of the Historical-Grammatical Method

Christian News, October 30, 1989

The essayist has the assignment to set forth the presuppositions of the historical-grammatical method and then later demonstrate how this method would be applied to the resurrection of Jesus pericope in the first paragraph of I Corinthians 15. That there are assumptions or presuppositions connected with the use of the historical-grammatical method is true, but it is just as true of the practitioners of the historical-critical method that as they employ this method they also start with presuppositions which in turn control the use of the method which then results in ultimate outcomes of their exegetical efforts. It is totally erroneous to depict the historical-critical method as simply a collection of tools and that this method can be employed without the user having assumed certain assumptions which control his methodology. I trust that before the exegesis of I Corinthians 15 is set forth by the essayist enjoined with the employment of the historical-critical method that he will clearly enunciate the presuppositions underlying this method as held by its recognized advocates.

Every method has assumptions and is teleological in character. It is true that a method is neutral in how it operates but it is controlled and directed by its assumptions and in the light of its assumptions the method must to be consistent achieve certain goals. The name of the historical-critical method has two descriptive terms: historical and critical. . . Further a method can be assessed by the consistency with which it follows its own presuppositions. Just as the historical-grammatical method has a preunderstanding a Vorverstandnis, so the historical-critical method has assumptions that guide the person who claims to be employing it.

The historical-grammatical method is primarily a product of the Reformation and post-Reformation periods of Western European Christianity.[1] While certain aspects of it were known and occasionally spasmodically utilized prior to Luther the historical-grammatical method is a development of Luther, Calvin, Zwingli, John Knox and other Protestant reformers.[2] After Luther's death it was the method used during the 17th and 18th centuries in Lutheranism, Calvinism and Arminianism.

The historical-grammatical method came out of the context of Western European Christianity and was developed in reaction to the allegorical method which had more or less dominated the history of the Church of Latin Christianity for over a thousand years.

Those theologians and exegetes that developed, propounded and defended the historical-grammatical method brought with them a number of presuppositions which had controlled previous methodology in the church. These they kept but other presuppositions were also adopted whose acceptance made necessary a new interpretative methodology, which in many respects was radically different from the method that controlled the Roman Catholic Church during the first decades of the 16th

657

century and in the centuries prior to 1517.[3]

Before giving the main presuppositions of the historical-grammatical method, it is necessary to describe how it operates and what its goals are. The majority of books that contain a history of Biblical hermeneutics do not have a special section dealing with the historical-grammatical method.[4] During the time that the Christian Church has been in existence, which has been over 1900 years, different methods of interpretation have been in vogue.[5] In the course of that long history a number of different kinds of schools in interpretation have arisen upon the scene utilizing methods which were significantly different from each other. The consequence of this situation resulted in different understandings and promulgations of what the Holy Scriptures truly taught and intended to teach.

Allegory, taken over from Greek secular literary interpretation, invaded the church already in the pre-Nicene age as well as in the centuries following Nicene Council.[6] Both Origen and St. Augustine were proponents of a manifold-sense of Scriptures concept. Eventually a fourfold sense was practiced in both the Eastern and Western branches of Asiatic and European Christendom respectively. After Augustine's death allegorism came to be the controlling method of Biblical interpretation. In addition to its use, there developed the claim by the Bishop of Rome that only the Church has the God-given right to interpret the Scriptures and that the Church alone had the privilege and ability to interpret Scriptures and determine its true meaning. The Roman Catholic believer was to believe a doctrine or dogma not because it was taught in the Scriptures but because the Church determined a doctrine of belief. All Christians were to recognize the teaching magisterium of the Church; although a dogma was not in the Scriptures it was nevertheless to be accepted. In addition, the Vulgate of Jerome, in many respects a fine translation, yet containing mistakes in translation, was made the definitive text, when matters of doctrine and ethics were concerned. Furthermore, the Old Testament canon was enlarged to include ten of the fourteen books regarded as apocryphal by both the Jewish synagogue and the Protestant Churches.[7]

The allegorical method had been opposed by the School of Antioch which stressed a historical interpretation as opposed to the allegorical.[8] In Paris the school of the Victorians emphasized a methodology not in sympathy with allegorical method.[9] Nicholas of Lyra also sponsored hermeneutical views that were contradictory of what was standard hermeneutical procedure in his day. Luther was influenced by Nicholas of Lyra.[10]

However, it was in the 16th century that there occurred a hermeneutical revolution or revolt which Luther initiated and fostered, a revolution that changed the course of Western European history. The Protestant Reformation would have been impossible apart from this change in the hermeneutics that was employed to interpret the Holy Scriptures of both the Old and New Testaments.[11] Luther, Calvin, Zwingli and other reformer's rejected the fourfold meaning of a Biblical text or pericope. Luther realized that permitting the Scriptures to be interpreted by this method was to make of the Bible a waxen nose, which could be twisted to give any meaning any way that an interpreter desired to give a passage. It was declared that a passage had only one intended meaning. Furthermore, it was the contention of Luther and other reformers that only the Scripture determined the meaning of a text and not the Church, and if church doctrine or dogma contradicted the Bible, the church teaching was to be rejected.[12] For the 16th century that truly was revolutionary. The Protestant movement which made great inroads on the numerical strength of the Roman See and resulted in the loss of millions of adherents was made possible by the adoption of a new system of Biblical interpretation by the Reformer. A system of hermeneutics was developed and utilized that differed radically in many points from the systems in use in both the Eastern and Western branches of Christianity as represented by the Roman Catholic and the Greek Orthodox Churches.[13]

Luther became the proponent of a methodology which in essence was the historical-grammatical method. Melanchthon employed it in his teaching at the University of Wittenberg. Since Luther and Melanchthon wrote the majority of the Lutheran Confessions, the Large and Small Catechisms; the Smalcald Articles (Luther), the Augsburg Confession and the Apology of the Augsburg Confession (Melanchthon), the *Formula of Concord* was the only book not authored by these two professors of the University of Wittenberg. A perusal of the hermeneutics of the *Formula of Concord* reveals that it also uses the principles of the historical-grammatical method.[14]

In the post-Reformation period, during the 17th and 18th and 19th centuries the historical-grammatical method was employed by the Lutheran theologians. A number of scholars refined the method and defined some of its aspects more clearly. Professor Terry, who lived prior to the twentieth century, and did not witness the development of the newer sub-methods of the historical-critical methods, which was to develop from a radical type of literary criticism into form criticism, tradition criticism, redaction criticism and content criticism, described in his 1890 Biblical Hermeneutics the historical-grammatical method as follows:

> In distinction from all the above-mentioned methods of interpretation, we may name the Grammatico-Historical as the method which most fully commends itself to the judgment and conscience of Christian scholars. Its fundamental principle is to gather from the Scriptures themselves the precise meaning which the writers intended to convey. It applies to the sacred books the same principles, the same grammatical process and exercise of common sense and reason, which we apply to other books. The grammatico-historical exegete, furnished with suitable qualifications, intellectual, educational, and moral, will accept the claims of the Bible without prejudice or adverse prepossession, and, with no ambition to prove them false, will investigate the language and import of each book with fearless independence. He will master the language of the writer, the particular dialect which he used, and his peculiar style and manner of expression. He will inquire into the circumstances under which he wrote, the manners and customs of his age, and the purpose or object which he had in view. He has a right to assume that no sensible author will be knowingly in-

consistent with himself, or seek to bewilder and mislead his readers.[15]

Some of the presuppositions that were used by the developers and promoters of the historical-grammatical method had been used in the interpretation of the Bible according to the allegorical method and because they were valid were not abandoned. Yet other presuppositions were adopted in order to truly justify the elimination and rejection of the past weaknesses and errors in the exegesis of Holy Scriptures.

1. A basic presupposition kept by Luther, Calvin and many other reformers was the historic position of Latin, Western and Eastern Greek Christianity that the Bible was the Word of God in its entirety.[16] Even though the Roman Church of Luther's day held that there were two sources for revelation: Scripture and tradition, they did teach that the Bible in its entirety was the inspired, inerrant Word of God. Christian scholars down through the centuries have held it a presupposition that the Bible is a unique book because the Holy Spirit was its author. In the *Table Talk* Luther is reported as saying: "We ought not to criticize the Scriptures, or judge the Scriptures by our mere reason, but diligently, with prayer, meditate thereon, and seek their meaning."[17]

2. Another presupposition of the developers of the historical-grammatical method was the recognition of only those canonical books which were employed as Scripture by the Jewish synagogue and as also reflected in the New Testament, both of which give no evidence of having acknowledged any of the apocryphal books, now a part of the official Old Testament canon of Roman Catholicism and of Eastern orthodoxy.[18] The rejection of books like Maccabees, Tobit, the Wisdom of Solomon and other writings had implications for the establishment of the kind of doctrines were to be placed into a systematic theology as true doctrine God would have His people hold and teach. The elimination of ten of the fourteen apocryphal writings as given in Protestant apocryphal lists, has implication for Biblical interpretation, especially when the principle is used, namely, that Scripture alone in the source for the formulation of divine truth.

3. A third presupposition of the Luther and the other Protestant Reformers was that only the text in the original languages was the determinative one. This meant the non-recognition of the Vulgate, a translation in Latin, as the Scriptural text that decided the meaning of a certain text. The mistranslation of the pronoun **hu** in the Hebrew text of Gen. 3:15, in the Protevangelium, as **hi**, "she" was utilized to support Mariolatry. Both the Council of Trent and the Vatican Council of 1870 affirmed the authoritative character of the Latin Vulgate as the deciding authority in establishing doctrine and morals. The Reformers' insistence on the use of the Hebrew Old Testament and the Greek New Testament made possible a scholarly exegesis of the Biblical text and fostered the philological method of the interpretation of the Bible which came to characterize the historical-grammatical method. Only by the use of the original text could exegesis truly be scholarly and grammatic.[19]

4. A fourth presupposition was the conviction, based on the Word of God itself, that the supreme and final authority in theological matters was the Bible. Ramm stated Luther's position as follows: "The Bible is

the supreme and final authority in theological authority. Its teaching cannot be countermanded nor qualified nor substantiated to ecclesiastical authority whether of persons or documents."[20]

5. A fifth important presupposition of the historical-grammatical method as developed by the Protestant Reformers was the principle that the literal meaning was the usual and normal one. The Scholastics had developed their hermeneutics into two divisions: literal and spiritual. The Spiritual was divided into: allegorical, anagogical, and topological. Luther contended for the primacy of the literal meaning of a text. Dean Farrar quoted Luther as holding: "The literal sense of Scripture alone is the whole essence of Christian faith and of Christian theology."[21] C. A. Briggs cites Luther as writing: "Every word should be allowed to stand in its natural meaning and that should not be abandoned unless faith forces us to it."[22]

The literal meaning could only be adequately attained by the use of the original text in Hebrew and Greek. Luther gave the following advice: "While the preacher may preach Christ with edification though he may be unable to read the Scriptures in the originals, he cannot expound or maintain their teaching against the heretics without this indispensable knowledge."[23] It is generally acknowledged that Luther played an important role in sponsoring the revival of Hebrew and Greek studies.

6. The proponents of the historical grammatical method operate with the presupposition that the **autographic** text is the authoritative text and that since errors have crept into the transmission of the text, it is necessary to practice textual criticism, also known as lower criticism. Part I of Fuerbringer's little hermeneutical manual, by means of which thousands of pastors were introduced to the science of Biblical hermeneutics, deals with Biblical Criticism, establishing the text of the Bible. Dr. Fuerbringer wrote: "The exegete must for this reason, first of all, endeavor to ascertain the original form of the text. (Textual criticism, verbal criticism, lower criticism.)"[24] Fuerbringer calls attention to the fact that Luther already realized the necessity of textual criticism, and sites IX, 1086; VIII, 1719, 1849, 1852; XIV, 600.[25] Historical Lutheranism has not opposed the proper use of lower criticism and not rejected the legitimate findings of a reliable type of textual criticism.

7. Another presupposition of the employers of the historical-grammatical method was the recognition that the Biblical books were literary documents and therefore there was a proper place for literary criticism.[26] After the textual critic has determined either for himself or because he is persuaded that the text of printed critical editions substantially contain the correct text, he then on the basis of such a text as an exegete studies a Biblical book in terms of authorship, time of writing, place of writing, purpose of writing, integrity and historical background. Sometimes these isagogical questions are answered clearly by the text of the book, sometimes they are not. The literary critic uses both internal evidence and external evidence in dealing with these questions which often determine the interpretation of a given book or books. For example, the rejection of Mosaic authorship in favor of the documentary hypothesis

has many implications for the interpretation of the first five books of the Old Testament and sometimes also for the book of Joshua. (Hexateuch theory). The Unity of Isaiah versus multiple authorship of Isaiah again has implications as to where in the progress of Old Testament revelation the 66 chapters of this book are to be placed, how chapter 13 and 14 and 39 are to be understood, chapters which the text assigns to Isaiah but denied by historical-critical proponents to the prophet Isaiah. There are New Testament statements in which there are quotations from chapters 1-39, 40-55, and 56-66 and are all ascribed to Isaiah the prophet.

8. Another assumption of the users of the historical-grammatical method as employed by Luther, the Lutheran Confessions and those who have remained faithful to the hermeneutics of the Lutheran Confessions is the assumption of the unity of the Holy Scriptures.[27] God ultimately is the Author of the 66 canonical books. The Old and New Testaments are one complete revelation of God and are not to be separated; the Old Testament is not to be treated as if there were no New Testament for which it was preparatory. Luther cited the ancient maxim: Novum Testamentum in Vetere latet, Vetus Testamentum in Nova patet (Luther III, 1882, 1884).[28] The New Testament is hidden in the Old and the Old Testament is revealed in the New. Sometimes the true intended meaning of a given Old Testament text is first made explicit by the New Testament where the Author, the Holy Spirit reveals what had been the intended meaning of a given Old Testament text. Psalm 110 would be an example, where David speaks about Yahweh's Messiah. Jesus and other New Testament writers clearly state that David wrote Ps. 110, a view which commentaries written by proponents of the historical method do not accept; instead they claim this psalm was used at the coronation of a new king in Judah or Israel and in no way was predicative of the Messiah.

9. Related to the presupposition of the unity of the Scriptures is the presupposition that Scripture can be used to interpret Scripture. This presupposition is found in the New Testament and for this reason Luther, the authors of the Lutheran Confessions, and later Lutheran theologians and pastors that accepted the hermeneutical principles practiced and employed what the theologians described as "Scriptura **Scripturam interpetatur**."[30] The Old Testament frequently receives clarification as to its God-intended meaning, from the New. By virtue of the validity of this presupposition which is employed as an interpretative principle, the Biblical interpreter uses parallel passages to understand given passages. This rule is also useful in dealing with dark passages or those that are susceptible of more than one meaning, because to our age there are factors unknown that were known to the original recipients. The classical formulation of Scriptura Sacra sui ipsius interpres is already evident in Luther's writings as early as 1519.[30] This was a principle that was employed by various writers before Luther's time. In a general way, the principle that an interpreter uses the writings of a given author to explain statements in a book is a principle of general literature. That Scripture can and does interpret Scripture is also related to the fact of the clarity of the Holy Scripture and with the fact that God is the ultimate

Author of all books comprising the Biblical canon and that the Scriptures are the only source and norm of doctrine and morals. Dr. Ralph Bohlmann wrote concerning this matter:

> The fact that the Scriptures were authored by God suggests that the principle **Scriptura Sacra sui ipsius interpres** is simply an extension of the general hermeneutical principle that the passage must be considered and explained in terms of this context of any Bible passage is ultimately the entire Scripture. That the "context" of Scripture can give a true explanation of any passage rests on the fact of its divine authorship, by virtue of which Scripture is held to be in agreement with itself.[31]

10. It was and is an assumption of the Lutheran exegetes following the teachings of the Bible that the Scriptures in their autographic text are inerrant and do not contain contradictions as they employ the historical-grammatical method. Because God is the author of the Scriptures Luther and the Lutheran Confessions held that they did not have errors or contradictions. In the Large Catechism Luther wrote: "that God does not lie" (IV 57), and "God's Word does not err," (IV, 57). Therefore Luther urges: "Believe the Scriptures. They will not lie to you" (LC V 76). The *Formula of Concord* rejects as an opinion the errancy of Scripture because "in this way it would be taught that God, who is eternal Truth, contradicts itself" (SD XI 35). The preface to the Book of Concord describes the Scripture as "the pure, infallible, an unalterable Word of God".[32]

Frederick C. Grant, a well-known critical scholar in *An Introduction to New Testament Thought* stated that the Scriptures testify about themselves as follows:

> Everywhere it is taken for granted that what is written in Scripture is the work of divine inspiration, and is therefore trustworthy, infallible, and inerrant. The Scripture must be "fulfilled" (Luke 22:37). What was written for our instruction (Rom. 15:4; I Cor. 10:11); what is described or related to the Old Testament is unquestionably true. No New Testament writer would dream of questioning a statement contained in the Old Testament, though the exact manner or mode of its inspiration is nowhere stated explicitly.[33]

11. A fundamental and basic presupposition of the Lutheran exegete employing the historical-grammatical method is the centrality of justification by faith as the chief article of the Biblical revplation.[34] No interpretation of the Bible dare violate or be in disagreement with this Biblical teaching. This has been called the **Hauptartikel Principles**.[35] We may say of it that it is a presupposition as well as a hermeneutical principle. The **Hauptartikel** presupposition or principle is referred to often in the Lutheran Confessions. In Apology IV, 79-80 we read: "We prove the minor premise as follows. Since Christ is set forth to be the propitiator, through whom the Father is reconciled, we cannot appease God's wrath by setting forth our own works. For it is only by faith that Christ is accepted as mediator. By faith alone, therefore, we obtain the forgiveness of sins when we comfort our hearts with trust in the mercy promised for Christ's sake." In Apology IV 2 (German text) Melanchthon calls the doc-

trine of justification by faith as "der vornehmste Artikel (praecipuus locus)," an article valuable for determining the clear correct understanding of the entire Holy Scriptures, and alone able to point the way to the unspeakable treasures and right knowledge of Christ, and thus alone shows the true meaning of all of the Bible. In the Smalcald Articles the Wittenberg Reformer calls Christ and faith in Him as "the first and chief article."

12. A presupposition closely allied with this **Hauptartikel** for the Lutheran exegete is the Christocentricity of the entire Bible.[36] This Christocentricity of the Scriptures, the Old Testament, is regarded basic by those interpreters who do not question the reliability of the Biblical text. For Luther Christ permeates the Old Testament Scriptures and this fact was emphasized by Luther in his writings as well as throughout the Lutheran Confessions. One does not truly understand the message of the Old Testament, if Christ is not found there by modern exegetes but as many of the New Testament writers do. Luther stated that all the promises of the Old Testament find their ultimate fulfillment in Jesus. The Angel of the Lord who comes to the patriarchs of the Old Testament and blessed them was Christ. When Yahweh is depicted in the Old Testament times as redeeming His people, the reader must think of Christ, so Luther contends. The Old Testament saints were not merely saved by implicit trust in the mercy and grace of God but by Christ, who was the object of the faith of the Old Testament believers. Commenting on Gen. 3:15, Luther says:

"Here it is written that Adam was a Christian long before the birth of Christ. For he had the same faith in Christ that we have. For in matters of faith, time makes no difference. Faith is of the same nature from the beginning to the end of the world. Therefore he, through his faith, received the same that I receive. He did not see Christ with his eyes, neither did we, but he had Him in the Word. The only difference is this: at that time it was to come to pass, now it has come to pass. Accordingly all the Fathers were justified in the same manner as we are, through the Word and through faith and in this faith they also died."

When Luther finds Christ in the Old Testament he is not allegorizing as some might contend, but merely reading the Old Testament in the light of the New and thus finds a deeper meaning than an exegete does who ignores the New Testament. This would also be an application of the use of the analogy of faith. In response to the objection to Luther's Christological interpretation that he was making a text utter something originally not intended by the text, Luther would reply that the New Testament fulfilment of the Old Testament promise is a part of the larger historical context of Old Testament passages, because God, the Author of all Biblical books, therefore can be set forth what the true intended meaning of Old Testament passages has reflected in the New Testament.

13. A fundamental presupposition of the Lutheran exegete employing the historical-grammatical method is the belief that in the Holy Scriptures God speaks a word of Law and a Word of Gospel, a word of condemnation and a word of forgiveness.[37] It is a fundamental presupposition

that these two doctrines must not be confused but their messages kept distinct from each other. Without the proper distinction between Law and Gospel the central message of Holy Scripture cannot be ascertained. Malanchthon's whole argument in the Apology is closely bound up with the recognition and use of the Law/Gospel dichotomy. The *Formula of Concord* stated: "The distinction between Law and Gospel is an especially brilliant light which serves the purpose of that Word of God may be rightly divided and the writings of the holy apostles may be explained and understood correctly." The distinction of Law and Gospel is no Lutheran doctrine for "since the beginning of the world these two proclamations have continually been set forth side by side in the church of God with the proper distinction." The patriarchs knew this distinction as did David.

Footnotes

1. L. Berkhof, *Principles of Biblical Interpretation* (Sacred Hermeneutics) (Grand Rapids; Baker Book House, 1950), p. 27.

2. Bernard Ramm, *Protestant Biblical Interpretation* (Grand Rapids: Baker Book House, 1970). pp. 48-51.

3. Raymond F. Surburg, "The Significance of Luther's Hermeneutics for the Protestant Reformation," *Concordia Theological Monthly*, 24:241-261, April, 1953.

4. Cf. James D. Wood, *The Interpretation of the Bible* (London: Gerald Duckworth, 1958). Frederick W. Farrar, *History of Interpretation* (London: Macmillan and Co., 1886).

5. E. C. Blackman, *Biblical Interpretation* (London: Independent Press, 1957), pp. 65-158; Henry Preserved Smith, *Essays in Biblical Interpretation* (Boston: Marshall Jones and Company, 1924), pp. 33-167; George Holley Gilbert, *Interpretation of the Bible, A Short History* (New York: The Macmillan Company, 1908), pp. 1-292.

6. Farrar, **op. cit.**, pp. 127-158.

7. Cf. *Biblia Sacra Juxta Vulgatam Clemetinam* (Romae-Tornaci-Parisiis: Typis Societatis S. Joannis Evang., 1956) pp ix-xii.

8. Ramm, **op. cit.**, pp. 48-51.

9. **Ibid.**, p. 51.

10. Farrar, **op. cit.**, p. 277; **op. cit.**,

11. Surburg, **op. cit.**, p. 242.

12. Ramm, **op. cit.**, p. 55.

13. Cf. Farrar, **op. cit.**, p 325ff.

14. Ralph A. Bohlmann, *Principles of Biblical Interpretation in the Lutheran Confessions* (St. Louis: Concordia Publishing House, 1968).

15. Milton S. Terry, *Biblical Hermeneutics - A Treatise on the Interpretation of the Old and New Testaments* (New York: Eaton and Mains, 1890), p. 70.

16. Ramm, **op. cit.**, pp. 55,58.

17. As cited by Ramm, **op. cit.**, p. 54.

18. Dr. M. Reu, *Luther and the Scriptures* (Columbus: The Wartburg Press, 1944), p. 13-48; Rupert E. Davies, *The Problem of Authority in the Continental Reformers* (London: Epworth Press, 1946), p. 107.

19. (missing)

20. Ramm, **op. cit.**, p. 53.

21. Farrar, **op. cit.**, p. 327.

22. C. A. Briggs. *History of the Study of Theology* (New York: Charles Scribners and

Sons, 19), II, p. 107.

23. As cited by Ramm, **op. cit.**, p. 54.

24. L. Fuerbringer, *Theological Hermeneutics* (St. Louis: Concordia Publishing House, 1924), pp. 4-8.

25. **Ibid.**, p. 3.

26. A Berkeley, Michelsen, *Interpreting the Bible* (Grand Rapids: Wm. B. Eerdmans Publishing Company, 1963), pp. 99-337; Charles Augustus Briggs, *General Introduction to the Study of Holy Scriptures*. Revised Edition. (Grand Rapids: Baker Book House. 1970, reprinted from the revised edition of 1900), pp. 293ff.

27. L. Fuerbringer, **op. cit.**, pp. 14, (par 28), 30 (par 29&30), p. 17.

28. **Ibid.**, p. 16.

29. **Ibid.**, p. 15; Wm. Dallmann, W.T. Dau and Th. Engelder, *Walther and the Church* (St. Louis, Concordia Publishing House, 1938), pp. 124, 125.

30. Bohlmann, **op. cit.**, pp. 99-100.

31. **Ibid.**, p. 108.

32. Bohlmann, **op. cit.**

33. Frederick Grant, *An Introduction to New Testament Thought* (New York: Abingdon Press, 1950), p. 75.

34. Robert David Preus, "How is The Lutheran Church to Interpret and Use the Old and New Testaments?" *The Lutheran Synod Quarterly*, 14:23-24, Fall, 1973; Bohlmann, **op. cit.**, p. 73-79.

35. **Ibid.**, p. 23.

36. Preus, **op. cit.**, p. 29.

37. Holsten Fagerberg, *Die Theologie der lutherischen Bekenntnisschriften* von 1529 bis 1537, trans. Herhard Klose (Gottingen: Vandenhoek & Ruprecht, 1965), pp. 91-96: Edmund Schlink, *Theology of the Lutheran Confessions*, trans., by P.F. Koehneke and H. J. A. Boumann (Philadelphia: Mulenberg Press, 1961), pp 136-137.

Questions

1. The historical-grammatical method is primarily a product of ____.
2. The Bishop of Rome declared that only the Church has the God-given right to ____.
3. What made the definitive text? ____
4. Luther recognized that the allegorical method made the Scriptures as ____.
5. Luther became the proponent of a methodology which in essence was ____.
6. The Roman Church of Luther's day did teach that the Bible was ____.
7. Luther contended for the primacy of the ____ meaning of the text.
9. Luther played an important role in sponsoring the revival of ____ and ___ studies.
10. Textual criticism is also known as ___ criticism.
11. Who is the ultimate author of the 66 books of the Bible? ____
12. The New Testament is hidden in the ___ and the Old Testament is revealed in the ____.
13. The preface to the Book of Concord describes the Scripture as ____.
14. What is the Hauptartikel? ____
15. For Luther ____ permeates the Old Testament?
16. What two doctrines must not be confused? ____

In Defense of Luther

Christian News, November 12, 1990

(Ed. The October 15 *Christian News* in a page one story titled "Gordon Winrod — Former LCMS Pastor: 'LUTHER WAS FORERUNNER OF ANTI-CHRIST — HATED JESUS— AND WAS PRO-JEW'" published a large part of the October, 1990 *Winrod Letter* which was sent to many pastors and congregations in The Lutheran Church-Missouri Synod. Several asked *CN* to respond to Winrod's attack upon Luther and what Winrod says about the Jews. The November 5 *CN* published a letter defending Winrod.)

A Rebuttal of Winrod's Attack Upon Luther as "the Fore-runner of Anti-Christ"

Pastor Gordon Winrod of Our Savior Church and Latin School, Gainesville, Missouri, has for a number of years published his *Winrod Letter*. His most recent one, October, 1990, No. 300 contains a vicious attack upon Dr. Martin Luther, whose birthday Lutherans will observe on November 10th. The reader of letter 300 will find it difficult to search out statements about Luther, about the Wittenberg Reformer that are more vicious and scurrilous than those of Winrod, who calls Luther "the fore-runner of Anti-Christ." The *Winrod Letter* misrepresents the facts of the Bible, ascribes actions and deeds to the Jews that are not true. This letter is anti-Semitic in character. Winrod accuses Luther of beliefs he did not subscribe to, shows an abominable ignorance of secular and European history. His hermeneutics as used in Revelation and other Scriptures is erroneous. His knowledge of textual criticism is extremely faulty. His interpretation of 2 Thessalonians 2:1-12 is totally wrong. His claim that Luther hated Christ and sided with the Jews against Christ must be classified as a lie.

The strange and sad fact about Pastor Winrod is that he once enjoyed a theological training at one of the two seminaries of The Lutheran Church-Missouri Synod, for he is acquainted with the Lutheran Confessions and especially the teaching on the Anti-Christ, as expressed by Melanchthon and Luther in separate confessional writings.[1] He also refers to the fact that many Lutherans believe that the teachings of the Lutheran Confessions are true because (quia) they are in agreement with the Word of God and not merely in so far as (quatenus) with The Bible.[2] He also stated that his views are not taught in Lutheran seminaries or preached in Lutheran pulpits.[3]

Winrod's Letter No. 300 Has No Real Theological Content
Although he makes a great deal about the alleged claim that Luther was against Christ, that he expunged the name of Jesus from numerous passages and also asserted: "The chief doctrine of the Bible is that Jesus

is God every time He is considered in the Scriptures, by whatever He is known other than Jesus. He who would take away Jesus is anti-Jesus (cf. I John 2:22,"[4]). He never tells his readers what Jesus has done for mankind. The Lutheran Reformation emphasized the fact that Christ was crucified for the sins of the world and that those who repent of their sins and are brought by the Holy Spirit to believe and trust in Jesus, will have eternal life. That is what Martin Luther taught. Not a word in the *Winrod Letter* about salvation by grace through faith in Christ is even hinted at in this long attack on the Reformer.

Winrod's Hatred of the Jews

This is the way Letter 300 begins: "The Jews, the conspiratorial international Sect of Pharisees, are the workers of the world system of communism. They are creators and workers of communism. They work through their fronts, from behind the scenes, the great lie of the Jews is that they are God's people of the Book, and that those Christians, who kept the Jews down and out of power for a thousand years (Ap. 20) are the kingdom of anti-Christ."[5] According to Winrod, Jesus and the Apostles denominated the Jews as the kingdom of anti-Christ. By contrast averred Winrod: "On the other hand, Martin Luther (1483-1546) A. D.) taught that the earthly kingdom, in which Christ's Church was comprised (dominated by Christ for more than a millennium), known as the Catholic Church, is the world system of anti-Christ."[6] Luther, however, contradicted the New Testament by teaching that the Catholic Church is the anti-Christ. The Reformation was a huge mistake according to Winrod, because Luther, "a Jew-promoted leader of anti-Christian Jewish revolution said the Catholic Church is the world-system of anti-Christ, and that the Pope himself, is the anti-Christ."[7]

According to the Gainesville, Missouri, preacher the greatest achievement of the Lutheran Reformation was the emancipation of the Jews. That supposedly was its first purpose according to Winrod. This allegedly was the fulfillment of 2 Thessalonians 2:3.[8] Winrod interprets the latter Pauline passage as predicting that Christ could not come until there would be a falling away from Christ's truth and a great revolt occur, which would free the workers of iniquity. Eventually, those workers would rise to world power. For a thousand years Christianity would rule with the Devil and the Jews bound. This Winrod found in Revelation 20:2-3.[9] But the sixteenth century loosed Satan. The 16th century Reformation of Luther emancipated the Jews, who were anti-Christ. Luther and Jews were in league with each other. The Roman Catholic Church was infiltrated by this Jewish group of anti-Christ and the Christian organizations were unable to resist this Jewish revolution.

The Fruits of Luther's Revolt as Alleged by Winrod

Thus Winrod wrote on page 2B, lines 15ff.: "The entire world eats the fruits of Luther's revolt today. Germany, did then; immediately, more than a thousand monasteries and castles were levelled to the ground; hundreds of villages were laid in ashes, the harvests of the nation destroyed, and 100,000 were killed. Germany suffered a Jewish reign of terror. But this is not told in the Lutheran seminary or pulpit." Because of Luther many people suffered. When the Jews were liberated secret organizations, like the Freemasons sprang up in Europe (1717 A.D.). The French Revolution in 1789 A.D. was sponsored by Jews and allegedly resulted in the killing of millions of Christians. It's cry of liberty, equality and fraternity was Jewish inspired. Luther's Manifesto "The Freedom of the Christian Man," written 250 years before the French Revolution had inspired all negative, subversive and baneful movements in European History.[10] In 1776 the Jewish experimental democratic revolution came to the American shores, to the 13 colonies. Then in 1917, Jews from the U.S. descended upon Russia and with Jew U.S. dollars supported communism. Socialism is Jewish. The practice of insurance was unknown throughout the Christian centuries was promoted with a vengeance. Woman's liberation is a Jewish innovation. Women today dominate the homes of America, with 60% divorce rate.[11] The Catholic Church has been affected by Judaism which infiltrated the Catholic Church. In fact, since Vatican Council of 1965 A.D. it is forbidden to say anything derogatory about the Jews.[12] Luther's Reformation was directed against the Christian Church which kept under control the anti-Christ Jews.

Winrod's Condemnation of Luther

Inasmuch as Luther was fighting for the anti-Christ, Luther must be labelled the fore-runner of anti-Christ. One must ask the Gainesville pastor, how could Luther be a forerunner of that heresy which already had existed for over 1,000 years?

Winrod asserts in Letter 300, p. 2: "Luther's crowning crime, securely dealing forever his eternal damnation, was what He did to God's Word. There is proof, more than any other thing, that he was against Jesus. His German 'Bible' is the evidence against him."

Before beginning the discussion about Luther's Bible translation, some of his previous assertions need to be rebutted and Winrod shown to be a misinterpreter of Biblical and church history, of Luther's life and activity, as well as his misuse and misinterpretation of the Bible.

Who Is the Great Anti-Christ of 2 Thessalonian 2

Winrod rejects the teaching of the Lutheran Confessions that the office of the papacy is the great Anti-Christ foretold by Paul in Thessalonians.[13] The New Testament Scripture speaks of many anti-Christs who appeared in the second half of the first century A.D. In 1 John 2:18 the beloved Apostle wrote: "little children it is the last hour, and as you have heard that the Anti-Christ is coming, even now many anti-Christs have come, by which we know it is the last hour," and in verse 22 of chapter 2 he explained: "Who is a liar but he who denies that Jesus is the Christ? He is anti-Christ who denies the Father and the Son."[14] This means that any person, whether he be a Jew, a Mohammedan, a Buddhist, or a Taoist, an unbelieving pastor or theological professor; in fact, any person who rejects Christ or any major doctrine taught by Jesus is an anti-Christ. In

John's day the Gnostics denied Christ's humanity; today modern anti-Christs reject his deity.

Lutheran theology has distinguished on Biblical grounds that the term "anti-Christ" is employed in a general and in a specific sense.[15] Koehler wrote: "In the broader sense it applies to all false teachers within the Church who teach doctrines contrary to the Word of Christ. This spirit of anti-Christ was in the world at the time of John (I John 4:1-3)."[16] But St. John distinguishes between the many anti-Christs of his day and the one anti-Christ who was to come in whom the spirit of the many anti-Christs would culminate. Paul agreed with John: "that day shall not come, except there comes a falling away first, and that man of sin be revealed the son of perdition (2 Thess. 2:3)." Both apostles speak of the same individual whose coming was to be a sign of the last time. Both teach that the spirit of anti-Christ (1 John 4:3), or the mystery of iniquity, was at work even in their day (2 Thess. 2:7), but would in the course of time become more pronounced and recognizable.

The Marks of the Great Anti-Christ, the "Man of Sin"

2 Thessalonians 2:1-12 has listed six marks of this great anti-Christ.[17] Paul told the Thessalonians there will be "a falling away," i.e. there will be a falling away from the Gospel by the teaching of false doctrines. Because of this falling away from faith in Christ by individuals who follow anti-Christ, there would be great loss to the true invisible church.[18]

Furthermore, Paul informed his readers that the Antichrist will sit in the temple of God (2 Thess. 2:4). Christ has many enemies outside the Church, but this individual would be in the visible Church of Christ. Luther and the Reformers believed that the Roman Catholic Church by its official position has condemned the Pauline doctrine of justification by faith as set forth by Paul in Romans 4:15. The Biblical teaching that sinners are saved solely through faith in Christ is officially condemned in Canons, 9.11,12 of the Council of Trent.[19] This doctrinal stance is supported by the Papacy.

Paul further taught that the Antichrist would sit in the temple of God. Many exegetes have found many different personalities who were outside the Church of God as Antichrist, men like Julian the Apostate, Mohammad, Napoleon, Hitler, communism and others as the predicted Antichrist.[20]

However, all of them did not sit in the temple of God and their opposition was performed openly. The real Antichrist is called by Paul "a mystery of iniquity" and that he works secretly, giving the impression that he was working with Christ, coming with all deceivableness of unrighteousness (2 Thess. 2: 9-10). This Antichrist operated within the Church of Christ and not outside of it.

A third feature of the Antichrist according to Paul is that "he opposeth all that is called God or that is worshipped, so that he as God sitteth in the temple of God showing himself that he is God." Lenski said of this characteristic: "The phrase points out what is the extreme of lawlessness; opposition and self-exaltation against mindless than every God 'said' to be God, plus every reverenced object said to be reverenced (Lenski on 2 Thess. 2:4)."[21] The Pope has claimed to have received from Christ the promise that the Church would be built upon. "Thou art Peter and upon this rock will I build my Church, and the gates of hell will not prevail against it" (Matthew 16:18). However, this interpretation is a serious interpretation for the context shows that Christ was going to build His Church on Peter's, confession "That Christ was the son of the living God" and not on the personality of Peter, or Simon, bar Jonas.

Koehler has pointed out that this phrase points out the extremes of lawlessness are: opposition and self-exaltation against no less than every God 'said' to be God plus every reverenced object 'said' to be reverenced,[22] Koehler explained as meaning: "Over all these antichrist exalts himself, claiming authority and lordship over them, as vice regent of God on earth, to whom the God-appointed estates are subordinate."[23] With the decree of Vatican Council setting forth infallibility of the papacy, the Roman pontiff has claimed that He alone is Christ's representative and has usurped for himself the authority of God, who must be obeyed by all Christendom as though he were God himself. Since the death of Luther the world has seen the promotion of Mary as born without sin (decree of the immaculate conception), as well as her assumption into heaven, both teachings that have no warrant in God's Word.

The fourth characteristic of the Antichrist is his rise to full form and stature. The spirit of antichrist was already at work in the days of the apostles (1 John 4:3; 2 Thess. 2:7). Already Peter had to warn the elders against being lord's over God's heritage (1 Peter 5: 1-3). From the very outset there were ambitious persons in the church who endeavored to lord it over others. In Corinth there were those willing to exalt one pastor over the other (I Cor. 1:12). However, at Peter and Paul's time, there was something to check ecclesiastical ambition (2 Thess. 2:5-7). For one, there was the authority of the apostles (Acts 20:29,30); and furthermore, there was the powerful pagan empire, which between 49 A.D. and 313 A.D. persecuted the church at least ten times.[24] It was only after Constantine had declared the Christian faith a licensed religion and the same emperor favored Christianity, that there then developed the power of the bishops of Constantinople and Rome especially, when the three other bishops came under the influence and control of the Muslims. Gradually the Roman bishop made the claim that he was the head of Christendom.[25] Church history bears out the analysis of Koehler: "Slyly, surreptitiously, but persistently, men would strive for power and authority in the Church, until one would succeed in exalting himself above all that is called God and is worshiped, so that he as God sitteth in the temple of God showing that he is God."[26]

In one's identification of this great Antichrist, it is necessary to take all marks into account. The entire composite picture must be used. A study of the last nineteen hundred years of church history reveals the fact that there is only one institution that matches them, namely the Papacy. The fifth mark of the Antichrist according to Paul was that Satan himself was the force behind this ambitious striving for primacy and pre-

671

eminence in the Church. This unchristian movement Satan will support with "all power and signs and lying wonders, and with all deceivableness" (2 Thess. 2:9,10). The Antichrist or "man of Sin" will use miracles, outward displays, pomp and success to blind people as to his real character.

The sixth mark of the Antichrist is that he will continue in the visible Church until the end of time. When Christ finally comes, teaches St. Paul "whom the Lord will consume with the spirit of his mouth, and shall destroy with the brightness of His coming" (2 Thess. 2: 8).

While the New Testament does not specifically inform us who this "man of sin" is, it does describe him in detail so that when he appears true believers will recognize him. In one's identification of this great Antichrist, it is necessary to take all marks into account. The entire composite picture must be used. A study of the last nineteen hundred years of church history reveals the fact that there is only one institution that matches them, namely the Papacy. For a justification of this interpretation, the reader should consult Koehler, *A Summary of Christian Doctrine*, pp. 275-278 or Theodore Hoyer's *The Papacy* in Volume II of *The Abiding Word*, pp. 709-767.

Winrod's Misinterpretation of the Book of Revelation

The interpretation of John's vision or apocalypse has been a battleground for centuries. There are at least four principal schools of interpretation: (1) Preterist; (2) Historical; (3) Futurist; (4) Spiritual.[28] The first interprets the vision as having reference to episodes in Jewish history and in Christian history up till the fall of Jerusalem and the fall of Rome. The second, takes the position that we have in the vision the entire course of the centuries of Christian era. The third postpones the significance of the vision to the events accompanying the second coming of Christ. The fourth holds that in sign and symbol we have the never-ending conflict between good and evil. Winrod has adopted a literal interpretation and fails to realize that the numbers in Revelation are symbolical.[29] For the Gainesville pastor the thousand years of chapter 20 are literally a thousand years.[30] Before the Protestant Revolt according to Winrod, the Catholic Church was the repository of the truth. This was the time when Satan was bound and the Jews as anti-Christ were bound.[31] This is based on Revelation 20. The millennium correctly, according to St. Augustine, was the entire period between the two comings of Christ. According to the premillennialists the thousand years are still in the future when Christ will come to establish a physical worldly kingdom in Palestine.[32] All Jews will be converted and accept Christ as their king. Winrod, therefore, is in a Class by himself when it comes to the interpretation of the Book of Revelation. He claims that the number of the antichrist is 666.[33] Since the Reformation the Devil has been loosed and the Jews freed, thanks to their friend Martin Luther.[34]

Luther and The Jews Partners in Crime

In recent years a number of Lutheran denominations have passed resolutions at their national conventions condemning the writings of Luther relative to what he wrote about the Jews. Winrod has totally distorted the relationship of Luther to the Jews of his time. Jewish writers have vigorously condemned Luther's assertions about the Jewish people and certainly believe that Luther was their enemy.

Winrod and the Roman Catholic Church

Thus Winrod wrote: "Prior to the Jewish revolt, beginning with Luther's theses on the church door of Wittenberg, Germany in October, 1517 A.D., the Holy Repository of Sacred Scripture and God's Christians for a millennium was a Catholic Church. Its Dominator was Jesus. Its faith was Christian, its common tongue was Latin Vulgate."[35]

Nowhere does he say anything derogatory about the Roman Catholic Church, except that Vatican II should not have forbidden to criticize the Jews. Luther however, was the perverter of God's Word because he did not accept the Latin Vulgate as God's Word directly.[36]

Winrod and Church History

There never was a united church under one head. The Eastern Orthodox Churches used a Greek Bible and the Patriarch of Constantinople did not recognize the pontiff of Rome's claim to be the head of Christendom.[37] Winrod needs to be reminded that between 593 A.D. and the present time many false doctrines have entered the Roman Church.

Here are some of them: 593-Purgatory; 754-the Pope's claim to also have temporal power; 847-the decretals of Isidore; 858-the donation of Constantine; 1075-the greatest divorce in history, decreed by Gregory VII; 1100-money for masses; 1184-the Inquisition, which also persecuted Jews; 1190-The sale of indulgences; 1215-the doctrine of transubstantiation; 1226,-adoration of the host; 1229-the Bible placed on the Index of forbidden books, 1475-the cup denied the laity; 1545-the Council of Trent which labelled justification by faith apart from works as a heresy; 1608-The invention of scapulars; 1854-The Immaculate Conception of Mary; 1864-Condemnation of separation of church and state; 1870-Papal infallibility; 1950-the assumption of Mary into heaven.[38] It was Luther who protested most of these theological doctrines and issues. Luther endeavored to restore the Church back to the doctrines of the New Testament.

Winrod's Promulgation of the
Vulgate as God's True Word

The German Bible and the King James claim to be translated from the original languages.[39] Winrod, however, claims that this is a lie, for we no longer have the original manuscripts.[40] However, he contends that the Vulgate made by Jerome between 390-410 A.D. was based on better MSS than the present transmitted text of the Old and New Testaments.[41] That Vulgate used better MSS is not true. The Vulgate is a translation and-as a secondary version is not superior to the present text used in the *Biblia Hebraca* and Nestle's 26th edition of the *Greek New Testament*. It is an axiom of textual criticism that a primary translation is superior to a secondary version.

For the first three hundred years the Latin Church used the Itala, Old Ita Zian, of which there may have been different versions and it was a translation from the Greek Septuagint, a translation of the Hebrew text.[42] This became corrupt in the course of time, so finally, Pope Damasus asked Jerome to make a new translation.[42a] First he corrected the New Testament and then over a fifteen year period translated from Hebrew MSS, with the help of Jewish rabbis the Old Testament. The Vulgate also contains the Apocrypha.[43] Thus by his advocacy of the Vulgate Winrod is employing a Bible which does not contain in 14 books God's Word! Because Winrod believes that only the Vulgate contains the true Word of God, he maintains a Latin school connected with his church.

Winrod does not seem to know the history of the text of the Vulgate, or if he does know, is not divulging damaging evidence against his mistaken position. While Jerome's Vulgate is considered a good translation, it contains errors and mistakes. Thus Genesis 3:15 makes Mary the person who would crush the serpent's head.[44] The English translation of the Vulgate was the Rheims-Douay version, made to counteract the various English renderings of the Bible, made from Hebrew, Biblical Aramaic and Greek. A whole series of Bibles were made available for the English reading world, beginning with Tyndale's New Testament 1525 till the completion of the Authorized or King James Version.[45] The Roman Catholic Jesuit scholar McKenzie wrote about the Vulgate as follows: "The problem of the Vg (Vulgate) can be said only to have begun with its production. It was multiplied by careless copying, and the recensions of Cassiodorus (579), Alcuin (800), Theodolf (821), Lafranc (1089), and Stephen Harding (died 1134) failed to establish a reliable text."[46]

There are significant differences between the Vulgate and Luther's German Bible, which in its entirety was translated from the original languages. As an aid in textual criticism the Vulgate, together with the Septuagint and the Peshitta can be of service where problem verses exist in our transmitted MSS. Winrod condemns Luther as perverter of the Word of God because he did not use the Vulgate,[47] with which the Reformer was well acquainted from his youth.

Council of Trent Declared the Vulgate
As Final-Count of Appeal

By his insistence that the Vulgate is the original and reliable text of Holy Writ, Winrod is promulgating the canon of the Council of Trent that in matters of doctrine and life the final court of appeal is the Vulgate text. Such a stance is scientifically to be rejected and according to the best canons of textual criticism indefensible and wrong. The fact is that Luther's German Bible is a primary version; the Vulgate a secondary one. Winrod is slandering Luther when he writes in letter No. 300 that Luther was committing a great sin by perverting the Word of God.[48]

Luther Allegedly Opposed to Christ

Luther is labelled an anti-Christ because he was opposed to Jesus Christ. Winrod claims that Jesus was not loved by Luther, because he refused to place the name of Jesus in the Old Testament the way the Vulgate did. He cited Habakkuk 3:17, where in the Vulgate the name of Jesus is found. The Luther Bible renders Habbakuk 3:17 like this: "Denn der Herr, dein Gott is bei dir, ein starker Heiland . . . Er wird sich ueber dich freuen, und dir freundlich sein und vergeben und wird ueber dir mit Schalle froelig sein."[49] The Hebrew text does not have the name of Jesus in it. In fact, the name Jesus is Greek and not Hebrew. The Vulgate inserts the name of Jesus in numerous passages and because Luther did not follow this interpretative method of the Vulgate, Winrod accused Luther of hating Jesus and consequently was an anti-Christ.[50] Because the Jews in their translation of the Old Testament do not place the name in numerous Old Testament verses, and Luther does not either, Winrod argues that Luther and the Jews are in league with each other and are antichrists.

So Luther loves the Jews more than he does love Christ and, therefore, must the Reformer be labelled a Christhater.[51] Because Luther does not follow the Vulgate in its translation of numerous Old and New Testament passages Winrod, invokes against Luther the passages that warn against adding or detracting from the Word of God such as Deut. 12:32; Deut. 4:2; Prov. 4:2; Prov. 30:6. These passages only apply to the original text, and not to a translation. However, as already stated Winrod is working with a wrong view as to which MSS constitutes the transmission of God's words and which MSS and version really represent the autographic texts of the Bible.

Who Is the Real Bible Twister?

The charge brought by Winrod against the German Bible as not constituting the Word of God, is in fact the one that must be brought against him. He claims that where ever the name of God appears in the Old Testament it must be Jesus.[52] He fails to distinguish the Biblical truth that there are three distinct persons in the Trinity, yet one divine essence. Both the Old and New Testament distinguish between the Father, the Son and the Holy Spirit. He appears to espouse a monotheism limiting God to Jesus and ignores the Father and the Holy Spirit.

The Jewels of the Reformation

Instead of Luther being the fore-runner of the great Antichrist, Luther exposed the antichristian character of much of Roman Catholic theology. The following are some of the benefits of Luther's Reformation. **1. The open Bible.** All men have the right to read the Scriptures, where the plan of salvation is clearly delineated. The Reformation put the open Bible into the hands of the people. **2. Justification by faith.** It was the key to the understanding which Dr. Martin Luther, by God's providence was allowed to find. As Paul taught: "For by grace are ye saved; and that not of yourselves: it is a gift of God: not of works, lest any man should boast (Ephesians 2:8-9)." **3. The right of private judgment.** The authority to decide religious beliefs is in the hands of every reader, it does not belong to any man or any organization. **4. Universal education.** A great principle of Protestantism is the general enlightenment of people. Every public school and Christian Day School is the gift of the Reformation. The concept of universal education is directly traceable to the Reformation. **5. The Complete Sacrament.** Here is another treasure of the Reformation. There are two things to be received in the Lord's Supper:— "Take eat, this is my body; 2. – Drink you all of it, this is the cup of the New Testament in my blood" (Matthew 26:26; Mark 14:22; I Cor. 11:24). **6. Christian Hymns.** The Reformation was literally sung into the hearts of people. Luther wrote a number of hymns and became the inspiration for many Christian hymn writers. **7. The evangelical parsonage.** Luther made it possible for the clergy to marry and enjoy family life and have a legitimate place for the God pleasing use of sex. 8. (Civil and. religious liberty.[53]) Our modern freedom is the fruit of the tree planted by Martin Luther. The priceless blessings of liberty and the rights of conscience recognized and enjoyed, and guaranteed in our great republic, are directly and indirectly, the result of the truths so clearly and forcibly proclaimed by Martin Luther over four hundred years ago. **9. The restoration of the doctrine of the general priesthood of all believers.** Peter in the first epistle told the congregations of Asia Minor that they were a royal priesthood and described the privileges such priesthood entailed. A Christian believer has direct access to God and does not need a version of the Old Testament priesthood to act as intermediary between him and God.

Luther a Devoted Devotee of Christ

The allegation of Winrod that Luther hated Christ is the height of irresponsible writing. The *Weimar Edition of Luther's Works* (100 volumes) has thousands of statements by Luther showing his great love and devotion to Jesus Christ. The *American Edition of Luther's Works* of 55 volumes likewise has thousands of statements in which Christ is confessed and adored as God, Creator, Redeemer, Judge and the world's only Savior from sin, death and the devil. In all the Christological literature of theology, there is not a finer expression of Luther relative to the vital importance of Jesus Christ to sinners than that found in the Reformer's Explanation of the Second Article of the Apostles' Creed.

Footnotes

1. Gordon Winrod, *The Winrod Letter*, Issue No. 300, October, 1990 A.D. p. 1 B, lines 7ff.
2. **Ibid.**, 1 B, line 23.
3. **Ibid.**, p. 2-B, lines 20-21.
4. **Ibid.**, p. 4 B, lines 40ff.
5. **Ibid.**, p. 1 A, lines 1-8.
6. **Ibid.**, p. 1 A, lines 44ff.
7. **Ibid.**, p. 1 A, lines 44ff.
8. **Ibid.**, p. 2 A, lines 72ff.
9. **Ibid.**, p. 2 A, lines 72f.
10. **Ibid.**, p. 2 A, lines 58-59.

11. **Ibid.**

12. **Ibid.**, 2 B, lines 56ff.

13. **Ibid.**, p. 1 B, lines 3ff.

14. *Holy Bible - The New King James Version* (New York: Thomas Nelson Publishers, 1979), p. 1195.

15. Cf. "Antichrist," Erwin Lueker (Editor), *The Lutheran Cyclopedia* (St. Louis: Concordia Publishing House, 1954), p. 37.

16. Edward A. Koehler, *A Summary of Christian Doctrine* (Detroit and Oakland: The Rev. L.H. and the Rev. A.W. Koehler, 1939), p. 273.

17. Cf. the interpretation of the Pauline periscope in Paul E. Kretzmann (St. Louis: Concordia Publishing House, 1924), *The New Testament*, Volume 2, pp. 361-364.

18. Theodore Hoyer, "The Papacy," Theodore Laetsch (Editor), *The Abiding Word* (St. Louis: Concordia Publishing House, 1947), II, p. 750.

19. Koehler, **op. cit.**, p. 274. Philip Schaff, *The Creeds of Christendom with a History and Critical Notes* (New York: Harper and Brothers, 1919), II Greek and Latin Creeds, II 1,90-99.

20. R. Ludwigson, *A Survey of Bible Prophecy* (Grand Rapids: Zondervan Publishing House, 1951), pp. 25-26.

21. Lenski, *The Epistles of St. Paul to the Thessalonians* (Columbus, Lutheran Book Concern, 1952), on 2 Thess. 2:4.

22. Koehler, **op. cit.**, p. 275.

23. **Ibid.**, pp. 275-276.

24. **Ibid.**, pp. 275:-277.

25. Boniface VIII (c. 1235-1303) in his *Unum Sanctum* claimed absolute authority over kings. Elgin S. Moyer, *Who Was Who in Church History* (Chicago: .Moody Press. 1962), p. 50a.

26. Koehler, **op. cit.**, p. 274.

27. **Ibid.**

28. Everett K. Harrison, *Introduction to the New Testament* (Grand Rapids: William B. Eerdmans Publishing Company, 1968), pp. 435-438.

29. D. A. Hayes, *John and His Writings* (Cincinnati: Methodist Book Concern, 1917), p. 296.

30. *Winrod Letter* No. 300, p. 1 A, 9 lines from bottom of the column.

31. **Ibid.**

32. **Ibid.**

33. **Ibid.**, p. 2 B, line 7.

34. **Ibid.**, p. 2 A, line 14 from the bottom of the column.

35. **Ibid.**, p. 1 A, 12 lines from bottom of column.

36. **Ibid.**, p. 3 A and p. 4 A and B.

37. "Eastern Orthodoxy," Jeril C. Brauer (editor), *The Westminster Dictionary of Church History* (Philadelphia: The Westminster Press, 1971), pp. 282-283.

38. *The Split Between Roman Catholicism and Christ* (New York: The Lutheran Press, no date); pp. 1-26; Theodore Hoyer, *Why I Am Not a Roman Catholic* (St. Louis: Concordia Publishing House, 1953), 44 pp.

39. Winrod, **op. cit.**, p. 3A, lines 10ff.

40. **Ibid.**, line 10.

41. **Ibid.**, 3 A, lines 31ff.

42. H. F. D. Sparks, "The Latin Bible," H. Wheeler Robinson, (Editor), *The Bible - In*

Its Ancient and English Versions (Oxford: At the Clarendon Press, 1940), pp. 100-110.

42a. Merrill F. Unger, *Introductory Guide to the Old Testament* (Grand Rapids: Zondervan Publishing House, 1951), pp. 171-172.

43. Cf. Biblia Sacra, *Juxta Vulgate Clementinam* (Romae et Parisiis: Desclee at Socii, 1956), pp: v-vii.

44. The Vulgate reads in Gen. 3:25: "Ipsa conteret caput et tuum, et tu insidiaberis calcaneo ejus." Cf. also Knox, *The Holy Bible. A Translation From the Latin Vulgate in Light of the Hebrew and Greek Originals* (New York: Sheed and Ward, 1956), p. 3: "she is to crush thy head, whilst thou dost lie in ambush," a translation that translates the Hebrew text incorrectly.

45. Jack P. Lewis, *The English Bible From KJV to IV* (Grand Rapids: Baker Book House, 1981), pp. 17-38.

46. John L. McKenzie, *The Dictionary of the Bible* (Milwaukee: Bruce Publishing Co., 1965), p. 917.

47. Winrod, **op. cit.**, p. 4B, lines 18ff.

48, **Ibid.**, p. 2 A, 12 lines from bottom of page.

49. Ehrenfried Liebich, *Die Bibel oder die ganze Heilige Schrift Alten und Neuen Testaments nach der deutschen Uebersetzung Martin Luther* (Konstanz: Buchhandlung Carl Hirsch, 1765), p. 293.

50. Winrod, **op. cit.**, p. 4 A, line 50ff.

51. **Ibid.**, p. 4A, line 48.

52. **Ibid.**, p. 3 B, lines 24ff.

53. Most of these were taken from *Jewels of the Reformation* (New York: Lutheran Press, no date), pp. 1-3.

Questions

1. Gordon Winrod called Luther ____.
2. Winrod once enjoyed ___.
3. There is not a word in the *Winrod Letter* about ____.
4. What did Winrod write about the Jews? ____
5. The Lutheran Reformation emphasized ____.
6. The Antichrist will sit in the ____.
7. Since the death of Luther the world has seen the projection of Mary as ____.
8. The numbers in Revelation are ____.
9. The Council of Trent labeled ____.
10. What does Winrod say about the Vulgate? ____
12. Who is the real Bible twister? ____
13. What are some benefits of Luther's Reformation? ____

Answering Winrod

November 1990
Dear Brother Otten:
In my rebuttal to *Winrod's Letter 300* I noticed as soon as I read it in print that I had been inaccurate in stating that the Vulgate was not a primary translation.

I spent the last 3 days writing this article on the Vulgate and how Roman Catholics are teaching Winrod that the Vulgate is the only text that can today be employed as really representing God's Word.

If you feel that you cannot use my article, please print some where the opening page (1), so that any person who recognizes my inaccurate answer will realize that I know better.

Since the 2nd Sunday in December has often been observed as "Bible Sunday" you might use it to show how the Vulgate, an influential Bible translation originated and its handling in the Roman Catholic Church.

My article would show how wrong Winrod is with regard to the view that the Vulgate is the only authentic text of God's Word that Christendom has.

May you and your family have a blessed Thanksgiving, and that the New Church Year will see many blessings bestowed upon you for your efforts to proclaim and defend God's Word.

Yours in Christ,
Raymond F. Surburg

Correction and Supplementation On the Vulgate

Christian News, December 10, 1990

In my rebuttal of *Winrod's Letter* No. 300, which appeared in *Christian News*, November 12, p. 10 column 1,[1] I inaccurately called the Vulgate a secondary version. What I should have written was that the Rheims-Douay and Challoner Translation in English using the Vulgate text as basis for their translations was not a primary version. The Septuagint, the Peshitta, and the Vulgate are important primary versions, originating between circa 250 B.C. and 405 A.D. Any translations made from the original Hebrew and Aramaic texts of the Old Testament and the Koine Greek New Testament are primary versions.[2] A "daughter translation" or version would be the Old Itala and Rheims-Douay Bible, which are translated from a translation. The Authorized or King James Version and the Luther Bible of 1534 are primary versions. This writer would emphasize that the Vulgate is a primary translation.

Winrod's Emphasis on the Vulgate

Since Pastor Winrod makes so much of the Latin Vulgate and judges Luther for failing to use it for his German translation, it might not be out of place to give the history of this important Latin translation of the Bible. Many of our readers might find the following presentation useful in appreciating the great influence which the Vulgate has had for at least fifteen hundred years of church life and of church history.[3] The strictures in my recent article did not intend to denigrate the Vulgate but were directed at English translations based on the Vulgate as being superior to good translations made from the original languages of Holy Writ. The argument of Winrod that the Latin is superior to Luther's Bible, whose language created the new high German language, and as Norlie's *The Translated Bible* has shown was to have inspired a host of new translations in a number of European languages.[4]

Jerome, the Translator of the Vulgate

The Bible of the Old and New Testaments has been available since the early Christian centuries. The Vulgate was the last in a series of Latin versions made in the Early Christian Church. While Greek was the language of communication in the Roman Empire, there were countries in this Empire that used Latin exclusively. Such lands were Spain, Italy, Gaul and North Africa, thus necessitating a Bible in Latin.[5] A translation was made into Latin in North Africa, which employed the Septuagint, which some even contended was inspired. McKenzie claimed that the origin of the Old Latin Version is unknown; it was probably that it arose in North Africa; it was likely that a number of versions arose in N. Africa, Gaul or N. Italy. A document of 180 indicates the existence of a Latin version in Africa. The same Roman Catholic scholar also believed that the variations in the MS tradition are so great that scholars disagree. Whether there was one Lt. version or several.[6] If there was only one old Latin version it seems that quite early it was divided into two text types; the African and the European.[7] It is quite possible that the European version cited by St. Augustine was the next type known as the Itala.[8] Since the Old Latin was soon displayed by the Vulgate the extent MSS are few and incomplete. The Old Testament was rendered into Latin from the Septuagint around A.D. 150. Unger claimed that the Old Latin was so faithful to the LXX, that the latter's evident blunders were reproduced.[9] The Apocrypha from the Old Latin were added to the Vulgate, who did not consider the Apocrypha as Word of God.[10]

The Origin of the Vulgate

The Vulgate is the great translation of the entire Bible and was accomplished by Jerome (Eusebius Hieronymus).[11] The New Testament was revised from 383 onward and the Old Testament was produced between A.D. 390-405. Jerome undertook the revision of the New Testament at the charge and suggestion of Pope Damasus, who was greatly disturbed by the inaccuracies that had crept into the Old Latin. Thus the

Vulgate New Testament was a revision and later went under the guise as having been newly translated from the Greek by Jerome.[12] Before embarking on the translation of the Old Testament from Hebrew and Aramaic, Hieronymus revised the Psalms, which played such an important role liturgically in the Roman cultus. The North African scholar made two revisions of the Psalter; the first in 385 which was a cursory revision of the Old Latin, known as Psalterium Romanum. A second made after 385 revised the Book of Psalms according to the Hexaplaric text of Origen, and was named *Psalterium Gallicum* (Gallican Psalter), so called because it was used in Gaul.[13]

Jerome at Bethlehem, in Palestine

Pope Damasus had been dead a number of years when Jerome settled in Bethlehem, where he secured the services of Jewish rabbis and obtained portions of the Hebrew Old Testament. Please note at this juncture the help from Jews whom Winrod denounced as enemies of Christ. Thus Winrod wrote: "Shall we set aside the Holy Scriptures of the Holy Church in favor of a creation of the so-called Hebrew by Massoretic Jewish-anti-Christian devils, sex-perverts and liars (as Jesus called them)."[14] Unger claimed that as a result of study under the rabbis in Palestine, Jerome was enabled to see the unsatisfactory condition of the Septuagint and the Old Latin texts and substantial agreement among Hebrew manuscripts.[15]

The Old Testament was recorded for the most part in Hebrew with Biblical Aramaic found in Daniel 2:4-7:28 and in Ezra 4:8-6: 18; 7:12-26. It is to Jewish or Hebrew scribes that we owe the transmission of the text of the 39 books in our European Bibles or the 24 according to the arrangement of the present Hebrew Bible.[16] It was only because the Jews, whom Winrod so denounced, that Luther and the Bible translators of Protestant Bibles could have the original text to render into another language.[17] That is a debt Christianity owes Judaism. This is a fact of the history of textual criticism that Winrod cannot appreciate but denounces.

Jerome did not consider the books of the Apocrypha on a par with the inspired and canonical books of the Scriptures of the Old Covenant. Upon the urgent insistence of his friends he translated Judith and Tobit, together with the rest of Esther and the uncanonical additions to Daniel.[18]

Unfavorable Reception Given Vulgate

Jerome's Vulgate was a private translation and when it appeared it was met with great opposition by the majority of laity and clergy, all of whom were satisfied—with the Old Itala or whatever version they used, especially with the Septuagint. It took nearly four hundred years when it won out over the Old Latin and ultimately became the version of Western Europe.[19] Alcuin, a great scholar at the court of Charlemagne, especially promoted the Vulgate, because of its superior character. In McKenzies's opinion "Jerome had learned Hebrew well, and did not hesitate to ask Jewish opinions on interpretation."[20] Unger further noted that Jerome "justified his endeavor to put the Hebrew Scriptures as a source for New Testament quotations into the best and most intelligent rendering by demonstrating that not all these quotations were taken from the Septuagint, but that many were taken direct from the Hebrew. Few, however, wise and honest enough to admit the necessity of having the purest possible text of the Bible."[21]

The Triumph of the Vulgate

From the time of Charlemagne on till the Reformation the Vulgate became the Bible of Western Europe.[21a] In the course of time, many corruptions entered the text with a number of revisions resulting. The following scholars tried to purify the Vulgate, namely, Cassodorus (570), Alcuin (800), Theodulf (821), LaFranc (1089), and Stephen Harding (died 1134) but all failed to establish a text faithful to the original text of Jerome.[22] In 1450 it was the Vulgate which had the honor of being the first book printed by Gutenberg using movable type.

Erasmus, the Roman Catholic humanist, honored by many Popes, printed the first Greek New Testament. With him began the development of the science of textual criticism that has culminated in a number of critical texts of the New Testament. Erasmus' Greek New Testament exercised a tremendous influence on subsequent Bible translations.[23] The effort of Erasmus was denounced by Winrod as a person who really worked to denigrate the best text of Holy Writ, the Vulgate by publishing this Greek New Testament. Thus Winrod has pontificated: "The Latin Bible was the Bible of the Church from 400 A.D. until the present time. Shall we set aside it for a Greek creation of non-Christian humanist, the early sixteenth century? Shall we set aside the Holy Scriptures of the Holy Church in favor of a creation of the so-called Hebrew by Massoretic Jewish anti-Christian devils, sex perverts and liars (as Jesus called them)?"[24]

Council of Trent and the Vulgate

The Council of Trent in 1546 decreed that a new and corrected edition of the Vulgate be made. This new revised Vulgate was begun at Louvain under private auspices and a commission was appointed in Rome and only under Pope Sixtus V (1585-1590) was this done. The Sixtine edition was unsuitable for reproduction. The Trentine decision was carried out under Pope Clementine VIII and published in 1592-1593). Pope Pius X has appointed a commission to prepare a critical edition and the monks of the Benedictine monastery of Jerome are carrying out this project.[25]

"The Council of Trent passed a decree that the Vulgate is the authentic text to be employed in the Latin Church."[25a] According to Pope Pius XIII (1943) the authenticity is to be understood that the Vulgate was not intended to be juridical not critical. This means that the Vulgate is free from error regarding doctrine or morals. According to McKenizie "the original texts have that superior critical authenticity Which is theirs by nature and translations into vernaculars for common use are not only permitted but encouraged, in Afflante Divino (Pius XIII, 1943)."[26]

The Rheims Bible and the Douay Bible

Between 1525 and 1611 there was a great deal of Bible translation going on in England. Thus there appeared the Tyndale Bible, The Miles Covdale Bible, The Cranmer Bible, The Great Bible, The Geneva Bible, The Bishops Bible and the Authorized or King James (1607-1611).[27] Since there were many Catholics in England, Scotland and Wales there was felt a need for the Bible based on the Latin Vulgate.[28] The result was the Douay Version, the first official, English translations for English-speaking Catholics. The New Testament was issued as early as 1582 by the English College located at Rheims and was known as The Rheims New Testament. The Old Testament, for the most part the work of Gregory Martin, a translation of the whole Vulgate was published in 1909, when the English College returned to Douay and hence is called The Douay Bible, a work that was characterized by a heavy influence of Latin.[29] The poorest part was the Psalter. The Douay Bible was "a translation of a translation, of a translation."[30]

The reader will find in the original Douay a heavy emphasis on ecclesiastical terms. Repentance is rendered penance. Some unfamiliar words are exianited, donances, and commersation. Deacon is translated minister, and elder is rendered as priest. Ephesians 3:9 is made to "the dispensation of the sacrament." The King James translators used this version in about 3,000 places.[31] The Old Testament appeared too late to be consulted or used. The Douay Bible did not see too many printings.

The Revision of the Rheims-Douay by Challoner

Since the publication of the Rheims-Douay Bible the English language changed considerably, so it was felt that the English of the Douay had to be updated. This was done by Bishop Richard Challoner, Coadjutor he the Vicar Apostolic of London. He revised the Douay Bible between 1749 and 63. Challoner updated the work of Dr. Martin's Douay Bible. For two hundred years the Challoner Bible was standard for English-using Catholics.[32]

The Knox Translation of the Vulgate

Twentieth century Englishmen were presented with a new translation by Msgr. Ronald Knox who was a gifted linguist and is supposed to have produced a fresh readable translation of the Vulgate which consulted the Hebrew and Greek originals. This was authorized by the Hierarchy of England and Wales and the Hierarchy of Scotland.[33]

Recent Roman Catholic Translation
Based on the Original Languages

Pius XII in his encyclical *Divino Afflunte Spiritu* encouraged Roman Catholic scholars to deal with the sources.

This was done in The Westminster Version of the New Testament and was the work of Lattey and Keating. Already in 1898 Fr. F. Spencer rendered the Four Gospel from Greek into English. The Confraternity Version of the New Testament was an updating of the Challoner-Rheims Bible.[34]

Winrod claimed that Mother Church had the true Word of God in the Vulgate, and that the Greek New Testament and the Hebrew Old Testament are not better or more reliable than the Vulgate, which allegedly had better manuscripts from which to translate.[35] The Roman Catholic Church has not taken this position, for in the twentieth century Roman Catholic scholars have made not only translation of the Gospels and the New Testament from the original Greek,[36] but The Catholic Biblical Association, sponsored by the Episcopal Committee of the Confraternity of Christian Doctrine produced a four volumes, which appeared in 1952, 1955, 1961 and 1962. The New Testament has also been rendered into English.[37] Heidt believes it will supplant all other translations. Those who worked on the translation of The Confraternity Bible were under instruction to translate from the original languages with critical use of all the ancient sources.

Another Bible which made available to Roman Catholics and other Christians the Holy Bible in modern English, using the original languages was the Jerusalem Bible. The inspiration for this new Bible was the French Jerusalem Bible. The English Jerusalem Bible is not a translation of the French but as its editor stated, the new Bible has been directly rendered from the Hebrew and Aramaic of the Old Testament[38] and the Greek of the New Testament.

Winrod's opposition to the use of the Biblia Hebraica and the last critical 26th edition of the New Testament, the Nestle-Ahland edition as containing for the most part the actual Word of God as deposited in the autographs. His rejection of the principles of textual criticism places him in a class by himself to which no recognized conservative or critical scholar would subscribe but would denounce as theological ignorance.

Footnotes

1. H. S. Miller, *General Biblical Introduction - From God to Us* (Houghton: The World Bearer Press, 1944), pp. 210-211.
2. **Ibid.**
3. Merrill. F. Unger, *Introductory Guide to the Old Testament* (Grand Rapids: Zondervan Publishing House, 1951), p. 175.
4. O. N. Norlie, *The Translated Bible* (Philadelphia: The United Lutheran Publication House, 1961), 1934), pp. 72-192.
5. Arthur Weiser, *The Old Testament: Its Formation and Development* (New York: Association Press, 1961), pp. 178-179.
6. John McKenzie, *Dictionary of the Bible* (Milwaukee: Bruce Publishing Company, 1965), p. 916.
7. **Ibid.**
8. Unger, **op. cit.**, p. 170.
9. **Ibid.**, p. 170.
10. McKenzie, **op. cit.**, p. 917.
11. H. F. D. Sparks, "The Latin Bible," in H. Wheeler Robinson, *The Bible In Its Ancient and English Versions* (Oxford: At the Clarendon Press, 1940), pp. 110-115.
12. Unger, **op. cit.**, p. 173; Sparks, **op. cit.**, p. 111.
13. F. F. Bruce, *The Books and the Parchments* (Old Tappan, N.J.: Fleming H. Revell Company, 1963), Third Revised Edition, p. 205.
14. *Winrod Letter*, No. 300, as reprinted in *Christian News*, October 15, 1990 l, p. 9.

15. Unger, **op. cit.**, p. 172.
16. Ernst Wuerthwein, *The Text of the Old Testament*. Translated by Erroll F. Rhodes (Grand Rapids: William B. Eerdmans Publishing Company, 1979), pp. 12-21.
17. Winrod, Letter No. 300, as reprinted in *Christian News*, Oct. 15, 1990), p. 9.
18. McKenzie, **op. cit.**, p. 918.
19. Unger, **op. cit.**, p. 174.
20. McKenzie, **op. cit.**, p. 918.
21. Unger, **op. cit.**, p. 173.
21a. Bruce, **op. cit.**, pp. 201, 211.
22. Sparks, "The Latin Bible," op cit., pp. 115-121.
23. Bruce Metzger, *The Text of the New Testament* (New York and Oxford: Oxford University Press, 1968); Second Edition, pp. 98-105.
24. Winrod, **op. cit.**, p. 9.
25. McKenzie, **op. cit.**, p. 918.
25a. Bruce, **op. cit.**, quotes the decree of the Council of Trent relative to the Vulgate.
26. McKenzie, **op. cit.**, p. 918.
27. Cf. the overview of translations from the Greek and Hebrew and Aramaic versions of Protestant Bibles between 1525-1611 in Wilburg Smith, "The Bible and Its Development," in *The Holy Bible - The New American Standard, The Open Bible* (New York: Thomas Nelson Publishers, 1978), pp. 1239-1252.
28. William Heidt, *Inspiration-Canonicity-Texts-Versions-Hermeneutics* (Collegeville, Minnesota: The Liturgical Press, 1970), p. 83.
29. Smith, **op. cit.**, p. 1251a.
30. Jack P. Lewis, *The English Bible From KJV to NIV. A History and Evaluation* (Grand Rapids: Baker Book House, 1981), p. 27.
31. William Carlton, *The Part of Rheims in the Making of the English Bible* (Oxford: Oxford University Press, 1902).
32. Heidt, **op. cit.**, p. 84.
33. Ronald Knox, *The Holy Bible - A Translation from Latin Vulgate in the Light of Hebrew and Greek Originals* (New York: Sheed and Ward, 1956), cf. preface, pp. vii-vii.
34. Heidt, **op. cit.**, p. 84.
35. Winrod, **op. cit.**, p. 9.
36. Heidt, **op. cit.**, pp. 84-86.
37. *The New American Bible* (Cleveland: The Catholic Press Publishers; distributed by The World Publishing Company, 1970), pp. 1-232.
38. *The Jerusalem Bible - Reader's Edition* (Garden City, New York: Doubleday & Company, 1966), cf. preface of two pages.

Questions

1. The Septuagint, the Peshitta, and the Vulgate are ____.
2. The Vulgate was the last in a ____.
3. The Vulgate was accomplished by ____.
4. Jerome settled in ____.
5. What debt does Christianity owe Judaism? ____
6. In 1450 the Vulgate had the honor of ____.
7. Who printed the first Greek New Testament? ____
8. The Douay Bible was ____.
9. Winrod's rejection of the principles of textual criticism places him in ____.

The Hermeneutics of Theodore Laetsch, Professor of Concordia Seminary, St. Louis From 1927-1947

Christian News, October 7, 1991

The faculty of Concordia Seminary, St. Louis, founded in 1839, during the one hundred and forty year history of The Lutheran Church-Missouri Synod has exercised a great influence on the doctrinal practice of the pastors and congregations of the Synod.[1] Some of the greatest theologians and scholars of the LCMS have been members of its faculty. However, between 1958-1974 most of the faculty exercised a baneful influence on the LCMS by adoption of the historical-critical method and helped to bring about a division in the church body which resulted in eventually about 110,000 people leaving the church body.[2]

The one hundred and forty-two years of existence of the St. Louis faculty might be divided into five periods: 1. 1839-1877, with C.F.W. Walther its prominent leader; 2. 1877-1931, with Francis Pieper the outstanding leader of this period; 3. 1931-1947, with W.A. Maier, Sr., Louis Fuerbringer, W. Arndt, J.T. Mueller, Theodore Graebner, Th. Laetsch, P.E. Kretzmann, W. G. Polack, John Fritz, Th. Hoyer as leading professors; 4. 1947-1974, with A. Fuerbringer, Repp, Caemmerer, Roehrs, Von Rohr Sauer, E. Lueker, Scharlemann, F. Danker, Jones, Graesser, Franzmann, and others constituting the faculty, and during this period well over fifty individuals served on the faculty, which did, with the exception of R. Preus, Klann, Wunderlich and Scharlemann, walk out early in 1974;[3] 5. 1974 till the present. Under Ralph Bohlmann and Karl Barth an attempt was made to rebuild a new orthodox faculty.

Much has been made, and rightly so, of the contributions of C.F.W. Walther. His birth and death have been remembered in a number of anniversary celebrations since 1887.[4] Although Francis Pieper perpetuated the theology and memory of Walther and he so far has been the great systematician of the LCMS and his three volume *Christian Dogmatics* has been the standard textbook at both the St. Louis and Springfield-Ft. Wayne seminaries of the LCMS, Pieper has been somewhat neglected as compared with Walther.[5] During the period between 1931 (death of Pieper) and 1947 (the year of Synod's centennial) three prominent Old Testament scholars were: W. A. Maier, Sr.,[6] L. Fuerbringer.[7] and Theodore Laetsch. [7a] The latter has as a professor influenced between one thousand and two thousand students during his teaching career and still influences pastors and students through his commentaries, his articles in *The Concordia Theological Monthly* and his many sermon studies and sermon outlines that have appeared between 1927-1947. It would seem fitting that the contributions of Laetsch should not be forgotten. It will be the purpose of this essay to discuss "The Hermeneutics of Theodore Laetsch," some of whose hermeneutical principles and theology this writer has heard criticized within the last five years.

The Professional Life of Theodore Laetsch

Theodore Laetsch (1877-1962) was a professor of Old Testament interpretation from 1927-1947. When the writer was a student at Concordia Seminary St. Louis (1929-1933), Laetsch was one of a faculty numbering fourteen instructors in 1933. Prior to assuming the professorship at Concordia Seminary, St. Louis, he had been pastor at Chippewa Falls, Doer Park, Eau Claire, Pleasant Valley and Sheboygan, all located in Wisconsin. As an Old Testament scholar, he rejected all forms of the higher-critical method as propagated in his day. He was a conservative Lutheran scholar, completely in agreement with the hermeneutical principles of Luther, of the Lutheran Confessions, of Walther, Pieper, L. Fuerbringer, G. Stoeckhardt and A.L. Graebner.

In addition to lecturing students for twenty years, he also influenced his students and fellow pastors with his literary productions. His two commentaries, *The Minor Prophets*[8] and *Jeremiah*[9] were two of the three volumes of the Old Testament commentaries planned by Concordia Publishing House some sixty years ago which were to cover the whole Bible. Only Maier, Sr. wrote the other Old Testament one to appear, namely, Nahum[10] and William Arndt's the commentary on Luke.[11]

Laetsch authored many major articles for *The Concordia Theological Monthly*.[12] Here are his articles, covering the areas of exegesis, pastoral theology, Biblical theology, Old Testament theology, apologetics preaching and homiletics. "Administration of the Sacraments," *CTM*, 10:401-415, June, 1930; "Behold, He Shall Come," *CTM*, 4:427-935, December, 1935; "Catechism in Public Worship," *CTM*, 5:234-241, March, 1934; "Catechism in the Christian Home," *CTM*, 5:596-604, August, 1954; "D. Pieperals Prediger,"*CTM*, 2:276-771g, October, 1931; "Divorce and Malicious Desertion," *CTM*, 3:850-55; 923-933, 4:35-38, 127-133, Nov.-December, 1932; January and February 1933; "In Memory of Prof. George Metzger, D.D., *CTM*, 3:127-132; February, 1932; "Malicious Desertion," *CTM*, 4:19-205, March, 1933; "Mosis Lied am Roten Meeer," *CTM*, 11:89-99, 169-178, February-March, 1940; "Pastor's Professional Bible Study," *CTM*, 9:81-89; February, 1938; "Preaching on the Augsburg Confession ," *CTM*, 1:280-285, April, 1930; "Privileges and Obligation," *CTM*, 12; 721-743, October 1941; "Prophets and Political and Social Problems," *CTM*: 11:241-268; 337-351; April-May, 1940:

"Schriftlehre von der Verstockung," *CTM*, 3:7-11. 108-113g., January-February, 1932; "Streitet die Verstockung Pharaohsnicht mit Gottcs Gerechtigkeit und Gnade;" *CTM*: 569-574g. August, 1932; "Studies in Hosea," *CTM*: 2:909-920; 3:33-45; 120-127; 187-196; 262-268; December, 1931, January-April, 1932; "Wer ist Der Prophet in Deut. 18:15-19;" *CTM*, 2:424-437, June, 1931; "What Was Written on the Two Tables of the Covenant?" *CTM*: 9:746-751, October, 1938.

In the area of sermonizing and homiletics Laetsch published sermon textual studies in both German and English. In the *CTM*, there are no less than fifty-four sermon studies. A majority of them deal with New Testament texts. He authored two articles dealing with Lenten sermons, "Brief Lenten Outlines," *CTM*: 8:202-205, March 1937 and "Entwuerfe zu Passionspredigten," *CTM*: 6:208-214; 286-289g., March-April, 1935.

Purpose of This Study

It is the purpose of this presentation to examine the exegetical writings of Theodore Laetsch and establish the principles of interpretation taught by him to his students, and the hermeneutics that controlled his commentaries and exegetical writings. The brief study will reveal that Laetsch employed principles of interpretation that had been used for at least a hundred years in the writings of other LCMS theological professors and pastors. Laetsch's hermeneutical principles will be shown to follow those of Luther, the Lutheran Confessions, C.F.W. Walther, Pieper, Stoeckhardt, A.L. Graebner, Louis Fuerbringer, W. Arndt and Mennicke.

Editor of the Abiding Word

The Abiding Word, Volumes 1 and 2, contain an anthology of doctrinal essays, delivered in 1946 by various professors and pastors in connection with the centennial of The Lutheran Church-Missouri Synod, originally known as Die Synode von Missouri, Ohio und Andere Staaten. Laetch was chosen to be the editor of the 35 essays comprising the two volumes of The *Abiding Word*. [13] They were intended to show the world that in 1946, after a hundred years what the theological position and doctrinal practice of a church body was that had grown to nearly two million souls. The reader of these two volumes will see exactly what the LCMS held on the entire gamut of Christian doctrine, beginning with predestination and ending with the locus on eternal life. Thus the entire plan of salvation, the ordo salutis was clearly enunciated.

In the preface to volume 2, Laetsch wrote: "A close study of these doctrinal essays in this second volume, which like those of volume one are based on the writings of the fathers and founders of our Synod, has confirmed the conviction of the editor that the title of these volumes do not intend to bring any new doctrine of God's Word as they have been taught in our midst during the past century, the theology of the Word. In the second place, on that account it is the abiding Word of God Himself declares that the Word of our God shall stand forever (Is. 40:8), that it liveth and abides forever" (I Peter 1:23).[14]

Laetsch found himself in complete agreement with these theological essays, all following historical Lutheran principles of interpretation. He used the statement of Solomon in Proverbs Chapter 25:1 to characterize these essays: "A word fitly spoken is like apples of gold in pictures of silver." Here is Laetsch's evaluation of Volume I: "In the early literature of our Missouri Synod there is presented in silver receptacles to all who will read a rich selection of chosen golden apples worth more than their weight in gold. These golden apples were gathered from the tree of life, from God's Holy Word, that Word of which Christ says: 'Thy Word is Truth' (John 17:17). That Word which Peter called the incorruptible seed, the Word of God that liveth and abideth forever. (I Peter 1:23). That Word of Holy Scripture which is able to make us wise unto salvation though faith which is in Christ Jesus and which is profitable for doctrine, for reproof, for correction, for instruction in righteousness and for comfort (2 Timothy 3: 15-17)."[15]

Specific Sources of Laetsch's Hermeneutics

In volume II of the *Abiding Word* there is an essay entitled "Bible Interpretation," by Victor Mennicke, father of the present first vice-president of the LCMS.[16] The books consulted by Mennicke in setting forth historical Lutheran principles of interpretation, as seen from the bibliography concluding the essay, were the works of Luther, the Lutheran Confessions as found in *The Book of Concord of 1580*, Pieper, Baier, Quenstedt, Rambach and L. Fuerbringer, all Reformation, post-Reformation, nineteenth and twentieth century orthodox Lutheran hermeneuticians.[17] Inasmuch as Laetsch gave praise and endorsement to the essays of volume II, he must also be referring to Mennicke's "Bible Interpretation," it would be thus fair to assume that he was also subscribing and endorsing the hermeneutical principles of historic Lutheranism as set forth by Mennicke. Finding fault with certain aspects of Laetsch's hermeneutics, therefore, would mean that those Laetsch followed were also being rejected by his critics. This would mean that Luther, the Lutheran Confessions, Gerhard, Quenstedt, Baier, Rambach, Walther, Pieper and Stoeckhardt and Mennicke were in error on some of their basic principles of Lutheran interpretation.

As this writer presents Laetsch's hermeneutical principles they will be compared with Lutheran exegetes and dogmaticians and preachers whose hermeneutics he had repeated and adopted. The reader's attention will especially be called to the hermeneutical principles of C.F.W. Walther, who clearly enunciated the interpretative principles he followed in all his teaching, preaching and writings, as set forth in Theses XII-XXI of his work, *The Lutheran Church the True Visible Church of God*."[18] Reference will also be made to Louis Fuerbringer, L. Fuerbringer's, *Theological Hermeneutics*,[19] the writings of Stoeckhardt and the works of Francis Pieper and other Lutheran exegetes.

Bible Can Be Readily Understood

Laetsch would agree that just as a person reading a newspaper can understand what he reads, so in general the Bible is clear and what it communicates can be understood. "Thy word is a lamp unto my feet and light unto my path" (Psalm, 119:5). In his *Old Testament Isagogical Notes*, used at the seminary in an Old Testament course, he held that when God speaks to Moses, this is exactly what occurred.[20] In Leviticus the assertion is made numerous times "and Yahweh spoke to Moses," this could not be interpreted as Wellhausen has done in his *Prolegomena of the History of Israel* to mean, that the laws and regulation that Moses received from God were actually post-exilic concepts placed into the mouth of Moses.[21] Laetsch rejected all higher criticism that denied clear statements of the text. This would also hold true of all miracles reported in the Old and New Testament, which higher critical scholars reinterpret and deny their historical reality. In his article: "What Was Written on the Two Tables of Stones?" Laetsch rejected the fact that there was any conflict between Exodus 20:17 and Exodus 34, which higher critics placed in opposition to each other.[22]

The Bible and Certain Principles of Interpretation

There are two kinds of rules used by the Biblical hermeneutician: those distinctive ones found in the Bible itself and those derived from the normal processes of thinking, logical rules not in conflict with the Bible.[23] In contradistinction to modern secular hermeneutics, the person faithful to the Scriptural text will remain with those principles clearly used by the Holy Spirit who inspired writers and eschew interpretative principles that reject those of Holy Writ. The method of allegorization, so prominent in the Christian Church for over a thousand years, was rejected by Luther and those who followed the Wittenberg Reformer's rules of interpretation.[24] For instance the blood and water which came out of the side of Jesus when the Roman soldiers pierced Jesus side (John 19:34) do not refer to the Lord's Supper and Baptism.

Laetsch agrees with Walther's thesis XIII which stated: "The Ev. Lutheran Church recognizes the written word of the apostles and prophets as the only and perfect source, rule, norm and judge of all teaching — a. not reason, b. not tradition, c. not new revelations."[25] When Laetsch became a clergy member of the Lutheran Church and later when he assumed his St. Louis Seminary professorship, he publicly declared that he also accepted the Lutheran Confessions. Relative to the principles enunciated in Walther's thesis XIII, he accepted the Comprehensive Summary of the *Formula of Concord* and also the statement of Luther in the Smalcald Articles: "The Word of God shall establish articles of faith and no one else, not even an angel."[26]

Human Reason Rejected as a Criterion
for the Establishment of Interpretation

Human reason as an arbiter and judge of the contents of God's Word was totally rejected by Laetsch. The Documentary Hypothesis or Theory he insisted was governed by human reason and was repudiated by him as may be seen from his *Isagogical Notes on the Old Testament.*[27] A number of faulty presuppositions, anti-Scriptural and anti-supernatural, controlled this theory which has gone in the course of the 19th century through so many changes. The whole higher critical approach was invented, controlled and continued by false assumptions and procedures and deductions made from the use of a human reason, and was opposed to the infallibility and clearness of the Bible. Reason has a proper place in interpretation, however, not as a master over God's Word, but rather as an instrument for its comprehension.

The Purpose of Holy Scriptures According to Laetsch

Laetsch would contend that the main purpose of the Bible was to give God all glory (I Cor. 10:31). With the Apostle St. Paul, Laetsch would declare: "Whatsoever things were written aforetime were written for our learning that we through comfort and patience of the Scriptures might have hope" (Romans 15:4). Laetsch was in agreement with Gerhard, who in his *Loci Theologi* expressed the view for the purpose of Biblical interpretation to be observed, "it must glorify and extol the divine goodness, wisdom, righteousness, truth and power and confirm the basis of our Christian faith and increase our zeal in godliness."[28]

The Main Purpose of Holy Writ, to Bring People to Faith in Christ

The Bible, Old and New Testaments, knows of but one plan of salvation, namely to cause people to believe in Christ Jesus as Savior and Redeemer.[29] Christ is the heart of Holy Writ. 2 Timothy 3:15-17 clearly sets forth the true and only purpose of the Old Testament, namely, "to create faith in Christ Jesus." The New Testament citing the words of Jesus: "I am the Way, the Truth and the Life, no person comes to the Father except by me." John 3:16 announces the truth that if a person does not believe in Christ, he will be condemned.

The Christology of the Old Testament

In his sermons, articles and commentaries Laetsch strongly came out for the existence of prophecies and promises about the Messiah in the Scriptures of the Old Covenant. The only hope that mankind has for eternal life has been furnished by Christ. Laetsch certainly had the New Testament Scriptures on his side, for as Peter testified: "All the prophets from Samuel and his successors have spoken of these days" (Acts 3:24), namely, of the redemptive work of Christ and the establishment of the Christian Church. Laetsch accepted Deuteronomy 18:15-19 as a passage, where Moses as a type, clearly also predicted the coming of Christ as a Prophet whom the Israelites should accept and obey.[30] Peter quoted Deuteronomy 18: 15-19 as a prediction of Christ, fulfilled in the life of Christ (Acts 3:21-23). This interpretation was also held by Luther, Walther, Pieper, Stoeckhardt, and others in the LCMS for at least a century. Laetsch wrote in his article: "Wer ist der Prophet in Deut. 18:15-19," as follows: "According to the analogy of faith only Christ could be meant despite the general higher critical denial of the New Testament's interpretation." Laetsch was convinced that in the writings of Moses, the Former and Latter Prophets and in Writings of the Old Testament there were many predictions about various facts about Christ's life and ministry and that these were fulfilled as the New Testament writers amply attest.[31] In Jeremiah 23:5-6, in which the Messiah is called "Righteous Branch," also called "Yahweh Is Our Righteousness," Laetsch contended the Old Testament here possessed a Messianic prophecy.[32] The Hebrew term **zemach**, "branch," he argued was one of Holy Scripture's titles for the Messiah (Is. 4:2; Zech. 3:6; 6:12).[33] In his exposition of Jeremiah 23:5-6 Laetsch wrote as follows: "It is the righteousness which the Seed of David who is the Woman's Seed of Genesis 3:15, procures for mankind by bruising Satan's head. As the Servant of the Lord he bore the sins of man (Is. 53:11), which the Lord laid on Him (53:6) who had done no

691

wrong (v. 9) and who suffered all the penalties mankind had deserved (vv .5-6). By His vicarious substitutionary death Christ fulfilled all the demands of the mandatory and punitive Justice of God. He became 'Our Righteousness' establishing this righteousness as the norm to be followed in His kingdom. Since this righteousness was procured by him whom God calls 'Jehovah is Our Righteousness,' it is a righteousness procured by Jehovah, it is as timeless as the Lord, retroactive (Heb. 9:15), accepted by them (Gen. 4:1), by Lamech (Gen. 5:29), it was counted as righteousness to believing Abraham (Gen. 15:6); it became the hope and joy of all believers in the Old Testament (Heb. 11:1:40), it was the basis of blessings, spiritual and maternal, temporal granted in the Old Covenant. It is that vicarious atonement on account of which the Righteousness Servant throughout the ages justifies many (Is. 53: 12), makes them righteous children of God heirs of salvation for the sake of the salvation he has procured. For this reason 'righteousness' is so frequently linked up with salvation."[34]

This long quotation and others which might be cited show that Laetsch followed Luther, [35] The Lutheran Confession,[36] Walther,[37] Pieper,[38] Stoeckhardt[39] W. A. Maier, Sr.[40] in their understanding that the Old Testament had many prophecies about Christ as promised Messiah.[41]

Scripture Interprets Scripture

It is a Biblical principle of interpretation that Scripture interprets Scripture. (Scriptura scripturam interpretatur).[42] Just as Christ refuted Satan's misinterpretation of Psalm 91:11-12 by citing the entire passage and not leaving out key words, so Peter in his Pentecostal sermon (Acts 2:29) asserted that Psalm 16:10 does not apply to David, but to Christ. A perusal of Laetsch's commentaries and other writings shows that he has followed the Scriptural principle that Scripture interprets the Scripture, especially where the New Testament clearly defines and Old Testament texts. On the strength of Matthew 2:6 Laetsch interpreted Micah 5:2 as a prophecy of Christ's birth in Bethlehem. In his Micah commentary, Laetsch wrote: "Scripture speaks of the Child, born of a human mother. God Himself speaking of the Anointed, the Messiah tells Him Psalms 2:7. Wisdom, the Son of God, speaks of his birth before all times (Prov. 8:23-31). Because of this birth the future Messiah is Immanuel, God with us (Is. 7:14), the Mighty God, Everlasting Father (Is. 9:6; cf. also John 1:1-3; 9:35- 38; Col. 1:15-17, Heb. 1:1-12). It is to this birth that Micah refers here. This generation from all eternity distinguishes the Child of Bethlehem from all other descendants of David, and thus alone qualifies Him for the work of Ruler of Israel His Church."[43]

Holy Spirit Speaks Through the Words of the Bible

Laetsch held together with Pieper,[44] Engelder,[45] J.T. Mueller,[46] P. E. Kretzmann,[47] that the Holy Spirt speaks through the words of the Biblical text. The intent of the Holy Spirit is recorded in the words written in the sixty-six books of the Old and New Testaments'. God's message and intentions are not to be separated from the writings of the Old Testament prophets and the written books of the Evangelists and Apostles. In his article commemorating the life of Professor Metzger, Laetsch praised his colleague's faithfulness to the text of the Word of God, and that he could not permit any person to change the text.[48] As homiletician, catechist, and exegete Metzger practiced faithfulness to the text. Thus Laetsch wrote: "And the class taught in the manner outlined by Metzger, will be like Timothy of old, be made wise unto salvation through faith in Christ Jesus and be thoroughly furnished unto all good works." Like Metzger, averred Laetsch, handling of the text should be thorough, Scriptural, textual and Christocentric. In his articles "The Pastor's Professional Bible Study" the readers were admonished by Laetsch to be faithful to the text and by all means were to employ the original Biblical text, besides considering the primary Bible versions like the Septuagint, the Peshitta, and Vulgate and also to consult Luther's translation of the Bible as well as the Authorized English Bible, in order to get at the real meaning of the text.[49]

Laetsch held together with Engelder, P. E. Kretzmann, J.C. Fritz, Maier, Sr., Pieper L. Fuerbringer that the old Lutheran principle that to challenge the teachings of the Bible was the same as challenging the Holy Spirit who had inspired the Holy Scriptures. Luther in the Smalcald articles stated that only the Holy Spirit spoke through Holy Scriptures.[50]

Interpretation Must Be According to the Analogy of Faith

In his writings Laetsch espoused the Lutheran hermeneutical rule that all Scripture must be interpreted according to the analogy of faith. He agreed with Gerhard's Loci when the latter wrote: "By the rule of faith we mean the passages of Scripture in which articles of faith are set forth in plain and clear terms."[51] The Apology states: "Besides examples ought to be interpreted according to the rule, i.e., according to plain and clear passages of Scripture not contrary to this rule, that is, contrary to Scripture."[52] *The Formula of Concord* declares: "First (then we receive and embrace with our whole hearts) the Prophetic and Apostolic Scriptures of the Old and New Testaments as the pure, clear fountain of Israel, which is the only true standard by which all teachers and doctrines are to be judged."[53]

That teachings must agree with the analogy of faith is also an interpretative principle set forth clearly in God's word. Thus Paul asserted "Hold fast the form of sound words which thou hast heard from me, in faith and love. (2 Timothy 1:13) The same apostle instructed Timothy: "If any man teach otherwise and consent not to the wholesome words of our Lord Jesus Christ and to the doctrine which is according to godliness." Laetsch held that Adam and Eve, taken from Adam, were the first human beings created by God and asserted that the direct creation of Adam and Eve by God was a teaching demanded by the analogy of faith. The rejection of the Mosaic authorship was against the teachings of both the Old and New Testaments.

No extra Biblical conceptions and ideas were to be used against the analogy of faith. The Roman Catholic Traditions were not to be employed to deny the doctrines and truths clearly set forth in Holy Writ. Human reason cannot be employed to repudiate teachings in harmony with the analogy of faith. Philosophy is basically the employment of reason to promote things contrary to the analogy of faith. Human feelings and human experiences cannot be utilized to deny teachings in harmony with the analogy of faith. Higher criticism applied to the Bible by modern scholarship violated many teachings of the Bible. Questioning or rejecting the Mosaic authorship, the authorship of Davidic psalms, the division of Isaiah among a number of different authors, the historicity of Jonah, the miracles, his staying in the body of the great fish, various miracles of the Old Testament referred by Christ and Saul of Tarsus are rejected although such interpretations reject the clear assertions of the New Testament and called into question the deity of Christ and St. Paul as an inspired apostle of Jesus Christ.

The Importance of Using the Original Languages

To correctly interpret God's inspired Word, Laetsch agreed with Lutheran scholars before, as well as during his lifetime, to the effect that the original languages must be employed, that is Hebrew and Biblical Aramaic for the Old Testament and Koine Greek for the New. That Laetsch did this may be readily seen from his commentaries and exegetical articles. Laetsch took seriously the dictum of Luther, who asserted: "In the same measure that the Gospel is dear to us should we zealously cherish the languages."[54] Only when the Scriptures are correctly translated can the doctrines of the Bible be accurately established. In this respect Laetsch was following Walther, who in thesis XVI, A said: "The Ev. Lutheran Church lets the original text alone decide."[55] Walther quoted Pfeiffer: "This must be maintained over against the papists, who ascribe canonical authority to their Latin version, the Vulgate."[56] Fuerbringer in his Hermeneutic also teaches the importance of using the original Biblical languages.[57]

Each Passage of Holy Writ Has One Intended Sense

Beginning with Luther, Lutheran exegetes have followed the following principle: "The Bible should be interpreted with the assumption that the author had only one intended sense: 'Sensus literalis unus est.'" Fuerbringer, Laetsch's collegue on the faculty, took the same stance that a Biblical verse has only one intended sense.[58] Walther in thesis XVI, C. stated: "The Ev. Lutheran Church holds the literal sense has but one sense."[59] The latter cited Luther, 18: 1307 and 4:1304f. Mennicke makes the same point and cited Lieber, *Legal and Political Hermeneutic*: "No sentence or form of words can have more than one true sense and this is the only one we have to inquire for. This is the basis for all interpretation. Interpretation otherwise has no meaning. Every man or body of persons making use of words does so in order to convey certain meaning, and to find this precise meaning is the object of interpretation. To have two meanings is the equivalent to have no meaning. The interpretation of two meanings implies absurdity.[60]

Return to Numerous Senses of the Bible Rejected

Arguing that many of Old Testament prophecies are not rectilinear prophecies of events and happenings in the life of Christ, appears to be a return to the Middle Ages when the church usually could find a fourfold sense in Bible passages; in fact at one time as many as seven different senses were found, later reduced to four. To find two completely different meanings in Isaiah 7:14 contradicts the New Testament which clearly asserts that Mary's becoming with child was foretold by the prophet Isaiah in 7:14. Critical scholars contend that what the prophet Isaiah was telling King Ahaz was that a young woman of this time was going to bring forth a child, whom she would call Immanuel, i.e. God is with us![61] When conservative scholars who accept this interpretation come to Matthew one the original meaning of Is. 7:14 has been given a different meaning, namely, referring to Mary's being pregnant and calling her child "God is with us."[62] Thus Isaiah 7:14 is given two different meanings. The same holds true of Micah 5:2, where critical scholarship believes that Micah referred to the coming of a future Israel ruler but rule out the twofold miraculous birth of a Ruler, whose goings forth are from eternity. Micah 5:2, according to Matthew, was a prophecy of the place where the Messiah was to be born and also a statement of His deity and Virgin birth (v. 3).

Pieper wrote: "It can also be proved a posteriori in the light of the New Testament that the intended sense of the Old Testament text is none other than the one expressed in the New Testament.[63] In a long footnote, Pieper[64] referred to the series of Stoeckhardt with the title "Weissagung und Erfuellung," where the latter treated the following Matthean passages Isaiah 7:14; Matt. 1:18-23; Micah 5:2; Matthew 2:6; Hosea 11:1; Jer. 31:15; Is. 8:22-Matt. 9:1-3; Zech. 6:12; Matt. 2:23; Is. 40:3; Matt. 3:1-3; Is. 40:3 and a host of other passages in the Old Testament is directly fulfilled in the New Testament.[64]

A perusal of Laetsch's writings would reveal that he agreed with Stoeckhardt,[65] Pieper,[66] L. Fuerbringer,[67] and Mennicke[68] that many Old Testament texts are erroneously misunderstood because of the refusal to accept the intended sense of the New Testament which the Holy Spirit has caused to be recorded. Passages do not have two intended senses but only one.[69] In this matter Laetsch was following Luther who wrote: "The Holy Spirit is the most simple writer in heaven and earth; accordingly His words cannot have more than one meaning." "We should not say that Scripture or God's Word, has more than one sense" (IV: 1305; XVIII:1307),[70] C.F.W. Walther in theses XVI D asserted: "The Ev. Lutheran Church acknowledges only the literal sense has but one sense."[71]

The Clarity of Scripture

Like Walther,[72] Pieper,[73] L. Fuerbringer,[74] and J .T. Mueller[75], Laetsch held to the clarity of Scripture, which meant that there are no "views" and "open questions." The psalmist declared: "Thy Word is a lamp unto my feet and a light unto my path," (Ps. 119; 105). Peter calls it "a more sure word of prophecy that shineth in a dark place," (2 Pet. 1:19). Paul denominated it: "The light of the glorious Gospel," (2 Cor. 4:3,4).

The doctrine of the clarity or perspicuity of Holy Writ is important for Laetsch and he held that to utilize reason to explain a clear passage by another clear passage is wrong. The perspicuity of the Bible is its own proof. "Thy word is a lamp unto my feet and a light unto my path" (Psalm 119:5). Laetsch agreed with the proposition that the Bible is clear and in most cases there is no reason for explaining clear passages by still more clear ones. The perspicuity of the Word of God can only be apprehended and accepted as long as the heart and mind of the exegete or expositor are captivated by the Word of God and subject to it.[76] When one employs human reason or makes accommodations to higher criticism the real intent of Scriptures will be negated or reinterpretation will occur.[77]

Laetsch agreed with Luther that the plain, simple doctrine must be upheld, when the text is plain and clear. Luther wrote: "Of course they do not agree, that is why you lose it if you consider it without the Word. This knowledge is too high. My mind cannot grasp it. Yours even less."[78] He would have agreed with an earlier author in an article appearing in the faculty journal, *Lehre und Wehre* who wrote: "We shall let the Scriptures be its own interpreter, and the worry how these matters agree we shall leave to Him in whose hands our salvation rests securely."[79] Laetsch would suggest following Luther's advice: "Kneel down in your own room and in true humility sincerely pray that he would give you Holy Spirit through His dear Son soon to enlighten you and give you understanding."[80]

The Bible Is Written in Human Language

Laetsch recognized that the Bible is composed in human language, and that the Holy Spirit used Hebrew, Biblical Aramaic, and Koine Greek in having His Word recorded by human writers, in sixty-six books over at least sixteen centuries. So like Luther, Walther, Stoeckhardt, Pieper, he contended that the historical grammatical method was to be used, and rejected the historical-critical methodology.[81] Laetsch was opposed to those who ignored the grammar of the text. This can easily be seen if one reads his commentaries, exegetical writings and homiletical contributions. For this practice he had the support of *The Apology of the Augsburg Confession.*[82]

The Bible must correctly be interpreted according to its grammar, before the correct doctrine can be elicited from a Scripture passage, paragraph or chapter. Thus Paul in the Letter to the Galatians emphasized the proper use of grammar. In Chapter 3:16 Paul asserted: "He saith not, and to seeds, as of many, and to thy seed which is Christ." A very important doctrine is established by using the rules of human grammar.

When higher critics ignore the clear text and reject it, this leads to erroneous and soul-destroying teachings. Laetsch in his exegetical endeavors followed the advice of Luther who said: "We should stay with the clear words of Scripture and its natural style and peculiarities, as is customary to the rules of grammar, the common usage of language, the natural way of speaking, just as God gave language, to mankind."[83]

696

The Usage of Parallel Passages

Since the Bible in all its parts is the work of the Holy Spirit and the latter is the real author of the Bible, it is not surprising that in Holy Writ the same teachings are set forth in different books, and where that is the case the interpreter will find parallel passages. The assertion that the Pentateuch or Law of Moses is referred to in a number of Bible passages in both the Old and New Testaments can be established from numerous passages in the Old and New Testaments.[84]

Law and Gospel Must Be Distinguished

Laetsch followed Luther that the exegete must properly distinguish between the law and Gospel, a hermeneutical method followed by him in his commentaries, exegetical essays and sermonizing. Here he was in agreement with Walther who under thesis XVIII 8 asserted: "The Ev. Lutheran Church distinguished between Law and Gospel, John 11:17;10:4; 2 Tim. 2:11."(85) This was also the stance of the *Formula of Concord*, Epitome V, par. 2.

The Guiding Star of All Interpretation

Since Christ is the world's only Savior, Laetsch made the teaching of justification the foundation and guiding star of all teaching. This is the view Walther set forth in thesis XVIII, A.[86] *The Augsburg Confession* in articles XXVI, par. 4 and XXVII, par. 48 clearly enunciated this important truth which has characterized the exegesis of the LCMS for over a hundred years.[87]

Laetsch and the Lutheran Symbols

Laetsch followed Walther, who in thesis XXI, A wrote: "The Ev. Lutheran Church is sure that the teaching contained in its symbols is the God's truth because it agrees with the written Word of God in all points."[88] Laetsch's love for the confession was shown by the fact that he published three articles in which be encouraged parents to study and use *Luther's Small Catechism* in the home[89] and in the church services[90] and called upon pastors to preach on the doctrines of the *Augsburg Confession*.[91]

Footnotes

1. For a history of Concordia Seminary from 1839-1964 cf. Carl S. Meyer *Log Cabin to Luther Tower* (St. Louis: Concordia Publishing House, 1965), 322 pp.
2. Cf. issues of *The Lutheran Witness* beginning with 1974 and following years.
3. Meyer has given a list of all individuals who served on the St. Louis faculty between 1939-1964, pp. 297-299.
4. Walther Sesquicentennial, 1811-1961. *Handbook for Pastors and Congregations.* Prepared by the Walther Sesquicentennial Committee of The Lutheran Church-Missouri Synod, 1961; Aaron Kopf, *Our Great Heritage* (St. Louis: Concordia Publishing House, 1961. 16 pp. Among the Minor Festivals of the Church Year, *Lutheran Worship* (St. Louis: Concordia Publishing House 1982), May 7 is to be observed as the date C.F.W. Walther is to be remembered, p. 9.
5. Francis Pieper, Index, *Christian Dogmatics.* Prepared by Walter W.F. Albrecht (St.

Louis: Concordia Publishing House, 1937), IV, pp. 995b-998b.

6. W. A. Maier, Sr., Erwin Lueker, *Lutheran Cyclopedia* (St Louis: Concordia Publishing House, 1975), p. 512.

7. **Ibid.**, p. 818.

7a. **Ibid.**, pp. 455-456.

8. Theo. Laetsch, *Bible Commentary, The Minor Prophets* (St. Louis: Concordia Publishing House, 1956), 566 pp.

9. Theo Laetsch, *Bible Commentary, Jeremiah* (St. Louis: Concordia Publishing House, 1952), 412 pp.

10. Walter A. Maier, *Bible Commentary, The Prophet Nahum* (St. Louis: Concordia Publishing House, 1959), 356 pp.

11. William F. Arndt, *Bible Commentary, The Gospel According to St. Luke* (St. Louis: Concordia Publishing House, 1956), 523 pp.

12. Cf. Index to *Concordia Theological Monthly*, (1930-1959), Compiled by Theodore Allwardt (St. Louis: Concordia Publishing House, 1963), 127-129a.

13. *The Abiding Word*. Edited by Theodore Laetsch (St. Louis: Concordia Publishing House 1946), 593 pp. Vol. I, 593 pp. *The Abiding Word*, **op. cit.**, II, 783 pp.

14. Laetsch, *The Abiding Word*, **op. cit.**, I, preface.

15. **Ibid.**, Vol. I, preface.

16. Victor Mennicke, "Bible Interpretation," *The Abiding Word*, 11, pp. 35-68.

17. **Ibid.**, p. 768.

18. Dallmann, Wm. Dau, W.H.T. and Engelder, Th., *Walther and the Church* (St. Louis: Concordia Publishing House.)

19. Louis Fuerbringer, *Theological Hermeneutics - An Outline for the Classrooms* (St. Louis: Concordia Publishing House, 1924), 24 pp.

20. Theodore Laetsch, *Old Testament Isagogical Notes* (St. Louis: Concordia Seminary Print Shop, 1929), pp. 1-10.

21. Julius Wellhausen, *Prolegomena to the History of Israel* (New York: Meridian Books, 1969).

22. Theo. Laetsch, *What Was Written on the Two Tables of the Covenant? Concordia Theological Monthly*, 9:746-751, October 1938.

23. Cf. Raymond F. Surburg, *The Principles of Biblical Interpretation* (Ft. Wayne: Concordia Seminary Press, 1980), pp. 48-63.

24. Cf. Raymond F. Surburg, "The Significance of Luther's Hermeneutics for the Protestant Reformation," *CTM*, 22:246-269.

25. *Walther and the Church*, **op. cit.**, p. 123.

26. *Concordia Triglotta* (St. Louis: Concordia Publishing House, 1921), p. 467.

27. *Isagogical Notes on the Old Testament*, **op. cit.**

28. *Loci Theologi*, ed. of Preus (Berlin, 1865), p. 237.

29. Theodore Laetsch, "In Memory of Prof. George Metzger, D.D.," *CTM*.

30. Th. Laetsch, "Wer ist der Prophet in Deut. 18:15-19?", *CTM*, 2:424-437.

31. **Ibid.**

32. Laetsch, *Commentary, Jeremiah*, **op. cit.**, p. 191.

33. **Ibid.**

34. **Ibid.**, p. 191.

35. *Weimar Edition of Luther's Works*, 47:16; *St. Louis Edition of Luther's Works*, 7:1924.

36. *Formula of Concord, Solid Declaration*, Art. VII, Theodore Tappert, *The Book of*

Concord (Philadelphia: Fortress Press, 1959), p. 596; *Apology of the Augsburg Confession*, Art. XXI, Tappert, p. 231.

37. *Walther and the Church*, **op. cit.**, Thesis XVIII, A.

38. Francis Pieper, *Christian Dogmatics* (St. Louis: Concordia Publishing House 1950), I, p. 215.

39. George Stoeckhardt, *Adventspredigten, Augslegung Der vornehmsten Weissagugen* (St. Louis: Concordia Verlag, 1887), 241 pp.

40. Walter A. Maier, Sr., *Selected Psalms* (St. Louis: Concordia Seminary Mimeo Company, 1930).

41. *Concordia Triglotta*, **op. cit.**, p. 881.

42. Fuerbringer, *Theological Hermeneutics*, **op. cit.**, pp. 17-18.

43. Th. Laetsch, *Bible Commentary - The Twelve Minor Prophets*, **op. cit.**, p. 272.

44. Pieper, *Christian Dogmatics*, **op. cit.**, I, pp. 228-231.

45. Th. Engelder, *Scripture Cannot Be Broken* (St. Louis: Concordia Publishing House, 1944).

46. J. T. Mueller, *Christian Dogmatics* (St. Louis: Concordia Publishing House, 1955), p. 106.

47. P.E. Kretzmann, *The Foundations Must Stand* (St. Louis: Concordia Publishing House, 1936), chapters 24, pp. 24-61.

48. Theo. Laetsch, "In Memory of George Metzger, D.D." *CTM*, 3:331, February, 1932.

49. Theo. Laetsch, "The Pastor's Professional Study:" *CTM*, 9:31-89, February, 1938.

50. Smalcald Articles, Part III, Art. VIII, *Triglotta*, **op. cit.**, pp. 495-497.

51. Gerhard, *Loci De Interpretatione Scripturae* par. 75.

52. *Concordia Triglotta*, **op. cit.**, p. 441, par, 60.

53. **Ibid.**, p. 851, par. 3.

54. *Weimar Edition of Luther's Work*, 11:455f.; *St. Louis Edition of Luther's Works*, 19:1336f.

55. *Walther and the Church*, **op. cit.**, p. 124.

56. **Ibid.**, p. 124.

67. Fuerbringer, *Theological Hermeneutics*, **op. cit.**, p. 4.

58. **Ibid.**

59. *Walther and the Church*, **op. cit.**, p. 1240.

60. Lieber, *Legal Hermeneutics and Legal Hermeneutics*, 3rd Edition p. 74f was quoted by *The Theological Quarterly*, 1902, p. 110.

61. Walter R. Roehrs and Martin Franzmann, *Concordia Self-Study Commentary* (St. Louis; Concordia Publishing House, 1971), p. 450a.

62. Laetsch, *Commentary on the Twelve Minor Prophets*, **op. cit.**, p. 572 (Micah 5:2).

63. Pieper, *Christian Dogmatics*, **op. cit.**, I, p. 248.

64. **Ibid.**, I; p. 248, note 50.

65. G. Stoeckhardt, *Der Prophet Isaiah* (St. Louis: Concordia Verlag, 1902), p. 87.

66. Pieper, *Christian Dogmatics*, **op. cit.**, I, p. 248, Note 50.

67. Fuerbringer, *Theological Hermeneutics*, **op. cit.**, p. 17.

68. Mennicke, "Bible Interpretation," **op. cit.**, p. 47.

69. Cf. Laetsch, *The Twelve Minor Prophets*, **op. cit.**, p. 88; also *Commentary, Jeremiah*, **op. cit.**, p. 250.

70. *St. Louis Edition of the Works of Martin Luther*, vol. 4, 1305; 18:1307.

71. *Walther and the Church*, **op. cit.**, p. 124, XVI D.

72. **Ibid.**, Thesis XIV, p. 123.

73. Pieper, *Christian Dogmatics*, I, p. 319.

74. Fuerbringer, *Theological Hermeneutics*, **op. cit.**, p. 20.

76. Mueller, *Christian Dogmatics*, **op. cit.**, p. 318.
76. *Lehre und Wehre*, 1907, p. 72.
77. The *St. Louis Edition of Luther's Works*, VII, p. 1175.
78. **Ibid.**, XII, p. 1605.
79. *Lehre und Wehre*, 1907, p. 534.
80. *St. Louis Edition of Luther's Works*, XIV, p. 434ff.
81. Cf. His Old Testament Isagogical notes, op.
82. *Concordia Triglotta*, **op. cit.**, p. 282, Par. 9.
83. The *St. Louis Edition of Luther's Works*, **op. cit.**, XVII, p. 1820.
84. L. Fuerbringer, *Introduction to the Old Testament, An Outline for the Classroom* (St. Louis: Concordia Publishing House, 1925), pp. 20.
85. *Walther and the Church*, **op. cit.**, p. 126.
86. **Ibid.**, p. 125
87. Wm. Arndt, "The Doctrine of Justification", in *The Abiding Word*, I, **op. cit.**, II, pp. 235-257; Ralph A. Bohlmann, *Principles of Biblical Interpretation*. Revised Edition (St. Louis: Concordia Publishing House, 1983), pp. 99-112.
88. *Walther and the Church*, **op. cit.**, p. 127.
89. Theodore Laetsch, "The Catechism in the Christian Home," *CTM*, 5:596-604, August, 1934.
90. Theodore Laetsch, "The Catechism in Public Worship," *CTM*, 5:234-241, March, 1934.
91. Theodore Laetsch, "Preaching on the Augsburg Confession" *CTM*, 1:280-285, Apr.

Questions

1. What faculty has exerted a great influence on the Lutheran Church-Missouri Synod? ____
2. What happened at this seminary between 1958-1974? ____
3. How many left the LCMS? ____
4. Surburg was a student at Concordia Seminary, St. Louis from ___ to ____.
5. Laetsch rejected all forms of ____.
6. Laestch is the author of ____.
7. What is the *Abiding Word*? ____
8. The blood and water which flowed out of the side of Jesus does not refer to ____.
9. What did Laetsch insist about the documentary hypothesis? ____
10. Deuteronomy 18:15-19 refers to ____.
11. Psalm 16:10 does not refer to David but to ____.
12. The rejection of the Mosaic authorship was against the teachings of both ___.
13. Higher criticism applied to the Bible violates ____.
14. Laetsch, Luther, and Fuerbringer were among those who emphasized the importance of the ____ languages.
15. A Bible verse has only ____ intended ____.
16. Does Isaiah 7:14 have two different meanings? ____
17. Laetsch contended that the ____ method must be used and rejected the ____ methodology.
18. According to Laetch, the teaching of justification is ____.

The Life and Writings of Carl Manthey Zorn

Christian News, December 12, 1994

Christian News of September 19, 1994, announced the fact that Carl Manthey Zorn's *Manna, Meditations on the Life and Teachings of our Lord Jesus Christ for Family Devotions*, Second Edition, 1906, has been translated by Dr. John Sullivan, a book having about 700 pages.[1] Dr. Zorn, 1846-1928, was one of the stalwart Missourians who lived during the first seventy years of the existence of The Evangelische Lutherische Synode von Missouri, Ohio und Anderen Staten, now called The Lutheran Church-Missouri Synod (LCMS). He was one of the leading churchmen between 1876 to 1911. He was active during the times of Carl F. Walther, George Stoeckhardt, A. L. Graebner, Louis Fuerbringer, Francis Pieper and other greats of the first seven decades of the LCMS's history. It would certainly be instructive to know more about this early theological giant and of his worthwhile contributions to the spiritual life of the LCMS.

Zorn's Life Until His Miraculous Conversion

Carl Manthey Zorn was born at Sterup, Schleswig on March 18, 1846.[2] His father was a pastor and his mother a devout Christian. As he grew to manhood, to quote Zorn himself he was "ein wilder Bursche", a wild and wayward young fellow. While a student at Erlangen University, he claimed "to hell I fast was sinking."[3] His religious professors did not believe in the inspiration of the Bible. Zorn averred: "Theology became abominable to me, all poppycock."[4] His teachers so influenced him that he gave up going to church. He told his shocked mother: "Mother, I believe in a God, but not in Jesus, but not in the Jesus revealed in the Bible. The Bible is out of date. It's too much you expect me, a man of the 19th century, to believe in it." In fact, he did not even possess a Bible. At the Gymnasium in Kreuznach, Grabau, a teacher of mathematics, told the young Zorn: "There is no God. But everything else said about religion is nonsense." At Erlangen, Zorn joined the fraternity, called Germania, whose slogan was: "Freedom—Honor—the Fatherland." Many of the Burschen drank heavily. They engaged in duels. In 1867 Zorn suffered a severe head wound which took a half of a year to heal. Zorn himself confessed: "I was a wild and careless fellow if not immoral. I found no pleasure in getting drunk. But I did not attend church. I was going down, down, down. One teacher said: "With God nothing is impossible—except to convert Zorn."

Zorn's Miraculous Conversion

In his book **Aufwaerts** (Upwards) Zorn tells of his conversion. Leaving Erlangen, he became a tutor of a private family, where he instructed his wards about God, virtue and immortality. An old pastor remarked to

Zorn, "Zorn, if that is all you believe and teach you will surely go to hell and take others with you." Then, one night Zorn relates: "Although I had no vision I was aware of God's presence and anger. I was afraid of the judgement, fully aware of inability to stand in it. I realized I was an abomination to God. Throughout the night I ran to and fro in my room. I was in the hands of God's crushing hands and cried out: 'O God, be merciful to me'. I then thought of Christ. But he remained foolishness to me. God in three persons and one in three to become man? Nonsense!" The next night the same thing happened. Thereupon Zorn went to a pastor to whom he related his experiences. The latter told Zorn to read the four Gospels with the desire to find Christ. This advice was followed. Like in St. Paul's case, the scales fell off his eyes. Zorn reported: "I learned to know Jesus and the glory of His saving love and power. With a loud outcry I jumped on the table, then knocked the chairs over and began to praise God. I wanted to sing but could only remember my confirmation hymn: 'Now I have found the Firm Foundation.'"

> *Now I have found the firm foundation*
> *Which holds mine anchor ever sure;*
> *Twas laid before the world's creation*
> *In Christ my Savior's wounds secure;*
> *Foundation which unmoved shall stay*
> *When heaven and earth will pass away.*
> *It is that mercy never ending.*
> *Which human wisdom far trenscends.*
> *Oh Him who loving arms extending.*
> *To wretched sinners condescends.*
> *Whose heart with pity still doth break*
> *Whether we seek Him or forsake.*

Zorn Enters India Mission Field

Zorn, a man six feet and two inches, making an imposing figure, after his conversion had a great desire to become a missionary in India. He was now convinced of two things: 1. I have forgiveness of sins through Jesus Christ. 2. The Bible is God's Word because it revealed Jesus to me. These were two truths that had been revealed to him through his experiences connected with his conversion, truths he formerly had totally rejected. Up to this time he had been a member of the State Church which taught the Reformed doctrine of the Lord's Supper. He became a Lutheran, he studied Luther's *Small Catechism* and the other Lutheran Confessions. Zorn won over the children of the family he was tutoring, yes, even their parents.

Study at the Leipzig Mission House

The Leipzig Mission House prepared missionaries for India. For at least 150 years this organization sent out evangelists to India. At this institute also Fritz Zucker was a student, who later taught at Concordia, Ft. Wayne, later becoming its president. In 1870 Zorn entered the training school and graduated in February, 1871.

After his ordination in June 1871, he sailed for India. Somewhat later Mariechen Hengstenberg, daughter of a Reformed pastor, became a Lutheran and joined her spouse in India. The Zorns were subject to violent storms and endured great heat. On page 202 of his book, *Dies und das aus dem Leben eines ostindischen Missionars,* he said that dangerous wild animals, buffaloes and leopards often threatened their lives. They often had to contend with murderous robbers who wanted to harm them. False teachers in the Christian churches were also numerous.

Originally Zorn came to Madras, but from there he headed for Tranquebar, way down in south India, even at one time he proceeded down to Trivandrum. The Leipzig missionary mastered the Tamil language, which has 200 letters (compared with 26 in English) in seven months. He served in the small kingdom of Puttekottai, whose king was Rama Chandra Behauder. Zorn tried to convert the king to Christianity, but failed. Still the king admired Zorn and became his friend. In south India Zorn worked zealously having dealings with Mohammedans, Bramins, and the caste peoples. In Pudukottai he worked from 1871 to 1876, five years, of which one was nearly spent in language study.

Zorn's Resignation From the Leipzig Society

Some of Zorn's teachers at the Leipzig Missionary Institute were of the same theological stripe that his professors at Erlangen University had been. Kahnis of the Leipzig Society denied the doctrine of the Trinity; F. Delitzsch taught that Genesis 1-3 were myths. Luthhardt held that man had a free nature and was not dead in trespasses and sins. Zucker, Grubert, Willkom, Schaeffer objected to the false theology of the Leipzig Society and that its missionaries could teach what they wanted to. All, except Schaeffer left.

Zorn Emigrates to the United States

The Leipzig Society refused the way home for those who resigned. Zorn appealed to Carl Ferdinand Walther for help. The latter sent 3,000 dollars after Zorn left India. His sister also had refused to help her brother. When Zorn arrived looking like a beggar in disheveled clothes, even Walther was embarrassed. But in a short time, Zorn proved himself and was accepted as a valuable addition to the clergy of the LCMS. In 1876 he became a pastor at Sheboygen, Wisconsin, and remained there until 1881. In 1878 Zorn received a call from the prestigious Trinity Church of St. Louis, Missouri but declined the call.

Zorn Becomes Pastor of Zion, Cleveland

In 1881 he accepted a call to Zion Lutheran Church of Cleveland, Ohio, where he served 30 years, until 1911, when he retired at the age of 65. Although not very old, he was worn out from a strenuous life. A number of times he unsuccessfully tried to introduce English at Zion.

Zorn as Theologian and Author

Besides being a missionary in India and a pastor for 35 years, he authored a number of books. The list in The Concordia Historical Institute, St. Louis claims he wrote 52 books and writings. As a writer Zorn exercised an important influence on Lutherans and other Christians. His various theological writings are worth studying today, as will be the case when Christian people purchase and use his *Manna*.

Zorn's Concerns for Missions

Zorn wrote a number of books to create interest in foreign missions. He published two volumes relating to his experiences in the East Indian mission field, namely *Diesund das aus dem Leben eines ostindischen Missionars*[5] and a continuation of the latter book, entitled *Dies und das aus fruehem Amlsleben.*[6]

Exegetical Writings

No other pastor wrote more volumes in which various books of the Bible were explained than did the Cleveland pastor. George Stoeckhardt authored a number of scholarly commentaries, as those of on Romans, Ephesians, 1 Peter and Selected Psalms. These were the volumes available at Zorn's time. However, Zorn made available to the general Christian public, clergy and laity alike expositions, written in German, which covered most of the books of the New Testament, such as the *Der Heiland*, a harmony of the life of Christ,[8] *Die Apostelgeschichte und Kirchengeschichte fuer Kinder und Eltern*,[9] *Romans*,[10] *I and II Corinthians*,[11] *Galatians*,[12] *Colossians*,[13] *I Thessalonian*,[14] *The Pastoral Epistles*,[15] *James*,[16] *II Epistle of Peter and Jude*,[17] *The Epistle of Hebrews*,[18] and *Revelation.*[19] In the Old Testament he wrote expositions on the *Psalms*,[20] *Proverbs*,[21] *Ecclesiastes*,[22] and *Song of Solomon* (in German called *Jesus-minne.*)[23]

A number of his exposition were lengthy. *Der Heiland* went through four editions between 1907-1914 with 80,000 copies being printed. It was supplied with pictures of outstanding artists and had 403 pages.[24] It probably proved to be his most popular work which helped in making Christ real to thousands of Christians in Europe and in America. His *Commentary on Colossians* was his most extensive New Testament commentary and was intended for clergy and laity alike.[25] Although avoiding using within the body of his writings the original text of the Bible, in footnotes he would take note of the Hebrew and Greek texts of Holy Writ to clarify a point of exegesis.[26] Zorn's expositions were published by three different publishing houses, namely, Der Verlag und Druck von Johannes Herrmann, Zwickau, in Saxony, Northwestern Publishing House, Milwaukee, Wisconsin and Concordia Publishing House (in German: Concordia Verlag), St. Louis, Missouri.

Zorn's Doctrinal Writings

Utilizing the principles of the analogy of faith and the ones which states that Scripture is to be interpreted by Scripture, he argues that all fundamental doctrines may be found in Genesis, Chapter 1 to 5. In his *Die ganze christliche Lehre* (Mos. 1-5) he finds the major doctrines of the Bible. He listed over twenty-five teachings that can be found in the opening chapters of Holy Writ.[27]

Zorn was a pastor during the years of the controversy regarding election and conversion, which began to rage in 1872 and lasted for decades. In 1881 Missouri adopted the Thirteen Theses.[28] The Cleveland Pastor contributed two volumes to this voluminous literature produced in The Synodical Conference of North America. His contributions were called *Bekehrung und Dnadenwahl: Erster Teil:* Bekehrung; Zweiter Teil: Gnadenwahl. Its substitute was: Fuer jeden Christen aus der Schrift erklaert (179 pages).[29]

Handbuch fuer den ersten Selbstunterricht in Gottes Wort was composed for those individuals interested in the fundamental doctrines of God's inerrant written revelation. In this book Zorn made use of Luther's *Small Catechism* and emphasized the person and work of Christ, warming the reader's heart for Jesus.[30] In this book also confirmands had a volume which furnished a solid foundation for the Christian faith.

Over the years Pastor Zorn received questions about difficult teachings of the Bible and the Lutheran faith. He answered these theological concerns in *Christenfragen, Aus Gottes Word beantworted.*[31]

Inasmuch as most Calvinistic and Arminian Churches denied and rejected infant baptism, Zorn published *Von de Taufe.*[32] In the interest of converting people, Zorn wrote an 80-page monograph, entitled: *Wie werde ich gewiss selig.*[33] Pastor Schneller of Cologne (Koeln) said of it: "Fresh, gripping and stirring, the author knows how to deal with an old but eternal theme."

A study entitled Das Gesetz, dealt with the word "nomos," (the Greek for "law") as used in the New Testament.[34] This work might be classified under Zorn's exegetical or Biblical expository writings or under doctrinal contributions. The employment of "law" in thirteen books, involving a study of over two hundred passages, is the subject of this writing. It was intended for theologians and non-theologians. All passages in the New Testament that treat of "nomos" are examined. It is a valuable contribution to the exegetical literature of the LCMS.

Zorn's Sermon, a Source for His Biblical Doctrinal Beliefs

In 1914 the Ohio pastor published his *Kleine Hauspostille,* purported to be a series of short sermons for all Sundays and festivals of the church year.[35] This book could have been classified with the devotional writings of Zorn or placed in the doctrinal category. A great deal of Christian doctrine is presented in the sixty-five different sermons that compromise The *Kleine Hauspostille.* A little dogmatics could be extracted from these sermons which cover the Lutheran ecclesiastical year once preached in Zion Lutheran Church, Cleveland, Ohio.

This volume of Lutheran sermons, solidly Biblical, was furnished with a foreword, in which the author sets forth his views as to what should be involved in the writing and delivery of a sermon. One might term the latter, "Brief Thoughts About the Science of Homiletics".

Zorn's Devotional Writings

Besides issuing *Manna* (960 pages) already referred to in the introduction, he also made available a volume entitled *Brosamen*, which contains devotions for the entire year.[36] A cheap edition was issued specifically for the European market, a book of 500 pages. There also appeared a large octave edition, furnished with pictures. A survey of Zorn's literary contributions reveals that he was concerned with all levels or strata of his congregation. *Weide Meine Laemmer* (Feed My Sheep) was composed for children and adults, in which are 552 Bible stories, that began at Creation and ended with Christ's Second Return.[37] Each devotional is accompanied by a prayer and is supplied with a hymn verse. Another important devotional book came from Zorn's facile pen, called *Lasset die Kindlein zu mir kommen!* It was composed of 298 devotions based on the four gospels.[38] Here also each devotion is concluded with a prayer and hymn verse.

Pastoral Theology

In the early history of the LCMS the question of the intimate dance became a matter of religious concern. Relative to this matter Zorn penned the booklet *Vom Tanz*.[39] Another theological concern was the question of whether a man might marry his dead wife's sister (called Schwagerehe). Concerning this ethical issue, Zorn wrote a brief study on Leviticus 18: "Darf Ein Witman die Schwester seiner verstorbenen Frauheiraten?"[40] The sin of masturbation was also discussed by the Ohio pastor.[41] The Cleveland pastor was also concerned about the senior members of his flock. For them he issued in print a sermon on Romans 8:18: "Ich halte es dafuer, dass dieser Zeit Leiden der Herrlichkeit nicht wert sei, die an uns soli geoffenbart werden."[42] The Missouri Synod was opposed to the various lodges who promulgated a religion of work righteousness and Zorn wrote *Ein Kurzes Wort ueber die Logen*.[43]

Biographical Works of Zorn

A biographical volume also came from his fluid and prolific pen, called *Grossvaters Jugenderrinerungen*, issued in two parts: 1. *Abwaerts* and 2. *Aufwaerts*. It claimed to be written for his children and nephews.[44]

Like any Biblical interpreter, preacher, counselor, missionary or evangelist, Zorn followed some system of Biblical interpretation or hermeneutics. Here are the basic hermeneutical principles that controlled the Ohio pastor's exegesis:

1. The Bible must be interpreted according to its own claims that it is the inspired Word of God in all its parts.[45]
   In his writings Zorn makes every effort to impress the reader with the fact that only the Word of God established doctrines.
2. Only the Bible is the true source for instruction for faith and life."[46]
3. The Bible canon is a unit as a whole and in all of its parts and therefore does not contradict itself. Like Luther, Zorn believed that God

does not lie or deceive.[47]

4. Since the Bible is God's Word in human language, it must he interpreted according to its human side. This does not mean that the historical method may be employed to question truths normally contrary to human experience, as miracles or prophecies.[48]

5. The interpretation is never an end in itself, but the purpose is the glorification of God.[49]

6. The true interpreter of the Bible is a Christian who possesses the gifts of the Holy Spirit.[50]

7. Biblical hermeneutics presupposes that God's Word is found in the original Biblical languages; in the Hebrew and Aramaic for the Old Testament, and Greek for the New Testament. Zorn believed that Luther's translation in the German Bible of 1534 and later revised, contained in general the reliable original text.[51]

8. In determining the words of Holy Writ, Zorn assumed that the author used the word in its common meaning (usus loquendi), until it is obvious that the Biblical writer is employing it in a different manner.[52]

9. No interpretation is correct, that is not according to grammar and syntax of the language in which it was written.[53]

10. The interpretation of every word and passage of Scriptures must be in agreement with the context.[54]

11. Every interpretation of Scripture must be historically correct, that is, the Bible must be understood as a historical book, and be interpreted according to its historical circumstances both of the Bible itself and the world in which it is written.[55]

12. The Bible must be interpreted with the assumption that the author had only one intended sense in mind when he wrote the given Word or passage. (Sensus literalis unus est).[56]

13. The New Testament interpretation of an Old Testament passage quoted in the New Testament is definitive for the original intended sense of the Old Testament Word or passages.[57]

14. Scripture interprets Scripture. Scripture radiates its own light.[58]

15. All formulations of Christian doctrine must agree with the analogy of faith and must never contradict the analogy of faith.[59]

16. All Biblical interpretation must have Christ as its center, teach Christ, and glorify Him as Lord and Savior.[60]

17. Any interpretation which violates the doctrine of justification by faith is erroneous and must be rejected.[61]

18. In the interpretation of figurative language the interpreter seeks the point of comparison and does not go beyond it.[62]

19. In the interpretation of prophecy, the interpreter seeks its fulfillment in the New Testament and shows how the prophecy was fulfilled.[63]

20. In the interpretation of types, the interpreter designates those portions of Scripture typological which Holy Writ itself indicates as typical.[64]

21. To the doctrines of Scriptures belong also the valid and the neces-

sary deductions from Scripture; not all doctrines of the Bible are taught in expressed words.[65]

22. The interpreter must distinguish between explanation, exegesis, and application.[66]

Zorn's Hermeneutics Like That of Luther, Walther, and Lutheran Confessions

An examination of Zorn's principles of Biblical interpretation reveals they are those of Luther and the Lutheran Confessions.[67] Zorn's hermeneutics agrees with those principles outlined by C. F. W. Walther as Theses XIII XX of the latter's *The Lutheran Church the True Visible Church*.[68] They are consonant with Louis Fuerbringer's *Theological Hermeneutics* [69] or with Victor Mennicke's "Bible Interpretation," setting forth the LCMS's Position on Scriptural interpretation at its centennial in 1947.[70]

Footnotes

1. *Christian News*, Vol. 32, No. 34, Monday, September 19, 1994, pp. 1, 22.
2. Cf. Karl Ehlers, "Life and Ministry of Dr. Carl Manthey Zorn," *Concordia Historical Institute Quarterly*, August 1971, Vol. XLIV, Number 3, p. 129. Ehlers wrote: "He was greatly troubled by increasing unfaithfulness to God's Word. Cf. *Bekehrungund Gnadenwahl* which stated that they are only based on Holy Writ.
3. Kari Ehlers, "Life and Ministry of Dr. Carl Manthey Zorn," *Concordia Historical Quarterly*. XLIV, 122, August l971
4. The data on the life of Manthey Zorn found in this essay are based on the Ehler's article, footnote 3; cf. also *Lutheran Cyclopedia* (St. Louis: Concordia Publishing House, 1975), p. 845.
5. Published by Verlag des Schriftvereins (E. Klaemer) Zwickau, in Saxony, no date).
6. **Ibid.**
7. In the 1966 ties H. W. Degener translated from class notes the following comments of George Stoeckhardt, *First Epistle of Paul to the Corinthians, The Epistle to the Philippians, The Lectures on the Second Epistle of St. Paul , Exegetical Lectures on the Epistle of Titus* and *Lectures on the Revelation of Saint John*. All made available by Concordia Theological Seminary Bookstore, Fort Wayne.
8. *Der Heiland*, 4th Auflage (Milwaukee: Northwestern Publishing House, l909), 403 pp.
9. Carl Manthey Zorn, *Apostelgeschichte iuid Kirchengeschichte in 81 und 52 Andachten* (Zwickau: Verlag und Druck von Johannes Herrmann, No date), 335 pp.
10. C. M. Zorn, *Der Brief an die Roemer. In Briefen an Glaubensbrueder* (Verlag und Druck von Johannes Herrmann, no date), 190 pp.
11. C. M. Zorn, *Die zwei Epistein St. Paul an die Corinther* (Zwickau: Verlag des Schriftvereins (C. Klaemer), no date), 312 pp.
12. C. M. Zorn, *Die eistliche und selige Freiheit eines Christenmenschen, Der Brief an die Galater* (Zwickau; verlag des Schriftvereins (C. Klaemer), no date), 120 pp.
13. Carl Manthey Zorn, *Der apostolische Brief an die Kolosser* (St. Louis: Concordia Publishing House, 1915), 545 pp.
14. C. M. Zorn, *Der erste Brief und die Thessaloniker* (Zwickau: Verlag des Schriftenvereins (C. Klaemer), no date), 55 pp.

15. C. M. Zorn, *Vom Hirtenamt. Die Briefe Pauli an Timotheus, Titus und Philemon* (Zwickau: Verlag und Druck von Johannes Herrmann, 1921), 264 pp.

16. C. M. Zorn, *Der Brief des Jacobus* (Zwickau: Verlag des Scriftvereins (C. Kiaemer), 192), 120.

17. C. M. Zorn, *Die 2, Epistle St. Petri und des St. Judae* (Milwaukee: Northwestern Publishing House, 1918), 30 pp.

18. Carl Manthey Zorn, *Die Epistle und die Hebrarer* (Milwaukee: Northwestern Publishing House, 1917), 68 p.

19. Carl Manthey Zorn, *Die Drei Episteln St. Johannis* (Zwickau: Verlag und Druck von Johannes Herrmann, 1914), 39 pp.

19a. *Die Offenbarung St. Johannes* (Zwickau: Verlag und Druck von Johannes Herrmann, 1961), 406 pp.

20. C. M. Zorn, *Die Psalmen. Der Himmelspilger Kost* (Zwickau: Verlag des Schriftvereins (E. Klaemer), 1921), 755 pp.

21. C. M. Zorn, *Weissagimgen und Wamungen atis dem Sprueche Salomonis* (Zwickau: Verlag und Druck von Johannes Herrmann, no date), 128 p.

22. C. M. Zorn, *Gottestrost. Der Prediger Salomonis* (Zwickau: Verlag and Druck von Johannes Herrmann, no date), 128 pp.

23. C. M. Zorn, *Jesusminne. Das Hohelied* (Zwickau: Verlag des Schriftvereins (E. Klaemer), no date), 132, Peter C. Krey, *Lo! The Bridegroom, The Song of Heavenly Love* based his fifty meditations on Zorn's *Jesusminne*, 1966, l39 pp.

24. Cf. footnote 8.

25. Cf. the title and subtitle of the book.

26. Zorn, *Der Brief and die Galater*, **op. cit.**, pp. 49,61,62,64,74,76,86,92,l02,l05.

27. C. M. Zorn, *Die ganze christliche Lehre in 1. Mose 1-5* (Zwickau: Verlag von Johannes Herrmann, no date).

28. Erwin Lueker, *Lutheran Cyclopedia* (St. Louis: Concordia Publishing House, 1954), pp. 1057-1058.

29. C. M. Zorn, Bekehrung und Gnadenwahl. Erster Teil Bekehrung. ZweiterTeil: Gnadenwahl (St. Louis: Concordia Publishing House, 1902), 64 and 100 pp.

30. *Handbuchfuerden Ersten Selbatunterricht in Gottes Wor* (Zwickau: Verlag des Schriftvereins (E. Kiaemer, no date).

31. *Christenfragen. Aus Gottes Word beatwortet* (Zwickau: Verlag des Schriftvereins, no date), 314 pp.

32. C. M. Zorn, *Von der Kindertaufer* (Zwickau: Verlag des Schriftvereins, no date).

33. C. M. Zorn, *Wie werde ich gewiss selig?* (Zwickau: Verlag des Schriftvereins, no date).

34. Carl Manthey Zorn, *Dase Gesetz* (Milwaukee: Northwestern Publishing House, no date), 207 pp.

35. Carl Manthey Zorn, *Hauspostille. Kurze Predigten auf alle Sonntage und die gebreuchligsten Festtage des Kirchenjahres* (Milwaukee: Northwestern Publishing House, 1914) 202 pp.

36. Carl Manthey Zorn, Manna. *Meditations on the Life and Teachings of Our Lord Jesus*, Second Edition, 1906, translated by John F. Sullivan, originally published by Zwickau: Verlag des Schriftenvereins, 1906, 960 pp.

37. C. M. Zorn, *Weide meine Laemmer* (Zwickau: Verlag des Schriftenvereins, no date).

38. Carl Manthey Zorn, *Lasset die Kindlein zu mir kommen* (Zwickau: Verlag von Johannes Herrmann, no date).

39. C. M. Zorn, *Vom Tanzen* (Zwikau: Verlag des Schriftvereins).

40. C. M. Zorn, *Darf ein Witman die Schwester seiner verstorbenen Frau heiraten?* (Zwickau: Verlag des Schriftvereins, no date).

41. C. M. Zorn, *Die heimliche Selbstbeflckung, Eine wahre Geschichte* (Zwicliau: Verlag des Schriftvereins, no date).

42. C. M. Zorn, *Ich halte es dafuer, dass dieser Zeit Leiden der Herrlichkeit nicht wert sei, die ans uns soil geoffenbart werden*. Predigt ueber Roln. 8,18 (Zwickau: Verlag des Schriftvereins, no date).

43. C. M. Zorn, *Ein kurzes Wort ueber die Logen* (Zwickau: Verlag des Schriftvereins, no date).

44. C. M. Zorn, Grossvaters Jugenderrinerungen (Zwickau: Verlag des Schriftvereins, 1921).

45. Cf. Ehler's statement about Zorn's position, **op. cit.**, "He was greatly troubled by increasing unfaithfulness to God's Word by professors at the Leipzig Mission Institute. Cf. Zorn's argument in *Bekehrung und Gnadenwahl*, **op. cit.**, p. 129. In all his writings the source for his theological beliefs was Holy Writ and only God's Word, Cf. *Hauspostille*, p. iii.

46. Zorn never cited the Apocrypha or Pseudepigrapha as source and basis for authentic divine teachings.

47. Zorn, *Vom Hirtenamt, Der Brief Pauli an Titus*, pp. 195-196.

48. Zorn totally rejected the historical-critical method which directly opposed the historical-grammatical method of interpretation, in all his writings and preaching he supported the historical-grammatical method. Cf. *Hauspostille*, iii. See how he uses it in his magnum opus, *Der Kolosserbrief*. Zorn believed in miracles, *Hauspostille*, p. 32 and in Biblical prophecy, *Hauspostille*, p. 4.

49. *Der Brief an die Roemer*, **op. cit.**, pp. 187-188.

50. Zorn, *Brief an die Thessaloner*, **op. cit.**, pp. 5-7.

51. For his German audience the best possible German translation was used, but he sometimes referred to the original languages to clear up a point.

52. Cf. Zorn, *Der Brief an die Galater*, op.cit., p. 50.

53. When the Biblical text said that Christ rose from the dead, that meant exactly what the words said. It is not mythological or figurative language. Zorn, *Die Korintherbriefe*, pp. 130-131.

54. This principle is followed in all his exegetical writings.

55. Proverbs, the Psalms and the Pauline Letters follow this hermeneneutical rule.

56. Psalm 2, quoted four times in the New Testament, speaks of the Messiah. Matthew 1:18 agrees with Isaiah 7:14 as describing the virginal Birth Zorn, Die Psaimen, op cit., pp. 3-6.

57. Zorn in *Der Heiland*, p. 29 claimed that Jesus' return from Egypt was the direct fulfillment of the prophecy in Hosea 1:11. Cf. also Zorn, *Der Brief an die Galater*, pp. 54-57.

58. Zorn, *Der Zeite Brief an Timotheus in Hirtenamt*, p. 171 (on 3:16); Zorn, *Der Brief an die Hebraer*, p. 43.

59. Cf. his explanation of James' justification by works in *Der Brief an Jacobus*, pp. 54-58.

60. Cf. Zorn, *Die Psalmen*, his interpretation of Psalm 2 and 8 is thoroughly Messianic; Der Heiland, (Vorwordt, p. iii; Hauspostille, p. 178.

61. Zorn, *Hauspostille*, p. 178.

62. Zorn, *Der Heiland*, pp. 238-239 believes the account of The Rich Man and Lazarus was not a parable, but an actual occurrence. Cf. Zorn's discussion of Christ's parables, *Der Heiland*, pp. 86-87.

63. Zorn, *Apostelgeschichte*, pp. 2, 7, 9. Whenever a New Testament writer quotes an Old Testament text, and claims it was a prophecy, Zorn expected this interpretation, Cf. Also *Der Heiland*, pp. 4-12.

64. Zorn, *Der Brief an die Galater*, pp. 75-78.

65. Zorn, *Die drei Epistein St. Johannis*, pp. 30-31.

66. Zorn distinguished between interpretation and application. However, he contended that Scripture must be applied to the reader so that the heavenly manah of God's Word can carry out its fourfold function as stated by Paul in 2 Timothy 3:16-17.

67. Ralph Bohlmann, *Principles of Biblical Interpretation in the Lutheran Confessions* (Revised Edition: St. Louis; Concordia Publishing House, 1983), 163 pp.

68. Wm. Dallmann, W. H. T. Dau and Th. Engelder, *Walther and the Church* (St. Louis: Concordia Publishing House, 1938, pp. 122-126; cf. also Raymond F. Surburg, 'Walther's Hermeneutical Principles," in Arthur Drevlow's, *C.F.W. Walther, The American Luther* (Mankato: Walther Press, 1987), pp. 95-114.

69. Louis Fuerbringer, *Theological Hermeneutics* (St. Louis: Concordia Publishing House, 1924).

70. Victor Mennicke, "Bible Interpretation," in Theodore Laetsch, Editor, *The Abiding Word* (St. Louis: Concordia Publishing House, 1947), pp. 35-58.

Questions

1. When did Carl Manthey Zorn live? ____
2. While a student at Erlangen University, he claimed ____.
3. What happened to Zorn? ____
4. The Leipzig Mission House prepared missionaries for ____.
5. Zorn mastered the ____ language.
6. What did some teachers of the Leipzig Mission Society deny? ____
7. Zorn appealed to ___ for help.
8. He served at ____ for thirty years.
10. The Concordia Historical Institute claims Zorn wrote ____.
11. ____ copies of Zorn's Der Heiland were printed.
12. Zorn argued that all fundamental doctrines are to be found in ____.
13. What was the Schwagerehe? ____
14. ____ is the true source for instruction for faith and life.
15. What does Sensus literalis unus est mean? ____
16. Scripture interprets ____.
17. Zorn's Hermeneutics is like that of ____.

The Influence of Eugene Nida On Bible Translators And Bible Translations

Christian News, May 5, 1997

The founder of the Wycliffe Bible Translators was Cameron Townsend, who had the ambitious vision to make available to the people of the world the Word of God in their respective languages.[1] This is surely a great vision. However, with this ambitious undertaking there developed simultaneously a method of translation that resulted (either knowingly or unknowingly) into the relativization of the Bible by a new system of Bible translation.

A significant contributor to the current philosophy and method of Bible translation has been Eugene Nida, an expert in Biblical language and a specialist in linguistics, which he developed and incorporated in his theory of Bible translation. A Dutch evaluator of Nida stated: "Eugene Nida is the most influential person in the field of Bible and translation in our time."[2] This fact found its expression in his position as "Translations Research Coordinator for the United Bible Societies." He has been the Executive Secretary for the American Bible Society. He is the author of a considerable number of important and scholarly books dealing with Bible translation and the science of communications.[3a] Through Nida's influence modern Bible translation employs the principle of "dynamic equivalence."[3b] The United Bible Societies have officially adopted this theory of Bible translation as their guide for making the Scriptures available to the nations of the world. The Bible Societies have set as one of their priorities to use their funds primarily for the translation of the Bible into colloquial languages. Paul Ellingsworth wrote in the *Bible Translator*, 23 (1972): "Since Bible Societies never have enough money for everything, this means that it is unlikely that they will in the future support translations in traditional ecclesiastical languages."[4]

Nida and Dynamic Equivalence

Nida has exercised a great influence on Bible translators and their translations by his sponsorship of the theory of "dynamic equivalence," a concept which existed long before Nida's times. However, he appears to be credited with its promotion and given special credit for its usage. As Van Brugge has noticed: "In dynamic equivalence translation the focus in Bible translation has been shifted from the text to the response of receptor."[5] Thus Nida has asserted: "The older focus in translating was the form of the message. . . The new focus, however, has shifted from the form of the message to the response of the receptor. Therefore, what one must determine is the response of the receptor to the translated message."[6]

Wycliffe and Nida's Objectives in Bible Translation

One might compare Nida's objective in translating the Bible with that of John Wycliffe (1320-1384) who made the first translation into English from the Latin Vulgate. "Since the laity should know the faith, it should be taught in whatever language it is most easily comprehended. Men ought to desire only the truth and freedom of the holy Gospel, and to accept man's Law and Ordinances only in as much as they have been grounded in Holy Scripture."[7] Nida defined translation in this way: "To translate is to try to stimulate in the new reader in the new language the same reaction to the text the original author wished to stimulate in his and immediate readers."[8]

Wycliffe and Nida Compared

Wycliffe, who believed in the sovereignty of God and the verbal inspiration of the Bible, wanted to provide English Christians, ignorant of the Bible, the Word of God in their vernacular, so that they might compare God's Word with the teachings the clergy-dominated Church taught. From the Wycliffe translation from Latin into English, it became apparent to the English readers of the fourteenth-century that many teachings and practices of the Roman Catholic Church were either not found in Scripture, or even contradicted God's revealed truth.[9] The problem with Nida's proposal in translating, according to Heldenbrand, is "that the translator creates the readers' response by manipulating the text of the Scriptures and so results in the fact that it makes the missiologist and the translator into experts who have the power to define the Scriptural message for the masses, a situation parallel to the one Wycliffe faced with the fourteenth century clergy. This approach ignores the sinfulness of man when it relies so completely on the abilities and integrity of the missiologist and translator. God is the only one worthy of such trust because he is omnipotent, omniscient, and holy."

Nida's Communication Theory and Dynamic Equivalence

For many Biblical students the term "dynamic equivalence" simply means any non-idiolect method. An idiolect translation endeavors to preserve the idiom of the Hebrew, Aramaic and Greek texts in translation. To some people "dynamic equivalence" simply means that the translator takes into account the distinct manner of expression in the language into which he translates, often called the "receptor language."[10] The manner in which Bible Societies have used the "dynamic equivalence" principle reveals after close scrutiny that more is involved in their translation methodology. Van Bruggen claimed: "The latter emphasis reflects the fact that the theory involves more than a view of language. It entails a certain perspective on both the nature of communication and the character of the Bible."[11] There have been those who have pleaded for freer translations; the new and distinctive element in the theory of "dynamic equivalence" is in its concept of man and the Bible. It is the new Nida theory of dynamic equivalence that has led Bible societies to place emphasis on Bible helps, aids on Bible translation, on reading helps, and similar interpretative aids to promote different meanings for Biblical texts under the guise of aiding the receptors.

An Examination of Nida's Views on Communication

According to Nida the purpose of translation may be said to establish contact between the author and the ultimate reader by means of a message. The aim of the translator is to promote communication.[12] However, it must be recognized that a person's theory of communication influences the direction of his translational effort. Nida developed certain views about communication which have affected the manner the original Hebrew, Aramaic, (Old Testament), Koine Greek of the New Testament are rendered. It is Nida's position that because of altered views about communication that new translations are needed. Nida's theories about Bible translation were not determined by modern linguistics, as many believe, but by his theories about communication. Because of his views on communication, Nida has insisted that all old Bible translations needed to be revised and in all translations for those not having a Bible, that his views needed to be followed. Nida thus claimed that the altered theories of Communications had implications for Bible translations. Previous to the introduction of Nida's views on communication, that the latter occurred at the level of information-transfer, but now Nida contended the communication process must occur within a total cultural pattern.[13] In the past, a translator had sole regard for the message to be communicated, but in the last years, the message of the text is connected with the receptor, whether at the individual or group level. According to Nida's article "Implications of Contemporary Linguistics," it is necessary that the message must be set forth in such a way that receptors may decode it "within the limits of their channel capacity."[14]

Take for example the preaching of an eighth century Hebrew prophet to his audience, that same message will not communicate to the twentieth-century readers what it did to the eighth century audience. To make the Bible communicate, it must take into consideration the culture of the twentieth-century which must be presented in such a way as to be communicating and speaking to today's problems. Communication according to this theory involves the circle of the speaker, the listener, the message, and this circle is closed by time and culture. This circle of communication is broken when the difference between Biblical and modern culture is not considered. Thus Nida declared: "Similarly, in the biblical account the holy kiss, the wearing of veils, women speaking in the church, and wrestling with an angel all have different meanings than in our own culture."[15] The problem with Nida is that he fails to recognize that the historical-grammatical method of interpretation takes into account the historical and cultural backgrounds of a Biblical text. Nida operated with a hermeneutical system different from that followed by conservative Protestant scholars.

Form and Message in Theological Construction

In developing what Nida calls "a Biblical view of communication," he postulated five "basic presuppositions about language communication."[16] They became the foundation of his theory of knowledge by drawing two deductions which he called "implications of the biblical view of communication." In his book **Message and Missions,** Nida asserted:

1. Verbal symbols are only labels and are of human origin.
2. Verbal symbols, as labels for concepts, have priority in communicating of truth.
3. Language and symbols reflect a meaningful relationship between symbol and behavior.
4. Communication is power.
5. Divine revelation takes place in the form of a "dialogue."

From these five presuppositions Nida drew the following conclusions: 1. The Bible revelation is not absolute, and 2. All divine revelation is essentially incarnational.[17]

Critique of Nida's Views

Relative to the declaration that the "Bible revelation is not absolute," Nida is claiming that all human language is a human invention and essentially labels Biblical statements as relativistic. Human language is said to have human limitations and so also do the statements of the Bible, and consequently they are not authoritative. His second presupposition averred that all revelation is essentially "incarnational."[18] These positions of Nida turn out to be of such a nature as to limit God as to what he can say and what mankind can actually consider what God would have them believe and what He can reasonably expect them to do. Nida's communication theory assumes that God cannot really communicate with his creatures in a meaningful way and mankind cannot really ascertain God's will.

Christ certainly never gave the impression, as revealed in the Four Gospels, that his contemporaries could not understand the Old Testament or that they could not comprehend what He taught them. The Lord and His Apostles understood statements made by Moses just as the latter intended them to be understood and heeded. As the receptors of the Mosaic message they grasped exactly what Moses had intended to convey. The Lord and His disciples quoted from the Psalms, Isaiah, Jeremiah and other Old Testament Scriptures and assumed that the Jews could correctly know, as the receptors, what the God-inspired writers had set forth.

The Importance of Words

Words make up sentences. Sentences make up paragraphs; paragraphs are organized into segments, segments are an essential component of a section and sections are the main divisions and constitute the literary structure of a Biblical book. The meaning of the Ten Commandments did not change over the centuries. There never has been doubt about their words and what they teach. They have the same meaning at Christ's time as when first spoken and later recorded on two tables of stone.

Nida's Violation of the Analogy of Faith

The analogy of faith is that hermeneutical principle that sets forth the total Divine Teaching on a doctrine.[19] It is the claim of the Holy Scriptures that the canonical Scriptures of both testaments was given by the Holy Spirit and is as Paul said "God-breathed" (2 Tim. 3:15). The words of the Old and New Testaments were God's words and had one intended meaning.[20] The clarity of and perspicuity of the Bible are clearly enunciated.[21] Paul instructed the Corinthians that "the unspiritual man" cannot receive the things of the Spirit of God, which by contrast would aver that the "spiritual" man can receive the teachings of the spirit of God. The God-spirited Words of the Bible can be understood and comprehended and there can be expected on the part of reader or hearer a response and obedience to the instruction given. If the Bible cannot be correctly understood, why would the Psalmist describe God's Word as "a light to our path and a lamp to our feet." God's revelation is clear and can and should be responded to. The Bible presupposes that the regenerate person can understand and respond to God's revelation. If the Word of God were unclear and difficult to understand, one might ask how could Christ say that on judgment day people would be judged by the Word of God He had given His followers? If God's message was not comprehensible, how could people be judged for failure to keep it as will be the case on Judgment day?

The Place of the Holy Spirit in Effective Communication

Jesus promised His disciples the Holy Spirit who would guide them in the correct comprehension of the Divine Message. Jesus informed His disciples that: "I have many more things to say unto you, but you cannot hear them now." These words uttered on the night before He died, stated that His revelation was not yet complete, but that He would give them further revelation. Thus in 14:25-26 it is stated: "These things I have spoken unto you, while abiding with you, but the Helper the Holy Spirit, whom the Father will send in My name, He will teach you all things and bring to your remembrance all that I have said unto you." Again in John the Savior informed the disciples: "I have many things to say to you but you cannot bear them now. But when, He, the Spirit of Truth comes. He will **guide you in all truth;** for He will not speak on His own, He will speak to you what is to come" (John 16:13).

Jesus claimed adequate sufficiency for His teachings. In the post-Ascension period Christ through the Holy Spirit, made known what mankind needed to know. Christ while in Galilee on a mountain commanded His disciples to preach the Gospel and to teach **all things** He had given them to proclaim (Matthew 28:20).

Nida's Attacks on the Words of the Bible

In his book **Message and Missions** Nida attacked the words of Holy Writ when he wrote: "Even if a truth is given only in words, it has not been translated into life. Only then does the Word become life to the receptor. The words are in a sense nothing in and of themselves."[22] It is true that the Word of God benefits only when correctly understood and its words are believed and the receptors live and perform according to it.[23]

716

However, the receptor's response does not vitiate the content and the reliability of the objective Biblical text. The Bible is true and authoritative irrespective of whether it is disobeyed or obeyed. The Biblical reader needs to keep in mind and separate: 1. the text; 2. its communication or content; 3. the receptor or the text's reader. The text is a God-given reality and is the norm of judgment for a person's life and deeds. Nida's debasement of individual words is dangerous.[24] The Bible teaches that its words were taught by the Spirit of God Himself. Thus Paul declared: "This is what we speak, not in **words** taught by a human wisdom but in **words taught by the Spirit of God.** Expressing spiritual truths in spiritual words (I Cor. 2:13)."

All words in a sentence are important. In Galatians Paul bases his argumentation on the singular of the word "seed." "Now the promises were given to Abraham and his seed (sperma). It does not say "and to seeds" referring to many, but to your seed (Gen. 12:27), referring to one—and this is Christ (Gal. 3:16-17)." In Revelation the Apostle John warns the readers not to add or detract from the Christ given messages, otherwise there would follow serious and dire consequences (22:18-19). Paul calls the Old Testament words the "oracles of God (Rom. 3:2)." Paul argues that even though the Bible is a human document, it is to be treated with respect and confidence, and the Word of God cannot be set aside or added to. Here are passages which emphasize the importance of adhering to the text: Deut. 4:2; 12:32; Prov. 30:6, Rev. 22:18-20.

Nida's Concept of Incarnational Revelation

Nida asserted: "All divine revelation is essentially incarnational."[25] Here the word "incarnational" is derived from the word "incarnation," a theological term which meant that God's Son took on himself human form, human flesh and blood. During the State of Humiliation Jesus accepted human limitations. For instance, Jesus stated that he did not know the day of the Second Coming. There were occasions when he abstained from using the divine power which he possessed by virtue of the communication of attributes and the unity of the God-Man.[26] When the Bible is described as incarnational that is interpreted as meaning that the Bible as a human-divine book has limitations. So God cannot reveal Himself to mankind in the Holy Scriptures. So the Bible, though God's Word, cannot completely reveal God's will to mankind infallibly and errorless.[27] This position of Nida does not agree with the Bible's claim to be the truth. Paul's assertion in 2 Timothy 3:15-17 with its fourfold purpose of God's intended revelation would not be true.

Nida argued that the Bible, though God's Word, is in human form and this implies that the Bible has human limitations and further would mean that God cannot completely reveal Himself to mankind in language of fallible men.[28] This position of Nida does not agree with the Bible's claims. Since the Bible is Spirit-breathed and its Spirit guided authors were born along by the Holy Spirit (2 Peter 1:21) it is as Paul assured the Roman congregation that the Old Testament was given for hope and as the same Apostle instructed Timothy that the Bible of the Old

Covenant made people wise unto salvation by creating faith in Christ Jesus. The same Scriptures were able to prepare and aid men and women to live God pleasing lives (Romans 15:3; 2 Timothy 3:15-17).

The Origin of the Theory of Dynamic Equivalence

An investigation of the theory of dynamic equivalence reveals that it has grown out of views developed by modern anthropology, sociology and was further determined by certain forms of linguistics as developed by Nida. Van Bruggen defined dynamic equivalence as: "Quite simply, the theory of dynamic equivalence says that the translator must consider not only the difference between the **language** and the prophets and their meaning but also the difference in the conditioning of the cultural pattern of the two periods. We are faced with not only with a different language, but also with different receptors."[29]

Nida's Erroneous Concept of the Nature of Man

Heldebrand sees in Nida's view of language an attack on God's creation of man. God created man in His own likeness and His own image. God endowed Adam with the gift of language. Man's linguistic ability was a gift of the Creator.[30] Adam and Eve were able to speak and communicate with God. Eve also understood the lies uttered by Satan through the medium of a snake. God gave Adam and Eve directions for the continuation of life and they also grasped them. After the Fall Cain understood Yahweh's remarks to him and showed that he could totally grasp what God had told him. Nida has assumed that language is a human creation and not a divine gift. Nida postulated that language symbols reflect a meaningful relationship between symbols and behavior. He reduced the Biblical revelation to the Neo-orthodox concept of "the event," and reduced Biblical revelation to that which is "apprehendable by men." In his book, *Message and Missions* he wrote: "The focus of the Biblical revelation is the event, God is revealed as one who acts, speaks, and performs miracles, but He does not describe His essence. From the Biblical point of view, the ultimate reality apprehensible by men is not to be found in isolated qualities in Biblical assertions but in behavior relationships expressed by concrete actions in the realm of time. Language is seen thus as a set of symbols to describe behavior, not a mystical code to the eternal essence. In this sense Nida's Biblical view of epistemology is strikingly contemporary, for symbols are being more and more viewed in terms of their **functional relationships,** rather than on the basis of any hidden conceptual reality."[31] Nida's claim that human language is unable to convey God's essence must be labelled as false and dangerous. The truth is that many Biblical verses assert God's essence. "The Lord, our God, is one Lord. (Deut. 6:4;" "God is Love (1 John 4:16)." Christ said: "I am the Light of the World '(John 8:12).

Heldenbrand correctly rejected Nida's views when he responded:

"While it is no doubt true that human language can never express the complete essence of God, it is patently false to say with Nida that language can therefore be unable of expressing anything at all about God's essence."[32]

When Nida claims that words cannot reveal the divine essence, that is the very objection the Mohammedans have and still make against the doctrine of the Trinity, in *Practical Anthropology* Nida took up the question: "Are we really Monotheists?" and answered in this manner: "In following the Biblical symbols which grant full attributes of personality to all persons of the Trinity, we almost immediately lead people to conceive God, Christ, and the Holy Spirit more as three than one." According to Nida God did not give eternal truths, but God accommodated Himself to the times in which the Biblical books were written. Thus Biblical revelation is expressed by time-bound forms of communication. God revealed Himself through the imperfections of language. Nida warns that it is wrong to canonize the imperfect form recorded in Scripture. Thus when the Bible is translated, it must give expressions in different cultures that had their own limitations. Because of the time-boundedness of the Biblical writings the European Bible Societies adopted the following statement: "In this dialogue between the Bible Societies and developments in biblical studies, we may well find the authority of the Bible being questioned. This need not disturb us, for the Bible is not a collection of recipes or dogmatic statements; it speaks for itself."[33]

The Denial of the Absolute Character of the Bible

Nida claimed in *Message and Missions* that Biblical criticism is not "absolute," citing as proof Paul's statement "now we see through a glass darkly" (1 Cor. 13:12) and the Bible cannot, because it is incarnated, can have no absolutes. Because human language is limited, it cannot be a vehicle for supernatural and eternal truths. Literal accuracy is not deemed important for Nida.[34] Correctly Van Bruggen has said about this view: "To them the power of a translation does not lie in its literal association with the original text, but in its reaching modern man. Loyalty to the revelation of the incarnate Word, then means that the needs of the receptor are given priority over the original form of the message."[35]

For Nida and his followers the central focus is not so much what the text says but in its transmission to the receptor's response as to what the Biblical text asserts. Van Bruggen claimed that "it is therefore, a deliberate formulation of principle when the Bible societies today say that they support the churches in the communication of the biblical message in all its aspects."[36] At the World Council of Churches Assembly, held in Nairobi, 1975, the following positions were taken as representing the purpose and activity of the Bible societies and also discussed the matter of principles for Bible translation.[36] The question was raised: What is the role of our present context for the interpretation of a Biblical text? In answering this question the representatives of the UBS claimed the original context must be ascertained. The original languages needed to be mastered and the historical background determined. But the UBS executives averred, that the translators and exegetes had their own social and cultural contexts. Bible translators supposedly are aware of this fact. The result has been that now Bible translators have come to realize the importance of the receptor-language and of dynamic equivalence in translation.[37] The UBS further reports "Some exegetes and theologians still tend to ignore this important influence on their own context. There is no such thing as a timeless, objective understanding of the Bible and the Christian faith. All exegesis and interpretation of biblical texts are colored by our dogmatic and cultural presuppositions, by the questions of our time. This is not simply a statement of fact, but a recognition of the very nature of God's Word. Biblical texts lose their quality as God's living Word if they are not continuously reinterpreted for new times and situations. Such new interpretations can of course be false, just as it would certainly be false to "freeze" biblical texts in their form of past interpretation.[38]

The presuppositions of dynamic equivalence are to be rejected for four reasons according to Van Bruggen: 1. It rejects the orthodox doctrine of the unity of unchanged divine and human natures of Christ by making words subject to the limitations of the first century. 2. It denies that the Bible transcends the time it was written. God's revelation aims to restore communication between God and man but cannot itself be described as a past communication event. 3. It confuses the people present and the people addressed and thus limits the horizon of God's speaking in the Bible to the centuries of the past. 4. It fails to account for the creation of man in God's image, the unity of the human race in Adam, and thus its unity in guilt and punishment.[39]

Heldenbrand in his book, *Christianity and New Evangelical Philosophies,* made this evaluation of Nida's dynamic equivalence: 1. It is an expression of relativism. 2. It makes the limitations of human language absolute. 3. It relativises the Bible by submitting #2. 4. It relativises God by submitting His revelatory activity to #2. 5. Theologically, it is to be classified as an example of the New Hermeneutic, a mutation of Neo-orthodoxy. 6. It is indivisibly linked to other emphases of ethnotheology such as contextualization, and to its method which is adapting the Gospel by borrowing from non-Christian religious systems. 7. It is an attack on the grammatico-historical approach to the interpretation of the Bible.[40]

The Good News Bible, A Product of Dynamic Equivalence Theory

The American Bible Society, under the influence of Nida's supervision, completed in 1976 The Good News Bible, also called Today's English Version. According to a statement of the United Bible Societies this version is to be used throughout the world and it may be considered the best example available of the use of dynamic equivalence methodology. Van Bruggen in *The Future of the Bible* has shown on pages 85-96 some of the weaknesses and errors of the TEV. Not only does the TEV differ greatly from the *King James Version,* but it is also much freer when compared with *The Revised Standard Version* of 1946, 1952 and 1960. The Old Testament was the cooperative effort of seven critical Old Testament scholars, who allowed their higher criticism to affect their rendering of the 39 books of the Old Covenant Scriptures.[41]

720

Translations employing the dynamic equivalence hermeneutic produce translations often far removed from the original Biblical texts. This was the judgment of Steiner and Weber about the German version of TEV."[42]

Footnotes

1. Ethel Emily Wallis and Mary Angela Bannett, *Two Thousand Tongues to Go. The Story of the Wycliffe Bible Translation* (New York: Harper and Row Publishers, No Date), p. vi.

2. Jacob Van Bruggen. *The Future of the Bible* (New York: Thomas Nelson, I.C., 1878), p. 68.

3. **Ibid.**, pp. 69-84.

3a. Eugene Nida, *God's Word in Man's Language* (New York: Harper & Brothers, 1951). Eugene Nida, *Bible Translating* (New York American Bible Society, 1947). Eugene Nida, *Toward a Science of Translating* (Leiden: E.J. Brill, 1964). Eugene Nida and Charles R. Taber. Published for the United Societies by E.J. Bill, Leiden, 1974). Eugene A. Nida, *Translating Meaning English Language Institute* (San Dimas, Cal. English Language Institute, 1982); Eugene A. Nida, William D. Reyburn, *Meaning Across Cultures* (Maryknoll, New York: Orbis Books, 1981); Jan De Waard, Eugene A. Nida *From One Language to Another* (New York: Thomas Nelson, Publishers, 1986); Eugena A. Nida, *Signs, Sense, Translation* (Roggebaai, Cape Town, South Africa, 1984; E. A. Nida, J.P. Louw, A.H. Snyman, J.V.W. Cronje, *Style and Discourse* (Roggebaai: Cape Town, South Africa, 1983. Eugene A. Nida co-authored with a number of scholars Handt for Translators; also *Guides for Translators*. He has also written a plethora of articles for scholarly journals.

4. Paul Elligsworth, *Bible Translator*, 23 (1972), p. 220.

5. Bruggen, **op. cit.,** cf Appendix I, pp. 151-168; also pp. 67-83.

6. Eugene A. Nida, *Message and Mission* (New York: Harper and Brothers, 1960), p. 224.

7. *Wycliffe New Testament, Sexcentenary Edition* (Printed in England, International Bible Publications: Kinprint International, 1986), p. vii., as cited by Richard L. Heldenbrand, *Christianity and New Evangelical Philosophies* (Second Edition, Completely Revised, Warsaw, Indiana Words of Life, 1993), p. 38.

8. Heldenbrand, **op. cit.**, pp. 40-41.

9. **Ibid.**

10. Eugene H. Glasman, *The Debate Translation. What Makes a Bible Translation Good?* (Downers Grove, 111; Intervarsity Press, 1951), pp. 52, 66-67, 75-76.

11. Heldenbrand, **op. cit.**, pp. 41-42.

12. Eugene Nida, *Bible Translating* (New York: American Bible Society, 1947), p. 12.

13. Eugene A. Nida, and Charles Taber, *The Theory and Practice of Translation*, **op. cit.**, p. 12.

14. Eugene A. Nida, "Implications of Contemporary Linguistics for Biblical Scholarships," *Journal of Biblical Literature*, 91 (1972), pp. 73-89, especially p. 76.

15. Van Bruggen, *The Future of the Bible*, **op. cit.**, p. 70.

16. Eugene A. Nida, *Message and Mission* (New York: Harper & Brothers, 1960), pp. 224-225.

17. **Ibid.**, p. 225.

18. Louis Matthew Sweet, *The Study of the English Bible*, (New York: Association Press, 1914), pp. 96-125.

19. George Schodde, *Outlines of Biblical Hermeneutics* (Columbus: Lutheran Book Concern, 1917), pp. 192-193.
20. William Dallmann, W.H. Dau and Theodore Engelder, *Walther and the Church* (St. Louis: Concordia Publishing House, 1938), p. 124.
21. Francis Pieper, *Christian Dogmatics* (St. Louis: Concordia Publishing House, 1950), I, p. 320.
22. Nida, *Message and Mission*, **op. cit.**, p. 226.
23. **Ibid.**, p. 226.
24. Nida, *Message and Missions*, **op. cit.**, p. 226.
25. **Ibid.**, p. 225; Heldenbrand, **op. cit.**, pp. 42-43.
26. Francis Pieper, *Christian Dogmatics* (St. Louis: Concordia Publishing House, 1951), H, p. 82.
27. Heldenbrand, **op. cit.**, pp. 45. 48.
28. Bruggen, **op. cit.**, p. 76.
29. **Ibid.**, p. 71.
30. Heldenbrand, **op. cit.** p. 45.
31. Nida, *Message and Missions*, p. 224.
32. Heldenbrand, **op. cit.**, p. 46.
33. Nida, "Are We Really Monotheists," p. 50.
34. Bruggen, **op. cit.**, p. 76.
35. **Ibid.**, p. 76.
36. *Working Plan for Europe*, p. 12.
37. *Bulletin of the United Bible Societies 101* (1975), p. 21.
38. **Ibid.**, p. 21.
39. Bruggen, **op. cit.**, p. 84.
40. Richard L. Heldenbrand, *Christianity and New Evangelical Philosophies* (Warsaw, Words of Life, 1993), p. 54.
41. Eugene A. Nida, *Good News for Everyone* (Waco, Texas: Word Book Publishers, 1971), p. 48.
42. R. Steiner, *Neue Bibleübersetzungen vorgedtellt, verglichen und gewerted* (Neukirchen: Neukirchener Verlag, 1975), pp. 105-115; K/Weber, *Bibleübersetzungen unter der lupe. Handbuch für Bibleleser* (Wetzler: Schulte, 1972), pp. 142-151.

Questions

1. Who founded Wycliffe Bible Translators? ____
2. Who was Eugene Nida? ____
3. In dynamic equivalence translation the focus has been shifted from ____ to ____.
4. Who made the first Bible translation from the Vulgate to English? ____
5. The problem with Nida is that he fails ____.
6. Nida operates with a hermeneutical system different than that ____.
7. Nida concluded that Bible revelation is not ____.
8. Jesus promised His disciples that the Holy Spirit would ____.
9. Nida's debasement of individual words is ____.
10. Nida's dynamic equivalence is an expression of ____.
11. The American Bible Society in 1976 completed the ____.

A Jewish Book
The Jewishness of the New Testament:
Jews and Judaism in the New Testament

Christian News, June 16, 1997

Liberal Protestant, liberal Lutheran, liberal Roman Catholic and Jewish critical savants have advocated wrong views about Jews and Judaism and their relationship to data of the New Testament.[1] Their views are in conflict with what Holy Writ teaches about the Jews and their relationship to Jesus and St. Paul. The authors of the 27 books of the New Testament were penned between A.D. 45 and A.D. 100. Although orthodox and liberal Jewry ignores, reinterprets, and often rejects what the New Covenant Scriptures say about Jesus and Judaism, it will be the purpose of this presentation to show that the New Testament is truly a Jewish book and that anti-supernaturalistic scholars have not set forth who Jesus was and what he taught and, have not correctly set forth the truth relative to Christ's relationship to His nation. Twentieth-century liberal Protestantism and anti-Christian Judaism have rejected the inspired character of the New Testament, repudiated the deity of Christ and His saviorhood. This essay will also show that there were Jews who accepted the fact that the Messianic prophecies of the Old Testament were fulfilled in Jesus of Nazareth. In order to understand the New Testament writings, the reader needs a good knowledge of the 39 books of the Old Testament as well as a thorough knowledge of the 27 books of the New Testament.

Different Names for Abraham's Descendants

There are different names employed in the Old Testament for Abraham's descendants. The names of "Hebrew,"[2] "Jew,"[3] and "Israelite" are all used as designations for the descendants of Abraham, Isaac and Jacob. "Hebrew" appears before the name "Jew" appears in the Old Testament revelation. The plural "Israelites" is found at least 16 times in various Old Testament books. The word "Hebrew" is employed for the earlier "Hebrew person." Goddard wrote: "I Samuel 14:21 may suggest that the terms are to be equated. Jewish people quite uniformly have 'Israel' and the children of Israel' (later Jews) in referring to themselves, finding in such terminology treasured religious and national associations. Foreigners spoke of them as "Hebrews" (Ex. 1:16; 2:6) and they so identified Abraham's descendants when speaking to non-Jews (Gen. 40:15; Ex. 10:3; Jonah 1:9) in contexts involving contrasts between Israelites and those of other nations, also the same phenomenon appears (Gen. 43:32; Ex. 1:15;2:11; I Sam. 13:3; 14:21)."[4]

The Designation "Jew"

The word "Jew" refers to a descendant of Judah, the name was applied to members of Judah (2 Kings 16:8; 18:26,28; 25:25; 2 Chron. 32:18; Esther 2:5; 3:4; 5:15; 6:10; 8:7; Jer. 32:12; 38:19; 52:228). The word "Jew" was applied to Hebrews who were members of the Southern Kingdom (2 Kings 16:6; 25:25), but later was extended to any person who returned from the Babylonian Captivity. As most of the exiles came from Judah and as they were the main historical representatives of ancient Israel the term "Jews" finally came to comprehend all the Hebrew race throughout the world (Esther 2:5; Matthew 2:2). As early as the time of Hezekiah, the language used by the Hebrews was called "Jewish." The adjective "Jewish" was only applied to the Jews' language or speech (2 Kings 18:26; Nehemiah 13:24; Isaiah 36:11-12).[5]

Jews in the New Testament
In the Gospels "Jews" (always in the plural) is the usual term for Israelites and Jews and Gentiles are often contrasted (Mark 7:3; John 2:6), thus Paul warns against "Jewish fables" in Titus 1:14 and writes about Jewish religion in Galatians 1:13-14. The New Testament also employs the term "Judaize" which Paul utilizes to designate Jewish teaching which was added to the Gospel of justification by faith.[6]

The designation "Israelite" occurs twice in the New Testament, in John 1:47 and Romans to designate descendants of Abraham.

The Jewish or Hebraic Character
of the New Testament Scriptures
The New Testament may be called a "Jewish book," for all of the writers of the New Testament were Jews, with the exception of Luke, who was a proselyte of righteousness. Matthew, Mark, John, Paul, James, Jude, the author of Hebrews, were all descendants of Abraham, Isaac and Jacob. The New Testament presupposes the Old Testament to be the Word of God. Not only in the New Testament are direct quotations and allusions found, but Old Testament personalities are part and parcel of New Testament literature. A number of New Testament books would be meaningless without a knowledge of the Old Testament as well as references in the New would be meaningless without a knowledge of the Old Testament Scriptures. In fact, the New Testament purports to be a continuation and fulfillment of the Old Testament teachings and theology. The Messiah foretold in various Old Testament writings, is said by Christ and His apostles to have been fulfilled in Jesus of Nazareth. The three major divisions of the Old Testament, the Law, the Prophets, and the Kethubim (whose first books' was Psalms) spoke about Jesus death and resurrection (Luke 24:25-27; 44-46; 1 Cor. 15:3).

How the New Testament Writers Employ
the Old Testament The Gospel of St. Matthew
The first Gospel was written by a publican, by the name of Levi, or Matthew. He penned his memoirs of Christ's life to show that many of the Old Testament prophecies were fulfilled in Jesus of Nazareth. The purpose of Matthew's Gospel is disclosed in part by the fact that it was written for Jewish readers and is thoroughly Jewish in complexion. [7] The

object of the writer seems to have been to connect the Law with the Gospel; to show the relation of the Old Dispensation to the New; "to connect the memories of his readers with their hopes; to show that the Lord of the Christians was the Messiah of the Jews." Whenever there is an event or happening, a prophecy about the Messiah, Matthew begins the reference to it with the phrase: "This happened which was spoken by the prophet." This assertion occurs over 30 times in the First Gospel.

The Relation of the Gospels to the Old Testament

No one can read the Gospels without realizing that their story had its beginning somewhere else.[8] The first verse in Matthew speaks of David and Abraham. The second and third verses in Mark refer to "the prophets" and quotes from Malachi and Isaiah. The fifth verse of Luke mentions Abia and Aaron. The seventeenth verse in John speaks of Moses, and the twenty-first verse of Elijah, and without some knowledge of the Old Testament these assertions could not be understood. The Four Gospels are replete with many quotations and allusions to many different books of the Old Covenant Scriptures. Although Matthew's Gospel was probably not the first to be composed, Matthew is placed first as being most intimately connected with the Old Testament.[9] The truth is that Matthew's Gospel is saturated with the Old Testament. The purpose of Matthew's design was to prove the Messiahship of Jesus, and to prove that truth, he had to secure his proofs from the Old Testament.

References to the Old Testament may be divided into two classes, **citations** and **allusions;** citations being quotations, and allusions being references. Scroggie approximates about 130 references with 53 quotations and 76 allusions. There are approximately 129 Old Testament references: 53 of them are citations, and 76 are allusions. Every part of the three-part canon: The Law, the Prophets and Psalms (Luke 24:44) are cited or mentioned. These references are taken from 25 of the 39 books. The Books referred to are: The Pentateuch, I Samuel, I Kings, 2 Chronicles, Nehemiah, Job, Psalms, Proverbs, Isaiah, Jeremiah, Ezekiel, Daniel, Hosea, Amos, Jonah, Micah, Zephaniah, Zechariah, and Malachi. The frequency of quotations in certain books is Psalms 29, Deuteronomy 27, Isaiah 26, the prophet Jeremiah has 13, Leviticus 13, Exodus 12, to Genesis and Zechariah 9 each, to Daniel 9, and 3 each to Numbers, Ezekiel, Micah and Malachi.[10]

Luke's Gospel and the Old Testament

Some have made the claim that Luke has little in it of the Old Testament, but this is not correct. There are said to be about 130 references, that is quotations and allusions in Matthew and between 90-100 in Luke.[11] It has been pointed out that the difference between Matthew's and Luke's use of the Old Testament is determined by their character and purpose. Matthew, being the Gospel of the Jews, builds heavily upon the Old Testament, and often such expressions occur as "that it might be fulfilled," which was spoken," "was said," "this was done that," but in Luke little is said about fulfillment of prophecy, because that would not greatly interest readers (3:4; 4:21; 21:22; xxii, 37; 24:44). In Luke the Old Testament references may be classified as 1. direct quotations; 2. direct references, but not citations, and 3. echoes of Old Testament passages.

John, the Apostle and Evangelist, and the Old Testament

Dr. Plummer claimed that the Fourth Gospel is saturated with the thoughts, imagery, and language of the Old Testament.[12] Likewise Bishop Westcott has said "that without the basis of the Old Testament, the Gospel of John is an insoluble mystery." Biblical scholars' estimates vary as to the number of references in the Fourth Gospel's references to the Old Testament.[13] Thus Dr. S. Davidson claims that there are 26; Westcott and Hort list 20; yet another gives the high number of 44. Scroggie believes that there are probably no less than 124 references which are not understandable apart from books of the Old Testament.[14]

Some of the Old Testament references are found in Christ's assertions, others are found in the assertions of the Evangelist, of John the Baptist, of Philipp, of Nicodemus, of Nathanael, of Peter, of Pilate, of Martha, the Jews, the People, the Pharisees, certain Samaritans and the woman of Samaria.

In the quotations and allusions there are references to Abraham, Jacob, Joseph, Moses, Elijah, David, Isaiah, Micah, Zechariah and the Prophets.[15] Some of these names occur in quotations, others are found in allusions, some are evident in references particular and general, both direct and indirect. There are in John's Gospel 19 quotations and there are references to the Books of Exodus, Numbers, Deuteronomy, Psalms, Isaiah and Zechariah. There are about 105 allusions and they are from 12 books: Each book of the Pentateuch, 2 Samuel, Psalms, Proverbs, Isaiah, Micah and Zechariah.[16]

Seven times the author of John's Gospel calls attention to the fact that an event or saying in Christ's life is fulfilled in the Old Testament (12:38; 13:18; 15:25; 17:12; 18:9; 19:24,28,36). "This happened that it might be fulfilled" is a formula also found in the Matthean Gospel and has suggested to some scholars that there may have been a written source, containing a Jewish collection of statements predictive of the coming Messiah, possibly called **The Testimonies,**[17] a possible source used by Matthew and John.

There are over 20 quotations, found in John's Gospel in nine different chapters that relate to the Forerunner of Christ, to Christ's zeal, to the manna in the wilderness, to Christ the Divine teacher, to the authority of His witness, to the Deity of Christ, to Christ being welcomed as He entered Jerusalem, to the manner of His entrance, to the people's rejection of Him, and the reason for it, to the treachery of Judas, to the world's causeless hatred of Christ, to the casting of lots for His garments, to His bones not being broken, and to the people beholding Him on the Cross.

The Old Testament quotations and allusions are important because they show that Judaism was a preparation for Christianity, and that Messianic types and prophecies were fulfilled in Christ. As one scholar has said: "The Christian theology of the Evangelist is based upon the theology of the Old Testament (1:45; 4:22; 5:46; 8:56)." There were a number of events that were typical of happenings in Christ's life, such as the brazen serpent, the manna, the pascal lamb, the water from the rock, the pillar of fire (8:12), the shepherd, and the vine. Professor Luthardt has called attention to the fact that "there is a striking agreement between the Fourth Gospel and the Second half of Isaiah, chapter 40-66."[18]

Old Testament Data in the Pauline Epistles

Of Paul's 13 letters, nine were sent to Churches, one to Rome, two to Corinth, one to the Galatian group of Churches, one to Ephesus, one to Philippi, one to Colosse, two to Thessalonica; and four were sent to individuals, one to Philemon, one to Titus and two to Timothy. Paul, who once was a member of the Pharisees, knew the Old Testament Scriptures well. Romans, considered Paul's most theological letter, and one of his longest, contains more quotations from the Old Testament than in all other Epistles together.[19] There are 70 direct quotations: These are from at least 14 of the Old Testament Books; and the books most often quoted are the Psalms and Isaiah.[20]

Romans, 1 and 2 Corinthians and Galatians, the second group of distinctive Epistles, contain 140 references. Romans has 74,1 Corinthians 30, 2 Corinthians about 20, and Galatians about 13. That means that the Big Four Pauline Epistles have a total of 140 references, and the references are mainly from Genesis, Deuteronomy, Isaiah and the Psalms.[21]

The Epistle of the Hebrews and the Old Testament

The Epistle to the Hebrews was penned specifically for Hebrew Christians.[22] This anonymous letter had as its purpose to show that Christianity was better than Pharisaic Judaism and that Jesus was better than the angels (ch. 1), greater than Joshua and Moses, that Christianity was superior to the Old Testament's sacrificial system, that in Christ the Old Covenant had been fulfilled. Twice the covenant written about in Jeremiah 31:31-34 has been realized in Christ and His Gospel. The author of Hebrews begins his Epistle like this: "In many and various ways God has spoken of old to our fathers by the prophets, but in these days he has spoken by a Son, whom he appointed the heir of all things, through whom, he created the world." He reflects the glory of God and bears the very stamp of His nature, upholding the universe by His word of Power" (1:1-2).

One of the purposes for the penning of Hebrew was to warn Jewish Christians against returning to the old and antiquated Judaism. The recipients of Hebrews were in danger of falling back into Judaism and drifting away from the one and only saving faith (2:2:1; 3:6,14; 4:1,11; 5:1-8,11, 12;9:9,10; 10:23; 36-39; 13:9-12).[23]

Hebrews is characterized by contrasts which are profoundly striking and significant. These contrasts are between the Son and Angels (1-2); between the Son and Moses (3:1-11); between the rest of Canaan and the rest of God (3:12-4:13), between Christ and Aaron (4:14-5:10); between babyhood and maturity (5:11-14); between apostasy and faithfulness (vi); between the Melchisidecean and Aaronic priesthoods (7); between the

Old Covenant and the New (8); between the offerings of the Law and the Offering of Christ (9-10:18); between punishment under the Law and under the Gospel (10:19-39); between faith and sight (11); between sons and bastards (12:5-13); between the earthly and the heavenly congregations (12:18-29); and between the old and new altars (13:10-15).[24]

The Epistle of James and The Old Testament

The Epistle of James reads like an Old Testament wisdom book. In this respect it is reminiscent of the Sermon on the Mount. Like other New Testament books it has a number of references to the Old Testament. The writer makes reference to Abram, Rahab, Job, and Elijah; to the Law, and some of the commandments; and there are other references or allusions to passages in all Books of the Pentateuch, Joshua, I Kings, the Psalms, Proverbs, Ecclesiastes, Isaiah, Jeremiah, Ezekiel, to Daniel and to no less than seven of the Twelve Minor Prophets.[25]

Scroggie claims that there is remarkable evidence that besides James' letters references to the Old Testament, he had an acquaintance with the Apocrypha especially the Book of Ecclesiasticus, to which he claims there are no less than 15 allusions; in fact, some scholars have claimed the existence of 32. Twelve uses of the Wisdom of Solomon are allegedly found. Some Biblical students believe that James is very close to the Old Testament, in point of spirit, compare James 4:7-10. James may be the first book to have been written, the beginning of the New Testament canon.[26]

The Epistle of Jude and The Old Testament

Jude, a one-chapter book of 23 verses, is replete with references and allusions to the Old Testament.

This one-chapter book is one of the most Hebraic books of the New Testament, written either by the Apostle Jude or by one of the brothers of Christ. From the contents it is apparent that it was addressed to Jewish Christians. Scroggie pertinently remarked: "The Epistle, having regard for brevity, contains more allusions to Jewish history, except 2 Peter, which so closely resembles it, and perhaps the Epistle to the Hebrews."[27] It may also have been sent to a Christian Church in Palestine for instance, localize the occasion or the letter.

First Peter and the Old Testament

Peter addressed his First Epistle to the churches of Asia Minor, comprised both of Jews and Gentiles.[28] No person can completely understand this Petrine book without a knowledge of the Old Testament. The Rock Apostle, Peter, in his First Epistle presents Christian truth in Jewish mould. Averred Scroggie: "Like the writer of Hebrews he shows how all the essentials of Judaism are reflected in Christianity, and so, in chapter 1:1-2:10, the first main division of the Old Testament there are reflected references to election, inheritance, a chosen generation, a royal priesthood, a people of God's own possession, Temple, Altar, Sacrifice." There are in this Epistle proportionately more quotations than in any other Book of the New Testament.[29]

728

Second Peter contains one of the important passages about the Old Testament's content and inspiration. Verses 19-21 show the high regard the Apostles had for the Old Testament Scripture.[30] Chapter 2 is similar to Jude and Peter, and contains the same Old Testament references as does Jude.

Revelation and the Old Testament

No person can understand the Apocalypse unless he or she has a thorough knowledge of the Old Testament. The symbolism is neither Greek or Roman, but Hebrew. "The originality of the Writing is, for the most part, not in the presentation of new ideas, but in a combination of old ideas." Every figure employed in the Book is drawn from the Old Testament. Of Revelation's 404 verses, 265 contain Old Testament language and about 550 references to Old Testament passages. Without reference to the Old Testament, the Apocalypse would be an enigma.[31]

The Majority of Proper Names Are Jewish

The documents of the New Testament mention many individuals, male and female, having Jewish names. In the infancy narratives in Luke and Matthew the majority of characters are Hebraic. Thus the first man in Luke was Zechariah, a Jewish priest and his wife Elizabeth, a Jewess. The latter's cousin was Mary, the mother of Jesus' and her husband Joseph and their children were descendants of King David. Simeon and Anna, devout believers, were of the same race as Christ for whom they waited. The 12 disciples were likewise descendants of Abraham; Ananias and Sapphira (Acts 5) were Jews, as were many companions and followers of Paul, a Jew proud of his ancestry. Aquila and Priscilla were Jews practicing the same trade as St. Paul. Barnabas, "son of exhortation" (consolation) was a Jew from Cyprus and was a teacher at Antioch with Paul. A relative of Barnabas was John Mark, Jew, who was a helper of Barnabas and Paul on their journey to Cyprus and Asia Minor. Lazarus was a Jew, brother of the Jewesses Mary and Martha, one of three people Jesus raised from the dead. All the Marys mentioned in the New Testament were daughters of Abraham, Isaac and Jacob. Mary Magdalene, out of whom Jesus drove seven devils, was from Magdale. Mary Magdalene was present with other Jewish women at the crucifixion, burial and resurrection; two members of the Sanhedrin, Nicodemus and Joseph of Arimethea, were Jews. The women who served Jesus during His evangelistic tours, such as Mary Magdalene, Mary, the wife of Joseph; Mary, the mother of James, Salome and Martha of Bethany were descendants of Sarah, wife of Abraham.[32]

Jesus of Nazareth, a Jew of the Davidic Line

Jesus was born of Mary, the wife of Joseph, both of whom were of the house and lineage of David. The Matthean genealogy (Matt. 1:1-18) stresses the fact that Jesus' origin was of kingly descent. His parents were faithful Jews who observed the laws and customs of the Old Testament. Thus when Jesus was eight days old, they had him circumcised.

As Jews faithful to the Mosaic Law, Luke reports: "And when the days of their purification according to the Law of Moses had passed, they took him to Jerusalem, to present him to the Lord, as it was written in the Law of Moses (Ex. 13:2)."Christ's parents offered a sacrifice as commanded by the Law of the Lord, a pair of turtle doves or two young pigeons (Lev. 12:1).

Jesus parents must have attended the major feasts of Judaism. When Jesus was 12 years old. His parents took Him up to Jerusalem to be at the yearly festival of the Passover (Luke 2:41-47).

When Jesus had grown to manhood and began His public ministry, it is reported by John's Gospel that He attended three passover festivals and one feast of Tabernacles.[33] He loved the Temple which He is depicted as having visited a number of times. He attended the synagogue in Nazareth and visits to the synagogue were a part of His religious observances.

Jesus held the Law in great esteem. He declared that He had not come to destroy the Law but to fulfill it. His high regard for the Law is shown by the assertion that "not one tittle or iota should be destroyed or pass away until it all would be fulfilled." He believed that the Old Testament Scriptures was the Word of God and quoted a number of times from it. He contended that the three major divisions of the Old Testament—the Law, the Prophets and the Writings (Kethubim) spoke about Him, the Messiah. Especially the Messiah's suffering, death, burial and resurrection from the dead had been foretold. Until the time of the resurrection Jesus observed the ceremonial and moral laws of the Pentateuch. He asserted to His enemies: "But the Scripture cannot be broken," which means the Word of God cannot be changed.

Jesus' Dealings With His Fellow Jews

Christ for most of the three year ministry devoted it to the Jews. To a Gentile woman He said: "I am sent to the lost sheep of Israel." He traversed the provinces of Galilee, Samaria and Judea as well as the Decapolis preaching the Good News of the Kingdom of God. He preached to individuals and crowds. Matthew records that Jesus addressed crowds on the shores of Galilee, when He uttered the Sermon on the Mount. In the Temple Jesus contended with the Scribes, Sadducees and Pharisees. The Lord showed compassion, healing many sick, miracles were part and parcel of His ministry (beginning in A.D. 26 and ending in A.D. 30).[34]

Christ loved all men and women and children, especially He showed His concern for the less respected people, including the tax collectors and publicans. Christ offered freely the blessings of the Kingdom of God or Kingdom of heaven to all who repented of their sins, believed in Him as their redeemer from sin. For the continuance of His ministry He chose 12 Jewish men, establishing a first-century apostolate, which ended with the death of John around A.D.100. These men after His ascension had the command to make disciples of all nations by baptism (Matt. 28:18-20) and the teaching of all things revealed them by the Holy Spirit, who was to guide them in all truth.

The Jewish Response to Christ's Invitations

A study of the Four Gospels reveals that a number of Jews in 5 B.C. accepted Jesus as the promised Messiah (Luke 1 and 2). Such was the case with Zechariah, Elizabeth, Mary, wife of Joseph, Anna, Simeon, the shepherds (Luke 2:15-22), the various Marys, Nicodemus and Joseph of Arimathea. The 12 Apostles first became His disciples before being appointed to the Apostolate. The parents of James and John, Zebedee and Salome, were early followers of Jesus. At the crucifixion of Christ a number of women, who had followed Jesus from Galilee, namely, Mary Magdalene, Mary the mother of James and Joses and the mother of Zebedee's sons, were on Calvary (Matt. 27:55-56). Cleophas and another man believed in Jesus as is evident from Luke 24:32. After the ascension as a result of Peter's preaching 3,000 people were baptized. As the days went by, the Lord kept adding to the Jerusalem Church "daily those that were being saved" (Acts 2:47). In the days following Pentecost, many people became followers of Christ. Luke also recorded the fact that many priests accepted Christ as the promised Messiah. Luke wrote: "And the word of the Lord continued to spread; and the number of the disciples was increasing" (Acts 6:7). The Book of Acts, the great missionary book of the New Testament, showed how the Gospel of Jesus Christ was established in Judea, Samaria, in Damascus, in various provinces in Asia Minor, in Greece, Illyricum, Italy and probably in Spain.

The Rejection of Christ by Most First-Century Judaism

Opposition to Christ the Son of God began in babyhood when Herod the Great endeavored to have Him killed (Matthew 2:1-12). Throughout the three-year ministry the Scribes, the Pharisees, the Herodian are depicted by the Evangelists as opponents of Jesus, rejecting Him as the Messiah foretold in Old Testament prophecy. Not only were His enemies rejecting His teaching, they were also envious of the influence Christ wielded over the minds of the people. The Pharisees accused Jesus of blasphemy (Luke 5:21), of being in league with the devil (Matt. 9:34), of breaking of the law (Matt. 12:2), and often planned to destroy Him. After the miraculous resurrection of Lazarus by Christ, a meeting of the Sanhedrin was called and it was decided, with Caiaphas presiding, that Jesus should be killed (John 11:50-51). The chief priests and the Pharisees gave orders that any person knowing where Christ was, should report it, so that He might be arrested (John 11:57). Matthew 23 contains denunciation of the Scribes and Pharisees as hypocrites and as blind leaders of the blind. After Palm Sunday Scribes, Pharisses and Sadducees made every attempt to discredit Jesus and find reason for having Jesus apprehended for false teaching. Through the treachery of Judas Iscariot they were able to take Jesus captive. At an illegal night session of the Sanhedrin Jesus was condemned to death on the grounds that He claimed to be the Son of God. They sent Jesus to Pontius Pilate, claiming that Jesus was a rival to Caesar and worthy of death. Matthew in chapter 26 reported: "Then the chief priests and the elders of the people met together in the court of the palace of the high priest who was called Caiaphas, and they plotted together to get Jesus into their power by a trick and put him to death," however, they believed that this should not be done during the upcoming Passover feast (Matt. 26:3-5).

Jewish Opposition to Christ and His Gospel after Pentecost

As a result of Peter's preaching on the day of Pentecost, when the apostle showed how the great Old Testament Messianic prophecies were fulfilled in Jesus of Nazareth and also declared:

"Therefore let the whole House of Israel know assuredly that God has made him both Lord and Christ, this Jesus whom you have crucified (Acts 2:36)," opposition by the Sadducees developed.

Priests, the commander of the Temple and the Sadducees opposed Peter and John's preaching, had them seized and put in jail. The elders, and scribes, Annas, the high priest Caiaphas, John and Alexander and all the members of the high priest's family demanded Peter and James to state by what power they had healed a lame man. This group forbade the disciples to preach the message of the death and resurrection of Christ. Because of their success in winning converts and healing sick people, the Sadducees had Peter and John cast into prison. Stephen was lynched and stoned to death because he identified Christ with Old Testament Messianic prophecy (Acts 7:52).

After the death of Stephen, Luke in Acts chapter 8 records the fact that on "this very day" there broke out a great persecution against the church in Jerusalem, and all except the apostles were scattered throughout Judea and Samaria. Paul of Tarsus was laying waste the church of God, searching out men and women to cast them into prison.

Jewish Opposition to Paul Since His Historic Conversion

Between A.D. 33 and 60 Paul periodically was persecuted by Jews. After his completely being turned around by Christ, he preached in the synagogue in Damascus. When Paul was very effective in showing his countrymen that Jesus was the promised Messiah, the Jews sought to kill him (Acts 9:23). After escaping out of Damascus, the Tarsian went to Jerusalem, where he preached Christ to Grecian Jews (Acts 9:29), but the Jews tried to kill him (Acts 9:2). In Antioch in Pisidia Paul preached in the synagogue showing by the use of many Messianic prophecies that they were fulfilled in Christ. As a result of this sermon many Jews and devout proselytes believed Paul's Christian message. The next Sabbath the whole city came to hear Paul's Christological message. When the Jews saw the crowds, they were filled with jealousy and began to contradict Paul's statements. Later Jews urged on certain women and some prominent citizens who stirred up persecution that Paul and Barnabas were driven out of the district of Iconium (Acts 13:50-51). At Iconium Paul preached in the synagogue and it resulted in a number of Jews and Gentiles believing. Again, embittered Jews stirred up the souls of Gentiles, and also embittered people against Jews. A plot was formulated to maltreat and stone Paul, Barnabas and Christians (Acts 14:1-6). When the apostles got wind of it, they fled to the Lycaonian towns of Derbe and

Lystra.

On his second missionary journey Jews opposed Paul and his message. At Thessalonica, Jews moved by jealousy, formed a mob and assaulted the house of Jason where they failed to find Paul and brought charges that Paul was upsetting the habitable world with his anti-government message. A number of Jews were won over for Christ's kingdom. Jews from Thessalonica came to Berea and stirred up trouble and troubled the crowds. In Corinth, Jews accused Paul before the proconsul of Achaia, Gallio. From Corinth Paul proceeded to Ephesus, where he entered the synagogue and preached Christ crucified (Acts 18:5).

On his third missionary journey, Paul preached fearlessly for three months in the Jewish synagogue (Acts 19:8). Some Jews were hardened and disobedient and spoke against "the Way," Paul who withdrew his disciples and held discussions in the hall of Tyrannus. As a result Paul's preaching for two years, Luke records this fact: "This went on for two years, so that all inhabitants of Asia heard the Lord's message, Jews as well as Greeks." After spending three months in Greece (Acts 19:10) he planned to return to Jerusalem. While in Macedonia, as he was about to sail for Syria, Jews made a plot against Paul (20:3).

One reason for returning to Jerusalem was to fulfill a vow. It was suggested to Paul that he should associate himself with four men under a vow, that he purify himself with them, pay their expenses that they could have their heads shaven. By this action all Jews in Jerusalem would know that Paul was not against the Hebrew OT faith. Thereby Jews would know that Paul was not against Moses or against circumcision. Paul did what was suggested to him by the leaders of the Christian Church at Jerusalem. On the seventh day of carrying out these suggestions, Jews from Asia saw Paul in the temple and began to stir up the crowd against Paul. The result was that a mob surged on the apostle and dragged him outside the Temple, and this resulted in the imprisonment of Paul in Caesarea, which lasted two years and his appeal to Caesar and ended in Paul's first Roman imprisonment (A.D. 60-62).

Paul and First-Century Judaism

Next to Jesus, Paul, the Jew, predominates as an important character in the New Testament. He was born in Tarsus of Cilicia, lived in a busy Graeco-Roman city, which may have had a university.

Of central significance was Paul's strong Jewish heritage, being fundamental to all he was and later became. He was never ashamed to call himself a Jew (Acts 21:39; 22:3) and was justly proud of his Jewish heritage and background (2 Cor. 11:21) and retained a deep and abiding love for his brethren according to the flesh (Rom. 9:1-2; 10:1). By becoming a Christian he did not feel that it was a conscious departure from the religion of his forefathers as set forth in the Old Testament Scriptures (Acts 24:14-16; 26:6-7). His racial affinity with the Jews enabled Paul with great profit to begin his missionary labors to each city in the synagogue, for there he had a prepared audience.

Born of purest Jewish blood (Phil. 3:5), the son of a Pharisee (Acts

23:6), Saul was cradled in orthodox Judaism. At the proper age, probably 13, he was sent to Jerusalem and completed his studies under Gamaliel (Acts 22:3; 26:4-5). In the year 33 Paul became a fanatic in opposing people of "the Way." The followers of Christ were considered "heretics" who needed to be exterminated. He consented to the lynching and stoning of Stephen (Acts 7:59-8:3; 9:1-2).

According to Luke, Jesus of Nazareth appeared to Paul on the Damascene road and changed the whole course of Paul's life. In two addresses Paul discussed his miraculous conversion (Chapters 22,26). Saul was baptized by Ananias of Damascus, who befriended him. Jesus appointed Paul to be the apostle for the Gentiles. As a new follower of the Nazarene, Paul at once proclaimed the deity and Messiahship of Christ in the synagogue of Damascus. On his missionary journeys, in cities where there were synagogues, Paul would visit them and show how the Messianic prophecies of the Old Testament were fulfilled in Christ, whose atoning death and resurrection all Jews needed to accept. With Barnabas and Mark he visited Cyprus and cities of Asia Minor. He embarked on three different missionary journeys with Barnabas, Timothy and Silvanus, and was instrumental in founding congregations in Corinth, Berea, Thessalonica, Philippi, and other cities of Asia. A number of the congregations with whom Paul had dealings had both pagans and Jews. Every possible occasion where he could meet with Jews were taken by Paul. One of the latest references of Paul's reasoning with the Jews is found in the beginning of his first Roman imprisonment: "Testifying from morning till evening, testifying to the kingdom of God about Jesus both from the law of Moses and from the prophets" (Acts 28:23). Some were converted, but most were not.

Paul's Great Love for the Jews

That Paul loved the Jews is clear from the beginning of Paul's Epistle to the Romans (9:1-3).

The central portion, Chapters 9-11, deals with the great refusal and their unbelief and the saving of a remnant[34] of the Hebrew people with this assertion: "I am speaking the truth in Christ, it is no lie. My conscience bearing me witness in the Holy Spirit (Romans 9:1) that I have sorrow and incessant anguish in my heart. For I was on the point of praying to be accursed from Christ on behalf of my brethren according to the flesh" (Romans 9:2-3). In the beginning of chapter 10 Paul declares: "Brothers, the longing of my heart and my prayer is that they may be saved." Judaism, Paul claimed that Jews had a wonderful religious heritage: "For they are the Israelites: To them belong the sonship, the Shekinah glory, the covenants, the giving of the law, the service of the Temple, and the promises; theirs are the patriarchs, and of them, as according to the flesh is Christ, who is over all, God blessed forever" (Rom. 9:4-5). Although in general Jewry rejected Christ, Paul taught that a remnant would be saved. And thus Gentiles and converted Jews will be saved (Rom. 11:26).[35]

Even though chosen by Christ to be the Apostles to the Gentiles, Paul, whenever possible, would attend Jewish synagogue where he found Jews and presented Christ to them as their Savior and Redeemer, offering Jews the plan of salvation.

Twentieth-Century Judaism and the New Testament

Numerous Jewish writers have discussed John the Baptist, Jesus or Jeshua, James, the brother of Jesus and Paul of Tarsus. Divergent views are held about Jesus of Nazareth and the harm that Saul of Tarsus did to Christ and Judaism. Learsi and others claim that John the Baptist was an Essene. Averred Learsi: "His manner of address, the food he ate, and the importance he attached to ritual abolution, all point to that conclusion."[36]

Klausner wrote a lengthy book on Jesus of Nazareth and concluded his volume with the question:

"What is Jesus to the Jews?" The eminent University of Jerusalem professor asserted "no step in life-story of Jesus, and no line in his teaching on which is not stamped the seal of Prophetic and Pharisaic Judaism and the Palestine of His day, the close of the Second Temple. Hence it is somewhat strange to ask. What is Jesus to the Jews? Klausner accepts the judgment of Wellhausen, "Jesus was not a Christian," He was a Jew, and as a Jew, His life story is that of one of the prominent men of the Jews of his times,[37] while his teaching is Jewish teaching of a kind remarkable in its truth and its imaginativeness.[38]

Schweitzer, in *A History of the Jews, Since the First Century,* a book sponsored by Anti-Defamation League of B'nai B'rith, claimed that the life of Christ was one of a number of crises between 135 B.C. and A.D. 70.[39] Schweitzer completely ignored Christ in his discussion of Judaism during the Roman period, which was a surprise that a Roman Catholic professor should completely ignore Christ.

Chaim Potok claimed that "modern scholars of the Bible study the sacred text of Christianity in the same way as they do that of Judaism in an effort to understand the historical Joshua, son of Joseph, whose name in Aramaic was Jeshua."[40] Potok, on the basis of reading the Gospels, Acts wrote: "Behind the many enigmatic and conflicting traditions of later generations, added after Christianity had severed itself from Jewish beginnings and was increasingly involved in the destiny of Rome, there emerges from an impartial reading of the gospels of Matthew, Mark, and Luke the picture of a Jew who was probably a rabbinical student, a Pharisee, became a preacher and wonder worker, taught a gentle ethic not unlike that of Hillel, and in the final year of His all-too-brief life felt Himself to be at first a prophet and then Messiah—and became an apocalyptic Pharisee."[41]

Relative to the trial and execution of Jeshua, Laersi claimed that our information is dependent upon the four Gospels of the New Testament. It is Learsi's opinion that not only do the witnesses not agree with each other because they contradict each other, and furthermore, it is doubtful whether they were unprejudiced. The accounts of Christ's trial and crucifixion were written at a time when feelings ran high against the Jews and when Christians were bitter against the Pharisees.[41a] Learsi contended this when Jesus turned over the tables of the money changers, that was tantamount to sponsoring a riot. Jesus was arrested, tried before a court of the Sanhedrin, and convicted of blasphemy. The evidence which led to His condemnation was his claim, that in a special sense He was "the son of God." Learsi made the charge that the Gospel records about Jesus' death strain ordinary credulity to the breaking point. Jesus was condemned to death by Pontius Pilate, wrongly portrayed as kind and lenient, on the grounds that He claimed to be the king of the Jews.[42]

Other Jewish writers present a better picture of Jesus. Max Dimont, *Jews, God and History,* devoted pages 134-139 to Jeshua, son of Joseph and gave a very sympathetic picture of Christ. The Jews had Jesus arrested after the episode of turning over the tables and driving out the sellers of doves, to protect him against the Romans. It was Romans who demanded that Jesus be turned over to them so that they might kill Him.[43]

Abba Hillel Silver declared that the contemporaries of Jesus did not reject Him, who was a great treasure God gave the Jews, but they did refuse to accept His Messianism, Paul's onslaught on the law, the Gospel of redemption through the atoning death and resurrection and the doctrine of God incarnate in man.[44] Klausner made this significant evaluation about the Nazarene. We cannot imagine a work of any value in the time of Second Temple which does not also include the history of Jesus and an estimate of his teaching. As far as Klausner is concerned Jesus **was not** a Christian but **became** a Christian. But He "was a light to the Gentiles," a nationalist, a great teacher of morality and an artist on parables. For the Hebrew people today, the same Hebrew scholar asserted: "To the Jewish nation he can neither be God nor the Son of God, in the sense conveyed by belief in the Trinity. Either conception is to the Jew not only impious and blasphemous, but incomprehensible. Neither can He, to the Jewish nation, be the Messiah: The Kingdom of God has not yet come. Neither can they regard Him as prophet."[45]

Modern Judaism's Condemnation of St. Paul

Modern Judaism considers Paul as the founder of Christianity.[46] Klausner claimed that it can be said with finality: "Without Jesus no Paul and no Nazarenes; but without Paul no world Christianity." "Thus it may be said that Christ was not the founder of Christianity, but St. Paul the apostle of the Gentiles," despite the fact that Paul's religion was based on Jesus's theological views and what he also derived from the Jewish Church in Jerusalem.[47] Dimont claimed that the Christian Church sprouted out of the mind of Paul.[48] It was St. Paul's ingenuity which was responsible for transforming the humanism into religious dogma, in Paul's Epistles he succeeded to shape the world of Christianity.[49] In order to win converts for his new creed Paul abrogated the immemorial laws and practices of Judaism. The ceremonial laws were made obsolete, Sabbath and other festivals need not to be observed. Circumcision was unnecessary for Gentiles.[49]

Margolis and Marx in their *A History of the Jewish People* devoted less than page to Paul of Tarsus.[50] They portray Christianity being created at Antioch when Paul won over conservative Peter by proclaiming the abrogation of the Mosaic law. According to these two scholars Paul is supposed to have envisaged the Church of God as one and dual at the same time, in which Jew and Greek had each had a place. "He therefore left the prerogatives of Israel untouched; the ancient gifts of grace and of the election were irrevocable."[51] However, the Pauline position resulted in the dethronement of the Jewish people. Christians claimed the election for themselves. They appropriated the Old Testament for themselves. And it was no longer a solely Jewish possession. Thus the daughter despoiled the mother. Margolis and Marx claimed that Christianity was a transformed Judaism.[52]

Klausner claimed that "the foundation of Paul's teaching lay in Jewish beliefs and opinions, which took on a new, half-pagan complexion from foreign influences, and thus became non-Judaism and anti-Judaism."[53] Although Christianity gave birth to Christianity and was accepted by half of the world, it was emphatically rejected by Judaism itself. Klausner has this sharp evaluation of Paul's teaching and of Christianity: "In spite of the fact that the foundations of all the teachings of Paul are Jewish, his own teaching is both the contradiction of the Jewish religion and the rejection of the Jewish nation."[54]

The Jewish Remnant, Chosen by Grace

Paul asked: "Has God rejected his people? By no means! (Rom. 11:1) God has not rejected his people whom he foreknew" (11:2).By inspiration Paul was made to write: "So too at the present time there is a remnant chosen by grace. But if it is by grace" it is no longer of works; otherwise grace would no longer by grace (11:5-6). Today Jews for Christ are bringing many to Christ, recognizing Christ as the promised Messiah.

Footnotes

1. Cf. various essays in Marc H. Tannenbaum, Marvin R. Wilson and James Rudin, *Evangel and Jews in An Age of Pluralism* (Grand Rapids: Baker Book House, 1984), pp. 29-47; 85-104; 226-238; Marc H. Tannenbaum, Marvin R. Wilson and A. James Rudin, *Evangelicals and Jews in Conversation* (Grand Rapids: Baker Book House, 1978), pp. 2-33; 54-75; 142-153.
2. B. L. Godard, "Hebrew" Hebrews, *Zondervan Pictorial Bible Encyclopedia* (Grand Rapids: Zondervan Publishing, 1963), pp. 342-343.
3. Steve Baarabas, "Jew," *Zondervan Pictorial Bible Dictionary*, 1963), pp. 429-430.
4. Goddard, "Hebrew" Hebrews," *Zondervan Pictorial Bible Dictionary*, **op. cit,**, 342.
5. **Ibid.**
6. "Judaitzo," G. Abbott-Smith, *A Manual Greek Lexicon of the New Testament* (New York: Charles Scribner's Sons, 1929), pp. 217-218.
7. Charles R. Erdman, *The Gospel of Matthew* (Philadelphia: The Westminster Press, 1930), p. 12.
8. W. Graham Scroggie, *Know Your Bible*, Vol. II. Analytical, The New Testament (London: Pickering & Inglis, No Date), p. 37.

9. W. Graham Scroggie, *A Guide to the Gospels* (London: Pickering Inglis, 1948), pp. 267-268.

10. **Ibid.**, p. 270.

11. Scroggie, *A Guide to the Gospels*, **op. cit,**, p. 365.

12. **Ibid.**, p. 426.

13. **Ibid.**, p. 426.

14. **Ibid.**

15. **Ibid.**

16. **Ibid.**

17. **Ibid.**, p. 426.

18. **Ibid.**, p. 429.

19. Scroggie, *Know Your Bible*, New Testament, **op. cit,**, p. 171.

20. **Ibid.**, p. 171.

21. **Ibid.**, p. 173.

22. Charles Erdman, *The Epistle to the Hebrews* (Philadelphia: Westminster Press, 1934), pp. 17-18; George Hadjiantonious (Chicago: Moody Press, 1957), p. 296.

23. **Ibid.**, p. 298; Scroggie, *Know Your Bible,* New Testament, **op. cit,**, p. 296.

24. **Ibid.**, p. 273.

25. Hadjiantoniou, **op. cit,**, p. 304.

26. Scroggie, *Know Your Bible*, **op. cit,**, pp. 296-297.

27. **Ibid.**, p. 302.

28. **Ibid.**, p. 315.

29. **Ibid.**, p. 315.

30. **Ibid.**, p. 302.

31. **Ibid.**, p. 372.

32. For a more complete listing of prominent characters of Hebrew descent mentioned in the New Testament, cf. H. Wayne House, Chronological and Background Charts of the New Testament (Grand Rapids: Zondervan Publishing House, 1981), pp. 44-46.

33. **Ibid.**, p. 105.

34. For a listing of Christ's Miracles, **Ibid.**, cf. pp. 112-117.

35. Cf. C. M. Zom, Der Brief an die Romer (Zwickau, Veriag und Druck von Johannes Herrmann, No Date), p. 155-158. William Hendriksen, "And So All Israel Shall Be Saved" (Grand Rapids: Baker Book House, 1945), 36 pp.

36. Rufus Learsi, *Israel, A History of the Jewish People* (New York and Cleveland: The World Publishing Company, 1949), p. 158.

37. Joseph Klausner, *Jesus of Nazareth, His Life, Times, and Teachings* (New York: The MacMillan Company, 1925), p. 413.

38. **Ibid.**, p. 413.

39. Frederick M. Schweitzer, *A History of the Jews Since the First Century* (New York: The MacMillan Company, 1971), p. 31.

40. Chaim Potok, Wanderings. *History of the Jews* (New York: Fawcett Crest, 1978), p. 371.

41. Learsi, **op. cit,**, p. 160.

41a. Learsi, **op. cit,**, p. 161.

42. **Ibid.**, p. 161.

43. Max I. Dimont, *Jews, God, and History* (New York: New American Library, 1962), p. 139.

44. Abba Hillel Silver, **op. cit,**, p. 96.

45. Klausner, *Jesus of Nazareth*, **op. cit,**, pp. 413-414.

46. **Ibid.**, pp. 413-414.

47. Joseph Klausner, *From Jesus to Paul* (New York: The MacMillan Company, 1943), p. 590.

48. Max I. Dimont, *The Indestructible Jews* (New York: New American Library, 1971), p. 241.

49. **Ibid.**, p. 194.

50. Max L. Margolis and Alexander Marx, *A History of the Jewish People* (Philadelphia: The Jewish Publication Society of America, 1927), p. 228.

51. **Ibid.**, pp. 228-229.

52. **Ibid.**, p. 229.

53. Klausner, *From Jesus to Paul*, **op. cit,**, p. 591.

54. **Ibid.**, p. 591.

Questions

1. Who has advocated wrong views about Jews and Judaism? ____
2. The 27 books of the New Testament were penned between ____.
3. The New Testament is truly a ____ book.
4. Who has repudiated the deity of Christ? ____
5. To understand the New Testament writings the reader needs a good understanding of ____.
6. What are some different names for Abraham's descendants? ____
7. The term "Jews" finally came to comprehend ____.
8. May the New Testament be called a Jewish book? ____
9. All the writers of the New Testament except Luke were ____.
10. The New Testament purports to be ____.
11. The first Gospel was written by ____.
12. What assertion appears over thirty times in the First Gospel? ____
13. Matthew's Gospel is saturated with ____.
14. Judaism was a preparation for ____.
15. The Big four Pauline Epistles have a total of ____ to the OT.
16. The purpose of Hebrews was to show ____.
17. James reads like an Old Testament ___ book.
18. James may have been the beginning of ____.
19. No person can understand the Apocalypse unless he has a ____.
20 Jesus of Nazareth is a ____ of Davidic line.
21. Jesus came not to ____ the Law but to __ it.
22. "The Scriptures cannot be broken" means ____.
23. Jesus was condemned to death on the grounds that____.
24. Why did the Jews seek to kill Paul? ____
25. Paul never was ashamed to call himself a ____.
26. Where did Paul begin his ministry from city to city?____
27. Jesus appointed Paul to be ____.
28. "Some were converted but most were ____."

The Contribution of Biblical Archaeology to Biblical Studies

Christian News, March 9, 1998

A little over a century and a half ago the Bible reader's knowledge of the Ancient Near East, where Old Testament and New Testament events occurred, came ultimately from the Bible. The former Assyriologist Steele wrote a number of years ago: "Nearly all history of Egyptian, Babylonian, Hittite and Persian Empires and monarchs was derived either directly from ancient literature, which itself went back to early biblical records."[1] How the situation has changed in the last one hundred years is a fact that many present-day students of the Bible do not realize. It is difficult to comprehend this fact since at present Bible students have available to them thousands of original documents from these lands, some going back to at least 3200 B.C.[2] In addition, the major museums of the world contain fabulous collections of utilitarian and artistic objects, fashioned by people living in the Near East, where cities and sites go even beyond 4,000 B.C.[3]

Archaeology has furnished Bible readers with information about peoples and lands once known only from Biblical references and, strangely enough, which were considered mythical and not historical.[4] Now the Biblical reader has documents and artifacts which have verified names and places mentioned in the Bible. With the new discoveries it is now possible to reconstruct in remarkable detail the ritual worship of Egyptian priests,[5] the curriculum of Sumerian schoolboys[6] and the court life of Assyrian kings who lived and died ages ago. In truth, much of the world of Abraham, Moses, David and Daniel has come alive again through the diligent skills of the excavator's spade and the scholar's pen.

The findings as well as the conclusions of archeology have had bearings on the interpretation of the Bible.[7] The data from archaeology have been used against as well as for the defense of the Bible. Concerning this issue, Steele wrote:

> In general, there are two opposite opinions. Some hold that although many historical statements of the Bible agree with the facts determined by archaeological studies, in at least as many instances the new findings point up errors in the Bible especially in the earlier periods and the prophetic books. Others believe that there is perfect and complete agreement between the two sources of data.[8]

Steele disagreed with both positions. Thus he adverred: "In fact, however, both positions are incorrect. The fundamental error of the first is its assumption of equal or superior validity and consequent authority for the partial data of science over the records of the Bible. The fallacy of the second is its assumption that human interpretation of observed data in archaeological science is as reliable as divine revelation concerning historic events recorded in the Bible."[9] On the basis of these false assumptions opponents and proponents of the Bible made improper use of archaeological data in relation to the Biblical text.

As an example of the misuse of both positions Steele cited the fact of such a statement that recent excavations of Jericho have shown that this city did not exist as a significant settlement at the time of Joshua 6 is false, or the claim that the flood layer found by Woolley at Ur proves the fact of the Biblical Flood. Both of these interpretations are not so certain and should not be advanced as positive proof.[10]

According to Steele there are two main uses of archaeology, which others have pointed out from time to time. Declared Steele: "It provides the Christian with abundant material to fill in the background of Biblical history, thus giving a better perspective. It also helps us correct many mistaken concepts regarding biblical history, which have raised honest questions in the minds of persons seeking to understand the Bible."[11]

Other scholars have pointed out there are a number of other uses for Biblical archaeology.[12] A number of these will be the topic of this presentation.

The History of the Use of the Word "Archaeology"

The word archaeology (sometimes written archeology) has had an interesting history as to its meaning. At Josephus' time the word was used in the sense of "history."[13] Flavius Josephus wrote an "Archiologia of the Jews," usually translated "The Antiquity of the Jews." After some introductory matters Josephus begins his history with the Creation." It is organized around twenty books and takes the reader into his own time, when the Romans controlled Palestine.[14]

In the nineteenth century the word "archaeology" came to be used with the meaning of "antiquities."[15] In the last one hundred years there have appeared a number of books with the title "Biblical Archaeology." Berkhof, author of *Biblical Archaeology*,[16] employed the word "archaeology" in this sense as did Franz Delitzsch,[17] Kalt,[18] Benzinger[19] and others. Berkhof defined Biblical archaeology like this: "The study of Biblical archaeology is an important aid to the correct understanding of the Bible, since it gives a description of the social, civil and religious customs of the people among whom God's revelation was given, especially of Israel which was pre-eminently the people of God."[20] Berkhof further said about Biblical archaeology (in the second sense): "This study differs from Biblical history in that it does not aim at a genetic description of the ever changing facts of history, but portrays the more constant conditions of life."[21] In his book, Berkhof discusses all phases of the economic, social, political and religious conditions of the Bible.

The third and latest use of the word "archaeology" is the current use and is related to the uncovering of the past by means of the spade, through archaeological excavations.[22] Scholars have given many and varied definitions for this third use of "archeology." One writer defined archaeology "as the study of ancient things, that have been excavated and belonging to a former era."[23] Books and articles dealing with archaeology have defined "archaeology" in different ways. Thus Schoville wrote: "A search for existing literature will produce numerous definitions of ar-

741

chaeology, ranging from the scientific study of material remains of past human life and activities,"[24] from a currently popular dictionary to the candid assessment of the British scholar, P.R.S. Moory in *Archaeology, Artifacts and the Bible*, who stated frankly that "archaeology is the study of durable rubbish."[25]

Other definitions of the word include "the study and historical interpretation of all the material remains that vanished civilizations have left in the ground," and "the study of the things men made and did, in order that the whole way of life may be understood."[26]

Schoville suggested as a definition: "Archaeology is the systematic recovery, analysis, and interpretation of the surviving evidence of human activity."[27]

Biblical archaeology may be defined "as the examination of ancient things which have been lost and found again, as those recovered objects relate to the study of Scripture and the portrayal of life in Bible times."[28]

Archaeology is basically a science. Knowledge is obtained by the acquisition of systematically observed data, and facts are discovered, evaluated and classified, then are organized into a body of information. Archaeology employs the help of other disciplines, such as chemistry, anthropology, zoology, architecture, photography. Some subjects studied by archaeology have never been lost, as temples, the Parthenon, and the pyramids, ziggurats, obelisks but perhaps a knowledge of their original form and the purpose and the meaning of inscriptions on them have been lost.

The investigation of archaeological ancient life includes the study of monuments, inscriptions, languages, literature, art, architecture, implements, houses, cities, and all other remains of man and his activities.

Biblical archaeology is a part of Near Eastern archaeology which covers all the countries of the Fertile Crescent, beginning with Eygpt, on the latter's western end and including Canaan, Syria, Aram Naharaim, Mesopotamia, Elam and Persia on the eastern side. Palestinian archaeology which begins with prehistoric times and ends usually with the Byzantine or Islamic and Crusader times.[29]

The General Functions of Archaeology

Vos has correctly called attention to the fact that archaeology performs the very useful service of helping us to understand the Bible. It reveals what life was like in biblical times, it helps often to clear up obscure passages, showing us what they really mean and how historical narratives and context of the Bible are to be understood.

Critical scholars generally contend that the findings of archaeology should never be utilized to prove that the Bible is true. Critical scholars contend that archaeology should never be used to confirm the accuracy of the Bible. Those who frown on the plenary inspiration of the Bible are opposed to resorting to archaeological evidence to show the Scripture's reliability. Not only is the employment of Biblical archeology frowned upon but denounced as unwarranted.

Christians who believe God's Word is the truth and that the Jesus of the Bible is "the way, the truth, and the life," believe that archaeology has been of service in supporting Holy Writ and can be a valuable tool in some instances of attaining to a clearer understanding of the Bible's message and teachings. There are a number of areas, as Free has pointed out, where archaeology has and will continue to serve the Bible student in his study and application of the Bible's facts and truths.

I. Archaeology and Biblical History

The history of the Bible may be divided into the following time periods. They are: 1. The Primitive Period (Genesis, chapters 1-11); 2. The Patriarchal period, as found in Genesis 12-50, containing accounts about the lives and activities of Abraham, Isaac, Jacob and Joseph; 3. The Mosaic period, covering the Books of Exodus, Leviticus, Numbers and Deuteronomy. They speak about the Jewish Egyptian bondage, the exodus from Egypt, the 40-year stay in the Wilderness, the march from Kadesh Barnea to Moab; 4. The conquest of Canaan under Joshua (Book of Joshua); 5. The Period of the Judges (Book of Judges, I Samuel 1-8); 6. The Establishment of the Undivided Monarchy (I Samuel 9-31; II Samuel; I Kings 1-2) Kings Saul, Ishbaal, David and Solomon; 7. The History of the Northern Kingdom (I Kings 12- II Kings 18) with 19 kings, 9 dynasties; 8. The History of the Southern Kingdom, 19 kings, all a part of the Davidic dynasty, who ruled from 930-587; I Kings 18 - II Kings 25; I Chronicles 10-36; 9. The Exile and the Return from the Babylonian Captivity; 10. The Intertestamental Period, 400-63 B.C.; 11. The Roman Period, the New Testament and especially the life of Christ and Founding of the Christian Church (63 B.C.-A.D. 100).

Practically every Bible period has received light shed upon it by archaeological discoveries. Each period has been broadened and deepened by archaeological discoveries. For example, the Patriarchal period has been especially illuminated by archaeological work at cities like Jericho, Shechem, Bethel, Beersheba, Gerar, Dothan, Jerusalem, Eblaor Tell Mardikh. Mesopotamian discoveries at Nuzu, Mari and Chagar Bazar have been very helpful in shedding instructive light on social and economic conditions of this period of Biblical history. Bible readers now have answers to questions that past generations could ask and had no answers for. Why did Isaac not revoke the oral blessing which he bestows on Jacob, when it was apparent that he had practiced deception in order to get the blessing? (Genesis 27:34-41). The Nuzu or Nuzi tablets in cuneiform show that in Mesopotamia that an oral oath would stand up in court as a valid one, even though only spoken. Formerly, readers wondered why Laban, when he caught up with his son-in-law Jacob and family, could say of the latter's offspring: "These are my children (Genesis 31:43)." The Nuzu tablets reveal that in Jacob's day a grandfather exercised control over his grandchildren.

The adoption of Eliezer, Abraham's trusted servant, whom he wanted to appoint his legal heir because of Sarah's childlessness, was according to the practice of Near Eastern custom, as evident from Nuzu, the Code of Hammurabi set forth the need of a childless wife to offer unto her husband a slave woman who would serve as surrogate wife for the purpose of raising offspring. This practice was followed by Sarah when she gave Abraham her Egyptian slave Hagar as substitute for her to bear children and thus to perpetuate Abraham's name.

Robert Dick Wilson, formerly professor of Semitic languages at Princeton Theological Seminary and Princeton University, claimed that already by 1926 archaeology had confirmed the names of 40 Biblical kings, Israelite and non-Israelite. This shows that in the Old Testament the authors have been dealing with true historical happenings and would lend credibility to the trustworthiness of the historical books of the Old Testament canon.

The Hittites, mentioned at least 46 times in various books of the Old Testament, a hundred years ago were said never to have existed and the Biblical references to them were erroneous. Since Winckler's excavations at ancient Hattushash or Bohgazkeui, where the German scholar uncovered about 20,000 tablets, written in a number of different languages, of which one turned out to be an Indo-European language, deciphered by the Czech scholar Hrozny.

II. Archaeology Acts as a Commentary to the Bible

It has been said that the best commentary on the Bible would be a trip to the Holy Land. The Bible is a book of 66 books coming from a time period covering easily 6,000 years of recorded history. Genesis 1-11 covers the span from the Creation (thousands of years ago) and not millions of years ago and the time of Abraham, 2166-1989 B.C. While critical scholarship labels these early chapters as a myth, the Bible itself in many places of both the Old Testament and the New Testament refers to persons, events and places mentioned in Genesis 1-11 as historical and its events from having transpired in calendar time. Babylon, Accad, and Sumer, the Tigris and Euphrates, countries, cities and people alluded to in Genesis have been discovered or are known from ancient canonical documents to have existed.

Before the age of archaeology (beginning about A.D. 1840) there were statements that puzzled Bible readers. The prohibition to Israel: "Thou shalt not seethe a kid in its mother's milk," has puzzled Biblical students; the reason for this prohibition was not apparent until the discovery of the Rash Shcamra or Ugarit cuneiform tablets in 1929. Within a year these texts, written for the first time in a cuneiform language using an alphabet of 30 signs, turned out to be a Canaanite language closely related to Hebrew. These finds at Ugarit constituted firsthand evidence for the fertility cult of the sex-oriented Canaanite fertility, so often and fiercely denounced in the Old Testament. The prohibition found three times in The Pentateuch "not to seethe a kid in its mother's milk" was directed against a pagan ritual practice designed to placate a pagan god. Thus Moses warned Israelites not to engage in such a heathen practice.

Entire books have been written from an archaeological perspective treating various periods more fuzzy. H. Vos has written a volume titled *Genesis and Archaeology*. L. Woolley has authored books titled *Abraham,*

Ur of the Chaldees. John Garstang, *Joshua and Judges.* Bruce Vawter has been the general editor of a 12-volume series called "Backgrounds to the Bible."

III. Archaeology and the Dating of Biblical Books

Archaeology has helped to correct a number of misconceptions and erroneous theories about the dating of Biblical books. Critical scholars have dated many portions of Biblical books late. Wellhausen's documentary hypothesis is still generally accepted today as the correct manner in which the books Genesis to Deuteronomy have come into existence. These Mosaic books are dated between 850 B.C. and 390 B.C. One of the major arguments advanced by Wellhausen was the objection that Moses could not have written the Pentateuch because writing was not available at Moses' time. There is nothing, except Deuteronomy 34, which could not have been written by Moses.

The Nuzu, Mari, Alalakh, Chagar Bazar and Ebla tablets show that much material found in Genesis comes from a time before Moses, that it originated in the pre-Patriarchal and Patriarchal periods of Old Testament history. Writing in the Near East goes back to 3200 B.C.; documents from various Sumerian cities of the Mesopotamian Valley come from the third millennium B.C. For von Rad in his little monograph **Moses,** to question the historicity of Moses is now unjustified in the light of archaeology.

Critical scholarship in the past has denied psalms to David and the writing of Proverbs to Solomon. The proverbial literature has been assigned to around 450 B.C. Chapters 1-9 are usually considered the latest part of Proverbs, dated around 400 B.C. Critical scholars reject the assertion of the author of Kings, namely, that Solomon wrote 3,000 proverbs, 1,005 songs in his life time (I Kings 10:28-32).

Why must the Biblical proverb collection be late when archaeological discoveries have revealed different forms of wisdom literature prevalent throughout the Near East anywhere between 2450 to 1,000 B.C.? Tablets uncovered from Sumerian cities in the southern Mesopotamian Valley have shown the existence of proverbs. Cyrus Gordon has published a collection of Sumerian proverbs. It has been reported that among the nearly 20,000 tablets found at Ebla that there existed a wisdom literature in this North Syrian city. From Egypt have come a number of **Instructions** classified as part of the gnomic literature of Egypt, dated between 1800 B.C. and 600 B.C. *The Wisdom of Amenemopet* has been dated by Egyptologists as originating between 1000 and 600 B.C. There is some similarity between this Egyptian proverbial collection and Proverbs 22:17-24:22. The Near Eastern wisdom of literature, including the proverb genre, was not late but from the second millennium B.C. Solomon lived in the tenth century B.C. and the Bible compares the Solomonic wisdom writings with other people of the Near East depicted as contemporaneous with David's son, Solomon.

The lateness of the origin of the Book of Psalms was advocated in the early part of the twentieth century. Many psalms were even assigned to the Maccabean era (165-63 B.C.) Briggs, in the *International Critical Commentary on the Psalms*, makes many psalms late. The earliest psalms were assigned to the Persian period (539-331 B.C.) or even to the Greek period (331-63 B.C.). However, the archaeological discoveries at Ugarit or Rash Shamra have necessitated a re-evaluation of the critical position on the date of the writings and publishing of the Psalter. Since similar poetic patterns, the use of different kinds of parallelism and poetic imagery are found in the poetic epics hailing from Ugarit, dated as originating between 1600 and 1200 B.C., it is now recognized that there need be no objection rendered about the idea that psalms were written by David. In fact, one scholar went so far as to believe that some psalms come from about 1200 B.C.

Another archaeological discovery affording a change in the thinking of critical Old Testament scholars was the finding in the Dead Sea Caves of a collection of non-canonical psalms, named the **Hodayot**. These are psalms written in imitation of the Biblical Psalms. Since the **Hodayot** are dated around 150 B.C. and since the Biblical Psalms were the model, it is argued that the Biblical Psalm book must have been in existence at a much earlier time, thus definitely ruling out the Maccabean dating of Biblical Psalms, so popular years ago.

IV. Archaeology and the Dating of Deuteronomy

George Mendenhall of the University of Michigan has shown that in the historical documents coming from the New Hittite Empire (1600-1200 B.C.) that there were two kinds of covenant made by the Hittite kings. The Suzerainty and the parity covenants were employed by various of these rulers. The Suzerainty covenant had a certain structure; it was an agreement which the Hittite sovereign made with subject kings, princes and cities. The basic elements of the Suzerainty covenant (berith) can be shown to be found in Exodus 20, Leviticus 27, and Joshua 24 and the entire book of Deuteronomy. Merdith Kline claims that the following are the components of the Suzerainty covenant: (1) the preamble which introduces the speaker (cf. Deut. 1:3-4); (2) the historical prologue describing the previous relations of the author of the covenant (cf. Deut. 1:3-4); (3) the stipulations detailing the obligations of the vassal state (cf. Deut. 24:7); (4) document clause providing for the safekeeping and regular public reading of the agreement (cf. Deut. 27:8); (5) the gods who are witnesses to the treaty (cf. Deut. 32:1; Is. 1:2; Ezekiel 17:13-21); (6) the blessings and curses formula (cf. Deut. 28). For a more extensive discussion of the treaty covenant in Near Eastern literature, the reader is advised to consult Dennis J. McCarthy, *Treaty and Covenant*.

Kline has organized his brief commentary on Deuteronomy for the one-volume *Biblical Wycliffe Commentary* as follows:

I. Preamble: Covenant Mediator (i. 1-5).

II. Historical Prologue: Covenant History (1:6-4:49).

III. Stipulations: Covenant Life (5:1-26; 19).

IV. Sanctions: Covenant Ratification (27:1-30:20).

V. Succession Arrangements: Covenant Continuity (31:1-34:12).

The form used by the author of Deuteronomy is paralleled to the 1600-1200 B.C. forms of the covenant as found in the Hittite historical documents. This would certainly substantiate the second millennium character of Deuteronomy. Critical scholarship claims that the Book of Deuteronomy is not a unity, making only chapters 5-26 a unit. But the outline of Kline shows that the claims of the Book that Moses was the author of the entire book shows that the book in its entirety is a unit, held together by the various aspects of the Suzerainty covenant structure.

V. Archaeology and Exegesis

Free contends "Archaeology not only throws light on the general historical situation but frequently clears up for the exegete the meaning of a particular verse or even words." Free cites as an example the statement of Moses' eye was not dim nor his natural force abated (Deut. 34:7). Many interpreters have been puzzled by this translation of the King James Version. The Word in the Hebrew of Deuteronomy is **le(a)h.** This word is similar to the word for "jaw." In view of this meaning some translators have rendered it as "extension of teeth." This is what Jerome did in the Vulgate. Discoveries from Rash Shamra show that in the Ugaritic texts this word is twice employed in the sense of "manly vigor" or "natural force." Most modern translations have not adopted the Jerome interpretation.

Philip Hyatt in his article "Archaeology and the Translation of the Old Testament" has given a number of areas in which archaeology has helped in the area of exegesis or interpretation.[30] In the Old Testament the reader will find the names of many objects, both religious and secular. In a number of cases the translators did not know exactly what was meant. Archaeology has discovered some objects mentioned in the Old Testament which now it is able to identify more precisely. Thus in the Old Testament there is an object referred to called **hamman.** There are eight different places where it is referred to namely, in Lev. 26:30; 2 Chron. 14:5; 34:4,7: Is. 17:8; 27:9; Ezek. 6:4,6. Because of the fact that the object was associated with idolatrous worship. The King James translated the word as "Image" in every case except one (2 Chron. 34:7), where it is rendered "idol." *The American Standard Version* always translates it as "sun-image." A few years ago there was found at Palmyra, Syria, an altar of incense which had this very word inscribed upon on it. Thus the word should be translated as "incense altar," and the meaning is also supported by the etymology of the Hebrew word. Hence, in the *Revised Standard Version* it always appears as "incense altar" (or in one place "altars of incense").

Especially in the field of New Testament interpretation the Greek papyri and ostraca have opened a new field of study with the revelation that the Greek of the New Testament was not a special kind of "holy" Greek, but the common language of the Roman world of Jesus' and Paul's day. Helpful light and insights have been furnished relative to the grammar, lexicography and syntax of the New Testament. New insights have also been given to the Greek of the Septuagint, which is frequently quoted by the inspired New Testament writers. Adolph Deiszmann has made very important contributions to New Testament studies. Moulton and Milligan have made available a dictionary based on the use of words employed in the New Testament as found in the Greek papyri and ostraca.

VI. Archaeology and Hermeneutics

The science of hermeneutics which enunciates the rules for the interpretation of Scripture depends largely on a correct knowledge of the historical, geographical and linguistic features when explaining Biblical texts. Archaeology is a necessary adjunct in all these areas. For instance when interpreting Deuteronomy 34:7, for a correct interpretation of that verse, it is necessary to know whether it was Moses' teeth or natural strength which was not impaired.

In the area of New Testament studies a great number of words have been amplified and in some cases the former interpretation has been changed by the papyri and inscriptions.

VII. Archaeology and the Historical Setting

To correctly understand and to interpret the Bible it is vital to possess a knowledge of the historical milieu in which these events took place. Before the discovery of the Nuzu texts Bible readers were probably puzzled by Laban's pursuit of Jacob to Canaan in order to recover the household gods (or penates).

Laban believed that his son-in-law had stolen them. Texts from Nuzu have revealed that according to the custom of the times the person who had the household gods could lay claim to the patrimony on Laban's death. Rachel wanted it for her husband and not for Laban's sons.

Another example would be the visit of the Queen of Sheba in the tenth century B.C. Formerly critical scholars questioned the historicity of the Queen of Sheba's visit to Solomon as recorded in I Kings 13:1. Assyriological records give us details about the land of Sheba early in the first millennium B.C. Professor James Montgomery, former professor at the University of Pennsylvania, in his book *Arabia and the Bible,* has shown the reality of the Queen's visit to Jerusalem. Montgomery claims that the historical setting as given in I Kings is "quite correct."

VIII. Archaeology and Biblical Geography

It has been well said that the two eyes of history are "geography and chronology." To know the places where events transpired make the understanding of a Biblical narrative meaningful. Blacklock asserted about Biblical geography as follows:

Any reader of the Bible will be struck by the contrast to place names, sometimes even to precise geographical allusions set in the narratives. It is of value to the devotional reader, as well as the serious student of the Bible to cultivate a geographical awareness of the environments associated with it. For the testimony of geography in the framework of Biblical history is essential to the chain of events and indeed is an integral part of the divine revelation.[31]

The writer of the article "Ancient Cities and Biblical Archaeology" *Pictorial Biblical Encyclopedia* wrote:

"Archaeological data have often served to correct misconceptions about the identification of certain places based only on similarities of name. Thus it has been shown that the present day Khirbet Burj'as Sur is not the site of Beth Zur, although it preserves the name. The true site of the ancient town and its Hasmonean system of walls is at Khirbet-et-Tubeiza nearby.[32]

Topographical research has also contributed to the general biblical history. For example, evidence has been found to confirm the Biblical narratives by showing that during the period of the Patriarchs (Middle B Bronze Age) most of the people lived in the plains and valleys, leaving the tree-covered hills as populated pastures. In the same way, the study of the ruins of Transjordania confirmed the impression given by Genesis 14 that the "king's highway" was an important line of communication as early as the 18th century. B.C.

IX. Archaeology and Literary Criticism

Literary criticism is concerned with the authorship, date, purpose and the integrity of the books of the Bible. These literary questions can be variously answered, depending upon presuppositions with which the Biblical student approaches the Bible. Authorship as stated by given books will be denied on the basis of rationalistic presuppositions. The rejection of the intervention of God is history, the denial of prophecy, the repudiation of divine revelation and inspiration has produced a system of literary criticism hostile to the Bible's own claims.

Formerly, it was argued that Moses could not have written the Pentateuch because writing was not in vogue in Moses' day. Archeology has shown that at the time that Moses lived, he could have one of five different scripts which archaeology has shown were current in the 15th century B.C. Another reason against the Mosaicity of the Pentateuch was the fact that the background in the Pentateuch was too late to have originated in the Mosaic age. Once again the Nuzu, Mari and Alalakh tablets have revealed the reverse. Furthermore, the cities that are mentioned in Genesis like Jerusalem, Beersheba, Dothan, Bethel and others are cities archaeological discoveries have shown were in existence in the 21st to 19th centuries, agreeing with the geographical references of the Genesis account.

Exodus, Leviticus, Numbers and Deuteronomy have laws and cultic regulations that have parallels in Near Eastern law codes and in tablets from Ugarit-Rash Shamra. The Code of Hammurabi, the Eshnuna Code, the Lipit Ishtar Code, Assyrian, Babylonian and Hittite Law Codes (available in remnants) are early and antedate many laws of the Pentateuch.

The discoveries at Ugarit or Rash Shamra have revealed that the various Sheathen epics, such as the Baal, Daniel, and Achat ones, have references to at least 15 ritual terms, which are similar and even identical to the ritual and sacrificial terminology used by Moses in Leviticus and the ritual portions in Exodus and Numbers. Leviticus has been assigned to the Holiness Code dated to the time of Ezekiel (592-571 B.C.) and the Priestly Code coming even from a later time, dated as originating between 500-450 B.C. Yet the same ritual terms were employed before 1200 B.C. The epics were contemporaneous with the time of Moses. Why then could not Moses have utilized the same terminology for different sacrifices and objects of the cultus?

Archaeologically speaking, discoveries from the Near East support the Mosaicity of the Pentateuch, which New Testament writers, including Christ, espoused. Albright has asserted that archaeology has time and again rejected and left unsupported the hypercriticism made against Biblical literature. The Dead Sea Scrolls have furnished evidence for the early dating of the Gospel of John. Thus the use of "didaskalos" was supposed to be evidence for a late date for the Gospel of John, placed by critical New Testament scholar ship around A.D. 150. The word "didaskalos" has been found on an early ossuary inscription hailing from the first part of the first Christian century.

X. Archaeology and Theology

The theologian deals with different doctrines of the Bible. One doctrine the theologians come to grip with is the doctrine of the goodness of God. How is the theologian to deal with those statements in Deuteronomy, Joshua, and Judges in which the children of Israel are commanded by Yahweh to drive out the pagan Canaanites from the Promised Land. (Deut. 7:1-5) The Book of Joshua records how at times a city like Jericho was declared **chrem,** that is completely devoted to destruction. How can episodes in Joshua and Judges be harmonized with the goodness of God?

Unger and others believe that the Rash Shamra tablets and archaeological finds supply answer to this difficult question. From Ugarit have come first hand evidence of the beliefs and practices of the Canaanite fertility cult which was associated with sexual orgies and human sacrifice, both an abomination of the God of Israel, who claims to be the God of all mankind. The alphabetic cuneiform texts from Ugarit have shown that Baalism was a licentious and corrupt kind of worship. The worship practices and theology of Baalism constituted a stench in the nostrils of the Lord. Yahweh used his people Israel as the punishers and executioners of His wrath against man's unrighteousness and perversions. Free declared concerning his issue: "The systematic theologian works with a body of revealed truth. If this revelation is shown to be inaccurate, historically incorrect, filled with contractions, what has the theologian to build on? The results of archaeological research show the firm support that exists for revelation accept and for the theology which derives from it."[33]

Footnotes

1. Francis R. Steele, "Archaeology and the Bible," *Christianity Today*, 2:16, November 25, 1957.

2. James L. Kelso, "Archeology's Role, in Bible Study," *Christianity Today*, 2:9, July 1957. Howard F. Vos, Genesis and Archaeology (Chicago: Moody, Press, 1963), p. 9.

3. Samuel Noah Kramer, *The Sumerians - Their History, Culture and Character.* (Chicago: University of Chicago Press, 1963), p. 229ff.

4. Merrill F. Unger, *Archaeology and the Old Testament* (Grand Rapids: Zondervan Publishing House, 1953), p. 15.

5. Joseph P. Free, *Archaeology and Bible History* (Revised and Explained by Howard F. Vos (Grand Rapids, Zondervan. 1992), pp. 15-16.

6. Kramer, **op. cit.**, p. 229ff.

7. Joseph P. Free, "Archaeology," Baker's *Dictionary of Theology* (Grand Rapids: Baker Book House, 1960), p. 61. 8. Steele, **op. cit.**, p. 16.

9. **Ibid.**

10. **Ibid.**

11. **Ibid.**

12. Howard Vos, *Introduction to Biblical Archaeology* (Chicago: Moody Press, 1983), pp. 14-15).

13. L. Berkhof, *Biblical Archaeology* (Grand Rapids: Smitter Book Co., 1928), pp. 15-16.

14. William Whiston, *The Works of Flavius Josephus* (London: Ward, Lock, & Co., no date), p. 26.

15. **Ibid.**, pp. 26-536.

16. L. Berkhof, *Biblical Archaeology* (Grand Rapids: Smitter Book Store, 1928), p. 17.

17. Franz Delitzsch, *Biblical Archaeology*.

18. Edmund Kalt, *Biblische Archeologie* (Zweite, vermehrte Auflage; Freiburg im Breisgau, Herder & Co., 1934),' 147 Saiten.

19. Benzinger, *Biblische Archaeologie* (Leipzig: 1894).

20. Berkhof, **op. cit.**, p. 17.

21. **Ibid.**, pp. 17-18.

22. H. F. Vos, *Archaeology - Wycliffe Bible Encyclopedia* (Grand Rapids: Zondervan Publishing House, 1975), I, p. 125.

23. Keith, N. Schoville, *Biblical Archaeology in Focus* (Grand Rapids: Baker Book House, 1978), p. 16.

24. **Ibid.**, p. 16.

25. **Ibid.**, p. 16.

26. **Ibid.**, p. 16.

27. **Ibid.**, p. 16.

28. Howard F. Vos, *An Introduction to Bible Archaeology* (Chicago: Moody Press, 1983), pp. 14-15.

29. **Ibid.**, p. 14.

30. J. Philip Hyatt, "Archaeology and the Translation of the Old Testament," in *An Introduction to the Revised Standard Version of the Old Testament* (New York; Thomas Nelson and Sons, 1952), pp. 49-55.

31. E. M. Blaiklock, *The Zondervan Pictorial Bible Atlas* (Grand Rapids: The Zondervan Publishing House, 1969), p. 2a.

32. "Ancient Cities, Excavated Sites Biblical (Archaeology and Archaeological Sequence)," Gaalyahu Cornfeld, *Pictorial Bible Encyclopedia* (New York: The Macmillan Co., 1964), p. 45b.

33. Free, "Archaeology," Baker's *Dictionary of Theology*, E. F. Harrison, Editor-in-Chief (Grand Rapids: Baker Book House, 1960), pp. 62-63.

Questions

1. The major museums of the world contain ____.
2. What has archeology furnished? ____
3. The third and latest use of the word "archeology" is related to ____.
4. Archeology is basically a ____.
5. Biblical archeology covers all the countries of ____.
6. Palestinian archaeology begins with ____ and ends with ____.
7. What do Christians who believe God's Word is the truth believe about archeology? ____
8. What is the first period of the history of the Bible? ____
9. What is the last period? ____
10. What do the Nuzu tablets reveal? ____
11. Robert Dick Wilson claimed that by 1926 archeology had confirmed ____.
12. What was said about the Hittites a hundred years age? ____
13. The Bible in many places refers to persons, events, and places in Genesis 1-11 as ____.
14. What do the Nuzu, Alalakh, Chagar Bazar and Ebla tablets show? ____
15. Archaeology shows that there need be no objections that Psalms was written by ____.
16. The Greek of the New Testament was ____.
17. Why did Rachel want the household gods? ____
18. James Montgomery's Arabia and the Bible shows the reality of ____.
19. Archeology has shown that at the time of Moses ____.
20. What did Christ espouse about the Mosaicity of the Pentateuch? ____
21. Now can episodes in Joshua and Judges be harmonized with the goodness of God? ____

The Hermeneutics of Robert Preus

Christian News, October 5, 1998

Dr. Robert Preus was one of the outstanding scholars of world Lutheranism in the twentieth century.[1] He was considered an authority on the theology of the post-Reformation period of Lutheranism. That this was the case may be seen from his doctoral dissertation, titled *The Inspiration of Scripture - A Short Study of the Theology of the 17th Century Dogmaticians* (1955)[2] and his two-volume work, The Theology of Post-Reformation Lutheranism, vol. I (1970) and vol. II (1972)[3] and various essays dealing with the Symbols of the Lutheran Church, especially the *Book of Concord* and in the latter, *The Formula of Concord.*[4]

A graduate of Lutheran College, Decorah, Iowa, he attended Luther Seminary in St. Paul, followed by graduation from Bethany Lutheran Seminary (ELS), Mankato. He did postgraduate studies at Oslo, Washington, Chicago and Harvard Universities. Dr. Preus was well acquainted with the history of theological ideas beginning with the Ancient Church till modern times, was well-versed in the theology of Karl Barth[5,] Emil Brunner, Rudolf Bultmann[6] and the post-Bultmannians. Preus was conversant with the history of hermeneutics, as well as being regarded as an authority on the Lutheran Confessions as well as the doctrine of Justification by faith[7], the doctrine of the "standing or falling church." He was well-informed about the theology of Walther[8], Pieper and the doctrinal theology of The Lutheran Church-Missouri Synod. The same was also true about his acquaintance with the theological literature of the Wisconsin Evangelical Lutheran Synod and the Evangelical Lutheran Synod.

Dr. Preus was a prolific writer. A bibliography of his publications was printed when he assumed the Presidency of Concordia Theological Seminary, Springfield, Illinois, and later Fort Wayne, Indiana, in 1974. Forty-eight books and articles had been published between 1955 and 1974.[9] He wrote mostly in English, one in German and a number in Norwegian. Another bibliography appeared covering the years 1974-1984, and showed that 25 more materials were in print.[10]

When the higher critical scholars and liberal scholars endeavored to get control of the LCMS, Preus was one of a number of scholars who fought this attempt by liberal scholars at St. Louis, River Forest and other colleges of the Concordia University System (as now known). Preus showed the unLutheran Character of those attempting to follow the liberal tendencies of world Protestantism. As President of The Springfield and Fort Wayne Seminary, he endeavored to promote the theology of Luther and the Lutheran Confessions.[11]

As a competent exegete and dogmatician, Dr. Preus realized the great importance of knowing and practicing a sound system of Biblical hermeneutics.[12] In a number of his published writings Preus set forth what he believed were the true Biblical principles of interpretation and also criticized wrong principles of interpretation, of which certain scholars were guilty of advocating and

753

practicing in their exegetical endeavors.[13]

The Hermeneutics of Robert Preus as given by him in the following contributions:

Robert Preus, *The Theology of Post-Reformation Lutheranism* (St. Louis: Concordia Publishing House, 1970), Vol. I, pp. 315-339; Volume II, pp. 136-138; 150; 234, 257, 257-258.

Robert Preus, *"Guiding Theological Principles,"* in P. A. Zimmerman, Editor, *Rock Strata and the Bible* (St. Louis: Concordia Publishing House, 1970), pp. 12-23.

Robert Preus, "Biblical Hermeneutics and the Lutheran Church Today,*" Proceedings of the Twentieth Convention of the Iowa District West of The Lutheran Church-Missouri Synod*, 1966, pp. 29-61. Robert Preus, "How Is the Lutheran Church to Interpret and Use the Old Testament?" Bethany Lutheran College, Mankato, Minnesota, 1973 (Bethany Lutheran College Reformation Lectures, 1973).

Robert D. Preus, "Notes on the Inerrancy of Scripture," in John Warwick Montgomery, *Crisis in Lutheran Theology* (Grand Rapids: Baker Book House) II, pp. 18-47.

Robert Preus, "Biblical Hermeneutics and the Lutheran Church Today," Grand Rapids: Baker Book House, II, pp. 81-120.

Robert D. Preus, "The Hermeneutics of the *Formula of Concord*," in Arnold J. Koelpin, *No Other Gospel* (Milwaukee: Northwestern Publishing House, 1980), pp. 309-331.

Earl Rademacher and Robert Preus, *Hermeneutics, Inerrancy and the Bible. Papers from ICBI. Summit II* (Grand Rapids: 1984).

Robert Preus, "Response: Unity of the Bible," Rademacher and R. Preus, *Hermeneutics, Inerrancy and the Bible* (Grand Rapids: Zondervan Publishing House, 1984, pp. 671-690).

A Summary of Lutheran Biblical Principles of Interpretation as Found in the Writings and Books of Preus

Preus's Definition of Hermeneutics

In his discussion of the hermeneutics of the *Formula of Concord* Preus gave this definition: "Hermeneutics may be defined as the art of interpreting the Scriptures. Hermeneutics includes the presuppositions the interpreter brings with him as he studies the Scriptures, his doctrine concerning Scripture and his attitude toward it as he carries the principles of interpretation to the intelligent reading of all literature in general. Hermeneutics deals with the method as well as the tools of exegesis."[14] The late and former President of Concordia Seminary, Springfield-Fort Wayne, would agree with the description of hermeneutics as found in the *Concordia Cyclopedia*, which stated: "That part of theological study which deals with the fundamental rules of apprehension and interpretation of Bible texts, partly on the basis of general logic and grammar, partly with reference to each particular book, always on the principle that the Bible is the Word of God."[14a] Preus drew his hermeneutical principles from the New Testament, from the writings of the Early Church Fathers, from Luther's writings, also from the hermeneutical principles employed by the authors of the Lutheran Confessions and from certain writings of the theologians of the Lutheran Age of Orthodoxy. In addition to his observations on the statements of over 20 some theologians of the Age of Lutheran orthodoxy, Preus was acquainted with the heremeneutical principles of C.F.W. Walther and various leaders of the Lutheran Church-Missouri Synod. He also relied on the hermeneutical principles enunciated by Hoenecke and various Wisconsin and Norwegian Churches' theologians in the United States and also in Norway.

Preus agreed that the Lutheran Church had a special Biblical hermeneutic. Thus he asserted "The Lutheran emphasis upon the doctrinal unity of Scripture, the divine origin, and authority of the Bible—all such emphases constitute a series of hermeneutical presuppositions of gigantic proportions, presuppositions which will totally determine the interpretational attitude to the sacred Scripture."[15]

Presuppositions Determining Hermeneutics

Preus claimed that the hermeneutics of the 1570s among Lutheran was the same as had been in the 1530s. In the *Formula of Concord* the exegesis of Luther is adduced. One could follow and predicate that it was the hermeneutics of 1570-1580. Chemnitz, Selnecker and Chrytaeus wrote many exegetical works and upon their bases it would be possible to formulate the hermeneutics of the *Formula of Concord*. The writers of the *Formula of Concord* let Luther's exegesis and hermeneutics speak for themselves. They were open to the tremendous advances made by the humanists and later by Christian theologians.[16]

The Doctrine of Scripture As Presupposition for Hermeneutics

It has been claimed in certain circles that the Lutheran Confessions had no doctrine of Scripture.

But Preus cited the *Formula of Concord* as giving a thorough and comprehensive doctrine of Scripture and that this doctrine of Holy Writ is presented in its introductory chapter titled "Rule and Norm."[17] The *Formula of Concord* supports the doctrine of Biblical inspiration, authority and inerrancy. The *Solid Declaration* teaches that the Word of God is the sole rule and norm of doctrine in the *Formula of Concord*, indiscriminately calls Scripture the Word of God which would involve the inspiration of the Bible's 66 books. In this document, writers of the *Formula of Concord* state that no human idea should be used to establish doctrine. The Word of God and Scripture are employed synonymously in the *Formula of Concord*. Article III of the *Solid Declaration* says that the Holy Spirit opens the hearts to understand the Scriptures and adheres to its teachings.[18a] In one place the *Solid Declaration* attributes the Word of God or Scripture to the activity of the Holy Spirit.

The *Formula of Concord* and the *Solid Declaration* teach that God is the author of Scripture and that it is divine.

Did the Post-Reformation Theologians follow the Same Hermeneutics as Luther and the Lutheran Confessions?

To answer this question one needs to turn or consult Robert Preus' *The Theology of Post-Reformation Lutheranism* (2 volumes). In this major and definitive work Preus has examined over 20 theologians of the 16th and 17th centuries. Exegesis is necessary to determine the doctrinal teachings. Hermeneutics, in turn, determines how these dogmaticians understood the Holy Scriptures. A number of theologians of the Lutheran Age of Orthodoxy have written books on the discipline of Hermeneutics.[18]

Relative to the Post-Reformation period of Lutheranism Preus made this judgment: "In general the spirit and the rules of the reformers became the guiding principles of Protestant orthodox interpretation."[19] To name the scholars who followed the footsteps of Luther and Calvin would be to name most of the great exegetes from Reformation times till now. In Preus' judgment that the dogmaticians of Post-Reformation Lutheranism considered themselves as promoting sound Lutheranism, and was bound not only to the doctrines, but to the hermeneutics. To abandon the latter which was believed to be Christ's hermeneutics, they held, could result in abandonment of Christian doctrine.[20]

Basic Rules of Hermeneutics as Found in the Writers of Lutheran Orthodoxy

In his *Post-Reformation Theology of Lutheranism*, 2 volumes, Preus has discussed in detail the major and primary principles of Biblical Interpretation. Preus made the general observation about this period of Lutheran history: "But the hermeneutical approach to Scripture which we have among post-Reformation Lutherans was not something which could just be discarded or even modified, for it was a part of the heritage of the Reformation and of the Lutheran Confessions. There is no doubt the question that the dogmaticians we have studied considered themselves and genuine Lutheranism bound not only to a doctrine but to hermeneutics. To abandon that hermeneutic would result abandoning the Christian doctrine as well.[21]

Preus cited the position of the Socinians who departed from traditional hermeneutics of the Reformation and the Church Catholic, which resulted in the abandonment of the doctrines of the Holy Trinity and the deity of Christ. The Lutheran hermeneuticians, exegetes and dogmaticians were greatly opposed to the Socinianism.[22] Socinians rejected the hallowed hermeneutics of the past. The attacks of 16th and 17th Lutheranism rejected Socinians Exegesis. The Lutherans were motivated by the conviction that Socinian hermeneutics was responsible for a number of false doctrines. Socinians refused to read the Old Testament in the light of the New, played down the analogy of faith and refused to find the Trinity in the Old Testament.[23]

The importance of Lutheran Orthodoxy which lasted for three hundred years, upheld and defended the doctrines of Scripture and the Lutheran Symbols, and thus made possible the existence of the Lutheran Church today.[23a]

Writers of Orthodoxy on Hermeneutics

Preus called special attention to Andrew Hyperius, Book II of his *De Theologe de Ratione Theologi Libri III* (Basel, 1556).[24] In the second section Hyperius gives guides for Scripture reading. Another good source would be Flacius, *Clavis Scripturae*.[25]

Preus believed that the *Formula of Concord* contains all the necessary presuppositions for exegesis and pointed out the principles of hermeneutics[26] which the *Formula* authors held uniquely biblical and therefore necessary for essential and Biblical Study and therefore necessary for Biblical reading and exposition.[27]

The *Formula* taught that the Bible was the written Word of God or that the Bible is the authoritative source and norm for all teaching in the Church. Thus the *Solid Declaration* declares:

"We clearly pledge ourselves to the prophetic and apostolic writings of the Old and New Testaments as the pure and clear fountain of Israel, which is the only norm according to which all teachers and teachings are to be judged and evaluated" (Rule and Norm. 3).[28]

Wrote Preus: "It is a fundamental and prerequisite hermeneutical principle in reading any piece of literature purporting to speak authoritatively on any subject to determine who is the author of the piece and the degree of authority to be accorded to it.[29]

C. Biblical Authority and Biblical Infallibility

The same section of the *Formula of Concord* which claims that Holy Writ is the source and norm of teaching refers to the truthfulness of Scriptures. The two concepts entail each other.[30] To hold that the Bible is errant and fallible contradicts the statement that Sacred Scripture is "pure, infallible, and the unalterable Word of God." Throughout the *Formula of Concord* it is asserted that the Word of God is "pure doctrine," taken from Scriptures and emphasizes the truth of the divine Word.[31] Asserts Preus: "And throughout the Formula this belief in the infallibility of the Bible comes through as the confessions interpret Scripture and confess their doctrine. God's Word is not false and it does not lie (Epit. VII, 13). In its discussion of the words of institution of the Lord's Supper the *Formula of Concord* insists that these words are clear and true. They are the words of Christ who said: "I am the Truth."[32]

The expression "true" and "infallible" as attributed to Holy Writ are the best possible terms for the concepts of the reliability and inerrancy of Holy Writ. The Word of God is **autopistos** (i.e., self-authenticating).[33] The value of Scripture's inerrancy and agreement, opined Preus, gives with itself the offer of total comfort and assurance to the Christian who interprets and rests on the words found there (*Solid Declaration*, XI, 36).[34] If Scripture contradicts itself, we would no longer trust the promises of God therein. Yes, one could not practice serious exegesis.[35] It would be impossible to determine the intended sense. In this sense the inerrancy of Scripture undergirds serious exegesis.[36]

The Bible itself provides rules for its interpretation, understanding and application. Some of these principles will pertain to the posture, or preunderstanding the hermeneutic and his relationship to God. At other times they will resemble grammatical and linguistic principles found in ancient literature. The authors of the *Formula of Concord* were convinced that they considered the principles they employed were fundamental.

A. Search for the Sensus Literalis

The first purpose of an exegete is to determine the meaning of the Biblical text. This is evident when the *Solid Declaration* is read. The authors of the *Formula of Concord* wish to ascertain the sensus literalis (literal sense) and when the writers of the *Formula* used it, they believed that the teaching they were advocating was "according to the Word of God," that it was drawn from the Word of God (S.D. II, 6,8; III, 8: IV, 28; VIII, 51, 53: 60:669). Their purpose was to find **the Meinung Verstand vera et genuina** of a given text (SD III, 36; VI, 36; VI, 5; VIII; 7,22,23,50,51).[37]

Finding the intended sense of a passage is a fundamental principle of any literature, ancient or modern. When human writings do not seem to make sense, an attempt is made by interpreters to harmonize them if the intended sense does not agree with human reason, human empirical evidence or even to reinterpret the words or find a more plausible meaning.[38] But the Biblical hermeneutic dare not change the intended sense of a Biblical passage or paragraph. However, the Christian exegete committed to the divine origin and complete truthfulness cannot proceed in such a manner but as SD VII, 45; of 38) states the reader is to accept the words of Scripture: "in their strict and clear sense, just as the words read." Nothing should lead a reader faithful to God's Word to leave "the clear sense of the text." Preus agreed with the theologians of the Lutheran Age of Orthodoxy that an interpreter must be sensitive to the stylistics and **modus loquendi**. One must guard against a wrong literalism, which is done by failure to recognize figures of speech throughout the Bible. Like the 16th and 17th centuries exegetes, Preus avoided allegorization or fanciful interpretation. The former Concordia Seminary, Springfield- Ft. Wayne, president realized that even though God's Word was clear as well as truthful, it was not always easy to determine the **sensus literalis** and this was due to man's handicaps and weaknesses, because regenerate believers know of the profundity of the mysteries of the Christian faith. For example, John 6:48-58 was taken metamorphically as referring to faith and not to the Lord's Supper. With the Age of Lutheran Orthodoxy Preus held that in interpretation involved not only the meaning of individual verses, but also pericopes and whole books and the entire Scripture.[39]

In his article: "The Hermeneutics of the *Formula of Concord*" Preus took note of the problems Lutherans faced when endeavoring to ascertain the **sensus literalis** when it appears as if one Scripture were contradicting another dealing with the same subject. Preus cited *Solid Declaration VIII, 6-14,* with the doctrine of the personal union and the resultant communication of attributes. Article VIII of the *Solid Declaration* in its entirety is a good example of the use of hermeneutics and exegesis at this point: The Lutherans refused to permit the intended sense of one pericope to be used against another pericope dealing with the same subject. In this article the exegetical results or conclusions taken from the Biblical data are summarized. However, the summary appears to oppose all rational synthesis. Opined Preus: "The discussions in Article VIII illustrates with clarity the intended sense, that the intended meaning of a subject must be retained at all costs, and if paradoxes or tensions emerge from the comparison of these passages and their intended meaning, they must remain, and for all the biblical data dealing with the subject must be retained in tension."[40]

Another example of the consequence of the use of the sensus literalis happens when one article of faith seems to oppose another. In such a case, stated Preus, one article must not be employed to deny another. What God's Word teaches about conversion must not be used against justification by faith. The doctrine of election must not be employed to reject another Scriptural teaching.[41]

The theology of Scripture will manifest many lacunae, apparent paradoxes, mysteries that cannot be probed or harmonized. To disagree with clearly enunciated teachings stated in given passages would be tantamount to the rejection of the **sensus literalis**.[42]

B. The Unity of Scripture
(Analogical Exegesis)

From the divine character of Holy Scripture and its truthfulness is derived a second major hermeneutical principle, namely, the unity of Scripture. By the unity of Scripture is meant that the Word of God as found in the Old and New Testament teaches one message of law and Gospel, one way of salvation, one heavenly doctrine[43] (Cf Tappert, Preface, p. 5). The sixty-six books of the Bible (minus the Apocrypha) are not the product of many different writers, but has One Author, the Holy Spirit, are therefore, God's Word. This means that Sacred Scriptures agrees with itself and that Scripture can be employed to interpret Scripture. The agreement of Scriptures with itself is known as the analogy of faith. Passages of the Bible that treat of the same subject or article of faith do not contradict each other. Frequently passages that are unclear in one place are clarified by statements in another passage. Opined Preus: "In no way is the principle of the analogy of Scripture thought to be at variance with the basic exegetical task of finding and adhering to the intended meaning of the biblical text. Rather it appears to be an extension of just the first principle."[44]

C. The Gospel Principle (The Centrality of Justification)
1. The Proper Distinction Between Law and Gospel

One of the major principles of Lutheran orthodox hermeneutics is the proper distinction between Law and Gospel. This is the clear position of *The Formula of Concord*, which asserts that the proper distinction between Law and Gospel is an especially brilliant light and serves the purpose that the Word of God may be rightly divided (recht geteilt, recte secari) and the writings of the holy prophets and apostles may be explained (eigentlich erklaert). Law and Gospel should never be mixed. When the exegete fails to do this, it darkens the merit of Christ. By correctly separating Law and Gospel, Christians can comfort themselves in greatest temptations against the terrors of the law.[45]

A hermeneutic correctly distinguishes between these two forms of God's Word when he correctly understands what is Law and what is Gospel. The Formula says: "that the Gospel is for everything which comforts and which offers mercy and the grace of God to violators of the Law."

There are different ways in which Law and Gospel are confused. In the Apology of the Augsburg Confession, Melanchthon criticized the Roman Catholic Church for interpreting Law passages as Gospel (IV, 7,12, V, 11). In all Scripture Law and Gospel are found side by side. The Law works contrition and repentance, the Gospel tells what Christ has done for man's eternal salvation.

2. The Hermeneutical Function of the Gospel

Closely related to the function of Law and Gospel is the emphasis on the centrality of justification by faith.[46] Luther and Melanchthon attached primary importance to the doctrine of justification by faith and only as this doctrine is seen in both Testaments can Holy Writ be correctly understood. In the *Smalcald Articles* (11,1) Luther termed the work of Christ and His Word and faith in Him in Him der **Hauptartikel.** He employed this article to reject work righteousness as a method of salvation and also used it to reject all papal aberrations and unevengelical practices (SA II, 1, 8,24,31; IV, 3). *The Solid Declaration* agrees with Melanchthon's *Apology of the Augsburg Confession, The Apology* agrees with Luther relative to the centrality of the doctrine of justification by faith. The *Apology* asserted: "This is justification by faith is the chief article of the entire Christian doctrine without which no poor conscience can have any abiding comfort or rightly understand the riches of the grace of Christ."[47] Likewise Luther declared: "Where this single article remains pure, Christendom will remain pure, in beautiful harmony and without any schisms. But where it does not, it is impossible to repel any error or heretical spirits (SD III, 6)." Preus believed that the *Formula of Concord* used justification by faith as a hermeneutical principle. His discussion of hermeneutical principles showed how it was employed in a number of articles.[48]

However, it was Preus' contention that the Gospel principle was not to be utilized to mitigate the clear intention of any Scripture or articles of faith.[49] Articles V and VI of the *Formula of Concord* shows that the Gospel in no way detracts from God's law, even though in God's economy the Law serves the Gospel.

Article VI is a polemic not only against antinomianism but against Gospel reductionism. Declared Preus: "In the case of all the articles of faith Scripture must be the only source of the article, this is apparent in every single article of the Formula, and significantly in article IV dealing with justification."[50]

In the *Formula of Concord* the chief article is employed as

760

Melanchthon had done in the *Apology* and Luther in the *Smalcald Articles*. In all three symbols the chief article was resorted to in order to counter false and unevangelical practices which denied the Gospel and positively to combat rationalistic or legalistic exegesis which undermines the Gospel and positively to set forth a setting for the presentation of the articles of faith.[51]

Preus shows how this principle was utilized in Articles IV, X and especially in article XI "On Predestination." It was also utilized in Article X, dealing with Adiaphora."

D. Biblical Realism, as a Presupposition for Biblical Hermeneutics[52]

Preus rigorously opposed classical liberalism and twentieth century secularism. This included the new orthodoxy of aberrant Protestantism and the theologians who deny the reality of the supernatural birth of Christ, that God assumed human nature, the Virgin Birth, the resurrection from the dead. His Ascension and session of God's right hand, Christ's twofold nature. His return for judgment and the resurrection of all who have died. He rejects the liberal denial of the miracles of Christ who portray the miraculous accounts as didactic tales or myths. For the perversions of Scripture, Preus would argue that they rejected the intended meaning of God's Word. For the unregenerate exegetes they did not believe that Adam and Eve ever existed, that Adam's offspring were born in sin, inherited from their progenitors and ultimately needed the atoning work of Christ. Although the practitioners of the new hermeneutic claimed they were faithful to the **sensus literalis**, "They did not believe in the historic or ontological reality underlying biblical assertions."[53]

The Lutheran theologians of the 16th and 17th centuries were cognizant of this problem of denying the reality of events dealing with mankind's redemption and they rejected all efforts to deny the reality of any text or pericope[54] that questioned the vicarious atonement, death, resurrection, ascension and second coming of Christ. They would have repudiated texts or pericopes that were portrayed as allegorization and such interpretations calling salvation events as aetiological saga, didactic tales, symbolical history, faith events, and midrash.[55]

The *Augsburg Confession* emphasized Scripture's realism and asserted that the Trinity is not only God but is God. (AC 1,2) when it proclaims that original sin is truly sin (vere peccatuk), when it speaks of Christ as true God and true man and says that Christ suffered (AC III, 2, Latin text) and arose (AC III, 3, German text) and when it declares that the body and blood are truly present in the Lord's Supper (AC X). The **vere** is added to underline the fact that **est** expresses reality as used in the Lord's Supper, even when figurative language is employed. Even though the right hand of God is figurative, it still denotes a reality. Preus contended that this expression was nevertheless used in a realistic sense.[56]

This same realistic understanding of the theology of the Sacred Writings was recognized by the *Formula of Concord*. The Word of God teaches the communication of attributes, not merely a verbal one (SD VIII, 31,

56-59, 63). God dwells in the believers (SD III, 65). The fact that the body and blood are distributed by a wicked priest shows that the Post-Reformation Lutheran theologians believed in true theological realism. This principle of realism is brought out wherever the **manducatio indignorum** (the eating of the unworthy) is stressed (SD VII, 8, 18, 53). The very doctrine of the real presence in Holy Communion is evident as a classical expression of the maxim of reality.[57]

The *Augsburg Confession* and the *Formula of Concord* emphasize the reality of original sin as recorded in Holy Writ. Although rejecting Strigelian or Pelagian diminution of sin, the *Formula of Concord* stressed the reality of sin which corrupts and was the result of the Fall in Eden and held also true about the present condition of mankind (SD, I, 6,9,ii, 13,27; V, 32). "Since the fall" and "through the fall" occur as a refrain in the *Formula*. Luther stressed the Fall as the reason human beings are lost and subject to eternal damnation. Article I of the Formula has this as its central point, namely, the reality of original sin.[58]

E. The Purpose of Scripture

The *Solid Declaration* (XI, 12; Rom. 15:4) teaches that it is the purpose of Sacred Scriptures to lead to repentance and hope. The purpose of the Bible is Soteriological (justification through faith).[59] Asserted Preus: "No article of faith can be taught or interpreted against this saving purpose of God's Word. Thus the doctrine of predestination must be related to the central doctrine and must be taught so as to not engender despair. It is improper to speculate about election and endeavor and probe the hidden wisdom of God."[60] The purpose of Holy Writ is to show mankind that the Law serves the Gospel and all articles should be coordinated to the article of redemption and salvation (14-32).

All Biblical interpretation should be pursued in the light of Scripture's purpose. The *Solid Declaration* declares: "It is certain that any interpretation of Scripture which weakens or even removes this comfort and intent (SD XI, 92) is contrary to the Holy Spirit's intent and will: It is important to realize the relationship between the purpose of Scripture and the unity of Scripture as another principle of interpretation.[61]

F. The Holy Spirit and The Interpretation of Scripture

While the writers of the *Formula* knew that the Holy Spirit is the interpreter of Sacred Scriptures and although the Bible does not explicitly assert this truth, they believed that the Holy Spirit was the final interpreter of the writings which He caused holy men of God to record. Since the Holy Spirit is the ultimate author of Holy Writ, He must be relied upon to interpret the writings He intended to be understood. The Holy Spirit does not prevaricate or lie. One of the functions of the Holy Spirit is to help in the interpretation of Holy Writ. There is no conflict between the *Formula of Concord's* statement previously set forth as Biblical principles of interpretation, and the Holy Spirit's guidance.

Throughout the Lutheran Confessions there is emphasized the sanctifying office of the Holy Spirit to help the regenerate exegete understand the intended sense of the Holy Spirit, the third Person of the Godhead.[62] Thus the *Solid Declaration* claims that the Holy Spirit "opens the intellect and the heart to understanding the Scriptures and to heed the Word" (SD II, 26,27; V. 12; C f Luke 24, 25; Acts 16:14.) Averred Preus: "Notice, he leads us to understand Scripture (this means exegesis) and to heed the Word, (this means faith and application) the two aspects of exegesis."[63]

What the *Formula of Concord*, the longest and most theological of all Symbols of Lutheran Church, appears to assert was that it believed that its exegesis was firmly based on Scriptures and that the authors of the *Formula of Concord* were not aware of any serious inconsistency in their hermeneutical method. This was Preus' evaluation of their hermeneutical method.[64]

Robert Preus and the Historical Critical Method

The historical Critical Method became prominent in the first half of the Twentieth Century and was adopted by many Protestants, Lutherans and Roman Catholics. Lutheran scholars in Europe and in America became seriously involved in its use. Connected with this interpretational method were **Sachkritik** (content criticism), form criticism, demythologization, redaction criticism and midrash, the fanciful interpretation given by the rabbis, who often made up stories, presented in a certain literary form.[65] Preus was well-versed in the arguments the new hermeneutic found in the writings and works of some of the prestigious scholars of world Protestantism. In a number of presentations Preus took up their views and refuted them on the basis of Scriptural hermeneutics and the hermeneutics of Luther, the Lutheran Confessions and also the writings of Post-Reformation Lutheran Orthodoxy. In 1966 Preus delivered at Iowa District West, Twentieth Convention of the Lutheran Church-Missouri Synod, the following essay: "Biblical Hermeneutics and the Lutheran Church Today," also as part of his 1973 Reformation Lectures at Bethany Lutheran College, Mankato, Minnesota, presented a critique of the higher critical method of Bible interpretation in "How Is the Lutheran Church to Interpret and Use the Old and New Testaments?"[66] The adoption of the Higher Critical Method has had important implications for the doctrine of Scripture, affecting its inspiration, authority, inerrancy.[67] Eventually each important Christian doctrine was subject to attack. The practitioners among Lutherans who used the Historical Critical Method attacked the exegesis of the Lutheran Confessions and the doctrine based on their exegesis. In a contribution in Rock Strata and the Bible Record by Paul Zimmerman, titled "Guiding Theological Principles. A Lutheran Confessional Approach to the Doctrine of Creation," Preus evaluated the critical doctrine of creation, using as basis for judgment the basic Lutheran Hermeneutics which Preus has set forth   clearly.[68] The Lutheran Confessional Approach entails employing and practicing the following rules:

1. The Holy Spirit as the true interpreter of Scripture; 2. The Scripture as the Word is God Himself; 3. This involves the divine origin, authority,

and sufficiency of Scripture which are assumed throughout the Lutheran Confessions and are the fundamental presuppositions to all Lutheran exegesis.[69] This is the position found in all Lutheran Confessions and is the stance of the *Formula of Concord*, which says in the *Solid Declaration* (D. II, 26): "But to be born anew, to receive inwardly a new heart is a part of the entire work of converting and enlightening and sanctifying man. It is through the Word that the Spirit comes to us, and it is through the Word—not merely Scriptures, of course, but the Gospel—that He brings us to faith (AC V; Ap. XII, 42)." This means only a Christian can read Scripture with complete understanding in the sense of acceptance, although even a Jew or a Turk can often understand the meaning of the words.

2. A fundamental presupposition, assumed throughout the Lutheran Confessions, is the belief in the divine origin, authority, and sufficiency of Holy Writ.[70] These principles are basic to sound Biblical interpretation. Another important hermeneutical rule is the Christocentricity of all of Scripture," beginning with Genesis 3:15 and running like a red thread through the sixty-six Biblical books of the Biblical canon. (Apol. XXIV, 55, 57; IV, 57)

All Scripture can be divided into two major parts, to teach two works of God to mankind, namely. Law and Gospel, to either terrify or comfort people. All Holy Writ must be read in the light of these two major doctrines (Ap. IV, 218-222). The epitome of the Gospel is the doctrine of justification by faith and is the chief doctrine of the Bible. Under no circumstances should this teaching, a hermeneutical principle be misrepresented (AP IV, 2). If this happens, then all is darkness, even though the grammatical sense of the Bible may well be understood. Opined Preus: "All doctrinal unity is maintained by the Lutheran Confessions along with the Christological unity of Holy Writ, for all Christian doctrine has its center in the doctrine of the Gospel."[72]

The Lutheran Confessions declare the clarity of Scripture, for the most part passages are cited to support Christian doctrine with little or no comment. That does not mean that there are not dark passages, but the confessors assumed that doctrine must be established from clear passages (Ap. IV, 314; LC V, 45; PC II, 87; Ap. XXIV, 94; FC SD VII, 50" AC XXII, 2). For reliable exegesis there is the necessity of grammatical exegesis; finding the literal sense, which is one. In the Lutheran Confessions the authors try to determine as to what was the intended sense. This is accomplished by the use of grammar, lexicography, and any historical tools available to determine the literal and intended meaning of a text on pericope. Etymologies, Biblical usage, even extra-Biblical data are brought to bear in the effort of determining the intended meaning of a Scriptural text or pericope (Ap. XXIV, 23, 81-83; FC 7-9; III, 17; AP. IV 246-253).

From the clarity of Scripture there is also obtained the principle that Scripture interprets Scripture, derived also from the truth that God is the principle author of the Word of God. The authors of the Confessions draw from all over Scripture, both the Old and New Testaments, when

764

they wish to establish a certain point (Ap. XII, 44-52; IV, 272- 285; 2562-63 FCSD II, 9-17.26; VIII, 70). The clear passages are employed to clear up difficult passages using these Biblical and hermeneutical principles. Preus judged the variant forms that the historical critical method took. Under no circumstance Preus argued that the historical-critical method could be harmonized with the theology of the Lutheran Confessions.

To be able to evaluate satisfactorily the historical-critical method, Preus claimed that one must know what the historical-critical method is in terms of its goals and assumptions and know where it conflicts with the Lutheran Confessions. Here is Preus' definition of this popular and current method: "The historical-critical method of studying Scripture (or any piece of literature) by using all the criteria of historical investigation. The analysis Scripture in terms of language, literary form, redaction criticism, source criticism, as well as historical, archaeological and other relevant data. The purpose of the method is not merely philological and linguistical: Namely, to learn the meaning of texts and verses of Scripture. The overarching of the method is historical, namely, to discover the history and history of the form and content of any given portion or unit in Scripture and to trace thehistory of the given unit through every step of its development until it finds its way into Scripture as we have it.[73]

This procedure can be applied to any Old Testament texts, to any parable and discourse of Jesus, any action or miracle of our Lord. The overarching purpose, the ultimate goal of the method, is to find the word or event behind the Biblical text, to ascertain the historicity or truthfulness of what the Bible asserts, to discover the historical origin of the contents of a text or pericope.[74]

For Lutherans and the exegetes influenced by the Reformer, as evident from the Lutheran Confessions and the post reformation Lutheran divines' exegesis was primarily a philological disciple and for the users of the historical-critical method a historical movement. For Luther and the Lutheran Confessions Biblical and historical investigation was undertaken to determine to aid in the determination of the canonical text, the prophetic and apostolic Word as such. Historical criticism is employed to ascertain history that may or not be behind the text.[75]

The historical-critical method was worked out by scholars in the 17th and 18th centuries, by individuals who rejected the traditional doctrine that the Bible contained God's revelation. The divine origin and the inspired character of the Bible was rejected as well as its authority. The historical data and events of Holy Writ must be treated as the historian did with secular history.[76]

Those Lutherans who applied these criteria to the historical events of the Bible were required by their false assumptions to reject many doctrines and facts of the Lutheran Confessions. They denied the historical events associated as a part of Jesus' life. New Testament scholars have refused to accept as actual historical events the miracles, sermons and discourses, the miracles of His resurrection, ascension and sitting at the right hand of God.[77]

The historical-critical method has wrong assumptions in its approach of Holy Writ. These assumptions are clear to any competent purveyor of the exegesis propounded by the historical-critical practitioners. The earlier and later developers of this hostile approach to God's Word have accepted views and rejected the possibility of revelation coming directly from God, attributing the contents to man's thinking and cogitations, thus ruling out the existence of God's actual words and consequent lacking authority to command human beings as to how truly to be saved and lead a God-oriented life. It is the judgment of Preus that the historical-critical method conflicts with every principle of Biblical interpretation as set forth in Scripture, in Luther's views about hermeneutics and in the New Testament's use of hermeneutical principles.[78]

Those interested in how Preus deals with the historical-criticism's view of Genesis Chapters 1-3 should read his discussion in *Rock Strata and The Bible Record*, pp. 16-23. In his essay "Biblical Hermeneutics and the Lutheran Church Today," he has set forth the views of form criticism, demytholization and Midrash. This essay also has a discussion of the faulty interpretation of Genesis 1-3, containing the doctrine of creation of everything in the universe, the creation of Adam and Eve and also the fall of man in paradise and the beginning of sin in the world.[79]

Conclusions of Preus' Hermeneutical Studies

In his Reformation Lectures at Mankato, Minnesota, Preus wrote in "How Is the Lutheran Church to Interpret and Use the Old and New Testaments?": "The historical-critical method conflicts with evangelical hermeneutics in every single point that we have discussed."[80] Again in another place in this essay, Preus claimed: "I need only mention that the results of the historical-critical method have at crucial points contradicted the doctrines of the Lutheran Confessions."[81] Preus concluded his Mankato Reformation lectures with this assertion: "Today those of us who wish to maintain the Gospel and our evangelical Lutheran identity have one clear course of action open to us. We must restudy and affirm our evangelical Lutheran hermeneutics. We must reaffirm the true Reformation principle of **Sola Scriptura**. And we must on doctrinal grounds and on the basis of the biblical and Christian idea of history reject as such as the historical-critical method of the investigation in the Scriptures."[82]

Footnotes

1. K. Marquart, "Doctor Robert Preus; An Appreciation," in K. Marquart, John R. Stevenson, Bjarne Teigen, *A Lively Legacy: Essays in Honor of Robert Preus* (Ft. Wayne: Concordia Seminary Press, 1985), pp. ix-xiii.
2. Robert Preus, *The Inspiration of Scriptures. A Study of the Theology of the Sixteenth Century Dogmaticians* (Edinburgh: Olive and Boyd, 1957), 216 pages.
3. Robert Preus, *The Theology of Post-Reformation Lutheranism* (St. Louis: Concordia Publishing House, Vol. I (1970) and Volume 11(1972).
4. Robert D. Preus, *Getting Into the Theology of Concord* (St. Louis: Concordia Publishing House, 1977); Robert D. Preus and Wilbert H. Rosin, *A Contemporary Look at the Formula of Concord* (St. Louis: Concordia Publishing House, 1978), cf. Arti-

cles XI "Predestination and Election," pp. 271-277.

5. Robert Preus, "The Theology of Karl Earth," *Concordia Theological Monthly*, XXXI, No. 2 (February 1960), 174-183; R. Preus, "The Prolegomnea to Karl Barth," *Concordia Theological Monthly*, XXX, No. 3 (March, 1960) 174-183, R. Preus, "The Christology and Soteriology of Karl Barth," *Concordia Theological Monthly*, No. 10 (October, 1960), 627-632.

6. Robert D. Preus, "Biblical Hermeneutics in the Lutheran Church Today," in John Warwick Montgomery, *Crisis in Lutheran Theology* (Grand Rapids: Baker Book House, 1967), pp. 100-101.

6a. Robert Preus, "Confessional Subscription," in Erich Kiel and Waldo Werning, *Evangelical Directions* (No publisher given, Chicago, 1970), pp. 43- 52.

7. Robert Preus, "The Justification of a Sinner Before God, as Taught in Later Lutheran Orthodoxy," *Scottish Journal of Theology*, Vol. XIII, No. 3 (September, 1960), pp. 262-277.

8. Robert Preus, "Walther and the Scriptures," *Concordia Theological Monthly* XXXII. Nu. 11 November, 1961), 669-691; Cf. also Proceedings of the Thirty-Eighth Convention of the Lutheran Church Missouri Synod, 1961, pp. 30-56.

9. Robert D. Preus, "Bibliography," *The Springfielder*, Vol. XXXVIII, No. 2, September, 1974, pp. 95-98.

10. Robert D. Preus: "A Bibliography 1974-1984," *Concordia Theological Quarterly*, Vol. 49, Numbers 2 and 3,83, 115.

11. Robert D. Preus, "Biblical Hermeneutics in the Lutheran Church Today," in Montgomery, *Crisis in the Lutheran Theology*, **op. cit.**, pp. 81-120.

12. Robert D. Preus, "The Hermeneutics of the *Formula of Concord*," in Arnold J. Koelpin, *No Other Gospel* (Milwaukee: Northwestern Publishing House, 1980), p. 309.

13. Cf. Preus, "Guiding Principles," in P. A. Zimmerman, Rock Strata and the Bible Record (St. Louis: Concordia Publishing House, 1970), pp. 12-17.

14. Robert D. Preus, "The Hermeneutics of the *Formula of Concord*," in Koelpin, **op. cit.**, p. 11.

14a. "Biblical Hermeneutics," in L. Fuerbringer, Th. Engelder, and P. E. Kretzmann, *Concordia Cyclopedia* (St. Louis: Concordia Publishing House, 1927), p. 82.

15. Preus, "The Hermeneutics of the *Formula of Concord*," **Ibid.**, p. 311.

16. **Ibid.**, p. 311.

17. **Ibid.**, p. 311.

18. Robert Preus, *The Theology of Post-Lutheranism* (St. Louis: Concordia Publishing House, 1970).

18a. **Ibid.**, pp. 316-317.

19. **Ibid.**, II, p. 257.

20. Preus, Vol. ii, pp. 257-258.

21. Preus, *Theology of Post-Lutheranism*, II, p. 257.

22. **Ibid.**, II, p. 114.

23. Preus, **Ibid.**, Vol. I. p. 21

23a. **Ibid.**, p. 21.

24. **Ibid.**, I, pp. 82fr.

25. **Ibid.**, I, pp. 236-237.

26. Preus, "The Hermeneutics of the *Formula of Concord*," **op. cit.**, p. 313.

27. **Ibid.**, p. 314.

28. **Ibid.**, p. 310.

29. **Ibid.**, p. 317.

30. **Ibid.**, p. 317.

31. **Ibid.**, p. 316.

32. **Ibid.**, p. 317-318.

33. **Ibid.**, p. 318.

34. **Ibid.**, p. 321.

35. **Ibid.**, p. 318.

36. **Ibid.**, p. 318

37. **Ibid.**, p. 319.

38. **Ibid.**, p. 323.

39. **Ibid.**, p. 321.

40. **Ibid.**, pp. 323-324.

41. **Ibid.**, p. 324.

42. **Ibid.**, p.324.

43. **Ibid.**, p. 325.

44. **Ibid.**, p. 325.

45. **Ibid.**, p. 331.

46. **Ibid.**, p. 331.

47. **Ibid.**, p. 331.

48. **Ibid.**, p. 331.

49. **Ibid.**, p. 331.

50. **Ibid.**, p. 331.

51. **Ibid.**, p. 331.

52. **Ibid.**, p. 332-333.

53. **Ibid.**, p. 333.

54. **Ibid.**, p. 333.

55. **Ibid.**, p. 334.

56. **Ibid.**, p.334; Preus, in John Montgomery, *Crisis in Lutheran Theology* (Grand Rapids: Baker Book House, 1967), pp. 101-113.

57. **Ibid.**, p. 334.

58. **Ibid.**, p. 334.

59. **Ibid.**, p. 335.

60. **Ibid.**, p. 335.

61. **Ibid.**, p. 335.

62. Robert Preus, "Biblical Hermeneutics of the Lutheran Church Today," Montgomery, *Crisis in Lutheran Theology*, **op. cit.**, 107-112.

63. Preus, "How the Lutheran Church Is to Use and Interpret the Old and New Testaments" **op. cit.**, as reproduced in *The Christian News Encyclopedia* (Washington, Missouri, Missourian Publishing Company, 1971), 1, p. 220.

64. Preus, "Guiding Principles, A Lutheran Confessional Approach to the Doctrine of Creation," **op. cit.**, pp. 12-23.

65. **Ibid.**, pp. 13-16.

66. "R. Preus, "The Hermeneutics of the *Formula of Concord*," In Koelpin, *No Other Gospel*, **op. cit.**, pp. 318-334. Preus, *The Theology of Post-Reformation Lutheranism* (St. Louis: Concordia Publishing House 1970. 1970), I. p. 338.

67. **Ibid.**, p. 338. Preus, "A Lutheran Confessional Approach to the Doctrine of Creation," Zimmermann, **op. cit.**, p. 15.

68. R. Preus, "How Is the Lutheran Church to Interpret and Use the Old and New Testaments?" Mankato Reformation Lectures, **op. cit.**, p. 220.

69. **Ibid.**, p. 220.

70. **Ibid.**, p. 220.

71. **Ibid.**, p. 220.

72. **Ibid.**, p. 221.

73. **Ibid.**, p. 221a.

74. **Ibid.**, p. 221a.

75. **Ibid.**, p. 220a.

76. **Ibid.**, p. 221a.

77. Preus, "Biblical Hermeneutics and the Lutheran Church Today," in Montgomery, **op. cit.**, p. 9.

78. Preus, "How Is the Lutheran Church to Interpret the Old and New Testaments?" Mankato Reformation Lectures, **op. cit.**, p. 220.

79. Preus, "Guiding Theological Principles," P. A. Zimmerman, *Rock Strata and the Bible Record*, (St. Louis: Concordia Publishing House, 1970), pp. 16-20.

80. Mankato Reformation Lectures, *Christian News Encyclopedia*, I, p. 220a.

81. **Ibid.**, p. 221a.

82. **Ibid.**, p. 221a.

Questions

1. The doctoral dissertation of Robert Preus was titled ____.
2. Preus was well versed in the theology of ____.
3. What did Preus do when higher critical and liberal scholars endeavored to gain control of the Lutheran Church-Missouri Synod? ____
4. What is hermeneutics? ____
5. Preus drew his hermeneutical principles from ____.
6. Does the *Formula of Concord* support the inerrancy of the Bible. ____
7. The Socinians rejected ____.
8. The *Formula of Concord* taught that the Bible was ____.
9. The first purpose of an exegete is to ____.
10. John 6:48-58 refers to ____ and not to ____.
11. What is the sensus literalis? ____.
12. The Books of the Bible have one ____.
13. What is the analogy of faith? ____.
14. The Law works ____ while the Gospel tells ____.
15. What is the chief article of the entire Christian faith? ____.
16. ____ is the ultimate author of Holy Writ.
17. When did the historical Critical Method become prominent? ____
18. What runs like a red thread through the entire Bible? ____
19. Scripture interprets ____.
20. Historical criticism is employed to ____.

What Significance Do *The Dead Sea Scrolls* (DSS) Have for the Understanding of the New Testament?

Christian News, November 29, 1999

The Dead Sea Scrolls (DDS) found between 1946 and 1956 have significance for three different areas of Biblical studies: 1. For the textual criticism of the Old Testament;[1] 2. For the history and literature of the intertestamental period,[2] and 3. For the background and religious milieu of the time the books of the New Testament were being written.[3] An extraordinary large literature has been published dealing with these three areas of Biblical study. Many books and thousands of journal articles have appeared in the last 48 years.[4] Christian Jewish and humanistic scholars have discussed hundreds of aspects suggested by *The Dead Sea Scrolls*. The 1994 Exegetical Symposium of Concordia Theological Seminary, Ft. Wayne, held January 18-19, had chosen at its general theme: "the World of Qumran and its implications for the Study of the Bible." Three of the essayists dealt with "The Righteousness of Qumran's Teacher of Righteousness," and "the Pauline Righteousness of God," but there was no presentation that dealt with all the alleged implications of Qumran for the New Testament. A number of scholars have expressed the belief that Qumran had considerable influence on the theological views of various individuals and also on New Testament authors.

It will be the purpose of this essay to examine the validity of the assertions that the Qumran sect's influence was rather pronounced, especially when comparisons are made between the DSS documents and the writings of the New Testament.[5] As soon as the DSS were found and read and interpreted, a number of European and American scholars quickly made the claims that the Essenes, who usually are believed to have been the people who lived as a select community at Qumran,[6] that these sectaries had contributed significantly to the beliefs and practices of nascent Christianity.[7] No sooner were the DSS translated, then the claim was made that John the Baptist and Jesus of Nazareth were said to have been members of this esoteric community or at least had sufficient contact with them so that they had acquaintance with their distinctive religious ideas.[8] So that a number of distinctive doctrines and practices were borrowed from the Essenes. Proponents of the School of Comparative Religions quickly jumped on the bandwagon of those who held that Christianity was a mixture of religious ideas borrowed from many different sources. The Four Evangelists had borrowed terminology as well as theological concepts from the Essenes.[9] The Sermon of the Mount supposedly had been employing ideas found in Essene literature. The sacraments of Baptism and the Lord's Supper were definitely appropriated from books now found in the Dead Sea caves. Some of the organizational Christian structures were suggested by those employed by the Qumranites. The Gospel of John, was contended, was influenced by its dualism and its many antimonies which characterize a number of Essenic works. Jesus supposedly was influenced to utilize theological concepts clearly found in Qumranic writings. The Apostle Paul is said to show the influence of the Essenes in his theology as reflected in a number of his epistles. For a number of critical scholars the New Testament does not show anything unique, but essentially was a refurbishing of what the Essenes had held many years before Christ had appeared on the scene in Palestine.

I. John the Baptist and Qumran

According to Matthew, John the Baptist was preaching in the wilderness of Judea.[10] John lived about ten to 12 miles from the Qumran monastery. He may have been aware of the existence of the Qumran community, but there is no reference in Biblical literature or in Josephus that he had any knowledge of their existence or that he spent time there. When investigators came[10] from Jerusalem, sent by the Pharisees to inquire about his message and mission, John replied: "I am the voice of one crying in the wilderness." Here the Baptists were referring to Isaiah 40:3. This passage was also used by the Qumranites to identify themselves with the group foretold by the prophet Isaiah. It cannot be established that John the Baptist preached in the same wilderness where Qumran was located.

Differences Between John The Baptist and Qumran

A comparison of John the Baptizer and the teachings and practices of Qumran show that John, the son of Zecharias and Elizabeth, who was an ascetic, that the latter's asceticism was different from that practiced at Qumran.[11] John's ascetical ideals did not agree with that of the Essenes. Qumranic texts say nothing of eating locusts and honey as John did. The Baptizer's abstinence from wine and strong drink was also characteristic of the Rechabites in the days of Jeremiah and of those taking the vow of Nazirites. Furthermore, John's freedom of movement does not comport with the strict discipline practiced by the Essenes. John baptized all hearers if they repented of their sins, whether they were soldiers, Pharisees, Sadducees or common people. John baptized only once and that was for the forgiveness of sins. The Qumranites practiced daily ablutions and thus their respective baptisms were much different when compared with John's baptism.[12]

II. Jesus Christ and Qumran

Christ Jesus is the heart of Christianity. To be able to demonstrate that distinctive beliefs and distinctive actions were borrowed from Essenism would remove the uniqueness of the Christian faith by making of Christ a borrower and plagiarist of views which, therefore, would not have been original with him and so discredit that which was distinctive. Yamauchi has noted that "exaggerated comparisons between the Teacher of Righteousness and Jesus were made by Du Pont Sommer, Edmund Wilson, Allegro and others."[13] Charles Pfeiffer claimed: "Since the time

771

of Renan, who termed Christianity 'an Essenism which succeeded on a big scale,' scholars have been intrigued with the possibility of Essene influence on Christ, John the Baptist and Christianity as a whole. Similarities have frequently been pointed out between the life of an Essene community and the life of the early church. There is the danger, however, of overlooking the differences which also exist. The contrasts frequently appear more significant than the comparisons.[14]

It has been surmised, though without the slightest evidence, that Jesus lived for some years amongst the Qumran sectaries. Professor F.C. Grant characterizes this as fantastic nonsense.[15] According to Larson not only did Jesus live among the Essenes, but he left them and proclaimed on the highways of Palestine theological views that he had obtained from the Qumranites.[16] The fact that Christ is allegedly supposed to have lived among them and borrowed his distinctive theological views is based on the fact that Qumran was a few miles from familiar places in the life of Christ, such as Jericho, Jerusalem and cities in the Jordan Valley. Without any proof for his position, Edmund Wilson, did much to popularize *The Dead Sea Scrolls* and called the attention of people to similarities between certain aspects of Essenic theology and the teaching and preaching of Jesus. J.H. Rowley states: "The idea that Jesus derived His teaching from the sect is one that cannot survive the most superficial examination."[17] Professor Stauffer has argued that many teachings of Jesus were directed especially against the sectaries and that their influence on later writers of the New Testament was greater than on Jesus Himself.[18] For instance in the New Testament we read: "Ye have heard that it was said, 'You shall love your neighbor and hate your enemy,' but I say unto you, 'Love your enemies and pray for those who persecute you.'"

It has often been pointed out by commentators that in the Old Testament we do not find the command to hate enemies. However in the Scrolls we do find such a command.[19] Relative to the Sabbath observance there was a great difference between the Essenes and Jesus who was criticized by the Pharisees for his views about the Sabbath observance. Jesus told the religious leaders that "the Sabbath was made for man, and not man for the Sabbath." The Qumranites would not help an animal which had fallen into a pit. If a man fell into a place of water, he was not to be helped and raised by a ladder or a rope. Jesus took the opposite position.[20]

1. The Teacher of Righteousness and Christ

The anonymous Teacher of Righteousness (TR) was not the founder of the Qumran sect, but appeared some 20 years later when the sect had been groping for a leader to give it a sense of direction.[21] Some scholars believe that the TR may have been the author of *The Thanksgiving Hymns* (Hebrew: **Hadoyoth**), which it is believed gives the greatest insight in to the Qumranic sect's ideas about sin and salvation.[22]

Little is the information that is available about the Teacher of Righteousness in *The Habakkuk Commentary*, *The Damascus Document* and the *Commentary* (Pesher) *on Psalm 37*. From these sources scholars have determined that the TR was a leader who was persecuted by the Wicked Priest (WP), by whom was meant the corrupt high priest. Du Pont-Sommer[23] and Allegro interpreted certain texts that spoke about the death of the TR as having been accomplished through crucifixion.[24] Later these scholars claimed that TR was raised from the dead. Yamauchi, however, contended: "Nowhere is it said that he was killed, let alone crucified as some have averred. Nor is there any justification in any scrolls for claiming the resurrection of the Teacher."[25]

2. Who Was and When Did the Teacher of Righteousness Live?

Exactly when the Teacher of Righteousness lived has caused a number of scholars to place him at different times, between 175 B.C. and 134 B.C.[26] Rowley and Black would place the TR and the WP in the period 175 B.C.-162 B.C., and they would identify the TR with the Zadokite high priest Onias III and the WP with Jason who favored Hellenism and his brother Menelaus. Stauffer suggested their placement into the years 165-162 B.C. and would identify the TR with Jose ben Joezer and the WP with Alcimus. The following scholars, Milik, Cross, Sutcliffe, de Vaux, Vermes, Winter and Jeremias believe the TR and the WP were active between 134-76 B.C. Winter, Jeremias, and Bruce believe the TR was some unknown person, and WP would be either Jonathan or his brother Simon.

On the other hand, Allegro and Brownlee do not believe we know who the TR was, but the WP was Alexander Jannaeus. With the Hasmoneans the high priesthood was taken over as well as the Monarchy. In the period 76-63, Du Pont Sommer would hold that Hyrcannus II was the WP. Between 76-63 B.C., at the time of the Jewish War (A.D. 66-70). Roth and Driver hold that the TR was the zealot Menaham and the WP, Eleazer, the son of Ananias, the high priest. Yamauchi holds the years 152-134 B.C. as the time of the unknown TR was active, with Simon as WP.

3. The Teacher of Righteousness' Alleged Crucifixion and Resurrection

When Du Pont Sommer, Allegro, Wilson and others interpreted certain Dead Sea texts as showing the TR being crucified and that later he was resurrected, this was, of course, a very startling announcement and deduction. Christianity, supposedly, had borrowed these two teachings and made it central in the teachings of Christ. St. Paul labelled these two Siamese doctrines as the very ABC of the Christian faith. However, a number of specialists on *The Dead Sea Scrolls* questioned the reading of the DSS texts as correct. Manson, an authority on the DSS, asserted: "There is nowhere any suggestion to the miraculous in the death of the Teacher of Righteousness."[26]

Students of the DSS know very little about the Teacher of Righteousness. The references to him in the Scrolls indicate that he lived in stormy times and was opposed by one who is called the Wicked Priest (WP). The Zadokite document speaks of his being "gathered in,"[27] and this expression is used in the Old Testament for natural death. There is one text in the *Habakkuk Commentary* which seems to state that the TR was martyred.[28] Still another text refers to the Lion of Wrath, who hung people alive.[29] This may refer to crucifixion and so it is concluded that the TR was crucified, just as Jesus was later in A.D. 30 or 33. Many people were crucified in Jesus' time by the Romans and not a few suffered martyrdom by being crucified. Van der Ploeg, an authority relative to the DSS, stated: "That the teacher was put to death is an assumption that still lacks confirmations from the texts."[30] In the Qumran texts the alleged death of the TR is not emphasized as it is in The New Testament, in which there are at least two hundred references to the resurrection of Christ. The New Testament ascribes centrality to the death of Christ, claiming that Christ came to give His life a ransom for many. Nowhere in the DSS is any value or importance assigned to the death of the Teacher. While the DSS says little about the death of the TR, the New Testament devotes many passages and chapters to Christ's sacrificial death.

Unlike the Essenes Christ did not withdraw from the world or refuse to meet other Jewish sects and mingle among Jews who were not members of the Qumran community. Only perfect members after a three-year waiting period could become eligible for reception in the Essenes,[31] but Christ welcome all who were heavy laden and in need of help. Jesus associated with Pharisees, Sadducees, Scribes and Herodian.[32]

IV. The Expectation of the Messiah in Qumran and in Christianity

The Jews in the pre-Christian era, in the intertestamental period looked forward to the coming of the Messiah, who was to be a king and descendant of the Davidic house. Qumranic literature seems to expect a number of different Messiahs. If the Teacher of Righteousness was to be the Messiah, he would be one of two or three, but not as the Messiah. For the Christians of the New Testament there was to be but one Messiah and Jesus claimed to be the Christos or Meshiach of various Old Testament prophecies. The New Testament identified the Messiah with the "Son of Man," a name never found in the Qumran literature as a designation for the Messiah. The Teacher of Righteousness is never referred to as divine; he is never called the "Messiah," "the Son of Man," "Son of God," and never is he addressed as "LORD." It is possible to discuss the Essene religion without consideration of its Teacher of Righteousness, but it is impossible to discuss Christianity apart from Christ.

There are significant differences between Christianity and Qumranic theology and practice. The Essenes were ascetics, Jesus and the early Christians were not. The Qumranite community was a closed fellowship, to which only those who had been voted in were allowed participation with the group and considered full-fledged members. By contrast, Jesus during his three-and-a-half-year ministry traveled in Galilee, Samaria, Judea, and Deapolis and some times in the Syrio-Phoencian territory. Jesus did not identify Himself with any of the known sects of Judiasm.

The Jews and the Essenes looked forward to the coming of the Messiah at Christ's time,[33] but in the New Testament He is portrayed as having come. Mansour asserted "For the Qumran sect the Messiah's coming was imminent, whereas for John the 'visitation' had taken place, the Messiah was there already and the Spirit was abroad (Luke 1:58; John 1:32-33). John's mission was to designate Jesus as being the realization of the expected events."[34]

V. Qumran and the Sermon on the Mount

The Sermon on the Mount, Matthew 5:3-7:27, has ideas and expressions for which parallels have been found in *The Dead Sea Scrolls*. A number of Qumranic sayings begin with "Blessed is he" as in the introduction of the Beatitudes. But the word "Blessed" is also found in Psalm 1.[34] Another parallel between Qumran and the New Testament is the expression "the ancients," expressed as "then of old times."[35] Similarities between Essene literature and the New Testament is the forbiddance of using oaths. Another would be the warning against judging or condemning a brother. There are possibly a number of similarities between *The Manual of Discipline* and the *Gospel*.[37]

Unger claimed "that a number of references in the Sermon of the Mount are echoed in the Qumran literature and illustrate how Jesus' message fitted into the age in which He lived."[38] For example, Jesus taught that one cannot serve worldly gain or mammon, and God at the same time (Matt. 6:2A).[39] Basic ideal of poverty in the Qumran Community reflects the spirit of Jesus, who forbade oaths (Matt. 5:33-37). The Jewish sect at Qumran did likewise.

Jesus denounced all adultery in its deeper meaning of looking at a woman with lustful intention (Matt. 5:28).[40] Both "the lustful eyes" and "lustful spirit" are warned against in Qumranic writings. Some of the teachings of the Sermon on the Mount were found in the Old Testament or in Jewish books produced in the inter-testamental period. The Qumran Community and Christianity, it must not be forgotten, had their roots in the Old Testaments and that there should be similarities of language and theological concepts ought not to surprise. But Christ was God's Son and He was the Revealer of God's will, so His sayings by virtue of this are definitive.

VI. Qumran and the Gospels

Larson, following the presupposition and conclusions of some of the earlier writers dealing with Dead Sea Scrolls, claimed that many ideas and religious concepts found in the Synoptic Gospels were taken from Qumran. Thus Larson asserted: "That many passages in the Synoptic Gospels (of Matthew, Mark and Luke) are similar to what is found in Essene literature is simply uncontestable."[41] Again, it must be pointed out that the Essenes and John the Baptist, Christ and His fellow compatriots had the Old Testament, its expressions, theological ideas and prophecies in common. That Jesus used certain terms and ideas embedded in the Scriptures of the Old Covenant was His right as the true Messenger from

God sent to reveal the Father's plan for man's salvation.

VII. Qumran and the Gospel of John

A number of scholars have expressed the view that John the Evangelist may have been influenced by the Essenes. Thus Unger asserted: "When we come to Qumran teaching with the Gospel of John, there is a striking parallelism of ideas and in general terms. The explanation of this is that the Qumran ideas were current in the world of the first century."[42] John the Baptist, John the Evangelist and Jesus used terms current in the first century A.D. While these New Testament preachers used terminology current in their day, they filled them with new and distinctive meanings.

Dualism is an outstanding characteristic in John's Gospel (Belief versus unbelief, darkness versus life, truth versus error, concern versus indifference, love versus hatred).[43] Some of these antitheses are discovered in various Qumran documents. The great difference between the Essenes and John and Jesus was that the people of Qumran were still under the old economy. They knew that "the law came by Moses, but not "that grace and truth came by Jesus Christ;" of this they were unfortunately ignorant (John 1:17). John set forth the Messiah as the Light of the world and those who believed on Him as the Light of the world will have eternal life.

The Dead Sea Scrolls have dealt a blow to higher criticism which placed John's Gospel into the middle of the second century A.D. It used to be held that John was a product of Hellenism and dated about A.D. 150.[43] However, Robinson and Albright alleged that the Fourth Gospel and John's Epistles came out of a Palestinian background and needed not to be dated later than A.D. 60.[44]

VIII. Qumran and Acts

The communal meals of Qumran have been compared with the Early Church's celebration of the Lord's Supper. The communal ablutions at Qumran were not celebrated as sacraments by the Essenes. Christian baptism was performed only once and was probably suggested by the baptism of converts into Judaism. In the communal meals the bread and wine do not represent anything or considered to bestow special forgiveness of the giving of the body and blood of some cult leader.

It was obligatory when a person became a full-fledged member of the brotherhood to turn over his belongings, money and property to the general fund of the Essene brotherhood. All was held in common. Christianity is alleged to have borrowed this idea from Qumran. But in the Church of the first century believers in Jerusalem and Judea a free-willing sharing was undertaken. Ananias and Sapphira were told by Peter that they did not have to sell all, as did some Christians, and give it to the apostles. This sharing of all on a voluntary basis was not continued. Qumran contributed nothing to this aspect of early Christianity, as some would have present-day Christians believe.

IX. Qumran and the Pauline Letters

Some scholars have found echoes of Qumran in Paul's Epistles. Thus Unger remarked: "In the same fashion that John the Baptist and Jesus did not speak in a vacuum but out of the historical context of their age, so Luke, the historian and Paul, the Apostle, speak forth from the contemporary scene in which they found themselves."[45]

The Apostle Paul before his conversion was a "Hebrew of the Hebrews" and "a member of the Pharisees." As such he was acquainted with Judaism as found in the New Testament and probably was also conversant with the different books produced in the Intertestamental period and also had a knowledge of the different sects of Judaism. It would be unthinkable that he knew nothing of the Essenes, when even the Romans, Philo and Josephus were aware of them and their distinctive beliefs. Since Paul and the Essenes had a common heritage, namely the Old Testament Scriptures, it should not surprise that Paul used words and ideas from the Old Testament also employed by the Essenes.

A technical term found in the Pauline writings is the word "mystery." Paul used the term "Mysterion" a number of times in the sense of previously hidden truths, now definitely known which God had designed to make known to the Church.[46] The word "mystery" had in it a supernatural element despite its now being known. For instance in Romans 11:25 Paul writes of Israel's spiritual blindness during this present age as a mystery. Again in 1 Corinthians 15:51-52 and I Thessalonians 4:14-17 Paul speaks about the mystery of the translation of the people, living at the end of the age. Another use is referred to by Paul in Ephesians 3:1-11; Colossians 4:3 that the church of Christ is constituted both of Jews and Gentiles. The presence of Christ in the believer is called a "mystery" (Gal. 2:20; Col. 1:26-27). In Colossians 2:2; I Cor. 2:7 Paul refers to the fact Christ was the fullness of Deity and calls it a "mystery."[47] In describing the "man of sin," he is called "the mystery of iniquity" according to Paul (II Thess. 2:7). In a famous Christmas text Paul speaks of "the mystery of godliness" (I Timothy 3:16). In Matthew 13, the great parable chapter, Jesus elaborated on the "mysteries of the Kingdom of God."

By contrast in *The Dead Sea Scrolls* the word "mystery" is employed to connote the hidden decree of the Community. Nonmembers are not to be told "the mysteries of knowledge."[48] There are also the mysteries of God's understanding. A comparison of the use of mystery with that of the Qumran shows that Paul has invested the term with its own distinctive meaning according to divine revelation.

Some scholars have argued that the office of bishop in the Pastoral Epistles indicates a late date. The function of the **Mebebagger** or "overseer" at Qumran was the same as those of the bishops in the Pastorals. This fact therefore invalidates the argument for the late date of the Pastorals.[49]

X. Qumran and the Epistle to the Hebrews

A document found in Cave 11 deals with the enigmatic figure of Melchizedek. This text describes Melchizedek as a heavenly deliverer

777

similar to the archangel Michael. He is also depicted as the "heavenly one" who proclaims God's salvation.[50]

Yamauchi opines that "this may help to explain why the author of Hebrews stresses not only Christ's superiority to the Aaronic priesthood but also to the angels (Heb. 7:3), which speaks of Melchizedek without parentage, is usually explained on the basis that his ancestors are not mentioned in Gen. 14, but may now be interpreted in the light that Melchizedek was regarded as a super human being."

This writer prefers the traditional interpretation.[51]

XI. Qumran and Possible New Testament Documents

A number of scholars have been attempting to find New Testament manuscripts among *The Dead Sea Scrolls*. In 1972, the Jesuit scholar Jose O'Callaghan claimed that he discovered fragments of the Gospel of Mark in Cave 7, dating about A.D. 50.[52] Cave 7 (there are 12 caves that have yielded MSS) explored in 1955, is unique among the Qumran caves as a site which yielded only Greek MSS. The 21 tiny fragments inscribed in Greek uncial letters were originally published by M. Baillet in 1962. At the same time, the only fragments which were identified were 7 Q1, 1-2 as Exodus 28:4-17 and 7Q.2 as the apocryphal epistle of Jeremiah 43b-44. These fragments were dated to 100 B.C. The tiny size of the fragments and the paucity of letters preserved have cast doubts on their possible identifications. Blai Klock gave this evaluation: "Inasmuch as O'Callaghan's identifications are based on his readings of a large number of uncertain letters, they cannot be accepted as incontrovertible evidence of NTMSS at Qumran."[53]

Footnotes

1. Millar Burrows, *The Dead Sea Scrolls* (New York: Viking Press, 1956), pp. 301-327.
2. **Ibid.**, pp. 326-327, William Foxwell Albright, *History, Archaeology and Christian Humanism* (New York: McGraw Book Company, 1963), pp. 294-295; G. Vermes, *The Dead Sea Scrolls* (Baltimore: Penguin Books, 1962).
3. Pp. 11-14.
4. Charles Pfeiffer, *The Dead Sea Scrolls and the Bible* (Grand Rapids: Baker Book House, 1969), pp. 101, 115-125, 97-100.
4. Cf. Joseph Fitzmeyer, *The Dead Sea Scrolls*. Mayor Publications and Tools for Study (Missoula, Montana: Scholars Press, 1977), 176 pp.
5. A list of the major Dead Sea Scrolls is found in Wayne House, *Chronological and Background Charts for the New Testament* (Grand Rapids: Zondervan Publishing House, 1981), pp. 82-83.
6. Menahem Mansour, *The Dead Sea Scrolls* (Grand Rapids: Baker Book House, 1983), 143-152.
7. Martin A. Larson, "The Essene Origins of Jesus' Teachings," "*The Journal of Historical Review*," (March-April, 1993), pp. 33-34.
8. Mansour, **op. cit.**, pp. 160, 162.
9. Larson, **op. cit.**, p. 34.
10. Biblical data on John the Baptist, cf. Luke 1:17,80; Matthew 3:1-17; Mark 1:1-13; Luke 3:3-23a.

11. E. M. Yamauchi, "*The Dead Sea Scrolls*," C. Pfeiffer, H. F. Vos, and J. Rea, *The Wycliffe Bible Encyclopedia* (Chicago: Moody Press, 1971), p. 441.

12. W. H. Brownlee, "John the Baptist in the Light of the Ancient Scrolls," *The Scrolls and the New Testament*, ed. By K. Stendahl (London: SCM. 1951); C. H. Kraeling, *John the Baptist* (New York: Charles Scribners, 1951) J. Steinman, *Saint John and the Eseret Tradition* (London: Longmans, 1958.)

13. Yamauchi, **op. cit.**, II, p. 441.

14. Pfeiffer, **op. cit.**, p. 97.

15. F. C. Grant, *Ancient Judaism and the New Testament* (1960), p. 133.

16. Larson, **op. cit.**, p. 34.

17. H. H. Rowley, "The Qumran Sect and Christian Origins," in *From Moses to Qumran* (London: Lutterworth Press, 1963) p. 250; Cf. Millar Burrows *More Light on the Dead Sea Scrolls*, (New York: Viking Press, 1958), pp. 88ff. M. Graystone, *The Dead Sea Scrolls and the Originality of Christ*, 1956, p. 89; D. Flusser, "Aspects of The Dead Sea Scrolls," (*Scripta Hierosolymtana*, IV), (Jerusalem: Magnes Press, 1958), pp. 215ff.

18. Ellen Stauffer, *Die Botschaft Jesu damals und heute*, (1959), pp. 13ff.

19. *Manual of Discipline*, col. I, line 10, IX, line 21f cf. col. X, line 19f

20. C. Raben, *The Zadokite Document*, p. 56. Theodore Gaster, *The Dead Sea Scriptures* (New York: Garden City: Doubleday Anchor Books. 1956), p. 87.

21. Mansour, *The Thanksgiving Hymns* (Grand Rapids: Wm. B. Eerdmans Publishing Company, 1961), p. 45.

22. Mansour, *The Dead Sea Scrolls*, **op. cit.**, pp. 45,65,91ff, 106,132,150,156.

23. Millar Burrows, *The Dead Sea Scrolls* (New York: Viking Press, 1956), on *Habakkuk Commentary*, pp. 123-206; On The Damascus Document, pp. 349-364; Manual of Discipline, 390-399.

24. According to Yamauchi, **op. cit.**, p. 441.

25. **Ibid.** The following information about the different views on the TR and WP as researched by Yamauchi, **op. cit.**, "Dead Sea Scrolls," in *Wycliffe Bible Encyclopedia*, I, p. 440.

26. **Ibid.**, p. 440.

27. *The Zadokite Document*, IX, p. 21 (p. XX, line 1,) IX, 39 (p. xx, line 14.)

28. *Habakkuk Commentary*, vol. XI, line 5.

29. J. Allegro, *Journal of Biblical Literature*, LXXXV, 1956), pp. 89ff.

30. J. Van der Ploeg, *The Excavations at Qumran*, (London, 1958), p. 202.

31. A. R. C. Leaney, *The Rule of Qumran and Its Meaning* (Philadelphia: The Westminster Press, 1966), pp. 33, 112, 114, 118fr, 168, 171, 190ff.

32. Luke 7:36,37; Matthew 15:1; 16:1; John 8:3.

33. Stauffer's *Jesus and the Wilderness Community at Qumran* (Philadelphia: Fortress Press, 1964), listed eight differences between Christ and the Essenes, pp. 12-18.

34. Mansour, **op. cit.**, p. 156.

35. Unger, **op. cit.**, p. 37.

36. **Ibid.**

37. **Ibid.**, p. 37.

38. Unger, **op. cit.**, p. 35.

39. **Ibid.**, p. 39.

40. **Ibid.**, p. 39.

41. Larson, "The Essene Teachings of Jesus," *The Journal of Historical Review*, March-

April, 1993, p. 34.

42. Unger, **op. cit.**, p. 43.
43. Howard F. Vos, *Archaeology in Bible Lands* (Chicago: Moody Press 1977), p. 92.
44. John A. Robinson, *Can We Trust Our New Testament* (Grand Rapids: Wm. B. Eerdmans Publishing Company, 1977), pp. 33, 65.
45. Unger, **op. cit.**, p. 47.
46. **Ibid.**, p. 54; **Ibid.**, p. 55.
47. **Ibid.**, p. 54.
48. **Ibid.**, p. 55; **Ibid.**, p. 55.
49. H.H. Rowley, *From Moses to Qumran*, **op. cit.**, pp. 256-257. Clifford A. Wilson, Rocks, and Biblical Reliability (Grand Rapids: Zondervan Publishing House, 1977).
50. Yamauchi, *"The Dead Sea Scrolls,"* in *The Wycliffe Bible Encyclopedia*, I, p. 441.
51. **Ibid.**, p. 441b.
52. "Qumran Fragments," E.M. Blacklock, R. K. Harrison, *The New International Dictionary of Biblical Archaeology* (Grand Rapids: Zondervan Publishing House, 1983), pp. 379-380.
53. **Ibid.**, p. 380b.

Questions

1. When were the Dead Sea Scrolls found? ____
2. What did proponents of the School of Comparative Religions say about the Essene and the Dead Sea Scrolls? ____
3. Is there any evidence that John the Baptist had any knowledge of the existence of the Qumran community? ____
4. How did John's baptism differ from the Qumranites? ____
5. Who is the heart of Christianity? ____
6. Is there evidence that Jesus lived among the Qumran sectaries? ____
7. What was a great difference between the Essenes and Jesus? ____
8. Do any scrolls speak of a resurrection of the Teacher of Righteousness? ____
9. What is a difference between the Teacher of Righteousness and Jesus? ____
10. What is an outstanding characteristic in John's Gospel? ____
11. The Dead Scrolls dealt a blow to ____.
12. The presence of Christ in a believer is called ____.

Method in the Study of the Bible

Christian News, April 2, 2001

The failure to employ proper method in the study of the Bible can be a deterrent to a derival of the utmost benefit from Biblical study. "The secret of success with any study is in the discovery and proper use of a correct method. Where this is neglected, no matter how industrious, or energetic, or brilliant the student may be his efforts are doomed to failure."[1] While there is no royal road to learning, it does not follow that the student will be successful if he plunges energetically into the trackless wilderness and wanders aimlessly in the vast forest of truth. A definite and correct procedure must be employed if he is to make worthwhile progress, and yet as Adeney says, "It would be better to be hindered by any amount of impediments than to be blindly and obstinately adhering to a totally wrong method, since in that case the more progress we made the farther we should be from the goal."[2]

It is tragic when a student goes astray in the study of the Bible because of the great importance of the subject matter it contains. Although the Bible is a clear book and as the psalmist says "a lamp unto our feet," yet there are peculiar difficulties which beset the study of the Bible. Not only are the truths of religion a revelation from God, but the form in which they are presented demand close consideration. Despite the fact that the Bible is written for the common people in non-theological language, we nevertheless cannot ignore the fact of its origin in antiquity and the Oriental and Eastern character of much of the book. Without the proper background and understanding of the circumstances under which the authors of the Biblical library wrote, misunderstandings as well as misinterpretations are bound to arise.

Bible study is the most profitable of all types of study from the perspective of eternity; it certainly is the most useful to the student from the standpoint of the development of the mind as well as from the development of a person's moral and spiritual nature. This does not mean all Bible study is profitable or useful to the student. Dr. Torrey unhesitatingly asserted: "There is much so-called 'Bible Study' that is utterly profitless and not a little so-called 'Bible Study' that is positively injurious to the student."

A British scholar and lover of God's Word, the Reverend Astey brings the following accusation against so many interested and earnest students of the Bible:

"The habit of confining one's attention to the study of selected portions viewed by themselves apart from their relation to the context, in which they are found, is in some degree responsible for the lack of interest which many Christians experience when the Bible is read in this way. It is necessary to survey the whole field in a systematic, consecutive, comprehensive way, if the interest of Bible study is to be deepened and maintained."[3] Henry Dunn, an author who wrote a hundred years ago, in the opening chapter of his book asked the question: "Why is it that Christian people read the Bible so differently?" that conflicting sects alike appeal to it as the sole authority for their respective views? that Doctrines the most diverse are supposed to be equally well sustained by its statements?[4]

In answer to these questions Dunn enumerated a whole series of failures in procedure or method on the part of churches and Bible students. His criticisms are admirable and deserve to be given, although the quotation is somewhat lengthy. Thus he wrote:

In searching for an answer we have been led to the conclusion that the true explanation will be found in that prevailing neglect of the Bible, *as a whole*, which arises from its being almost always read in mere fragments; in forgetfulness of any particular purpose for which the book was given; in confusion regarding its inspiration; in errors relating to the Holy Spirit; in the confounding of revealed facts with human inferences; in bias of one kind or another; in reading, either for edification or from the kindling of devout feeling, without first ascertaining the **meaning** of that which is read; in the habit of **accommodating** Scripture, or of **perverting** it, by exaggeration, projection, or rather of misapplication of texts, in **allegorizing**, under the influence of an unbridled fancy; in the **abuse** of Parallel passages or references, in that darkening of the sense which is frequently occasioned by injudicious division into Chapters and Verses, in the acceptance of interpretation drawn only from Hymns; in the neglect and consequent abuse of unfulfilled Prophecy; in **inattention** to the character of the particular dispensation under which we are living; in errors to Church Authority, and the value of Tradition in undue reliance on the professional labors of the clergy; in turning helps into hindrances, and above all, in **habitual indifference** to the demand of Scripture makes on every man for prolonged study, as an essential prerequisite to the elevation by its means of moral character.[5]

Dr. Stevens, formerly a professor of Yale University in his contribution many years ago to a symposium titled "Hints on Bible Study" also stressed the importance of method relative to Bible study.[6] For a better understanding of the Bible he advocated what he termed "the literary method," a method which other savants have called "The book method." This method in Steven's opinion is an important method for a better and more rewarding way of studying the Word of Life. As a method it is opposed to a piecemeal study of passages, which at times may be useful, but which is helpless in fostering an intelligent knowledge of biblical literature in terms of whole books in their individual character and unity. Here we are not interested to set forth the basics of this methodology, but to emphasize its great utility as an effective method for thorough and beneficial Bible study.

The Importance of System

Method has been defined as "the way of doing things." In Biblical study the student should be systematic. In business system it's important. System counts in house work. The person who has system when he undertakes a specific task or type of work will be found to accomplish much more than the person who operates without system. There is no place where system is as valuable as in the study of the Bible. Many pastors, teachers and laymen devote much time to Bible Study, but since they read at random without system, they accomplish very little.

A serious student of the Holy Scriptures should be systematic and regular, setting apart a special time each day for Bible Study. Without such an arrangement, inertia and sluggishness, the natural enemy of us all, will gain the victory and precious hours will not be used to the best advantage. Many ministers and laymen dedicate a choice part of the morning when the mind is fresh and alert, to this endeavor. "And not only are the movements in our mental chamber at that time still unobstructed by the numerous cobwebs which, owing to strenuous exertion, worry, and disappointments hardly ever fail to establish themselves there in the course of the day, but through Bible-study the soul is given the nourishment it requires not to falter when as the hours go on, toils, debates, scenes of wretchedness and misery, and the harrowing experiences at the bedside of the sick and dying people are threatening to crush it." The ministry of a pastor and the teaching of a teacher will be the better for regular, daily Bible study.

In addition to fixing regular hours for Biblical study there should also be a definite system of work.

Desultory and aimless reading should be avoided. The poet Lowell once said: "Desultory reading, except as conscious past time, hetetates the brain and slackens the bowstring of the will."[7]

G. Campbell Morgan, who up to the time of his death, was one of the leading evangelical Scriptural expositors of Great Britain, a zealous student of the English Bible, claimed that Bible study requires system.[8] "No man is in any sense a Bible student who takes up the Bible and reads it by a method which can only be described as haphazard. To open it at a page and read to take certain portions allotted for each day by others, may be perfectly justifiable method for pleasure and may result in profit but such a procedure does not constitute study, in the true sense of the word."[9] Professor Riddle, formerly of the Western Theological Seminary, averred: "To study the gospels aright one must learn how to study."[10]

Study in Riddle's estimation is to be distinguished from getting a lesson which consists in committing answers to certain formulated or anticipated questions; it is different than reading which is passive listening to what has been written. Study involves and demands active inquiry on the part of the student.

In Riddle's opinion "learning how" is far more important than knowledge of the best and available for Bible Study. "For one who cannot use books aright, there are no good helps. To feel this is the first step in learning how to study the Gospels, as well in all, other branches of intellectual activity."[11]

Former Professor Willis Beecher warns against the "mistaken methods of some who want to study the Bible reverently and profitably." In his paper, titled "Right Spirit in Old Testament Study," he enumerated the following wrong methods of Old Testament study.

1) The study of selected passages which diverts from a thorough study for the complete meaning of a passage; 2) Not using the best version, the version that faithfully rendered the best attainable text of the autographs; 3) Not studying the Old Testament continuously; 4) Ignoring the literary character of a Biblical book, or where there are different literary genre within a Biblical book; 5) Not approaching the Old Testament in teachable spirit, and failing to ask the Holy Spirit for guidance.[12]

Bishop John Vincent at the end of the last century complained of improper use of method relative to Bible study when he wrote:

> We do study it, but in text and for texts. We quote it in disconnected fragments, we misquote through lack of accuracy in committing, we mislead in quoted texts, we quote human sayings of general literature as Scripture sayings, we put old constructions on old passages and assume that our views, because they are old must be true. But as for the study of literature what do we know about that process?[13]

Dr. Adney, formerly of New College London, in the preface to his book on Bible study declared:

> So perverse have been the methods of popular exposition and so long have they been pursued as of unquestionable validity, that the mention of some of the simplest rules for a right study of the Bible - rules that are accepted without question and applied almost automatically in the case of other books will no doubt strike some people, who are in a way very familiar with their Bibles, as a daring innovation.[14]

It is a common fault among many professional students of the Bible to consult commentaries before they have ever read the text of Scriptures, grappled with it, thought it over, before taking recourse to a *Bible Commentary*. Ellicott himself, the author of many commentaries on various Biblical books, calls attention in his essay, "How to Use Bible Commentaries" to this wrong method of Biblical study. Here again it resolves itself as far as Biblical study is concerned with the right method versus a wrong method of procedure. [15]

R. F. Morton distinguished between two different ways of reading the Bible. The one, he claims, is essential for all Christians, while the second in his opinion is optional. He termed the two methods as: 1) devotional, 2) critical. Morton advocated two different Bibles be employed by the student. Regarding the devotional reading, necessary for the nourishment of the spiritual life in man, he made the following suggestion: "When you are reading in this way, do not stop at the difficulties; go by them. It is of no use to stop in our approach to God because you see a boulder in the way, or because a swollen brook crosses the path. Press on, let the boulder alone; look a moment and you will see stepping stones across the brook."[16]

Commentaries in the past as well as other Biblical helps dealt with method in Bible study. Dummelow's one-volume *Bible Commentary* has an article titled "The Study of the Bible," which is concerned specifically with method, although numerous statements of Dummelow give erroneous suggestions of the study of the Bible.[17] The *Abingdon Commentary* of 1929 also has an article on "How to Study the Bible."[18] *The Holy Bible with a Devotional Commentary* by Jamieson and Bickersteth has an article called "*Helps and Hints of Bible Study. The Cambridge Companion to the Bible* was issued in the interest of fostering Bible study."[19] In the preface of the latter volume it is stated: "The present volume is intended to supply such information on the Structure and the Text of the Bible as may enable the English reader to understand questions now largely discussed."[20]

In the preface to James Gray's *Christian Workers Commentary on the Old and New Testaments* the author gives various suggestions as to method in Bible study. The very first suggestion is an important one, emphasized also by other articles dealing with methods of Biblical study, and reads: "Fundamental to any firsthand knowledge of the Bible is the reading of the Holy Book itself, and all the commentaries in the world are no substitute for it."[21]

From what has so far been presented, the primary importance of proper method is evident. It will, therefore, be of advantage to be acquainted with proper procedure in working with the world's most important Book, God's very Word.

Webster has defined method as follows: "Method may denote either an abstract or a concrete procedure in working with an abstraction or a concrete procedure but in both cases it implies orderly, logical and effective arrangement as of one's ideas for an exposition or an argument, or of the steps to be followed in teaching, in investigation ... or in any kind of place of work."[22] The educator Kilpatrick had defined method as "the most economical way of teaching or learning anything."[23] Dr. Horne of New York University has described method as follows: "In the last analysis, method is but the way of doing a thing."[24] The reasoning which Dr. H. H. Horne has applied to teaching may be with the same effectiveness applied to Bible study. He claims that a teacher must have some method in setting about his work. To cast method out, in the opinion of the former New York University professor, would be tantamount to casting teaching out itself. In teaching there is a right method which the teacher must discover. "The teacher must not excuse his inertia in discovering right method."[25] The same holds true of method in apprehending the argumentation of Biblical books.

Dr. Horne has enumerated six kinds of different methods which the student and Biblical reader should know. He listed them in pairs in one of his educational writings.[26] There is the pair of general and special methods. In general method the student will find an account of those principles which may be applied to any subject, while in the special he will and a description of those that are applicable to a specific subject.

The second pair is the inductive and the deductive methods. In the inductive the student goes from the particular to the general principle. The deductive method is just the reverse; there the student goes from general principles to particular applications.

The third pair of methods was designated by Horne as the empirical and the scientific. In the empirical the basis is found in imitation, habit, tradition, accident or experiment, while in the scientific is due to the union of the subject and the law in the mind. Dr. Horne contrasts the two methods as follows: "Empirical method is based on limited observation, is limited in its application, and is uncertain in its conclusions; scientific method is based on wide observation, is practically universal in its application, and is practically certain in its conclusions."

John Dewey has defined method as "the way of doing things in a given case."[27] It is thoroughly individualistic. In the use of a method certain main steps must be taken and at the crucial points conditions of growth have to be carefully maintained and fostered. According to Dewey there are five factors which must be remembered. These are: 1) The existence of a situation which appeals to an individual as his own concern or interest because arousing desire and effect; 2) Condition must be such as to stimulate observation and memory in locating the means, obstacles and resources that must be reckoned with in dealing with the situation; 3) The formation of a plan of procedure; 4) Putting the plan into operation; 5) A comparison of what was to be accomplished with that which actually was.

Dr. Kuist of Princeton Theological Seminary in utilizing this definition of Dewey, set forth the crucial points in method as the following: 1) The importance of observation; 2) The distinction between historical and recreative criticism; 3) The relation of inductive to the deductive method; and 4) Definition of structure.

Footnotes

1. W.F. Adeney, *How to Read the Bible* (New York: Thomas Wittaker, 1879), p. 9.
2. **Ibid.**, p. 9.
3. R. A. Torrey, *Getting the Gold Out of the Word of God* (New York: Fleming H. Revell & Co., 1925). p. 5.
3a: Martin Anstey, *How to Master the English Bible* (London: Pickering & Inglis, 1931), pp. 32-34.
4. Henry Dunn, *The Study of the Bible* (New York: G. P. Putnam & Sons, 1871), p. 1.
5. **Ibid.**, pp. 1-2.
6. George B. Stevens, "Study of the Bible as Literature," *Hints on Bible Study* (Philadelphia: John D. Wattles & Co., 1898).
6a. William Arndt, "The Pastor as Bible Student," *Concordia Theological Monthly*, 8:891, December, 1937.
7. Cf. Lowell, *Essay and Libraries*.
8. G. C. Morgan, *The Study and Teaching of the English Bible* (New York: Fleming H. Revell, 1910), p. 28.
9. **Ibid.**, pp. 28-29.
10. "Hints on the Study of the Gospels": *Hints on the Bible Study*, **op. cit.**, p. 207.
11. **Ibid.**, p. 208.
12. "Right Spirit in Old Testament Study," *Hints on Bible Study*, **op. cit.**, pp. 177-178.
13. *Unattained Ideal of Bible Study. Hints on Bible Study*, **op. cit.**, p. 250.
14. Adeney, *How to Read the Bible* (New York: Thomas Wittaker, 1897), p. 7.
15. "How to Use Bible Commentaries," Hint on Bible Study, **op. cit.**, p. 162.

16. Cf. R.F. Surburg, *The Book Method of Bible Study* (Seward: Concordia College's Steno Bureau, 1959), p. 6.

17. J. R. Dummelow, *A Commentary of the Holy Bible* (New York: The Macmillan Company, 1947 (Reissuel), pp. cxxxiv-cxxxix.

18. Eislen, Lewis and Downey, *The Abingdon Bible Commentary* (New York: Abingdon-Cokesbury Press, 1929), pp. 3-15.

19. Published by James S. Vitue, City Road and Ivy Lane, London, 1890.

20. *The Cambridge Companion to the Bible* (London: Cambridge University Press, 1905), p. 1.

21. James M. Gray, *Christian Workers' Commentary on the Old and New Testaments* (New York: Fleming H. Revell Company, 1915), p. 5.

22. *Dictionary of Synonyms*, p. 545.

23. W. H. Kilpatrick, *Foundations of Method* (New York: The Macmillan Company, 1925), p. 3.

24. H. Home, *The Psychological Principle of Education* (New York: The Macmillan Company, 1908), p. 51.

25. **Ibid.**

26. **Ibid.**, pp. 51-53.

27. Cf. his article on "Method," *Cyclopedia of Education*, edited by Monroe (New York: The Macmillan Company), IV, p. 205.

Questions

1. What is the most profitable of all studies? ____

2. There is much "Bible Study" that is ____.

3. The person who has a ____ will be found to have accomplished much more.

4. The ministry of the pastor or teacher will be better for ____.

5. All the commentaries in the world are no substitute for ____.

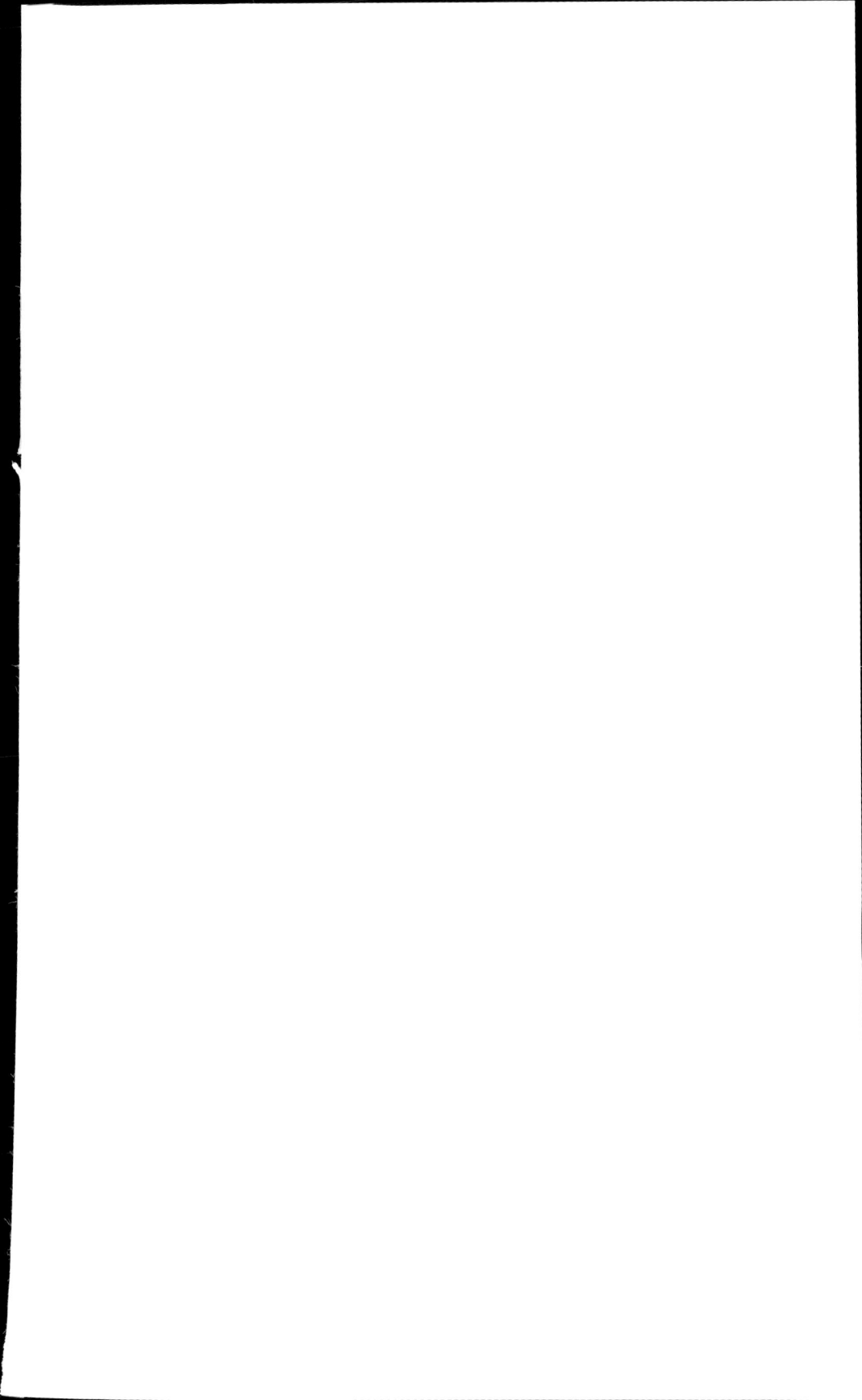

www.ingramcontent.com/pod-product-compliance
Lightning Source LLC
Chambersburg PA
CBHW030633150426
42811CB00048B/93